Praise for

LOUIS A
AN EXTRAVAGANT LIFE

which was on the Best Books of 1997 lists for
USA Today, the *Seattle Times, Publishers Weekly, Booklist,
Salon,* and the *San Francisco Chronicle.*

"By letting Armstrong speak for himself, Bergreen succeeds in shedding light on
a little-   ment."

"[Berg   of the
South   nd for
gangst

"Wha   is the
story

"Louis   wrote
himsel   rgreen
does n   seem
definiti

"Bergr   at an
entire I   . For
anyone   vill be
a great   sent to
become

"Bergreen's *Louis Armstrong* is the most balanced and complete account yet. One
of the reasons that Bergreen's book is so welcome is that it attends to Armstrong's endgame triumphs, of which there were many."

—*Newsday*

"Veteran biographer Bergreen once again demonstrates a gift for conveying the bone truth about an important figure while never sacrificing a core tenderness towards his subject's frailties and failings. Moreover, he makes us care anew about a misunderstood pioneer. Bergreen has probed more deeply than ever before into the textural milieu of the young Armstrong's New Orleans and the adult Satchmo's America. Thanks to Bergreen we meet a man who remained true to himself and his ideals, while making no attempt to disguise the quirks that kept him human."

—*Billboard*

"Even the most niggling music lover will respond to Mr. Bergreen's admiration for his subject's spontaneous, infectious humanity."

—*Economist*

"You can celebrate Satchmo's life with this wonderfully written and well-researched biography. Along the way you'll learn about America, too, during the Armstrong years, and the forces that shaped him and that he shaped."

—*Atlanta Journal and Constitution*

"*Louis Armstrong* is a loving memorial to a long, mythic career. More than any previous book on Armstrong, Bergreen's draws extensively on the man's own voluminous diaries and correspondence. Bergreen gets to the heart of the man."

—*Time Out*

"Bergreen has drawn deeply from [Armstrong's] autobiographical writings for his affectionate but flawed portrait of the man. . . . That alone sets him miles apart from [biographer] James Lincoln Collier, who considered Armstrong an 'unreliable' witness to his own life, but there is much more. Bergreen makes himself at home in Storyville, the New Orleans red light district where Armstrong was reared. With great relish he conjures up images of brothels and whores."

—*Los Angeles Times*

"Bergreen's biography is excellent when dealing with the colorful drama of Armstrong's career and, in his words, the trumpeter's 'distinctly American brand of optimism and striving.' "

—*San Francisco Chronicle Book Review*

"[Bergreen's] pleasure and enthusiasm show through on every page. . . . Describing individual [song] titles, Bergreen is always perceptive and makes you want to listen to that particular song."

—*Salon* magazine

BY THE SAME AUTHOR

Capone: The Man and the Era

As Thousands Cheer:
The Life of Irving Berlin

James Agee: A Life

Look Now, Pay Later:
The Rise of Network Broadcasting

BROADWAY BOOKS
NEW YORK

LOUIS ARMSTRONG

· an extravagant life ·

LAURENCE
BERGREEN

BROADWAY

A hardcover edition of this book was published in 1997 by Broadway Books.

LOUIS ARMSTRONG: AN EXTRAVAGANT LIFE. Copyright © 1997 by Laurence Bergreen. All rights reserved. Printed in the United States of America. No part of this book may be reproduced or transmitted in any form or by any means, electronic or mechanical, including photocopying, recording, or by any information storage and retrieval system, without written permission from the publisher. For information address Broadway Books, a division of Bantam Doubleday Dell Publishing Group, Inc., 1540 Broadway, New York, NY 10036.

Broadway Books titles may be purchased for business or promotional use or for special sales. For information, please write to: Special Markets Department, Bantam Doubleday Dell Publishing Group, Inc., 1540 Broadway, New York, NY 10036.

BROADWAY BOOKS and its logo, a letter B bisected on the diagonal, are trademarks of Broadway Books, a division of Bantam Doubleday Dell Publishing Group, Inc.

First trade paperback edition published 1998.

Designed by Claire Naylon Vaccaro

The Library of Congress has catalogued the hardcover edition as:
Bergreen, Laurence
　　　Louis Armstrong : an extravagant life / Laurence Bergreen.
　　　　　p.　　cm.
　　　Includes discography (p. 499), bibliographical references (p. 519), and index.
　　　ISBN 0-553-06768-0 (hc)
　　　　1. Armstrong, Louis, 1900–1971.　2 Jazz musicians—United States—Biography.　I. Title.
ML419.A75B47　　　1997
781.65'092—dc21
　[b]　　　　　　　　　　　　　　　　　　　　　97-13146　　CIP　　MN

ISBN 0-7679-0156-8

98 99 00 01 02 10 9 8 7 6 5 4 3 2 1

TO
BETSY,
NICK,
AND SARA

"My whole life has been happiness. Through all my misfortunes, I did not plan anything. Life was there for me, and I accepted it. And life, whatever came out, has been beautiful to me, and I love everybody."

LOUIS ARMSTRONG

"Shakespeare invented Caliban. Who the hell dreamed up Louis? Some of the bop boys consider him Caliban, but if he is, he is a mask for a lyric poet who is much greater than most now writing. Man and mask, sophistication and taste hiding behind clowning and crude manners—the American joke, man."

RALPH ELLISON

Contents

OVERTURE

n the beginning, he was a sound, and only a sound: a strange blend of happy cacophony and tormented caterwauling. Nothing like it had ever been heard before, not in New Orleans, where he was born in 1901, or Chicago or St. Louis, where he played as an emerging virtuoso cornetist, and certainly not in New York, where Duke Ellington said of his first exposure to that sound, "Nobody had ever heard anything like it, and his impact cannot be put into words." Nor had it ever been heard in Europe, or South America, or Africa, but everywhere it would be known as the sound of America.

With this sound, he established more popular songs than any other musician. The sound had two components. There was, initially, a cornet—and later a trumpet—that was more expressive than a mere instrument: sweet, stinging, lilting, cajoling, teasing, ebullient. And then there was his voice, the unforgettable voice that behaved like a huge instrument: growling, laughing, demented, soothing, fierce. The combination of the voice that sounded like an instrument and the instrument that sounded like a voice created the universally recognized persona of Satchmo. He looked and felt like a glowing lump of coal, hot and alive and capable of igniting everything around him. For him, music was a heightened form of existence, and he sang and he played as if it could never be loud enough, or last long enough, or go deep enough, or reach high enough. He believed there could never be enough music in the world, and he did his damnedest to fill the silence with all the stomping, roaring, screeching, sighing polyphony he could muster.

He was not just America's greatest musical performer, he was also a character of epic proportions: married four times, with countless romantic involvements in and around his marriages ("Take your shoes off, Lucy, and let's get juicy," he growls in "Baby, It's Cold Outside"); a lifelong believer in marijuana for the head and laxatives for the bowels; an accomplished storyteller who tossed off letters and memoirs with the same abandon he tossed off riffs; and an enthusiastic correspondent who as a young man turned to his typewriter to record his experiences and his glorious hard times, the record of a black man trying to make his way in twentieth-century America.

It would be pleasant to memorialize Louis this way, as a happy innocent, his life an unbroken arc from the streets, dance halls, and brothels of New Orleans to the nightclubs, vaudeville theaters, and concert halls of Chicago, and New York, and then on to the sound stages of Hollywood and all the other venues and cradles of popular culture from Scandinavia to Africa, where he is revered. It would be heartwarming to envision him effortlessly breaking "color barriers" everywhere he went, with audiences screaming, "Satchmo, Satchmo," as he smiled and blew his horn and wiped his perspiring brow with his spotless white handkerchief and sang "Ain't Misbehavin' " and growled a few words of filthy comic asides to the band, and then smiled again and eagerly pumped the valves on his gleaming trumpet, and raised it to his scarred yet indestructible chops, and blew his horn some more.

It would be convenient if his life were that simple, but of course it wasn't, not at all.

It was, in all externals, a wretched childhood, yet Louis was obsessed with it and returned to it throughout his maturity as the wellspring of his identity, of his music, of jazz itself. From the time he purchased his first typewriter in 1922, Louis tapped out his reminiscences, observations, dirty stories, bawdy puns and limericks, and most anything else that popped into his superheated mind. Sometimes he wrote in his hotel rooms, and sometimes he wrote between sets, in the dressing room of whatever nightclub or theater he happened to be performing in. He spent almost as much time pounding the keys of his typewriter as he did pumping the valves of his trumpet. And he told the same tales with each instrument, which only made sense, because in his mind, he *was* jazz; to prove his point, he titled the first chapter of his autobiography, "Jazz and I Get Born Together." He was driven to review and renew the sources of his inspiration whenever he could. The further his ambitions, accomplishments, and fame took him from his childhood, the more avidly he sought to return to it—to re-create it onstage night after night, to reminisce compulsively about it with friends, and to recapture it in an outpouring of letters and memoirs both published and unpublished, that spare nothing and relish every amusing, odd, or gruesome detail of his boyhood. His cherished memories preserve a vanished, and, to many, unknown way of life—that of poor black people in New Orleans in the early decades of this century.

Louis wrote as he spoke, in torrents of phrases linked by ellipses, as if he were writing an endless gossip column, the gossip of his life. He preferred to write on his stationery, in green ink on yellow paper, and when that was not available, on hotel stationery, even on the back of an envelope containing a letter inside. He distributed his confessional letters across the world to his correspondents, and some of them later appeared in popular magazines such as *True*, *Esquire*, and *Ebony*, which were willing to run his raw tales of his youth and sexual adventures pretty much as he wrote them. Many others have found their way into libraries and archives, and countless others languish in private hands. Eventually, in his early fifties, he summoned the confidence to write his autobiography, published under the title *Satchmo: My Life in New Orleans*. He wrote it by himself, without the aid of a ghostwriter, secretary, or amanuensis, and the book became a summation of all the letters he had ever written and stories he had ever told about the good old, bad old days in New Orleans.

The outcome of all this ceaseless literary activity, which neatly complemented his musical outpouring, was a kind of self-analysis, for his writing always returned to the same cluster of themes: how I became who I am; how my experiences, especially as a boy, have left indelible marks on me; and, implicitly, how I learned to turn adversity into happiness most of the time, and music all the time. Though confessional, his writing was never intended to be private. Except when he was intent on saving his energy for a performance, Louis was exceptionally gregarious—too gregarious to confine his writing to a diary, and too much of an exhibitionist not to tell everybody, if only for sheer shock value. Writing was for him a transactional process, a conversation with another person, and his conversation always came back to the same point: how the grim circumstances into which he had been born and raised in fact constituted a charmed life, the ideal childhood for a jazz musician.

Louis's consciousness was unique and all-encompassing. He held nothing back. People who knew him well invariably use the same word to describe him: "natural." He always said exactly what was on his mind, usually a mixture of music, sex, food, laxatives, and childhood memories. Even at the age of seventy, he boasted of his sexual prowess, and throughout his life he happily described who he had just gone to bed with, whether it was his wife or a girlfriend, and what they had done, and how he felt about it—usually delighted. He also reveled in his bowel movements. These were occasions for rejoicing, and he was not shy about sharing his enthusiasm for them with the world. His stationery, for instance, showed him sitting on a toilet, pants down around his ankles, grinning, glimpsed as if through a keyhole, with the legend underneath: SATCHMO SAYS: LEAVE IT ALL BEHIND YA! He urged his friends to take the strong laxative he used, Swiss Kriss, a herbal remedy sold by the physical culturist Gayelord Hauser, and he distributed small cellophane packages of it to everyone he met, enthusiastically explaining its benefits.

He loved marijuana, too. He smoked it in vast quantities from his early twenties until the end of his life; wrote songs in praise of it; and persuaded his musician friends to smoke it when they played. He planned to call an unpublished sequel to his autobiography *Gage*, his pet name for marijuana, but once his manager found out about the title and the subject of the work, he suppressed the manuscript, trying to protect Louis's reputation. Sections of the work that survived the censorship show that he regarded it as an essential element in his life and beneficial to his health.

Louis had many nicknames throughout his life. They were part of the legacy of New Orleans, where, he said, "it was a pleasure to nickname someone and be named yourself. Fellers would greet each other, 'Hello, Gate,' or 'Face' or whatever it was. Characters were called Nicodemus, Slippers, Sweet Child, Bo' Hog, so many more names. They'd be calling me Dipper, Gatemouth, Satchelmouth, all kinds of things, you know, Shadowmouth, any kind of name for a laugh. . . . I had a million of 'em. Then I got Satchmo and I'm stuck with it. I like it." After journalists dubbed him "Satchmo," a corruption of "Satchelmouth," in the 1930s, it became his more or less official nickname, and it was the one he printed on his canary yellow stationery. Record companies called him Satchmo, too, because they recognized that it was good marketing. Who could resist a name like Satchmo? It was almost a trademark. In private, around friends, he referred to himself as Gate or Dipper, and he called them Daddy and Gate to express his affection and recognition. Most everyone who knew Louis called him Pops.

He made few enemies, if any. He loved to amuse, to startle, and to entertain, but as Duke Ellington pointed out, he "never hurt anyone" along the way. Most everyone liked him, or loved him, or forgave his addiction to crude clowning, or gradually succumbed to it because Louis Armstrong was a genius as well as a jester, and part of his genius was his exuberant temperament. He occasionally raged or lost his temper, usually with good reason, but never for long; there was nothing malicious about him. At times, he could be naive and reckless, but he always relied on his buoyant personality to rescue him from any jam he happened to find himself in, and his irrepressible optimism usually came to his rescue. He was the pursuit of happiness personified.

The grin was so endearing, and the growl so comforting, that it is easy to overlook Armstrong's essential subversiveness. Although he seemed to belong wholly to the mainstream, his principal allegiances were to the underground of American existence, from which he had emerged. His whole life can be read as a rebuke to bourgeois proprieties. Louis played, smoked, ate, made love, and lived as he damn well pleased. Although he wanted everyone to love him, at the same time, he didn't care much what people, especially those in authority, thought of him. He welcomed everyone into his orbit, especially outcasts—pimps, hustlers, hangers-on, even critics. He loved whores, having grown up among them. "Yeah, those were my people," he said in their defense, "and still are. Real people who never told me anything that wasn't right." He loved whores so much that he even married one. They met when he was her customer, and she tried to keep him in line with a small arsenal of knives and razors. Although he wasn't religious in any explicit sense, he believed he saw the spirit as plainly in sinners, thieves, and whores as he did in more conventional people.

In all, his was a distinctly American brand of optimism and striving. By reexamining his childhood and recasting it in the best possible light, he became the persona he employed to beguile the world, "Laughin' Louie." But there was more to his laughter than simple mirth. There was power and even an edge of anger to the laughter. It was a cosmic shout of defiance, a refusal to accept the status quo, and a determination to remake the world of his childhood and by extension, the world at large, as he believed it ought to be. He thought he could accomplish this feat of legerdemain with his horn, his voice, and the jazz idiom, but in the end, it was Louis's animating spirit of joy, as much as his music, that was responsible for his transforming vision. No matter how much he suffered from the brutality of a caste system that consigned him to its lowest rank, he remained convinced his childhood was not the worst imaginable, but the best, overflowing with love, joy, and inspiration. "Every time I close my eyes blowing that trumpet of mine—I look right in the heart of good old New Orleans," he said. "It has given me something to live for."

To hear Louis tell it, or sing it, or blow it, no one else had ever enjoyed as privileged an existence as his New Orleans boyhood.

PERDIDO
STREET BLUES

t the time of Louis Armstrong's birth, New Orleans, the most international, least American of cities, was a world apart—a blend of French, Spanish, Canadian, British, Caribbean, and African cultures, customs, languages, religions, and cuisines. Located near the mouth of the Mississippi, where the river is widest and the surrounding terrain the swampiest, New Orleans nestles in a bend of the river a little over a hundred miles from the Gulf of Mexico. From its secure, partially concealed location, it derived its nickname the Crescent City. Although it seems inevitable that a major port city would flourish near the mouth of the Mississippi, New Orleans is an engineering marvel: a city built on water, even beneath the water, for its original site was actually several feet below the banks of the Mississippi. Water was—and is—everywhere, not only in the river, in nearby Lake Pontchartrain, and in the Gulf, but in the swamps surrounding the city. Earlier in the city history, these swamps bred malaria and harbored alligators; they still nurture lush vegetation, and they make a mockery of belowground burials. Even today, the dead are buried in aboveground vaults, a custom that had added to the city's superstitious ambience.

The oppressive heat and humidity made the city seem to rot around the edges. Visitors were seduced by its dreamy, slow-paced atmosphere, as if New Orleans were a little chunk of Europe that was unaccountably transplanted to the mouth of the Mississippi. In 1909, when Louis Armstrong was eight years old, Sir Henry Morton Stanley, the Anglo-American journalist and explorer, visited the city. He was struck by its "soft, balmy air, with its strange scents of fermenting molasses, semibaked sugar, green coffee, pitch, Stockholm tar, brine, mess beef, rum and whiskey-drippings." The inhabitants seemed just as remarkable and unusual to him, for "they had a swing of the body wholly un-English, and their facial expressions [were] different from those I had been accustomed to."

New Orleans *was* exotic, especially by the standards of white Protestant America, for the city was both predominantly Catholic and racially mixed. Founded in 1718 by Jean-Baptiste LeMoyne, New Orleans was originally a French city, in a French province, named for Philippe Duc d'Orléans, who was then the regent of France, and it was intended to protect French holdings from the British. Accordingly, the laws of the territory were not Anglo-Saxon in origin, as was the case in all other states. Instead, the laws and customs adhered to the Napoleonic code, tied to the canons of France and reaching back to the era of Roman occupation.

At first, settlers came to New Orleans in search of gold that turned out to be more mythical than actual. When that dream failed them, they turned to trading furs. At the same time, France was using the city as a dumping ground for its unwanted, especially its whores, thus planting the roots of prostitution deep into the city's culture and society. As more Europeans filtered into New Orleans, France secretly ceded the entire city to Spain in 1762; the transaction added a new cultural element to the populace. The following year, yet another group found their way to the city: Acadians seeking refuge from the British presence in Nova Scotia. Their descendants are known today as Cajuns. In 1764, the city finally learned that it had been severed from France—to which many of its respectable citizens proudly traced their ancestry—and the Spanish militia later suppressed a bloody rebellion to assert its dominance over the luxurious, sweltering city near the mouth of the Mississippi. In the following decades, the mixing and inter-marrying of the French and Spanish nobility in New Orleans gave rise to a new, indigenous culture, known as Creole, and their music, a blend of French and Spanish rhythms and motifs, also contributed to the music eventually known as jazz.

As the nineteenth century opened, New Orleans prospered, and France coveted the possession it had so rashly given to the Spanish. Napoleon badgered the Spanish into returning Louisiana to France in the clandestine Treaty of San Ildefonso, but New Orleans did not remain French for long. Only three years later, Napoleon sold the city and its territorial holdings to the United States; thus President Thomas Jefferson acquired New Orleans in the Louisiana Purchase. The Creoles of New Orleans, who had established a sophisticated, insular, and idiosyncratic lifestyle based on the twin pillars of religion and sexual freedom, were aghast, believing their city and their way of life had been sold out from beneath them. They dreaded an influx of barbarous, puritanical Americans who would condemn their Roman Church and old-world sexual customs.

New Orleans was an American city at last. However, the Creoles, French, Spanish, and Acadians who preceded the American parvenus were deeply entrenched and incredibly snobbish and clannish in relation to outsiders. They had settled in the exotic "Downtown" section of the city, while the newcomers—many of them Yankees—flocked to an equally prosperous "American" neighborhood known as "Uptown." When the British threatened to capture the city in 1814, General Andrew Jackson managed to raise an army of volunteers from both sides of town. In the Battle of New Orleans, January 8, 1815, the army defeated a common enemy, but the timing contained considerable irony, for the victory was won two weeks after the United States and Great Britain had signed a peace treaty, news of which had yet to reach the embattled city.

For the next forty-five years, the city flourished and luxuriated in its contradictions. New Orleans boasted the largest cotton and slave markets in the world, and because of slave labor, it emerged as the wealthiest city in the United States (on a per capita basis) in the years prior to the Civil War. Wealthy Creoles pursued their private, elegant, decadent lifestyle; enslaved blacks imported into the city supplied the labor necessary to make it all run. The races and cultures mixed occasionally, but only in ritualized ways, most importantly in the *bals de Cordon Blue*, usually known as the quadroon balls. (A quadroon was considered one-quarter black.) Here wealthy Creole gentlemen came in search of light-skinned black mistresses, quadroons, whom they would set up in separate households and maintain until they lost interest. These balls occurred at least four times a week in various hotels throughout the city. Except for the musicians, no black men were permitted to attend.

Considering themselves socially superior to dark-skinned blacks, quadroons and other light-skinned blacks belonged to a small, but prominent minority of free blacks in New Orleans known as *gens de couleur libre*, some of whom actually owned slaves themselves. Their offspring with dark skin were known as *Griffes*, and those with white as octoroons—one-eighth black, or even less. The octoroons and quadroons were reputed to be more sexually advanced than their white counterparts and were supposedly familiar with the full panoply of Parisian sexual practices, including whipping, fetishes, and bondage.

A visiting British tourist, appalled at the quadroon balls, disdainfully recorded her impressions of the custom of keeping a quadroon mistress:

> *The girls are highly educated, externally, and are, probably, as beautiful and accomplished a set of women as can be found. Every young man selects one early, and establishes her in one of those pretty and peculiar houses, whole rows of which may be seen in the Ramparts. The connection now and then lasts for life; usually for several years. In the latter case, when the time comes for the gentleman to take a white wife, the dreadful news reaches his quadroon partner, either by letter entitling her to call the house and furniture her own, or by the newspaper which announces the marriage. . . . Every quadroon woman believes that her partner will prove an exception to the rule of desertion. Every white lady believes her husband has been an exception to the rule of seduction.*

The system of maintaining a second family was widespread in New Orleans; Creoles referred to it as *plaçage*, or placement, and in practice it contained elements of both marriage and prostitution. It was, of course, inherently unstable, and the men often tired of their second families. Once expelled, many octoroon and quadroon women, without a secure place in society or a means of earning a living and accustomed to trading on their looks and sexual prowess, opened brothels. Thus the city's intricate social hierarchy only promoted what it sought to deny: a mixing of all races and cultures. It was often impossible to tell who belonged to what race, and doctors often altered birth certificates to suit a family's request.

Through such customs, New Orleans developed an international reputation for licentiousness, but its real and lasting sin lay in the crucial role the city played in the slave trade. New Orleans was the site of a dozen flourishing slave auctions. The city sought to protect its status as the slave auction center of the Western Hemisphere by seceding from the United States in 1861. The infamy lasted until 1862, when Union troops took control of the city and remained an army of occupation for fifteen years. Not until the 1880s did New Orleans begin to recover a semblance of its former self.

Although its wilder excesses and wealth never returned, it remained a multiracial city, a locus of licentiousness, and home to over a quarter of a million blacks, many of them freed slaves and their descendants. They were dark-skinned blacks, looked down on by whites, Creoles, octoroons, quadroons, indeed, by anyone with skin of a lighter shade. Like other descendants of recently freed slaves, Louis Armstrong considered himself neither French nor Spanish nor Creole. He did not speak French, nor did he identify with France, as Creoles of color did. He was, as he often said, an *American*, even though his ancestors came to America in chains and traced their roots to Africa.

> *. . . Now, if you's white, you's all right . . . If you's brown, stick aroun' . . . But if you's black, oh, brother, git back! . . . git back! . . . git back! . . .*

Prior to the Civil War, New Orleans was relatively hospitable to Creoles of color and even some blacks. Louisiana's *Code Noir*, designed to govern black behavior in public, was actually more liberal than British or American customs. In fact, blacks in New Orleans had more rights than their counterparts in any other city on the American continent, even those up north. Black life flourished in New Orleans, and the focal point for blacks was the *Place Congo*, later Congo Square—and today called Louis Armstrong Park.

Congo Square, one of the cradles of jazz, was hardly more than a field edging a swamp, where blacks, both slave and free, mingled, danced, and played their music. Even at this early date, the dances mingled African and European elements, prefiguring the mixture that would become jazz. The scene attracted many white visitors, and one left a vivid description of the astonishing energy and transforming power of the spectacle:

> *The favorite dances of the slaves were the Calinda, a variation of which was also used in the Voodoo ceremonies, and the dance of the Bamboula, both of which were primarily based on the primitive dances of the African jungle, but with copious borrowings from the* contredanses *of the French. . . . For the evolutions of the latter, the male dancers attached bits of tin or other metal to ribbons tied about their*

ankles. Thus accoutred, they pranced back and forth, leaping into the air and stamping in unison, occasionally shouting, "Dansez Bamboula! Badoum! Badoum!" while the women, scarcely lifting their feet from the ground, swayed their bodies from side to side and chanted an ancient song as monotonous as a dirge. Beyond the groups of dancers were the children, leaping and cavorting in imitation of their elders, so that the entire square was an almost solid mass of black bodies stamping and swaying to the rhythmic beat of the bones upon the cask, the frenzied chanting of the women, and the clanging of the pieces of metal which dangled from the ankles of the men.

The rites of Congo Square gradually became more sophisticated. The music incorporated French quadrilles and military musical motifs. The instruments evolved as well; black musicians traded their primitive, homemade drums and horns for European drums, woodwinds, and brass. They began to play the bugle and then the cornet. They played with Creole musicians, who excelled in the clarinet, the musical equivalent of a French accent. French folk songs collided with field hollers and improvised shouts of levee workers, all of this music slowly evolving into rags, shouts, stomps, rambles, and what was later called, simply, jazz.

In this relatively liberal atmosphere, the number of free blacks in New Orleans steadily increased, and by the Civil War, thousands of blacks were five or ten generations removed from Africa and slavery. No wonder they felt more American than African. Although they enjoyed considerable freedom, Louis Armstrong's ancestors didn't belong to this privileged class. They were, in stark contrast, slaves until the Civil War, raised on plantations, speaking English rather than French, with little idea of their origins and scant contact with other blacks. In the isolation imposed by slavery on plantations, they were stripped of their customs and identity, and it would be decades until they caught up with their own traditions, such as the rites in Congo Square, transplanted from Africa to America. In fact, poor blacks such as the Armstrongs had practically no official documentation of their past, or their ancestry, to which to cling. Louis was the grandson of slaves, and slaves, in general, were deprived of birth certificates, marriage licenses, and other proof of their existence. They took their masters' names as their last names, and if they showed up on records at all, it was as chattel; sometimes their names—usually just first names—appeared in bills of sale, and in inventories of holdings of the masters' estates. Under slavery, a fine piece of furniture was likely to be more fully documented than a slave.

When Armstrong's ancestors, and other slaves like them, were finally freed, they left their plantations for New Orleans and the often frustrated hope of employment. Although they spoke English, they were frequently uneducated, illiterate. If they did find work, it was usually in the form of manual labor. Creoles of color were especially disdainful of the freed slaves, and they continued speaking French to distinguish themselves from the blacks who flocked to their own neighborhood, "Back of Town." After the Civil War, this was the poorest, shabbiest part of the city, and it was here that Armstrong's grandparents settled, and his parents lived, and where he would be born and raised.

During Reconstruction, the fortunes of all the city's blacks declined. *Gens de couleur libre*, who had enjoyed more liberty than blacks anywhere else, suddenly found themselves stripped of their rights. The effect was traumatic. Some migrated to South America; others managed to pass as whites. Meanwhile, Armstrong's ancestors were condemned to poverty by new legislation enforcing segregation not only in schools but in all public gathering places. In 1896, the United States Supreme Court, in its Plessy vs. Ferguson ruling, upheld a Louisiana statute calling for "separate but equal" railroad carriages. With that ruling, an issue that had originated several years earlier as a local matter in New Orleans became a statewide and then a national policy. Segregation spread from railroad cars to schools, places of employment, every public space and transaction imaginable. In practice, "separate but equal" meant very separate and very *un*equal facilities for blacks and whites.

At the same time, "Jim Crow" legislation (the name derived from an old minstrel song), which aimed to disenfranchise all people of color, spread throughout the South. The effect of Jim Crow on black voter registration was especially striking. In 1897, four years before Louis's birth, it reached a peak of 95 percent. By 1901, it was reduced to just 1 percent.

Under these circumstances, the lot of *all* people of color in New Orleans declined dramatically after the Civil War, and in many ways, Louis's parents and grandparents were no better off than they had been in slavery. Plessy vs. Ferguson and Jim Crow remained in effect in New Orleans, and everywhere else in the South, until the 1954 Supreme Court decision, Brown vs. Board of Education, declared the doctrine of "separate but equal" to be unconstitutional. For most of Louis's life, "separate but (un)equal" was the defining reality. For him, ever-increasing segregation meant he came into the world as an outcast, at the very bottom of the social ladder, with scant hope of resisting legislation and customs designed to keep him and his kind in a state of ignorance, poverty, and disenfranchisement. New Orleans, once a great city, was now a social and political ruin, shorn of its prosperity. To be sure, it retained its air of decadence and its peculiar combination of Creole indolence and American enterprise, but it also suffered from an increasingly poisonous relationship among races and nationalities competing for dwindling resources and shreds of former glory. This was the wonderful, dreadful, divided city that gave birth to jazz—and to Louis Armstrong.

According to his own, cherished tradition, Louis Armstrong was an all-American jazz baby, born in New Orleans, Louisiana, on the Fourth of July 1900. He believed this to the end of his days, and so did everyone else, until a baptismal certificate confirming his actual birth date as August 4, 1901, surfaced and in the name of scholarship silenced one of the happiest legends in American popular music. Exactly three weeks after his birth, the infant was taken to Sacred Heart of Jesus Church at 139 South Lopez Street to be baptized "according to the rite of the Roman Catholic Church." The baptismal card, signed by the Reverend J. M. Toohey, described Louis as "*niger, illegitimus,*" apparently because his father had by that time abandoned his mother and was living with another woman. So it was that Louis Armstrong, an illegitimate black child, was baptized into the Catholic Church. Since his grandmother, Josephine, was a practicing Catholic, she was most likely the one responsible for arranging the baptism, and the earliest religious influence over him, though limited, was largely Catholic. Although baptized as a Catholic, Louis never thought of himself as a member of the Church. He remained similarly aloof from Protestantism, the religion of his mother and other family members. Even so, he was vaguely religious, and, at times, deeply spiritual, but his approach to religious matters was always unorthodox, and he took what he wanted from Catholicism, Baptism, and Judaism, and, under his grandmother's influence, voodoo.

Although he really was born on August 4, 1901, Louis's lifelong conviction that his birthday coincided with the Fourth of July was telling. It was the custom for poor blacks to adopt an honorary date as their birth-day—often Christmas, or New Year's Day, or the Fourth of July. The year was equally flexible, depending on the vagaries of memory or legal con-straints. By insisting on the Fourth of July as his birth date, Louis demon-strated his identification and his pride in a country and a region that wanted nothing to do with his kind.

At the time of Louis's birth, the Armstrongs lived in a small, single-story dwelling at 723 Jane Alley—sometimes called Jane's Alley, or James Alley. Their house was simple, but it was not a run-down, dilapidated shack. It sat squarely on a lot that was about 30 feet wide and 140 feet long, and since it had been constructed less than ten years earlier, it remained in fairly good condition. Like the adjacent homes, it was painted a pastel shade of white or yellow. There was one large shade tree in the yard in front of the house, and within, there were only two rooms. The kitchen dominated the interior. His mother, Mary Albert, whom everyone called Mayann, was just fifteen when he was born, and his father, William, known as Willie, was not yet twenty. Louis was their first child. As an adult, he recorded his impressions of his earliest years: "When I was about four or five, still wearing dresses, I lived with my mother in Jane's Alley in a place called Brick Row—a lot of cement, rented rooms sort of like a motel."

In their neighborhood, he also noted, "a row of Negroes of all charac-ters were living in rooms which they rented and fixed up the best way that they could. We were *all* poor. The privies (the toilets) were out in a big yard, one side for the men and one side for the women. They were pretty good size privies. Toilets with wooden seats (holes). Also a yard of a big size. . . . Oh, *everything* happened in the Brick Row. That was the famous name for the row of houses which was made of all bricks. I remember one moonlit night a woman hollered out into the yard to her daughter. She said (real loud), 'You, Marandy, you'd better come into this house, you laying out there with nothing on top of you but that thin nigger.' Marandy said, 'Yassum.' " Louis also recalled "churchpeople, gamblers, hustlers, cheap pimps, thieves, prostitutes, and lots of children. There were bars, honky-tonks, and saloons, and lots of women walking the streets for tricks to take to their 'pads,' as they called their rooms."

Even before Louis was born, his parents' relationship was fraying, and after his arrival, "they used to quarrel something awful." Immediately after his birth, Willie and Mayann Armstrong separated. The cause of the breakup was simple enough: Willie had found himself another woman, and he moved in with her. From then on, Mayann became an outcast, even from her own people. She moved out of the house on Jane's Alley, leaving her two small children with their grandmother Josephine, and found herself a shanty at Liberty and Perdido streets. It would be hard to name a worse address in all of New Orleans at that time. She lived in a neighborhood filled with "cheap prostitutes," the ones who couldn't afford to live in the city's designated red-light district, Storyville. There is a strong likelihood that Mayann herself turned to prostitution at this desperate moment. "Whether my mother did any hustling, I cannot say," Louis writes, but he strongly suggests that Mayann became one more prostitute in a neighborhood renowned for sheltering them. "If she was, she certainly kept it out of sight." Her circumspection enabled her to keep her son's love and a measure of her dignity. "One thing, everybody from the church folks to the lowest gave her the greatest respect, and she was always glad to say hello to anybody, no matter who," Louis wrote. "She held up her head at all times. Nothing excited her. What she didn't have, she did without. She never envied no one, or anything they may have. I guess I inherited that part of life from Mayann."

With his father gone and his mother on the streets, the infant Louis was thrown on the mercy of two very different households. Much of the time, he was sheltered by his maternal grandmother, Josephine, who cared for him lovingly. Occasionally he spent time in the house of his father's brother, Isaac, who had his own large brood to contend with and let Louis fend for himself. Because of these continual displacements, young Louis never got a clear sense of where he belonged in his family. He regarded his father, Willie, who was living with his second wife, Gertrude, as a stranger. Willie's habit of devoting all his attention to his second family, and none to him, was always a source of great pain to Louis. As for his mother, Mayann, she was an even bigger mystery to her son. No one talked about her, although he knew she was alive and living somewhere in New Orleans. "From the time my parents separated I did not see my father again until I had grown to a pretty good size, and I did not see my Mayann for a long time either."

In his parents' absence, Louis's crucial first experiences in love, work, punishment, play, and white folks came while he lived with his grand-mother, Josephine.

Josephine clothed him, fed him, and, most importantly, loved him during those early years. "Ever since I was a baby I have had great love for my grandmother. She spent the best of her days raising me."

Josephine passed her days washing and ironing clothes for white folks, and it was Josephine who, through simple necessity, gave him his first lessons in the value of work. "The only person who ever made his living sitting down was the shoemaker," she told him. And she gave him a nickel just to pick up and deliver her wash loads. It was enough money to make him feel rich.

Josephine punished him. "Whenever I did something she thought I ought to get a whipping for, she sent me out to get a switch from the big old Chinaball tree in her yard," Louis remembered. "You have been a bad boy," she would tell him, "I'm going to give you a good licking." His eyes filling with tears, he would reluctantly approach the tree and search its branches for the one likely to do the least damage, and when he returned to her with it, his grandmother would burst out laughing. But when she was genuinely angry, she would release weeks of pent-up frustration in a single sound thrashing.

Josephine took him to school and church, occasionally with her mother, Louis's great-grandmother. Like many other blacks in Back of Town, he attended both Baptist and Catholic churches, as well as a Baptist Sunday school, and even a church choir, where he "did a whole lot of singing" and "acquired my singing tactics."

Josephine first told him about slavery days. She had been a slave, and she told Louis just enough to excite his curiosity about this unfathomable condition. In those days, she said, the blacks spoke French. And they gathered every Sunday afternoon in Congo Square to dance to African music, African drums, African rhythms. "All the slaves came in their finest clothes," he recalled her telling him. "The women mostly had on calico dresses, and their hair was bound in tight bandannas. Some colored musicians played African music, and we would dance the Bamboula or the Conjaie until we had to go back to our quarters. . . . One would beat the drums, another would scrape a cow's horn with a key, a third would blow into an instrument with slides, a fourth sat on his haunches and rang bells." The way the old lady described slavery days, they seemed to have taken place centuries ago, in biblical times, yet their remnants were everywhere to be found.

Like many of her generation, Josephine was uncomfortable with blacks who rushed headlong toward freedom. "Them that kicks over the traces too quick," she warned her grandson, "forget that I have seen the days when we were slaves, when we were sold on the hoof like dumb cattle. Them that goes too fast gets nowhere. Them that shines and makes a lot of fuss in Perdido are goners. The gamblers, the drunkards, the no-good women, the pimps—they'll all be in jail before you grow a beard."

Josephine afforded young Louis his first exposure to whites, with whom he felt comfortable enough to play. "Days I did not have to go to school Grandmother took me with her when she had to do washing and house-work for one of the white folks. While she was working I used to play games with the little white boys out in the yard. Hide-and-go-seek was one of the games we used to play, and every time we played, I was It. And every time I would hide those clever little white kids always found me." Louis tired of being found whenever he tried to hide, and one day he hit on the idea of concealing himself inside a layer of his grandmother's Mother Hubbard skirt as she did her wash, and for once he managed to stump his white playmates, whom he heard dashing around, frantically trying to find him, until he stuck his head out and called attention to himself.

Finally, Josephine introduced the young boy to voodoo and told him of its most famous practitioner, the Queen of the Voodoos, Marie Laveau. Early one Sunday morning, she took Louis to visit Laveau's famous tomb in St. Louis Cemetery. With this visit, voodoo became part of the spiritual ambience of his youth.

Voodoo in New Orleans was everywhere and nowhere. Even blacks who professed not to believe in it and regarded it as pure superstition were afraid of its spells and curses and evocations of spirits, to say nothing of its obsession with feminine powers. Unlike Catholicism and Protestantism, which are distinctly patriarchal and unchanging, voodoo is woman-centered and constantly in flux. It is a very personalized and eclectic form of belief, aimed at righting personal wrongs and obtaining personal goals. No two priestesses practiced it in the same way; voodoo was whatever you made it. Its journey to New Orleans began nearly two hundred years earlier, with the importation of the first slaves from the West Coast of Africa, from the Fon, Yoruba, and Kongo tribes. Some of the enslaved were snake worshipers, some believed in other religions or sects, but they also believed in their spirit, Vodu. Few slaves went directly from Africa to the United States. Instead, they came by way of the Caribbean—Haiti, especially—where the enslaved tribes mixed African rites with Caribbean customs to create voodoo—a religion, cult, and culture that was ancient and new, sacred and profane, cruel and delicately nuanced. In the process, the name of the African spirit, Vodu, was gradually corrupted into "voodoo," "hoodoo," and other variants.

Voodoo superstitions proliferated in New Orleans. When Louis was a young man, it was not unusual for blacks or Creoles in New Orleans to change their clothes frequently, lest they wear a garment to which a potion had been applied. They took similar precautions regarding the food they ate, in case it was mixed with menstrual blood. They gathered fingernail clippings and hair that fell from their heads; if these items fell into the wrong hands, they could be used to control them. They were constantly on the lookout for *gris-gris*—sachets containing powders or animals parts that might cast an evil spell. *I don't want no black woman puttin' sugar in my tea,"* an old song about voodoo warned, " *'Cause I'm scared she might poison me."*

Voodoo, New Orleans-style, blended African, Caribbean, Catholic, and Protestant elements. It gradually incorporated Christian saints and prayers; it was not unusual to see a statue of the Virgin Mary placed prominently at voodoo altars, along with snakes and candles and desiccated animal parts. Its rites included wild dancing, animal sacrifices (chickens, especially), chants, charms, casting spells, and sexual orgies. With its strong appeal to the imagination and the emotions, voodoo became part of the inner life of New Orleans, especially among its women of color and Creoles of color. A number of important priestesses, including the famous Marie Laveau of Louis's childhood, acquired immense followings.

Actually, there were two claimants to the title of "Queen of the Voodoos." The first Marie Laveau was born about 1800 and lived on North Rampart Street. When she was young, she worked as a hairdresser for whites and especially for Creoles, calling herself "the widow of Paris." Once she became a *Voodooienne*, a voodoo queen, she distinguished herself by taking her rites into the open air and by claiming that she was a Christian. Laveau drove out her rivals and became increasingly influential over the blacks of New Orleans, especially the women, who dared not disobey her edicts. During her reign, voodoo beliefs evolved to the point where many followers adopted a two-tiered structure consisting of an omnipotent God on high, and on a lower, more personal level, local spirits, or Loas, that influenced every part of life. Louis's grandmother explained that her late husband took part in voodoo rites. She boasted that he had gone with Marie Laveau to Lake Pontchartrain at night and participated in her furious, mysterious ceremonies of life and death. Louis heard about a clearing in the swamps known as Fig Place, where Marie Laveau maintained an altar, and where her followers met by night to boil potions in a cauldron under the flickering light of torches. They would toss in lizards and snakes and herbs and even a live black cat. The practice upset young Louis a great deal. Josephine also informed Louis—and everyone who believed in voodoo knew this—that Marie Laveau could even bring the dead back to life.

The reign of Marie Laveau lasted until her retirement in the 1880s, when her daughter, the *second* Marie Laveau, took over the title, "Queen of the Voodoos," thereby becoming confused with her illustrious predecessor. The first Marie Laveau had earned the loyalty of her people with acts of charity and frequent visits to condemned prisoners and the sick. The second Marie Laveau seems to have been a much more haughty and vain priestess. To her critics, she was a madam and con artist who charged credulous clients, both black and white, small fortunes to cast spells and bring about the deaths of rivals. The second Marie Laveau was also an important personage in New Orleans, a power broker and celebrity whom the white establishment was reluctant to challenge. While she continued her reign, her mother, the founder of the voodoo dynasty, lived on in obscurity and died quietly in her eighties. She was buried in St. Louis Cemetery, and her daughter was eventually interred with her.

This was the tomb that Louis's grandmother took him to see. It is likely that Josephine, following the custom of all true believers, crossed herself with a stone used by the faithful for that purpose and marked the tomb with a red X both to placate the restless spirits within and to bring good luck—a practice that voodoo believers follow to this day. While Louis watched, she deposited a dime on the tomb, and explained that the moment they were out of sight the old Voodoo Queen herself would rise from her tomb and snatch it away. Louis had a notion to linger and watch this feat with his own eyes, but his grandmother hurried him away before grave diggers appeared as if from nowhere to brush this and many other dimes into their pockets.

Some of Josephine's voodoo beliefs rubbed off on Louis. Although he was not a dedicated follower of voodoo (and men tended to fear it rather than follow it), he believed, or at least some part of him believed, that the dead could come back to life, especially during wakes. And like many other musicians in New Orleans, he brought the influence of voodoo—particularly its mesmerizing chants and its use of childish or meaningless language—to jazz. His early singing, with its uncanny intensity, sudden growls, and scatting (nonsensical chanting) reveals voodoo influences. Although Louis used these mannerisms basically for comic effect, other musicians occasionally found them alarming. They could be so compelling that when he was a rising young jazz musician some of his colleagues thought they detected a voodoo ethos about him; it was nothing they could put their finger on, exactly, just a sense that he was in touch with something deep and spiritual that spoke through him and his music, especially his singing. And when he was a young man, he looked on women with a certain awe and treated their wishes with deference. Time and again, his behavior and remarks revealed that he considered women possessed of some extra powers that men did not have, and it was best not to challenge them.

While Louis lived contentedly with his grandmother, his parents attempted to resolve their differences. Two years after he left Mayann, Willie Armstrong returned to his wife. If she had been "hustling" to make ends meet while she was on her own, she ceased with the return of her husband, and they soon had a second child, a girl named Beatrice, whom everyone, including Louis, would call by her nickname, Mama Lucy. Although his parents had reunited, Louis remained with his grandmother. He expected to live indefinitely with her until a series of painful events separated him from this one anchor in his world. When he was five years old, his tightly circumscribed, stable life entered a time of convulsion.

As he returned from fetching water one day, he heard that a friend of the family, a stern middle-aged woman, had brought word that his parents had split up once again. Even worse, his mother was seriously ill and unable to care for her little girl, Mama Lucy. No one knew where Willie Armstrong was, or if he would ever return. The family friend also brought a message from Louis's mother, begging him to return and take care of her and Mama Lucy. It was a rather extraordinary request to make of a five-year-old boy, but Louis and his grandmother decided the time had come for Louis to return to his mother, sick or healthy.

"I really hate to let you out of my sight," Louis recalled her telling him that painful day, and he told her how sorry he was to leave. After he told his grandmother how much he loved her, the family friend took him by the hand, and as they turned the corner out of Jane Alley, the young boy stole a last glimpse of his beloved Grandmother Josephine waving good-bye to him, and he burst into tears.

L isten here, Louis, if you don't stop crying at once I will put you in that prison," said the woman taking him away to his new life, as they walked passed the House of Detention to the Tulane Avenue Trolley. "That's where they keep bad men and women. You don't want to go there, do you?" Still young enough to believe her threat might actually be carried out, Louis assured her that he did not, and he followed her on to the trolley. He was wearing his best clothes, a white Lord Fauntleroy suit with a Buster Brown collar.

This was an important event, his first trolley ride, but it was not the thrill it might have been, for he was stunned to see segregation in practice aboard this trolley. "It was my first experience with Jim Crow," he recalled, and the practice made a searing impression on his youthful, incredulous mind, like a red-hot iron being pressed into wax:

> *Since I was the first to get on, I walked right up to the front of the car without noticing the sign on the backs of the seats on both sides, which read: FOR WHITE PASSENGERS ONLY. Thinking the woman was following me, I sat down in one of the front seats. However, she did not join me, and when I turned to see what had happened, there was no lady. Looking all the way to the back of the car, I saw her waving to me frantically.*
>
> *"Come here, boy," she cried. "Sit where you belong."*
>
> *I thought she was kidding me so I stayed where I was, sort of acting cute. What did I care where she sat? Shucks, that woman came up to me and jerked me out of the seat. Quick as a flash she dragged*

me to the back of the car and pushed me into one of the rear seats. Then
I saw the signs on the back of the seats saying: FOR COLORED PASSEN-
GERS ONLY.
"What do those signs say?" I asked.
"Don't ask so many questions! Shut your mouth, you little fool."

After this bewildering lesson in inequality, Louis and his family friend got off the streetcar at Tulane and Liberty streets, in a crowded neighborhood strongly reminiscent of Jane Alley. They walked two blocks and entered a little shack belonging to Mayann, the mother he had scarcely known, and Mama Lucy, the sister he had never met.

The place was so simple—just a single room tucked away in an over-looked courtyard—that it occurred to young Louis for the first time that he might belong to a poor family. Even worse, his mother lay in bed with some unknown sickness, and here he was, supposed to take care of her somehow. "Oh God, a very funny feeling came over me and I felt like I wanted to cry again." The "funny feeling" led to Louis's lifelong preoccu-pation with health and home remedies, some sensible and some not, to cure all types of illnesses, a practice he began to learn that day from his mother.

"Always remember when you're sick nobody ain't going to give you nothing," his mother admonished, "so try to stay healthy. Even without money your health is the best thing. I want you to promise me you will take a physic at least once a week as long as you live. Will you promise?"

He promised, and then Mayann, sick as she was, asked him to fetch a box of "Coal Roller Pills." He didn't know what to make of them; they looked to him like Carter's Little Liver Pills, only they were about three times larger. Under her orders, Louis swallowed a few and said farewell to the stern woman who had brought him here. His mother then gave him a brief shopping list: meat, red beans, rice, and bread from the bakery, two loaves for a nickel. This was the Fred Staehle Bakery at 408 South Rampart, about three blocks from where he now lived, and locally renowned for selling fresh-baked bread every hour, on the hour. The odor of its baking permeated the neighborhood.

He wandered out in the street, alone in the great teeming city for the first time in his life, and headed toward Rampart Street, where the food shops were located. Along the way, he passed a group of tough-looking older boys, and when he tried to slip past them with a simple "hello," one of them stopped him dead in his tracks and called him a "mama's boy." This was a bully named One Eye Bud, he would later learn.

One Eye Bud spattered a handful of mud on Louis's white Lord Fauntleroy suit. "I was young," he said, "but I saw the odds were against me; if I started a fight I knew I would be licked." But then, without thinking, he hurled himself at One Eye Bud and "smashed the little snot square in the mouth." To his amazement, he drew blood. In fact, One Eye Bud and his little gang were all so startled they turned and ran, "with One Eye Bud in the lead." And little Louis, dirty and victorious after his first scrape in his neighborhood, went off to do his mother's shopping.

When he returned, he found his mother's house filled with cousins, virtual strangers he barely remembered from his infancy. This was the Myles branch of the family: Isaac ("Uncle Ike"), his young wife Frances, and their children—Jeremiah ("Jerry"), Louise, Sarah, Flora, and Edward. From now on he would be living with them all here, in the confined space of his mother's home. The arrangement was simple: the Myles branch of the family lived on the right side of the house, while Louis, his mother, and sister occupied the left side.

The head of the family, Uncle Ike Myles, worked exhausting days as a stevedore on one of the levees. The pay was inferior, but enough to feed and clothe all the children. That night, and for many nights thereafter, Louis slept in a bed between Edward and Uncle Ike, and his baby sister was sandwiched between Louise and Sarah. The rest slept on the floor. Accustomed to his grandmother's fastidious housekeeping, Louis was shocked that the children smashed their plates to pieces instead of washing them after meals, and when the plates were destroyed, Uncle Ike fed them out of tin pans, which were never washed at all. The Myles family's crude behavior earned Louis's contempt: "They were about as worthless as any kids I have ever seen, but we grew up together just the same."

His mother's recovery from her illness came as a mixed blessing for Louis, for she was now gone from the little house for days at a stretch, and when she returned, she warned him not to fall sick, because she couldn't afford the fifty cents or dollar that a visit to the doctor might cost. He felt her absence keenly.

Where did Mayann go? Did she return to her "hustle," prostitution?

Find work as a domestic? Live with a man? Her son had no idea, and no one told him. So he was left in a little house filled with people whom he scarcely knew, smashing plates and sharing beds. He yearned for the simple, wholesome, loving life he had led with his grandmother. In the space of a brief trolley ride, he had gone from being the center of the universe to an extraneous, unwanted element in it. Never again did he wear his spanking white Lord Fauntleroy suit or earn shiny nickels for making deliveries. When he looked back on those early days in his mother's cramped quarters, he marveled that he survived this unsupervised period of his life, far from the protection of his father, mother, or grandmother. That he did stood as proof that "the Lord takes care of fools."

Louis knew exactly whom to blame for his miserable lot. Not Mayann, whom he saw as a victim, but Willie, his conspicuously absent father. At least his mother returned to the one-room house from time to time, to lecture him on "physic" and to concoct home remedies out of the pepper grass that she collected down by the railroad tracks. But Willie never had the courtesy to appear, let alone attempt to support the two children he had with Mayann. Louis always resented his father's absence, even in old age, when he wrote, "The man who Mayann told us was our father left us the day we were born. The next time we heard of him he had gone into an uptown neighborhood and had several other children by another woman. Whether he married the other woman, we're not sure. One thing—he did not marry Mayann. She had to struggle all by herself, bringing us up. MAMA LUCY AND I WERE BASTARDS FROM THE START."

In reality, Willie Armstrong was not far away. He was living at 611 South Roman Street with his wife Gertrude and at least one child, Willie Jr. He worked as a charcoal burner at a nearby turpentine factory. Despite Willie's proximity, young Louis caught fleeting glimpses of his father only in parades— "He made the chicks swoon when he marched by as the grand marshal in the Odd Fellows Parade. I was very proud to see him in his uniform and his high hat with the beautiful streamer hanging down by his side"—glimpses that made him ache for paternal attention and affection, but there was none to be had from Willie. Eventually Louis became so indignant over his father's lack of interest, let alone love, that he simply blanked the man out of his mind.

His father became a phantom. He could have been anyone—or no one. "Down South the iceman was likely to be your father," Louis told himself.

"Or the mailman, or any mother-lover. My mother and grandmother were the people who raised me, specially my mother. She said, 'Son, you got a chance. Don't waste it.' " His father had given him nothing, not a word of advice, no legacy, no acknowledgment that he even was his father, only a lingering sense of failure, frustration, and anger. For that, the boy felt he owed the old man nothing in return.

Louis's life took a turn for the better when Mayann found "a good job working for a nice white family. She was very much relieved over it. . . . These people had a couple of kids. We would play hide-and-go-seek, while Mayann did her day's washing and ironing. Had a good time—every time. The Lord kept his arms around us all the time."

Now that she was in regular attendance at home, the two of them began to form a much-delayed bond, and Louis learned to trust his young and long-suffering mother. Much of their relationship revolved around food, which became a lifelong obsession for Louis, and Mayann's idea of "physic," based on a mixture of Southern and African folk remedies. He never forgot the lessons she taught him about his digestion. "Mayann told Mama Lucy and me you must take a good purge and clean your little stomachs out thoroughly. That will keep the germs away. We both gave Mayann our word that we will stay physic-minded for the rest of our lives. Mayann would take a purge right along with the rest of us, every night before going to bed. Every morning when we went to the toilet we would all have a cleaned stomach." Although Mayann's advice sounds wrong-headed by modern standards, it belonged to an era when slaves and their poor descendants had little to eat but spoiled or discarded food, when there was food at all to still their hunger pangs. After ingesting potentially harmful substances, a purgative was necessary to expel toxins from the system. So Louis acquired the habit of "staying physic-minded" for the rest of his days.

From Mayann, Louis heard still more about slavery and its effect on his family. Uncle Ike contributed to the discussion, but as Louis came to realize, the older generation tried to soften the harshness of slavery for his benefit. "My mother Mayann and my Uncle Ike Myles said slavery wasn't half as bad as some of the history books would like for you to believe." As an adult, Louis took their assertions as evidence of their slave mentality. "Mayann and Uncle Ike had a little touch of slavery," he decided, "because their relatives before them came right up in it." Despite their efforts to play down the devastating nature of slavery, young Louis was aware of its insidious effects. He learned how slavery sowed hatred and envy among blacks. "They couldn't keep a secret among themselves," he heard. "They would make plans among themselves, and one Negro would double cross them by sneaking back and telling the white man everything they had planned to do. Quite naturally that would make him the head nigger." In sum, "Slavery was just like anything else. B.S."

And as for the callous whites who enslaved his people, "it seemed as though the only thing that they cared about was their shotguns which they had strapped around them. So they get full of their mint juleps or that bad whiskey the poor white trash were guzzling down like water, then when they get so damn drunk until they'd go out of their minds, it's Nigger Hunting time. Any Nigger. They wouldn't give up until they would find one. From then on, Lord have mercy on the poor darkie. Then they would torture the poor darkie, as innocent as he may be. Then they would get their usual ignorant Cheshire cat laughs before they would shoot him down like a dog."

This was the vision of whites that Louis received from his elders, a legacy of slavery, malice, jealousy, and hate dividing the races. But it was not the legacy he would transmit.

When he was six years old, Louis began attending the Fisk School for Boys, located at 507 South Franklin, near his house. The only educational institution he ever attended, the Fisk School was a decidedly separate and unequal facility, but nonetheless quite remarkable. It was indelibly identified with its head, Arthur P. Williams, a strict disciplinarian. (Williams's wife ran the Fisk School for Girls, right next door.) Louis learned to read and write at Fisk, and he probably gained his first exposure to music there. Music was an integral part of Fisk; the school boasted choirs, staged operettas, and several distinguished Creole musicians taught there. Despite this potentially stimulating environment, school never really engaged young Louis, and he was often absent.

When not in school, Louis passed his days in hazardous barefoot play on the streets. "In our neighborhood there were always a number of houses being torn down or built and they were full of such rubbish as tin cans, nails, boards, broken bottles and window panes. We used to play in these houses, and one of the games we played was War," he said. "One Eye Bud made himself General of the Army. Then he made me Sergeant-at-Arms. When I asked him what I had to do he told me that whenever a man was wounded I had to go out on the battlefield and lead him off."

Discharging his orders, Louis was knocked out cold by a piece of slate falling from a roof. "When I was taken home Mama Lucy and Mayann worked frantically boiling up herbs and roots which they applied to my head." They put him to bed, gave him another dose of "physic," and he "sweated out good all night long." In the morning, Louis felt well enough to go to school "just as though nothing had happened."

As the incident and his speedy recovery suggest, he had learned to love and trust his errant but well-meaning mother and to abide by the homespun lessons she taught him. He had always tried to see the good in people, he said, because that is how his mother taught him. To illustrate her point, she told him a story he always remembered. One Sunday, she said, a strange minister substituted for the church's beloved preacher, Reverend Cozy. But the congregation didn't take to the stranger, except for one sister, who appeared to enjoy the substitute just as much, if not more, than the regular preacher. As soon as the service ended, members of the congregation asked her why she enjoyed the substitute so much. "Whenever our Reverend Cozy was preaching," she said, "I looked right straight through him and saw Jesus. When the substitute preacher was preaching, sure, I realized that he wasn't as good as our own pastor, so [I] just looked over him and saw Jesus just the same."

In conclusion, Mayann told her son, "That's the only way I've wanted to be, just like that sister."

And that was how Louis wanted to be.

2.

MAHOGANY
HALL STOMP

He came of age in a city dominated by music, in public places and public spaces. Louis Armstrong's New Orleans rattled, shook, clamored, clanged, and reverberated with parades, balls, carnivals, and funeral processions. And the ubiquitous music spoke to him, excited him, made the world seem special. "It was like a phenomenon, like the Aurora Borealis," said Danny Barker, who came from an old New Orleans musical family. "The sounds of men playing would be so clear, but we wouldn't be sure where they were coming from. So we'd start running—'It's this way!' 'It's that way!'—And, sometimes, after running for a while, you'd find that'd be nowhere near that music. But the music could come on you any time like that. The city was full of the sounds of music."

There was never more music in New Orleans than on the Tuesday— "Fat Tuesday"—before the beginning of Lent. The custom of Mardi Gras originated in Europe several hundred years before, and the French imported it to New Orleans. Since the self-denial of Lent ran counter to the ambience of the city, Mardi Gras became a time of complete self-indulgence, a Carnival of decadence and excess embraced by Creoles and blacks alike. It was proof of just how remote New Orleans was from the austere sensibilities that dominated the rest of the American continent, and outsiders took it as further proof of the city's decadence. As early as 1791, a government report warned that "people of color, both free and slaves, are taking advantage of Carnival, going about disguised, mingling with the Carnival throngs in the streets, seeking entrance to the masquerade balls, and threatening public peace." As time passed, things only got more extravagant, as "krewes"— social organizations devoted to masking and parading—entered floats in the sixty or so parades held in the weeks prior to Lent and held countless balls.

In Louis's childhood, the most celebrated of these ad hoc organizations was the Krewe of Rex, formed in honor of the Russian Grand Duke Alexis Romanoff, said to have chased Lydia Thompson, a famous actress, through the Mardi Gras madness. Those who aspired to identify with the House of Romanoff adopted its hues—purple, green, and gold—as their Carnival colors, while every variety of Creole and black expressed an affinity for other brilliant hues, particularly magenta and red. Blacks became renowned for their unbelievably gaudy costumes, often inspired by Native American dress. Ever since a few dozen slaves had escaped and found shelter among the local Chickasaw Indians in 1790, black neighborhoods formed Carnival "tribes" to honor various Indian tribes; there was even a "Creole Wild West Tribe," symbolizing the mixture of races and love of regalia that could be found only in New Orleans. Some black Carnival societies were known as "Pleasure Clubs," who traced their lineage back to the musical rites of Congo Square. As they became more respectable, the associations evolved into burial societies and fraternal orders, called "Aid and Pleasure Clubs," the most prominent of which was known as the Zulu Social Aid and Pleasure Club.

"I can remember the Mardi Gras [as far back] as five years old," Louis said of the prolonged revelry. And he recalled his young mother's wholehearted participation as she gave herself over to the spirit of Carnival. "You talking about a sharp masquerader or masqueradess, I'll never forget how sharp my mother was. In those days the women would go the limit to look good on Mardi Gras day. They would buy the very best in silk, satins and laces. The best silk stockings that were made in those days. They wore masks [in] the image of a face. And they would carry a small switch in their hands. That's what they use to let you know that they know you, then they'll give you a little peek from under their masks, and, from then on they'll take you into a saloon and buy you a drink, well, some drinks. . . .

". . . Anyway, I was sure proud of my mother in her short silk Mardi Gras outfit . . . With her li'l ol' big leg self, her silk stockings running all up to her—you'd be surprised how beautiful those women used to look."

While his mother displayed her once-a-year finery, young Louis, perpetually aware of the need of money, tried to wring some coin from the Mardi Gras parades. Along with other boys in the neighborhood, he went to the freight sheds on Calliope Street to retrieve an oil lamp, which he would carry in the hope that someone would pay him a "nice taste of change" to light the way of a nighttime parade.

This was not an easy way to make money. To get a lamp, Louis, and everyone else with the same idea, arrived at the shed at about five o'clock, just as it was getting dark, and had to confront "Captain Joe," who stood there "with a big stick that was made from a shovel handle . . . And every black sumbitch that sticks his head into that gate, saying, 'Here I am, Captain Joe,' as he goes through that gate, Captain Joe whales him right across his big head with that stick. Ha ha ha. That cat'll only smile in appreciation, as if to say, 'Cap'n Joe, you's a mess.' All that cat wants is that loot." Little Louis wanted it badly enough that he was willing to run that painful gauntlet to get it. "Lot of people see those guys carrying those lamps, and [think] they're happy, having lots of fun," Louis said, "but let me tell you those cats have to go through an awful set of head whippings in order to get [them]."

Equipped with a light, and oil to burn, Louis and the other light bearers donned white robes to participate in the night parade, which began at eight o'clock. It was a sight Louis never forgot: "To watch those old timers (those good old hustlers) strut in the parade in those white gowns (I call 'em) with the belt holding that big ol' lamp in the pit of their stomachs." And of course there was music every step of the way. "When that band starts to swing, those cats would swing up a *mess*, no foolin'." When it was all over, close to midnight, he saw the lights floating across the city, converging on the freight yard, where their bearers returned the lamps to the shed. Even then, along the way, he could make a little extra money by selling the unused lamp oil to housewives and small businesses. And when he and the others finally did return the lamps, Captain Joe, mercifully, was nowhere to be seen.

The music was everywhere! A matter of life and death! Brass bands, Creole and black, marched through the streets of the city at any time for funerals. They were the New Orleans version of a West African custom. In West Africa, the Dahomeans and the Yoruba enlisted musicians to accompany the deceased to his final resting place, and they serenaded his spirit. In New Orleans, their slave descendants kept the tradition alive. Beginning in the eighteenth century, black funeral musicians adopted American military band instruments—drums and tubas and trumpets, the same as John Philip Sousa used. They even played some of the same songs—"English" airs of the late nineteenth century and hymns such as "Nearer, My God, to Thee." And they dressed in quasi-military apparel, with smart-looking caps, white shirts, and dark pants. A traditional funeral always began the same way, with the band assembling in the morning, then beginning with stately slow numbers, a few hymns, and the inevitable "Flee as a Bird" to accompany the deceased to his grave; this was a soft, lilting lament mingling sadness and release from mortal cares. These brass bands resembled the Salvation Army marching for the glory of Temperance, but the resemblance ended there. Although the New Orleans brass bands played their music soberly and respectfully at the start of a funeral, they soon allowed the rites to take wing and to become a dancing, singing celebration.

To hear Louis tell it, New Orleans funerals were about the least somber to be found anywhere, with the singing and carousing starting even before the funeral. "Night before a funeral," he said, "they have a wake, everybody sitting all night around the body singing. You come in there, lead off a hymn and go right back in the kitchen and get cheese, crackers, whiskey, beer. Boy, they shouting! Brother's rocking that coffin."

Rocking the coffin: there was a New Orleans superstition, and one to which Louis claims to have subscribed. In the days before embalming became prevalent, it was held that "some bodies used to come back to life. The body would raise up and sit there on that slab, and imagine all them people trying all at once to get out of one little bitty door." Louis also liked to tell a story that mocked this superstition. At the wake of a deceased Elks Club member, Brother Jones, another brother touched the departed's forehead, which felt a trifle warm for a corpse. He went to the kitchen, where they were serving food and liquor, and he found the widow there. "Mrs. Jones," he told her, "I just touched Brother Jones's forehead and he seemed a little warm to me." The widow, who had been crying, suddenly stopped, dried her eyes, and looked right at him. "Hot or cold," she declared, "he's going out of here tomorrow."

As a young boy, Louis followed a locally renowned drummer, Harry Zeno, in many a funeral procession. On the way to the cemetery, Zeno would play softly. But on the way back, when things were considerably more lively, he "would pull the handkerchief from under his snare drum. . . . He would actually thrill me when he'd make a long clean roll on his snare. . . . Harry Zeno would start the march, then he'd get his cue from the cornet player—the leader to start 'em up, and old Black Benny"—this was the bass drummer, who later loomed as a superhuman figure in Louis's life—"would hit that bass drum three times to be exact—Boom Boom Boom."

On the way back from the graveyard—or, to be more precise, the aboveground vaults, those Cities of the Dead that gave New Orleans its otherwordly, mythical air—the band would break into the other inevitable funeral song, the hair-raising, mournful, "Didn't He Ramble":

> *"Didn't he ram-ble? . . . Didn't he ram-ble? . . . He was a good man 'til the Butcher cut him down . . ."*

The music of New Orleans never stopped. "There was so much music when I was growing up in New Orleans that you couldn't help but hear it," Louis recalled. And nowhere was the music more concentrated than in his own dangerous and wonderful Battlefield neighborhood. "There was all sorts of honky-tonks on every corner of Liberty, Perdido, Franklin, and Poydras streets. Mostly, they just had a piano player working there, but sometimes they had other instruments as well. There was Spano's, Red Onion, Kid Brown's, Henry Ponce's, and Matranga's. Just around the corner on Perdido Street was the Funky Butt Hall. On Saturday night the band would play for about half an hour outside to advertise themselves, so the people would know about it. Then they would come in for the dance. It was a beat-up old place with big cracks in the wall and we would go down and look through the cracks and see all them chicks dancin' and shakin' everything."

The music they played wasn't called jazz, not in those days. "When I was a little boy, five years old," Louis recalled, "it was called ragtime music," by which he meant the syncopated melodies popular since 1899, when the ragtime craze swept the land. Ragtime's irregular, conversational rhythms, the result of its "ragged time," introduced a compelling tension and informality that became one of the foundations of jazz, but at that time, it held sway on its own. Louis listened intently to it. "Whenever there was a dance or a lawn party the band, consisting of six men, they would stand in front of the place on the sidewalk and play a half an hour of good ragtime music. And us kids would stand or dance on the other side of the street until they went inside. That was the only way that we young kids could get the chance to hear those great musicians such as Buddy Bolden, Joe Oliver (my idol), Bunk Johnson, Freddie Keppard . . . and a whole lot of the other players who will forever live in my mind as the greatest musicians that I have ever heard since I was big enough to realize what was happening."

Buddy Bolden! Young Louis was in the thrall of this legend, the prototypical jazz horn player. "So far as any of us know who were born and brought up in New Orleans," Louis wrote, "this boy was really the first of them."

Bolden was the original Pied Piper of jazz, an alluring, doomed figure, half-man and half-myth. Like every other New Orleans musician, Louis knew the Bolden legend by heart. "He blazed himself into New Orleans with his cornet, as early as 1905, and they tell me people thought he was plumb crazy the way he tossed that horn." It was said that "Bolden used to blow so loud and strong that, on a still day . . . you could hear him a mile away." Improbable as it seems, the sound of his cornet may have been able to carry that distance, for another account claimed, "When Buddy Bolden played in the pecan grove over in Gretna, he could be heard across the river throughout uptown New Orleans." That was more like two miles. It was entirely possible that before the age of the automobile, especially late at night, when all was quiet, Bolden's piercing notes reverberated across the sleeping, silent city to stun those who listened.

At close quarters, the sheer force of his playing overwhelmed the competition. The reigning band at the time was the John Robichaux Orchestra, Creoles of Color whose style was more sophisticated and sweet than Bolden's rough, improvised power. Robichaux was considered *très distingué*, the epitome of the suave Downtown "musicianer," while Bolden was pure Uptown, a rough-edged "player." The rivalry between the Robichaux and Bolden forces was actually a clash of cultures, pitting the Downtown Creole population—a clannish, secretive group who identified strongly with France—against blacks, who had settled Uptown. To one old-timer, "the Creole people are slow. Maybe they depend a little too much on their pride. Don't mix with everybody. Don't trust everybody. They always in for society." In contrast, "Uptown, in the American part, other side of Canal Street, people had a different way. . . . They were sociable and more like entertainers. They played rougher, more *head* [improvised] music, more blues."

Buddy Bolden was Uptown to a tee. A crowd pleaser. He could be heard over at Miss Cole's Lawn Parties (actually an open-air dance pavilion), and, more often, in dance halls throughout the city's black districts, in places like Tin Type Hall, on Liberty Street. The Tin Type—now there was a place for jazz. By day, it served as a petty criminals' morgue, and every two-bit hustler and pimp who came to an early end was laid out there. By night, social clubs such as The Buzzards and The Mysterious Babies rented the Hall and hired Bolden's band to make the place jump. He played the city's Uptown dance halls, and he played the Downtown dance halls. Buddy Bolden's music was everywhere, delighting blacks and Creoles alike.

The Bolden Band and the Robichaux Orchestra often went head to head, with the winner determined by the audience. One night, down at the Mix Saloon, which was in Robichaux territory, the bands got into a fierce battle. At first Bolden prevailed, relying on his earsplitting volume, and blew the Robichaux men away, but then the Robichaux clarinetist, George Baquet, started in. He had this trick of twisting off a piece of his instrument as he played on it, and then another, and another, pretending all the while to play as if he held the entire instrument in his hands. When he was done, he was playing only the *mouthpiece*. Baquet's dexterity won the audience to his side, and as they cheered, a dismayed Bolden mouthed, "George, why did you do it?"

More often than not, though, Bolden was able to lure the audience away from his chief rival with a few strategically timed blasts of his instrument. It was said he could close a Robichaux dance by 10:30 simply by playing his cornet within earshot of the crowd. "Bolden used to put his horn out the window and start blowing the minute he got into the place, and they'd all leave Robichaux and traipse over to Bolden's," said one veteran of the New Orleans musical scene. "They said he was calling the children home."

There was more to account for Bolden's enduring appeal than musical virtuosity or volume. In addition to his music, he juggled a boisterous ménage of girlfriends. Buddy was catnip for women, and everybody knew it. "You was always hearing, for example, how he had three or four women living with him in the same house," said Sidney Bechet, the clarinetist, who also idolized Bolden. "He'd walk down the street and one woman, she'd have his trumpet, another, she'd carry his watch, and another, she'd have his handkerchief, and maybe there'd be another one who would have nothing to carry, but she'd be there all the same, hoping to carry something home." Buddy Bolden, the ladies' man, glamorized the image of the jazz musician in New Orleans. No wonder he made an impression on Louis, Sidney, and every other aspiring musician in New Orleans. Even Jelly Roll Morton, the jealous, self-proclaimed "inventor of jazz," paid tribute to Bolden, describing him as a unique phenomenon, "the most powerful trumpet in history . . . the blowingest man since Gabriel." Morton also left perhaps the clearest description of what Bolden actually looked like; he was a "light brown-skin boy from Uptown. He drank all the whiskey he could find, never wore a collar and tie, had his shirt busted open so all the girls could see that red flannel undershirt, always having a ball." The man set an example.

The memory of Buddy Bolden was preserved in his theme song, which reverberated along the streets and alleys of the city, across the outlying swamps, and through the opalescent mists drifting off the river:

> ". . . I thought I heard Buddy Bolden say . . . 'Dirty nasty stinky butt, take it away . . . Dirty nasty stinky butt, take it away . . . And let Mister Bolden play. . . .'"

If anyone played that song at the wrong time or in the wrong place, for example, out in the open where it was liable to cause a ruckus, the police would throw the offender into jail. But when Bolden played it at a dance, women wrapped change in their scented handkerchiefs and tossed them at him, and fights broke out as they competed for his attention. Bolden blew more than mere notes from his cornet; he seemed to blow magic, calling the children home.

The fact that he never made a recording—Buddy came along about ten years too early for that—only added to his mystique, because everyone was free to imagine the sound of the first great jazz musician without having to contend with a wax cylinder that might puncture his legend. Bill Matthews, a New Orleans trombonist who heard him often, captured the Bolden aura best: "Buddy Bolden always had his cornet with him, would pull it out in a barroom and play, him and his derby, when he'd get drunk. Buddy was the loudest trumpet player we ever had in the city of New Orleans." But, at the same time, "He was one of the sweetest trumpet players on waltzes and things like that, and on those old slow blues, that boy could make the women jump out the window. On those old, slow, low-down blues, he had a moan in his cornet that went all through you, just like you were in church or something. Everybody was crazy about Bolden when he'd blow a waltz, schottische, or old low-down blues. . . . He found those things to put in a blues . . . [that would] make a spiritual feeling go through you. He had a specially made cup that made that cornet moan like a Baptist preacher." Matthews insisted, "Not even Louis Armstrong had a tone like Bolden."

Louis never claimed outright that he actually heard Bolden play. What Armstrong did say was that if he had heard Bolden, it would have been in about 1906, when Louis was a small child. He might have passed a hall when Bolden was playing outside to advertise an upcoming dance. Anyway, no one could say Louis *hadn't* heard Bolden play the cornet.

Although his music was never recorded, his image was. There is one—and only one—extant photograph of Bolden; he is posing with his band and balancing a cornet in one hand. He appears to be a tall, dignified young man clearly proud of his instrument. He looks entirely contemporary, unaffected, casual, confident, not at all like the other musicians in the photo, whose stiff poses consign them to their time and place.

Buddy and the fellows in the band made a saloon on Gravier and Rampart their headquarters. It was a hole-in-the-wall place run by a man known only as "Mustache," and Buddy jokingly referred to it as his "office." Bolden's group, one of the first jazz bands, consisted of Bob Lyons, who played bass; Sam Dutrey on clarinet; Jimmie Palao on violin; Henry Zeno, the snare drummer whom Louis idolized; Frankie Dusen on trombone; and the guitar player, Brock Mumford. Buddy, who could make up a song about practically anything, even worked up a little tune for him, "The Old Cow Died and Old Brock Cried," that would survive under the title "Muskrat Ramble."

For a time, Buddy Bolden reigned as the first cornet king of New Orleans. Eventually, he ran into trouble, some of his own devising, some beyond his control. For starters, Buddy wasn't very good about paying the other musicians. He'd stall by telling them he had to cash a check, or agreeing to meet them at a certain time and place, and then failing to show up. Finally, the men decided they'd had enough of this treatment, and when they were playing the Masonic Hall, one of the rougher venues around town, they replaced Buddy Bolden with a fellow named Edward Clem, just like that. Buddy arrived late for the gig, as usual, and when he saw Clem blowing the cornet, he turned to Frankie Dusen, the trombonist, and asked if they were using two cornets now. Dusen shook his head. "What're you gonna do with the King?" Bolden said, meaning himself.

Dusen shot back, "You can go back home."

"You're gonna put me out of my own band?"

"I'm the King now," Dusen announced.

And that was how Buddy lost his band.

In 1906, he started showing signs of mental instability, muttering to himself and acting peculiar. He might have been suffering from severe manic depression or the effects of syphilis, but whatever the cause, he suffered a breakdown. While marching in the 1906 Labor Day parade, he went on a rampage. Several days later he was arrested. He was soon freed, but his dementia quickly advanced to the point where he lost his interest in his music and his barbershop. He rarely ventured outside. His charisma vanished, and he fell prey to paranoid fantasies. The following year, when he was only twenty-eight years old, he was confined to the East Louisiana State Hospital, an insane asylum, where he lived in a docile, befuddled state until his death in 1931.

Tears never lasted long in the New Orleans of Louis's memories and reveries, and distractions abounded. Even the pimps and hustlers who populated the Battlefield took time out from their occupations to field a respectable baseball team that participated in an informal black league. Louis always remembered a special Sunday when he joined up with a group of kids from the neighborhood to follow their league out to Algiers, a small town across the Mississippi River in rural Louisiana. The only thing at stake in the game, aside from neighborhood pride, was a keg of beer. "McDonald Cemetery was just about a mile away from where the Black Diamonds (my team) was playing the Algiers team," Louis wrote. "Whenever a funeral from New Orleans had a body to be buried in the McDonald Cemetery, they would have to cross the Canal Street ferry boat, and march down the same road right near our ball game. Of course when they passed us, playing a slow funeral march, we only paused with the game and tipped our hats to pay respect. When the last of the funeral passed, we would continue the game."

This particular game was well underway when the Onward Brass Band, a marching outfit led by Joe Oliver, retraced their steps from the cemetery, pounding out a jubilant "It's a Long Way to Tipperary" as they went. "They were swinging so good until Joe Oliver reached up into the high register, bearing out those *high notes in very fine fashion*, and broke our ball. *Yeah*." No wonder Louis was impressed—who else could blow his horn loud enough to shatter a baseball? The youngsters lost all interest in the game and followed the Onward Brass Band back to town.

"My favorite was Joe Oliver," Louis decided after that startling incident. "Joe was so good to me, even when I was a kid. When he was marching with the Onward Brass Band, they'd stop for a rest, and he would let me hold his horn. He knew this meant a lot to me, so he showed me how to put my mouth to it and get a note. Joe was always real nice to me." Even as a boy, Louis sensed that Joe Oliver possessed larger intellectual and emotional capacities than other cornet "kings" of New Orleans, and his instincts proved accurate—so accurate that his admiration for Oliver, sustained over many years, eventually led to the partnership that secured the reputation of both men. Of all the musicians Louis heard as a youth— drummers, hornmen, clarinetists, and string players—Oliver was the one who influenced him most. "Joe Oliver was the baddest sombitch in Storyville on cornet—*B'lieve* that," Louis insisted. He was unique, in Louis's estimation, because he was a "creator, with unlimited ideas, and had a heart as big as a whale when it came to helping the underdog in music, such as me. I was just a kid, [but] Joe saw I had possibilities and he'd go out of his way to help me or any other ambitious kid."

Music was coming at Louis from all directions by this time. In addition to meeting Joe Oliver, he developed a fascination with the notorious Funky Butt Hall, at 1319 Perdido Street, in the middle of an area teeming with prostitutes. Officially called Union Sons' Hall, or Kinney's Hall, Funky Butt, as everyone called it, was the closest dance hall to Louis's home, and it was the first place where he heard the music later called jazz. As the name indicated, Funky Butt was a tight, smelly, dirty place. And it drew Louis and his young friends like a magnet. "On Saturday nights, Mama couldn't find us 'cause we wanted to hear that music. Before the dance, the band would play out front about half an hour. And us little kids would all do little dances." Once the music moved inside, "we'd go look through the big cracks in the wall of the Funky Butt." Cracks, Funky Butt—as Louis was the first to admit, this spawning ground of the great American art form "wasn't no classyfied place, just a big old room with a bandstand."

More than music drew him to Funky Butt. There were those precious glimpses of forbidden adult rites. "To a tune like 'The Bucket's Got a Hole In It,' some of them chicks would get way down, shake everything, slapping themselves on the cheeks of their behind. Yeah!" But amid the licentiousness, the patrons of the Funky Butt participated in moments of surprising elegance. "At the end of the night, they'd do the quadrille, beautiful to see, where everybody lined up, crossed over—if no fights hadn't started before that. Cats'd have to take their razors in with them, because they might have to scratch somebody before they left there." Fighting was only to be expected. If a cat wanted to show respect for his chick, which was rare but not unheard of, he would ask her to stick out her elbow, and he would balance his hat on it. The hats were Stetsons, brand new, and very expensive, as much as six months' salary. And if anyone so much as grazed that Stetson balancing precariously on a chick's shivering elbow, there would be hell to pay. "Did you touch my hat?" the offended party would demand. And if the other cat admitted he did, which was the manly thing to do, "he hit him right in the chops."

Louis relished these spectacles, but his family was still desperately poor, and when he wasn't gawking at the pimps, whores, and hustlers in the neighborhood, he was scrapping for pennies and nickels. So many of his childhood memories return to this theme, the necessity of earning money, and all the ways he went about trying to get it when he had nothing to hustle but energy and enthusiasm. From the time he could go about the city on his own, he spent most of his free time thinking about ways of bringing money into the house. He remembered himself no more than a "li'l ol' kid, selling newspapers up and down Baronne Street, St. Charles Street, Canal

Street, in fact all those busy streets." He'd get around by hopping street-cars, "selling and hollering, 'Paper! Paper! Read the New Orleans *Item*! Paper! Paper!' And sometimes, the streetcar would not slow down, and the first time I went to jump off one of them, I wasn't hip to trotting a little bit when jumping off, and, my Gawd, I couldn't sit down for a week."

Despite everything, his hustling newspapers and his mother's work as a laundress, the family remained destitute. He resorted to collecting discarded potatoes and onions, which he sold to restaurants for a few pennies. He even found employment in the flesh trade. "Us kids would pound up a bucket of red brick dust and sell it to the prostitutes on Saturday mornings, make maybe fifty or seventy cents. Every Saturday they'd scrub their steps down with pee and then they'd throw the brick dust on the sidewalk in front, and that brought them luck Saturday night. That was their superstition." With the little bit of money he earned, he often bought himself a poor boy sandwich: "a half a loaf of that long bread, real dry, and a real thin slice of ham between it. You get it for five cents, and I've seen days in New Orleans when a poor boy sandwich would seem just like a chicken sandwich."

Desperate for money, Louis's mother returned to prostitution—"selling fish," or "her little hustle in the white folks' yard," as her son called it. Throughout her life, Mayann impressed everyone who knew her, especially her children, as dignified and private, and for her to resort to selling herself could only mean that she was in dire straits, with no other way to put food on the table. Whatever she did in order to earn money to feed herself and her two young children, it was private, and limited. She herself was not a creature of the New Orleans red-light district known as Storyville, trying to lure customers to her crib; the only men she allowed into her home were her hapless boyfriends—whom Louis called "stepfathers"—not those who paid for sex. Throughout his life, Louis knew who was responsible for his mother's turning to "selling fish": the father who had fled the day he was born.

At this desperate impasse, young Louis had the good fortune to find a job that earned a few pennies and nickels and, more importantly, that brought him into close contact with an entire family that showed him the possibility of another way of life in New Orleans. Through their association with this child, the Karnoffskys inadvertently became one of the earliest and most important incubators of American jazz. Louis, in turn, remained indebted to them throughout his life; indeed, their importance to him only increased as the years passed and he became ever more removed from New Orleans. In the autobiographical writings of his middle years, he scarcely mentions the Karnoffskys, but in his last years, when he felt the hand of death upon his shoulder, his memories turned again and again to the Karnoffskys with a fond obsessiveness as he explored their importance in his emotional life, racial perceptions, and musical development. The family captured his heart and his imagination. From the time he was a small boy to the end of his days, Louis was infatuated with Jews as a result of his association with the Karnoffskys.

Louis painstakingly recorded the family's history. "The Karnoffsky family came to America from somewhere in Russia [actually, it was Lithuania] a long time before I was born. They came to New Orleans as poor as Job's turkey. They settled in a neighborhood which was nothing but a gang of old run-down houses with the privies out in the backyard. If they rented the house or bought it, I did not know for sure. . . . The house was old, but since things were so tough for them at that time, they made the best of it and fixed it up real nice."

Their sons—Morris, who was twenty, and Alex, nineteen—went into business as junk peddlers, and Louis joined in their humble rounds. "I alternated with the two sons," he proudly recalled. "One went out into the street buying old rags, bones, iron, bottles, any kind of old junk. Go back to the house with the big yard, empty the wagon, pile up the old rags in one place, the bottles, bones, and the rest of the junk, all in separate places. Soon there would be big piles of everything. There was enough room for piles of stone coal which the older son, Morris, sold in the streets also. Especially in the red-light district—mostly in the evenings way into the nights. He sold it for five cents a water bucket to lots of the sporting women standing in the doorways. Hell, I was singing selling coal: *'Stone coal, lady! Nickel a water bucket! Stone coal, nickel a water bucket!* . . .'

"The bottoms of those buckets was all pounded up so maybe three or four big lumps would fill it. The women would be standing there in the doorways to their cribs wearing their 'teddie'—that was a famous uniform they had, all silk, like baby bloomers only transparent. One of them would call, 'Commere, boy. Bring me three buckets.' And it was for me to go in them cribs and for a quarter extra start them fires. And I'd take my little quick peek, you know, scared she'd catch me, slap me and shove me out of there. But they didn't pay me no mind. Just a stone-coal boy—breathing like a bitch, man."

Louis realized he was entering forbidden territory, here in Storyville, partly because of his age—"I only could get a quick peep at the girls while they were standing there at the door almost naked"—and partly because of his color—"Since the red-light district was strictly all white, we Negroes were not allowed to buy anything sexy. Some of those girls who were standing in the doorway of those cribs they looked just like a bunch of girls who had just finished high school or just received their diplomas from college. They looked *so* young. They all had pimps to give their money to."

Young as he was, Louis realized his glimpse of life in Storyville came solely as a result of his association with the Karnoffskys. "As long as I was working for the white man, I could witness all of this." He enjoyed his peculiar status, for "even the tough cops didn't bother me. And believe me, they were really tough"—tough enough to whip the heads of the hapless whores in the district or break Louis's leg if they had a mind to. After a while, though, he became a familiar sight to the cops, the industrious child on the coal cart, who helped deliver nickel buckets of coal to the whores.

Prostitution loomed large in Louis's life because it was fundamental to New Orleans. The city had long enjoyed a reputation for licentiousness found nowhere else in the United States. The first women in the city were prostitutes who sold their bodies to leather-clad frontiersmen skimming along the Mississippi on flatboats and to sailors arriving at the port of New Orleans at the end of a long journey at sea. From the start, the authorities attempted to contain prostitution or to endow it with a pretense of respectability. When the French ceded control of New Orleans to the Americans in 1803, laws sprang up to prevent prostitutes from plying their trade on the ground floor of buildings. By midcentury, they were required to apply to the city for licenses; in fact, the mayor was personally responsible for approving their applications.

Police and local officials tolerated prostitution, but they tried repeatedly to find some way to contain it as they danced around social hypocrisy. An ordinance calling for compulsory medical examinations of prostitutes was well on the way to becoming law when the women of New Orleans banded together to condemn the proposal as an "insult to Southern womanhood," and the plan died. Thus prostitution persisted, fed by the city's insatiable appetite for entertainment and gratification and by a constant influx of sailors from the Mississippi and the Gulf of Mexico.

In 1897, Sidney Story, a city alderman who had made a study of the issue, cajoled the City Council into adopting another ordinance, inspired by European models, to identify an area in the French Quarter as the "official" red-light district of New Orleans. So began a remarkable experiment in social engineering. Beginning in October of that year, any "prostitute or woman notoriously abandoned to lewdness" could live and work only within carefully prescribed boundaries: "From the South Side of Customhouse Street to the North Side of St. Louis Street, and from the lower or wood side of North Basin Street to the lower or wood side of Robertson Street. . . . And from the upper side of Perdido Street to the lower side of Gravier Street, and from the river side of Franklin Street to the lower or wood side of Locust Street." After adjustments to its borders, the district eventually consisted of thirty-eight blocks given over to brothels, saloons, gambling dens, and honky-tonks. Although a few prostitutes refused to be herded like cattle and departed, the overwhelming majority remained, and their wages helped to double rents in the district, which became known as "Storyville."

Louis considered the name a pointless euphemism, "just like someone telling a joke and beating around the bush when they get to the punch line because it is risqué." Storyville was, he said, "a phony name . . . which has never registered with me like the magic word, 'red-light district.' It sounds more musical to say the real thing." In time, Storyville became synonymous around the country, and later the world, with prostitution, a development that absolutely appalled Sidney Story. The alderman had intended to throw a *cordon sanitaire* around the district, to limit if not strangle it. Instead, his measures glorified and institutionalized prostitution in his city.

With its new, legally sanctioned status, prostitution in New Orleans prospered as never before. A single block in Storyville boasted as many as fourteen brothels, some of them small town houses, others large hotels. The largest of them all, Josie Arlington's well-known establishment at 225 North

Basin Street, employed hundreds of working girls. Her customers were exclusively white, as were all the customers in segregated Storyville. Some years later, in 1917, the City Council instituted a smaller, black Storyville, not far from its white counterpart, but whenever Louis described the sights and sounds of Storyville, he was invariably referring to the larger and more lurid white Storyville. Although the *customers* were whites only, the prostitutes were mixed: black, white, and Creole. (Creole women of color were the most desirable prostitutes in Storyville, considered the most beautiful and passionate, much to the horror of the city's old established Creole families, who raised their daughters in virtual seclusion, under strict Catholic guidelines lest they fall into a life of shame.) Inside, however, the establishments were rigorously segregated. Brothels offering white whores lined one side of a street, brothels featuring blacks the other. If they shared the same side of the street, the white brothels were designated by even street numbers, and blacks by odd ones. Jim Crow ruled even here.

By the time Louis was selling coal in the district, Storyville had become a national scandal and tourist attraction. Popular songs celebrated its vices (*Gimme a pig foot . . . An' a bottle of beer . . . Send me gate I don't care . . . Gimme reefer . . . An' a gang of gin . . . Slay me 'cause . . . I'm in my sin*) and its notorious characters (*Did you ever hear about Cocaine Lil? . . . She had cocaine hair on her cocaine head . . . She had a cocaine dress that was poppy red . . . But the cocaine blues, they made her sad . . . Oh, the cocaine blues, they made her feel bad*). The city fathers who had expected that creating a special district would contain prostitution were proven wrong, and whores of every color, variety, age, and inclination flourished within its borders as never before. Madames routinely placed a dollar on their doorstep each day to ensure the continued cooperation and goodwill of the police.

Storyville's entire cast of characters advertised in a well-organized, handsomely printed, widely distributed register known as *The Blue Book*. The annual edition, running to fifty pages, listed virtually every brothel in the district, complete with addresses, phone numbers, and photographs. Every prostitute was listed in alphabetical order, in separate columns for "white" and "colored women," each with her address. (There were a few men, but the prostitutes were nearly all female.) *The Blue Book* proclaimed its importance to readers for several reasons: "First, because it is the only district of its kind in the States set aside for the fast women by law. Second, because it puts the stranger on a proper and safe path as to where he may go and be free from 'Hold-ups' and any other game usually practiced upon the stranger. Third, it regulates the women so that they may live in one district to themselves instead of being scattered over the city."

Many bold new styles of music resounded throughout the crowded quarters of Storyville, but the real soundtrack of Storyville's revelry and debauchery and merriment and drug-taking and amorality and sensuality and freedom and decadence, its unique mixture of pleasure and perversity, was jazz. Or to be more precise, the music that would later come to be called "jazz." The larger brothels featured pianists, often playing ragtime, and a small dance orchestra playing through the night.

Street musicians, usually adolescent boys, were another important feature of the Storyville musical scene. They roamed through the streets in small groups, six or seven of them, playing a wild, improvised brand of music not heard anywhere else. The best known of these groups was the seven-man Spasm Band, and soon other spasm bands sprang up throughout Storyville. This was the era before recordings, so there is no way to know exactly how the spasm bands sounded, but on the basis of descriptions left by those who heard them, they were early, primitive jazz bands, short on sophistication but long on novelty. They featured harmonicas, fiddles, and brass, drums of every description, whistles, cowbells, gourds, and bizarre homemade instruments. When they blew, the hornmen often placed hats over their trumpets or stuffed whatever objects they could find into them, even a toilet plunger—anything to modify the sound. They played while dancing, or standing on their heads, and shouting "hi-de-ho" and "ho-de-ho," expressions imported from old Mississippi River songs. They frequently punctuated their music with howls and growls and wild calls to one another, or to their audiences gathering on the sidewalk outside the brothels and gambling joints, their rude cacophony drowning out the sweet sounds emanating from within. The spasm bands would play for a quarter, a nickel, even a penny.

By the time Louis started working in Storyville, spasm bands were everywhere. Much of the adult Armstrong's characteristic stage act, the laughing, joking, and singing, to say nothing of his distinctive growl, owes a distinct debt to the antics of the spasm bands he saw on his early treks through Storyville.

. . .

Young Louis embraced the music, women, tonks, and musicians of his raucous neighborhood. Above all, he was mesmerized by Joe Oliver. "I was just a youngster who loved that horn of King Oliver's," he said. "I would delight delivering an order of stone coal to the prostitute who used to hustle in her crib right next to Pete Lala's Cabaret. Just so's I could hear King Oliver play . . . I was too young to go into Pete Lala's at the time. And I'd just stand there in that lady's crib listening to King Oliver. And I'm all in a daze. That was the only way we kids could go into the district—I mean Storyville. I'd stand there listening to King Oliver beat out one of those good ol' good ones like 'Panama' or 'High Society.' My, what a punch that man had. And he could shout a tune. Ump.

"All of a sudden it would dawn on the lady that I was still in her crib very silent as she hustled those tricks, and she'd say, 'What's the matter with you, boy? Why are you still here standing so quiet?' And there I'd have to explain to her that I was being inspired by *the* King Oliver and his orchestra. And then she handed me a cute one by saying, 'Well, this is no place to daydream. I've got my work to do.' So I'd go home very pleased and happy that I did at least hear my idol blow at least a couple of numbers that really *gassed* me to no end."

At the time, there were at least a hundred nightclubs and brothels and tonks where jazz was played in Storyville. Many emerging jazz performers had their favorite joint, but for young Louis, Pete Lala's was the most important one. Maybe it was because King Oliver and the rest of that gang hung around there. "What a band he had at Pete Lala's. Oh, that music sounded so good. In that band he had Buddy Christian on the piano, Professor Nicholson on the clarinet, Zoo Robinson on the trombone, himself on the cornet, and Henry Zeno on drums." Louis got to know them all. To hear him tell it, they considered him special, perhaps because he regarded them with undisguised hero worship. "They seemed to treat me (as a youngster) so much nicer and take more time with me than the others. Then, too, I didn't go around any other place at all, because I was always a King Oliver disciple, ever since I could tell one note from another."

Oliver was a large solidly built man with one bad eye, the legacy of a fight, it was said. He was in his midthirties when Louis first encountered him, and just coming into his own as a cornet player. Like other musicians in New Orleans, he could not earn his living from performing alone. He worked as a butler for a prosperous white family, and it was easy to see him in that role, for his dignified bearing carried over into his music. From the start, young Louis was attracted to him, and cast Oliver in the role of adoptive father. "He had a good heart," Louis always insisted, and throughout his life, Oliver's goodness and generosity were articles of faith.

Although others dwelled on Oliver's seriousness and sense of self-discipline, Louis found him to be "full of jokes in those days. He played a good one on his piano player Buddy Christian. One night Buddy came to work all dressed up in a beautiful white suit he had just bought. It being a real hot summer night Buddy wore this suit. And at that time King Oliver used to chew tobacco even while he played his cornet. (Of course, I tried to adapt every little trait that King Oliver had, but honest, I just couldn't go for that tobacco chewing jive. *Oh, yass*, I tried it, and it damn near killed me. At least I thought I was dying, it made me so sick.) Anyway, Buddy came to work looking all pretty 'n' everything, and King Oliver waited until Buddy got ready to sit down at the piano, and just before he sat, the King reached up and got his big wad of chewed tobacco out of his mouth and sat it on Buddy's chair, and Buddy (all smiles greeting everybody) sat right down on this wet tobacco. Ump. Of course, it was over half an hour before he began to feel something penetrating through his pants, and when he turned around and looked, the whole cabaret laughed real heartily over it. Buddy was such a good natured guy he laughed it off, and King had his suit cleaned. King Oliver said as he apologized that white suit was so tempting he just couldn't resist it."

Louis drew a little moral from the story. "You see, in those days, musicians weren't so sensitive and didn't carry chips on their shoulders like you might among these present day musicians. Nowadays, if you tell a youngster the right way pertaining to playing your music, or ask him not to break certain rules you have as far as your orchestra, you're liable to get sapped up."

Of all the sidemen in King Oliver's band, Henry Zeno, the drummer, whom Louis remembered from funerals, fascinated him the most. The man seemed to have it all: musical ability, women, and a magnificent aura of danger about him. "Ah, there was a drummer for ya. He had a press roll that one very seldom hears nowadays. And was he popular with all the prostitutes, pimps, gamblers, hustlers, everybody. Most of the pimps were good gamblers also, and Henry Zeno was in there with them. He even had several prostitutes on his staff working for him. By that he would handle more cash than the average musician. And he was a little short dark sharp cat and knew all the answers. He even was great in a street parade. He also played in the Onward Brass Band, which was made up of the top-notch musicians and featuring on the cornets Emanuel Perez and King Oliver. And you never heard a brass band swing in your whole life like those boys . . . Ump Ump Ump."

Zeno and his type congregated at the "famous gambling joint" known as "25," which Louis observed closely. "That was the place where all the big-time pimps and hustlers would congregate and play 'cotch' (that's a game they played with three cards shuffled and dealt from the bottom of the deck). And you could win or lose a whole gang of money. These pimps and hustlers, et cetera, would spend most of their time at '25' until their girls would finish turning tricks in their cribs. Then they would meet them and check up on the night's take. Lots of the prostitutes lived in different sections of the city and would come down to Storyville just like they had a job. There were different shifts for them. Sometimes, two prostitutes would share the rent in the same crib together. One would work in the day and the other would beat out that night shift. And business was so good in those days with the fleet of sailors and the crews from those big ships that come in the Mississippi River from all over the world—kept them very busy."

If Louis learned anything from the scenes he observed in "25," it concerned human nature rather than gambling. Louis rarely gambled; instead, he watched the dramas played out all around him, each one a free-form morality play about love and death.

There was his friend Joe Jones, a young drummer who was one of "25"'s regular cast of characters. Jones fell "madly in love" with a beautiful young whore. Her name was Neeta, and to Louis's surprise, "she made him put down those drums, never to play again." Jones "automatically left me and the rest of the youngsters to be a big-time pimp at '25'." For a time, Joe Jones seemed to have it all, "living the life of ease, neglecting his music entirely," until "this chick ran out from under him. She fell in love with another pimp and nixed him out all of sudden. Then Joe Jones actually fell in love with another gal from Storyville. He even married her. And after a while she did the same thing as Neeta did. This, Joe Jones couldn't take. He got so despondent he tried committing suicide. He took a razor and slashed his throat. He came pretty near doing a good job of it." Louis saw the pattern repeated endlessly in Storyville: "a good-looking young boy would get excited at the idea of a young woman giving him money to put in his pockets every day, which automatically made him feel that he was really somebody important. So I'd say the women weren't to blame. It's those weak-minded youngsters."

There were so many other characters in and around "25"! There was Big George Callioux, a pretty fair hustler, as was his brother Jean. There were the Moore brothers, Morris and Godfrey, and Chinee Morris, and that blistering drummer, Redhead Happy. And then there was the man known simply as Crook, if only because "he wore his mouth one-sided all the time. Evidently he must have had a stroke somewheres through life." Crook was so tough "he would catch the boys from other neighborhoods and beat them to a pulp. Even the cops of Storyville were afraid to tackle him. Only one youngster had nerve enough to jump him and that was Black Benny, who lived in the Third Ward, the part of the city where I came from." That's how tough Black Benny was—even tougher than Crook! "He would go anywhere he wanted in New Orleans and wasn't afraid of nobody living. He and this character Crook tied into each other one night, and believe me, it was something. Black Benny being a dern good man with his dukes as well as beating a bass drum to a perfection. He took ol' Crook just like Grant took Richmond."

Louis came to understand how fragile life was, how suddenly it could end, especially in a place like "25." There, "you could run into . . . Clerk Wade, who was so great a pimp in Storyville that he wore diamonds in his garters. He was a sharp black boy. Of course, Clerk was killed by one of his whores when he was standing at the bar in '25' and she came in to ask him to take her back, and he shunned her and abused her lightly in front of the other pimps. She stood back and pulled out a shiny pistol and emptied it into his body. Clerk died right there on the spot. The district was very sad about it for days and days."

In Storyville, the death of a big pimp and gambler like Clerk Wade became the occasion for an extravagant New Orleans funeral, and Louis never forgot the spectacle. "The day Clerk was buried, I never saw so many girls crying over one man in my whole life. All the pimps turned out, also all the prostitutes—colored and white. Some of the pimps were pall-bearers. He was so famous even the respectable people of the city [and] the churches were all sad over his death." As for his murderer, the woman he'd scorned, she went before the judge and pleaded guilty, explaining in her defense that she "supported him and hustled for him and gave him every nickel she could rake and scrape." This being New Orleans, she was acquitted.

Big as Clerk Wade's funeral was, the funeral of Henry Zeno, who died not long afterward, "of natural causes," was even bigger. "The day of the funeral there were so many people that gathered from all sections of the town you couldn't get within ten blocks of the house where Henry Zeno was laid out," Louis recalled. "There were as many white people there to pay their last respects for a great drummer man and his comrades, and the people who lived the same life as he did, and the people who just loved to go to funerals no matter who dies. Although I was only a youngster, I was right in there amongst them. I had the advantage over the other kids by meeting great men such as Henry Zeno and King Oliver, so it broke my heart, too."

In the seventy years since the demise of the Storyville of Louis's boyhood, historians and scholars have made a determined effort to place a fig leaf over the origins of jazz and have argued strenuously against the obvious, that it was born in whorehouses and on the sidewalks in front of whore-houses, and that it came of age in these establishments. They have tried to drag it into the concert hall, the radio studio, the church, the nightclub, anywhere but the down-and-dirty honky-tonks, dives, brothels, gambling and dope dens described by the emerging jazz figures of New Orleans, all in the hope of conferring legitimacy on it. But legitimacy would have been the death of the authentic American music known as jazz. It was the bastard child of several colliding, overlapping cultures, of ethnic groups often at war with one another, and its isolation from the academy or the Establish-ment was precisely why it was so lively. The written, oral, and recorded reminiscences of those intimately involved in the early days of jazz are silent on the subject of stately nightclubs or dignified concert halls. Instead, they relentlessly emphasize two kinds of locations where they performed: dance halls and whorehouses.

Jelly Roll Morton, the self-proclaimed "inventor of jazz," was as responsible as anyone for popularizing it, and when he discussed its origins, and his own youth, he dwelled on his apprenticeship playing piano in Storyville brothels, which were respectable enough for him. In fact, he couldn't imagine jazz coming into being in any other kind of environment. Storyville, to his way of thinking, and to Louis Armstrong's, was the logical breeding ground for this music. Louis accepted the social environment of jazz in a matter-of-fact manner (after all, he grew up next to Storyville), but Jelly Roll was enthralled by the scenes of debauchery swirling endlessly around him. He could never quite get over the gaudy sights and sounds of the place. It was, he said, "something that nobody has ever seen before or since. Hundreds of men were passing through the streets day and night. The chippies in their little-girl dresses were standing in the crib doors singing the blues. . . . Police were always in sight, never less than two together, which guaranteed the safety of all concerned. Lights of all colors were glittering and glaring. Music was pouring into the streets from every house." He supposed the scene outdid Paris, what with every type of prostitute selling herself in Storyville, "some very happy, some very sad, some with the desire to end it all by poison, some planning a big outing, a dance, or some other kind of enjoyment. Some were real ladies in spite of their downfall and some were habitual drunkards and some were dope fiends as follows: opium, heroin, cocaine, laudanum, morphine, et cetera. I was personally sent to Chinatown many times with a sealed note and a small amount of money and would bring back several cards of 'hop'—opium."

When a girl became a prostitute, she usually shed her name and was known only by her nickname to customers and to the police. Flamin' Mamie, Crying Emma, Bucktown Bessie, Big Butt Annie, Bird Leg Nora, Gold Tooth Gussie, Yard Dog, Sugar Pie, Cherry Red, Buck Tooth Rena, Boxcar Shorty, Tenderloin Thelma, Lily the Crip, Three Finger Annie, and Miss Thing were some of the better-known whores in circulation when Louis was a boy. The brothels were as varied as their inhabitants. They included "creep joints where they'd put the feelers on a guy's clothes, cribs that rented for about five dollars a day and had just about room enough for a bed, [and] small-time houses where the price was from fifty cents to a dollar and they put on naked dances, circuses, and jive." At the other end of the spectrum, the big famous houses boasted mirrored parlors and the best piano players in New Orleans.

The most famous of all the establishments was Lulu White's. Like other madams, Lulu published a "souvenir booklet" to extol the charms of her establishment, and a handsome piece of work it was. It proclaimed that her house, "unquestionably the most elaborately furnished house in the city of New Orleans," was "built of marble and is four story; containing five parlors, all handsome furnished, and fifteen bedrooms." There was even an elevator "built for two," hot water, and steam heat. It was, the brochure claimed, the only brothel "where you can get three shots for your money— The shot upstairs, the shot downstairs, and the shot in the room." A biographical sketch of Miss Lulu explained that she was a thirty-one-year-old "West Indian octoroon" who, shortly after arriving in New Orleans, quickly learned "what the other sex was in search of." Not only that, but she was well-educated (so the brochure said), "having made a lifelong study of music and literature." Furthermore, "it would not be amiss to say that besides possessing an elegant form she has beautiful black hair and blue eyes, which have justly gained for her the title of the 'Queen of the Demi-Monde.'"

Like so many others in New Orleans, Louis was in awe of Lulu, and he described her appeal. "Lulu White was a famous woman of the sporting world in Storyville. She had a big house on Basin Street called Mahogany Hall. The song was written after her house had gotten so famous. Rich men came there from all parts of the world to dig those beautiful Creole prostitutes. And pay big money." Jazz thrived in other famous brothels, and the musicians lucky enough to find work in them earned more money than they ever thought possible while the gig lasted. "Around the corner from Lulu White was the famous cabaret of Tom Anderson. All the racehorse men went there during their stay and the racing season in New Orleans. In those days a band who played for those places didn't need to worry about salaries. Their tips were so great they did not have to even touch their nightly gappings. Most of the places paid off the musicians every night after the job was over instead of the weekly deal. That was because those places threatened to close any minute so the musicians and the performers didn't take any chances."

Colored madams, Creole whores, white patrons: that was Storyville, layer upon layer of sexual and social hypocrisy. Louis wasn't particularly upset about the racial games played at Lulu White's, though he conceded the arrangement was a "crazy deal." Mainly, he saw the place as a fabulous venue for a musician, where he could make so much money playing from the tips alone that he needn't worry about his salary. The piano was the brothel instrument par excellence, refined and cultivated, and a good brothel pianist played rags, and, occasionally, blues. "It was sweet, just like a hotel," said Clarence Williams, the pioneering black musical entrepreneur, of the Storyville nights of his youth. Many of these whorehouse pianists also doubled as pimps, sticking close to their girls by playing piano in the brothels. For many musicians, piano-playing was a sideline, except for Jelly Roll Morton, who supposed his claim to fame would rest on his musical accomplishments rather than his career as a pimp.

Not all the music in Storyville was sweet ragtime. "Why, you should have seen the [jam] sessions we had then," said Williams. " 'Round about four a.m., the girls would get through work and meet their P.I.'s (that's what we called pimps) at the wine rooms. Pete Lala's was the headquarters, the place where all the bands would come when they got off work, and where the girls would come to meet their main man. . . . Some of the P.I.'s would wear diamonds the size of dimes. And . . . you could buy all of the cocaine, morphine, heroin, and hop you wanted in the section, almost right out in the open. But I never knew hardly any musicians that took dope. It was mostly the girls who were out to destroy themselves if their man left them." Whatever their condition, "Everybody would gather every night and there'd be singin' and playin' all night long. The piano players from all over the South would be there, in for the races, and everybody would take a turn until daylight."

For all the excitement of Storyville and its rites, young Louis remained an observer rather than a participant. He continued to labor for the Karnoffsky family, and it was they, in a roundabout way, who provided him with his first opportunity to blow his horn.

He actually enjoyed the work and the routine. "They couldn't pay me much money. But at my age and as times were so hard I was glad just to be working and very happy so I could help my mother and sister. She [Louis's mother] had a job at a beat-up paper place where they bundled up old newspapers and made bales with them and sold them to some other company. She was paid fifty cents a day, and with my little fifty cents from each brother we managed pretty good. Mama Lucy [Louis's younger sister] was five years old. Too young to work, so we gave her the job of a housekeeper. One thing that I couldn't help but notice about the Karnoffskys, was poor as they were they weren't lazy people." Louis admired their quiet determination to overcome the obstacles facing immigrant families. "They suffered so badly in their early days in New Orleans. I shall always love them. I learned a lot from them about how to live—real life and determination. God bless them. Whatever they accomplished they certainly deserve it."

Watching the Karnoffskys struggling against prejudice, Louis came to identify with them. "With [the] little money they had, they bought two small horses [and] two small wagon harnesses. Alex would go out early in the mornings on his junk wagon—stay out all day, me right alongside of him." These were long days, since the Karnoffskys prepared for work as early as five o'clock in the morning, but, "working for these fine people, I learned to be an early riser just like them. I noticed they believed in being on the move. Up early every morning, making hay while the sun shined." Nonetheless, "I began to feel like I had a future and 'It's a Wonderful World' after all."

Eventually, the brothers decided to see if young Louis could attract attention to the Karnoffsky junk wagon. Rather than ringing a bell, or shouting, Louis decided to blow on a simple tin horn ("the kind the people celebrates with"). It was a crude instrument, scarcely better than a noisemaker. Louis said the horn cost him a whole dime, but it turned out to be a "great asset to the junk wagon. I even learned to play popular tunes on it."

He played the horn day after day, all day long. "When I would be on the junk wagon with Alex Karnoffsky," said Louis, "I would blow this long tin horn without the top on it. Just hold my fingers close together and blow. It was a call for old rags, bones, bottles, or anything that the people and kids had to sell. The kids loved the sound of my tin horn." Louis kept experimenting with it. "One day I took the wooden top off of the horn, and surprisingly I held up my two fingers close together where the wooden mouthpiece used to be and I could play a tune of some kind. Oh, the kids really enjoyed that. Better than the first time. They used to bring their bottles, Alex would give them a few pennies, and they would stand around the wagon while I would entertain them."

The brothers Karnoffsky urged him on, especially Alex, who would "applaud me every time." He told Louis that he "made a beautiful tone" with the little tin horn. "As a young boy coming up, the people whom I worked for were very much concerned about my future in music. They could see that I had music in my soul. They really wanted me to be something in life. And music was it. Appreciating my every effort." This was a startling discovery, that he was capable of pleasing others, white and black, young and old, with the sound he produced by blowing his horn; it was a discovery that led to his revolutionizing jazz, and by extension, American music.

Another employer might have sacrificed Louis's accidental interest in music to the demands of business, but the brothers encouraged him. "After blowing my tin horn so long I wondered how would I do blowing a real horn, a cornet was what I had in mind." At this point, the Karnoffskys intervened. "One day when I was on the wagon with Morris Karnoffsky—we were in Rampart and Perdido streets—we passed a pawn shop which had in its window an old tarnished beat-up B-flat cornet. It only cost five dollars. Morris advanced me two dollars on my salary. Then I put aside fifty cents each week from my small pay, finally the cornet was paid for in full. Boy, was I a happy kid.

"The little cornet was real dirty and had turned real black. Morris cleaned my little cornet with some brass polish and poured some oil all through it. Which sterilized the inside. He requested me to play a tune on it. Although I could not play a good tune Morris applauded me just the same, which made me feel very good. After blowing into it a while I realized that I could play 'Home, Sweet Home,' then 'Here Comes the Blues.' From then on, I was a mess and tooting away. I kept that horn for a long time. I played it all through the days of the honky-tonks."

The Karnoffskys' benign influence over the extraordinary youth who had come into their midst extended well beyond the horn. He learned to appreciate the singing he heard in their home, a deeply felt vocalizing that he would recall and emulate for the rest of his life. "I was relaxed singing the song called 'Russian Lullaby' with the Karnoffsky family when Mother Karnoffsky would have her little baby boy in her arms, rocking him to sleep. We all sang together until the little baby would doze off." So went his life with the Karnoffsky family: days of blowing a tin horn on the junk wagon, nights of helping to sing their infants to sleep, until, "when I reached the age of eleven, I began to realize it was the Jewish family who instilled in me singing from the heart."

Louis's first exposure to the horn and singing occurred within the Karnoffsky family circle, but no one in the family was especially musical, and none of the Karnoffskys endeavored to teach him. Louis taught himself. Furthermore, this prototypical jazz artist was gaining his first musical experiences with a white family, and adapting it to his black idiom. Until he met the Karnoffskys, his impression of whites was based on the stories he'd heard from his mother and his Uncle Ike—stories of the white man's cruelty toward blacks, the bitter and apparently endless legacy of slavery. Now, in the Karnoffsky family circle, Louis began to think and feel differently about whites. Here was a family that looked after itself, that was willing to accept him as he was, and that wanted to help him in simple, practical ways. And because the earliest encouragement he received in music happened to come from this white family, Louis always remained open to whites and willing to express himself to them through his music. He was convinced that his music, jazz, had no cultural or ethnic limits; it was neither black nor white nor Creole, but an admixture of all these elements, and more. Indeed, one of the most interesting aspects of jazz was the way it leapt like a flame from one culture to another.

After a while, the Karnoffskys virtually adopted young Louis. He spent more time with them than with his own family. He described his daily routine with them this way: "After a day's work in the hot sun, buying everything that we could buy, we would finish up, unhitch the horse and wagon, pile the rags + bones in one corner to dry, freshen up, have a good Jewish meal, relax for the night route." This route took him "through the red-light district selling stone coal a nickel a water bucket," and as he was forever reminding people, "in 1907 the New Orleans red-light district was in its blazing glory. Although I was just a young kid the police did not bother me. I was working for a white man. It was reason enough." Not only that, but, "Everybody knew me by my right name," and in addition to working night and day, "I managed to go to school through it all. Of course not like I wanted to. But I did a pretty good job pertaining to my studies." Louis was in more or less regular attendance at the Fisk School through the fifth grade, when he was ten years old, but as he suggests, his last years in school were marked by his increasing truancy. His real education during these years took place with the Karnoffskys, on their junk wagon and in their home.

As time passed, his relationship to the family deepened. He became aware of their outcast status as immigrant Jews. "I was only seven years old but I could see the *ungodly* treatment that the white folks were handing the poor Jewish family whom I worked for," he wrote. He pitied them, because, he believed, "The Jewish people has such wonderful souls." And he was grateful for the attention and affection he felt in their midst. "They were always warm and kind to me which was very noticeable to me . . . something that a kid could use at seven and just starting out in the world."

What's more, "I liked their Jewish food very much." Always obsessed with food, Louis was transfixed by the Karnoffsky cuisine. "Every time we would come in late on the little wagon from buying old rags and bones, when they would be having supper, they would fix a plate of food for me, saying, 'You worked, might as well eat here with us. It is too late, and by the time you get home, it will be way too late for your supper.' I was glad because I fell in love with the food from those days until now." To Louis, the Karnoffskys' diet seemed part and parcel of their striving for success. "Their food was always pure—the best. I noticed whenever I ate with them I would even sleep better. Much different from the heavy foods Mayann, Mama Lucy, and me had to eat." In the last years of his life, he wrote, "I still eat their foods, matzos. My wife Lucille keeps them in her bread box so I can nibble on them any time that I want to eat late at night." Old and famous, he still remembered the Family Karnoffsky with every bite.

As he came to know and love the Karnoffskys, he realized that the Jews and blacks had much in common. "Of course, we are all well aware of the Congo Square, slavery, lynchings and all of that stuff," he said, and "maybe the Jewish people did not go through all those things, but they went through just as much. Still they stuck together."

Meanwhile, he said, there were all too many older black men "in an alley or in the street corner shooting dice or nickels and dimes, etc. (mere pittances) . . . gambling off the money they should take home to feed their starving children or pay their small rents, or very important needs. Many kids suffered with hungers because their fathers could have done some work for a change. No, they would not do that. It would be too much like right," he complained bitterly. "They'd rather lazy around and gamble." In contrast, it seemed that "Jewish people always managed to put away their nickels and dimes, profits which they knew would accumulate into a *nice* little bundle some day."

His people, Louis wrote, actually made it harder on themselves than necessary, and their tendency to tear down those among them who did succeed all worked to their detriment and only served to widen the gulf between races. Louis didn't blame whites alone for conditions in the South; the way he saw it, blacks also conspired in their own servitude and diminished the possibility of righting ancient wrongs. Although Louis's estimation of the way blacks coped with discrimination appears harsh, he was not alone in his beliefs among New Orleans musicians of his day. Johnny St. Cyr, the banjo and guitar player, and one of Louis's closest friends, said, "The mulattos were actually more prejudiced than the whites were at that time." And "Pops" Foster, a jazz bassist who was born on a plantation, was indignant over the way one group of blacks discriminated against another. "The lighter you were the better they thought you were."

Louis occasionally found social justice among some whites, who he believed were capable of being fair-minded. "A white man may not care about *all* Negroes," he said, "but they all had a Negro they liked and respected." Which was what he wanted to be: a black man whom whites liked and respected, because he liked and respected at least *some* of them— Jews, in particular—to whom he felt a personal debt. "If it wasn't for the nice Jewish people, we would have starved many a time," he declared, and as a result, "I will love the Jewish people all of my life."

Although his father's departure inspired rage in Louis and affected his perceptions about blacks, he never copied whites. He knew himself, he knew that many of his special strengths and abilities came from being black, and he was even aware that his being black actually appealed to some whites. No matter how harsh the criticisms he leveled at his own people, he reveled in everything black—in black music, black cooking, black speech, black humor, black neighborhoods, and black women. At the same time, he was acutely aware of the tragic dimensions of black life in America. He accepted these conditions, as he accepted almost everything that came his way, good or bad, because it was in his nature to accept whatever life placed before him. This was his own racial credo, his core belief, and it remained remarkably consistent through decades of social upheaval and changes of fashion, and he always welcomed people of any color to join him in it.

When he was eleven years old, Louis dropped out of the Fisk School, in the middle of fifth grade. It was a decision he bitterly regretted later in life, when he realized how much he had missed. He had enjoyed school, but his decision was motivated by economics, for he was often hungry and dressed in rags. He was exhausted, as well, after four years of working for the Karnoffsky family at dawn, attending school haphazardly, and returning to work at night only.

Now that he was on his own, he joined a quartet of Uptown boys, all of them out of school and desperately in need of money. The others were "Little Mack," the lead singer; "Big Nose" Sidney; and "Redhead Happy" Bolton. The preadolescent Louis sang in a sweet tenor. They practiced in an abandoned lot on Freret Street, and when they felt ready went out on the streets to perform and pass the hat. Louis perfected a funny little jig, a real crowd-pleaser, and Little Mack astonished passersby with his somersaults. They staked out a spot on Poydras Street, near Maylie's restaurant, hoping to catch the attention of the swells with their repertoire of "Swanee River" and "Mr. Moon, Won't You Please Shine Down on Me?" Once a crowd gathered, the group performed a ridiculous skit in which Louis knelt in front of Redhead Happy and sang of his undying love for "her" as he rolled his eyes and drew laughter, applause, and coins from their audience.

The group quickly made a name for themselves in New Orleans music circles. They even came to the attention of Bunk Johnson.

Bunk was the most controversial trumpet "king" to come out of New Orleans. "Of the three," Louis said, meaning Bunk, Bolden, and Oliver, "Bunk Johnson had the most beautiful tone, the best imagination and the softest sense of phrasing." And unlike the shadowy Bolden, everyone knew Bunk, Louis included. "You really heard music when Bunk Johnson played the cornet with the Eagle Band," he said. "I was young, but I could tell the difference." Unlike Buddy Bolden, Bunk actually recorded, but the pressings came after years of enforced retirement and poor health, after he had lost his teeth and was playing with dentures, so you couldn't tell from these records how he'd played in his heyday. Yet everyone who heard Bunk when he was a younger man, decades before these lackluster recordings, said he was a scintillating and innovative musician, a man who inspired and informally taught a generation—not only Louis but Jelly Roll Morton, Bessie Smith, and King Oliver.

Bunk was also a drunk, and he was known to chase a skirt now and then. He was tall and slender, with a dignified face and bearing. He had a quiet, mysterious way about him, but the facts of his life were widely known. Willie G. "Bunk" Johnson was born in New Orleans in 1879. His parents were former slaves, and he was one of fourteen children. He studied music as a boy, and then, when still a teenager, he joined Buddy Bolden's band. Or said he did, anyway. Bunk had this way of tailoring his reminiscences to suit the interests of his interviewers, and everyone was avid to hear about the fabled, tragic Buddy Bolden. Bunk, for his part, had a gift for gab and was eager to please. In 1895, he claimed, Bolden and his merry band "had the whole of New Orleans real crazy and running wild behind it"—including Bunk, who got close enough for Bolden himself to notice a green bag that Bunk was carrying. His mother had made the bag, and it held the boy's cornet.

"What you got there, boy?" Bolden asked.

"A cornet."

"Can you play it?"

"I can play it," Bunk replied with confidence.

"Can you play the blues, boy?" And Bunk said he could. "What key you play the blues in?"

"Any key you've got."

Bunk played, Bolden hired him, end of story.

"King Bolden and myself were the first men that began playing jazz in the city of dear old New Orleans," Bunk insisted. "And I was with him and that was between 1895 and 1896." After leaving Bolden's band, Bunk claimed he toured the world, and then he resurfaced in New Orleans. By the time Louis encountered him, Bunk was forty-two—a well-known if enigmatic figure on the local musical scene and the butt of many jokes about his boozing and erratic behavior. Despite his tall tales, other musicians regarded him as the genuine article.

In his quiet way, Bunk liked to scout young musicians and offer them a helping hand, a rare thing in the tightly knit fraternity of New Orleans instrumentalists, where the older generation tended to exclude up-and-coming virtuosos who might start competing with them for jobs. Impressed by Louis Armstrong's fledgling quartet, Bunk enthusiastically recommended them to a clarinetist named Sidney Bechet, who was seventeen and on his way to becoming a brilliant musician and globetrotter. At the moment, though, Bechet was living at home in New Orleans, trying to gain as much experience as he could before he journeyed to that fabled place known as the North. "I was having an itch to go," he said of that period in his life. "I stayed on there a while, playing along with many great musicianers, growing into the music, thinking I'd be going off one of those days, but wanting to take the most I could with me. There was so much to play, so much to listen to." And Bunk told him, "I want you to go hear a little quartet, how they sing and harmonize."

Sidney went to hear them, came away impressed by their ability to harmonize, just as Bunk said, and returned over and over to listen. "I got to like Louis a whole lot, he was damn nice. . . . At that time, he sort of looked up to me, me playing in bands and being with the big men."

Bechet required that sort of deference to feel at ease. Later, when Louis came into his own as a trumpeter, a bitter rivalry characterized their relationship, but for now, Bechet enjoyed playing the role of sponsor.

Louis's insecurities made Sidney feel all the more secure. He remembered well the time he invited Louis and the rest of the quartet to his home for dinner and then to sing for his family. Louis reacted strangely, "he sort of hemmed around, and said he couldn't make it." Finally he admitted, 'Look, Sidney, I don't have any shoes. These I got, they won't get me there.' " Bechet said he "gave him fifty cents to get his shoes repaired, and he went off promising me he would come." But Louis never appeared for dinner, as Bechet recalled, and the memory of his broken promise always rankled him. "It's a little thing, and there's big things around it, but it keeps coming back. You're playing some number and it starts going—sometimes it goes right back to the street and those shoes."

After this disagreement, Bechet expected to have nothing more to do with Louis, but then began hearing from the drummer Black Benny about an impressive young cornet player. "You think you can play," Black Benny told Bechet, "I know a little boy around the corner from my place, he can play 'High Society' better than you." Bechet knew this was a clarinet part, just about impossible to play on the cornet, so he had to go hear for himself. And when he saw the cornetist, who should it be but that same little Louis who conned him out of fifty cents! And yes, he was able to play the part on a cornet brilliantly. Beyond that, he gave the impression that he was capable of stretching the cornet's musical limits and that he could do things with it that other musicians assumed were impossible.

As Louis's facility increased, he came to appreciate the finer points of Bunk's musicianship. "Buddy Bolden had the biggest reputation, but he just played loud," Louis said. "Don't think he really knew how to play his horn right. Bunk Johnson was very different. He had a beautiful tone, the best imagination and the softest sense of phrasing."

And Bunk, for his part, recalled Louis following him, just as Bunk himself had once followed Buddy Bolden. "Louis was eleven years old, and when he seen a parade, Louis tramped the street all day long, right with me. When the band stopped playing, he's worrying me to carry my horn and wanted me to learn him how to play. And Louis done that, done that for a long while. Then I seen that he were really interested in learning. I told him that I would. I'd learn him. But he'd have to do like I tell him. So he told me, 'Bunk, I sure will do like you tell me.' He say, 'All I want to do is learn.' And I told him, I say, 'Well, all right now. You want to learn how to read music?' He said, 'No. I want to learn how to play 'Pallet on the Floor,' 'Salty Dog,' 'Didn't He Ramble,' and 'Ball the Jack.' " These were the essential tunes of the New Orleans honky-tonk, many of which Louis later recorded and performed throughout his career. Bunk taught Louis a tradition as well as technique—the tradition of the New Orleans honky-tonks and parade musicians.

Louis followed Bunk all the way into the Storyville tonks. These were rough places, serving cheap whiskey, five cents a shot, most of the bottles erroneously labeled. If a customer became drunk, which was usually the case, he might be robbed and thrown out into the street, where thieves would strip him of his clothing. The tonks were no place for a child to pass idle hours, but Louis managed to gain entry.

"I was at Dago Tony's," said Bunk, naming one of the worst dives. "Louis was in short pants, he couldn't go in. But he would steal in there in the early part of the night, sleep behind the piano 'til I would come on. Then after he'd get in there, well, then I would show him and show him 'til he begin understandin' me real good. It was a short while before Louis could play the blues." Bunk taught him a few tunes, and then "music became easy to him—by head, by ear. And Louis could play anything that he could whistle."

Louis even managed to get his hands on Bunk's precious cornet. "He would fool with my cornet every chance he could get until he could get a sound out of it. Then I showed him just how to hold it and place it to his mouth and he did so and it wasn't long before he began getting a good tone out of my horn. Now that was every time he could get a chance to steal in[to] 'Dago Tony's.'" Bechet backed up Bunk's account of how the older musician taught the younger. "He'd stay behind the piano, mostly, keeping out of sight," Bechet remembered. "He did that because people used to come visiting from all over . . . some of them with police escorts . . . and if the police saw kids in short pants, they chased them out!" He even named the tonk, Dago Tony's on Perdido and Franklin streets, where "Louis used to slip in . . . and get in on the music standing behind the piano," precisely as Bunk recalled.

Although Bunk later wanted the world to know he was the first to teach Louis how to blow ("Now I've just said a lot about my boy Louis and just how he started playing cornet. He started playing it by head"), his approach was fairly casual. He called his method of instruction "showing Louis," which implies that it was not formal training, and certainly had nothing to do with written music, but was more of a spontaneous show-and-tell: hold it this way, do as I do, put your instrument to your lips not like *that* but just like *this*, get your tongue behind your teeth, try it up, try it down—and now blow it, blow that infernal thing, blow it so it comes to life! This was how Louis obtained a rudimentary understanding of embouchure, the way to hold his chops—his lips, cheek, mouth, and tongue—when he blew his horn.

By the time he was eleven, Louis had accomplished a great deal. He had begun earning money and had already formed a clear idea what he wanted to do for a living. He'd found a surrogate family, the Karnoffskys, to care for him. He'd formed relationships with influential musicians such as Joe Oliver and Bunk Johnson. And he'd seen a fair amount of the wilder side of Storyville. Throughout his youth, he'd deftly performed a juggling act, playing the bad boy or the good when he felt like it, or as circumstances required. Still, he generally avoided real trouble. His most serious offense consisted of sneaking into Storyville to hear the music and peek at the prostitutes. As criminal behavior flourished all around, he remained protected by his innocence, his lack of anger, and his association with the Karnoffskys. He appeared destined to become another fixture in Storyville.

But now that he had dropped out of school and had time on his hands and was surrounded by every sort of vice, Louis began looking for trouble. Soon enough, he found it, and things began spinning out of control faster than Buddy Bolden used to blow his horn.

3.

AIN'T MISBEHAVIN'

remember running around with a lot of bad boys which did a lot of crazy things. As the saying goes, your environment makes you," Louis said of this uncertain period, when he hovered on the verge of adolescence. "You must realize it was very shaky all the time during my days coming up in New Orleans. Especially those early ones. They were rough. You had to fight and do a lot of ungodly things to keep from being trampled on. Sure I had fights and did a number of rough things, just so I could have a little peace or elbow room." These fights could be lethal because his adversaries, who were from the notorious Third Ward, carried pistols "in holsters just like those real cowboys. And you think they won't shoot to kill? Huh!"

The issue of guns was especially sensitive in New Orleans. Ten years earlier, a deranged black man named Robert Charles, inflamed by a recent "Back to Africa" movement, got into a shoot-out with police and in the ensuing battle killed twenty-seven people. The tragedy left the city traumatized, and it altered the delicate balance of racial relations. Whites lived in fear of blacks, which meant that blacks lived in fear of whites and endured a tightly circumscribed existence. They were forbidden to enter many neighborhoods, especially after dark. Louis grew up in this charged atmosphere; it was all he had ever known of life in New Orleans.

Time and again, his mother, fearful for his safety, warned him, "Don't fight, don't fight," but when Louis took her advice, he didn't get the expected result. One day in school he quarreled with another student. In exasperation, Louis told him, "Since you want to start a fight, hit me." The boy punched him in the eye—"damn near blinded me." Heedless of his mother's words, Louis went after his adversary. "I swung on that so-'n'-

so's jaw and head. . . . From that time on I got the name of being a bad boy."

His precarious situation worsened drastically on New Year's Eve, 1912. It was—and is—the custom in New Orleans to greet the New Year by firing pistols into the night sky. That night, Louis planned to sing with his quartet to earn a little money. At the start of the evening, he decided to "borrow" a .38 that one of his "stepfathers" stored in a trunk in the Armstrong home. With the gun tucked into his belt, under his shirt, he joined up with Little Mack and the others, and the four of them paced along the stones of Rampart Street from Gravier to Perdido and back again, two by two. All around him, people were discharging pistols and shotguns, shooting off roman candles, and firing cannon. He remembered what they sang that night—"*My Brazilian Beauty down on the Amazon . . . That's where my baby's . . . Gone, gone, gone.*" In those days it never occurred to him there actually *was* such a place as Brazil, it was just a word in a song. He was excited and was showing off some funny little moves he'd been working on. He placed his hand behind his ear and started wagging that big Dippermouth of his, making some "beautiful tones." The quartet solicited requests from their audience. As the quartet sang and fetched money from the crowd, Louis anticipated dropping a few shiny coins into his mother's lap at the end of the night.

His happy little reverie ended when, "all of a sudden a guy on the opposite side of the street pulled out a little six shooter pistol and fired it off." The quartet, knowing Louis carried a pistol, shouted: "*Go get him, Dipper!*" How could he resist?

"Without hesitating," he recalled, "I pulled my stepfather's revolver from my bosom and raised my arm into the air and let her go. Mine was a better gun than the kid's and the six shots made more noise. The kid was frightened and cut out and was out of sight like a jackrabbit. We all laughed about it and started down the street again, singing as we walked along." They joyfully proceeded along Rampart Street, and Louis boldly reloaded his pistol, so excited with his loud new toy that he decided to follow New Orleans custom and shoot it into the air. "I had just finished firing my last blank cartridge when a couple of strong arms came from behind me. It was cold enough that night, but I broke out into a sweat that was even colder. My companions cut out and left me, and I turned out to see a tall white detective who had been watching me. Oh boy! I started crying and making all kinds of excuses: '*Please mister, don't arrest me . . . I won't do it no more . . . Please . . . Let me go back to Mama . . . I won't do it no more . . . '* "

His pleas fell on deaf ears. "When I looked around, those arms were hugging me, and I thought, 'Oh, Lord!' "

The arms belonged to Detective Edward Holyland, who, with his partner, George Dellman, had just finished arresting another man when the crack! crack! crack! of Louis's pistol caught their attention. Holyland got behind Louis, gripped him in his arms, wrestled him to the ground, and charged him with firing a gun in a public place. It was a very serious offense, even for an eleven-year-old.

What had begun as an ill-advised prank turned into a nightmare. The detectives escorted the boy to the New Orleans Juvenile Court at 823 Baronne Street. He was "locked up in a cell where, sick and disheartened, I slept on a hard bed until the next morning." This was a segregated detention cell on the third floor of the Court, and since Louis was the only black youth arrested that night, he was confined there alone. No sound echoed in the empty corridors, no laughter, no cornet. There was no one, black or white, for him to charm, only a profound institutional stillness. Every truant's nightmare was happening to him. He'd lost the freedom he'd always taken for granted; he wouldn't be going home to his mama and her red beans and rice that night, or the next. Or the next. The possibility that he had ruined his entire life loomed.

The following morning, New Year's Day, 1913, Louis was led downstairs to the courtroom, where Judge Andrew Wilson heard evidence from the arresting officer. After a trial lasting no more than fifteen minutes, the judge sentenced him to the Colored Waif's Home, a reform school located on the outskirts of New Orleans.

Louis was appalled and terrified. He was a boy, a child, he hadn't hurt anyone, he realized his mistake now—surely they wouldn't treat him as a common criminal? Although he would never have believed it at the time, the judge who had pronounced this sentence was, by the standards of his day, a progressive jurist who took an interest in the welfare of the boys who came before him, whether they were black or white. A graduate of Tulane Law School, Andrew H. Wilson had devoted years of service to his local school board, and when he ran for head of the Juvenile Court three years earlier, in 1909, he rode to victory on his reputation for honesty and his distance from the corrupting influence of City Hall. It was a position he was to hold until his death in 1921.

At ten o'clock that morning, an orderly came by, unlocked the cell, and said, "You are going out to the Colored Waif's Home." Louis was led to the prison yard, where he saw a horse-drawn wagon. He entered, and a "door with a little bitty grilled window was slammed behind me and away I went." He still could not believe the swiftness and severity of what had happened to him. "I was just a kid, twelve years old," he said. "Oh, but I cried."

To add to his shame, the incident came to the attention of the *Times-Picayune*, where the entire city read about Louis Armstrong for the first time, not as a musician, but as a youthful offender sentenced to jail for his crime.

FEW JUVENILES ARRESTED

Very few arrests of minors were made Tuesday, and the bookings in the Juvenile Court are no more than the average. Six white boys were arrested in Canal Street for disturbing the peace. The most serious case was that of Louis Armstrong, a twelve-year-old negro, who discharged a revolver at Rampart and Perdido streets. Being an old offender he was sent to the negro Waif's Home.

It is not clear what misdeeds qualified Louis as an "old" (presumably previous) offender. Possibly he had had minor run-ins with police, who knew him as a troublemaker, and he did describe himself as having earned a reputation as a "bad boy" at the time, but nothing approaching the gravity of this event had ever happened to him before.

The Colored Waif's Home had long been a fixture in New Orleans history and philanthropy, but had only recently come into its own. Designed in 1870 by a prominent Creole architect, Jacques N. B. de Pouilly, it was originally called the Girod Asylum, after Nicholas Girod, the mayor of the city during the War of 1812. His will had called for it to be built and provided the initial money. The asylum was intended to house French orphans, but bitter legal contests over the disposition of Girod's estate delayed the plan for over forty years, until the city of New Orleans stepped in and supervised its construction. By the time the building was completed, no one wanted the responsibility of running it, and the Board of Health, recognizing that it was surrounded on all sides by a fetid malarial swamp, condemned it before it was occupied. Finally, at the turn of the century, the swamps were drained, and in November 1906, more than seventy years after the institution's original benefactor had died, the city turned over the building, now fallen into severe disrepair, to the Colored Branch of the Society for the Prevention of Cruelty to Children, which oversaw its rebirth.

From this time, the Home's destiny was inextricably linked to that of its new leader, Joseph Jones—Captain Jones, as he was invariably called. Captain Jones was a black man whose calling was looking after orphans and juvenile delinquents—the overflow of New Orleans's streets and alleys. Born in New Orleans on July 15, 1880, and educated locally, Jones was still young, not yet twenty-seven, when he took over the institution, but he knew he had found his life's work. "In those days," he said later, "there were a great many youngsters in the city who were supposed to be 'bad,' but it seemed to me they were just kids who never had a chance." Until this time, white boys were sent to their Waif's Home, but "the colored boys went to the parish jail." Moved by their plight, Jones went to see Judge Wilson, who set the wheels in motion for a "colored" counterpart to the white Waif's Home. Though segregated, it offered a much better chance to black youths than mingling with the adult population of a jail. Jones then approached black lawyers, farmers, and other community leaders to back the project, and to fund it through the Society for the Prevention of Cruelty to Children. Louis had the good fortune to arrive near the inception of what became a successful social experiment. If he had been arrested only four years earlier, and sent to an adult jail instead of the Waif's Home, the outcome of his entire life might have been drastically different.

Nearly everyone who passed through the place, including Louis, looked on Captain Jones with gratitude and respect, tinged with fear. "He was very firm with the boys," said his wife. "When he'd say, 'Don't do it,' you better not do it. He had some kind of signal to silence the boys. He wasn't cruel, but if he told you, 'You're not going,' you were staying." Though he was stern, the boys understood that they were being treated as little soldiers rather than miscreants, and for all his emphasis on discipline, everyone who came into contact with him was aware of his genuine concern for the welfare of his boys, and they were also grateful to him, for he was doing a job no one else knew how to do, or was willing to do.

With aid from the city, local businessmen, and eventually from the Home's wards, Captain Jones renovated the building so it was habitable, though far from luxurious. The boys slept on bare bunks and had but a single blanket to warm them on chilly nights. The meals were similarly Spartan; a typical dinner consisted of dark bread and molasses, without meat or milk. The boys occasionally feasted on vegetables, especially beans, grown in the Home's garden, but if meat was ever served, no one has left a record of it. The Home's location was remote, about five miles from Louis's neighborhood in New Orleans, and when his parents and sister wanted to visit, they would have to take a long trolley ride, and then walk the final four blocks to the Home. The main building housed about 115 boys and a small staff consisting of three or four "keepers" to oversee them. A gardener raised the vegetables the boys ate, with the exception of sweet potatoes, which did not grow well in the marshy soil. At the time Louis was sent there, the Home loomed incongruously above a mixture of graveyards and farms, whose chickens invariably awoke the boys before sunrise. Louis remembered a "great big dairy farm where hundreds of cows, bulls, calves and a few horses were standing. Some were eating, and some prancing around like they wanted to tell somebody, anybody, how good they felt." But the animals were free, and Louis was in confinement. Despite its bucolic appearance, the entire complex was surrounded with barbed wire.

Louis arrived as the boys—actually, they were inmates—were having lunch. He traversed a corridor leading to the mess hall, where he took a place at the end of a long table and submitted to the stares of the others. A few muttered sardonic greetings, but, said Louis, "I was too depressed to answer." The food, when slapped down in front of him, sickened him. White beans without rice on a tin plate.

Disgusted, he staged a hunger strike, refusing to eat the simple fare placed in front of him: bread, molasses, and beans. He managed to hold out for three days, while Captain Jones looked on silently. On the fourth day, Louis admitted, "I was so hungry I was first at the table." The captain burst out laughing, but the best Louis could muster was a "sheepish grin," for he "did not share their sense of humor"—especially when it concerned him.

In the weeks to come, Louis discovered life in the Home was never less than strict and often harsh. Captain Jones ran his Home on a military model, and he wanted to instill patriotism in his boys. Each morning a delegation raised the flag, and promptly at six o'clock in the evening they lowered it. Most mornings he drilled the boys in the courtyard, teaching them to handle wooden weapons. Other instructors taught the boys gardening, carpentry, camping skills, and music—all considered vocational training. The keepers observed the boys' every move. Dormitory lights were extinguished promptly at nine o'clock, though the boys often stayed up late whispering in voices soft enough to avoid detection.

There was no prospect of escape from the institution. The few hapless youths who tried to flee returned to the Home in less than a week, traumatized by the ordeal of living on the lam and in serious trouble with the Juvenile Court. Captain Jones made one runaway into a particularly gruesome object lesson for the other boys. When he returned, hungry and afraid, the captain ordered four boys to hold him down and administered no less than "one hundred and five lashes" to his naked buttocks. "All of the boys hollered," Louis recalled, "but the more we hollered the harder he hit." Another runaway received an astounding five hundred lashes for his trouble. The punishment was so awful that Louis decided he would never try to escape, no matter how desperate he felt. He had no idea how long he would be in the Home. The Juvenile Court had considered his case serious enough to commit him "for an indefinite period," which could last until a judge set him free or "some important white person vouched for me and my mother and father." Since both possibilities appeared extremely remote, he had no choice but to make the best of the grim situation.

Louis turned his attention to the tasks at hand, and he took pride in his handiwork, no matter how menial. "The Waif's Home was surely a very clean place, and we did all the work ourselves," he said. "That's where I learned how to scrub floors, wash and iron, cook, make up beds, do a little of everything around the house." Cleanliness began with the boys themselves. "The first thing we did to a newcomer was to make him take a good shower, and his head and body were carefully examined to see that he did not bring any vermin into the Home. Every day we lined up for inspection." Those who did not pass had to change their clothes or wash themselves until they were up to snuff. Some youths arrived in truly pathetic condition, and it was up to Louis and the others to take care of them. "One day a couple of small kids had been picked up in the streets of New Orleans covered with body lice and head lice. Out in the backyard there was an immense kettle which was used to boil up our dirty clothes. Those two kids were in such filthy condition that we had to shave their heads and throw their clothes into the fire underneath the kettle."

Despite the hardships and cruelties he suffered at the Home, Louis always insisted that "the place was more like a health center or a boarding school than a boys' jail." He experienced a rebirth there because he learned to thrive on the discipline and finally received the attention—especially from older men—that he craved. His firing of the gun on New Year's Eve had been a cry for help, and the Juvenile Court had replied. "That shot, I do believe, started my career," he reflected twenty years later. "My whole success goes back to the time I was arrested as a wayward boy of thirteen. Because then I *had* to quit running around and began to learn something. Most of all, I began to learn music."

Music mattered a great deal at the Home. As Louis discovered, daily life ran according to the calls of the bugle. "A kid blew a bugle for us to get up, to go to bed, and to come to meals. The last call was the favorite with us all. Whether they were cutting trees a mile away or building a fire under a great kettle in the yard to scald our dirty clothes, the boys would hotfoot it back to the Home when they heard the mess call. I envied the bugler because he had more chances to use his instrument than anyone else." Louis naturally set his sights on the role of bugler.

The director of the Home's music program was a quietly remarkable man, Professor Peter Davis. (The title was honorary; most anyone who taught music at the time called himself a professor.) Within weeks, Louis was pestering Professor Davis to let him play in the Waif Home's orchestra, the pride of the institution. Louis wanted to be in the band partly because he loved music and partly because he was drawn to Davis, whom he came to regard with something approaching hero worship. "He was one of the finest persons I have ever met in my life," Louis said later. "Even when he would get angry with you, there would be a little something that would make you feel you would definitely do the right thing next time without him saying another word to you. He was the type of man you'd want to please at all times."

It took some doing, however, for Louis to win the professor's trust. At the beginning, Professor Davis assumed that Louis was going to be a major troublemaker simply because he came from around Liberty and Perdido streets, "full of honky-tonks, toughs and fancy women" (that is, brothels, pimps, and whores), and as a result, "he made it awful tough for me." In fact, when Louis broke a minor rule, Professor Davis gave him "fifteen hard lashes on the hand," said Louis. "After that I was really scared of him for a long time."

Louis wanted to watch the band practice in the worst way, but he kept his distance for fear of receiving more lashes from Professor Davis: "He made me feel he hated the ground I walked on." Still, the boy stole a few moments to listen in, and the sound of the music brought back memories of his musical heroes—Buddy Bolden, Bunk Johnson, and Joe Oliver. He no longer took music, or any of life's pleasures, for granted, and so it acquired the utmost importance. Music became synonymous with life, freedom, joy. He conceived what he called "an awful urge to learn the cornet," but he was convinced that the professor's dislike—no, *hatred*—of him stood in the way.

As time wore on, Louis's patience and devotion were rewarded, and he thought he detected a slight softening in the professor's attitude. One day the man even smiled at him, and then started talking to him, saying, "You're not as bad a kid as I thought you were. You were only mixed up in bad company," and finally, Professor Davis came up to him at dinner and said, "Louis Armstrong, how would you like to join our brass band?" The boy was too surprised to answer, and Professor Davis repeated the question. Louis ran from the mess hall, hurriedly washed, and dashed to rehearsal, where instead of the shiny cornet he expected to play, a tambourine was thrust into his hand. He began to beat it in time with the piece they were playing, "At the Animals' Ball." At last he was in the band.

His second piece of luck occurred when the bugler was released from the Home, and Professor Davis appointed Louis to take his place. This was a rare honor, and he decided to make the best of it. Under its previous owner, the bugle had become so badly tarnished that it was a dull green. Louis polished it until it gleamed, and everyone seemed to take heart from this demonstration of *esprit de corps*. As a result, Louis's morale soared. "I felt real proud of my position as bugler," he said. "I would stand very erect as I would bring the bugle nonchalantly to my lips and blow real mellow tones." When this happened, "the whole place seemed to change."

Impressed by the notes Louis coaxed from a simple bugle, Davis finally bestowed a cornet on the lad and taught him to play "Home, Sweet Home." "Louis came to me one day, saying, 'I believe I can blow that cornet, let me try,'" Davis recalled. "I looked at the boy who was only thirteen at that time and I saw nothing but sincerity filled with eagerness written all over his face. I said to him, 'If you want to learn I will begin you on the bugle first. It was all right with Louis. From a youth he always had a pleasant personality. Louis soon mastered this bugle and was ready for the cornet."

Davis's instruction has long been considered the first formal training Louis received on the instrument, and on the strength of this encounter he was later celebrated as Louis Armstrong's first music teacher. Although the guidance he gave Louis was far more rigorous than anything the young man had previously experienced, it was not his first exposure to the cornet. As Louis and so many others have recounted, he had been playing brass instruments, off and on, ever since his rides on the Karnoffsky junk wagon six years earlier. "People thought that my first horn was given to me at the Colored Waif's Home for Boys," he noted later in life, when he was eager to correct this long-standing misapprehension, "but it wasn't." According to Sidney Bechet, Louis had pushed the boundaries of cornet playing even before he entered the Waif's Home and had studied informally with Bunk Johnson, who was justly proud of the fact that he had influenced Louis a year before Davis.

The real lessons Louis learned from Professor Davis had more to do with self-respect and discipline than with musicianship. Even more important, Louis formed a positive relationship with an older male, a father figure, whose discipline, however strict, he was willing to accept. Louis's recollection of his study with the professor describes no *musical* break-throughs—Louis accomplished these on his own—but it marked the dawn of his moral judgment. Until this time, he had more or less acquiesced to the life into which he'd been born, a world of pimps, thieves, hookers, and gamblers, of random violence and enigmatic jolts of good fortune. Now, for the first time, Louis realized he could make choices about his behavior, choices about his environment, and that the choices he made would have immediate consequences for him. Another boy might have hated Davis for inflicting fifteen lashes for no real reason; it says much about his temperament that the young Louis automatically resisted the temptation to succumb to a justifiable rage and instead welcomed the attention he received, no matter how harsh, and accepted the challenge this treatment implied. If he could win over a taskmaster such as Professor Davis, there was no telling what he might accomplish in the world at large. Again and again during his life, Louis reacted to cruel and unfair people and situations, most notably to bigotry, in precisely the same way. He rarely responded with anger, and he usually tried to find some way to win over his adversary. Often, he succeeded.

His willingness to turn the other cheek was a singular facet of his character, and there is no simple explanation for it. He did not learn it from his mother, father, or sister. Whatever gave Louis the patience to withstand these challenges, it wasn't timidity on his part, as critics, both black and white, have frequently charged. Louis never turned a blind eye to cruelty. Each time he recounted an experience with injustice, the point of the story was always the same: he accepted cruelty and evil as a part of life, but he always sought ways to overcome them. Sometimes he employed his personal charm and musical ability; other times, he simply had good luck. These personal qualities were the tools Louis used to control his would-be masters; they were his revenge and his delight in a society that wanted nothing to do with him and would have been content to push him to the margins for the rest of his life. The rite of passage he underwent in the Waif's Home—from outcast to band member—became the story of his career in microcosm, the story of a soul cheerfully but resolutely determined to make his way in the world. In fact, Louis's autobiographical writings, shorn of their bawdy jokes and reflections on jazz, can be seen as a series of moral lessons, the fruit of a lifetime's experience as a black man and black musician in twentieth-century America.

Once Louis won Davis's trust and became a full-fledged member of the band, he blossomed under the professor's regimen. He practiced regularly, using his instrument to accomplish many ends: to master himself, to charm the world into being a less cruel place, and to advance his own ambition. In time, Davis paid his young protégé the ultimate compliment by naming him the leader of the Colored Waif's Home Band. In this role, Louis began to come into his own as a performer, an entire *personality*, not just a compelling musician. "I remember Louis used to walk funny with his feet pointing out and at the first note of music he'd break into comedy dances," Peter Davis said. "He could sing real well as a boy, too, even though his voice was coarse. I'd play the horn and he'd dance, then I'd put down my horn and he'd pick it up and start playing it." Here, at the age of only twelve is a snapshot of Louis as a mature entertainer, musician, and show-business personality: laughing, singing, dancing, joking, and playing, unable to confine his exuberance and playfulness to any single activity.

The appointment as band leader opened up new worlds to young Louis. For the first time in his life, he was somebody, for he had distinguished himself in something other than rule-bending and the acquisition of street knowledge. The most immediate benefit was that his title got him out of the confines of the Home on a regular basis, whenever the band performed in greater New Orleans. "Now I would get a chance to go out in the streets and see Mayann and the gang that hung around Liberty and Perdido streets."

One day, Professor Davis entrusted Louis with his greatest responsibility yet: to lead the band in a formation to a ferry that would carry them to a picnic on the banks of the Mississippi near Baton Rouge.

"Louis, I know I can count on you," he told the young man.

"Yes, Mr. Davis, you sure can," Louis replied. It was an exchange that only a few short months before Louis would never have imagined hearing.

It was a beautiful summer day when the band arrived at the picnic, with azaleas and magnolias in brilliant bloom and the air steamy and fragrant with their perfumed essence. The band, under Louis's direction, played for the picnic group, and then, to his astonishment, they were invited to eat right alongside the people they had just entertained. The band gratefully set upon a feast of ham, fried chicken wings, spoon bread, potato pie, and biscuits laden with pecan butter.

After the meal, Louis wandered off by himself into the refreshing coolness of a cypress swamp, where it was so quiet that even his footfall was soundless. Spanish moss dangled ominously from branches high over his head, and Louis remembered tales of runaway slaves, possibly his own ancestors, who hid from their masters in swamps like these. Drowsy from the rich food and the moist heat, he found a comfortable niche between two overarching cypress trees and fell fast asleep.

He awoke with a start, in the dark, and began stumbling blindly through the swamp, his feet slapping through the black water, his imagination teeming with stories of unlucky folks who had wandered into swamps such as these and never emerged. Weak with fear, he sank to his knees, and in the dismal stillness, he thought he heard a shout. "I got up and after a while followed the shouts, stumbling here and there over the weeds and pulling up short when I'd run my face into some hanging moss. Pretty soon I got to the edge and I was surprised! It was just late sunset outside! The folks were all packed up and ready to go."

Louis apologized profusely and caught up with the ferry just before it left. "I didn't play any more music that day," he glumly recalled of that intoxicating taste of freedom and danger.

Despite this brush with disaster, Louis continued to march and to play, and he made an impression whenever he put his cornet to his lips. Chester Zardis, who played with Louis in the band, recalled, "I loved Louis's style. Louis could make some positions there and sound so sweet there, it'd make you shake your head." The larger New Orleans musical community was gradually discovering him, as well. Kid Ory, a trombonist with his own band, remembered the first time he set eyes on Louis. It was Labor Day, 1912, and the Waif's Home band was parading right behind Ory's group. It was just a kid's band, Ory thought, until "I heard this trumpet behind me, you know, good solid tone. We stopped for a beer break and a sandwich, and he's still blowing. I said to him, 'Come here, I want to tell you something, you're doing a good job.' " Louis replied, "Thank you, Mr. Ory." "You're going to be all right some day, you keep that up," Ory said. "So I kept him in mind all the time."

In the months to come, Louis led the Waif's Home band at more private picnics and in parades throughout New Orleans: "Uptown, Back o' Town, Front o' Town, Downtown." Wherever the band went, its distinctive uniform attracted attention: "long white pants turned up to look like knickers, black easy-walkers, or sneakers as they are now called, thin blue gabardine coats, black stockings and caps with black and white bands which looked very good on the musicians." As the leader, Louis wore a special uniform consisting of "cream colored pants, brown stockings, brown easy-walkers and a cream colored cap." He even posed for a photograph with the band. In it he is surrounded by more than a dozen other youths, many of them holding their instruments—a tuba, French horn, trombone, and cornet are visible, as is a large drum. It is a serious, even somber group portrait, depicting youthful pride and ambition rather than revelry or high spirits. It shows an obviously disciplined unit.

The parades in which the band performed were generally daylong affairs, and they could be exhausting—not that Louis would ever admit to feeling fatigue when he was on display; he performed, therefore he was. When the Merry-Go-Round Social Club hired the band to march out to Carrolton, a journey of twenty-five miles, he claimed, "Playing like mad, we loved every foot of the trip." And perhaps they did, in retrospect.

Finally, Louis got his chance to march with the Waif's Home band through his old neighborhood, and as he loved to recall, word of their presence around Perdido and Liberty streets drew many well-wishers and curiosity-seekers. Even better, "all the whores, pimps, gamblers and beggars were waiting for the band because they knew that Dipper, Mayann's son, would be in it. But they never dreamed I would be playing the cornet, blowing it as good as I did," he wrote.

"They ran to wake up Mama, who was sleeping after a night job, so she could see me go by. Then they asked Mr. Davis if they could give me some money. He nodded his head with approval, not thinking that the money would amount to very much. But he did not know that sporting crowd. Those sports gave me so much that I had to borrow the hats of several other boys to hold it all. I took in enough to buy new uniforms and new instruments for everybody who played in the band. The instruments we had been using were old and badly battered." His self-esteem, almost nonexistent when he arrived at the Waif's Home, rose as his public successes multiplied.

Louis's victory march through Storyville illustrates why he felt he owed so much to the Waif's Home. He had gone back to his neighborhood, not in disgrace, but with a newly enhanced status, in a uniform, with a shiny cornet in hand, and showed them all how far he had come. Then, even more remarkably, he had turned around and used the resources of its gamblers, hookers, and thieves, whom he never scorned or despised, who were his people, to better the lot of the boys in the Home. In so doing, Louis had accomplished something far more interesting and complicated than simply renouncing his past. He incorporated it into the expanding terrain of his new life and his music. He was never one to deny his past, no matter what others thought of it. He preferred to return to it, to reexamine it, to reclaim it, to turn it into a source of entertainment and even joy.

Throughout his time in the Waif's Home, Louis's parents, though living separate lives, worked quietly to obtain his release. His mother, Mayann, beseeched one of her employers, who was white, to speak on behalf of her son with Judge Wilson. His father, who had never had anything to do with Louis, promised to take Louis into his home and to provide for him upon his release from the Home. At first, these appeals failed to move the judge. In June 1913, he adamantly refused to release Louis, but a year later, his attitude changed. He was impressed by the fact that Willie Armstrong was fully employed, in charge of the boiler at a turpentine factory. Louis had posed no serious disciplinary problems in the Home, had distinguished himself in the band, and even helped to raise funds for the institution. In the face of all this evidence, Judge Wilson released the young man to the custody of father and stepmother on June 16, 1914.

The delicate negotiation took place without Louis's knowledge. When his father and stepmother came to retrieve him, he was content in the Home, happy to stay indefinitely. It was a beautiful summer evening, "when the air was heavy with the odor of honeysuckle. How I loved that smell! On quiet Sunday nights when I lay on my bunk listening to Freddie Keppard and his jazz band play for some rich white folks about half a mile away, the perfume of those delicious flowers roamed about my nostrils." Keppard was yet another cornet king of New Orleans, an eccentric crowd-pleaser. "Those nights when I lay on my bunk listening to Freddie play the cornet and smelling the honeysuckles were heaven for a kid of my age. I hated to think I was going to have to leave it." He planned to ask his father to allow him to remain at the Home, where he was happy. He knew what awaited him in Willie's house: neglect, an empty stomach, and no time or place for his music. If he were permitted to bring his cornet with him, it would probably disappear within a week. Here, he was among friends and admirers ("Everybody there loved me, and I was in love with everybody"), but in his father's house he would be a stranger. His father's sudden interest perplexed him. After all, he had "never paid me a single visit" during the year-and-a-half he had lived at the Waif's Home. "I did not even know his wife. What kind of woman was she? Would we get on together? What kind of a disposition did she have?" Despite all these misgivings, he could not disobey the judge's orders.

While he packed his bags, the band played songs of farewell. And then it was time for the final leave-taking. "Mrs. Jones kissed me good-bye, and I shook hands with every kid in the place as well as with Mr. Jones, Mr. Davis, and Mr. Alexander. I was unhappy when I left the Home and walked to City Park Avenue to take the streetcar into town."

Twenty years after his departure, in the first flush of his fame, he wrote a telling letter to the Home's by now venerable director: "I shall never forget the people who have done everything for me. I feel as though although I am away from the Waif's Home, I am just on tour from my own home, I feel just that close at all times. I've never felt any different. . . . Am always proud to tell the world of the place [that] started me out as a first class musician." He signed it, "Yeowsuh."

His lifelong loyalty to the Home was a source of amazement to those who knew him. After all, he had been confined to a boys' jail with a bunch of other juvenile delinquents, eating a subsistence diet of bread and molasses, getting whipped if he stepped out of line, yet he claimed to love it. He bragged about the bad things right along with the good, and he had the courage to describe both sides, so folks would understand what the experience meant to him.

The day after he left the Home, Louis began looking for a job. He was fourteen years old, and for all practical purposes, his childhood was over.

4.

COAL CART
BLUES

ouis gave every indication of landing back in the Waif's Home before the next bugle call sounded across the swamps. For one thing, he truly wanted to return. He had felt safe in the Home with Captain Davis; life there was orderly and predictable. Louis had enjoyed a measure of status and re-spect, as well as food on the table. Now he faced the prospect of living amid a chaos of prostitutes, gambling, pimps, cocaine, and illicit pleasure—all the elements that had contributed to his arrest and sentence.

In fact, the next three years were the wildest and most traumatic of Louis's life, and it took him a lifetime to come to terms with all that happened during this period, and to be able to talk about it freely. Each time Louis returned to these crucial years in letters or reminiscences, he elaborated on the events that made such an impression on him; some were learning experiences, others unbearably painful, and all of them contributed to his growing up in a hurry. The first time he tried to remember and discuss this period, he simply said that he did not play the cornet between the ages of fourteen and seventeen and spent most of his time hauling coal on a horse-drawn wagon. Later, he returned to this grim period, but only to make light of it. Finally, near the end of his life, he wrote a much fuller account of his adolescence and laid bare the grief, violence, and uncertainty that accompanied his coming of age in New Orleans.

My father and stepmother lived at Miro and Poydras streets, right in the heart of The Battlefield. They were happily married and they had two boys, Willie and Henry," Louis recorded. Willie had lobbied hard to get his son released from the Waif's Home, but he had no more use for him now than he did at the time of Louis's birth. Although Louis had formed an unusually close and satisfying bond with his mother—all the more precious to him because it had been postponed until several years after his birth—nothing of the kind ever took place between Willie Armstrong and his oldest son. In keeping with his father's phantom presence, Louis's impressions of him are fleeting, incomplete. He recalled a "tall nice looking Guy. Brown Skinned. With holes in his back." These marks were, in all likelihood, smallpox scars. "He was working for a big turpentine company keeping fire in those big furnaces for a very small pay. He also had other children by another woman who lived in the Uptown section of New Orleans. I had two stepbrothers, a stepsister, and stepmother named Gertrude." Repelled by his father's icy remoteness, Louis turned to his stepmother for affection and hospitality. "I did not have to wonder long about Gertrude, my stepmother, because she turned out to be a very fine woman, and she treated me just as though I were her own child. For that alone I will always love her. Henry was nice too. He was very kind to me at all times, and we became good friends." His other brother—Willie—"was about as ornery as they come. He deliberately would do everything he could to upset everybody."

Young Willie proceeded to make the new arrival's life miserable. "My parents, who both had jobs, discovered I could cook and that I could make particularly good beans. They were therefore glad to leave me with the two boys and to let me cook for them. Since I was the oldest they thought the kids would obey me. Henry did. But oh, that Willie! He was such a terrible liar that sometimes I wanted to throw a whole pot of beans at his head." Finally, young Willie succeeded in making Louis lose his temper and hit him in the face. "It was a hard blow and it hurt him." Louis expected that when his father and stepmother returned that night, Willie would rush to tell them what had happened, "but the little brat did not even open his mouth to them," much to Louis's surprise and relief.

He had little time away from his domestic chores to attend to music. Whenever he found a few minutes to pick up his cornet and blow, basking in the remembered glory of his days in the Waif's Home, Willie and Henry "used to laugh like mad." Eventually, they stopped laughing and offered advice and suggestions. Despite his demonstration, the family persisted in regarding him as their cook. No one imagined he could earn much of a living playing that thing.

Louis stayed with his father and Gertrude for several months, until his stepmother gave birth to a girl, little Gertrude, and Willie decided that he could not feed four children, only three. And so, without a further thought, he kicked Louis out of the nest, in violation of the promise he had made to Judge Andrew Wilson. If Louis was hurt by his father's change of heart, he did not admit it at the time. By way of explanation, he offered, "In those days common laborers were barely paid, and though both Pa and Ma Gertrude were working they could barely make both ends meet." Willie's actions marked the second time his father had rejected him, and from this time forth, Louis ceased to think of Willie Armstrong as his father.

For a time, his future was entirely uncertain, until his mother appeared one night. She talked privately to Willie for what seemed to Louis to be an excruciatingly long time, and when they were at last done, she said to her son, "Louis, would you like to go home with your mother?" Louis instantly agreed, although he refrained from saying how delighted he would be to get as far away as he could from young Willie's torments and cooking chores. "He's a fine kid," Willie said to his ex-wife.

"He sure is," Mayann replied. Louis smiled through all this adult hypocrisy and left the house in the company of his mother.

Before I realized it," said Louis, "I was back living with them again in that great big room where the three of us happily lived. No great luxuries, you understand, we were poor people, but we were always dressed up and clean. No toilets where you pulled the chain, only one outside privy for everyone to use and emptied once a week." Mayann returned to ministering to Louis after her fashion, which meant a regular "physic" of dried herbs to purge his system. "She'd go over the other side of the railway tracks and pick up what we'd call pepper grass. . . . I remember my mother firmly believed in old-fashioned remedies. She always said never worry about things you can't get. We didn't know about cold cream and all that; in the winter time if you looked a bit ashy and scratched your legs, . . . she'd put axle grease on us. Wasn't gonna waste that food money on cold cream. She'd go and grab one of those wheels and stick her fingers in the nuts and rub it on your ankles." For the next three years Louis lived in close quarters with his mother and sister, sharing not only the same privy with the two women, but the same bed.

Home at last, he returned to "Liberty and Perdido streets, my old stomping ground," and set about picking up where he had left off. It was exhilarating to be back on the border of the District, back on the street, skirting trouble, sure to meet old friends—and just beginning to get interested in girls. Two sisters stole his heart for a brief, haunting period. They were Orleania and Wilhemina, the daughters of the Martins, the caretakers of his old school, Fisk. Orleania resisted his overtures, no matter how he tried to get her attention. As Louis recalled, the hapless young woman later "got carried away by show business and fell in love with an actor (and a beat up one at that) who never did get to the big time in show biz. Why, he never did get into any kind of time at all, because he could not act in the first place." Nonetheless, Orleania thought he was "heaven on earth," but he led her to "destructions" up north, where she turned tricks for him, only to see him spend all the money she'd earned on other women. Eventually, Orleania returned home, sadder but wiser, but still not interested in her devoted admirer, Louis Armstrong.

Women! He was beginning to love them, but he didn't understand them, especially the stately Wilhelminia, whom all the boys adored. Louis was so in love with her that he was afraid to tell her, even when she flattered him by saying, "Dipper, don't you never stop practicing your cornet. You are going to be real good someday." How could anyone top that? How could he fail to love Wilhelminia? Not only that, she was a "perfect virgin . . . never been kissed." Louis was in agony. "I probably wouldn't have known what to say to a nice girl like that anyway. . . . It was a useless thing to even think of trying to marry a girl as nice as Wilhelminia . . . and a virgin, too."

Then Wilhelminia suddenly died. Grief-stricken, Louis mourned briefly, and tried to distract himself with other girls. "My luck always ran with the girls that came to the dances where I was playing. Lawn parties or some kind of social function. Most of them were already master minded and had already [been] laid and schooled by the elderly (cheap) pimps, gamblers, etc., which made them sort of feel they were a little more superior to a young musician like me. It was the cornet and the musicians that I wanted to be around mostly anyway. And if I never had a sex session with a girl, it really didn't make any difference with me." At least, he tried to persuade himself that was the case.

. . .

ven if he wasn't successful with girls, he was always sociable, and he
never lacked friends. Soon after he returned home he came across
Cocaine Buddy Martin, who was working at Segretta's, one of the neighborhood tonks. Louis remembered Cocaine Buddy as a kid in short pants,
but he had grown formidably and seemed to be a young adult. "I slipped up
behind him when he was sweeping out the joint from the night's gappings
and happenings, and put my hands over his eyes."

"Guess who?" Louis asked and after Cocaine Buddy struggled for a
while, removed his hands.

"Dipper! Man, you've been gone a long, long time."

Louis told Cocaine Buddy about his fine time at the Home and the
wretched time at his father's house, cooking for all the little children. And
then he came to the point: he was desperate for work. It never occurred to
him that he could be anything other than a cornet player. It never occurred
to him to return to school. It never even occurred to him to look for work
in a different part of town. If he couldn't earn his living from music, he
knew, he'd become a laborer like his father, toiling throughout the days,
and gambling away what little money he had managed to earn on Saturday
night, running on the fringes of the pimp-and-whore subculture he knew so
well, until he was too sick to work, and wound up in a pauper's grave. At
that time, in that place, there were few other paths open to a black man with
scant education, and the *lack* of choices focused him on his musical aspirations with a healthy desperation.

Fortunately, Cocaine Buddy knew of an opening at another tonk, Henry
Ponce's, located right across the street. According to Cocaine Buddy, Ponce
was one of the biggest men in the district, and he wasn't afraid of anyone,
which could only mean that his Mafia connections were solid. What Cocaine
Buddy failed to tell Louis was that Segretta and Ponce, despite their proximity, belonged to rival syndicates and so were mortal enemies.

The Mafia had long been a potent force in the Third Ward. For years,
authorities suspected that immigrants from southern Italy were turning the
city into a Mafia outpost. In 1890, amid this atmosphere of mistrust, the
city's superintendent of detectives was shot to death, possibly by an Italian,
and authorities tried a large group of Italians, whom they termed conspira-
tors. The trial publicized a term new to American ears—*Mafia*—but the

jury found all the defendants innocent. The city, indeed, the whole country was outraged by the acquittal. After the trial, the city kept the defendants in jail, supposedly for their own protection. Meanwhile, enraged white supremacist organizations vowed to exterminate every Italian in New Orleans. Four weeks after the verdict, they held a rally and incited a riot that led to the storming of the jail where the acquitted defendants were held. They were lynched, and so were other Italian bystanders, a total of eleven men, shot down or strung up from lampposts. Even this atrocity failed to drive the Italians from New Orleans or to end the Mafia's influence on the city's commerce. The crime syndicate coalesced into two warring factions, the Matrangas and the Provenzanos, and most Italian-owned groceries and tonks were compelled to take sides.

Despite Ponce's ties to organized crime, Cocaine Buddy made the job sound tantalizing. He told Louis, "All you have to do is to put on your long pants and play the blues for the whores that hustle all night. They come in with a big stack of money in their stockings for their pimps. When you play the blues they will call you sweet names and buy you drinks and give you tips." That was sufficient for Louis. He went to see Henry Ponce and got the job, where he played cornet for the whores, pimps, and their johns. He even played for Joe Oliver himself. "He got off at 12 o'clock at night, and seein' they threw the key away where I worked, he'd come up there and sit down and listen to me play and he'd blow a few for me, you know, and try to show me the right things."

During the next several months, Louis became acquainted with some of the city's roughest citizens: Jimmy Maker, Yellow Lugene, Dirty Dog, Red Devil, Cheeky Black (Louis would barely escape with his life from Cheeky several years later), Long Head Willie Logan, and Roughhouse Camel. "They fought each other because of hate, jealousy, and rivalry," Louis said. They also fought because of women—razor-wielding, hard-drinking women who were as tough as the men, if not more so. Big Vi Green, Mary Meat Market, Funky Stella, Foote Mama, Cross-Eyed Louise, Alberta, Steal Arm Johnny, and, the baddest woman of them all, the ferocious Mary Jack the Bear. "A notorious group," he said, with considerable understatement.

This was the cast of rowdy, shady characters who hung around the dance halls and saloons where jazz was heard. Louis never forgot these places, and in his later years, he drew up a list of them, beginning with the famous dance halls and moving down to the humbler, forgotten, Italian-owned tonks, such as the one where he played as a fourteen-year-old:

> The Economy Hall (downtown across Canal Street), Co-Operators Hall (ditto), the Winter Garden (up from Canal Street), the Roof Garden (Rampart Street), the Sans Souci Hall (uptown), the Butcher Hill Hall (near the Protection Levee up in Charlton), Bradens Astoria Hotel dance hall (Rampart and Gravier), the Pythian Temple Roof Garden (located on Gravier and Saratoga streets opposite the old Parish Prison), Pete Lala's Cabaret in Storyville (where Joe Oliver played for many years), Mrs. Cole's Willow Lawn (uptown), where Kid Ory's Band played for a long time. . . . The Fairgrounds Battlefield Hall, they also held horse races there. The Artesan Hall (all Creoles) in the 7th Ward, the Perseverance Hall (ditto), the Francs Amis Hall (Creole Section), the Independence Hall (ditto, Elmira Street near St. Claude St.), St. Mary's Hall (the same), Two Honky Tonks (3rd Ward), Savocca's (Poydras and Saratoga), and Spano's (Poydras and Frank-lin sts.), Pratts on Dryades + Perdido (later Howard Ave and Dryades St.), Henry Matrangas's Honky Tonk (Franklin + Perdido sts., 3rd Ward), where Armstrong came up.

To survive in this competitive, violent environment Louis needed a mentor and bodyguard, and he soon found his guardian angel in the person of Black Benny, the gambler and brawler of "25" fame. "Benny was a really different character from any of the would-be bad men I knew," Louis said. "Outside of being a great drummer and a good musician and our idol, he was a neat and handsome man with a well constructed body. Fearless. Would fight at the drop of the hat and *could* fight." Danny Barker, the New Orleans banjo player, said Benny was "six foot six—nothing but muscle. He was handsome in a sort of African way. He was all man, physically. He feared nobody. . . . Benny was also a ladies' man, a bouncer, and a prizefighter." He was so tough that he'd enter the battle royals without thinking twice. These were not musical battles; they involved fists. Five men, blindfolded, in a ring. Strike the bell, and chaos erupts. Everybody punches like mad, and whoever can stay on his feet the longest wins the prize, maybe as much as ten dollars. It was a terrible sight, like mules kicking each other, Barker said, bloody and bone-crunching. "You'd have to be an awful brave man to get in that ring." But Black Benny did, and he always won, leaving four defeated rivals groaning at his feet. About the only time Benny actually lost a fight was when he got into a fracas with a group of firemen. "He would have cleaned them up if one of them had not sneaked up behind him with a wagon shaft and knocked him cold," Louis wrote. "That was the only way Benny could be subdued."

For all his physical prowess, Black Benny considered himself a peacekeeper—of sorts. "Benny was the musicians' friend. Whenever one of us was in hard luck Benny would help him out," Louis gratefully noted. Kid Ory, the bandleader who remembered Louis from a Waif's Home parade, described their partnership. "One evening, Benny brought Louis, who had just been released from the Waif's Home, to National Park, where I was playing a picnic. Benny asked me if I would let Louis sit in with my band. I remembered the kid from the street parade and I gladly agreed. Louis came up and played 'Ole Miss' and the blues, and everybody in the park went wild over this boy in knee trousers who could play so great." John Robichaux, the renowned Creole orchestra leader who'd actually beaten Buddy Bolden in a cutting contest, was impressed by the cornet prodigy's facility that day: "If Louis wanted to play something fast he played the blues fast, and when they wanted somethin' slow he'd play the blues slow. I mean he was strictly a blues man then."

Kid Ory was so impressed that he issued Louis a standing invitation to sit in with the band, and the cornet prodigy did return to play several times, always in the company of Black Benny. "In the crowded places, Benny would handcuff Louis to himself with a handkerchief so Louis wouldn't get lost," another band member recalled. When Louis joined the band in a funeral or street parade, Benny tied himself to the boy with a length of rope, and the two of them would march through the streets of New Orleans that way, Benny pounding on his bass drum, and Louis blowing the cornet. And what music they made! Mutt Carey, the youngest of seventeen children who had grown up to become a superb trumpet player, never forgot the revelation of the youngster's musicianship. "I was playing trumpet with the Kid then and I let Louis sit in my chair. Now at that time I was the Blues King of New Orleans, and when Louis played that day he played more blues than I ever heard in my life. It never did strike my mind that blues could be interpreted so many different ways. Every time he played a chorus it was different and you knew it was the blues, yes, it was all the blues."

As he became better acquainted with Black Benny, Louis learned about his "devilish" streak. For example, Benny consumed beer with a superhuman thirst. "If anyone made the mistake of passing that growler to him first he would put it to his chops and all we could see was his Adam's apple moving up and down like a perpetual motion machine. We heard a regular google, google, google. Then he would take the can from his mouth with a sigh, wipe the foam off his mouth with his shirtsleeve and pass the can politely to the guy next to him as though it still had plenty of beer in it. Nay, nay, Black Benny with his asbestos throat had drunk every drop of that beer." Louis also recorded that Black Benny's notion of a prank was to load a .45-caliber pistol with blanks on New Year's Eve and, while standing in front of a church, empty the gun at an old neighborhood drunk known as Jesus. "And when all the church sisters and everybody was screaming, 'Oh, Lord, he killed him, he killed him!' Jesus got up and run." This miraculous resurrection of Jesus proved an instance of Black Benny's singular sense of humor.

Naturally, everyone in the district knew the remarkable Black Benny, especially the cops, who "liked him so much they never beat him up the way they did the other guys they arrested." When an old policeman tried to arrest him, Black Benny politely refused, explaining, "I played cards last night, and I won enough to get this suit out of pawn. Ain't been dressed up for a year. Now you can suit yourself, I ain't going to jail today." Furious, the cop grabbed Benny by the back of his pants—"You know how they do when they're going to take you to jail," Louis said—and Benny *dragged* the policeman after him, through the mud, until the cop gave up.

Although he avoided arrest on that occasion, Benny did spend many nights behind bars. "When Benny was serving time in jail the captain of the Parish Prison would let him out to play in funerals," Louis noted approvingly. "When the funeral was over he went back to prison just as though nothing had happened. This went on for years, but Benny never served more than thirty days at a stretch. He was never in jail for stealing. It was always for some minor offense such as disturbing the peace, fighting or beating the hell out of his old lady Nelly." Black Benny, as it happened, was married, in addition to his pimping duties, and, "When he was not in jail for fighting, he would be in the hospital recovering from a carving she had given him."

The odd arrangement apparently suited everyone—Benny's wife, the girls he ran, and law enforcement authorities. His violent domestic life was hardly unusual by the standards of Storyville, where women wielded razors as enthusiastically as the men did their knives and guns. Although men *seemed* to have the upper hand in this bloody battle of the sexes, many women held their husbands and boyfriends and pimps hostage with the threat of cutting and stabbing. Nelly was among the most violent. She was "as tough as they make them," Louis recalled, a "small, good-looking, light-skinned colored girl who was not afraid of anybody, and when she and Benny got mixed up in a fight they were like two buzz saws." She was so tough, in fact, that when they brawled, Louis's sympathies were with Black Benny, despite his superior size and strength.

He never forgot the time Black Benny was marching along in a parade, beating his drum. Nelly saw her husband and began hurling insults at him. He called her names right back, as he continued to march. "I don't think they could even spell the words they used," Louis said. When Nelly refused to relent, Benny took his drum off the strap around his neck to show that he meant business now and wouldn't take any more jive. Nelly suddenly turned and darted off across a stone slab covering a gutter filled with stagnant water. Benny broke ranks and took off after her, fixing to give her a beating. He paused in front of the slab, lifted it with his immense strength, and as Nelly tried to duck, dropped it on her back. She crumpled to the ground, as still as death.

Nelly was tough, as Louis said. Just when everyone thought Benny had killed her, she got to her feet and drew a long knife from her stocking. Brandishing the blade, she started "calling Benny all the black so and so's she can think of." Now it was Benny's turn to run, but Nelly was fast, and she caught up to him and sliced his buttocks with that long knife of hers. The two of them wound up in Charity Hospital. Louis recalled that "When they were released they went home together, smiling at each other as though nothing had happened."

Despite the older man's outlandish behavior, Louis considered Benny an expert on the subject of women, although it is hard to imagine a worse source of advice on matters of the heart. Not surprisingly, Black Benny warned Louis that women, no matter how dainty and pretty, could be incredibly dangerous and voracious. He advised Louis against giving his heart and his loyalty to just one woman, for she would surely betray him. The best defense against the treachery of women, said Benny, was to have as many women as possible. That was how Benny handled his affairs, and he advised Louis to do the same: *always have more than one woman.* Louis never forgot Benny, and he followed his advice concerning women to the letter. For the rest of his life, Louis did his best to have *more than one woman*, despite the havoc created by his pursuit of multiple relationships.

It was now February 1915, and Louis had been working steadily at Henry Ponce's tonk for six months. The hours were endless. "Saturday the tonk stayed open all night, and on Sunday I did not leave before ten or eleven in the morning. The drunks would spend a lot of money and the tips were good as tips went in those days. I saved money all around. Mayann would fix me a big bucket to take to the tonk and eat in the early hours. This saved me the expense of eating at a lunch counter or lunch wagon. Mayann said that the meals in those places were not worth the money they cost, and I agreed with her."

Although Louis was able to save money, his mother and younger sister, Mama Lucy, were still in dire financial straits, so Louis set his sights on a day job to augment his income. He turned to the Karnoffsky family, with whom he had worked so happily on their junk wagon, but they no longer needed his services. He was too old to toot a tin horn on their wagon, yet he was not old enough to drive it, a chore that Morris handled himself. He was quickly running out of alternatives.

Finally, his mother's current boyfriend, Mr. Gabe ("the stepdaddy I liked best"), helped him land a job driving a coal cart for the C. A. Andrews Coal Company, located at Freret and Perdido streets, just two blocks from Henry Ponce's little tonk. Taking the job lashed him to an exhausting schedule. He played at the tonk until two, three, even four in the morning, for this was New Orleans, where the music never ended, and then he staggered home before sunup to sleep for a few hours, and then, "from seven in the morning to five in the evening I would haul hard coal at fifteen cents per load." Fifteen cents! The money stood between Louis's entire family and oblivion.

The only respite from work came at noon, when he and the other drivers tied up their mules in front of Gaspar's grocery and assembled at the lunch counter, where they devoured poor boy sandwiches. Here they could gossip and lounge for a while before filling their drinking cans with cool beer. When the church bells tolled one o'clock, they returned to their mules for the remainder of the afternoon.

Despite this punishing schedule, he thrived on the work. "I loved it," he insisted. "I felt like a real man when I shoveled a ton of coal into my wagon. Being as young and small as I was I could not make over five loads a day. But I was not doing so bad. The seventy-five cents I made in the day plus the dollar and a quarter tips I made in the tonk added up." One reason he found his grueling day job tolerable was that Mr. Gabe, a veteran coal hauler who earned three times what young Louis did, imparted various tricks of the coal haulers' trade: "He taught me the knack of loading up a cart so I would not hurt my back so much." And he took to heart Gabe's words: "Son, always have a kind word for your mule in the mornings when you go into his stall to hitch him up because a mule is a very sensitive and stubborn animal. . . . You might go into his stall one morning and find him nasty-feeling, just like a human being, and he's liable to kick your brains out." That was one piece of advice he never forgot.

Black Benny also worked for the Andrews Coal Company, and even on the job he kept the peace in his rough-and-ready way. "Once when he was driving his coal wagon," Louis said, "he saw some big fellows sapping a group of little kids. He jumped off his wagon at once and really made a stew of the bullies." Even in this mind-numbing work, Louis managed to find small consolations of companionship and common sense.

The coal-hauling job assumed vital importance to Louis when Henry Ponce's tonk suddenly closed down. Had Louis been a few years older and wiser, he might have been aware of the lethal rivalry between Ponce and his neighbor, Joe Segretta; as it was, he merely sensed a rising tension between them. One Sunday morning, after a night of blowing, Louis fell into a conversation with his employer, who walked him to the door, discussing the blues numbers Louis had played that night. "This surprised me because I had no idea he was paying any attention at all," he recalled. As Louis stood in the doorway, "beating my chops with Ponce," he noticed a group of tough young men congregating across the street at Segretta's, and they didn't look like they were on their way to church. He realized they were there to jump Ponce, who appeared to be oblivious to their intentions. "All of a sudden I saw one of them pull out his gun and point it at us. He shot twice and tore off toward Howard and Perdido streets just a block away. Soon the others were shooting at Ponce, as well, and running off. 'Well, I'll be goddamned,' Ponce said as the smell of gunpowder filled the air. 'Those black bastards are shooting at me.'"

He grabbed his gun and took off after his would-be assassins, leaving Louis alone on the sidewalk. Transfixed by the sound of Ponce squeezing off six shots in succession, Louis was terrified that both he and his boss would be gunned down in front of Henry Ponce's. A few minutes later, bystanders found him rooted to the spot. When they spoke to him, "it suddenly made me conscious of the danger I had been in. I thought the first shot had hit me." Before he could answer, he fainted.

As Louis regained consciousness, the sound of gunfire rang through the streets; he subsequently learned that the remorseless Henry Ponce had managed to wound each of his assailants, three of whom went to Charity Hospital, while not taking a single bullet himself. "When he stopped shooting he walked back to his saloon raging mad and swearing to himself." Louis staggered home and collapsed again. "It was days before I got over the shock."

When he did go back to work at Ponce's, he wrote, "I was always on the alert, thinking something would jump off at any minute." Nothing did. Ponce's tonk was now safe from thugs and guns, but not from politicians. In the next local election, the dangers surrounding tonks such as Ponce's became an issue, and law enforcement shut the place down. Ponce promised Louis he would reopen soon, but the closing stretched on and on. Finally, Ponce moved to an entirely new location at the other end of town, where he was transformed into a respectable haberdasher. Only then did Louis realize he had lost his coveted night job.

Louis entered a bleak period—dependent on his backbreaking coal-hauling job for an income, deprived of music. In his free hours, Louis and Isaac Smooth, whom he knew from the Waif's Home, roamed the District, savoring the music ("we were always looking for a new piano player with something new on the ball like a rhythm that was all his own") and mocking the drunks who could afford to while away the hours within their walls. Many nights they observed whores fight over pimps, and, one night, an especially ferocious brawl at the corner of Gravier and Franklin, in front of a popular tonk.

That was the night he first laid eyes on Mary Jack the Bear, one of the combatants. Mary Jack the Bear was reputed to be the toughest whore in New Orleans, which was saying quite a lot, and the other prostitute— Alberta, just out of high school—"sure was attractive." Alberta had recently been in love with Mary Jack the Bear's pimp, Joe Bright-Eyes, who promptly made her into a streetwalker. According to Louis, Alberta was so deeply in love with that man that she seemed not to mind the mistreatment. Then Joe Bright-Eyes dropped her. But Alberta never forgot her sweet man, and when she found him at the bar of a tonk, she did everything she could to attract his attention. Mary Jack the Bear took notice of her flirtatious display, and the two whores began insulting each other.

". . . Ain't nothin' tougher than an old hide, and nothin' better than a tender beefsteak . . ."

". . . I know you sluts that only sleeps with po' white trash . . ."

". . . Till yo' dirty hide gets you what I got here, you better keep that big mouth shut . . ."

". . . You low trash . . ."

Then Alberta said to Mary Jack the Bear, "He told me he was through with you. I guess it is your hustling money he gives me."

The entire place fell silent when this mortal insult was uttered. Mary Jack the Bear reflexively threw her drink into Alberta's pretty face, and Alberta responded in kind. "They grabbed each other and started struggling and waltzing and tussling around the floor until they were separated," said Louis. "When Mary Jack adjusted her clothes and reached the door, she stopped. 'Bitch,' she said, 'I'll wait for you outside.' " And Alberta, who appeared to be completely out of her league, replied, " 'O.K., bitch.' "

A little crowd gathered on the sidewalk to witness the confrontation, but Alberta cowered within the tonk for perhaps half an hour, and when she finally emerged, Mary Jack the Bear, who had been waiting and seething, leapt on her with a long knife, slicing her face, and Alberta produced a similarly vicious-looking knife and went after Mary Jack the Bear. "Every blow was aimed for the face, and every time one would slash the other, the crowd would go, 'Huh, my gawd!'" Louis said. They fought until they both fell to the sidewalk, groaning, disfigured, and bleeding, and an ambulance took them to the Charity Hospital, two wild, sad, sorry whores. Only one of them survived the fight: Alberta, the comparative innocent. Mary Jack the Bear, the toughest whore in town, died in the hospital that night. Her rival Alberta lived on for years, "but her face is marked up so badly that it looks like a scoreboard. The quarter has never forgotten that fight, one of the bloodiest anyone had ever seen."

On other nights, the whores made overtures to Louis and his friend Ike, "a very handsome child. . . . Like me he was afraid of those strong, bad women." Louis claimed he wasn't thinking about girls, not after witnessing the violent death of Mary Jack the Bear. He was terrified of being drawn into a relationship with a young razor-wielding prostitute; he had seen too many premature deaths on the streets of New Orleans to want that life for himself. Even so, it held him in its grip, for every night he walked the streets of the District with Ike in search of precisely what they declared they wanted to flee.

Louis's mother inadvertently contributed to his sense of crisis and uncertainty, as she drifted from one boyfriend to another. He had scant comprehension of the economic and emotional needs that drove her, but he sensed she was in peril, and rather than wallowing in disappointment, he felt protective of her. As for her boyfriends, they seemed to him as depersonalized and utilitarian as the trousers they left behind in the house: "I used to wear my 'stepfathers' trousers, rolling them up from the bottom so that they looked like plus fours or knickers. Mayann had enough 'stepfathers' to furnish me with plenty of trousers. All I had to do was turn my back and a new pappy would appear."

Not all pappys were alike, however. Mr. Gabe was his favorite, by far, and he wished that his mother and Gabe would somehow see their way to getting married, and rescue her from the likes of Albert, who abused Mayann horribly in front of her son. Louis never forgot the time he was playing near them, while they sat on the bank of the Galvez Street Canal, and Albert, without warning, called Mayann a "black bitch," and struck her in the face so hard that she fell into the water, and then callously walked away. "My God, was I frantic! While Mayann was screaming in the water, with her face all bloody, I began to holler for help at the top of my voice. People ran up and pulled her out, but what a moment that was! I have never forgiven that man, and if I ever see him again I will kill him."

Louis wrote about the incident more than forty years after it occurred, and still burned with indignation. Neither he nor Mayann ever did see Albert again, although Louis kept inquiring about him until he heard that Albert was, at long last, dead.

Although Albert managed to elude his fury, he did confront another rascal, known as Slim, who also abused Mayann. One morning, his pal Cocaine Buddy alerted him that his mother and Slim were brawling in Kid Brown's, a Franklin Street honky-tonk. As soon as he found them, "an idea popped into my mind: get some bricks. It did not take me a minute, and when I started throwing the bricks at him I did not waste a one. As a pitcher, Satchel Paige had nothing on me." At least one of Louis's bricks found its target, and Slim collapsed and was taken to the hospital. That was the end of Slim; Louis never saw him again, or he might have killed Slim. "He was a pretty good blues player," Louis said, "but aside from that we did not have much in common. And I did not particularly like his style."

Formative experiences were coming at him as thick and fast as bullets. Any more of them and he'd wind up in the Parish jail—or a pauper's grave —just as his life was beginning. Little wonder that the Waif's Home looked so inviting and secure in comparison with life on the streets of the District. Only Black Benny stood between the adolescent Louis and this intoxicating chaos, but Benny had problems of his own and could not always mind his young charge. He got into a celebrated fight with another well-known, popular gambler, who went by the name of Nicodemus. It began, inevitably, over a gambling dispute in yet another tonk. Neither antagonist was armed that night, so Nicodemus went home to retrieve his pistol while Louis and everyone else warned Black Benny to get the hell out of there before Nicodemus returned, or at least get a gun of his own. Instead, Black Benny foraged around in an alley until his hand fell on a four-foot-long lead pipe. When Nicodemus ran back to the tonk and prepared to deliver the *coup de grâce*, Black Benny brought the pipe crashing down on Nico's head.

Nico collapsed on the street, and the fellows in the tonk removed his piece, so the police wouldn't find it on him. "That's what I call sticking together," Louis commented. "We did not want the cops to mix up in our quarrels; we could settle them ourselves." Both men survived the incident, but for the rest of his life Nicodemus carried a fearsome scar on his jaw.

Although Louis felt reassured by Black Benny's protection, he realized how very different they were. Louis hadn't been in a fistfight since before the Waif's Home, and when he slapped one of his younger stepbrothers at his father's house, he had been appalled at himself for losing his temper and dreaded the consequences. He felt the potential for violence within himself, but he preferred to live out his hostile impulses vicariously, through Black Benny, or the various protector-thugs with whom he formed alliances through his life. Essentially, Louis was nonviolent, unwilling to use his fists, and reluctant to pick fights or even respond to taunts. He was perfectly capable of losing his temper, which he often did, and of shouting and swearing, but unlike most of the men and many of the women in the District, he went around unarmed. If Louis ever carried a knife or a pistol on his person at this or any other time of his life, despite the obvious danger surrounding him and the need for self-defense, there is no record of it. His way of negotiating his way out of peril was to run, or to laugh, or to find a Black Benny to act as his bodyguard.

Black Benny could do nothing to help his disintegrating family, however. Mama Lucy, the younger sister on whom he doted, left home to work in faraway Florida. "A large saw mill town down there was taking on a lot of hands to fill the orders that were piling up," Louis explained. "Workers on ordinary jobs could make a lot more money in Florida than they could in New Orleans, and Mama Lucy was among the hundreds of people who went. She stayed in Florida a long time and I began to think I would never see my dear sister again."

In Mama Lucy's absence, he transferred some of the attention and affection he had lavished on his sister to his cousin, Flora Myles, Uncle Ike's daughter. Flora and Mama Lucy had been inseparable and looked out for each other, but once Louis's sister left, Flora drifted into a rough crowd of teenagers who lived in the District. "They were a little more jive proof than the average teenager, and they did practically everything they wanted to without their parents' knowing about it." The teenagers led her to "an old white fellow who used to have those colored girls up to an old ramshackle house of his. I do not need to tell you what he was up to."

Flora became pregnant, and Louis was utterly bewildered by her condition. "All I could do was to watch Flora get larger and larger until a fine little fat baby arrived." She called him Clarence. The day she gave birth, August 8, 1915, one of the worst storms in years hit New Orleans. "The storm broke with great suddenness when I was in the street on my way home. The wind blew so hard that slates were torn off the rooftops and thrown into the streets. I should have taken refuge, for the slates were falling all around me and I might have been killed as a number of other people were." He arrived home drenched, terrified, exhausted, hugged his mother and another cousin, Sarah Ann, and looked around the small home, and that was when he saw Flora lying in the bed he shared with his sister and mother. "There I saw the baby Clarence, and it took all the gloom out of me."

Fair weather quickly returned to New Orleans, but in the days to come the city became the scene of numerous funerals to bury those whose lives the storm had claimed. Louis couldn't help but note that "Joe Oliver, Bunk Johnson, Freddie Keppard and Henry Allen [Sr.], all of whom played trumpets in brass bands, made a lot of money playing in funerals for lodge members who had been killed in the storm." Meanwhile, Clarence, the child of that storm, thrived.

Everyone in the neighborhood knew who was responsible for the unwanted pregnancy—the old white man who lured young girls to his house. Friends urged Flora's father, Ike, to get revenge, or at least see to it the old man was arrested, but Ike knew there was nothing he could do. "He was a white man," Louis explained. "If we tried to have him arrested the judge would have had us all thrown out in the street, including baby Clarence. We put that idea out of our minds and did the next best thing. There was only one thing to do and that was a job for me. I had to take care of Clarence myself and, believe me, it was really a struggle." Yet Louis never doubted that he had to take care of the baby, because "there wasn't anyone in the family who could take care of him properly. I just could do it myself. I had a little ol' beat-up job [that] wasn't paying much, but the kid liked me so much—and I was crazy about him, too—I used to take him every place I went."

That Louis accepted this burden at such a young age, and with so few resources at his disposal, was remarkable. Not even Flora's father, Ike Myles, was willing to accept responsibility for the child, but Louis never complained, nor did he think his assuming a paternal role was unusual. In fact, he became very attached to the child and regarded himself as Clarence's guardian and protector, for all intents and purposes his father. "Clarence became very much attached to me also," he said. "He had a very cute smile and I would spend many hours playing with him."

The role bound him to his coal-hauling job and to New Orleans. A large part of the reason why Louis did not leave the city in search of a better job or new experiences during these desperate years was his sense of responsibility for the infant Clarence. At the same time, he was deeply gratified to be able to provide for the baby; it meant that he was doing the work of a man and thus entering manhood. For Louis, being a man was synonymous with manual labor. "Nobody in my family had a trade, and we all had to make a living as day laborers," he said. "As far back as I can see up our family tree there isn't a soul who knew anything that had to be learned at school." Louis, at least, had the good fortune to be employed, "and when Clarence was born I was the only one making a pretty decent salary. That was no fortune, but I was doing lots better than the rest of us."

In addition to hauling for the Andrews Coal Company each day, he sold newspapers and, when he could, played a little music, "dances, picnics, funerals, and an occasional street parade on Sundays." When he was really up against it, and his family was going hungry, he scavenged through garbage bins for food that could be recycled and resold at a small profit. "I would go out to Front o' Town where there were a lot of produce houses. They sorted lots of potatoes, onions, cabbage, chickens, turkeys. . . . The spoiled products were thrown into big barrels which were left on the sidewalk for the garbage wagons to take away. Before they came I dug into the barrels and pulled out the best things I could find, such as half-spoiled chickens, turkeys, ducks, geese, and so on. At home we would cut out the bad parts, boil the parts thoroughly, dress them nicely and put them in a basket. They looked very tasty and we sold them to the fine restaurants for whatever the proprietor wanted to pay. Usually we were given a good price with a few sandwiches and good meal thrown in." Even then he wasn't done scavenging. He would follow the garbage trucks all the way to the Silver City dump, where many of the city's poor waited to see what prizes they might reclaim from the refuse. "This is one of the ways I helped the family raise the newborn baby Clarence," he noted without complaint.

• • •

Despite their poverty and the dearth of fresh food, Mayann managed to feed the family quite well at times. When they were able to scrape together fifteen cents, she sent Louis to Poydras Market to purchase fish heads, which she boiled and seasoned and served "with tomato sauce and fluffy white rice with every grain separate. We almost made ourselves sick eating this dish." She could also turn out a Creole gumbo that Louis considered "the finest in the world," cabbage and rice, and that New Orleans staple, red beans and rice ("It is my birthmark"). Hers was truly food for the soul as well as the stomach. When she had time, she urged Louis to improve his cooking skills, and he mastered her version of jambalaya, a "concoction of diced Bologna sausage, shrimp, oysters, hard-shell crabs mixed with rice and flavored with tomato sauce." If jazz were food, it would be jambalaya, and Louis was so in love with eating well, so intoxicated with fine cuisine, that he actually left the Andrews Coal Company to work for Thompson's restaurant at Canal and Rampart. He wasn't able to land the sought-after job of waiter at this establishment—the best he could do was dishwasher—but, "I was permitted to eat all the ice cream puffs, doughnuts and ice cream I wanted." For two weeks, he gorged himself. He became so sick of these heavy sweet foods that "the very sight of them nauseated me," and he returned to his former job, hauling coal, and in a free hour or so he jotted down a number called "Coal Cart Blues." Years would pass before he had the opportunity to perform it in public.

Although Clarence thrived, Flora Myles, his mother, never regained her strength. Louis ascribed her loss of health to the shock she had suffered giving birth in the ferocious storm. She moved in with her sister Sarah, and the little family tried to take care of her as best they could, but they could not afford the two dollars a visit to the doctor would have cost, and even the Charity Hospital "was filled to overflowing and patients had to be left in the yard." As her strength ebbed, she began to look to Louis as the permanent guardian of her child. "Flora must have felt that she was going to die for just before she passed away she made his name Clarence Armstrong and left him in my care." The short, tragic life of Flora Myles—at once mystery, burden, and miracle—ended, and Louis became the only real parent Clarence would ever know.

To Louis's surprise, Mama Lucy returned from Florida to attend Flora's funeral. He expected his sister would have plenty of money after working at a good job all these months, but he was dismayed that she had little to show for all her travel and labor. "She did everything she could to help us with food and other essentials," but "she had not brought back much money with her." The struggling Armstrong family—Mayann, Mama Lucy, and now Clarence—looked to the teenaged Louis as their primary means of support. To sustain them, he embarked on a dangerous new career.

noticed that the boys I ran with had prostitutes working for them," Louis later recalled. "They did not get much money from their gals, but they got a good deal of notoriety. I wanted to be in the swim so I cut in on a chick. She was not much to look at, but she made good money, or what in those days I thought was big money." He became a pimp for a brief spell, joining the ranks of other young men in the District who had a string of girls hustling for them. Louis wanted to be like the other, more experienced pimps, a real man, flashing money wherever he went.

Louis never hid the fact that he had been a pimp; nor did he boast of it. In truth, he was a sorry excuse for a pimp. He admitted, "I was a green inexperienced kid as far as women were concerned, particularly when one of them was walking the streets for me." He lacked the guile, the ability to manipulate others (especially women), and the aura of menace the job required. Nor did he manage to run a string of girls; his pimping was confined to a single, unappealing prostitute. "She was short and nappy haired and she had buck teeth. Of course, I did not take her seriously, nor any other woman, for that matter. I have always been wrapped up in my music and no woman in the world can change that." Despite his determination to hold the girl and her trade at arm's length, it wasn't long before he found himself in the same situation in which he'd seen so many older, bolder men. Prostitutes, he soon found, were tougher than he was, and instead of intimidating them, he lived in fear of them and the sharp weapons they concealed next to their skin.

Louis's young whore had designs on him, and she insisted he go home with her. "I wouldn't even think of staying away from Mayann and Mama Lucy," he told her repeatedly, "not even for one night." He never understood how serious she was, or possessive, until she pulled a knife on him. "It was not the kind of large knife Mary Jack the Bear or Alberta carried, it was a pocket knife," he said. Nevertheless, she stabbed him in the left shoulder, and soon enough his shirt was drenched with blood. Louis was not the first pimp whose blood had been spilled on the sidewalks of New Orleans, nor the last, and if Black Benny, or any one of his friends had seen him in this condition they would have laughed knowingly, but the incident terrified him. When his mother found the bloody shirt and asked him what happened, he admitted that his "chick" was responsible. "What right has she cutting on you?" Mayann asked. Before he could reassure her that he would not let it happen again, she was on her way to confront the young girl who had wounded her only son.

The girl was getting ready for bed when Mayann came tearing into the house and lunged for her, holding her by the throat. "What you stab my son for?" she growled. Enraged, Mayann "threw her on the floor and began choking her to death." Convinced that his mother was going to kill the girl, Louis ran to find the one person who might be able to rescue him, his guardian Black Benny, whom he found in a nearby tonk, gambling. Together they ran back to the girl's house, where the fight continued.

"Don't kill her," Benny ordered when he strode into the house, his six feet six inches filling the room.

Mayann gradually eased up on the girl, and as she retreated, uttered a warning: "Don't you ever bother my boy again. You are too old for him. He did not want to hurt your feelings, but he don't want no more of you."

At a stroke, Louis reverted from a young adult caught in a dangerous and volatile relationship to a child relying unashamedly on his mother to extricate him from a nasty spat. His brief, unhappy career as a pimp came to an end, but not his fascination with prostitutes or his propensity for winding up in the clutches of tough and violent women.

Despite overwhelming evidence to the contrary, Louis held fast to his belief that it was a wonderful world. A little rough around the edges, maybe, but wonderful, all in all. "I could go on talking about my home town like mad because I love it. I always will. It has given me something to live for. Those millions of memories. Even with those hard times I'd be willing to live them all over again if I could run into some more Joe Olivers

[and] those fine prostitutes and pimps and gamblers who told me, 'Son, you don't want to live this kind of life.' "

He didn't have much choice. When Louis was lucky, he found work marching in a funeral parade, blowing his cornet, but it was strenuous work, and he was always tired, and so was everyone else. "A lot of musicians would go out balling all night, then think they can give their best on the horn, but it catches up with them," he observed. "I'd see those boys play all night, then go to the Eagle saloon at seven on Sunday morning when they got a parade coming up at nine. Instead of taking a two-hour nap to break their tiredness so they could tough the day out, no, they'd stay up all night and drink! And at two o'clock in the afternoon, when the sun beat down on them, I've seen them drop dead in the parade. So I learned my lesson early." There was something biblical in the starkness in the life of the jazzman; if he wasn't careful, he could die in the course of discharging ordinary musical duties.

Louis blew for the love of it, certainly not for the money. Even the best-known musicians of the hour, people such as Alphonse Picou and Manuel Manetta, made no more than a dollar fifty a night, which meant playing from eight o'clock in the evening until four o'clock in the morning. The band leaders didn't do much better; the biggest star of them all, Joe Oliver, was making just twenty-five dollars a week at Pete Lala's cabaret. For years he had to work as a yard hand and butler to make ends meet.

One of the reasons that these fantastically capable and energetic musicians earned so little was the size of the talent pool. In New Orleans, it seemed that *everybody* played an instrument. Louis estimated there were over one hundred working bands, all of them competing against one another for the same gigs. To attract attention, the bands went about on flattops, giving free concerts in the hope of securing a paying job and making the city and the surrounding swamps resound with their boisterous music. "On Sundays, the bands would be out on the wagons, doin' the advertisin'," Louis said. "See, in those days, there were long wagons, pulled by maybe one horse, or two mules. They hauled furniture weekdays. On Sundays, a dance hall owner would hire a wagon for his band. And the wagon would go around the streets. Bass fiddle player and the trombone man sit on the tailgate, so they don't bump the others. Rest of the boys, drums, guitar, trumpet, and so forth sit in the wagon. So on Sundays, the musicians who wanted to work, not lay around and drink, went 'on the wagon,' and that's where that saying comes from.

"You see, they always had the big dances on Monday nights and the advertisin' the day before, Sunday. For instance, one gentleman is giving a dance at Economy Hall tomorrow, and another gentleman is giving a dance at the Funky Butt Hall." The Funky Butt was still going strong, just as raunchy as it was in the days of Buddy Bolden. "They named this kind of dancing they did there 'funkybuttin,' "—the girls out on the dance floor bending low, and shaking their asses, and slapping them—"and the hall was famous by that name. Anyhow, these two gentlemen are giving a dance, and each wants to draw a big crowd. So they send out their wagons, paradin' and advertisin.' Now finally these two wagons meet at a corner. Their wheels are chained together. Then the two bands blow it out. And the one that gets the big ovation from the crowd, that's the one that gets all the people Monday."

Louis might have been overwhelmed by the raucous competition he faced, despite his talent, but fortunately, his friendships with the older musicians were beginning to pay off. By 1916, when he was fifteen, Kid Ory was employing him on a regular basis. Ever better, Joe Oliver extended a helping hand, for which Louis was extremely grateful. After all, Oliver was, in Louis's words, a "powerful man. *The* top trumpet. I could play a whole lot of horn in my little way, but Joe was *the* King!"

Despite his reassuring air, there was something a little scary about Joe. It may have been his damaged eye. The legacy of a childhood mishap, the clouded eye roamed blindly in his head. People were never sure if he was looking at them or at something else, and many called him "Cockeye" behind his back. No one dared call him that to his face. There was a tough, unforgiving side to Oliver, revealed in flashes of temper. "I suppose some would say that Joe was arrogant," said one of his most fervent admirers, Johnny Wiggs. "If the band played a piece, one of the girls might go up and ask the name of the number. Whatever number they just played, Joe would say, 'Who struck John!' That was the title he gave everything." The one thing Oliver could not tolerate was being ignored, especially when he gave signals to his band by stamping his foot. When his thump went unheeded once too often, he brought a brick to the bandstand, and when it was time to give the signal, he smashed the brick into the floorboards.

Startled, the other musicians usually decided they'd best pay strict attention to his cues.

Louis himself received a bitter taste of Joe's wrath for only a slight infraction. Joe had made an arrangement with Louis. "If you ever get on the corner with the wagon, and *my* wagon comes up," Joe advised, "you stand up, so I can see you. That'll be our signal, you know." On one occasion, Louis accidentally overlooked the signal and failed to stand as told. In retaliation, the combined forces of Joe Oliver and Kid Ory drowned out Louis, and "the crowd went mad." After experiencing this public humiliation, Louis tried to explain his lapse to Joe, but before he could get a word out, the old man bared his teeth: *"Why in hell didn't you stand up?"*

"Papa Joe, it was all my fault. I promise I won't do it again."

Little Louis looked so humble and contrite that Oliver was persuaded to shrug off the matter and invite his protégé to join him for a beer. "This was a feather in my cap because Papa Joe was a safe man, and he did not waste a lot of money buying anybody drinks."

From then on, Louis and Joe Oliver had a real bond, and the young man became a frequent guest in the Oliver home and an avid admirer of his wife's cooking. Before long, Stella Oliver was serving him red beans and rice and treating Louis like her own son. She spoiled Louis by putting hock bones into the beans, and then, as they ate, Joe and Louis would eye each other playfully to see who would grab the last hock bone from her wonderful concoction. That was another thing they had in common: a love of food. Joe carried over 230 pounds on his short frame, and when Louis began to put on weight, he became a dead ringer for Joe Oliver. They could have been father and son, so much did they look and play and eat alike. The relationship between the two men was consecrated when Papa Joe bestowed one of his old cornets—a battered instrument he no longer played—on his grateful young acolyte. "I prized that horn and guarded it with my life," Louis remembered. "I blew on it for a long, long time before I was fortunate enough to get another one."

Despite the personal and professional guidance Oliver offered him, Louis was still an amateur, forced to supplement his meager musical income with manual labor. He went from one odd job to the next, always willing, trying to please his employers, but more often than not he was undone by appalling working conditions. "For a time I worked unloading the banana boats until a big rat jumped out of a bunch I was carrying to the checker. I dropped that bunch and started to run. The checker hollered at me to come back and get my time, but I didn't stop running until I got home. Since then bananas have terrified me. I would not eat one if I was starving."

Whenever one of Louis's schemes failed, he returned to hauling for the Andrews Coal Company, where the work, though dependable, was agonizingly difficult and the pay modest. "It was hard work shoveling coal and sitting behind my mule all day long, and I used to get awful pains in my back. So any time I could find a little hustle that was just a little lighter, I would run to it like a man being chased." Unfortunately, the "little hustles" never amounted to anything more than that, and it seemed to him that he would spend the rest of his life sitting behind his mule, "Lady," and, from time to time, marching in a funeral band to augment his income.

He rarely got a chance to play his cornet these days, and when he did, he seems to have made little impression, for the glowing reminiscences of his musicianship that mark other periods of his life are absent from this one. Instead, his limitations drew comment. "Why don't you try Dipper-mouth?" Bill Matthews, the trombonist, suggested to the members of his group, the well-known Excelsior Brass Band, who needed a good man on the trumpet. "Oh, man, he can't read," one of them said. Matthews said that even if he couldn't read, Louis would get along fine. Yet even Louis lacked the self-confidence to accept the job. "You know I can't make that, I can't make no brass band, not with the Excelsior Band." Matthews argued that if Louis would only try, he would learn how to read and play the music on the job, but the young man was still afraid. In his misery, Louis bought himself a nickel bottle of beer. "Then he had the cramps," Matthews said. "We had to lay Louis out. Louis got overheated and had the cramps from that . . . bottle. He stayed right there, so we went and played on throughout without Louis."

L ife became even tougher for Louis as Storyville and its opportunities began to wither. Since the outbreak of the Great War, a new breed of customer had drifted into the District—sailors who wanted to have sex as cheaply and quickly as possible, and music be damned. They became targets for predatory pimps, gamblers, and thugs. "There were an awful lot of killing going on," Louis noted. "Mysterious ones, too. Several sailors were all messed up, robbed and killed. That's one of the main reasons for the closing of Storyville. Those prostitutes commenced to having their pimps either rob or bash their brains in, anything to get that money. That's when the United States Navy commenced to getting warm, and brother, when they became warm, that meant trouble and more trouble, not only for the vice purveyors but for all the poor working people who made their living in Storyville such as cooks, waiters, maids, musicians, butlers, dishwashers. I'm telling you, it was a sad, sad situation for anybody to witness."

The growing public awareness of venereal disease did further harm to Storyville's reputation. "The law commenced to arresting all the prostitutes they caught standing in the doors and sent them over to the Isolation Hospital to be examined," Louis wrote. His sympathy lay with the diseased prostitutes, not with the customers they infected. "And if they had the least thing wrong with them—or if they're blood-bad [syphilitic]—they'd be sent away for a long time. And believe me, there were lots of prostitutes who had to be sent away for treatment. And of course reports from those cases helped the Navy to have a strong alibi to close her down."

In truth, Storyville's best days were long gone, and it is possible to trace its decline to 1909, when the District's most influential madam, Josie Arlington, retired from the business after making a fortune and losing her mind in the process. She died in 1914, her passing marked by a quiet, respectable funeral with nuns and priests in attendance. By that point, whatever decorousness had once been attached to the elegant brothels of Storyville was no more than a fond memory. Even without the government's intervention, the number of brothels and prostitutes declined precipitously. In Storyville's glory days, at the turn of the century, the police counted over 260 brothels and two thousand prostitutes in the District. In 1910, when Louis was delivering coal to the prostitutes for the Karnoffsky family, there were only 175 brothels and the number of active prostitutes had slipped to about eight hundred, many of them part-time. By the time the navy forced New Orleans to close down Storyville, there were fewer than 100 houses in operation and five hundred active prostitutes. The death blow finally arrived in August 1917, when Newton D. Baker, the Secretary of War, forbade prostitution within five miles of a local army base, and Josephus Daniels, the Secretary of the Navy, announced a similar edict for the navy. That same month, the Mayor of New Orleans, Martin Behrman, received a visit from Bascom Johnson, representing both the navy and the Department of War, who demanded that Storyville be shut down immediately. The good mayor actually went to Washington, D.C., to lobby on behalf of Storyville and its whores, but there wasn't a politician to be found who would publicly defend prostitution. Behrman's visit briefly forestalled the inevitable, but Daniels informed the mayor that if he didn't shut down Storyville at once, the combined forces of the army and the navy would step in and do it for him. Behrman finally yielded, and on October 17, he reluctantly introduced an ordinance designed to abolish Storyville. Calling prostitution a "necessary evil in a seaport the size of New Orleans," the ordinance lamely explained that "our city government has believed that the situation could be administered more easily and satisfactorily by confining it within a prescribed area. Our experience has taught us the reasons for this are unanswerable, but the Navy Department of the Federal Government has taught us otherwise." Within days, the resolution was adopted. On November 12, 1917, prostitution in Storyville was officially declared illegal.

On the appointed day, policemen circulated throughout the District, knocking on doors, telling the whores that they could stay if they liked, but they had to remove their red lights, and, of course, cease their prostitution activities, or they would be arrested. Nearly all the whores hung on until the end, and shortly before midnight, they finally grabbed their belongings, filled their carts, and walked out of the area, either to set up business somewhere else or simply to leave.

"The scene was pitiful," said a witness. "Basin Street, Franklin, Iberville, Bienville, and St. Louis became a veritable shambles of Negro and white prostitutes moving out. With all they had in the world reposing in two-wheel carts or on wheelbarrows, pushed by Negro boys or old men, the once Red Light Queens were making their way out of Storyville to the strains of "Nearer My God to Thee," played by a massed combination of all the Negro jazzmen of the Red Light dance halls. By nightfall, the once notorious Red Light District was only a ghost—mere rows of empty cribs. . . . The saloons and the old familiar wagons, with their wieners and hot hamburgers, remained for a time. Now and then a Negro organ-grinder came out to give one of Old Man Giorlando's untuned organs an airing, but the green shutters were closed forever. The old Red Light District of New Orleans became history."

5.

HOTTER
THAN THAT

For Louis Armstrong, the closing of Storyville meant more than the end of a bawdy diversion; it was the end of a way of life on which he had relied since he was a child. He spoke for many when he lamented the closing of Storyville. He regarded the end of the notorious career of Lulu White, his favorite madam, as a tragedy. "The law dragged her down like a dog until they broke her completely," he wrote with uncharacteristic choler. "It was a shame the way they snatched her mansion—furniture, diamonds galore, things worth a fortune." He consoled himself with the thought that the memory of her brothel, Mahogany Hall, and the street she made synonymous with sin, Basin Street, would live on.

Meanwhile, the prospect of unemployment loomed. He saw few alternatives to spending the rest of his days hauling coal or following a junk wagon through the suddenly quiet streets of New Orleans. "After Storyville closed down, the people of that section spread out all over the city, so we turned out nice and reformed," he remarked in a rare flash of bitterness. But the end of Storyville did not mean the end of prostitution in New Orleans, he discovered; it simply redistributed it and drove it underground. "Some [prostitutes] went into other neighborhoods kinda bootlegging the same thing, especially if the neighborhood were lively and jumped just a wee bit." For instance, "in the Third Ward, where I was raised, there were always a lot of honky-tonks, gambling, prostitutes, pimps going on, but all on a small scale, very very small at that. Where it would cost you from three to five dollars to see a woman in Storyville, it didn't cost but fifty cents or seventy-five cents to see and be with a woman in the Third Ward. There were no whites up this way at all. They were all colored. They weren't standing in the doors, either, because after Storyville closed that one situation wasn't to ever happen in New Orleans again. And it didn't.

"Now, after Storyville shut down, the girls could just call out the door for beer. But the wrinkle was, they could catch a 'John' (a sucker) and call down to whatever saloon they'd like to trade with and say these words: 'Oh, Bellboy, Oh, Bellboy.' And when the Bellboy from that particular saloon answers, this chick will say to him, 'Bring me half a can'—which means a nickel of beer. And he'll say, 'O.K.,' and go into the saloon and repeat the same thing, and [in] less than a few minutes he'll be on his way over this small-time whore's house with this half a can. She meets him at the door with her bucket or pitcher. He pours it in, collects the 'tack,' I mean the nickel, and returns to the saloon and sits outside on a beer barrel and waits for another order. He gets a salary just delivering drinks. If they desire a whole can, that's a dime of beer. So if you have more than two in the party, it's very wise to order a whole can. It wasn't anywhere near as handy for the girls as it was in the old days."

Louis didn't realize it at the time—nor did anyone else—but the end of Storyville marked the beginning of the jazz diaspora. Its disappearance forced the bands that once shook its dance halls and brothels to seek new venues beyond New Orleans, up the Mississippi River on riverboats, into northern recording studios, and then, on record, across the country and finally the world.

The closing of Storyville appeared to rob Louis of his last chance of becoming anything more than a part-time, semiprofessional musician. His mother and sister encouraged him to stick with his day job and had no interest in furthering his musical career. He stopped playing and practicing, but he did not stop thinking of music.

He briefly left New Orleans for Houma, Louisiana, to play in a funeral band supported by an undertaker known as Mr. Bonds. Here he earned a weekly salary and boarded in the Bonds's home. "He had a nice wife and I sure did enjoy the way she cooked those fresh butter beans, the beans they call Lima up north." When not committed to a funeral parade, he found time to play at local dances and to emulate Buddy Bolden: "When the hall was only half full I used to have to stand and play my cornet out of the window. Then, sure enough, the crowd would come rolling in.

That is the way I let the folks know that a real dance was going on that night. . . ."

Louis's independence proved short-lived. He gambled away his meager salary ("In less than two hours I would be broker than the Ten Commandments") and went home to Mayann, who fed him so well that he determined "never to leave home again." But soon he was off again, this time riding the rails up to Harahan—thirty miles from home. He had hatched a plan: he was going to work on a sugar cane plantation. It was the sheerest adolescent escapist fantasy. Older blacks, closer to sharecropping and slavery, knew what punishing, exhausting work cutting sugar cane was; it was a lonely, miserable life, with no relief but drinking on Saturday and church on Sunday. Even driving a coal cart in New Orleans was preferable. Eventually Louis had second thoughts about his scheme, and with every mile he traveled, he became lonelier and hungrier, "and the hungrier I got the more I thought about those good meat balls and spaghetti Mayann was cooking the morning I left." He made it home in time for dinner, never bothering to tell his mother of his aborted plan to work in the sugar cane fields.

Louis had no choice but to return to driving his coal cart. When he least expected it, he found a way to return to music. One evening, as he drove his coal cart home past Matranga's tonk, Clerk Wade, the Cotchplayer and pimp, hailed him inside for a drink. Matranga's was a dangerous place, and the reputation of its proprietor was so lethal that many people were afraid to utter his name. He belonged, as everyone knew, to one of the most feared Mafia clans in New Orleans. Louis had no idea of the danger surrounding Matranga and his tonk. As far as Louis was concerned, old Henry was all right, "he treated everybody fine, and the colored people who patronized his tonk loved him very much."

Matranga's little pleasure palace was a typical two-room tonk, with gambling in the back, while "the other room was for dancing—doing that slow drag, together, humping up one shoulder—maybe throw a little wiggle into it. Had a little bandstand catty-cornered, benches around the walls. Drinks were cheap—and strong." The patrons came in three varieties: gamblers, whores, and johns. Matranga managed to keep his rowdy customers in line without offending them. "Knowing how sensitive my people are when white folks shout orders at them and try to boss them around," Louis noted, "he left it to Slippers, the bouncer, to keep order." From the start, Louis was impressed by Slippers, "a bad M-F."

Like every tonk, Matranga's employed a small band. That night, the cornetist failed to appear, and Louis, for once at the right place at the right time, sat in. In fact, Slippers recommended him for the job. It had been months since he had played. He protested, "I'll have lips like a toilet bowl," yet Matranga offered him a steady gig on the strength of Slippers's recommendation. He even promised to finance a cornet for the young man. Louis naturally accepted the offer and savored the prospect of liberation from his coal cart.

Henry and Louis left Matranga's and walked to a pawnshop off Rampart Street. Most jazz musicians could not afford to own instruments, so pawnshops often rented them out for a night or two. But Matranga offered to buy a cornet for Louis on the spot and to reimburse himself by taking a fixed amount out of Louis's salary and tips over a period of weeks. They walked into a brightly lit pawnshop where Bob Lyons, who had once played with Buddy Bolden himself, stood behind the counter. Lyons and Matranga haggled over the price, settling on fifteen dollars. Louis's new employer peeled the full amount off his roll, and the two of them left the pawnshop with the instrument. When Henry wasn't looking, Louis kissed it.

His exhilaration faded as soon as he sat down to play with the other members of Matranga's band: Sonny Garbee, the drummer, and "Boogers," the pianist. Within minutes, his lips were sore; notes that had once come easily eluded him. To cover his embarrassment, Louis resorted to singing all the popular songs he knew, complete with risqué variants. He did well enough to obscure the memory of his faulty cornet playing.

Louis managed to keep his new job, but just barely, for the hours were burdensome, the pay nearly nonexistent, and his family skeptical. "At the end of the night I only received fifteen cents," he wrote. "I went home and divvied up with Mother, just the same. I told Momma that business was kinda bad last night and this fifteen cents was all that I had, and immediately my sister Mama Lucy awakened out of a sound sleep and said, 'Blow all night for fifteen cents? Ha ha.' Of course, it's funny now, but Sis made me so doggone mad." Mayann advised him to return to hauling coal.

. . .

Next morning, Louis rose at five o'clock, hitched up Lady, his regular mule, and resumed his day job. He still returned to Matranga's night after night, paying off the price of his cornet and regaining his facility. He soon won a raise to a dollar twenty-five a night, an amount that made an impression even on his mother.

He was tired all the time, but happy. He was finally back in his element, and he loved every brawling, sordid, dangerous, exhausted, reckless, bawdy minute of it. Matranga's was a magnet for the refugees from Storyville, who fortunately considered him off-limits. "They didn't bother with kids like us, but I knew Red Cornelius, carried anything he could get to cut you or shoot you. George Bo'hog [was] another one. There was Dirty Dog, Brother Ford and Steel Arm Johnny, Aaron Harris—always in trouble. That's all they lived for, gambling and that pistol and the pals. Cats used to come in from all the little old towns—Little Woods, Slidell, Bogalusa—in Saturday night. They'd be wearing their overall jackets, all pressed to look sharp . . . and a big .45 under the jacket. They'd just been paid off at the saw mill—cutting sugar cane, cotton, whatever, railroad-section gangs—and some of these cats would lose, try to raid the Cotch table. There'd be a shooting. And I used to see some of them—no money, no place to go, no sleep for days—trying to sleep standing up in a corner of the honky-tonk."

Louis studied the prostitutes so carefully that he considered himself an expert on their trade. "Around four or five in the morning, that's when all them whores would come into the tonk—big stockings full of dollars—and give us a tip to play the blues. . . . They'd get a little box of powdered chalk, buy fifteen cents' worth of perfume, pour it over the chalk and powder themselves with it. It was pink chalk. Couldn't stand white chalk—looked like you scratch your leg in wintertime." He noted how pimps victimized their girls. "These gals in the tonk would take their trick to a room and the pimp would hang around to see how long she stayed with the trick—and if she was a little too happy there, she gets a whipping after." After they had fleeced their tricks and fought with their pimps, they turned their attention to him. "We would play those lonesome blues and these gals could come trucking into the joint one by one with those short aprons on showing those fine 'gams' (their pretty legs) with those good silk stockings, showing a great roll of money they've swung all night for their daddy, and the first thing they would say to me was, 'How 'bout a drink, Dipper?' That's what my pet name was in those days. I was so small and cute (ahem) those ladies would sit me on their knees and buy me a glass of beer. They served real good cold beer in those days. It almost froze your goozle pipes. And as bad as those gals were, I never did get a scratch, and believe me, I've seen some awful fights around," Louis wrote.

Although he remained oblivious to Matranga's notoriety as a Mafia headquarters, Louis noticed that the tonk attracted a different type of crowd from the folks he had entertained at Ponce's. They were "tough sportin' people—we didn't even know the word gangsters then, we used the expression hoodlums. All those girls who kept their money in their stockings—they liked to hear me play the blues—but once trouble started between the bad cats someone would make sure I was safe."

All around him, though, people were dying in Matranga's. "This bad sombitch came in, played some Cotch and Georgia Skin, another game that nothing but the toughest of gamblers play. That's a game where the dealer pulls cards from the top, one at a time. And if the one he pulls happens to be your card, you lose, and have the privilege to select another if you wish to continue in that game. Well, the dangerous part about Georgia Skin is you're liable to be playing with a real smart gambler who knows how to carry the cub. The cub is the last card that comes off of the deck, which might be his card. In that way, he breaks every player. Of course, if someone digs him fixing those cards to that effect he's liable to be left there holding not anything but a nub," which meant that someone who didn't like losing to him might cut off his hand. "So the old saying went, 'If you don't want to carry a nub, don't carry the cub.'"

Through all the gambling and the drinking and the fornicating and the fighting Louis played his cornet. Slippers, the bouncer at Matranga's, told him, "We all like the way you blow that 'quail.' Boy, you sho' can blow that quail." And this was from Slippers, "a bad sombitch himself," who once killed a man in front of Louis. "This guy came to play Georgia Skin from this Levee camp," Louis recalled. "After losing he wanted to break up the joint. Slippers asked him out gently. He even put him out gently. This cat from the Levee camp, a sneaky sombitch, thought he'd wait until he caught Slipper's back turned and pulled out a great big forty-five and pointed directly at Slipper's back, and somebody hollered, 'Look out, Slippers,' and before a black cat could lick his own behind, Slippers pulled out his gun and beat him to the draw and shot him right in the belly. Ump. I wasn't good any more all night."

All this shooting was a little nerve-racking. In fact, Boogers was trembling and Garbee stammering after the outbreak. But by four o'clock in the morning, the whores were back, and they bought drinks for the band, and the music started up, and the shooting became just another colorful memory, a souvenir of good old New Orleans.

"I don't see how I didn't get it," Louis marveled of that night. "Just wasn't my time to die, man."

Louis managed to stay narrowly out of harm's way, but he still experimented with the assorted vices available at Henry Matranga's tonk, always within careful limits that he set for himself. He tried gambling, but he gave himself away easily. "I was too glad when I got a good hand so that everybody could tell." And he continued to flirt with the whores who flocked to Matranga's, although now he was torn by his desire for their tantalizing bodies and his fear of their violence and knives. They were so tempting and available and manipulative, especially so with an adolescent as their mark. "They would wear real short dresses and the very best of silk stockings to show off their fine big legs," he wrote. "As soon as we got off the bandstand for a short intermission the first gal I passed would say to me: 'Come here, you cute little son of a bitch, and sit on my knee.' Hmmmm! You can imagine the effect that had on a youngster like me. I got awfully excited and hot under the collar. 'I am too young,' I said to myself, 'to even come near satisfying a woman like her. She always has the best of everything. Why does she pick on me? She has the best pimps.' (I always felt inferior to the pimps.) I was afraid of the hustling gals because of my experience with the chick who pulled the bylow knife on me and stabbed me in the shoulder. Still the whores continued to chase me. Of course I admit I just couldn't resist letting some of the finer ones catch up with me once in a while."

About this time, Louis got drunk, "dead drunk," for the first time in his life—so drunk that friends had to carry him home to his mother, who ministered to her only son. "After she had wrapped cold towels with ice in them around my head she put me to bed. Then she gave me a good physic and told the kids to go home." The "physic" was one of her herbal concoctions, a powerful purgative.

"The physic will clean him out real good," she said. "After he has put one of my meals under his belt in the morning he'll be brand new."

When he came to his senses the next morning, Louis, highly embarrassed, apologized to his mother. Her reply, as he recounted it, revealed an understanding of his urge to explore the wilder side of life, combined with an unusual proposal for teaching him to hold his liquor. "Son," she said, "you have to live your own life. Also you have to get out into this world all by your lone self. . . . I would not dare scold you for taking a few nips. Your mother drinks all the liquor she wants. And I get pretty tight sometimes. Only I know how to carry my liquor to keep from getting sick. . . . I'll tell you what. Suppose you and I make all the honky-tonks one night? Then I can show you how to enjoy good liquor." Louis was only too happy to accept her offer.

Louis worked hard that week, hauling coal and blowing his horn and saving his tips. When his night off arrived, "I was loaded with cash." Mayann took him to Savocas' tonk, located at Saratoga and Poydras streets, where she began her lesson in drinking like an adult. Louis drank a few beers as he eyed the whores and pimps, and then they moved on to Spanol's, just around the corner. Here, the bartender was so delighted to see a mother and son making the rounds of the tonks together that he "kept pouring whiskey down into our stomachs"—raw whiskey, 100 proof, as powerful as a kick from a mule. All the while, Mayann "kept explaining to me how to hold my liquor," and Louis, growing increasingly unsteady on his feet, kept nodding and replying, "Yes, Moms."

Then it was on to Matranga's, where the boss told Mayann what a fine young man her son was. Said Louis: "That goes to show that no matter how tough an ofay [white person] may seem, there is always some 'black son of a bitch' he is wild about and loves to death just like he loves one of his own relatives." The praise was especially sweet after his mother had ridiculed the fifteen-cent salary he had brought home from his first night of work at Matranga's. But that was all forgotten now. Mayann lamented that she'd never been able to provide for Louis as she would have liked, "but I could not do very much about it except pray to the Lord to guide him and to help him," and she showered thanks on that fine and generous man, Mr. Henry Matranga, for employing her son at his matchless tonk. What better place for him to work than in the company of New Orleans's most discerning pimps and hookers? "The Lord will bless you for it," she exclaimed. "I shall remember you every night when I say my prayers."

At that moment, Slippers came in, and he recognized Mayann—from where, her son did not know, and did not ask—and Slippers, metamorphosing into a gentleman, invited them both to have a drink with him. "By this time, Mother and I were getting pretty tight," Louis said, "and we had not visited even half the joints. But we were determined to make them all." Meanwhile, Slippers, becoming more sentimental with every shot he poured down his throat, started telling Mayann how "that boy of yours should really go up north and play with the good horn-blowers." Louis was amazed. There was a crazy idea if he'd ever heard one. He expected to spend the rest of his life here, playing in a band or even leading one, like King Oliver, so long as he managed to dodge the hustlers' bullets and the whores' razors. He was aware that Jelly Roll Morton, Freddie Keppard, and a few other stars had gone up north, but it hadn't occurred to Louis that there might be a place for him beyond the boundaries of New Orleans.

"Thanks, Slippers," Mayann said, in an alcoholic haze. "Of course his no-good father has never done anything decent for these children. Only their stepfathers. Good thing they had good stepfathers, or else I don't know what those two children would have done."

Without warning a fight erupted in the back room, and Slippers suddenly left Louis and Mayann. "In less than no time, he was running the guy to the door by the seat of his pants. He gave him a punch on the chops, saying: 'Get the hell out of here, you black son of a bitch, and don't come back again, ever.' " The altercation brought Louis and Mayann back to their senses, at least temporarily. Finishing their round of drinks at Matranga's, they moved on to Segretta's at Liberty and Perdido, where the house served extract of Jamaica ginger for fifteen cents a bottle—enough to make a sailor sick for a week. "Everybody was buying this jive and adding half a glass of water, so Mayann and I joined in." The result was predictable: "It knocked you flat on your tail."

"Son, are you all right?" asked Mayann, her eyes glazed.

"Sure, Mother, I'm having lots of fun."

Louis claims that he and his mother consumed two bottles of extract of Jamaica ginger apiece. Whatever the amount, they were pickled. Even though Mayann offered to take him home, Louis wanted to visit his old stomping ground, Henry Ponce's, just across the street. Again, mother and son were received with open arms, effusive praise for Louis's playing, and more alcohol. A new three-piece band started to jump, and Louis danced with his mother on the cramped floor. By now Mayann was staggering, and as she went to say good night to Mr. Ponce "she fell flat on her face." Louis tried to pick her up, and when he bent over, he realized how drunk he was, and fell right on top of her. Everyone started laughing at the sight of these two falling-down drunks trying to get out the door.

Mr. Gabe, Mayann's steady beau, came to their rescue. "He straightened Mayann's hat and hair as best he could and led us to the door with a big smile on his face." He courteously thanked Mr. Ponce and shook his hand, and escorted Mayann and Louis home, only a block away. It was already daybreak, and the streets were nearly deserted at this hour. He carefully led them to the door, and into bed, where they slept the sleep of the deeply inebriated.

The next day, Mayann delivered her verdict on the adventure. "Son, I am convinced that you know how to hold your liquor. Judging by what happened last night you can take care of yourself," she declared. "You can look out for yourself if anything happens to me."

Louis's reaction was simple and forthright: "I felt very proud of myself." His mother was telling him, at last, that he was no longer her boy. He was a man.

For Louis, manhood meant two things: earning a living and keeping a woman. Now that he was making a dollar-twenty-five a week, plus tips, he was able to support himself for the first time. He was also able to indulge himself. With his newfound wealth, Louis purchased a Victrola, a wind-up model with a hand crank and large horn. On this machine, he heard recorded jazz and opera for the first time. "I had Caruso records, too, and Henry Burr, Galli-Curci, Tettrazini—they were all my favorites. Then there was the Irish tenor, McCormack—beautiful phrasing." These records opened his ears to music he would not have heard otherwise. He didn't just listen to Caruso and McCormack, he *studied* their recordings, their phrasing, and their burning *feeling*, all of which came to influence both his horn-playing and his singing. Louis Armstrong was not the only jazzman to appreciate operatic recordings, but he was the only one with the imagination and the daring to work operatic styles into his jazz.

He was becoming sexually adventurous, as well. He thought he knew something about women from observing the whores in Matranga's, so he decided to try his luck with a girl, Irene, whom he had admired from afar at Gaspar's grocery, during his lunch hours. She had always appeared oblivious to his interest. As time passed, he came to recognize her for what she was—one more jaded strumpet—but he was entranced all the same. Finally, she deigned to notice him, and Louis soon found himself so powerfully attracted to her that he thought about marrying her, even though he was only fifteen years old.

That wasn't a likely scenario. Irene was entangled with a hustler named "Cheeky" Black. Many nights, she came into Matranga's on Cheeky's arm, and the two of them asked the trio—Louis, Garbee, and Boogers—to play their favorite blues numbers. As he blew his battered cornet on the diminutive bandstand, Louis concluded that everyone in the joint was having a terrific time, except Irene. During an intermission when Cheeky was nowhere to be seen, Louis floated over and chatted her up. He learned that Cheeky had fleeced her of all her money, every last nickel. She hadn't had a thing to eat for two days. "She was as raggedy as a bowl of slaw," he said. Displaying his "soft heart," Louis started giving her most of his salary, night after night. Eventually, Irene and Cheeky went their separate ways, and that was Louis's moment to take over.

At twenty-one, Irene was more than five years older than Louis, the first of many older women to whom he was attracted. The difference in their ages suggests that Louis relied on her to usher him into manhood, and Irene brought her ardent young lover along quickly. She was passionate and devoted, as far as he could tell. His affair with Irene took off and soon overwhelmed him. "I had not had any experience with women, and she taught me all I know." This was love, true and everlasting—or so he thought. They endeavored to keep their relationship a secret at first, but eventually he revealed it to his mother, "who made no objections" as she watched her little Louis growing up so suddenly. Within weeks, the two of them were living together "as man and wife." Normally careful to give his addresses, Louis did not, in this instance, record where they set up housekeeping, but it was probably in Irene's digs. Most importantly, he was living on his own.

At this point, Louis reveals a development in their relationship that is open to various interpretations. Describing Irene as "very much dissipated by the life she had led," he tells how she fell ill with an unnamed "stomach trouble." She became dangerously sick, and "every night she groaned so terribly that she was driving me nearly crazy." Louis was desperate to help her find a cure.

In the midst of the crisis, as he hurried to Poydras Market to buy fish heads for a dish he was planning to cook for Irene, he bumped into King Oliver, who was on his way to play at a funeral. Louis told Papa Joe all about Irene's baffling illness, and he felt an enormous sense of relief as he poured out his cares. Louis trusted Oliver more than anyone else in New Orleans, because "he was always ready to come to my rescue when I needed someone to tell me about life and its little intricate things." When Louis finished his tale of woe, Joe generously offered Louis his chair—his chair!—at Pete Lala's for two nights. By sitting in for Oliver, Louis would make three dollars, enough to pay for a doctor. And, of course, he accepted.

Louis was anxious about his brief gig at Pete Lala's, for he wasn't sure that old man Lala, who was known to be nasty, would accept him in Oliver's place. Lala did, but he ordered Louis to play with a mute in his cornet. Louis found the demand unsettling; the use of the mute went contrary to his style, which was to play the melody clearly, cleanly, and loudly, the way Oliver did. The two quickly got into a contest of wills. Johnny St. Cyr, who played the banjo at Pete Lala's, remembered how "old man Lala had a limp and he would come across the floor, limping and shaking his finger at Louis." The admonition failed to stop the irrepressible cornetist, for "after he had turned his back, Louis would go into a little dance which would end up with him taking a few steps with a limp and shaking his finger just like the old man. This of course would bring the house down. Louis was always a comedian." Lala tolerated the youngster's antics for two nights, as agreed, then paid him off and sent him on his way. With his earnings, Louis dutifully took Irene to the doctor, and she soon recovered.

The real nature of Irene's malady is open to question. Was she indeed ill, or was she pregnant, and did the money he earned at Pete Lala's go toward an abortion? Whatever the cause of her malady, their love affair faltered. Louis saw her in a clearer, colder light; he realized that she was, after all, six years older than he and considerably the worse for wear. She wanted Louis to marry her, but the prospect, which had once filled him with joy, now seemed no more than a trap. His misgivings about Irene increased as he brooded over the sad tale of his "bosom pal," Joe "Seefus" Lindsay, whose unhappy experiences in love seemed an object lesson. The two had played in a pickup band from time to time, until Seefus inexplicably quit. He reappeared as a chauffeur married to an older woman. When the woman left him, Seefus "suffered terribly from wounded vanity and tried to kill himself by slashing his throat with a razor blade." Louis was terrified the same dreadful fate might befall him. First, he would be forced to give up his horn to support Irene, and then she would cheat on him and humiliate him.

Acknowledging that he was nowhere near ready for marriage, he "told Irene that since she was now going straight, she should get an older fellow," and he explained that since he was so "wrapped up in my horn I would not make a good husband for her." To hear Louis tell it, Irene accepted his decision with good grace and the two parted as friends.

As Louis knew—indeed, as *everyone* knew—Irene returned to her previous lover, Cheeky Black, who was, in Louis's words, one "real bad spade." In fact, Cheeky had earned his nickname because he had so much nerve. At the moment, he was nowhere to be seen, and Irene again spent time with Louis. The more Louis talked with Irene, the more he missed her. Irene invited him back to her place, but the invitation aroused Louis's suspicions. Wasn't she tight with Cheeky?

"Oh, no," she said. "I am no longer going with him."

So they went back to her place, and began kissing and hugging and making love, and as soon as he undressed and climbed into her bed, he heard a confident, menacing, insistent knocking on the door.

"Who is it?" Irene asked in a small voice.

"Cheeky."

Irene told her caller that she had company. "In those days," Louis explained of the protocol governing the delicate situation, "when a girl's Sweet Man or Pimp came to her door, and it was locked and she said she had company, he immediately would go away. Most of the times the gal is making money—and he's sure to get some of it." This time it was different. Cheeky had watched the two of them enter her house, and he had every intention of disrupting the tryst.

"Cheeky Black knew that Irene had never stopped loving me," Louis claimed, but the truth was that Louis had never stopped loving *her*, his first real love, the first woman he had ever been able to care for. "She never forgot how [I] had taken good care of her in my little country boy way when she was suffering with female trouble." No wonder it was "rather hard for Irene to just forget about me altogether for Cheeky Black."

Again, Irene reminded Cheeky that she had company, but Louis became increasingly nervous. Yes, he had locked the door, he reminded himself, but then, "like a flash of lightning, Cheeky Black broke the door down." She shrieked and ran into the street, "justa screaming and Cheeky Black pulled out his razor and started cutting at Irene's rear."

Louis frantically tried to get his pants on before Cheeky thought to come after him, and as soon as he was dressed, he tore out the door as fast as he could and ran all the way home—not to the home he had shared with Irene, but to his mother. When Mayann heard his account, she laughed right in his face, and Louis changed from a daring lover to a frightened little child fleeing a bully. "You'll know better next time never to go into a man's house and go to bed with his woman," she lectured her son.

"Mother," he vowed, "I will never do that again, as long as I am colored." It was one of his favorite expressions, his way of saying "forever."

Later on, he learned that a policeman had heard Irene's screams and rescued her from Cheeky's relentless razor. Louis kept his word. Taking this lesson in the limits of love to heart, he never again risked bothering her. In fact, he never saw her again, much to his relief.

While Louis was in the final throes of his affair with Irene, the influenza epidemic of 1918 descended on New Orleans. A city-wide ordinance banned the assembly of crowds, and by extension, musical performances, including tonks like Matranga's. Mayann took sick, then Mama Lucy, then Clarence. "With everybody suffering from the flu, I had to work and play the doctor to everyone in my family as well as all my friends in the neighborhood," Louis recalled. But with Matranga's shut down, he was out of a job and desperate for money.

He found work on a milk wagon, working side by side with a "very fine white boy." They delivered throughout the West End, out to Spanish Fort, all before dawn. Everywhere he went, he was barefoot, traveling across roads made of oyster shells, stopping to play craps and win, and coming home with so much money in his pockets that his mother worried about what he'd been up to. And then, one Sunday, he tripped while trying to mount the moving wagon. His toe ground under the wheel, whose weight forced tiny sharp pieces of shell into the tender skin. The pain was "terrible," and his solicitous employer took him to Charity Hospital, where a doctor removed the pieces bit by bit. "I like to have died," Louis said.

When he informed the doctors he was injured on the job, they wanted to know if he would sue his employer, the Cloverland Company, for damages. Louis knew he might win hundreds of dollars with a lawsuit, but he told them, "No sir. I think too much of my boss for that. Besides, it wasn't his fault." He simply wanted to heal and get back to work. His boss gave him a little present out of gratitude, and Louis returned to the milk cart— until the company laid off both him and his boss.

Fortunately for Louis, labor was in short supply in New Orleans, and he quickly found himself another job right in town, at a government construction site at Poland and Dauphine streets. He wore a big yellow identification button and jostled with tough Puerto Ricans, most of them so poor they were practically naked. "We were glad enough to work with them although they had the nerve to look down on us because we were colored," he noted. Nevertheless, he was glad to have the work. Even Kid Ory, locally famous, was working on this project, as was Joe Lindsay, now recovered from his frightening suicide attempt. At lunch, the three of them—Armstrong, Ory, and Lindsay—got together and swapped stories. Louis caught them up on his short-lived romance with Irene and his unexpected encounter with Cheeky Black. They all laughed about it and commiserated and laughed some more about women, work, money, and the hard times they shared.

When that job ended, Louis found another, this time with a wrecking company, and was buoyed by the hope of finding some hidden treasure in the house they were tearing down. "I worked away furiously with my crowbar hoping to be able to shout to the gang, 'Look what I found.' A lot of good my hard work did me; I never found a thing." Afraid of being crushed by a falling wall while tearing down a house, he concluded this type of work was not for him, and moved on to a job as a whitewasher, working with the father of his friend Isaac Smooth. To reach work, he had to negotiate the dreaded Irish channel, a New Orleans street populated with brawling Irish who'd as soon kill a black man as spit on him. And yet, "under old man Smooth's protection we had no more to fear than rabbits in a briar patch."

It was now 1918, and Louis's apprenticeship since leaving the Waif's Home had lasted four years—years of wandering, of evanescent accomplishments, of lucky escapes from danger and disaster, of furtive love with wild women. Although he claimed he was happy throughout these years of trial and error, an undercurrent of sadness, of missed opportunities, and of smoldering resentment at the lot of the black man in New Orleans filters through all his reminiscences, as if he were saying, "I made the best, the *very* best, of an awful situation." However, the prospect of being drafted into the United States Army to battle the Germans promised to give his life a sense of purpose. The previous April, President Woodrow S. Wilson had declared war against Germany and the Kaiser, and ever since then the country had mobilized at a dramatic pace. The size of the armed forces would increase from two hundred thousand to five million, and Louis Armstrong fully expected to be among them. For musicians, the motto of the hour was "work or fight." Louis expected to work *and* fight.

He went to his local draft board to register. He gave as his date of birth July 4, 1900, listed his occupation as musician, and his place of employment—though he could have chosen from many—as Pete Lala's on Conti Street. By calling himself a musician instead of a coal hauler, he might have been hoping that if he were drafted, he could play in a military band, not unlike the band he'd led in the Waif's Home. Technically, Louis was not yet eligible for the draft, since he was actually just sixteen years old that winter, and even the age he supplied to the board, based on what he believed to be his date of birth, still left him six months' shy of qualifying. But he had his card. "When I could feel that draft card in my hip pocket I sure was a proud fellow, expecting to go to war any minute and for Uncle Sam—or blow for him." For Louis the draft meant escape from his increasingly futile existence. Mayann and Mama Lucy were able to fend for themselves, he knew, and for the moment he was so tantalized by the prospect of leaving New Orleans for foreign shores that he forgot about the welfare of his adopted son Clarence.

Weeks later, his surge of patriotism was sorely tested when the police, looking for a robber, raided Matranga's, where he was having a beer. The police arrested everyone on the premises, including Louis, and took them all down to Parish Prison. Although the prison was a familiar place, only a short walk from his mother's house, he felt utterly isolated. It was apparent the police were looking for a black man, and any black would do, even him.

He endured a grim prison regimen, taking abuse from prisoners and guards alike, especially the dreaded yard captain, known to all as Sore Dick, who tripped him and soon had him sweeping the prison yard, an activity that boded ill, for "that was the way you get in the groove before you start serving a term." After several humiliating days in confinement, he was sprung as inexplicably as he'd been incarcerated, his deliverance arranged by Henry Matranga, who exercised his formidable connections on Louis's behalf. The lesson of that particular nightmare was not lost on him: in a world of prejudice and iniquity, he could survive with the help of a powerful white sponsor, especially one endowed with strong mob affiliations.

The day he left the jail, the city was in the grip of Mardi Gras fever— "It's a funny thing how life can be such a drag one minute and such a solid sender the next"—and he joined in the revelry. Life continued to look sweet when he found work "hopping bells," or delivering beer to prostitutes from a Third Ward saloon. This hardly seemed to be work at all, since he could ogle the whores to his heart's content, but the job, like so many before it, was short-lived. Soon he was back behind his mule, driving a coal cart, precisely as he had been doing for the past three years, and as it seemed that he would be doing for the rest of his working life. At least he had his former "stepdaddy," Mr. Gabe, to keep him company, and he was so fond of the man ("Any time I wanted it, I could always get a quarter out of him") that he tried to persuade his mother to take him back. Mayann refused, and eventually Louis acknowledged "I just could not run her life for her."

. . .

Finally, Louis's luck began to improve. In June, Joe Oliver, his mentor and father figure, joined the growing exodus of jazz musicians going north. Although he'd bootstrapped himself to the top of the musical hierarchy in New Orleans, he still didn't earn enough from his music to support himself, and if he remained in New Orleans, it seemed his situation would never change: butler by day, cornetist by night. Like every other musician in town, he'd heard of the success Jelly Roll Morton and Freddie Keppard had enjoyed up north, and he felt ready to enter their company.

At first, it appeared that Louis was losing his most important and powerful ally, and he had a difficult time imagining the New Orleans musical scene without Joe Oliver to anchor it. Furthermore, they had developed such a close personal tie that he considered Papa Joe more of a father to him than his real father had ever been. He took time off from his coal cart to see Papa Joe off at the train station, and he was overcome with melancholy. "I felt the old gang was breaking up," he lamented.

It was only after Oliver's train had left the station that Louis began to realize any benefit. Joe had vacated a crucial slot in the band, and Kid Ory, who managed the group, needed a replacement. "There were many good, experienced trumpet players in town, but none of them had young Louis's possibilities," he said. "I went to see him and told him that if he got himself a pair of long trousers I'd give him a job."

Louis was naturally elated. "To think that I was considered up to taking Joe Oliver's place in the best band in town!" he exulted, and rushed to tell his mother the great news. As for Mama Lucy, he still smarted from the way she'd belittled him when he'd brought home only fifteen cents from his first gig at Matranga's, and he decided she could just find out about his success on her own. Even when she did congratulate him, he acted indifferent, but inside he was trembling with excitement. "Within two hours," Ory continued, "Louis came to my house and said, 'Here I am. I'll be glad when eight o'clock comes. I'm ready to go.'"

His first night with the band he was determined to look and sound *exactly* the way Papa Joe did, so he draped a bath towel around his neck, the way Papa Joe did, and he played just the way his ear told him Papa Joe always played. The only problem was that he blew so long and loud that the other members of the band scarcely had a chance to be heard over his heroic cornet blasts. The other fellows figured he would settle down in time, and after his tryout night, Kid Ory formally invited Louis to join the band. Louis accepted; after four years of struggling on the fringes of the New Orleans jazz world, he suddenly arrived.

The band spread his reputation throughout New Orleans, but Louis's first taste of fame proved bittersweet. "When he hired me, Kid's last advice was, 'Work up a number so we can feature you once in a while,' " Louis recalled. This sounded like a good idea, "so I put a new piece together. Words and music. Even put in a little dance." The song was an unashamedly filthy thing called, variously, "Keep Off Katie's Head" or "Take Your Finger Outta Katie's Ass," possibly inspired by Kate Townsend, a Storyville madam who'd been barbarously murdered years before.

> . . . *Why don't you keep off Katie's head? . . . Why don't you keep out of Katie's bed? . . . It's a shame to say this very day . . . She's like a little child at play . . . It's a shame how you're lyin' on her head . . . I thought sure you would kill her dead . . . Why don't you be nice, boy, and take my advice . . . Keep off Katie's head . . . I mean . . . Get out of Katie's bed . . .*

When Louis sang this to a packed house at Pete Lala's one night, "Man, it was like a sporting event. All the guys crowded around and they like to carry me up on their shoulders." It wasn't just the song that got the crowd so excited, it was the dance Louis did with it, his version of the Shimmy, which was just beginning to appear in cities around the country, scandalizing proper folks. *Variety* denounced it as a "vulgar cooch dance, a lewd outgrowth of the jazz mania." Storyville, naturally, couldn't have cared less about the opinion of polite society, and Louis performed the song and dance regularly at Pete Lala's.

"One night, as I did the number, I saw this cat writing it all down on music paper. He was quick, man, he could write as fast as I could play and sing. When I had finished he asked me if I'd sell the number to him. He mentioned twenty-five dollars. When you're making only a couple of bucks a night that's a lot of money. But what really put the deal over was that I had just seen a hard-hitting steel gray overcoat that I really wanted for those cold nights. So I said, 'Okay,' and he handed me some forms to sign and I signed them. He said he'd be back with the cash. But he never did come back."

That man was named Clarence Williams, the first important black music entrepreneur in New Orleans, and as Louis's account shows, he was a sharpie who knew how to get things done. He was a relatively young man himself at the time, born in Plaquemine, Louisiana, on October 8, 1893. An all-American mixture of black, Creole, and Choctaw, he was exposed to the blues and ragtime piano during his Delta boyhood. In 1906, he discovered Buddy Bolden, who came through Plaquemine, and was stunned. "I had never heard anything like that before in my whole life," he said. About this time, he ran away from home and joined a minstrel show, found his way to New Orleans, and he worked as a shoeshine boy and tailor, while learning from the older musicians in Storyville. He taught himself to play the piano, to sing, and to read music, which put him at a great advantage. He played in dime stores, in restaurants, on street corners, and he probably crossed paths with little Louis a number of times during his apprenticeship because he was even better known as a manager and promoter than as a musician. In this capacity, he came up with the inspiration of the ham kick, a surefire crowd-pleaser. He suspended a ham from the ceiling of the tonk and invited the women present to kick it. Whoever succeeded won the ham. The catch was that the women could not wear underclothes during the contest. The idea caught on, and pretty soon underdrawer-less women were kicking hams all over town. There was even a Ham Kicker's Club.

In 1913, when he was twenty, Williams and Armand Piron, a violinist, opened the first black-owned music publishing business in New Orleans. This was years before anyone saw a future in black music, and he did what any number of songwriters of the period did: he adapted any promising folk tune that happened to catch his ear. When he heard Louis sing "Keep Off Katie's Head," he believed the song could become popular, but even Williams didn't realize how big a hit it would become.

For a long time, Williams and Piron let Louis's bawdy tune languish, but in 1919, they decided to capitalize on the growing acceptance of the Shimmy by publishing the song. They changed the music slightly, gave it a faddish title—"I Wish I Could Shimmy Like My Sister Kate"—cleaned up the lyrics, which now proclaimed, *"I might be late, but I'll be up to date*

. . . *When I can Shimmy Like My Sister Kate.*" Credit for music and lyrics was claimed by Piron alone.

The song became a hit, and it inspired other songs about the naughty Shimmy. By now Williams, his business instincts sharper than ever, had gone to New York and gotten into the burgeoning record industry. He arranged for an unknown young blues singer named Bessie Smith to record Louis's tune for the Okeh label, but the song was never released. Within months, other recordings of "I Wish I Could Shimmy Like My Sister Kate" appeared. Williams and Piron made an absolute fortune from it. Eventually, Louis heard the hit song and realized its derivation. In 1924, eight years after Clarence Williams had written it down while Louis sang it in Pete Lala's, the two men met again, this time in a recording studio. "I waited and I watched but all during those sessions Clarence never made a move to pay me the twenty-five," Louis said.

Although Louis Armstrong was now a name to be reckoned with in New Orleans music circles, he still had to rely on his day job for income. There was no way he could support Clarence, his mother, sister, and a girlfriend on the dollar-twenty-five a night he made blowing his horn. He spent more of his waking hours in the coal cart, staring at Lady's hindquarters, than in any other activity. Now that he had his seat with Kid Ory, he no longer wished to be drafted—he'd lose his chair to someone else!—and the best way to stay out of the draft was to keep his coal delivery job.

For a time he struck a balance between the two occupations. After a hard day's work, he threw himself into the merriment of Kid Ory's band. They played at Tulane University for dances and proms, and Louis reveled in the cheerful atmosphere he helped to create. "I worked up a little 'jive' routine," he said of those carefree days, "which was a little tap dancing and a little fooling around between my numbers to get laughs." Working with Kid Ory's band even satisfied his consuming appetite, for they often played at a country club for rich whites, who took delight in feeding the band the same food they ate. After the gig, he'd chat up a few of the waiters and waitresses, and persuade them to give him still more food to take home to his family.

Louis's ambition was not so easily sated. After only months in a job that many musicians in New Orleans would be content to hold for their entire careers, he became acutely aware of the band's limitations. He discovered that in the pecking order of New Orleans "musicianers," Kid Ory's outfit was not at the very summit; that honor belonged to the John Robichaux Orchestra, the haughty Creoles who had dominated the New Orleans musical scene since the days of Buddy Bolden. The key to their august reputation, at least among musicians, was that the Robichaux outfit was a *reading* orchestra, and Kid Ory's band, though acknowledged as sensational "hot" players, could not read. As a result, they were not considered acceptable in a dignified setting such as a funeral or a formal dance, where written music was required.

Louis, in contrast to the other members of his band, yearned to be counted among the leading musicians of the hour. He got his chance when the Ory outfit was invited to substitute for missing members of the Robichaux orchestra at a funeral. Louis was determined to show up "those big shots" on this occasion. From the moment the musicians congregated at the lodge, where the funeral procession was to begin, he "noticed all those stuck up guys giving us lots of ice." He gave Ory a conspiratorial poke in the ribs; they were determined to give these Creoles a little surprise.

When the funeral started, the Ory contingent started to play, it seemed to Louis, a damned sight better than the Robichaux "musicianers." Once they made it out to the graveyard, and interred the deceased, it would be time to swing into something hot. Finally, the drummer sent out a thrilling roll announcing a good old-fashioned rag, and Louis and Kid Ory tore into the music. As for the Robichaux fellows, "those old fossils just couldn't cut it." Even the second line—the "raggedy guys" following the procession— was impressed. Louis and the band took an encore, something that didn't happen every day. They played all the way back to the lodge hall, and swung into "Panama" just as they entered, where a crowd cheered them on, and Louis, recalling just how Papa Joe took the last chorus way into the upper register, where the sound cleared the sinuses and quickened the pulse, took it up, up, up, and *hit those notes*, every one of them, and damned if those old fossils from the Robichaux orchestra weren't patting him on the back! They even asked the Ory band to play at other funerals. "After all, we'd proved to them that any learned musician can read music, but they all can't swing."

Suddenly in demand as a musician, Louis spurned an offer from the Robichaux Orchestra. If he *had* joined, he would have had to deny his "hot" jazz style in favor of the sweet Creole manner. Instead, he accepted an offer from a rival outfit, the Tuxedo Brass Band, under the direction of Oscar Celestin, where he felt musically and socially compatible. Papa Celestin was a formidable trumpet man in his own right, popular with everyone. The son of a sugar cane cutter from rural Assumption Parish, he'd grown up in dire poverty and arrived in New Orleans in 1906, when he was about twenty-two. From approximately 1910 to 1925, his outfit reigned as the city's premiere marching band, with the possible exception of the Onward Brass Band and was known everywhere by the distinctive legend printed on its business card: MUSIC FURNISHED FOR ALL OCCASIONS. By the time Louis joined, Celestin's best days as a trumpet man were over; he was falling prey to ulcers, often unable to march with his own band, and he urgently needed a replacement cornet.

The Tuxedo Brass Band was a spit-and-polish outfit, and the first day Louis reported for work, he raised eyebrows. William "Baba" Ridgley, who played trombone with the band, was surprised when he saw a mere "boy" showing up to do a man's work. "He had on a police cap that looked as if it were too large for him, a little old blue coat, and a little dirty bag under his arm for his cornet." But as soon as this bedraggled youth began to blow, he allayed the fears of the band. Indeed, he learned their entire repertoire in a matter of days. "You couldn't learn what Louis learned as quick as he did," Ridgely said. "It had to be given to you. Louis had that from his birth."

As the Tuxedo Brass Band's second trumpet, Louis "felt just as proud as though I had been hired by John Philip Sousa. It was a great thrill when they passed out brass band music on stiff cards that could be read as you walked along. I took great pains to play my part right and not miss a note." However, he was not yet able to read the music placed in front of him, so he missed plenty of notes. Whenever he did, said a colleague, "he would bust out laughing, saying, 'Y'all watch me, I'm gonna get it this time. I was kidding you that time,' " and he would try again, and again. If he still had trouble with his part, Papa Celestin tutored him until he played through the rough spots as if he'd always known them. As a result of their close contact, Louis developed some reservations about Celestin's style of cornet playing. True, "he always delivered a real beautiful tone. Mellow and very pleasing to the ear," Louis decided, but Celestin "blew the cornet from the side of his lips, which was definitely not embouchure heaven."

The Tuxedo Brass Band put on a fine show; their uniforms consisted of white caps with black bands, blue shirts, white pants, and tan shoes. Marching through the streets of New Orleans, their instruments gleaming, they were a sight to behold, especially the eager young second trumpet, who danced, or even shadowboxed, as he played. According to Baba Ridgley, Louis's uniform was so extravagant that it caused problems for him when the band marched through rough neighborhoods. "The bad boys would follow Louis up, get right by him, call him everything they could think of, tell him: ' 'Cause you're playing with the Tuxedo Band you think you're somebody.' Louis would run them off down the street, for about half a block." Their taunts never bothered Louis, who knew that many celebrated musicians had been part of its ranks: Jimmie Noone, Johnny Dodds, Black Benny Williams, Alphonse Picou, Peter Bocage, Manuel Perez. He considered belonging in their august company his "best break down in N[ew] O[rleans]."

In time, Louis became so proficient that the other musicians began to urge him to take over the first trumpet, especially on those days when Papa Celestin was too sick to participate. One of his colleagues, Babe Phillips, said, "He told me he couldn't do that, because that was Celestin's band. He said, 'I can't go be a boss on that man. I just want my money.' And they was making money, too, because they had a first-class band, and they was playing almost every night."

His life underwent another upheaval on November 11, 1918, Armistice Day. He never forgot where he was when he heard the news that the Kaiser had surrendered. The day began routinely, Louis guiding his coal cart through the streets of New Orleans, chanting, "Stove coal, a nickel for a water bucket." At eleven o'clock in the morning, he reached Fabacher's restaurant on St. Charles Street, where he had a big delivery to make. He was groaning under the weight of the shovel, his face and neck and arms coated with gritty dust and "sweating like mad," when he saw automobiles roaring down the streets, trailed by tin cans. Children ran through the streets, shrieking. He asked a stranger what was going on, and the old gentleman told him the war was over. At that moment, Louis said, he felt "as though a bolt of lightning struck me all over." He automatically went back to shoveling coal from his cart when it occurred to him the war was *over*, and he didn't need to be doing this type of work anymore. "I immediately dropped that shovel, slowly put on my jacket, looked at Lady and said, 'So long, my dear. I'll dig you another time.' " He dashed home and told his mother he'd just quit his job and would devote all his time to his music. After nearly four years, his "Coal Cart Blues" were over.

The end of the war brought welcome changes to New Orleans. No longer subject to blackouts and rationing, the city sparkled at night, and dance halls and tonks reopened to accommodate patrons eager to celebrate. "Oh, the city sure did look good again, with all those beautiful lights along Canal Street." Henry Matranga was back in business, and he offered Louis his old job, but it was too late; Louis had very few free nights by now. He was even working Monday nights, normally the slowest night of the week, in a series of dances Kid Ory arranged at Economy Hall.

Saturday nights, he often played in a tonk known as the Brick House, in Gretna, an obscure hamlet near New Orleans. He took the Jackson Avenue ferry to the tonk, where he found the type of scene he knew all too well from his nights in the Third Ward, playing the blues in a three-piece band before a crowd of gamblers and prostitutes, where "you could get your head cut off, or blown off, if you weren't careful." He rated the place the most dangerous he'd ever played, which is saying a good deal. "It was the honky-tonk where levee workers would congregate every Saturday night and trade with the gals who'd stroll up and down the floor and into the bar. . . . Bottles would come flying over the bandstand like crazy, and there was lot of just plain shooting and cutting. But somehow that jive didn't faze me at all, I was so happy to have some place to blow my horn."

When he'd finished blowing for the night, leaving the Brick House proved an experience in terror, for the local drunks, black and white, were spoiling for a fight with one another, and he knew that if a racial confrontation erupted, he might be shot or lynched simply for being in the wrong place at the wrong time. His worst fear nearly came to pass when he was taking the ferry home early one morning, and an old white woman slipped and fell on the slick deck. A black woman exclaimed, "Thank God!" Louis froze, expecting the remark to incite a riot, but "the Lord was with us colored people that night, because nothing happened." He felt lucky to make it home alive.

Louis was willing to expose himself to these hazards because one of the prostitutes in the Brick House exerted a powerful spell over him. She was skinny, but something about her drew him back to the Brick House and its myriad hazards three Saturday nights in a row. She had a way of looking at him "with stuff in her eyes," and he began giving her "the righteous look in return." That was how their affair started, a drama of passion, knives, sex, and even love.

Her name was Daisy Parker.

Louis was under no illusions about Daisy. He knew she wanted him as a regular customer, and he was willing to pay for her favors. He went upstairs to see her, and she told him the price—she was selling herself cheap, he believed—and he told her he'd return after work to consummate the deal. All through the night, he played and thought about this hot, pretty "Creole" woman he was going to be with. When he finished the last set, he went straight to her room, bursting with anticipation.

She undressed, and, to his astonishment, stripped down to a pair of artificial hips designed to enhance her figure. Louis felt deflated. "As much as I've been admiring this chick and her shape, here she comes bringing me a pair of water wings." Daisy immediately explained that she didn't weigh much, less than a hundred pounds dripping wet, and thought she needed the hips to give her the curves that nature had failed to provide. Louis got over his shock and stayed with Daisy until five o'clock in the morning. Then they walked out on the levee, and looked at the Mississippi flowing past in the predawn darkness.

In the coming weeks, Louis returned again and again to Gretna, the Brick House, and Daisy's room, and they "commenced to fall deeply in love with each other." But as he knew from painful experience, life with a prostitute was never a simple matter, and Daisy had her share of complications. She was three years older than he was and had a common-law husband, whom she neglected to mention. Louis later learned he was a drummer in a nearby tonk in Gretna and lived with Daisy in the village of Freetown. At this point, he should have seen the warning signs of imminent trouble, but all he could think about was how much he loved this prostitute

Daisy with the bewitching eyes. His reminiscences of her also suggest she was a passionate lover who pleased him greatly. He wanted her more and more, especially during the long weeks when Kid Ory had booked the band into a plush country club gig and Louis couldn't make it out to the seedy little tonk in Gretna to see her. He even called her on the phone—a new experience for Louis, who was used to living in homes without phones—to try to arrange a meeting, but she claimed she was just a simple country girl who "didn't know how to get over to the New Orleans side of the river."

Daisy's coyness only intensified his desire to see her, so one afternoon he put on his best suit, his "sharpest vine" (in fact, his *only* vine), and took the ferry and bus to Freetown, to pay her a call. He found her living in a plain, four-room house, the rooms all lined up, so "you could stand in the front door and look all the way back to the kitchen." She placed his hat on the sewing machine table, and the next thing he knew, he was in her arms, kissing her passionately, for free.

Minutes later, there was a knock on the door, and then a bang, and who should come barging in but Daisy's old man, who knew all about her new boyfriend. Daisy jumped off Louis's lap and charged out the back door, with her husband in hot pursuit. "For a moment I thought of a million things," Louis wrote. "The first was the incident with Irene and Cheeky Black." But he didn't have time to dwell on his indiscretion, because Daisy's old man, having caught her, struck her so hard she fell to the floor in a heap. Louis looked frantically for his telltale hat, and as soon as he retrieved it, he ran out the door as fast as his legs would carry him. He dared not look back until he reached the ferry to New Orleans. "And I said to myself: 'Ump! Once again, never again.' Then I thought of how I'd said the same words when Cheeky Black caught Irene and me. But this time I meant it."

He kept his resolve for a month. He suffered pangs of longing and consoled himself by consuming his mother's red beans and rice. He decided the affair with Daisy really had ended, but "one day who should come around my neighborhood of Liberty and Perdido streets but Daisy!" This was the same woman who had claimed she didn't know how to get from Gretna across the river into New Orleans. Louis was aghast and suspicious: "I thought right away she was only using me for a playtoy." Yet he stood on the street corner, with Daisy imploring him to come back, telling him how she'd missed him, while all his old buddies getting off work from the coal yard stopped to watch the sight. She got to his head, and he realized he was signifying in front of his friends, "with a fine chick breaking down all over me." The others encouraged him. "Go on, Dipper!" they shouted. They were impressed with him, and he was getting impressed with himself.

Daisy and Louis strolled over to Rampart Street, where they took a room in Kid Green's Hotel, at the corner of Rampart and Lafayette, "so we could talk over many things." Kid Green was another outlandish New Orleans character, a former prizefighter who sank his winnings into a hotel, where he held court. Louis and Daisy took a room, where they spent the night talking about everything. He was aware of Daisy's shortcomings: she was a prostitute, illiterate, spoiled, jealous, and manipulative. But he was in love with her. Her hold on him was so strong that he finally gave up trying to resist. "She really did move me greatly."

The next day, when they finally left their room in Kid Green's Hotel, they went directly to City Hall and got married.

Are you going to let him marry that whore?"
This was the question that everyone asked Mayann. She did her best to appear unruffled by her son's choice of bride, telling him that he had his own life to lead. She wished both him and Daisy happiness in life. After they wed, Daisy returned to Freetown to pack her clothes, and Louis went home, where his mother anxiously questioned him about his impulsive actions. Inevitably, he defended his decision. "With my good sense and mother-wit, and knowing how to treat and respect the feelings of other people, that's all I've needed through life. You taught me that, Mother. And I haven't done so bad at it." His honeyed words reassured Mayann, and the neighborhood gossips fell silent for a time.

The first month of their marriage passed in a jumble of quick liaisons in hotel rooms and borrowed apartments, since the newlyweds had no place of their own. Eventually they found an apartment over an upholstering shop on Melpomene Street. It consisted of two rooms accessible by an exterior staircase facing an alley strewn with garbage. There were two sagging porches (called galleries), front and back; when it rained, they became dangerously slick. The plumbing consisted of cold water, an outhouse, and a bathtub in the alley. Even Louis, who was accustomed to modest quarters, found the apartment depressing. The one bright spot in the apartment was Louis's beloved Victrola, and his record collection.

From the start, their marriage was violent and tumultuous. To hear Louis tell it, Daisy was a ravenous beast who could never be satisfied for long, and who provoked the worst in him. "The way those tough men such as gamblers, pimps, etc., got along with their wives and whores," he wrote, "that was the same way that I had to get along with Daisy. That was to beat the hell out of her every night and make love in order to get some sleep. That was supposed to be love. . . . She was so mean and jealous."

Although he was irresistibly attracted to Daisy, Louis quickly discovered he had made a big mistake in marrying her. He occasionally sought solace in the arms of other women. Daisy invariably found out and retaliated. "To my surprise I awakened one morning and Daisy had a big bread knife laying on my throat, with tears dropping from her eyes, saying, 'You black son-of-a-bitch, I ought to cut your goddamn throat.' "

Terrified, he tried to bluster his way out of the situation, telling her she didn't have the nerve, and she let him go that time. He knew there would be a next time, and a time after that. From then on, Daisy virtually held him hostage with her knife and her razor and made him live in fear of his life. Although Daisy constantly threatened to cut him, she never actually used her knife on him. "That's why I always said the Lord was with me," Louis later observed. Nonetheless, their fights were so violent and bitter that "many times she and I went to jail from fighting in the streets, and my boss would have to come and get me out. Now you can see why I don't remember just how many times that I went to jail. It was a common thing in those days. I can proudly say though that I didn't steal—much. I didn't have to, and I was so busy trying to keep from getting hurt and blow[ing] my horn."

A number of times Louis moved out and hid in his mother's house, vowing never to return to Melpomene Street, but sooner or later Daisy always tracked him down, pleaded with him to return, and promised to let him blow his horn as much as he pleased. He always gave in.

L ouis kept his sanity during the tumultuous year he lived with Daisy by bringing his adopted son Clarence, now three years old, into their ramshackle apartment and lavishing as much care on the child as he was able. While the failure of his marriage to Daisy shamed Louis, he compensated by taking understandable pride in the bond he formed with his son. "Ever since Clarence was a little shaver in dresses," Louis boasted, "he obeyed me as if he was my son. He's called me 'Papa' all his life. . . . Am still devoted [to him] deeply. He's still the happiest youngster there is."

Louis failed to mention that his apartment was also the scene of tragedy for the child. The memory was so painful that Louis, who normally did not flinch from uncomfortable subjects, found it difficult to discuss the matter, which he termed an "unpleasant little thing." At the same time, he never denied the truth of what happened to Clarence. "He was playing on the back porch one day in New Orleans and it was one of those awful heavy rainy days," said Louis of the incident that changed the course of Clarence's life, "and this porch was awfully slippery and wet. And Clarence was out there playing by himself on this porch which was in the back yard and the porch was one story high from the ground. Thank God it was only one story, because Clarence fell off this slippery and wet porch to the ground and landed directly on his head. Ump. Ump.

"The only way we found out that he fell—he got up and got off the ground, came up the back steps justa crying. We ran to him immediately to see if he was hurt. Rushed him to a doctor. They had some of the greatest in the world examine him. All the doctors said the fall Clarence had set him back four years behind the average child. They called it 'feeble minded.' " For the rest of his life, Louis would take care of the partly disabled Clarence.

Trying to support his wife, adopted son, mother, and sister, Louis discovered that not even his two regular gigs, with Kid Ory and the Tuxedo Brass Band, sufficed. Rather than return to the coal cart, he spent his days peddling coal. He waited for schooners bearing charcoal to enter the New Basin Canal. From them, he bought lumps of charcoal wrapped in burlap. He took the charcoal home, chopped it into pieces small enough to fit in a water bucket, and sold it to prosperous homes for five cents a bucket. To rid himself of the grimy coal dust, he bathed himself every day in a tub in the alley. "In order to get real clean I would have to sit on the rim and wash myself from my neck to my middle. After that I would stand up and wash the rest of me. . . . Handling and selling charcoal was certainly a dirty job. My face and hands were always black, and most of the time I looked like Al Jolson when he used to get down on his knees and sing 'Mammy.' But with that job and playing music I made a good living."

Meanwhile, he fought with Daisy over an attachment he'd formed to another girl, Rella Martin. Whenever he came home, Daisy greeted him with shouting and curses, but he continued to see Rella. Louis always lived according to a double standard. He was not then, and would never be, interested in remaining faithful to one woman. Such behavior was alien to his experience and went against the advice he'd received from Black Benny, who had counseled him to maintain a string of girlfriends both to prove his masculinity and to protect himself against *their* unfaithfulness. Benny's own experience showed the folly of that advice, for, in the end, his girlfriend, a jealous prostitute named May Daughter, shot him. Black Benny, the most feared man in the Third Ward, the victor in countless battles royal, "lived for a whole week with a bullet in his heart," Louis said, before dying an agonizing death.

Louis's own love life finally came unraveled the day he acted as a pallbearer in a funeral for one of the brothers from the burial society he had joined, the Tammany Social Aid and Pleasure Club. It was now February 1919. While the funeral party was assembling at the church, he passed the time chatting with Rella and his old friend Little Head. He was wearing his best vines, out of hock just for the day: a black suit, patent leather shoes, and, most impressively, a brand new Stetson hat. His sense of calm and well-being dissolved the moment he saw Daisy approaching with a grim and determined look on her face. When she reached the group, she flourished her razor in his face, and Louis took off like a shot, his hat, the symbol of his *amour-propre*, tumbling to the muddy ground. When Little Head stooped to retrieve it, Daisy swiped his ass with her razor, and Little Head took off in the same direction as Louis. Crazed with jealousy, Daisy fetched his hat and ominously shredded it with her razor. "My Gawd! Did that burn me up!" He flew into a rage, and members of his club had to restrain him for his own protection, for she still wielded the razor. "You haven't even got a penknife," they reminded him.

Louis controlled himself, just barely, and fell in step with the funeral procession. As they struck up "Nearer My God to Thee," he was still fuming over the indignity he had suffered in front of his fellow club members. As soon as the body was planted, he broke ranks and ran home. As he put the key in the door, he found himself besieged by a shower of bricks. "I saw Daisy cursing and throwing bricks faster than Satchel Paige." He picked up a brick, threw it, and "it hit Daisy right in the stomach. She doubled up in a knot, screaming, 'You've killed me. You've killed me.'" The police appeared at the scene, Louis took off again, and Daisy was arrested; when she kicked an officer in the face, he split her scalp with a nightstick. "Daisy played it smart," Louis wrote, with venom. "She went to jail crying like an innocent babe regardless of all the hell she had just raised. Just like a woman."

As this drama was taking place, the funeral procession continued its unhurried course. Louis took up his position and resumed blowing as if nothing had happened, but as he marched, he received a message from Daisy, imploring him to free her. When his funeral chores were over, he went to a grocery store and phoned Henry Matranga, who worked his corrupt magic to spring Daisy. Louis went down to the police station to meet her. He pitied her, but also took silent satisfaction in her slight limp. They kissed, apologized, and walked slowly home.

The closer to their apartment they got, the more upset she became—he could see it on her face. "All of a sudden she turned on me and started to curse and call me all kinds of dirty names," Louis said. She accused him of crippling her and vowed to get revenge. "That struck me as a very, very strange thing for her to say to me, especially as I had begun to think that everything was all right." He prepared himself for another of her "cheap scenes," and by the time they reached their corner, they were trading insults and blows. Again, a policeman intervened, but this cop had heard Louis play. Instead of whipping their sorry heads with his licorice stick and taking them to Parish Prison, he advised, "Dippermouth, why don't you take your wife home off the street before some other cop comes along and arrests the two of you." Louis thought, Amen to that!

When they returned to their apartment, he told Daisy the time had finally come to "call it quits." Daisy broke down in tears, and Louis realized he was powerless to escape her grasp, her allure, and her razor, unless he left New Orleans altogether. Yet no matter what Daisy might do to him, he still found it unthinkable to abandon his hometown when he was working regularly and making a name for himself.

Louis was now first cornet in the Kid Ory Band and second trumpet in the Tuxedo Brass Band, fetching a dollar-and-a-half a gig. He was always busy, marching in funerals, playing until four o'clock in the morning, going out to swell country clubs, and riding on trucks with the bands to advertise their engagements. He even had the luxury of turning down offers from rival outfits—imagine! By the age of eighteen, Louis Armstrong had gone about as far as a jazz musician could go in New Orleans—a nonreading musician, that is.

6.

LAZY
RIVER

To read, or not to read: this was a major issue among New
Orleans musicians. For many, especially black musicians,
music was a tradition to be passed down by the ear, not the
eye, and they reflexively distrusted musicians who could
read music. There was a certain pride in *not* being able to
read music, because reading got in the way of *feeling* the music. Not only
that, but it got in the way of improvisation by confining musicians to a rigid
set of choices with given keys, and it got in the way of listening and
responding to the complicated rhythms and harmonies of other musicians.
In other words, reading music stifled the music inside the music, the notes
that only musicians heard, or thought they heard. And there were so many
notes in New Orleans-style music—notes that supposedly didn't exist,
notes that would later be called "blue notes," notes that the written octave
couldn't capture. Besides, no one ever played the same song the same way
twice in a row in the really hot, swinging bands. What would be the point
of that?

Although Louis was still a dues-paying member of the nonreading
school of musicians, he was slightly defensive about his lack of reading
ability. Like many of his colleagues, he assumed that following written
notes got in the way of true musical feeling and self-expression; it was
impossible to improvise and play "hot" while reading from a score. Even
jazzmen who could read pretended they could not, to stay in their peers'
good graces. At the same time, he admitted, "I wanted to do more than fake
the music all the time because there is more to music than just playing
style."

In the spring of 1919, Louis was presented with the opportunity to
learn to read music and redirect his fledgling career. It was a Sunday, and

he was riding through New Orleans along with the rest of the Ory band on the back of a truck, advertising their Monday night concert at Economy Hall. "We were playing a red-hot tune when another truck came along the street with another hot band," he said. "We came together at that same corner of Rampart and Perdido streets where I had been arrested five years before and sent to the Waif's Home. Of course that meant war between the two bands and we went to it, playing our strongest. I remember I almost blew my brains through my trumpet."

A man by the name of Fate Marable was watching Louis that day. Everybody knew who Fate Marable was. The tall, lean, redheaded, light-skinned black man was already a legend. He was *the* band leader on the Mississippi riverboats, conducting a crackerjack orchestra that entertained passengers on daylong excursions on the majestic vessels. And, as everyone knew, Fate's orchestra was a *reading* group, which excluded an astonishing number of gifted, even brilliant musicians from joining. Louis was intimidated by Fate's formidable reputation: "Fate was a very serious musician. He defied anybody to play more difficult than he did. Every musician in New Orleans respected him. He had seen the good old days in Storyville, and had played cotch with the pimps and hustlers at the '25' gambling house. He had had fine jam sessions with the piano greats of those days such as Jelly Roll Morton, Tony Jackson, Calvin Jackson, Udell Wilson, Arthur Campbell, Frankie Ahaynou, Boogus, Laurence Williams, Wilhelmina Bart Wynn, Edna Francis and many other of the all-time greats. He always won top honors with them."

On the riverboats, Fate transferred his keyboard prowess from the piano to the calliope, and quickly gained fame as the best-known calliope player on the Mississippi. When he played that instrument, a sister to the organ, he seemed a vision from another world, enshrouded in his raincoat and rain hat, huddled before a steam-powered calliope atop the uppermost deck of a riverboat gliding along the Mississippi, the instrument shrieking as he pounded on its waterproof keyboard. He seemed possessed by a demon when he played, inhumanly indifferent to the racket, the steam, and the water pouring down his face, dripping off the end of his nose onto the back of his ocher hands, as his fingers dashed through one tune after another. The steam-powered calliope made the damnedest sound, half organ, half Hell's bells, and all of it transformed into something otherworldly as it floated out into the night.

Danny Barker recalled hearing Marable at the calliope as early as 1915. "They didn't have all the noise that you have today, like automobile and trucks, it was quiet, and you could hear that beautiful calliope on the river," Barker said. Amid the quiet, Fate's calliope reverberated for miles around, the music reflecting off the surface of the water as it flowed around the riverboat. When the boat approached a landing, a crowd, drawn by the music, would gather to hear him play, and, if they could afford it, to board the boat when it docked, the better to listen to the celebrated Fate Marable, calliope player and orchestra leader extraordinaire. Those who could afford the price of admission spent the night dancing and drinking to the musical accompaniment of the Fate Marable Orchestra, for when Fate was done with his calliope calisthenics, he traded his oilskin raincoat for a tuxedo, sat before a piano, so serene and tame compared to the rough beast of the calliope. From this vantage point he led his "Colored" orchestra for an audience of white patrons aboard vessels owned by the Streckfus Lines, a name that was famous up and down the Mississippi and synonymous with swell times. Nothing was finer than spending an evening aboard one of the Streckfus Lines's riverboats, and of all their orchestra leaders, the most popular and sought after happened to be Fate Marable.

No one, not even Marable's own son, Fate Jr., knew the origin of the Marable name. There was speculation that it had originally been "Marble" and that Fate had changed it on a whim, but in any event it proved to be distinctive and instantly recognizable, as was Fate himself, with his shock of red hair and freckled face. His light complexion gave rise to rumors. "Marable had worked for Streckfus so long, and he looked so white, that people used to say he was Streckfus's son," said his drummer, Baby Dodds. In fact, Marable's light complexion derived from his mixed black and Irish ancestry. After spending his childhood in Paducah, Kentucky, he had taught himself music through force of will and immense self-discipline. Marable was just twenty-nine at the time he saw Louis performing on the back of the truck, but his reputation as an orchestra leader was already nearing its peak, and he seemed decades older than his musicians.

A perennial talent scout, Marable followed Louis since he had emerged from the Waif's Home. Impressed by the young cornetist in the fierce battle of the bands, Marable offered to sign Louis up on the spot, for short excursions on the *Dixie Belle*, where he led the orchestra.

The *Dixie Belle* resembled a giant floating wedding cake. She boasted three decks, all of them enclosed by ornate fretwork. With dark puffs of smoke rising from its stacks, the riverboat was visible for miles around. She was an even more impressive sight at night, when she shed countless splinters of light across the undulating black surface of the Mississippi. There were two huge paddle wheels on either side and deck space capable of holding a thousand paying customers. Marable's band usually played on the third deck, before a vast, gleaming dance floor. This was a big bunch, twelve musicians including Louis on cornet, a far more complex outfit than Ory's seven-man band, to say nothing of the three-man groups in the tonks. It was so big, in fact, that it was an *orchestra*, as Marable insisted on calling it. At precisely eight o'clock in the evening, the orchestra would start playing aboard ship, when she was tied up at the foot of Canal Street. Come eight-thirty, the ship would steam away, and after a night of dancing and good music, slip back into her berth by eleven.

Throughout the winter, Louis spent many an evening with Marable's orchestra on these brief excursions in and out of New Orleans, and he loved playing in this setting. It was a huge step up from the city's nightclubs and tonks. The crowd was orderly and appreciative, and the pay was predictable. But it could be hard work, for Louis was still trying to make a name for himself, and challengers were just as determined to stop him by outplaying him during spirited "cutting contests" in which instrumentalists battled to outdo one another. Louis could be fiercely competitive in the heat of these contests, and one of the most savage sprang up during one of his short excursions with Fate. When the boat tied up for a few hours, Marable's orchestra entertained the audience from a bandstand. Meanwhile, another band took up a position close by; it was smaller, only seven men, but it boasted Emmet Hardy, in those days a name to be reckoned with in New Orleans jazz circles. "Hardy was blowing so hard he split both his upper lip and his lower lip, too," said one astonished onlooker. "And when he would open up to let the water out of the horn, blood would come, where he'd split his lips. And when they got through, from the other bandstand, Louis made his bow and hollered all the way across the floor, 'You are the king!' Just like that. Recognizing Emmet."

Now that Louis was in Marable's orchestra, he had to begin the chore of learning to read music. Musicians regarded Fate as a demanding schoolmaster. Said Louis's pal, Zutty Singleton: "There was a saying in New Orleans. When some musician would get a job on the riverboats with Fate

Marable, they'd say, 'Well, you're going to the conservatory.' That's because Fate was such a fine musician and the men who worked with him had
to be really good." During intermissions, Fate tutored the hot young cornet
player in the rudiments of reading music. "Being a very apt young man,"
Louis boasted, "I learned whole lots of reading music real quick."

In the spring, Marable offered Armstrong a place with the orchestra for
the summer season. This meant Louis would have to leave New Orleans
and Daisy to sail up and down the Mississippi for months on end. "He
wanted me to come with his band in the worst way," said Louis, who
reveled in Fate's attentions. At the same time, "I was always afraid to leave
New Orleans," Louis confessed, "afraid, I guess, that I'd lose my job and
couldn't get back home." Instead of accepting Fate's offer outright, he
considered other possibilities. He wrote to the famous band leader Fletcher
Henderson about a job. "Smack" Henderson had already asked Louis to
join his orchestra in New York City, and Louis had turned him down. This
time, Henderson had no need of his services. Meanwhile, Joe Oliver, in
Chicago, kept up a lively correspondence with Louis, promising that some
day soon he would invite the cornetist to join his band. But Oliver's offer
had a way of never materializing.

That left Fate Marable as his only real suitor. "Fate had a way of his
own. He could see that I was very happy in his wonderful orchestra,
playing the kind of music I had never played before in my life and piling up
all the experiences I had dreamed of as an ambitious kid." So Fate got his
way, after all. "Things were jumping so good for me that the minute Fate
popped the question, I said 'yes' so fast that Fate could scarcely believe his
ears." It was even easier for Louis to say "yes" when Fate pressed an
advance payment into his hand.

In keeping with the spirit of courtship, Fate had "popped the question"
during a moonlight excursion, and once the boat docked, Louis dashed off
to tell his working wife the good news. Although he and Daisy were still
man and wife in the eyes of the law, their marriage was a sham, thanks to
her continuing employment as a prostitute and his philandering. By the
summer of 1918, he had returned to live with his mother, Mayann. Despite
these circumstances, he sought her blessing on his new venture. Daisy did
not share his excitement. She was nothing if not possessive, and liked to
keep all the men in her life close at hand. When she was done giving her
young husband a piece of her mind, "my feathers felt awful," Louis said.

Still, he was desperate for a chance at success, and, though he couldn't bring himself to admit it, just as desperate to get away from Daisy's world. "If I turn this offer down the way I have been doing with others I'll be stuck here forever with nothing happening," he told her. Recognizing the inevitable, Daisy forced herself to brighten, pecked her husband on the cheek, and tried to put the best face on matters. Relieved, Louis took her shopping in the high-class stores on Canal Street a few days later.

One night, not long before Louis left New Orleans, he ran into a "fine white boy" from Houston, Texas, who played trombone in a local band run by Peck Kelly. Jack Teagarden was a tall fellow, with a soulful voice and a relaxed, self-effacing manner. He first heard Louis play during one of the moonlight excursions and never forgot the experience. He had been wandering around the French Quarter with a pal, both of them drunk, when he suddenly heard a trumpet in the distance: "I couldn't see anything but an excursion boat gliding through the mist back to port," he remembered. "Then the tune was more distinct. The boat was still far off. But in the bow I could see a Negro standing in the wind, holding a trumpet high and sending out the most brilliant notes I had ever heard. It was jazz; it was what I had been hoping to hear all through the night. I don't even know if it was 'Tiger Rag' or 'Panama.' But it was Louis Armstrong descending from the sky like a god. The ship hugged the bank as if it were driven there by the powerful trumpet beats. I stayed absolutely still, just listening, until the boat dropped anchor. It was Fate Marable's orchestra. . . . I talked with the musicians when they landed and Fate Marable presented me to the unknown cornetist with the round open face: Louis Armstrong!"

"Tea" even got to blow a little horn for Louis that night. And Louis was equally appreciative. "The first time I heard Jack Teagarden on the trombone I got goose pimples all over; in all my experience I had never heard anything so fine," Louis said of that meeting. He took Jack around the boat, introduced him to Captain Joe Streckfus, and invited him into the special world of New Orleans jazz musicians. Their paths would cross again and again throughout their lives.

As Louis was the first to admit, his leave-taking of New Orleans was far from clean. It was complex and fraught with longing for women and for a way of life he realized was quickly passing into memory. The fragile set of conditions that had combined to produce jazz—the collision of cultures, the freedom from the constraints of bourgeois morality—had changed, just as he was changing and approaching adulthood. Nevertheless, he recognized the necessity of moving on.

"I will never forget the day I left New Orleans by train for St. Louis," he wrote of the journey, which he characteristically recalled in terms of the food he ate. "It was the first time in my life I had ever made a long trip by railroad. I had no idea what I should take, and my wife and mother did not either. For my lunch Mayann went to Prat's Creole Restaurant and bought me a great big fish sandwich and a bottle of green olives." Louis looked like the picture of an itinerant musician, with his slightly battered cornet, bulging suitcase, and "great big fish sandwich." His companion on the train was David Jones, who played the melophone, and whom Fate had also just snatched from New Orleans.

The St. Louis he found on his arrival was in many ways a city of the nineteenth century, its narrow streets lit by gaslight. The smell of slaughterhouses and packing houses wafted over it. The city was rigidly segregated. In 1917, when blacks began to take over some of the jobs in the packing houses, race riots broke out. White workers and their sympathizers went on a murderous rampage, shooting and lynching blacks, stringing them up from lampposts. Long after the city's white community decided it was best to forget the incident, it remained an urgent, burning memory for blacks residing in St. Louis and East St. Louis, and they lived in fear of another race riot. When Louis arrived here with his cornet in hand, he was treading on dangerous ground.

Marge Creath, a local pianist, remembered Louis on his first visit to St. Louis as uncertain and afraid, keeping his distance from whites and blacks alike. "Louis was so shy, as soon as he got off the stand he'd run down to the first deck—the band played on the second deck—and wouldn't talk to anyone. So one night a bunch of us said we were going to get him. He was down to the waterfront, and just kept his head down and didn't have anything to say. . . . I can see him right now; we were telling him how we loved his playing and he kept his head down, didn't want to talk."

He slowly began to emerge from his shell, but only in the company of fellow musicians. The reticence is not surprising. This was his first visit to a major city outside New Orleans, and he needed time to adjust, to feel his way. For the time being he focused on his work. The work ethic was deeply ingrained into Marable, and he was a martinet as well as a musician. He insisted on rehearsing the orchestra for an hour or two a day, incredible by the standards of New Orleans, where rehearsal was considered anathema. The other musicians told Louis terrifying tales of Marable's penchant for discipline. Drunkenness, missing a rehearsal, cutting up on stage, all of the shenanigans that went along with the music down in New Orleans, were grounds for dismissal from the orchestra. Fate understood how to motivate his men with fear and humiliation, and they all knew he could be one sly and mean son of a bitch when he felt like it. "If one of us made an error or played part of a piece wrong he would not say a thing about it until everyone thought it had been forgotten," Louis said. "When you came to work the next day with a bad hangover from the night before, he picked up the music you had failed with and asked you to play it before the other members of the band. And believe me, brothers, it was no fun being shown up before all the other fellows if you did not play that passage right; we used to call this experience our Waterloo."

Fate had a whole repertoire of tricks to keep his musicians in line. If he heard one of his men playing out of tune, he would rattle a big bunch of keys he carried with him and, laughing, toss them on the unlucky player's stand. And if Fate decided to fire one of his musicians, he turned the event into a spectacle. Clark Terry, the trumpet player, also played in this orchestra, and he was astonished by Fate's ingenious technique for humiliating his victim. "Whenever Fate would have occasion to get rid of somebody, the band would pass the word along to everybody to come one hour earlier. So if you knew rehearsal usually came at eight o'clock, everybody came at seven o'clock, except the person who's going to be fired.

"So all the people are there and they're on the boat and then all of a sudden, an hour later, here comes the guy who's going to get fired. When he gets on the boat, the band starts playing, 'They'll Be Some Changes Made, They'll Be Some Changes. . . .' All of a sudden the cat would realize, 'Oh my God! I'm late!' so he rushes up to the area where the band is playing and in his chair is the ax—you know, the fire ax." When he saw it, he knew he had just gotten the ax. After seeing this ritual, musician, Louis, and everyone else in the band dreaded receiving the same treatment.

Marable's emphasis on discipline accorded perfectly with the attitude of his employer, Captain John Streckfus. He was one of three brothers, all of them amateur musicians, two pianists and a violinist. The Streckfus Steamboat Line, which commenced operation in 1884, was originally designed to haul freight up and down the Mississippi until the fast-growing railroads began to steal its business. The captain decided to devote his company's fleet to excursions and, at one time or another, the Streckfus Steamboat Line operated eleven Mississippi riverboats under the slogan, "The most for the money is what the public gets." Based in St. Louis, Streckfus, of German-American parents, did his utmost to appeal to wealthy white patrons, "the very best class of people," according to company publicity, by serving the best food and liquor he could offer, and he maintained his ships in spotless condition. Streckfus was obsessed with providing a wholesome ambience aboard ship. "No gambling or disorder of any kind will be allowed," his company proclaimed. "There will be a lady attendant, and ladies and children will have the same protection and care they would receive in their own homes."

This polite environment was a long way from the whorehouses of New Orleans in which Louis and most other jazz musicians had come of age. Despite the social controls, the riverboats served as the next significant incubation chamber for the development of jazz since they brought the music to new audiences. Streckfus had very fixed ideas about the kind of music the boys in the band should play. "He would attend rehearsals, tap his feet with his watch in his hand, and if the band failed to keep proper tempo (sixty beats a minute for fox trots and ninety for one steps) somebody got hell. If it happened too often there were new faces on the bandstand," recalls Clarence Elder, a Streckfus employee.

Streckfus was also determined that there would be no stars in the orchestra. He paid his musicians a decent, uniform salary, fifty dollars a week, in addition to room and board. There was also a five dollar-a-week bonus payable at the end of the season; it was intended to encourage the musicians to stay on. The equality of pay eliminated envy and bargaining among the musicians, but it also blunted incentive. Why work harder, or blow harder, or spend time and effort developing new musical ideas, when the pay remained the same? Predictability mattered more than originality.

Even as he exposed his white audiences to black music, Streckfus carefully adhered to the Jim Crow customs of the day. Six days a week, the boats admitted whites only. Monday nights were set aside for black audiences. To distance himself from them, Streckfus delegated a black promoter named Jesse Johnson to book the Monday excursions, and Johnson made a name and good money for himself within this tightly circumscribed system. Marable's musicians found Monday nights to be special events, where they didn't have to please their white bosses. "It gave us an altogether different sensation because we were free to talk to people and the people could talk to us, and that's a great deal in playing music. We were less tense because it was our own people," Baby Dodds, the drummer, explained. The Monday crowd was, according to various reminiscences, wilder than Baby Dodds allowed. E. Simms Campbell remembered the Monday night excursions in which he participated this way: "Lodges and fraternal orders of all sorts would get together and have a benefit—to this day I have never found out what the benefits were for—but they always meant plenty of ice-cream and cake for us, and above all, music, the blues. Those boat rides usually ended up in fist fights, knife fights, and bottle-throwing contests. Drinking St. Louis corn, packed on the boat like cattle, bugging to the tunes of Jelly Roll Morton, some too ardent boy friend would cut in on another's girl, then fireworks! I can see an excited crew, redfaced and panting among a sea of black faces, trying to restore order." These spirited riverborne Monday nights went on for years, for the Streckfus Steamboat Line ships continued its policy of segregation until 1969, when the company finally relented under court order.

Fate Marable had signed on with the line in 1907, remaining loyal to it, segregation and all, until he retired in 1940. For Marable, at least, life under the Streckfus regime was good. His employer trusted and liked him. Of all the orchestra leaders Captain Streckfus employed, Marable was the only one permitted to hire his own musicians. In the early days, he employed whites willing to perform with a black leader aboard the flagship, *J. S.* (short for "Joseph Streckfus"), until that boat burned and sank in 1910. Later, he assembled a band consisting entirely of musicians from his home-town of Paducah, and it proved to be one of the dullest ensembles afloat.

Finally, a year before Louis's arrival, Marable, drawing on his decade-long acquaintance with the New Orleans jazz scene, started hiring black musicians for the orchestra aboard the *Sidney*. The others in this celebrated ensemble included Baby Dodds, who was revolutionizing jazz with his precise, feathery, intricately juxtaposed rhythms; Johnny St. Cyr, who played guitar and banjo; George "Pops" Foster, who played double bass with a bow (this was before plucking the strings became commonplace); David Jones on melophone; Boyd Atkins on violin; Fate himself at the piano, the most dignified of all the instruments; David Jones and Norman Mason on sax; and Lorenzo Brashear on trombone.

Even though this was a lineup of "hot musicians," they did not play "hot" aboard the *Sidney*. It was feared that Storyville-style antics would shock Streckfus's patrons, encourage lewd behavior, and tarnish the line's name. The Marable orchestra confined itself to dance tunes, waltzes, adaptations of melodies from classical music, and slow, easy tempos. To careful listeners, however, Marable's orchestra had a distinct sound. "It had a different kind of beat," said one. What it lacked in precision, it made up for in feeling, for their music was "bouncy," and cheerful. Louis believed that Captain Joe Streckfus "loved our music," and he remembered the old man smiling and chuckling "while he watched us swing, and he would order special tunes from us. We almost overdid it, trying to please him."

For the first time since his boyhood experiences with the Karnoffskys, Louis was spending considerable time in the company of whites, and trying against all obstacles to establish a healthy relationship through goodwill alone. But it wasn't easy under these circumstances. "We were not allowed to mingle with the white guests under any circumstances," Louis recalled of his years on the Streckfus riverboats. "We were there to play good music for them, and that was all." Louis tried to fathom the strange attitude of whites, telling himself that because he was from the South, he had a better understanding of racial relations than Northerners. On the one hand, he was not permitted any ordinary social interaction with them, while on the other, they loved his music, and if they talked to him, they often made it plain they liked *him*, as well. "I have always loved my white folks and they have always loved me and my music," he wrote. "I have never had anything to be depressed about in that respect, only respect and appreciation."

Before long, Louis and the other cats were receiving invitations to play in St. Louis for appreciative white audiences at the Grand Central Hotel. "It was the first time," he said, "that colored 'cats' had ever come North to play there. The people learned to like us right away. Every night, at the top of the program, Fate would swing us into the 'St. Louis Blues' and they would go crazy about our music."

One night, Louis, David Jones, and Fate himself were invited to hear a group of St. Louis musicians. "We three sat to one side of the band and listened to them play. We could see the boys in the band had heard about us. They kept looking over at us, in a curious way, but not letting on they were. We watched close to see what their music would be like, because we knew they had a big reputation in St. Louis, and naturally we were interested to see how our New Orleans bands, like Kid Ory's and the rest, would stack up against them. Well, we were surprised. In no time at all we could tell they were doing things that had been done down home years before." The revelation boosted his self-confidence. These northern cats weren't as great as he'd imagined them to be. "The leader would try to swing them away from the score but they didn't seem to know how." Later that evening, the leader graciously gave Louis a chance to strut his stuff. "After several numbers he had his trumpeter do a call to attention. When the room was quiet, he stepped out in front and announced: 'We are honored to have with us tonight three of New Orleans' most distinguished performers. They come from a town where they even have jazz music with their breakfast.' "

Louis shivered with anticipation, and then, "We cut loose with one of the very newest hot songs. . . . Every one of us was a natural swing player and didn't need any scoring at all. We almost split that room open— man, did we play! I got so hot I hardly knew there was a room. Davey threw that big horn of his around so you'd have thought he'd gone clean out of his head, and Fate kept right along with us. Boy! Could Fate make those keys sing! Well, they all liked it fine. They stood up and yelled out for more and the band boys were all on their feet, too, and the leader came over and shook our hands. We gave them an encore and then, as a courtesy to them, we played the 'St. Louis Blues' the way we had swung it back home. My, that was a big night for me," he exulted. "It was the first time I had an ovation like that in a really big city away from New Orleans."

Louis made himself conspicuous in the Marable orchestra in another, less exalted manner: his shabby clothes. "He reported for band rehearsal with his feet half out of his shoes," Captain Joe Streckfus remembered. Even Baby Dodds, the drummer, was taken aback by Louis's rustic outfits. "He used to wear jumpers, starched and ironed," said Baby Dodds. "It had been washed and faded so bad that it wasn't blue anymore. And it was stiff with starch. He didn't care, but I told him he would have to stop wearing that. Louis wore a shirt without a collar, but bought a celluloid one to fasten on." It was called a "hobo collar" because hoboes could remove them and wash them anywhere, even in a river. So there was Louis, in starched overalls, blowing on his trumpet so hard that the buttons popped off his hobo collar, first one side, then the other. The sight of the young rube from New Orleans busting his buttons made the others laugh. "He just sat there looking like the end man in a minstrel show," remarked Baby Dodds, who tried to coax Louis into wearing a regular collar, as everyone else in the orchestra did. Only low-class gamblers and hustlers wore those things, Dodds said, and if that's what Louis wanted to look like, there was nothing anyone could do about it.

Baby Dodds felt entitled to condescend to Louis for several reasons. He was seven years older, and his sensibilities were considerably more refined. Warren "Baby" Dodds's New Orleans childhood revolved around the church, not the brothel, and his father sent all his children to Sunday school. "If we weren't gentlemen on the street, we were gentlemen in church," Dodds said. His first exposure to music occurred not when he crept into some liquor-sodden tonk, but when he heard classical music. Such music was not easy for a person of color to come by. "Negroes were not allowed in the places where it was played, so I heard it by standing on the outside," Dodds said. He often stood in the lobby of the Tulane Theatre, listening to the orchestra playing for the white patrons seated within. His first love was the flute, not the drum or saxophone or banjo or any other instrument associated with jazz. "I don't see how in the world I ever wanted to play the flute," he later reflected, "because there was no field for colored people in classical music."

Still, his early love of symphonic music helped him in jazz. "Being a jazz man, when I hear a symphony I pick out different things which I feel I can use in jazz." He took up the clarinet, but the instrument was, to him, a poor substitute for the flute. Besides, his older brother Johnny had already taken up that instrument. For the rest of their lives, Baby and Johnny danced an intricate dance of sibling and musical rivalry.

Over his father's objections, Baby found his way to the drums. He learned from hearing or playing with such fabled New Orleans musical characters as Black Benny, Buddy Bolden, and even Jelly Roll Morton. No matter how deeply he entered into the jazz milieu, Dodds disdained these rough, unschooled characters. Throughout his life, he harbored the conviction that he had been meant for higher pursuits, which the white man's bigotry had prevented him from attaining. It is possible, however, that Baby contributed more to music as a jazz drummer than he would have as a flutist in a symphony orchestra. He added gadgets to the drums to develop new sounds and rhythms. He adjusted the foot pedals to shorten the stroke, so he could work out extremely intricate rhythms with his legs. And he demonstrated musical, as well as mechanical, prowess.

Baby had been married since 1912 to Odell Johnson, but the jazz musician's itinerant life had taken its toll on the marriage. During his time with the Marable orchestra, Baby and Odell separated, and they finally divorced in 1921. It is possible that their relationship was further complicated by Baby's wandering eye. Stories about his fondness for young men abounded. His manner was said to be effeminate, and he liked to surround himself with boys. He also made outrageous remarks designed to confirm the rumors. When the jazz critic Rudi Blesh came to see him for the first time and asked if he could remove his coat, Baby shot back, "You can take your pants off if you want to."

During his first summer, most of Louis's time aboard the Streckfus riverboats consisted of tramping along the Mississippi as far north as St. Paul, Minnesota. "Tramping" meant that Louis and the orchestra spent just a night or two in a town, played a few dances, and in the morning, as the mist rose from the placid river, steamed off to the next stop. Despite its brilliant musicianship and earnest desire to please, the Fate Marable Orchestra endured rebuffs. "The first year we went up the river we didn't do good at all. It was pitiful," Baby Dodds complained. "They'd advertise . . . that we were colored. So people wouldn't be disappointed. . . . They saw Negro roustabouts but had never seen a Negro with a tie and collar on, and a white shirt, playing music. They just didn't know what to make of it."

Absurdities abounded wherever they went. In Alton, Illinois, a young white customer bet his pals that he could jump from the deck of the riverboat and live to tell the tale. While the Fate Marable Orchestra played to a huge crowd, perhaps as many as eight hundred people, the youth tumbled into the water, sending the crew scurrying. The crowd ran to the railings to see what had happened, and the boat listed so far it was in danger of taking on water. Panic struck. Louis and the other musicians tried to remain upright on the badly tilting stage, and the captain, showing true Streckfus mettle, urged them to keep playing at all costs. "We played 'Tiger Rag' until we were blue in the face and eventually most of the people calmed down," Louis recalled. As for the reckless boy, he survived, but perhaps wished he hadn't. The enraged crew rescued him and would have beaten him senseless if he hadn't been so young; instead, they turned him over to the police, who arrested him.

So it went throughout the summer, from Alton to Hannibal, Missouri, the boyhood home of Mark Twain. Crowds came in droves to watch the black men in their fancy ties and shirts play. From Hannibal the riverboat worked its way north past Quincy, Keokuk, entered Iowa, and cruised along the Iowa-Illinois border, past Rock Island, playing one-nighters at every town that would have them. When Louis's riverboat reached Davenport, Iowa, he met a seventeen-year-old cornet player from that town. His name was Bix Beiderbecke.

He seemed completely out of place in the rough-and-tumble world of jazz, for he was the scion of a prosperous German-American family. A contemporary described him this way: "Bix was a raw-boned, husky, farmboy kind of a kid, a little above-average height and still growing. His frog eyes popped out of a ruddy face and he had light brown hair that always looked like it was trying to go someplace else." He seemed like the typical all-American teenager of the twenties; he was playful, liked girls, and enthusiastically experimented with booze, but Bix baffled anyone who tried to get close to him or understand what drove him.

The only quality that was apparent to all who knew Bix was his musical ability. He had inherited his talent from his mother, who played the piano and organ, and his grandfather, who led a German-American chorus in Davenport. When he was tall enough to reach the keyboard, he began to pick out classical melodies on the piano, and it was obvious to all that a child prodigy was in their midst. Given his cultivated musical background, he appeared destined for a life of music in a conservatory or a classical orchestra. Bix confounded his family's expectations. He listened to early jazz recordings and changed his musical direction. He tried to persuade his uncle, a band leader, to give him lessons, but was refused. Undaunted, Bix bought his own cornet (perhaps the only young jazz musician of the day who could afford to do so), repaired to his bedroom in Davenport, taught himself the rudiments, and in no time was playing with his high school band at football games.

Bix was still uncertain of his potential when the *Sidney*, bearing Marable's orchestra, tied up in his hometown of Davenport, and during the week the boat spent there, he went aboard whenever he could. Accompanied by a group of friends, he heard Marable playing the calliope, for no one could resist the spectacle, and listened to the orchestra, and especially its cornetist, Louis Armstrong. Normally, Fate's musicians did not socialize with the patrons, and they were downright wary of white jazz musicians. "We used to call white musicians 'alligators,' " Baby said, a private code word among Marable musicians. "That was the way we'd describe them when they'd come around and we were playing something that we didn't want them to catch on to. We'd say, 'Watch out, there's an alligator!' "

Bix was the exception; he managed to ingratiate himself with the orchestra, especially his new idol, Louis, whose confidence he quickly gained. According to Baby Dodds, "Louis told Bix he didn't have a horn, so Bix said, 'Well, meet me when I go out and I'll see if I can get you a horn.' And Bix took him out afterwards and helped him pick out a horn." This spontaneous act of generosity, so typical of Bix, sealed a friendship that would become increasingly important to the two young men who had nothing in common except musical genius and a spirit of generosity.

After the *Sidney* steamed away from Davenport, Bix returned to his home, picked up his cornet, and gradually transformed Louis's New Orleans-style of blowing into something new and unique, something that did not belong to any particular city, style, or tradition. On top of all this, he fell under the spell of modern composers, Ravel and Debussy and Stravinsky, and their influence put a whole new spin on Bix's idea of jazz. Although Bix often sounded like other hornmen, no one else sounded quite like him. In his hands, the cornet became the first cousin of the French horn that it was, soothing and elegant, but then, without warning, stinging, and blue.

It was in one of these little Iowa river towns that Louis's friend Baby Dodds nearly got himself killed. The incident began when Baby got roaring drunk—and not for the first time. He staggered onto the bandstand that night, late *and* drunk. Fate tried to cover for Baby's scandalous behavior by slowing the tempo—they were playing in front of white folks, after all, and needed to make the best possible impression—but Baby became so offended by Fate's maneuver that he started yelling at the band, calling them a "gang of black bastards" in front of the astonished patrons. Fate called an intermission and tried to talk sense to Baby, but the drummer just got more obstreperous. He threatened to punch anyone who came near him. At this point, Louis decided to see what he could do to settle Baby down.

"You wouldn't hit me, would'ja?" he asked.

"I'll hit you and I'll hit the boss," Baby roared.

Louis backed off, and Baby continued to flail and rant, until Captain John Streckfus himself showed his face and asked Baby to calm down. Baby promptly told the captain what he could do to himself, in full hearing of all the patrons. "God help Baby," Louis said to himself. All of a sudden Captain John, a large, powerfully built man, grabbed Baby's neck with two hands and started choking him. He kept him in a choke hold even after he stopped struggling, and his eyes turned red. "It was a gruesome sight," Louis recalled, "but nobody said, 'Don't choke him anymore.' " Only when Baby collapsed and fainted did Captain John relax his death grip. Fate apologized to the captain, and the orchestra returned to the bandstand, without Baby, to finish the evening's dance.

With incidents like this to teach him, Louis learned to be cautious and to mind his manners at all times. The closest he came to breaking the law, or getting into real trouble, was buying bootleg booze. In this regard, Louis was no different from millions of other law-abiding Americans who were also flouting the dry laws. The advent of Prohibition coincided with his arrival in the orchestra. Everywhere they went, Louis and his colleagues found bootleggers ready to cater to their thirst. Rather than discouraging his musicians from obtaining moonshine, Fate encouraged them. "Fate was the type of cat who loved to drink," said Clark Terry. "He would get up and put his clothes on and run to the nearest bar and order a shot and then hold his drinking hand with the other to get the drink down, and then it was like the fire went to his heart. Then he'd say, 'Okay, now let's get it on.' " Fate's thirst led him to participate in a big liquor buy with Baby Dodds and Louis. They arranged to meet a moonshiner during intermission, and the man showed them a whole suitcase of alcohol for sale, twenty-five dollars a quart, payable up front. Fate, Louis, and Baby paid their money and walked off with a heavy, clinking suitcase. "But when we got back on the boat we found out there was nothing in the suitcase but three bricks," according to Baby. "We had a real big laugh and kidded Louis and Fate a long while about it."

Louis was never one to let self-denial stand in the way of enjoyment of the world's bounty. All around him he saw examples of the folly of frugality. He observed David Jones (now "Br'er Jones" to him) starve himself aboard ship and save every nickel he could to send to his family, who needed the money for their cotton farm. And to what end? "The boll weevils ate all of his cotton before the season was over. He did not even have a chance to go down and look his farm over before a telegram came saying everything had been shot to hell. After that David Jones used to stand at the boat rail during every intermission looking down at the water and thinking about all of the jack he had lost." Louis became so concerned he warned Fate, "He's liable to jump in the water most any minute."

"This incident taught me never to deprive my stomach," Louis concluded. "I'll probably never be rich, but I will be a fat man." He succeeded. When he joined the orchestra, he weighed 140 pounds, but within a year he had to buy himself "a pair of fat man's trousers." Not that he minded—eating well, he told himself, was proof of living well. But this dramatic weight gain marked the beginning of a battle with weight and a love-hate affair with food that would preoccupy him for the rest of his life. During his riverboat journey, he also showed the first signs of another obsession: "physic," or self-medication. From his mother, Louis inherited a powerful conviction that you saw a doctor but twice in your life, when you were born and when you died, and sometimes not even then. Over the years, Louis would develop some exotic ideas about "physic," but for now he simply relied on a nostrum known as Scott's Emulsion, which he consumed by the bottle. "He had a cold all the time," Baby recalled of Louis, "and we used to kid him around, laughing and joking. Once he took a whole course of Scott's Emulsion. It cleaned him out perfectly." Large doses of Scott's Emulsion proved useless against the common cold. Louis became so sick—and his voice so raspy—that he was convinced he had developed tuberculosis and was sure to die. Eventually, "he got rid of the cold but the voice developed like that and he's been like that ever since."

Beyond these distractions, Louis focused on his instrument and gradually improved. He memorized all manner of melodies, from folk songs to popular tunes of the moment, and learned to adapt his playing to different audiences, white and black. He functioned as a showman as well as a musician. When Captain Streckfus, always eager to meddle in musical affairs, showed up with slide trumpets and slide whistles and all manner of blocks and triangles, the musicians, especially the haughty Baby, all turned away in despair. But Louis was game for anything. He'd play the slide whistle or any other damn fool instrument just to see what kind of a sound he could get from it, and what effect it would have on the music and the crowd. For Louis, that spirit of endless playfulness was the essence of performing.

His exuberance and creativity extended beyond music; his lingo also broke new ground. "Come on, you cats!" he'd urge as the orchestra played. "Cats?" Until this time, "cats" was a rather specialized term. One jazz musician referred to another as a "cat," but Louis took to referring to all blacks as "cats," and then some whites as "cats," until just about everyone was a "cat" as far as Louis was concerned. "Look out there, Pops," he'd holler while the orchestra played. "Pops?" Some old-timers like Bunk Johnson went by the honorific "Pops," but Louis took to calling everyone "Pops" at one time or another, including himself. He'd talk about "jive," another term new to many. Nor had they heard about "scat"—a funny babbling Louis would lapse into when the music seemed to transport him, and he just went with it, riding along with it in his private musical language. In fact, Louis was coining or popularizing some of the key words of the urban vocabulary of the late 1940s and '50s. He didn't sound hip at the moment, no one knew about hip yet, or cool, or other jazz attitudes—he sounded strange. More and more, though, he was beginning to sound like Louis.

Meanwhile, the riverboat followed its course to Clinton and Dubuque, across the Wisconsin-Minnesota border, then steamed all the way up to Prairie du Chien, LaCrosse, Winona, Red Wing, and its final destination, St. Paul, in time for the Fourth of July. The vessel served as a floating dormitory, mess hall, rehearsal space, and nightclub in the heat of the summer. "You couldn't get cool anywhere; it was just as hot inside the boat as up on deck," Louis recalled. "We boys and some of the deck-hands got half a dozen long ropes and fixed big loops on the ends and threw them out over the stern, making the other ends fast along the rail. Then we took hold of the ropes and let ourselves out into the water until we got down to the loops, which we would slip around our arms, and lay back and let the boat pull us along."

At the end of August, the riverboat steamed off to its home port of St. Louis, arriving in time for Labor Day and summer's end. After the holiday, which was always good for business, the winter season took Louis and the *Sidney* tramping back down the river. When they reached Cape Girardeau, Missouri, the boat docked. The captain and his wife went ashore and as they were walking down the main street of the town, they passed a store selling Victrolas and records. "An idea came to me," Streckfus wrote. "We purchased a record of 'Avalon,' which had one chorus in one key, then a few bars of modulation and into another key, with the second chorus in that key. That was the first record of its kind." He bought that record, plus a few others, and set up the Victrola aboard ship to play the records. "Soon the orchestra boys, who were napping in the texas, the deck above, heard a style of dance music that they had never heard before. They all came running down, and it wasn't long before we were in a rehearsal of these pieces, everyone playing by ear. Louis Armstrong, with his trumpet in hand, came over to the Victrola and would pick up on his trumpet the notes in the several chords in modulation, giving the saxophone section their chords, likewise the brass their changes in chords, and by repeating over and over again, all chords were down pat."

That night, they played "Avalon" to a crowd of over a thousand, and they were a huge hit. The captain insisted that he and the Victrola were responsible for their success. Fate Marable, of course, had a different opinion about who was actually responsible, but in any event, it was now clear that the orchestra had begun to bloom. "We were the first colored band to play most of the towns at which we stopped, particularly the smaller ones," Louis wrote. "The ofays were not used to seeing colored boys blowing horns and making fine music for them to dance by. At first we ran into some ugly experiences while we were on the bandstand, and we had to listen to plenty of nasty remarks. But most of us were from the South anyway. We were used to that kind of jive, and we would just keep on swinging as though nothing had happened. Before the evening was over they *loved* us."

South of Cairo, the climate, the accents, and the pace of life took on a familiar southern feel, languid, even genteel, as the riverboat paddled along the Arkansas-Tennessee border. In Dyersburg, Blytheville, and Memphis the orchestra drew enthusiastic crowds and then plunged further south into Mississippi, where the landscape became flat, swampy, and empty. When they hit Greenville and Vicksburg, they stayed aboard ship—no telling what trouble lurked onshore despite the Streckfus Line's generally successful efforts to bring black musicians and music before white audiences.

On they steamed, past Natchez, and into Louisiana at last, through little Morganza into Baton Rouge, where there was good money to be made. The Fate Marable Orchestra was nearly home, their riverboat awash with familiar swampy odors off Saint Gabriel and Vachérie, until one fine day in late January or early February they steamed into New Orleans. Fate himself perched atop the calliope, banging out a steam-driven tune to announce the arrival of the *Sidney*, its huge white bulk looming majestically above the sleepy, sensuous, welcoming city. They were home in time for Mardi Gras.

During Louis's stint with the orchestra, Fate Marable gradually changed the face of jazz, at least outside New Orleans. Hardly anyone was calling it jazz, yet, not even the musicians who played it. They called it New Orleans-style music, or even ragtime because of its kinship to the piano rags of Scott Joplin. In parts of the country where religion was a potent force, even Joplin's tranquil little sonatas were considered suspect. On June 17, 1917, when jazz, by then called "jass," was about to become a national craze, the New Orleans *Times-Picayune*, the voice of the city's establishment, inveighed against this degenerate form of music. Its editorial, "Jass and Jassism," made an "-ism" out of the music to equate it with modern evils like Communism and Bolshevism. "Why is the jass music, and, therefore the jass band? As well ask why is the dime novel or the grease-dripping doughnut. All are manifestations of a low streak in man's taste that has not yet come out in civilization's wash." The paper's editorial writer declared that jass belonged "down in the basement of the House of Music," in the "servants' hall of rhythm." The *Times-Picayune* declared that the main problem was the unfortunate emphasis on rhythm. "On certain natures," the paper theorized, "loud sound and meaningless noise has an exciting, almost intoxicating effect, like crude colors and strong perfumes, the sight of flesh or the sadic pleasures in blood." As a remedy, the *Times-Picayune* prescribed the "languor of a Viennese Waltz or the refined sentiment of an eighteenth century minuet." At the same time, the newspaper was forced to acknowledge that "jass" originated in New Orleans. However, "We do not recognize the honor of parenthood, but with a story in circulation it behooves us to be the last to accept the atrocity in polite society, and where it has crept in we should make it a point of civic honor to suppress it. Its musical value is nil, and its possibilities of harm are great."

Whites were not the only ones to condemn jazz. Creole musicians, who emphasized sweet music for public consumption, resented the uproarious new form of music. And many blacks were keenly sensitive to the depredations of prostitution and drugs, which were part of the jazz milieu, and wanted no part of it for their children. So the scandalous reputation of jazz was not exclusively a racial issue. Nevertheless, jazz had outgrown the restrictive southern social order and could no longer be suppressed.

In contrast, New York, the center of show business and commerce, had a completely different take on jazz. Maybe jazz *was* bad for morals, but it was fantastic for business. That's what New York understood. If jazz was born down in New Orleans, the jazz *business* began to flourish up in New York City. In 1917, at about the time the *Times-Picayune* tried to disavow jazz, a group of white musicians from New Orleans arrived in New York and began playing nightly at Reisenweber's, instantly turning an old Columbus Circle lobster palace into the epicenter of a musical revolution. They called themselves the Original Dixieland Jass (later Jazz) Band, but their music was, for the most part, fairly derivative. The most original thing about them was the fact that they had gotten themselves to New York, where they were suddenly in the right place at the right time and fully prepared to cash in on the public's hunger for jazz.

Until the coming of the Original Dixieland Jazz Band, it hadn't occurred to anyone that jazz could make much money. On March 25, 1918, in New York City, they waxed a tight, furious recording of "Tiger Rag" that instantly took the country by storm. All of a sudden, this old-fashioned, newfangled New Orleans music became a national phenomenon, part of popular culture and even show business. ODJB versions of "Lazy Daddy," "Clarinet Marmalade," "Ostrich Walk," and "Toddlin' Blues" followed in quick succession. Releasing one hit song after another, the band ignited a craze for jazz and incited college boys everywhere to take up the cornet and form jazz combos. Everyone could recite the name of their players: Nick

LaRocca, cornet; Eddie Edwards, trombone; Larry Shields, clarinet; Henry Ragas, piano; and Tony Sbarbaro, drums. These were the first men to become rich and famous jazz musicians.

Although they played with a demonic intensity thrilling to most ears, they clung to a set of mechanical formulas. They had learned their craft by listening to traditional New Orleans jazz musicians, many of whom couldn't read music. (Neither could the members of the Original Dixieland Jazz Band, for that matter, with the exception of Eddie Edwards, the trombonist.) The ODJB polished and arranged traditional tunes, many of which had been around since before the Civil War, copyrighted them, and made them into hits.

Let it be noted that the members of the group that brought the sounds of New Orleans jazz to New York and the country at large were white, not black. The fact they were white smoothed the way for widespread acceptance of their style of music. And their style of playing differed from black musicians in New Orleans. It was tighter, with little room for improvisation, and faster. There was often lots of splashy cornet playing and banjo twanging, and it was nearly always in 2/4 time, with a simple rhythmic order underlying its apparent intricacy. Critics came to call this jazz genre "Dixieland."

The commercial success of the Original Dixieland Jazz Band quickly spawned scores of other white jazz bands, notably the New Orleans Rhythm Kings. And Jimmy Durante, a musician before he became a comedian, concocted a so-called "New Orleans Jazz Band" in Harlem, a white man bringing black music to a white neighborhood that would soon become a black one. This type of cross-cultural exchange became part of the uproarious era that F. Scott Fitzgerald christened "the Jazz Age."

Not everyone agreed that jazz came about this way. Nick LaRocca, the left-handed cornetist of the Original Dixieland Jazz Band, proclaimed that his band had not just popularized jazz but *invented* the idiom, and that blacks had merely copied his innovations. "The Negro did not play any kind of music equal to white men at any time," he insisted. "Even the poorest band of white men played better than the Negroes in my day." In his embittered old age, he complained that legions of untrained black musicians had stolen the jazz mantle away from him and other Italian-American musicians and laid claim to music that did not belong to them. "I say the colored man has his rightful place in any music, but why not the white man?" He was convinced Louis Armstrong had simply based his style of playing on Nick LaRocca. Just because he was "one of the most outstanding of the colored musicians," LaRocca said, "that didn't make him [great]. It didn't make the other Negroes great."

LaRocca was motivated by envy and racism, and he exaggerated shamelessly, but jazz does contain important elements derived from Italian music, especially its emphasis on melody. There are French influences, as well, in its quadrille rhythms, not to mention Caribbean elements and Mexican flourishes picked up from military bands that came up to New Orleans, where they made a huge impression on local musicians. Even Mexican music contained within it South American-Indian motifs that influenced jazz. All in all, jazz boasted a very complex, mixed lineage, but it is essentially African-American music. You could remove the white elements—the French quadrilles, the Mexican military rhythms, the Italian melodies—and the music would still recognizably be jazz. But if you removed the black elements—the emphasis on improvisation, the polyphony, the complex rhythms, not to mention the all-important attitude that music was part of daily life—the remainder would not be jazz. The African-American elements defined jazz; they gave it substance and a framework to incorporate European and South American influences.

At the end of his season with Fate Marable, Louis collected his bonus and went ashore. He hadn't eaten a decent meal in six months, and he was determined to make up for lost time. He went straight to his old apartment on Melpomene Street, where Daisy greeted him with a kiss and a "big pot of red beans and rice." They talked a long time that night, as he told her of his adventures up and down the Mississippi, all the while thinking, "If Daisy would only always be as sweet to me as she is today. If only we would never have another fight."

After a few days, his mother invited him for dinner, which he shared with Clarence, and Mama Lucy—"the wrecking crew," Mayann called them. Trying to feed them all on a skimpy budget, his mother "went to Zatteran's grocery, and bought a pound of red beans, a pound of rice, a big slice of fat back and a big red onion. At Staehle's bakery she got two loaves of stale bread for a nickel. She boiled this jive down to a gravy, and I'll tell you that when we came we could smell her pot almost a block away." All of them, Mayann, Mama Lucy, Daisy, and Clarence, stuffed themselves. Feasting on his mother's cooking, he knew he was back, and he was glad.

Louis did not relax for long. In constant need of money, he was soon working in various honky-tonks and cabarets throughout New Orleans, until the riverboat season recommenced. His best gig, with Kid Ory's band, had evaporated, since Ory himself had left the city. "Pete Lala got mad when I didn't cut him in on the dances at the Economy Hall and the Co-operators Hall," said Ory, "so he got about fifty cops to go around and run my customers away. I felt I was going to lose my health down there." Ory's first notion was to go to Chicago, but one night he rounded up his pals, including Louis, Johnny Dodds, and Joe Lindsay. They convened at Ben Mulligan's saloon and drank until they all fell on their knees, right there in the saloon, and pledged they were going not to Chicago but to California, where the work was supposed to be plentiful and free of union control. Ory followed through, but Louis lost his resolve and stayed behind, preferring to wait for his next season with the Fate Marable Orchestra.

Between seasons, Louis found work at Tom Anderson's. Not just another tonk, Tom Anderson's was a big, boisterous, important place with the best location in the former Storyville, on Rampart Street, just past Canal. It was a carnival of jazz and lust and just about everything else that was enjoyable and forbidden in most other places. Louis's friend, the jazz writer Robert Goffin, noted that the saloon functioned as the "vice-City Hall as well as the City Hall of vice. This king of the underworld knew all his subjects—gangsters, gamblers, idle rich, perverts, and playthings of passion—and greeted them by their first names. They swelled his coffers with an unending flow of tainted gold. Much of this was diverted in turn to those who made their living by catering to the passions of others: barmen; dope-peddlers; ample-bosomed madames with pearl necklaces, prostitutes with faces ravaged by liquor, insomnia, and sin; scar-faced pimps, hustlers who could tell you the price of each miserable girl; white musicians; colored trumpeters with rosy lips; pianists who partially dismantled their instruments so that they made more noise and kept the customers awake."

Louis was back in his element at Tom Anderson's, and he loved working there. "That was a swell job if there ever was one," he said in a fond haze of nostalgia. Not only were the patrons rich white swells with lots of money to spare for tips, but the waiters, whom he made sure to befriend, supplied him with plentiful leftovers: steaks and quail and chops, all of the first quality. "I felt real important eating all those fine meals, meals I could not have possibly paid for then."

No matter how much he enjoyed this work, he knew he had to leave New Orleans again, for Daisy, after a brief period of tranquillity, reverted to her jealous rampages and threats to take her razor to him. In April 1921, he left for another summer-long tramp up and down the Mississippi, and once again, he was back by Labor Day. He calculated he had now traveled five thousand miles on the riverboats, playing and practicing jazz constantly, and gaining confidence as a musician. "I could read music very well by now and was getting hotter and hotter on my trumpet. My chest had filled out deeper and my lips and jaws had got stronger, so I could blow much harder and longer than before without getting tired. I had made a special point of the high register, and was beginning to make my high-C notes more and more often. That was the greatest strain on the lips."

He drifted further apart from Daisy. When he returned from his most recent summer season aboard the Streckfus Lines, she was no longer at the Canal Street dock to greet him. He felt both a sense of relief and disappointment in her absence.

By the fall of 1921, Louis was chafing under the limitations of Marable's formula for success in the music business. He was now twenty. He had been playing the horn for thirteen years, and he sensed the end of his apprenticeship approaching. Where he had once been content to accept Marable's teachings and discipline, he now wanted to play music his own way, but his boss was not about to allow that aboard the Streckfus riverboats. As his tenure with the Marable orchestra lengthened, Louis became the only instrumentalist to take solos, a practice that had crucial consequences both for his own musical development and the future of jazz, for it was here, on the riverboats, that the idea of the jazz soloist was born. "One day Louis rehearsed a trumpet solo," Captain Joe Streckfus recalled, "with Fate at the piano and Louis on the trumpet, the balance of the orchestra not playing. That night Louis Armstrong stood up alone and played his trumpet solo accompanied by the piano. This was the first time. The applause and requests for an encore were so great, they repeated the number." Until now, jazz performers, black and white, generally played together, occasionally taking turns, each man having his brief moment in the spotlight to show off the sound of his instrument and to introduce himself with a nod toward the audience. But Louis had something different in mind; he was beginning to work toward the idea of his cornet leading the entire orchestra. He was interested not in longer solos, which interrupted the flow of the music, but in directing the course of the music and filling it with his personality. Once Louis began to assert himself on stage, adding ever more solos of his own devising, Captain Streckfus himself ordered Marable to rein in his exuberant cornetist.

Louis's partner in rhythmic crime, Baby Dodds, the drummer, was also testing the limits with rapid, irregular beats. Because Streckfus was obsessed with tempo, Dodds was the most likely to incur his disapproval. Streckfus ordered the orchestra to play "toddle time," four beats to the measure, predictable as a grandfather's clock. "To me, four beats was all wrong," Dodds argued. "It has a tendency to speed up the music. But for older people it was easier since instead of dancing to a step, they would just bounce around." Dodds was soon sharply reminded that it was Streckfus's riverboat, and his word was law. If he didn't like things as they were, he could pack up and leave.

Dodds looked to Fate to intercede, but when the leader deferred to Captain Joe, Dodds bitterly concluded, "Fate Marable had been with Streckfus so long that anything Streckfus asked for he'd tell us to do, even if it meant breaking our necks." Dodds insisted he couldn't or wouldn't play that damned old "toddle time," and Louis, inspired by Dodds's rebellion, also refused to curb his musical flights of fantasy. "We were the stars on the boat," Dodds told himself, "why monkey with us?"

In unison, they wrote and delivered their resignations.

Marable quickly replaced Armstrong and Dodds with musicians of less inventiveness, and good old thump-thump toddle time prevailed on the Streckfus lines. Indeed, it became the trademark of the Fate Marable Orchestra in the post-Armstrong era.

Although they parted company with some acrimony, Louis, like nearly all musicians who played in Fate Marable's orchestra, remained grateful to his former boss and "schoolmaster." He had learned much during his two years tramping up and down the Mississippi aboard the *Sidney*—much about jazz, gambling, bootleg booze, and white folks. He was twenty, and many of the outlines of the mature man and performer were plainly visible. He was already hard at work willing the jazz solo into existence. He was as much a showman as a musician. His gregariousness, extending to both races, was apparent to all. He had struck up a solid rapport with the teenager who would become the other great cornetist of the era, Bix Beiderbecke, and with the young man who would become the preeminent trombonist, Jack Teagarden. His voice had acquired a startling new depth. He began to develop his lifelong obsession with "physic"—home remedies for whatever he imagined ailed him. He began to eat vast quantities of food, to become a "fat man," because his sense of life told him to seize on whatever pleasure was available to him, and next to music, food was the most reliable sustenance. And he began to display a love of playing with language, contorting familiar words into new meanings.

But he had much to learn. He remained impenetrably naive about money, gambling away most of his earnings, and about women, for he still held onto the hope that he could somehow concoct a satisfying life with Daisy, the whore with the heart of tin.

At the end of his final season with Marable, Louis returned to New Orleans, where great changes awaited him. Daisy had given up prostitution and found work as a domestic for wealthy white folks who lived in a fine house in Saint Charles. No sooner had he alighted from the train than he discovered that Daisy had moved out of their two-room apartment on Melpomene Street and now lived in servants' quarters in her employer's home. Not only that, but she'd adopted a thirteen-year-old girl named Wila Mae Wilson. Accordingly, Louis went out to this strange, white neighborhood to the unfamiliar "home" he shared with the wife he hadn't seen for months.

Very quickly, he realized the arrangement would never work. To reach the entrance to the servants' quarters, he had to pass through an alley, "and I was rather afraid when I came home in the wee hours of the night that I might be taken for a burglar." This was precisely what happened the first time he came home at four o'clock in the morning, after a long, exhausting streetcar ride. Just as he'd feared, a white watchman observed him entering the alley and followed him. Louis had the presence of mind to explain to the man that he actually lived here. "My wife works for some white folks and we're staying on the premises," he said. The watchman let him go, but Louis, who had taught himself to brave flying bullets and bottles in some of the toughest tonks in the South, and who traveled up and down the Mississippi to towns where few blacks ever went, knew he could never live this way. The second he walked in the door, he woke Daisy and Wila Mae and told them they were leaving right away.

Playing the complaisant wife for once, Daisy gave notice to her employers in the morning, and the little family moved into a three-room apartment at Saratoga and Erato that Louis found for them. That she behaved responsibly toward her adopted daughter, Wila Mae, surprised him to no end, because, as he saw things, "Daisy never did take to anybody very much. Lots of times she did not care very much even for me." Yet she doted on the child.

Only later did he discover that Daisy was also keeping company with a boyfriend, Louis "Shots" Madison. Louis knew Shots— he was a cornetist, too! Louis was deeply wounded. He would have been happier knowing she was working as a prostitute than engaged in a romantic liaison. He told himself that Shots was a *good* cornet player—not as good as he was, naturally, but the painful lesson showed him that Daisy, whatever her drawbacks, was consistent in her preference for a fine cornet man. "After all, a cornet is not a bad instrument to fall for." He resigned himself to her infidelity, and years later, noted in a matter-of-fact way: "Shots Madison and I were raised up around Liberty and Perdido street[s] together, and he was also Daisy's boy friend."

There had been one other important change in Louis's absence. His sister had gone off on her own, yet another sign that the world of his childhood was coming to an end. Mama Lucy returned to the Florida town where she had once labored in a saw mill and where, Louis discovered, she had a common-law husband. To make ends meet, the two of them ran a "little gambling joint." To hear her talk, it sounded so lush that Louis was tempted to ask her for a little taste, but he would never lower his pride to ask his younger sister for money unless he was desperate. "I would delight in giving my family as much money as I could, but I dreaded asking them for anything," he explained. He considered himself "the lucky one" when it came to making money. Word of Mama Lucy's venture into gambling spread, and neighborhood gossips said they were afraid for Mama Lucy when they heard she was dealing cards and running with hustlers, but Louis had no worries on that score. He knew his sister had seen it all and could handle herself. Furthermore, she carried a knife wherever she went, "and with that wide long blade she would soon carve up anybody who tried to get out of line."

By the summer of 1922, Louis, now twenty-one (and thinking he was actually a year older than that), assumed he had found his permanent place in New Orleans. His four-year-long marriage to Daisy, whom he had once loved so dearly, had finally ended, as he forced himself to realize.

Otherwise, he thought he was doing pretty well for himself. He had his steady gig in Tom Anderson's, and he was playing in a quartet with Albert Francis, Paul Domingues, and Edna Mitchell. All that in addition to his work with the Tuxedo Brass Band. Just when he thought his life, so often unstable, had at last fallen into a predictable pattern, he received a telegram, and it changed everything—his own life, the development of jazz, and the course of popular entertainment, even the face of American society. It was a telegram that would take him away from New Orleans, and help to bring him to the attention of the world at large, a world waiting for and fascinated with jazz, both the music itself and the idea of the jazz life, which he unconsciously personified. Louis's own life can be broken down into two distinct phases: everything that occurred before he received the telegram, and everything that occurred after.

It happened one afternoon in August 1922, when he was playing with the Tuxedo Brass Band at a funeral in Algiers. "It was terribly hot out on the street," he said, "and I remember my uniform almost choked me." After the funeral, Louis and the other musicians repaired to the Lodge house to quench their thirst. As they were saying their good-byes, Louis received the telegram from "Papa Joe." The world seemed to stop as he read it, for Louis instantly realized the offer's significance for him personally and professionally. There was no time to ponder; he knew that he must accept immediately. "I made up my mind just that quick. Nothing could change it. Joe my idol had sent for me—wow."

"Sorry boys," he suddenly said to the other members of the Tuxedo Brass Band, shaking the hand of every one of them. "I've got to go."

He would be making fifty-two dollars a week playing for Oliver in Chicago. That was serious money, more than he could ever expect to earn in New Orleans as a musician. It was enough to assure that he would no longer have to supplement his income from playing with work as a laborer, or coal cart driver, or anything else. That kind of money excited envy, and the other musicians in the Tuxedo Brass Band urged him to reconsider "because Joe Oliver and his boys were having some kind of union troubles," Louis later wrote. The controversy nearly prevented his leaving New Orleans. "When the Tuxedo Brass Band boys told me that King Oliver and his band were 'scabbing,' I told them, 'The King sent for me, and it didn't matter with me what he was doing. I'm going to him just the same.' And so, I went."

In addition to working with his beloved Joe Oliver, leaving New Orleans held another attraction for Louis. In Chicago, he would at last be safe from Daisy and her razors. No matter how far apart they drifted, or what other liaisons she formed, she remained irrationally possessive of Louis. On several occasions, she had appeared at cabarets where he was performing, brandished a blade, and accused him of flirting with other women. Louis had seen enough men in New Orleans die at the hands of jealous women to believe her capable of killing him. Since Daisy was a country girl who had a difficult time getting around New Orleans, he calculated that he would be safe from her up north. As it turned out, he was wrong. Regardless of the distance separating them, she always considered them man and wife, and would continue to haunt him.

The next day, at Matranga's, Louis broke the news of his impending departure to Slippers, the bouncer with a deep appreciation of jazz. "When he found out that I was leaving for Chicago, he was the first one to congratulate me. And while he shook my hand, here are the words that he said, which I shall remember til the day I die: *'When you go up north, Dipper, be sure and get yourself a white man that will put his hand on your shoulder and say, "This is my nigger."'* Those were his exact words." Louis never forgot this advice, for Slippers "was a crude sonofabitch, but he loved me and my music."

The notion of finding a white champion was already ingrained in

Louis's consciousness. It was a survival mechanism that he and other blacks had reluctantly developed in a society defined by Jim Crow. "If you didn't have a white captain to back you in the old days—to put his hand on your shoulder—you was just a damn sad nigger," he explained. "If a Negro had the proper white man to reach the law and say, 'What the hell you mean locking up my nigger?' then, quite naturally, the law would walk him free. Get in that jail *without* your white boss, and yonder comes the chain gang! Oh, danger was dancing all around you back then." In time, Louis would find the type of man Slippers recommended.

Several days later, a boisterous group burst into the New Orleans train station. Fate Marable was there, and so was old Papa Celestin, good sport that he was, and the rest of the Tuxedo Brass Band, whose members were still trying to persuade Louis to remain with them, safe from Oliver and his well-paid scabs up north. "Joe Oliver is my idol. I have loved him all my life. He sent for me and whatever he's doing I want to do it with him," Louis recalled telling them, but more likely, that is what he told himself. At any rate, he reluctantly said good-bye to them all. The train pulled in, and Louis gladhanded the Pullman porters aboard the gleaming cars. They all knew Dipper, they'd seen him tailgating around New Orleans. They were his people. They shouted to him, "Where are you goin', Dipper?" When he answered that he was going to Chicago, bound for glory, one of them replied, "You're a lucky black sombitch."

He said good-bye to his family, Mayann, Mama Lucy, Clarence, and his marriage to Daisy; to his neighborhood, the Parish Prison, the Charity Hospital, and the Fisk School; to all the tonks he'd played, Matranga's, Ponce's, and Tom Anderson's; to the Waif's Home; the Tuxedo Brass Band; to his many friends; to the women, Irene, Rella, and more whores than he could name; to voodoo; to his mangled Stetson; to the memory of Storyville and the Mississippi mists enveloping the city of his birth. Louis said good-bye to it all, and took it all with him to Chicago. "Just then I boarded the train with the fish sandwich (trout loaf) that Mayann, my dear mother, had fixed for me, and I was on my way to be with the man I musically loved—King Oliver. I did not rest until I saw his smiling face." So he began the journey north.

It would be nine years until he saw New Orleans again.

7.

CHICAGO
BREAKDOWN

arrived in Chicago about eleven o'clock the night of August 8, 1922 (I'll never forget it) at the Illinois Central Station at Twelfth and Michigan avenues," Louis wrote of his new life. "I was all eyes looking out the window when the train pulled into the station. Anybody watching me closely could have easily seen that I was a country boy." He had been hoping and expecting to see Papa Joe at the station, ready to greet him with outstretched arms, but when he reconnoitered the platform, he saw not one familiar face. Meanwhile, "all the colored people . . . who had come up from New Orleans were getting into their cabs or their relatives' cars." Just when he was thinking about turning around and going back home, a porter came up to him and said, "You are the young man who's to join King Oliver's band at the Lincoln Gardens."

His guide explained that since Louis had missed his train, and the King had to get to work, he took the precaution of tipping the porters to be on the lookout for the bewildered new arrival from New Orleans. The porter put Louis, grateful and dazzled, into a cab and told the driver to take the young man to the Lincoln Gardens Cafe. The great adventure was beginning at last; his life seemed to be starting over at this moment.

He arrived at the Lincoln Gardens at Thirty-First and Cottage Grove avenues, where he was confronted by an imposing canopy that seemed to run forever. From where he stood, the lobby looked "so long that I thought I was never going to reach the bandstand." As he paid the driver, he could "hear the King's band playing some kind of a real jump number, and believe me, they were really jumpin' in fine fashion . . . I said to myself, 'My Gawd, I wonder if I'm good enough to play in that band' . . . and hesitated about going inside right away." A wave of self-doubt assailed him.

Finally, the situation righted itself. "Somebody must have told Joe Oliver about my dumbness—standing out there and refusing to come in—so Papa Joe came outside and when he saw me, the first words that he said to me [were], 'Come on IN HEAH, you little dumb sumbitch. We've been waiting for your black ass all night.'" How good it was to hear that! "Then I was happy and at home just to hear his voice, and enjoyed every moment with him."

Between sets, he looked Louis over and muttered, "Why I've not seen that little slow foot devil in years." Slow foot! That was just what Papa Joe had called him down in New Orleans. Louis could scarcely believe that it was four years since they'd seen each other. So much had happened since then: Louis had married and nearly divorced Daisy, been up and down the Mississippi, and grown up. "You've been in some fast company since I last saw you," Joe said, inviting Louis to join in.

"I went on up to the bandstand and there were some of the boys I had known back home. They were glad to see me and I was tickled to death to see them all." There were, in addition to Joe Oliver, Baby Dodds and his brother Johnny, Honore Dutrey, and Bill Johnson. Once Louis joined their ranks, they would form the nucleus of the first important small band in jazz.

He went home that night with Joe, and ate a meal prepared by Joe's wife, "Mama Stella," Louis called her. He naturally remembered precisely what she fed him that night for his first meal in Chicago: red beans and rice, half a loaf of bread, and "a bucket of good ice cold lemonade." When dinner was over Joe took him by taxi—it was incredible, the way everyone got around in taxis up here in Chicago—to the boardinghouse he'd found for Louis. The address was 3412 South Wabash, and as their cab pulled up, Joe explained that Louis would have a room with a private bath.

"What is a private bath?" Louis asked

"Listen you little slow foot sumbitch, don't be so damn dumb."

"In the neighborhood where we lived," Louis recalled, "we never heard of such a thing as a bathtub, let alone a *private bath*." Louis reminded Papa Joe about the washtubs in the backyards down in New Orleans. Had he forgotten? Joe burst out laughing. Yes, he did, but they were up north now.

They reached the boardinghouse, run by Joe's friend, Filo. Louis thought she was a "Creole gal," but she was, in all likelihood, Filipino. She smiled as soon as she saw them. "Is this my home boy?" she asked.

"Yep," Joe told her. "This is old Dippermouth." By now, Louis was dying to "witness that private bath of mine." In the morning, he finally got his chance to use it.

Louis spent the next few days rehearsing with Joe Oliver's band, and then it was time to get down to some serious blowing. "Joe, with his big wad of chewing tobacco in his cheek, would go *pa-chooo* into a brass cuspidor, then he'd start beating his foot on top of that cuspidor, setting that tempo, and *blow*! And whatever Mister Joe played, I just put notes to it trying to make it sound as pretty as I could. I never blew my horn over Joe Oliver at no time unless he said, 'Take it!' " Louis recalled. "Sitting by him every night, I *had* to pick up a lot of little tactics he made—phrases, first endings, flairs." Indeed, he learned enough from Joe to last him a lifetime: "I'll never run out of ideas. All I have to do is think about Joe and always have something to play off of." Although he admired the creativity and spirit of Oliver's playing, he couldn't help but notice that Joe's chops had deteriorated during the four years they'd been apart—perhaps the result of his penchant for chewing tobacco—but he dared not say a word, because although Papa Joe was past his prime, he was still the King.

Their first night together, they played a number called "Eccentric," which featured several cornet breaks, or solos. Joe and the band alternated, and then Joe and Bill Johnson went into this crazy act. Joe made his cornet sound like a baby wailing, and Bill made his guitar sound like a nurse trying to calm the baby. Bill even managed to hit a note that sounded like a nurse saying, "Don't cry, baby." Then the two of them began fighting, musically, and needless to say, their stunt brought the house down. There was a floor show after that, and finally it was Louis's turn. He played hesitantly, mindful that he was the *second* cornet in the band.

In this midst of their intensive schedule of rehearsals and performances, Papa Joe suggested they drop in at the Dreamland Cafe to meet the pianist, Lil Hardin. It is entirely likely that Papa Joe, in suggesting this visit, had more than music on his mind. Months earlier, he'd sent Louis a photograph of his band when Lil was in it, and Louis remembered her as an "attractive-looking, brown-skinned girl." He even wrote back to Joe to say, "Tell Miss Lil I like her." Louis figured nothing would ever come of that stray remark, and now he felt a twinge of embarrassment at the prospect of meeting her in the flesh, but he overcame his shyness enough to accompany Papa Joe to the Dreamland at 3520 State Street.

When they arrived, Louis was impressed and intimidated. This was not just a nightclub, it was an institution. This was where King Oliver had played, and Alberta Hunter. The *Defender*, Chicago's powerful black newspaper, promoted it as a "first class resort owned by a member of the Race." He was Billy Bottoms, and he ran a tight ship. "Residents and businessmen of the Race throughout the city could feel safe in taking their close friends and the members of their families there with the knowledge that nothing would be allowed, by word or act, to cause complaint."

Joe took Louis over to Lil, introduced him, and then—nothing. "I was a little disappointed," she said. And surprised. "All the musicians called him 'Little Louis,' and he weighed 226 pounds! And I said, 'Little Louis?' Wonder why they call him 'Little Louis,' as fat as he is!" In fact, she was "disappointed all around because I didn't like the way he was dressed. I didn't like his hairdo. He had bangs. That was the style in New Orleans, he told me later, to wear bangs. And they were sticking right straight out!" Joe Oliver's protégé looked to her like a hick, just another youth from a sleepy southern city let loose in Chicago, whereas she, Miss Lil Hardin, jazz pianist extraordinaire, was slender, proper, and sophisticated, all the things that "Little Louis" definitely was not, as far as she could tell. This fat "Little Louis," she instantly decided, was not her type. Still, she took pains to conceal her reaction, and Louis, for his part, always thought, "Lil believed in me from the first."

Together, Louis Armstrong and Lillian Hardin would become the leading couple of jazz. They were very different, but were united by their energy and spirit. Both had traveled far and fought hard to get to where they were. Indeed, Lil had started as far back as Louis had, and had come even further.

Shortly after the Civil War, Lil's grandmother, Priscilla Martin, a freed slave, was living with her husband and their four children near Oxford, Mississippi. Her husband was a drinker, and the problem eventually became serious enough for her to pack up her three girls and one boy, and their worldly goods, in a mule cart and make the arduous trek to Memphis,

Tennessee. Time would show that she was the first in a line of three independent, strong-willed women.

In Memphis, Lil's grandmother put down roots, worked hard, and made enough money to acquire a house, where she raised her children, including Lil's mother, Dempsey. In the ensuing years Dempsey came of age, married, and remained in Memphis, where she gave birth to Lil on February 3, 1898. (Lil was three-and-a-half years older than Louis, a fact she strove to conceal throughout her life.) When Lil was seven, her father, Will Hardin, died. By this time the family was living at 32 Railroad Avenue and she was attending the Virginia Avenue School. The Hardin household was always a busy place, even after Will's death, for her mother remarried, and cousins constantly came and went.

Everyone worked, even the women and children. Lil's mother was employed by a prosperous white family, the Gastons, and as Lil came of age, she knew she would soon be working, too. When the Gastons moved away, her mother found a new job, as a maid in Union Station.

Dempsey was a determined woman, who wanted the best for her child—refinement, education, and class. Lil's first exposure to music came in the third grade, when her teacher, Violet White, gave her organ lessons. "My mother knew I was musical, so she got me a teacher," said Lil of that turning point in her young life. "This teacher was also one of my school-teachers, so she taught music in the afternoons, after school. I started taking lessons from her. Now that I've studied so much afterward, I knew she wasn't so good to begin with. Anyway, she taught me how to read the notes, but technique was some sort of a foreign word to her, because I remember I used my fingers anyway I wanted to." Lil quickly displayed her aptitude for music, and soon she was playing at school marches and hymns in her Sunday school at the Lebanon Baptist Church, where her playing caught the attention of the Reverend R. J. Petty.

"By the time I was eight or nine, I could play at church and school— the hymns and the little marches. And I was supposed to be the organist for the Sunday School and one piece especially I remember was 'Onward, Christian Soldiers.' I might have known I was going to end up in jazz because I played 'Onward, Christian Soldiers' with a definite beat! The kids would be singing, '*On-ward, Chris-tian Sol-diers*,' and it was real funny. And the pastor used to look at me over his glasses."

Dempsey was intensely proud of her daughter's accomplishments in conventional church music, however, and Lil recalled her "chest just bursting with pride." Somehow, her mother put by enough money to purchase an old organ, which she installed for her daughter to play at home. That wasn't enough for Lil; she wanted a piano, too, a new one. Dempsey made her wish come true, and Lil considered the arrival of her instrument as "one of the happiest days of my life." She guarded her new possession fiercely. She even wore the key to it around her slender young neck so that no one else in the large family could reach in and besmirch the ivory keys. Every night after her dinner, Lil unlocked the piano and delighted her family with her musicianship.

As Lil was the first to acknowledge, she could be a stubborn and willful child. Describing her young self, she used words like "nasty," "pushy," and "assertive." She also displayed a wide streak of vanity. She became fascinated, indeed, obsessed with clothes and with her appearance, and she developed a taste for fine things, expensive things, things her mother could not afford to buy. She grew into a slender, attractive teenager, with lustrous hair and large, seductive eyes, which she employed on men, usually to good effect. Despite her mother's lavish, selfless encouragement of her musical career, there was always a great deal of tension between Lil and Dempsey. As Lil matured, the two women became locked into a contest of wills. Later in life, Lil conceded she had been inclined to be "mean to my mother."

At sixteen, Lil enrolled at Mrs. Hick's School of Music, where her teachers allowed her to continue her idiosyncratic fingering technique. Despite this handicap, Lil managed to challenge the school's leading student, Bertha Dunne. At commencement, the two students were to perform in a contest. Lil was determined to outdo her rival, but near the end of her performance, she lost her place. She had the presence of mind to improvise her way to the end. The feat only made her seem more talented, and she was declared the winner on the spot. It was a moment of sweet triumph. All her life, she recalled that people called her a genius that day, and a child prodigy, although she was almost a grown woman. Bursting with self-confidence, she gave a concert at her church, bought herself new clothes for the great event, and arranged a big party afterward. She was learning to be a star.

Her musical tastes were changing rapidly. She became acquainted with another kind of music, the kind of music her mother and most respectable

Louis (left, at age seventeen), his mother Mayann (seated), and sister Mama Lucy pose for a formal portrait in 1918. At the time, Louis was making a name for himself in New Orleans honky tonks and marching bands. ARCHIVE PHOTOS/ FRANK DRIGGS COLLECTION

A "family" resemblance: Joe Oliver, the cornet "king," was young Louis's mentor and father figure. He is shown here in 1923, about the time he sent his famous telegram summoning young Louis from New Orleans to Chicago. ARCHIVE PHOTOS/FRANK DRIGGS COLLECTION

Louis (front row, head circled) proudly poses with the Waif's Home band in 1913. In the decades to come, he credited the reform school's strict regimen for rescuing him from an aimless life. FROM THE COLLECTION OF THE LOUISIANA STATE MUSEUM

The legendary first man of jazz, Buddy Bolden, back row, second from the left, strikes an insouciant pose with members of his band in about 1905. Back row, left to right: Jimmy Johnson, Bolden, Willie Cornish, William Warner. Front row, left to right: Jefferson Mumford and Frank Lewis. This is the only known photo of Bolden. ARCHIVE PHOTOS/FRANK DRIGGS COLLECTION

Louis Armstrong in 1925, not long after he began recording with King Oliver's Creole Jazz Band. ARCHIVE PHOTOS/FRANK DRIGGS COLLECTION

Lil Hardin, who became Louis's second wife, hams it up with the other members of King Oliver's Creole Jazz Band in San Francisco in 1921. Left to right: Minor "Ram" Hall, Honore Dutrey, King Oliver, Lil, David Jones, Johnny Dodds, Jimmy Palao, Ed Gorland. ARCHIVE PHOTOS/FRANK DRIGGS COLLECTION

Life on the Mississippi: Louis, third from right, takes his place with the Fate Marable Orchestra aboard the Streckfus riverboats. A stern taskmaster who liked to humiliate errant musicians, Marable is at the piano. HOGAN JAZZ ARCHIVE, HOWARD-TILTON MEMORIAL LIBRARY, TULANE UNIVERSITY

Louis, seated, holding record, with the members of the Les Hite Orchestra at the Cotton Club in Culver City, California, in 1930. Louis loved California, but after a marijuana bust there, he was forced to return to Chicago. Left to right: Luther Craven, Joe Bailey, Bill Perkins, Marvin Johnson, Lionel Hampton, Les Hite, George Orendorff, Henry Prince, Louis, Charlie Jones, Harvey Brooks, Harold Scott. ARCHIVE PHOTOS/FRANK DRIGGS COLLECTION

"The World's Greatest Trumpeter" — Chicago, c. 1931. As a young star, Louis's dapper style of dress set trends among his followers. HOGAN JAZZ ARCHIVE, HOWARD-TILTON MEMORIAL LIBRARY, TULANE UNIVERSITY

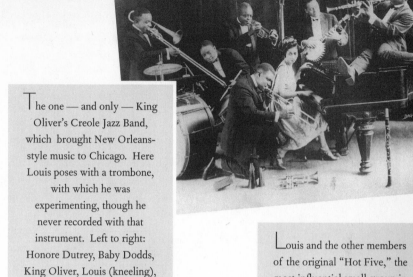

The one — and only — King Oliver's Creole Jazz Band, which brought New Orleans-style music to Chicago. Here Louis poses with a trombone, with which he was experimenting, though he never recorded with that instrument. Left to right: Honore Dutrey, Baby Dodds, King Oliver, Louis (kneeling), Lil Hardin, Bill Johnson, Johnny Dodds. ARCHIVE PHOTOS/FRANK DRIGGS COLLECTION

Louis and the other members of the original "Hot Five," the most influential small group in early jazz history, in Chicago in 1925. Left to right: Louis, Johnny St. Cyr, Johnny Dodds, Kid Ory, and Lil Hardin. ARCHIVE PHOTOS/FRANK DRIGGS COLLECTION

Louis' Armstrong's Hot Five, Exclusive Okeh Record Artists.

Louis Armstrong's "Secret 9," the New Orleans baseball team he sponsored during his triumphant return to his hometown in 1931. Louis is at right, his pride evident. HOGAN JAZZ ARCHIVE, HOWARD-TILTON MEMORIAL LIBRARY, TULANE UNIVERSITY

During his 1931 visit, Louis also made sure to visit the Waif's Home. Once an inmate, he was now a celebrity. Although his marriage to Lil was all but finished, she joined him in New Orleans, much to his chagrin. HOGAN JAZZ ARCHIVE, HOWARD-TILTON MEMORIAL LIBRARY, TULANE UNIVERSITY

Louis (left) with Johnny Collins, his abusive, thuggish manager, in Sheffield, England, in 1932. ARCHIVE PHOTOS/FRANK DRIGGS COLLECTION

Louis with his youthful girlfriend, Alpha Smith, who later became his third wife, in London, 1933. ARCHIVE PHOTOS/FRANK DRIGGS COLLECTION

Louis in 1937 with the two
men most responsible for
directing his career:
the tyrannical Joe Glaser (left)
and Cork O'Keefe (right).

ARCHIVE PHOTOS/FRANK
DRIGGS COLLECTION

people feared, the music of the brothel and devil, ragtime. Instead of the hymns and sonatas her family expected of her, Lil yearned to play popular songs. That would happen only over her mother's dead body. "She hated any form of popular music," Lil said. "I could play for the churches and things like that," but Dempsey considered songs like "St. Louis Blues" simply "sinful." Lil continued her campaign, and eventually her mother allowed her talented, headstrong daughter to buy polite sheet music such as Irving Berlin's recent hit, "Alexander's Ragtime Band." Lil purchased "St. Louis Blues" on the sly. Its composer, W. C. Handy, was black, and his inspiration came from a church in his hometown of Florence, Alabama, where the pastor used a distinctive chant to exhort his parishioners to come forward. Handy turned that chant into the lament of a woman who has lost her lover. One of the song's most celebrated lines—"That man got a heart like a rock cast in the sea"—derived from an equally unlikely source, a drunken woman whom Handy overheard singing about her own long-lost lover. When Handy asked the poor woman what that line meant, she explained, "Lord, it's hard, and gone so far she can't reach it." His distillation, a song of heartrending emotion, became one of the hits of 1914, in the days when sheet music for a popular tune routinely sold hundreds of thousands of copies. Dempsey later discovered that Lil had purchased and concealed the sheet music for this song, and beat her with a broomstick.

Just when Lil seemed to be drifting the way of the saloon and honkytonks, her mother sent her off to college, Fisk University in Nashville, Tennessee. Fisk had risen from the ashes of the Old South, during the Union Army's occupation of Nashville. In October 1865, government and charitable groups banded together to start a school to educate freed slaves and their children. In December, General Clinton Bowen Fisk found quarters for the fledgling institution in a former Union Army hospital, and he bequeathed his name to the new experiment in education. Several weeks later, the school welcomed its first students, emphasizing elementary education until the Nashville public schools reopened in 1867. At that time, Fisk Free School received a new charter, as Fisk University, and moved to new quarters, this time an abandoned Union Army camp, but was in dire need of funds to survive.

From its inception Fisk was known throughout the country for its student choir, the Fisk Jubilee Singers, who toured the country, and later, the world, to stimulate contributions to the university. They popularized

Fisk's name and mission, and the proceeds of their tour helped the university through difficult times. In 1888, the institution graduated its most influential student, W. E. B. Du Bois, who went on to become a sociologist, teacher, and Civil Rights leader. Although the student body of Fisk was overwhelmingly black, the administration, and much of the faculty, were white, and as time passed, the university became the target of charges of paternalism and racism. Not until 1947 did Fisk appoint its first black president, Charles S. Johnson. At the time Lil Hardin entered Fisk, she found an institution still struggling to reconcile the shoddy compromises of the Reconstruction era with rising black expectations.

For much of her life, Lil proudly maintained that she spent four years at Fisk, majored in music, and was her class valedictorian. (She led Louis to believe that, and he never doubted it.) She displayed a diploma from the university tacked to the wall above her piano and talked happily of singing with the institution's Mozart Society, and the Fisk Jubilee Singers, whose repertoire ran more to "Negro Spirituals" and Handel's *Messiah* than to Handy's "St. Louis Blues." Her time there seemed to be an idyll and a confirmation of her musical talent.

At other times, Lil told a very different story. She explained that her career at Fisk was actually far from happy. It was humiliating. She complained that her lack of fingering technique hampered her progress in music there, and the music department gave her "second-grade material" to study. With tears in her eyes, she forced herself to practice beginner's pieces, and no one called her a genius or child prodigy anymore. She became so enraged at her former teachers that she tore up the diploma she received from Miss Hick's School.

This second version of her time at Fisk is far closer to the truth. According to Fisk University records, Lillian Hardin was not the valedictorian of her class, nor did she graduate. In fact, she spent no more than a year at Fisk before dropping out.

As disappointing as the plain truth was, her life was about to take a dramatic turn precisely because she was no longer in college. In September of 1918, her mother moved with the entire Hardin family, Lil included, to Chicago, the emerging center of the jazz world. By joining her mother up north, Lil was shortchanged a fancy education, but she was ideally situated to indulge her passion for jazz and blues. The great irony is that her mother, who had always despised popular music and had beaten Lil when she discovered a copy of "St. Louis Blues" in her possession, inadvertently placed her daughter at the epicenter of jazz.

When Lil Hardin arrived in Chicago, Louis Armstrong was seventeen years old, still hauling coal in New Orleans and dreaming of becoming a full-time musician. No one outside that city had ever heard of him, or seemed likely to. While Louis seemed to take forever to uncover his musical and professional destiny, Lil homed in on hers within a few short weeks of coming to Chicago. To acquaint herself with the city, Lil took long walks and soon became caught up in the possibilities of her new life there, amid "its beautiful brick and stone buildings, excitement, people moving swiftly, and things happening."

On one of these expeditions, she discovered Jones's Music Store, at 3409 $^1/_2$ South State Street. "I stopped and gazed at all the sheet music in the window display, wishing I had every one of them but knowing how impossible that was. I decided to go in and buy one that I heard so many people whistling on the street." She went inside, and "they had it all right and they had a fella there named Frank who was supposed to demonstrate it to me." This was a salesman, Frank Clemons. "He sat down and played it over for me. Well, he didn't play it well, so I asked him if I might try it over. He readily consented and was very surprised that I played at sight as well as adding something to it. When I finished he had me try out other numbers and then asked if I'd like the job demonstrating music." Taking the job meant she would spend her days pounding out all the new tunes on the shop floor in the hope of luring customers into buying the sheet music. It also meant she would meet people constantly, especially musicians, who were likely to strike up conversations with an attractive young demonstrator.

Lil was briefly uncertain; she had been looking for sheet music, not a job. "I don't know," she said. "My mother wouldn't be too keen on me taking a job."

"Well, do you go to school?" Clemons asked.

"Yes," Lil ad-libbed.

"Well, you can play here in the afternoon—get a chance to learn all the music."

Lil told the man she would go home and ask her mother. "So I just went home, messed around a little bit," as she recalled. "Three o'clock, I came back and when I walked in, the lady said, 'Oh, Frank, she's nothing but a child!' "

The "lady" was Jennie Jones, the owner of the store; she was a tall, imposing woman, whose light complexion strongly suggested she was a mulatto. Working for this woman meant crossing a subtle social and color barrier that separated mulattos from other, darker blacks. But Clemons was insistent that Mrs. Jones hire the girl, young as she was. "She can play," he said, and turning to Lil, he asked, "Honey, want to play some music for me?" Not for nothing was Frank Clemons a salesman.

Mrs. Jones brought several sheets of music for Lil to play, and she handled them easily, sight-reading all the way, even improvising a bit, and at the end of the audition, Mrs. Jones declared, "She plays real well. Honey, if you want to work, I'll give you $3 a week." Lil gratefully accepted the offer without bothering to consider that it worked out to only sixty cents a day. "Oh, yes, yes, yes!" she squealed.

"I didn't *stroll*, I *ran* all the way home to break the news to Mother, who was naturally indignant."

"The very idea! Work! And for only three dollars a week! I should say not, young lady," Dempsey insisted.

"Well," Lil recalled, "in no time at all I sold her on the idea, just to learn all the music and have something to do until [it was] time to return to school. Off I went to work the next morning, thrilled beyond words over my first job. As soon as I got to the music store I got busy playing all the music on the counter and by two P.M. the place was packed with people listening to the 'Jazz Wonder Child.' I played on and on, all the music there, all my classics. My what a thrill. No wonder the people called me child, I looked to be about ten years old in my middy blouse and eighty-five pounds."

By the second day, Lil said, "I had learned everything on the music counter, because I didn't know how long my job was going to last, so I just got busy learning all the music, you know, but the people that came in to buy music, they would stop and say, 'Oh, gee, what a good piano player this little girl is.' They called me a little girl. I was quite a feature there!" She could play everything from Bach to W. C. Handy.

By the second week, Mrs. Jones saw fit to raise Lil's salary to eight dollars a week. It was a moment in life when it seemed anything could happen, and soon enough, it did.

During Lil's third week on the job, Jelly Roll Morton strolled in, his diamond-studded tooth gleaming. Lil was fully aware that Jelly Roll was Mister Hot Music himself. He was also one of the best whorehouse piano players who ever was, especially when there was a pretty girl to entertain. "Jelly Roll sat down, the piano rocked, the floor shivered, the people swayed while he ferociously attacked the keyboard with his long skinny fingers, beating out a double rhythm with his feet on the loud pedal. I was thrilled, amazed and scared. Well, he finally got up from the piano, grinned, and looked at me as if to say, 'Let that be a lesson to you!' And I said, 'It was a lesson.' "

The crowd that had gathered insisted that Lil—the Little Jazz Wonder herself—also play a tune. Lil was understandably reluctant to demonstrate her skills for the self-proclaimed "inventor of jazz." "Well, I'm really in for it," she thought, "and suddenly remembering that he had played nothing classical, I sat down to the piano very confidently, played some Bach, Chopin, and 'The Witches' Dance,' which they especially liked." Nonetheless, "I knew I could never beat Jelly Roll, but from that day on, I put all my eighty-five pounds to work trying to sound like him." After six years of playing piano, Lil had finally found her true style—jazz, not the classical music she had studied as a child. "I learned all the popular things, and I started adding my own stuff to it and playing loud and I was a sensation to people at the music store."

The next big name to appear in Mrs. Jones's music store was the New Orleans Creole Jazz Band. They appeared during Lil's fourth week on the job. *Everybody* knew these fellows. They were the first black New Orleans jazz band to make it big in Chicago, and now everyone wanted to be like them. They, more than any other group, had ignited the craze for New Orleans jazz in Prohibition-era Chicago, and they were in the vanguard of a wave of musicians emigrating north. From the comparative obscurity of marching in brass bands, they became celebrities at the De Luxe Cafe at 35th and State, where they played to standing-room-only crowds every night. It wasn't just their music that lured patrons; the band also featured several attractive female singers.

Instead of the robust, self-assured musicians Lil expected, she discovered that the members of the New Orleans Creole Jazz Band were skinny, sickly, and strangely aloof from their own quickly forming legend. There was "Sugar Johnnie" Smith on cornet, a "long, lanky dark man with deep little holes in his skinny face. He never had too much to say and I wondered about that, but how was I to know that he was dying on his feet with T.B.? Couldn't tell by his playing." Then there was the band's nominal leader, Lawrence Duhé, though Lil knew him as Dewey. "He was skinny, too, but much lighter in color and always smiling." As for the others, "Roy Palmer (trombone) was the darkest one, but jolly and happy-go-lucky violinist Jimmie Palao (a decided Creole with his olive complexion and straight hair) was skinny and coughed all the time. He died with T.B. also. The bassist was Eddie Garland, who was the healthiest of the skinny ones. Tubby Hall (drums) was as fat as the others were skinny, and the youngest of the band that left New Orleans to make jazz history."

The moment they swung into the music, Lil realized that these reserved, elegant, and frail gentlemen were superb, innovative musicians who could raise the roof. "When they started out on the 'Livery Stable Blues' I nearly had a fit. I had never heard a band like that, they made goose pimples break out all over me. I'm telling you they played loud and long and got the biggest kick out of the fits I was having over their music." Yes! "Sugar Johnnie played a growling cornet style, using cups and old hats to make kinds of funny noises. Duhé's clarinet squeaked and rasped with his uneven scales and trills. Roy was sliding back and forth on the trombone making a growling accompaniment to Sugar Johnnie's breaks. Jimmie's violin sighed and wheezed while he scratched the strings with his bow."

What Lil heard that day was actually an audition for her boss, Mrs. Jones, who also ran a booking agency out of her music shop. On the strength of their sensational performance, she booked the band at a Chinese restaurant on the North Side for a short gig for which they needed a pianist. Mrs. Jones started sending them local talent, all men, and all pretty fair ragtime pianists, but none clicked with the fellows from New Orleans. So one night, she decided to send over her eighty-five-pound Jazz Wonder Child in the company of Frank Clemons, the salesman who'd hired her.

Lil sat in with the boys, and, in her most proper voice, asked, "What number are you playing and what key is it in?"

"Key?" they said. The band exchanged looks, as if to say, who is this girl?

This wasn't a *reading* band; this was a real New Orleans jazz band, and they didn't worry about the *key*. They worried about the *feeling*. They worried about the rhythm. They worried about the tips. But they did not worry about the *key*.

"When you hear two knocks, start playing!" Sugar Johnnie told her.

They started in, and Sugar Johnnie suddenly said, "Boom! boom!" which was her cue to "just hit everything on the piano" in whatever key her ear told her the band was in. Blending in wasn't as difficult as it seemed, because when Lil listened carefully to what they were doing, she realized they were playing only four or five chords. She could find her way into their music with no trouble at all.

After that bumpy beginning, the rest of the tryout went just fine, and when it was her turn to solo, she thumped out a little Jelly Roll Morton thing, loose and fast, and before she knew it, the men were saying, "We're gonna keep this little girl with us." Duhé offered her $22.50 a week, and Lil was delighted to accept. Then they asked her how old she was, and she admitted she was a minor. This was a problem, because it was against the law for a minor to play in a cabaret such as the De Luxe Cafe, where they were still turning away crowds. The band decided to get around the problem by keeping her age secret, and she, in turn, kept her new job hidden from her mother.

And that was how Lillian Hardin went from a three-dollar-a-week demonstrator to a twenty-two-and-a-half-dollar-a-week "New Orleans" jazz pianist in one month.

At first, Lil's secret life with the band went exactly according to plan. "This was New Orleans jazz, and the people ate it up. Ah, what fun! What life! Everybody in town falling in to dig us. No dancing, just listen and be sent. De Luxe Cafe . . . deluxe business . . . deluxe jazz by the New Orleans Creole Jazz Band." Better still, she was making twenty dollars a night in tips in addition to her salary, which meant she was taking home well over a hundred dollars a week, and no one to spend it on but herself. She bought fancy clothes, hats, perfume, lived the high life, the jazz life, and never once regretted dropping out of Fisk.

They billed her as "The Hot Miss Lil," but truth be told, her playing was hotter than her love life. The musicians, as it turned out, were all gentlemen, and "they assured me no one was going to touch me," which came as a relief to Lil, but also as something of a letdown. The girl singers were the ones who gave her problems. The particular bane of her existence was a singer named Dovie, who had a mean mouth. When Dovie started raining curses down on Lil's head, the men would have to rush in to protect her.

For a time, she managed to conceal her job from her mother. Had she known that her daughter was playing in a jazz band consisting entirely of men from New Orleans, and breaking the law in the process, the old woman would have locked her in her room and thrown away the key *and* the piano. But then, during Lil's second week in the New Orleans Creole Jazz Band, a friend of Dempsey's happened to see her perform. The next day she told Lil's mother, "Saw your little girl at the cabaret."

Dempsey confronted her daughter, who broke down in tears. "What's the matter with you?" her mother asked.

"I'm working in a cabaret, and I know you're going to make me quit."

"What? A nasty, filthy, dirty cabaret!" Lil knew her mother well; she could have written the script for what her mother would be saying. "After all the money I've spent on you! Sending you to school to make you a lady and you end up in a vulgar, no good cabaret! You'll quit tonight." As far as her mother was concerned, being a jazz pianist was no better than being a madam of a whorehouse, and perhaps even worse, because it didn't pay as well.

That seemed to be the end of the matter, until Lil revealed the amount of her salary and tips and gave the money to her mother. Astonished and speechless, for once, Dempsey allowed Lil to keep her job under careful supervision. "We worked from 9:00 P.M. till about 1:00 A.M. Ten minutes to one, my mother would be standing at the door, and I'd say, 'Why don't you wait downstairs?' I didn't want the people to know that she had to come after me, after me being so 'hot' all night. But she came for me the whole time I worked at the De Luxe and then we got a job across the street at the Dreamland." Dempsey then arranged for a succession of handpicked escorts to walk Lil home every night after the performances. "From then on," said Lil, "it was all smooth."

But life in the precarious world of jazz was never smooth. That winter, Sugar Johnnie, the cornetist who'd told her to listen for the knocks, caught pneumonia and died. Mutt Carey came up from New Orleans to replace him, but didn't work out and left as quickly as he'd come. Mutt's replacement was Joe Oliver, whose formidable reputation mystified Lil, until he began to assert himself in the band. Oliver was nothing if not professional. Where most jazz musicians were interested in having a good time both on stage and off, Oliver insisted on discipline, deportment, and musicianship. He took an instant dislike to the trombonist, Ray Palmer, whom he accused of sleeping on the stand, and prevailed on Lawrence Duhé, the band's nominal leader, to fire him. After this altercation, Duhé himself quit, and the New Orleans Creole Jazz Band became Oliver's to command.

Lil survived the turmoil and played with the band in Chicago nightspots for the better part of 1920 and 1921. In June 1921, Oliver took the band on the road, all the way to San Francisco. By now he had strengthened the personnel with handpicked favorites from New Orleans, beginning with the trombonist Honore Dutrey. Although his musical ability was universally acknowledged, Dutrey suffered badly from shortness of breath. As a soldier in the Great War, he had inhaled poison gas, which weakened his lungs, but he refused to put down his horn. He often left the bandstand during performances to cough, and gasp for air, and spray his throat and nose, and when he recovered, he would return to his seat and blow as if nothing had happened. Oliver also brought in the immensely talented Dodds brothers: Johnny, the older of the two, on clarinet, and Baby Dodds, fresh from the Fate Marable Orchestra, on drums. During their travels, Lil kept a polite distance from these men, whom she found intriguing, but also slightly frightening. "Johnny Dodds was sober," as she recalled, but "Baby Dodds was kind of wild. He was the playboy of the orchestra. King Oliver was sober, too. He smoked cigars, but he didn't drink. None of them drank, hardly."

As it was now constituted, the New Orleans Creole Jazz Band, under the direction of Joe Oliver, was the leading jazz unit in Chicago, and one of the most important jazz forces in the country. Their name, of course, was something of a misnomer, for they played hot jazz rather than sweet Creole-style dance music, and their personnel was noticeably short on actual Creoles.

After six months on the road, Lil and the band parted company. She returned to Chicago alone and found employment at the prestigious Dreamland Cafe. Meanwhile, Joe Oliver brought the other members of the band to the Lincoln Gardens Cafe. In July 1922, he decided to fortify the band with a second cornet, and he had just the fellow in mind. He sent a telegram to New Orleans, inviting Louis Armstrong to join the Creole Jazz Band right away. And not long after that, he introduced her to Lil.

Even if Louis's countrified appearance disappointed Lil, it was easy enough to fathom her appeal to him: her education (if even she had spent only a year at Fisk, that far exceeded Louis's fifth-grade education), her musical experience in Chicago and California, her sophistication and familiarity with city ways, and her independent income. She had no need of someone like him, and even if she had, her mother would have thrown up as many obstacles as possible. Louis, on the other hand, urgently needed someone like Lil. Everything about Daisy represented his past, and everything about Lil represented his future. Without quite being aware of it, or able to articulate it, he was looking for a relationship *in* music, with a woman who understood jazz, and who understood *him*. This meant a woman who was as different from Daisy as possible. His relationship with Daisy, his almost ex-wife, had revolved exclusively around sex, and it quickly degenerated into a cycle of neglect, exploitation, and abuse. Of all the relationships with women that Louis would have in his life, his marriage to Daisy was by far the most passionate, but also the most reckless and antiromantic. She taught him hard lessons about love and loyalty and betrayal, the stuff of so many jazz songs, and if nothing good came of it, he had at least matured as a result of her repeatedly breaking his heart.

Louis's attitude toward women had matured, but there remained an important constant; he was still searching for a maternal figure to provide a home for him. He needed a woman to take care of him and to minister to him, while he functioned as the occasionally naughty but mostly adorable child. Daisy was a highly eroticized version of that maternal ideal, all sex and lingerie and razors, but her patience with Louis, or with any man, was extremely limited. With Daisy gone, Louis quickly recognized Lil as the musical and romantic fulfillment of his innermost needs. Like Daisy, she was three years older than he. Even better, she was at home in the world he wanted to enter—the world of Chicago jazz and northern sophistication.

Several great things were coming together in Chicago at the moment Louis Armstrong met Lil Hardin. They were part of the enormous and influential migration of southern blacks to the prairie metropolis, whose black population swelled from 45,000 in 1910 to 235,000 in 1930. The migration had been going on for some time, ever since the end of the Great War, and it increased in pace each month as thousands of blacks arrived in search of better pay, and found work, if not social equality, with amazing ease.

The wages were startling; men who had barely managed to scrape a few dollars together as sharecroppers now made a hundred, or even two hundred dollars a week in the Chicago slaughterhouses, factories, and rail yards. Their economic breakthrough prompted more and more blacks throughout the Delta to come north and try their luck in the Windy City.

Making good money, they quickly settled down—mainly on the South Side, in an area bounded by 12th and 31st streets. The newcomers had money but little to spend it on until restaurants, dance halls, gambling casinos, and shows catering to black patrons sprang up. They clustered around State Street, a major black thoroughfare characterized by the poet Langston Hughes as a "teeming Negro street with crowded theaters, restaurants, and cabarets. And excitement from noon to noon. The street was full of workers and gamblers, prostitutes and pimps, church folks and sinners. . . . For neither love or money could you find a decent place to live. Profiteers, thugs and gangsters were coming into their own."

Chicago in these boom years quickly became the new center of black American life. The *Defender*, the most important black newspaper in the United States, was based in Chicago. William Dawson, for years the sole black member of Congress, lived on the South Side of Chicago. Jack Johnson, the boxing champion, perhaps the most famous black man in America, celebrated his biggest victory, over Jim Jeffries, in Chicago. Bill Bottoms of the Dreamland and William S. Abbott of the *Defender* staged a black versus white football game in Chicago. (The blacks won, 7–0.) There was even a black "Royal Gardens Motion Picture Company," that produced three movies in Chicago.

Chicago had everything, including a thriving vice trade. The city's infamous red-light district, the Levee, had been shut down by the authorities, just as Storyville had, but it resurfaced as the "Vice District": twenty square blocks harboring five hundred saloons, one thousand concert halls, and five hundred brothels—a profusion of sex, music, flesh, and corruption that rivaled New Orleans. There was a harder edge to the vice trade in Chicago than in New Orleans; up north, business came first. There were as many as three thousand prostitutes in Chicago in these days, but few of them inspired songs or legends, as they had a way of doing down in New Orleans. They were cash registers on two legs.

Shortly after Louis's arrival, the city of Chicago installed lights on State Street, the center of the action, and even that mundane civic improvement affected black life. Now, the "Black Belt" pulsed with life twenty-four hours a day. Louis's black neighbors, hardworking porters, stevedores, postal clerks, and laborers by day, went home, rested, washed, and in the middle of the night—at 2:00 A.M.!—rose, dressed in their best, and went out to the streets to meet companions, to find women, to go to the joints over on 35th Street where New Orleans jazz was heard: the Dreamland, the Plantation, the Sunset, the De Luxe, and the Elite Cafe.

Money was flowing in to Chicago. Clothes, cars, women, furs, hip flasks, diamonds, spectacles, celebrities, and stunts proliferated. Nickelodeons became motion picture palaces, radio stations became networks, playing fields became stadiums, pistols became machine guns. Theaters, ballrooms, and department stores catered to various facets of black life, "supplying the needs of a cosmopolitan population," as the *Defender* put it.

The *Defender* promoted a vision of Chicago as the emerging center of black life in America. The paper's city and national editions celebrated all aspects of black life in Chicago, especially jazz. "Chicago's musicians"—many of whom were actually from New Orleans, and would soon return to New Orleans—"are way ahead of our group in other cities of the country," the *Defender* informed its readers. "Their achievements have been wonderful. . . . Let us make the world respect us. Ours is an art." The *Defender*'s pages overflowed with classic Chicago boosterism. "Chicago is the embodiment of the dream of Booker T. Washington," it declared, and the South Side, readers were told, was comparable to Rome, Athens, or Jerusalem. It was a place where blacks would have no fear of "racial embarrassment." Chicago had long been a mecca for conventions of white institutions, fraternities, and companies; now, the same thing was happening with black organizations. Encouraged by the *Defender*'s cheerleading, America's blacks wanted to come to Chicago, to gather, to see, and to be seen. "Work together, acquire real estate, and then you will be independent," the paper exhorted its readership.

Despite the flowering of black culture and commerce in Chicago, relations between whites and blacks were in many ways worse than they were down south. Prosperity did not bring blacks anything approaching social equality. Three years before Louis arrived, in 1919, Chicago had been the scene of a violent race riot, which demonstrated that blacks here, as in so many areas, lived a precarious existence and that racial tolerance was often illusory. In New Orleans, the races were at least close, not to say intimate, but up in prosperous Chicago, the races did not mix. They were profoundly uncomfortable with one another. They lived, worked, and played far apart. No blacks could gain admission to skating rinks, amusement parks, or nightclubs outside the Black Belt. No blacks found work driving the ubiquitous yellow cabs or buses or at major department stores in white areas. There was no such thing as a black policeman or fireman outside of black districts in Chicago at that time, and the police, hopelessly corrupt, rarely bothered to enforce the law in black neighborhoods.

The absence of law enforcement allowed shootings and stabbings to proliferate more or less unchecked, and numbers running evolved into the biggest independent business in the black community. It went by many names, "policy wheels" or just "policy," and took many forms. Most cruelly, the absence of law enforcement permitted prostitution to flourish, maiming many young lives. Young black women often faced the choice of taking a job involving drudgery, usually as a domestic, or walking the streets.

Many blacks were prominent and visible in New Orleans's public life, but Chicago's burgeoning black community tended to be invisible to white eyes. For most whites, black life was impossible to understand or decode— with one prominent exception. Because it was loud, because it was fun, and because they could participate in it, jazz became the one aspect of black life in Chicago that registered with whites. Jazz could never have come into being in polarized, commercial Chicago, but it was one hell of a place to popularize and sell it to the rest of the country. To satisfy the enthusiasm of blacks and whites alike for jazz, Chicago became the scene of the "black-and-tan" (the phrase harked back to Reconstruction days, denoting Republican coteries with both black and white constituents). Black-and-tans employed black musicians and singers to entertain black and white audiences. It would be stretching a point to say that black-and-tans were truly integrated, because blacks and whites were often seated separately, but they became arenas for social experimentation. Here, blacks danced with whites, prostitutes fished for potential customers, and the band played on, endlessly.

An observer who descended into the black-and-tans' electric atmosphere for an evening described an "atmosphere of sensuality," amid people who "find delight in seeing the intermingling of the races."

As part of the black migration from the South to Chicago, Louis collided with another great social upheaval, Prohibition, which gave rise to the illicit social environment in which jazz—and his career—flourished.

On January 16, 1919, the Eighteenth Amendment to the Constitution was ratified, and it became the law of the land one year later. It forbade the "manufacture, sale, or transportation of intoxicating liquors within, the importation thereof into, or the exportation thereof from the United States . . . for beverage purposes." Billy Sunday, a former baseball player turned preacher, greeted the arrival of Prohibition by conducting an enormous funeral of John Barleycorn—the personification of moonshine—in Norfolk, Virginia. In this grand production, a team of horses drew a hearse bearing a twenty-foot-long coffin. When the cortège arrived at Sunday's tabernacle, twenty pallbearers shouldered the coffin as the figure of the devil limped behind in defeat. "Good-bye John!" Sunday shouted to the cheering throng of ten thousand ardent Prohibitionists. "You were God's worst enemy. You were Hell's best friend. I hate you with a perfect hatred. I love to hate you. The reign of tears is over."

Emotions ran so high because forces behind Prohibition, a coalition made up largely of idealistic ex-suffragettes and self-righteous preachers, had been out campaigning and lobbying and marching and singing for the cause for decades, and the politicians who ratified the amendment were naturally reluctant to criticize clergymen and women (who had just gotten the vote). Will Rogers, the humorist, described the hypocrisy that engendered Prohibition this way: "If you think this country ain't dry, just watch 'em vote. If you think this country ain't wet, just watch 'em drink. You see, when they vote, it's counted. When they drink, it ain't."

Prohibition could not have arrived at a worse time for the country. If there is nothing so powerful as an idea whose time has come, there is nothing so ludicrous as an idea whose time has passed. By the time it finally became law, Prohibition was an anachronism, a vestige of the nineteenth century overwhelmed by the twentieth. The nation reacted to the law in sharply varying ways. The Midwest, dry by custom and local ordinance, generally for decades, remained staunchly so. The South, dreading tax men back to the days of the Whiskey Rebellion a hundred and twenty years before, defied the new law of the land, and so did the East, whose ethnic groups, especially Catholics, regarded the Eighteenth Amendment as a Protestant assault on their sacrament. Even President Warren G. Harding flouted the law and served alcohol in the White House, making it the nation's most prominent speakeasy.

Rather than stemming the flow of booze in Chicago, Prohibition opened the floodgates. The number of bars, honky-tonks, and speakeasies in the Windy City quickly doubled. Now that it was demonized and glamorized, alcohol consumption increased, especially among younger Americans. The law turned millions of normally law-abiding citizens into lawbreakers. Furthermore, it automatically delivered the huge liquor business, along with cabarets and nightclubs, into the hands of gangsters, who followed no laws except their own. Jazz had long been part of the New Orleans demimonde, and now it became part of the new underworld created by Prohibition. For Louis, and for so many other jazz musicians, this development meant that from now on, their employers would be hoodlums or quasi-hoodlums. No matter how respectable and mainstream he became, he would never be free of their influence, and once he came into their fold in Chicago, he was never able to leave.

The creation of an outlaw culture meant that jazz, which had enjoyed a brief period of respectability, was again synonymous with bootleg booze, nightclubs, and wild women—and so more popular than ever. This was the beginning of the Jazz Age, which coincided with a crucial demographic shift in the United States: in 1920, for the first time, the majority of the population was living in cities, rather than in rural areas "The evil which the old-fashioned preachers ascribe to the Pope, to Babylon, to atheists, and to the devil, is simply the new urban civilization, with its irresistible scientific and economic and mass power," wrote Walter Lippmann, the influential political commentator, in 1927. And no city better represented the Jazz Age in its glory and squalor than Chicago.

For a young jazz musician in search of his future, and in search of *himself*, there was no finer place on earth to be than Chicago. But progress meant loss, as well. Louis gradually realized that his sojourn in the

Windy City marked the beginning of a limitless exile from New Orleans and the world into which he had been born. The one constant in his life was Joe Oliver, who kept Louis under his thumb, as well as anyone else who threatened to upset the smooth operation of the band. On one occasion, Oliver broke up a harmless spitball fight among the musicians by threatening to shoot them. To demonstrate that he was absolutely serious, he opened his cornet case and displayed the gun it contained. "Things quieted down," Baby Dodds said of that incident. "He wasn't going to shoot anybody, but that was his way of stopping the spitball business. Joe may have carried that gun because he was afraid of holdups . . . but naturally we thought he was carrying the gun for us."

Joe made it clear to everyone that it was his band and no one else's. "There was a painted canvas sign about two by four feet square hanging outside the best-looking building that housed the Lincoln Gardens Cafe, a sign that read KING OLIVER AND HIS CREOLE JAZZ BAND," said a visitor. "From the looks of the place on the outside one would never guess that on the inside was the hottest band ever to sit on a bandstand, but once you got through the crowded hallway into the cafe proper it was a sight to behold. The thing that hit your eye once you got into the hall was a big crystal ball that was made of small pieces of reflecting glass and hung over the center of the dance floor. A couple of spotlights shone on the big ball as it turned and threw reflected spots of light all over the room and the dancers. Usually they'd dance the Bunny Hug to a slow blues like 'London Blues' or some other tune in a slow blues tempo, and how the dancers would grind away." The dancers were hot, the music was hot, the musicians were hot, too, from all that blowing. "They always had a water pail on the stand with a big piece of ice in it and a dipper. Anyone who got thirsty would just go over to the bucket and help himself to a drink. Usually this was after they had played for about an hour. The place was informal and if the boys in the band wanted to take their coats off and really get comfortable, they did." In the midst of the sweating, grinding, laughing, drinking, brawling crowd stood the King himself, calling the tunes, waving his arms, blowing his gleaming cornet, dominating his musicians and the entire hall.

Louis, meanwhile, took tentative steps toward independence. He found himself an apartment at 459 East 31st Street, complete with a private bath and shower. That was living. It seemed as though he had propelled himself forward in time until he joined the twentieth century. He now inhabited a world of ambition, high-pressure commerce, and sudden hazard—all of which made him wary of his new surroundings. In contrast, New Orleans seemed an endless daze of jazz funerals and honky-tonks and voodoo. Nevertheless, he missed it terribly. Desperate to remain in touch with those he had left behind, Louis bought a typewriter on which he wrote letters to his friends back home. His loneliness and nostalgia marked the beginning of his lifelong love affair with letter writing and the beginning of his never-ending attempt to recapture his astonishing, brutal, sensual youth. Louis liked writing; in fact, he liked typing, which he considered a hobby rather than a chore.

Isidore Barbarin was among the first to receive a letter from Louis-in-exile. Barbarin was a fixture in New Orleans music circles, a venerable member of the Onward Brass Band and the patriarch of a jazz dynasty; his sons Paul and Louis were important jazz drummers, and his grandson, Danny Barker, would make a name as a jazz guitarist. On September 1, Louis typed a letter overflowing with a bittersweet mixture of good humor and yearning for home. He had turned twenty-one just a month before, but his voice and persona were already apparent: his good-natured chiding, his endless nostalgia for New Orleans (he'd made it to Chicago but couldn't help believing that New Orleans was still the center of the action), and his delight in friendship. "You taken so long to answer," he began. "Well, I know just how it is when a fellow is playing with a red hot brass [band] and they have all the work. He don't have time to be bothered with writing no letters. Well, I understand, Pops. I heard all about you all having all those funerals down there. I'm sorry that I ain't down there to make some of them with you all. The boys give me hell all the time because [I'm] forever talking about the Brass Band and how I used to like to make those parades. They say, 'I don't see how a man can be crazy about those hard parades.' I told them that they don't go hard with you when you are playing with a good band." While he was working on the letter, Joe Oliver showed up to accompany Louis to their gig that night, and Louis began telling Isidore about him: "Joe Oliver is here in my room now, and he sends you his best regards. Also all the boys." Louis then wondered why another musician to whom he had written had not replied. "Ask him do he needs any writing paper, stamps, too. Let me know, and I'll send him some at once. Ha, ha." Louis would have continued typing on his new machine, but Joe was hovering over his shoulder, telling him it was time to go to work. He ended with a pun: "Good knight. All from Louis Armstrong." And then he was off to play the night away at the Lincoln Gardens.

At this time, the fall of 1922, Oliver began to give Louis more opportunities to display his youthful virtuosity, and the younger cornet player emerged as the real star of the Creole Jazz Band. Barney Bigard, a promising young New Orleans clarinetist who had also come to Chicago, recalls, "What really started Joe into giving Louis his own chorus, and this is what Joe Oliver told me, was that one night they were playing when this guy Johnny Dunn walked in, who was cracked up to be a hell of a trumpet man in those days. Johnny Dunn was with a big show and the people were clamoring to hear what he would play. He walked on to the stand and said to Louis, 'Boy! Give me that horn. You don't know how to do.' That made Joe Oliver real angry and he told Louis, 'Go get him.' " Despite his apparent shyness and insecurity, Louis was a veteran of ferocious cutting contests in New Orleans, and when his prowess on the horn was challenged, he never failed to rise to the occasion, as Bigard relates. "Louis blew like the devil. Blew him out of that place. They looked for Johnny Dunn when Louis was finished but he had skipped out. They never found him in there again. So that's when Joe started to turn Louis loose by himself."

Word of the new phenomenon from New Orleans spread quickly through the clannish fraternity of New Orleans jazz musicians in Chicago, and soon enough Louis became embroiled in a far more vicious cutting contest. His rival on this occasion was Freddie Keppard, renowned for the crowd-pleasing stunts he had perfected on the vaudeville circuit. Even Jelly Roll Morton raved about him: "I never heard a man that could beat Keppard—his reach was so exceptional, both high and low, with all degrees of power, great imagination, and more tone than anybody." Years before, Joe Oliver had triumphed over Keppard in a cutting contest in New Orleans, but Keppard had matured as a musician since then, and he was spoiling for revenge. He was more of a showman than a musician, because of a carefully guarded secret: he couldn't read a note of music. Jelly Roll, one of the few who knew the secret, was amazed by the stratagems Keppard employed to conceal the truth. He insisted on hearing the tune played first, and then he encouraged the other musicians to play it over and over until he'd learned it by ear. "He would be having valve trouble, fingering the valves, shaking the instrument, sitting it out; all the while he would be listening. Somebody would ball him out and he would say, 'Go ahead, I'll play my part!' Next time, he would pick up his horn and play right through."

So one night Keppard, without his instrument, dropped in at the Lincoln Gardens to hear Louis blow. He stood insolently beside the bandstand, as if it belonged to him. Then he had the temerity to walk up to Louis and say, "Boy, let me have your trumpet." It was one thing to try to outblow a man, quite another to take his instrument. After an awkward moment, Louis handed his shining instrument to Keppard. Lil, who was present that night, described what happened next: "Freddie, he blew—oh, he blew and he blew and he blew and then the people gave him a nice hand. Then he handed the trumpet back to Louis. And I said, 'Now get him, get him!' Oh, never in my life have I heard such trumpet playing! If you want to hear Louis play, just hear him play when he's *angry*. Boy, he blew and people started standing on top of tables and chairs screaming." As for old Freddie, "He eased out real slowly."

Louis, usually generous to other jazzmen, seemed to relish Keppard's subsequent decline, as though he had been responsible for starting his would-be rival on the path to oblivion that night. "A heavy drinker," he noted of Keppard. "His ego when he was a young man and [the] clowning that he did must have been rather amusing, to get the recognition he achieved. But he sure did not play the cornet seriously at any time. Just clowned all the way. Good for those idiot fans, who did not care whether he played correct."

After a series of such cutting contests, Louis's reputation soared. More musicians came to decide for themselves whether he was actually as good as they'd heard he was. Several suspected Louis plugged his horn with chewing gum in order to achieve his earsplitting highs. This was an old trick, and the giveaway was that a trumpet plugged with chewing gum could hit only the highs, and not the lows. Louis was happy to show his mouthpiece to anyone who cared to inspect it to scotch the rumor, and then wailed out on the bandstand. When Louis blew—hitting as many as two hundred high C's in a row—the effect was astounding, numbing, and exhilarating. Listeners thought they heard even more notes than he was actually blowing as the excitement spread from their ears to their brains and fingertips. Once he had everyone's attention, he proceeded to bend the notes, as if he were putting a spin on a ball; the notes were not merely loud and shrill, they were ravishing, the sound of molten brass poured with exquisite control and force. And this was still a very young Louis. His musical creativity was just beginning to catch fire.

Although they were initially attracted by his power (the earsplitting volume) and his virtuosity (his rapidly running notes), musicians stayed to listen because Louis taught them a new approach to jazz, a style his obliging nature made it easy for them to absorb. "I still remember the arrival of Louis Armstrong in Chicago," said one of his new devotees, Tommy Brookins. "The news spread like wildfire among the musicians who hurried that same evening to Lincoln Gardens. It wasn't that Louis's name was then known, but the musicians were aware of the fact that a young trumpet player had just arrived from New Orleans and was playing with Oliver. . . . Opposite young Louis, who was already prodigious, Oliver's style rapidly appeared to us to date a little and it was frequent to hear musicians among themselves talk of the 'old style.' Let's say, rather, that Joe's style was a little rougher than that of his young rival."

The musicians who flocked to the Lincoln Gardens soon realized he was doing a hell of a lot more up there on the bandstand than showing off. He was in the process of developing the vocabulary of modern jazz, taking it out of sleepy New Orleans and sticking it right in the fast-beating heart of Chicago. He was showing them a new way to be a jazz musician, inventing the idea of the modern jazz soloist right before their astonished eyes and ears. He was giving them a new musical *language*. Louis's breathtaking improvisations and freshly minted cadenzas were more than mere feats, they amounted to a new type of music. They were almost miniature compositions in themselves, musical dramatizations of Louis's fantasies and psyche.

His extroverted virtuosity appealed to all jazz musicians. It was as though Louis had taken their music out of its infancy and given it a powerful breath of new life and independence. He showed them ways to be inventive, to have fun, and strut their stuff as never before. No matter what their instrument, there was something in Louis's virtuosity for each of them. Within a few years, a generation of jazz musicians, black and white, would build whole careers on the new style of jazz that Louis began to forge in Chicago in the latter part of 1922. They would draw inspiration from his riffs and phrasing and beyond that, his overall conception of the triumphant, driven jazz soloist.

To be sure, Louis *did* have a few musical tricks up his sleeve to enhance the illusion of spontaneity, but they were subtler than plugging his horn with chewing gum. The big feature of those early days with the King Oliver orchestra were the two cornet breaks Louis and Joe took. They seemed to be improvised, but they carefully worked out the breaks in advance to give the illusion of spontaneity. "He'd tell me while the band was playing what he was going to play on top. Wah wah wah! And I'd pick out my notes, and that's why all the musicians used to come around and hear us do that," Louis said of their sleight of hand. "Whatever he was gonna do, he'd let me know about four, five bars ahead while the band was jumpin.' Musicians would be sitting right in front of the bandstand and they couldn't tell what break we were gonna take. We weren't reading any music." That was showmanship of a high order.

Louis didn't just play up on the bandstand, he grinned and he mugged. His spoken patter, which he had been developing ever since his days on Mississippi riverboats, was as extravagant and novel as his body language. Louis took the trouble to annotate jazz lingo for everyone, black and white, to demonstrate how it emerged from the music. He was the etymologist of jazz. Yes! For instance, he explained the word *Gate* like this: " 'Gate' is a word swing players use when they call out to one another in their own language, but most of them, I guess, don't know how it started. I have heard some of them explain that it came from the word 'alligator'—that is, the word we use for a person who is not a player himself but who loves to sit and listen to swing music. We will say about some new number we plan to play, 'The "alligators" will like that.' I may mention here that there are more than four hundred words used among swing musicians that no one else would understand. They have a language of their own, and I don't think anything could show better how closely they have worked together and how much they feel apart from 'regular' musicians and in a world of their own that they believe in and that most people have not understood."

Louis was determined to show everyone how their private language, both musical and spoken, operated.

Soon every musician in town, and lots of nonmusicians, picked up his *patois*.

". . . chops . . ."

". . . oh, play that thing . . ."

". . . swing it, Gate . . ."

". . . solid sender . . ."

". . . muggles . . ." (marijuana)

". . . vipers . . ." (marijuana smokers)

". . . jive . . ."

". . . mellow . . ."

". . . gutbucket . . ." (after the pail that caught the innards of cleaned fish, hence, lowdown, playing your heart out)

With his distinctive language, gestures, and musical genius, Louis remade jazz in his own image; it was surprising, colloquial, yet filled with emotional power and delicate nuance. The combination of all these elements made for an irresistible, influential new American music.

As Louis's reputation grew, Lil Hardin was forced to acknowledge there was more to him than his bangs and baby fat. He had extraordinary personal qualities: warmth, charm, humor, and generosity—not to mention a naïveté that would play right into her hands. In fact, he might even welcome her intervention in his life. Gradually, she began to think of him as both a potential suitor and protégé. Lil needed to be in control, she could often be assertive and willful, and the notion of shaping this diamond in the rough known as Louis Armstrong, both as a person and as a musician, appealed to her greatly. In fact, they both welcomed the possibility of a complex, unconventional relationship, in which stereotypical roles were reversed. Even Joe Oliver figured in the romantic equation as the father figure presiding over their union. With Lil acting as his surrogate mother and Joe as his surrogate father, Louis, the virtual orphan, found the emotional sustenance he so badly needed. Lil Hardin and Joe Oliver quickly became the two most important people in his life, as necessary to him as the air he breathed.

Louis began keeping constant company with Lil, on the bandstand, and off. He'd never met anyone like her. She was dazzling, sophisticated, and advanced; she even had her own car, which played a role in their courtship. "I had a secondhand Hudson which was a block long, and made a lot of noise, like you were going ninety miles an hour and you'd only be going about thirty," Lil said. "I invited King Oliver and Louis out to take a ride one afternoon. I was just learning to drive myself. I was going down Michigan Avenue and when we got to 35th and Michigan, I killed the motor right in the middle of all the traffic and the motorists was tooting the horns and Joe and Louis was sitting up in the back and snickering and laughing and neither one of them knew how to drive. And I didn't know how to start the car again. So a man had to get out of his car and came over and start it. I never could get them out riding anymore. I would ask Louis to go out and Louis said, 'No, no, no, no. If you want to go out with me, we'll have to walk.' Honest to God!" After this mishap, their relationship flowered. "Louis and I started going to dances and shows and things together and then we started to be sweethearts." That was the innocent expression they both used to describe this phase of their courtship: *sweethearts*.

King Oliver furthered their romantic and musical partnership by snatching her away from the Dreamland and installing her as the pianist in his Creole Jazz Band. She negotiated a salary of one hundred dollars a week, more than Oliver was paying Louis. It was an outstanding sum for a twenty-four-year-old musician to be making just four years after her arrival in Chicago.

Although they played together night after night, Lil remained oblivious to his musicianship, until she heard a chance remark made by Joe Oliver. "I probably would have never paid any attention to Louis's playing if King Oliver hadn't said to me one night that Louis could play better than he could," Lil recalled. "He said, 'As long as I keep him with me, he won't be able to get ahead of me, I'll still be the King.' After he told me that, I started listening. It was very difficult listening to somebody play who's always playing second to somebody else, but I started listening to Louis after that as much as I could." Now, finally, she was impressed by his playing, so impressed, she said, "I thought the main thing to do was to get him away from Joe. I encouraged him to develop himself, which was all he needed. He's a fellow who didn't have much confidence in himself to begin with. He didn't believe in himself."

Lil spun impossible dreams for Louis, dreams he enjoyed hearing but did not dare to credit. She insisted that "I could swing better than 'King' Oliver." Not only that, "I should have a chance to be first trumpet myself, and would never get it as long as I stayed with 'Papa Joe's' band." The prospect of leaving Joe was too much for Louis to contemplate at the moment. "I knew she was talking big, and just laughed at her. But I could see, too, that she was serious and thinking of me." To Lil, the situation was simple: "Though Joe Oliver was Louis's idol and he wanted to play like

Joe, that wasn't his style. He tried to play some of Joe's solos, but they sounded different. Joe always played with a mute, you know, and Louis played clear and straight."

She surreptitiously enticed him to try out her brazen ideas. "We used to practice together, 'woodshed' as we say (from the old-time way of going out into the woodshed to practice a new song). She would play on the piano and I, of course, on my trumpet," Louis said. "I had learned how to transpose from the piano part. We used to play classical music together sometimes. We bought classical trumpet music. Later on, we played in churches. All of this was giving me more and more knowledge of my music." The regimen cost Louis considerable agony. Lil recalled that before the church concerts, Louis "used to get so afraid and would sweat like anything before he went on. He would get nervous and excited before his solo." The anxiety betrayed his growing ambition and self-criticism. It was one thing to play with a big loud band up on a bandstand; if he blew the wrong notes or rhythm, only the other musicians knew. But in church, before a quiet audience, his playing—his tone, rhythm, and breath—was exposed to pitiless scrutiny; if he faltered, everything collapsed. Even Lil, banging sturdy chords on her piano, couldn't carry him. It was the kind of anxiety that drove so many other jazz musicians to drink. Louis discovered he couldn't play drunk; his fingers turned to blocks of wood, so he was determined to remain sober throughout the ordeal of learning to become a soloist.

His exposure to classical music made him appreciate "how much I had learned in the South. There were only a very few bands that played the way we did, and most of the good players, though not all of them, had come north from the lower Mississippi country, from Memphis down to the Delta." He took inspiration from his boyhood teacher, Bunk Johnson, forgetting all about how Johnson used the bottle to get him through his sets. He would fill Lil's ears with tales of the fabled Bunk and his wonderful tone. "He always said, 'You should have heard this fellow Bunk play,' " Lil remembered. Louis tried to demonstrate some of Bunk's style to her by whistling, because he couldn't make it happen on the trumpet yet. These days, he seemed to be whistling wherever he went. She could "hear him coming up the street, from two blocks off, whistling. He would whistle his head off, all these fancy runs that he later played." And he'd tell her again, "*You should have heard Bunk play!*"

Lil assumed that her boyfriend's sudden obsession with Bunk Johnson (the name meant nothing to her) was connected with Louis's trying to break free of Joe Oliver's influence. "Finally I figured out that Louis was wasting his time trying to copy Oliver and [was not] so good at it," so she advised him, "Go ahead and play your own way." Easier said than done. He kept at it, eventually producing beautiful riffs ("He had the most beautiful shrill whistle," Lil remembered), and at her urging he tried to make these sounds through his cornet. "That is where the great Louis Armstrong began to emerge," Lil said.

Bit by bit, he introduced the techniques he'd learned from Bunk into his trumpet playing. He entered "just a fraction behind the melody," as he told Lil, and then caught up to the other musicians and finally got out in front of them. Bunk's trick produced a real New Orleans sound. Sure, it was "wrong" by the standards of classical music, but in jazz, with its relaxed tempos and polyphony, the technique added tension to the music, as the ear waited for the soloist to enter. In Louis's hands, this was more than just a gimmick; he used it to imply notes that carried as much musical meaning as the actual notes. His horn engaged the ear and the mind, making the listener hear things that were only suggested, never stated. Eventually, he learned to alternate between the melody and his variations on it, until the melody gradually disappeared behind the notes suggesting it, and the ear supplied what his horn left out. His method was rebellious, yet it conformed to a ruthless inner logic. He embroidered and invented tunes within the tune, rhythms within the rhythm. He interpolated growls, comments, coarse jokes, his private language of feeling and perception and thought—crude, melancholy, subtle—that transformed whatever piece he happened to be playing into an extension of his psyche.

Louis tried to use his New Orleans tricks in a wild piece he'd been working on with Joe Oliver, the "Dippermouth Blues." It was Louis's most original contribution to the band's repertoire, so it had been named after him. Even so, he just couldn't get it right. He spent an entire week trying to get his solo down, without success. The trouble stemmed from his use of a mute to achieve the wah-wah sound he wanted—not just any wah-wah, but a dirty tone, or slurred wah-wah. No matter how many times he tried it, his solo failed to satisfy him. Nor could he ask anyone else for help, for this was his solo, his sound, and only he could tell if it was right or wrong. For now, it was wrong. He "got so disgusted," Lil recalled, that he "gave it up as impossible." But Louis kept returning to the troublesome solo, until it began to sound the way he imagined it should. It was a very conversational sound, this wah-wah—laughing, mocking, sighing, pleading. It sounded as though he were half-talking, half-singing through his trumpet, making a spoken as well as a musical statement. Other trumpeters could make their instrument sing, but Louis learned to make his talk, as well. With all this practice and study he was getting more confident in his abilities. In New Orleans, he seemed to be just another jazz musician, albeit a highly competent one, but here in Chicago, he was a rarity, and his self-esteem rose with Lil's encouragement.

Over the years, Louis often mused about Lil's responsibility for transforming him from just another hot cornet player into the first true jazz soloist. His impressions are wildly contradictory, and they suggest how ambivalent he was concerning Lil as a lover and a teacher. In his early reminiscences, written twenty or so years after the fact, he subscribed to her version of events—that she acted as his coach, almost his Svengali, and created a new, more assertive and musically sophisticated Louis Armstrong. In his later recollections, Louis grew increasingly skeptical of Lil, her musical ability, and her motives. In 1969, near the end of his life, he denounced her as an imposter who "did not know jazz [but] had the nerve to accept the title as a piano player, and at the same time sitting in with the most famous jazz men in the world! How she got that job I can't figure out to this day. Read music, yes, as an improviser, terrible." Disgusted with Lil's having made a career of taking credit for "creating" Louis Armstrong, he delivered a harsh denunciation. "This chick admits all she was interested in was the paydays, more money than she ever made."

By the time the two of them finished their hot little sessions in the woodshed, Louis no longer seemed like a hick to Lil, or to anyone else. He came to believe that his New Orleans childhood, far from being a detriment, actually equipped him to deal efficiently with the issue of making a career for himself in Chicago. There was no vice, no pressure, no extreme situation to which he was exposed in Chicago that he hadn't seen countless times before in New Orleans. He knew all about hustling and tough guys and cornet players who would cut him if he gave them half a chance. Furthermore, his years with Fate Marable had imparted a professionalism to

Louis. He was always prompt, he always knew his part, he knew how to get along with the other members of the band, how to hold his ground if they tried to subvert him, and most important, he knew to obey the leader of the band. Thanks to his days traveling up and down the Mississippi, he was at ease both with white audiences and with black. He could improvise and he could read—if not with the best of them, then at least when he needed to. All of this paid off handsomely in Chicago, where he instinctively understood that he had to market himself as performer and entertainer in its commercial culture.

He spent his nights as well as his days with Lil. In her accounts of her romance with Armstrong, Lil portrayed herself as a young innocent slow to awaken to the genius of the crude but endearing Louis. In fact, she was considerably more worldly than she admitted. During her time away from the Oliver Band, she had married a singer, but the relationship withered as soon as they wed, and, as Louis discovered, "they were on the outs when she and I started running together after work." Their respective unhappy marriages actually gave them some common ground, for they were both seeking escape with a kindred spirit. Inevitably, "the boys in the band commenced to get rather suspicious of she and I, and for a while they all gave us a lot of 'ice,' meaning they treated us rather cool when we went to work. But it wasn't one of those drastic hates. It was more of an astonishment than anything else"—an astonishment borne of jealousy and incredulity that "Little Louis" and "The Hot Miss Lil" could possibly be involved. "For instance," Louis recounted, "one of the boys in the band made an assertion, in other words, he made a crack: 'Just think, here we are, a bunch of hip musicians, been up north for years, making a play for Lil, and a real "country sumbitch" comes up here and takes her from right under our noses.' "

Ignoring their colleagues' scorn, Lil and Louis increasingly confided in each other. "She used to tell me her trouble concerning her married life, and I would tell her mine. It seemed as though we felt so sorry for each other we decided out of a clear sky to get together for good."

Their romance helped Lil to further Louis's education. Lil, in his words, "knew Chicago like a book" and led him into the city's boisterous nightlife. "I'll never forget the first time Lil took me to the Dreamland

Cabaret on 35th and State streets to hear Ollie Powers and May Alix sing," Louis wrote of this once-renowned duo. Powers and Alec blended spirited renditions of current hit tunes with vaudeville-style acrobatics and bawdy repartee. "Ollie had one of those high singing voices, and when he would sing songs like 'What'll I Do?', he would really rock the whole house." Louis and Lil fell in love to "sob songs" by Irving Berlin, like young lovers everywhere at the time.

"May Alix had one of those fine strong voices that everyone would also want to hear. Then she would go into splits and the customers would throw paper dollars on the floor and she would make one of those running splits and pick them up one at a time. I asked Lil if it was all right to give Ollie and May a dollar each to sing a song for me. She said sure, it was perfectly all right. Then she called them over and introduced me as the new trumpet man in King Oliver's band. Gee whiz. I really thought I was somebody meeting those fine stars." From then on, Louis was a fan of Powers's, and much later, played the trumpet at his funeral ("What a sad day that was").

Bill "Bojangles" Robinson made an even larger impression. Louis went to see him in the fall of 1922 at the Erlanger Theater, an occasion that launched his lifelong admiration for the premier black entertainer of the pre-Armstrong era. Known today primarily for his roles as an affable tap-dancing accoutrement in Shirley Temple movies of the 1930s, Robinson was actually a graceful, dignified, and amusing comedian and dancer who appealed to black and white audiences alike.

Finding time to see Robinson proved difficult. Louis was working nights at the Lincoln Gardens. Instead, "I had Bill Johnson take me to the matinee show one day so I could see this man whom I had heard and read about in my early days in N.O." Shortly after, Louis wrote an astute account demonstrating his growing skills as a writer and student of popular entertainment and fashion:

> As he came out of the wing on stage, the first thing that hit him was the flashlight. Sharp—Lord knows that man was so sharp he was bleeding (our expression when we mention someone that's well dressed). Anyway, he had on a sharp light tan gabardine summer suit, brown derby, and the usual thick-soled shoes in which he tapped.
>
> It was a long time before Bojangles could open his mouth. That's how popular he was and well-liked by all who understood his greatness

as a dancer and a showman. He waited after the thunderous applause had finished, and looked up into the booth and said to the man who controlled the lights—Bill said to him, "Give me a light, my color." And all the lights all over the house went out. And me sitting there when this happened, with the whole audience just roaring with laughter. When I realized it, I was laughing so loud, until Bill Johnson was on the verge of taking me out of there. . . .

Then Bojangles went into his act. His every move was a beautiful picture. I am sitting in my seat in ecstasy and delight, even in a trance. He imitated a trombone with his walking cane to his mouth, blowing out of the side of his mouth making the buzzing sound of a trombone, which I enjoyed. He told a lot of funny jokes, which everybody enjoyed immensely. Then he went into his dance and finished by skating off the stage with a silent sound and tempo. Wow, what an artist. I was sold on him ever since.

Louis was also impressed because Robinson "didn't need black face to be funny" or popular with both black and white audiences. His appearance was distinctively, aggressively contemporary ("the quality of his clothes, even from the stage, stopped the show"), and he avoided the trappings of minstrelsy. "He did not wear old raggedy top hat and tails with the pants cut off, black cork with thick white lips, etc." To Louis, fresh out of bangs and baggy pants, Robinson's persona had a liberating effect. This was the way *he* wanted to appear on stage—sharp, aggressive, compelling. Within weeks of his arrival in Chicago, Louis set his sights on becoming more than a jazz musician; he wanted to be an all-round performer who could play, sing, dance, joke, and beguile audiences into a trancelike state. Bojangles showed him how to be a star.

In the next few months, Louis did become a star, even to white musicians, who found him energetic, entertaining, and accessible. Their interest in Louis baffled Lil, who was accustomed to performing for largely black audiences, yet they turned out night after night to hear him blow. From the bandstand of the Lincoln Gardens, a puzzled Lil would often spot a "bunch of white musicians—ten, twelve, fifteen, sometimes twenty—and they would all go up right in front of the bandstand to listen, and I used to wonder to myself—what they were listening to? That's how much I knew about what we were doing, huh? Louis and Joe said Paul Whiteman's Band

and Bix Beiderbecke were in that bunch that used to come. But I didn't know their names, never even asked who they were. You see, the boys, they never talked to me anyway. They used to talk to Louis and King Oliver and Johnny Dodds, but they would never say anything to me."

Paul Whiteman was hard to miss, for he was as large as a house. The leader of his own, all-white band, Whiteman and his musicians came to catch the Creole Jazz Band at Lincoln Gardens nearly every night, as soon as their own gig ended. But they came more on business than pleasure. "They had tuxedos on," said Baby Dodds, "and on the cuffs of their sleeves they'd jot down different notes we played." To frustrate his white competition, Oliver scissored the titles off the music his band played. That way, "No one could come up and look at the number to get it for his own outfit. Sometimes they asked Joe what a certain number was called and he would say anything that came into his mind."

Lil continued to wonder why these nice young white boys were so fascinated with the band. "It was really funny to me, because I didn't know what they were trying to get or why or what they were trying to listen to. Now, I know." She would learn that Whiteman made jazz acceptable to white audiences by slowing it down, adding lots of symphonic-sounding strings, and perhaps most importantly, performing in symphony halls.

As for Bix Beiderbecke, the other regular visitor to the Lincoln Gardens, Louis hadn't seen the lad since they'd met in Davenport, Iowa. In the meantime, Bix had graduated from Davenport High and gravitated to Chicago to attend Lake Forest Academy. He started his own band as soon he touched down on the North Side, and joined up with every musical organization he could find, to the detriment of his studies. He was so busy, and drinking so hard, that Lake Forest, after bestowing a music award on him, asked him to leave. Nevertheless, everyone—his friends, his teachers— liked Bix, even though he was developing the pallor and seedy air of a speakeasy bum. Without the burden of school, Bix was free to take all the jobs he could find around Chicago, and to resume his fascination with Louis Armstrong.

Bix was one of the few white jazz musicians to whom black jazz musicians actually listened. Where Louis's phrasing consisted of endless bold and rousing declamations, Bix displayed a much lighter touch with the horn, and his phrasing seemed to pose endless musical questions, hesitations, and paradoxes. Louis's horn told you exactly what he intended; it was brilliantly clear, and there was never any doubt about his musical meaning. Every solo was a unit, a solid statement, from beginning to end, and wholly satisfying. But when Bix blew, you were never quite certain where he was headed. Was it jazz? Avant-garde? And what about his faux-Debussy piano compositions? Bix's cornet style seemed to define and redefine itself as a song went along, as if he had so many tricks that he could never decide which was the best, and so decided to try them all. The approach perplexed audiences—Bix would never win great acclaim in his lifetime—but musicians, who knew the enormity of the musical problems he wrestled with, were beguiled. Louis's reaction to the phenomenon was typical: "The first time I heard Bix, I said these words to myself: there's a man as serious about his music as I am. Bix did not let anything at all distract his mind from that cornet and his heart was with it all the time." Louis felt so deeply about Bix that he dedicated his first autobiography, *Swing That Music*, to him.

Bix, in turn, brought a friend with him to hear Louis blow. This was Hoagy Carmichael, a laconic, rangy lad from Indiana who was desperately trying to find his way into the popular music and jazz scene. Most of what he knew about music in performance came from his experience at college dances. Like Bix, he was fond of gin, which Prohibition made easy to come by, since it was illicit, plentiful, and cheap. He was also experimenting with marijuana. Hoagy never went anywhere without his hip flask of gin and his little package of carefully rolled muggles. "As I sat down to light my first muggle, Bix gave the sign to a big black fellow, playing a second trumpet for Oliver, and he slashed into 'Bugle Call Rag,'" Hoagy recalled. "I dropped my cigarette and gulped my drink. Bix was on his feet, eyes popping. For taking the first chorus was that second trumpet, Louis Armstrong. Louis was taking it fast. . . . 'Why,' I moaned, 'why isn't everybody in the world here to hear that?' I meant it. Something as unutterably stirring as that deserved to be heard by the world. Then the muggles took effect and my body got light. Every note Louis hit was perfection."

Hoagy was so moved he told Bix he just had to sit in with the band. So Bix conferred with Joe, who waved Lil away from the piano, and Hoagy plopped down in her seat, as the band swung into "Royal Garden Blues." "I had never heard that tune before, but somehow I knew every note. I couldn't miss. I was floating in a strange, deep-blue whirlpool of jazz. It wasn't marijuana," Carmichael thought. "The muggles and gin were, in a way, stage props. It was the music. The music took me and had me and it made me right."

By the end of September, it was apparent that Louis Armstrong, now twenty-one, had arrived. Everything seemed to work out perfectly. He was beginning to go places he'd never imagined he could reach, places where no black man had ever been—not just geographical locations, but places in American society and culture, places in the mainstream of music and popular entertainment that he was helping to redefine. He surveyed the city's burgeoning jazz life, much of it transplanted from New Orleans, with a sense of amazement. "Chicago was really jumping around about that time. The Dreamland in full bloom. The Lincoln Gardens of course still in there. The Plantation, another hot spot at the time. The Sunset was the sharpest of them all, b'lieve that. A lot of after-hours spots were real groovie, too. . . . All the musicians, night lifers and everybody plunged in there in the wee hours of the morning and had a grand time. I used to meet a lot of the boys there after we would finish at Lincoln Gardens." It went on that way night after night. Nobody slept. Everyone had money to spend. Everything seemed possible.

8.

DIPPERMOUTH BLUES

O n April 5 and 6, 1923, Louis Armstrong made his first recordings. More than any high C or high F he ever blew at the Lincoln Gardens, these recordings became the basis of his renown and influenced more musicians and audiences than he could possibly have entertained in a lifetime on the bandstand.

There were several reasons why Louis waited so long to record. For one thing, he had to overcome his early shyness and lack of confidence. And for another, the length of his wild solos surpassed the capacity of wax cylinders and early records. The most important reason, though, was that his boss, Joe Oliver, who was so farsighted in other matters, failed to grasp the significance of recording for jazz. Like so many of the early New Orleans jazz musicians, Oliver was reluctant to take his band into the studio. He believed—with good reason—that record companies would simply exploit his talents and that the recordings themselves would steal his audiences.

In fact, many early jazz stars feared recordings for the same reason. The cornetist Freddie Keppard, for instance, had passed up an opportunity to record as early as 1916 because, he claimed, "somebody will steal my stuff." Had he taken his horn into the studio, he would have waxed the first jazz recording. Nor was there much financial incentive, for the musicians received no royalties or copyrights for their performances or compositions. Generally, record companies paid a flat fee of twenty-five dollars for the entire band, and to earn even that pittance, they spent an entire day in the studio, to wax four to six songs. When they got into a studio—usually a stuffy "soundproof" room hardly larger than a closet—the musicians, who were accustomed to blasting away in the open air or spacious dance halls, felt uncomfortable and insecure. The constraints of recording technology meant they truncated their songs and virtually eliminated improvisation. Without an audience, without booze, without time to rehearse, they frequently played far from their best because it was only a *record*, after all, not the real thing. For all these reasons the early recordings fail to convey the power, style, and finesse of many New Orleans jazzmen.

Yet the recording industry was booming. Player pianos and sheet music, the primary sources of recorded popular music in Louis's youth, were yielding to wax cylinders, and then to 78 rpm records, which declined in price from over a dollar to about seventy-five cents. Several corporate giants dominated the field: Edison, Columbia, Brunswick, Okeh, and the Victor Talking Machine Company. All made huge profits, with the exception of troubled Columbia. The field was also crowded with many smaller, more specialized competitors, including a handful of black-owned companies. At the time Louis entered the studio, there were as many as two hundred recording companies generating annual sales of over one hundred million dollars, and *Variety* had recently begun to chart bestselling records. Victor, especially, reaped vast profits from its recordings of jazz performed by both black and white bands. (It would be years until integrated bands recorded regularly.) The popularity of jazz on disc caught everyone by surprise. Intended primarily for black listeners, jazz recordings instantly appealed to whites, as well, and "race records" quickly became desirable commodities, even collectors' items. For this reason, record companies were avid to record black talent wherever they could find it and market it to everyone.

The impact of recording on jazz was immense, varied, subtle, and complex. By 1924, the destinies of jazz and the recording industry were inextricably linked. Recordings naturally brought jazz into the homes of millions of listeners. More than that, they influenced the music itself. Jazz had been a preeminently aural medium, and its essence eluded even the most skillful notation. Jazz traditions, motifs, harmonies, and melodies were passed from one musician to the next. Now, with recordings, jazz musicians could study one another's performances, preserved with a faithfulness notation could never match. They could study not only the notes but the *style* of playing. The spread of recordings meant that performers could influence and learn from one another at a dizzying rate, and on a scale unimaginable in the days when jazz was heard only in New Orleans. From now on, it could penetrate everywhere, to an unlimited audience. There would be no more Buddy Boldens, whose playing was lost in the mist of legend. Even musicians with small followings, such as Bix Beiderbecke, who seemed destined to be forgotten, were able to leave a musical legacy to influence unborn generations of players. But of all jazz musicians who went before a microphone, none benefited from the power of recordings more than Louis Armstrong. Because of recordings, his style influenced virtually every other jazz musician of the day; no one could escape it. Without recordings, he would have continued to knock 'em dead at the Lincoln Gardens Cafe, but with recordings, he was able to delight and instruct listeners everywhere.

Louis's first recording dates came about when Joe Oliver took the Creole Jazz Band into the studio of a small but thriving record label, Gennett, in Richmond, Indiana. Gennett was actually the offshoot of the Starr Piano Company. In 1915, under the directions of its owner, Henry Gennett, the company began to manufacture phonographs, and from there it was a short step to establishing a record-making division. For a time, Starr stores sold Starr phonographs and Starr records exclusively, but this vertical integration threatened to isolate Starr products from the technological mainstream as determined by Victor, Columbia, and the other giants. To widen his distribution base, Henry Gennett launched a new label bearing his name. His company also began pressing records for other labels. Business boomed. By 1920, Starr was turning out fifteen thousand pianos, three *million* records, and three thousand phonographs a year. Inspired, Gennett opened its own recording studio, located in the midst of its manufacturing plant. However, musicians from Chicago were reluctant to make the five-hour train ride to Richmond to record. Responsibility for coaxing them fell to forty-one-year-old Fred Wiggins, who managed Starr's piano showroom in Chicago. Wiggins succeeded in talking some of its biggest names into recording for Gennett. Hoagy Carmichael, Bix Beiderbecke, and Jelly Roll Morton all went to Richmond, and the body of work they recorded in its studio became the first important collection of jazz, directly influencing at least two generations of musicians, and eventually millions of listeners. The company helped to foster a revolution in American music and popular culture.

Nothing could have been further from Henry Gennett's intentions. He simply wanted to lure customers into buying cheap records so that they would buy the much more expensive record players manufactured by his company. Jazz was just one of many lures. The Gennett label also recorded orchestras; it recorded singers, black, white, and blackface; and in 1923, the year Louis went before its megaphone, it recorded William Jennings Bryan making his famous "Cross of Gold" speech, the one that had electrified the Democratic National Convention back in 1896. In addition, Gennett served as the unofficial recording company of the Ku Klux Klan.

The Klan was very big in Richmond at the time. Indiana was said to have the largest membership of any state, and Richmond's klavern, or headquarters, boasted several thousand members, many of them prominent civic leaders. Klan parades were a common sight in Richmond, so when the black musicians of King Oliver's Creole Jazz Band came out to record, they were entering dangerous territory. Many Gennett employees were active Klan members (though not Henry himself), Klan literature was available in the factory, and the Starr company, when Louis Armstrong and the Creole Jazz Band first recorded there, had no black employees. The Gennett KKK records featured traditional hymns with new lyrics promoting a potent blend of white supremacy and biblical wrath, as well as original songs such as "Johnny, Join the Klan." Although a cross was not actually burning in front of the studio when King Oliver's Creole Jazz band arrived, it might as well have been.

The Gennett recording facilities were as hostile to musicians as Richmond's social climate was to blacks. It would be difficult to imagine a worse place to record music. The studio was housed in a single-story gray wooden shack located beside the noisy Whitewater River. A pumphouse adjoining the building also created a racket. But the rushing sound of the river was soothing compared to the cacophony created by the rail spur running not three feet from the studio's main entrance. Locomotives of the Chesapeake & Ohio Railroad lumbered along this track, hauling freight to and from the Starr manufacturing plant, and their din brought many recording sessions to a halt. It happened all the time: just when the band was starting to swing, along came a C & O locomotive, screeching and wailing down the tracks, drowning out the music and ruining the take. The musicians would have to wait for quiet before starting up again. Careful listeners of Gennett records swore they heard the trains on the recordings.

Inside, the studio was an acoustic nightmare. It measured 125 feet by 30 feet, with a glass window separating it from the engineer's tiny chamber. Soundproofing consisted of sawdust in the walls and draperies. It was an incredibly "dead" room. Despite its small size, a man standing at one end had to shout to be understood at the other, and musicians routinely complained that they couldn't hear one another when they played. Gennett's "chief engineer"—a title that really stretched the point—was Ezra Wickemeyer, an affable sort who endlessly fussed over the musicians' seating arrangements. A Catholic, Wickemeyer despised Gennett's Klan records, and he quit in protest at least once, only to return to his job soon after; the KKK records were usually made when he was not around. His policy was to make three takes of a song, from which he selected the best. There was no way to splice together sections of separate performances, or to combine instruments recorded separately. Gennett recordings, like others made in that era, are replete with flaws such as late or early entrances, flubbed notes, and incorrect key choice—not to mention various noises caused by instruments, bows, music stands, and coughing.

In 1923, recordings were still being made with a "mechanical" or "acoustic" system. When Louis and the other members of the Creole Jazz Band unpacked their instruments in Gennett's little studio they came face to face with a giant megaphone—it was about five feet in diameter and looked like a huge umbrella—designed to capture sound waves. The megaphone funneled the waves into a narrow cone, which transmitted them to a diaphragm, which in turn held a hair spring, which in turn held a stylus (a steel needle) that cut impressions on a rotating wax disc. Since the wax had to be soft to receive impressions, the studio was kept warm, year in and year out. Musicians compared making recordings in this studio to playing in a sauna—and a noisy one at that.

Such were the conditions in which Louis Armstrong, King Oliver, and the Creole Jazz Band spent two days making musical history.

t was something none of us had experienced and we were all very nervous," Baby Dodds said of the momentous occasion. "We were all working hard and perspiration as big as a thumb dropped off us. Even Joe Oliver was nervous. He was no different from any of the rest. The only really smooth-working person there was Lil. . . . She was very unconcerned and much at ease." Throughout, Dodds had to sip alcohol from his bottle to soothe his nerves. Louis took the process of recording in stride; to him, it was another way of playing a song, one with its own logic and possibilities. "We'd rehearse it on the job and when we got to the studio, all we had to do was cut it up and time it. Was no trouble at all to make them records. We'd just make one after the other."

During that session, they recorded several of their surefire hits: "Just Gone," "Canal Street," "Mandy Lee Blues," "I'm Going to Wear You Off My Mind," and "Chimes Blues." Now regarded as classics of pure New Orleans jazz, these versions were pale copies of the live music that King Oliver's Creole Jazz Band played at the Lincoln Gardens. Given the constraints of recording technology, the numbers are brief, all of them less than three minutes, which meant there was no time for extended solos. As a result, the band tamed the two cornet breaks for which Louis and Oliver were famous. Nowhere does Louis have a chance for extended solo displays; his vaunted ability to hit two hundred high C's would never fit on a record, nor was there any guarantee that the megaphone would be able to capture it even if he had tried. Nonetheless, these were Louis's first recordings, and "Chimes Blues," written by Joe Oliver, contains Louis's first significant solo. It is an astonishing piece of work.

The song contains both the past and future of jazz. Although the musical technique is far from perfect, the song ticks along nicely, with Johnny Dodds's clarinet elegantly weaving in and out of the predictable rhythm. Lil was supposed to produce the song's highlight, the sounds of chimes, by striking chords on the piano, but her playing was marred by slight hesitation. Then, near the end of the song, when Louis's trumpet takes over from the band, "Chimes Blues" suddenly fast forwards into the twentieth century. His bold, ascending, trilling, metallic notes streak over the creaky proceedings like a comet. Louis demonstrates great presence; as soon as you hear his horn—jarring, fresh, jagged, and sinuous—you know he has it. His horn sounds twice as loud as the rest of the musicians put together, and his subtle, suspenseful rhythmic shifts, combined with fleeting grace notes where least expected, impart drama to the song.

The confidence with which Louis attacked "Chimes Blues" suggested that, unlike his older, stodgier colleagues, he instantly grasped the possibilities of recordings. They could make him famous, if not rich, and they could *preserve* his playing. From the moment he stepped into a studio, he became a student of jazz recordings and jazz records, both his own and those made by others. He collected them, traveled with them, and listened to them endlessly. To the end of his life, he kept a record player—and when it became available, a tape recorder—at hand. He was the first important jazz musician to anticipate that his legacy would be actual recordings, not half-forgotten memories, and he devoted as much effort to building a recorded *oeuvre* as he did to his live performances. Alone among his colleagues, he *loved* the microphone. That thing could make him rich and famous, so he seized on it as his best and most faithful audience. He blew into it, played with it, made love to it, and later on, sang to it as if it mattered more than anything else in the world.

Then, too, he was lucky enough to play an instrument whose sound the era's primitive acoustic recording process was capable of capturing. The equipment's limited frequency range favored instruments with strong middle registers. The tuba was hopelessly lost; tuba players might just as well have not shown up in the studio, except that the other musicians needed to hear them. The piano fared only slightly better, and Lil's powerful, even heavy-handed thumping style barely comes through on these early recordings. The drums were hopeless. Baby Dodds's innovative drumming style was utterly lost to the megaphone. In fact, he was forced to dispense with the drums altogether and play *blocks* in the studio. The banjo, the clarinet, and most of all, the trumpet (or cornet) were the only instruments whose sound really registered.

On the first take, Louis's trumpet so overwhelmed the other members of the band that they moved Louis "way over in the corner—away from the band," said Lil. "And Louis was standing over there looking so lonesome. He thought it was bad for him to have to be away from the band, you know. He was looking so sad. And I would look at him and smile, you know. And that's the only way they could get the balance. Louis was, well, he was at least twelve to fifteen feet from us on the whole session, so then I was convinced, yes, he really can play good, because if his tone overshadows Joe that much, he's gotta be better. But I didn't know technically why it was better. I came to feel sorry for him that he was good, and people were trying to keep him back."

Despite all the difficulties of recording, the day proved to be furiously busy and productive. The Creole Jazz Band made twenty-seven takes. Gennett's engineers chose to release five and destroyed the others. The seven black musicians of the Creole Jazz Band could not stay in Klan-ridden Richmond overnight, so they rode the train out of town to a safe haven.

It is unlikely they returned to Chicago that evening, for they were back in the studio the next day, April 6, to record an even more ambitious set, which included "Snake Rag," another Oliver composition, and Louis's "Dippermouth Blues." Joe had a brief, shining moment here, when he took a solo that inspired countless imitations. He played with a mute, which imparts a seductive, plaintive, wailing quality to his cornet. He tickles the phrases, then wails and stomps, and *sends* them.

Although the band sounds tight on this recording of "Dippermouth Blues," they almost fell apart when making it. Baby Dodds, unnerved by the studio and perhaps befuddled by alcohol, forgot to take his solo on the drums—actually, the blocks—and Bill Johnson, in a high voice, called out, "Oh, play that thing!" to remind him. Concerning the distinctive spoken phrase, Dodds recalled that "the technician asked us if that was supposed to be there and we said no. However, he wanted to keep it anyway, and, ever since then, every outfit uses that same trick, all because I forgot my part."

The recordings brought Louis additional compensations. He received cocredit for writing several songs. And he received solo credit for at least one, "Weather Bird Rag," featuring a brief interlude in which Oliver and Armstrong whirl their way through a two-cornet break. The idea of composing songs was not new to Louis, but receiving credit was something of a novelty to him.

The recordings King Oliver's Creole Jazz Band made during these sessions were included in Gennett's 1923 catalog, titled, "Snappy Dance Hits on Gennett Records by Exclusive Gennett Colored Artists." Nowhere did the controversial word "jazz" appear. Gennett sold the recordings mainly in stores located in black neighborhoods. A few shops in white areas carried them, as well, but did not display them; they were kept in crates behind the counter, and customers who wanted them had to lean over the counter and, in a low, discreet voice, ask for them.

Nevertheless, the Creole Jazz Band's Gennett recordings were widely influential and admired. No other jazz recordings have been more carefully analyzed and copied than these, both for their representation of the "pure" New Orleans style of playing and for the individual performers in the band, especially Louis. They have been re-released countless times, and the original Gennett discs have long been important collectors' items documenting the birth of modern jazz, and, by extension, the Jazz Age itself.

. . .

Although the Gennett catalog described King Oliver's Creole Jazz Band as "exclusive," they were anything but. Now that its members had actually recorded, the band was more sought after than ever. Within weeks of the Gennett dates, the Okeh Record Company, a more high-powered label, snared their services. Like Gennett, Okeh was in search of black artists to exploit for the booming market in race records, but the resemblance ended there. Okeh had its own studio right in Chicago, in the Consolidated Talking Machine Company Building at 227 West Washington Street. The company's scouts caught up with King Oliver's Creole Jazz Band, featuring their exuberant second cornet Louis Armstrong, when they performed at a Music Trades Convention at the Drake Hotel.

Playing the Drake—Chicago's finest hotel—that was something to type home about! The location couldn't have been more prestigious, but the timing couldn't have been worse. The band performed a twenty-minute set at three o'clock in the morning, at the end of a bill that ran two hours overtime. Exactly what numbers King Oliver's Creole Jazz Band played that night is unknown. What *is* known, according to the trade journal *Talking Machine World*, is that their playing roused a "mob of admirers," who surged toward the stand at the end of the set to fawn over the musicians, "especially the little frog-mouthed boy who played cornet": Louis Armstrong. As the crowd rushed past Joe Oliver toward his protégé, the *second* cornet, it is easy to imagine the look on the King's face, a bittersweet mixture of pride, envy, and resentment.

As a result of the performance, the band won the Okeh contract, and several weeks later, they rerecorded many of the songs they'd waxed for Gennett, including Armstrong's show piece, "Dippermouth Blues." The performances were nearly identical and helped to promote the band's reputation. Within weeks the Chicago *Defender* announced:

KING OLIVER'S JAZZ ORCHESTRA, CHICAGO'S BIG FAVORITES,
MAKE FIRST OKEH RECORDS.

For years, King Oliver's Band has served up jazz to thousands at the Lincoln Gardens, Chicago's dazzling cabaret, but man alive, can't

these boys play it, say it in true blues harmony. Why, they are the ones
who put jazz on the map.

Remarkably, Gennett didn't take exception to the Okeh date, and in
October the company invited King Oliver's Creole Jazz Band back to
Richmond for another session. Later in the year, the band recorded for
Paramount and Columbia, improving with every date. At that moment, the
recording business was chaotic. Musicians were often cheated out of their
share of profits, but the field was wide open, and the chaos encouraged
flexibility, creativity, and spontaneity. Joe, Louis, Lil, and the rest of the
band seemed destined to become one of the most recorded jazz bands of the
era. This would have come to pass, had not dissension entered their ranks.
Their very success started to tear them apart. The fellows in the band
turned on Joe, and King Oliver's Creole Jazz Band began to disintegrate
even faster than it had made a name for itself.

Louis hardly seemed to notice the rumblings and discontent among his
colleagues, for during the summer of 1923, he could think of nothing
but the alluring Lil. For her part, Lil was thinking of both Louis and
business. She prodded him to become more independent. She simply
couldn't understand how he could allow Joe Oliver to treat him like a child
when it came to the serious business of pay. Papa Joe kept part of Louis's
salary, explaining that he was saving it so Louis could have something for a
rainy day. The arrangement was not something Louis discussed casually,
and Lil found out about it by accident, when she urged him to buy himself
some fancy new clothes, in keeping with the image of the star he wanted to
be. "You don't look right," she told him. "You've got to change your
clothes."

"What's the matter with my clothes?" Louis asked. Secondhand clothes
were a way of life to him.

"Got to have some new clothes," she insisted. "Where's your money?"

"Joe keeps my money."

"Well, Joe doesn't need to keep your money. You keep your own
money," she patiently explained, grooming him for maturity. "You go to
Joe and get your money."

The idea made Louis extremely uncomfortable. "Mr. Joe, you know he sent for me and he looks out for me."

"I'm gonna look out for you from now on," Lil said.

With that, Louis switched mentors, or rather, was told to switch. No longer would Papa Joe be his principal sponsor. From now on, it would be Lil. She had teased, cajoled, and pushed him in every way possible—romantically, musically, and now financially. If Louis could ever win his financial independence from Papa Joe, he would be free—free to be hers, that is.

Louis stalled. Lil insisted. "Anyway, I'm going to get you some clothes and you're going to give me my money back," she offered. Louis agreed to let her take care of him, and in purchasing fancy clothes for Louis, she took control of him, as well.

He allowed Lil to choose his entire wardrobe. He offered token resistance in only one instance, over a hat. Their dispute over it, though apparently trivial, came to stand for the larger issue of emotional control. Lil had to have it, and Louis was content to let her have it, if he could somehow retain his self-respect. "I went downtown and I bought him a marimba gray overcoat and a twenty-dollar velour hat and brought it back," Lil recalled of the intricate negotiation. "He tried the coat on and it fit perfectly. And he tried the hat on. Well, the hat, I measured his head with the tape measure and it fit as it should fit, but in New Orleans, they were used to wearing the hat sitting right up on top of the head."

"This hat is too big," Louis complained.

"No, no, no," Lil responded.

"Yes it is. This hat is not supposed to sit down like this, you know, around here. It's supposed to sit up here."

"Well, you go back down there now. You wear your coat and you go back down there and you try the hat on," Lil ordered him.

Louis returned to the store, and "he came back with the same size hat in another color. So, we would argue and argue and argue about this hat. But anyway, I let him keep this little hat." She told him, "The little hat is better than anything else."

That night, when Louis appeared for work at the Lincoln Gardens, his new clothing instantly attracted attention. Lil stood by, obviously pleased with her handiwork. Buddy Red, the manager, told Louis, "I knew if you fooled around, that chickie was going to change your appearance." More smiles and grins. Then Louis looked at Papa Joe for *his* reaction—but there was none. Joe set his jaw, and his walleye turned to stone. After an interminable wait, he let loose. He was shrewd enough to realize that Lil was the instigator, so he went after her. He called Lil "nothing but a spoiled kid" who "didn't have to give any money at home." He warned Louis that she spent all her money on "ice cream and clothes" and worse, she would "make him spend all of his money" the way she did. If he kept playing with "that crazy girl"—Joe couldn't bring himself to say her name—Louis would be broke in no time flat.

Louis was on the spot, torn between the man he loved like a father, who *was* his father for all intents and purposes, and the woman who held his future in her graceful, scheming hands. Louis looked at Joe and muttered, "Yeah, I know." But Lil could tell he liked the way he looked now, sharp and up-to-date. Why had Joe never thought to give him money to buy new clothes? Why didn't Joe care about his appearance the way Lil did? Louis liked looking good, liked feeling good, and he liked Lil.

After the quarrel with Oliver, Lil instructed Louis, "You just get all of your money from Joe and keep it yourself." Of his subsequent behavior, she simply remarked: "So he did. He asked Joe for the money, and then we decided to get married."

Although Lil had managed to pry Louis loose from King Oliver's grasp, they faced more complications. "Louis was already married to Daisy," Lil knew, "and he had to get a divorce. It took six months." Louis started formal divorce proceedings in the fall of 1923, charging her with "willfully deserting and absenting herself from the complainant, without any reasonable cause, for the space of over two years immediately prior to the filing of the Bill of Complaint in this cause." Lil's own marriage had ended by now, and it is easy to contemplate her egging him on, never letting the matter rest until it reached its conclusion.

"Armstrong vs. Armstrong" was filed in Cook County, Chicago, and if Daisy ever contested the proceedings, there is no record of it. Nor did Louis return to New Orleans to speak with Daisy or to file legal papers there. Lil would certainly not have let him go at this hazardous juncture in their relationship; anything might happen to him down there. He remained in Chicago with Lil and the band during the months his complaint worked its way through the courts. Two days before Christmas 1923, Louis received an early present in the form of his divorce decree after six years of marriage to Daisy. Louis was now free, but not for long. Lil was determined to lead him to the altar as soon as a proper wedding could be arranged.

Six weeks later, on February 5, 1924, the Chicago *Defender* informed its readers of the glittering nuptials of two local celebrities:

MISS LILLIAN HARDIN IS

BRIDE OF LOUIS ARMSTRONG

Miss Lillian Hardin, daughter of Mrs. Dempsey Miller, 3320 Giles Ave., was married to Louis Armstrong of New Orleans, La. . . . The bride was beautifully attired in a Parisian gown of white crepe elaborately beaded in rhinestones and silver beads, and Miss Lucille Saunders, a lifelong chum of the bride who was her bridesmaid, wore orchid chiffon with silver trimmings.

Oscar Young's seven-piece orchestra furnished music for the occasion. Mr. and Mrs. Armstrong are both members of King Oliver's Creole Band, who are recording for Gennett, Okeh, and Columbia records.

The band was there, of course—Joe Oliver, and his wife, and the Dodds brothers, and the rest of the fellows. They all wished the newlyweds well, as did Lil's friends and family. "The couple received many beautiful presents," the *Defender* noted.

For Louis, things were happening so quickly that he was in a daze, unable to stop and think, happy to go along with the show. Lil was the girl that every man in the band wanted, and Louis was the one who got her. He was launched into a new life. "When Lil and I got married we made the rounds of the night clubs, and everybody threw rice on us as we were getting in and out of the taxi cabs. And they all invited us out to their homes."

Lil liked real estate and quickly found a new home in Chicago. The speed with which she located the property suggests that she had located it before they were wed. The address of their new home was 421 East 44th Street, and Lil made certain to list it in her name. She also brought her mother to live with them, and Louis seems not to have minded Dempsey's presence. He was too busy marveling at his good fortune—he was not yet twenty-four, and he had a wife, a home, and a fast-growing reputation. For an itinerant jazz musician, his life was now remarkably stable and comfortable. He was catching up quickly to Lil, and appeared poised to overtake King Oliver himself.

Louis contributed one item to the household that was sure to please Lil, a baby grand piano—a sign of prosperity, status, and culture. Musicians who dropped in on the newlyweds always went to the piano first. Among them was Jelly Roll Morton. Louis's friend Zutty Singleton recalled the night that "we all went to Louis's place and Jelly sat down at that piano and really gave us a serenade. He played and played, and after each number he'd turn around on that stool and tell us how he wrote each number and where it came from. It was a real lecture, just for the benefit of me and Lil and Louis." So fond was he of the Armstrongs' new piano that Jelly Roll became a frequent visitor to their house.

For Louis, the most significant addition to his life at this moment was not the piano, or the house, or even Lil, but his adopted son. When Louis describes his sudden transition to maturity and married life, he emphasizes the arrival of Clarence, whose presence and ordinary daily activities gave him keen paternal pleasure. "I had the folks down in New Orleans whom I left Clarence to live with when I went to Chicago put a tag on Clarence, put him on a train, and send him to me. It was one swell, grand reunion," Louis recorded with evident satisfaction. This development was exceedingly important to Louis because he had never been able to savor a moment's happiness with his own father. Yet he was able to forge a mutually satisfying bond with young Clarence, and, in the process, he was able to lessen the pain of the psychic wounds he suffered when his father abandoned him. His relationship with Clarence, more than the trappings of success, made Louis feel proud. "Clarence had his own special room," Louis boasted, and he quickly found the child a "school where they teach the backwards." This turned out to be a happy circumstance for both father and son, for "there he turned out to be one of the best baseball, basketball, and football players in the whole school. And everybody knew him and called him Little Louis Armstrong."

Louis reveled in his ability to take care of his new family. "When Lil and I had our home together," he reminisced, "she, Clarence, and myself used to sit in our parlor evenings after supper, and she would run over some of the finest classics on that brand new baby grand piano I bought her. Lil's mother was very fond of me also. She had a stroke in one arm. I bought her a secondhand typewriter, and it was just the thing for her to pass the time away. She got pretty good typing with one hand."

Meanwhile, Mayann Armstrong lived by herself, not far from her son. She had come to Chicago to track down disturbing but false stories about Louis—and then decided to stay. According to the gossip she had heard in New Orleans, Louis was starving and sick in Chicago. As Louis later wrote, the tale "worried my dear mother almost crazy," and Mayann resolved to rescue her son from the depredations of life in Chicago and "immediately grabbed a train."

Louis was playing at the Lincoln Gardens at the moment of her arrival, and he relished telling the story of their unexpected reunion: "Just as we were getting ready to hit the show, we all noticed a real stout lady with bundles in her hands cutting across the dance floor. To my surprise, it was my mother, Mayann. The funny thing about it was, King Oliver had been kidding me that he was my stepfather for years and years. And when he saw Mayann (tee hee) he did not know her. So when Mayann came onto the bandstand I whispered into Joe's ear, 'Well, Papa Joe, Mother's here. Shall I tell her what you've been saying?' Oh, gosh, you should have seen Papa Joe blush all over the place, and she thanked him for being so swell to her son. I thought he'd just swoon."

When he asked her what on earth she was doing up here in Chicago, she explained, "Lawd, chile, somebody came to New Orleans and told me that you were up here awfully low, sick, and starving to death."

"Aw, Mama, how could I starve when I'm eating at King Oliver's house every day, and you know how Mrs. Stella piles up King's plate full of red beans and rice. Well, she fills mine the same way. Now, how could I starve?" Seeing that her son was well fed and among friends, Mayann relaxed and allowed Louis to introduce her to the members of the band, starting with Joe Oliver. As Louis joyfully recalled, "She smiled all over her face."

Mayann quickly felt at home in Chicago, and decided to stay for a while. This was fine with Louis. In days to come, he wrote, he "bought her lots of fine clothes, all kinds of silk lingerie."

She had lived in Chicago ever since, but now that her son was married and settled, she decided the time had come to return to her home. "Being a Christian woman, who belonged to Rev. Cozy's Church on Perdido Street, she just missed her congregation so dearly," Louis explained. "To make her happy to go back I agreed. Purchased her ticket to New Orleans, sold her apartment. The night before she left Chicago, we made the rounds of all the nightclubs and dances." That, of course, was Louis's idea. "I said, 'Mother darling, now that you are leaving me, how about you and me go out and have a real grand time just by ourselves—no one else.' She agreed right away, and the police had to show both of us where we lived the next morning, coming from those places. Mother and I laughed over that event a lot of times."

Mayann returned to New Orleans knowing that her precious son was enjoying all he could eat and drink. She showed off the finery she'd acquired up north, thanks to her son's generosity, and she took increasing satisfaction in religion. Whatever sinning she had done in her youth was behind her. Her search for love had been, at best, a mixed adventure, and she now had her eye on eternity, and, of course, on her son.

Shortly after she arrived home, Mayann exchanged a few words with Daisy Parker, delicately skirting the subject of Louis's remarriage. Daisy said she still loved that man, and she was determined to get him back. In fact, she was prepared to go all the way to Chicago to find him, if that was what it took.

There was another person who challenged Louis's newfound independence—Joe Oliver. He had warned Louis about Lil, and Louis had gone ahead and married her anyway. Joe tried to remain on cordial terms with the newlyweds—he had, after all, introduced them, and they were still in his band—but it was getting difficult. His visits to their new home crackled with tension. Knowing exactly what King Oliver thought of him these days, Louis felt extremely uncomfortable and tried to compensate with forced politeness. As Lil recalled, "Whenever Joe came to the house you'd think that God had walked in. Louis never seemed to relax completely with him around because he was so afraid of doing something that might upset him."

Despite Louis's best efforts to keep the peace among them all, Joe continued to complain about Lil behind her back. He continued to warn that she would take all his money and leave him broke. He taunted Louis horribly, telling the young man he would never make it on his own. "What does Louis think he's going to do?" Oliver would ask anyone who cared to listen. "He won't get anyplace. He'll find out." He even encouraged the musicians to turn on Louis. Baby Dodds, for one, got into a shoving match with Louis on the bandstand at the Lincoln Gardens. "We had been kidding and joking and when I said something the whole band would sway with me. Then Louis would say something else and the whole bunch swayed with him," Baby said of that night. "We were kidding during the intermission period, and it got pretty hot. Then we got up to each other and clinched and scratched each other and I tore his silk shirt. We all used to wear silk shirts then, white Japanese silk shirts. . . . It was stopped because we had to play music but our silk shirts were very ragged by then."

Despite the rising tension, the band continued to play nightly at the Lincoln Gardens. One night, who should turn up, looking for her Louis, but Daisy Parker, razors and all. She caused a ruckus at the entrance to the place, claiming to be "Mrs. Armstrong," when everyone knew perfectly well that Mrs. Armstrong was up on the bandstand, playing the piano alongside her husband.

Daisy tried to get Louis's attention by shouting and waving her fists. Up on the bandstand, he quickly noticed the commotion, and when he recognized Daisy, went to her, took her by the arm, and led her to an obscure bar. There, he tried to talk some sense to her, as he kept his eye fixed on the bulge of the razor she concealed in her stocking. She proved as difficult as ever to handle. She seemed to have forgotten all about their divorce and insisted they were still man and wife. "Quite naturally she tried to go through the same processions as she did in the old days down in New Orleans," Louis wrote of that volatile moment, twenty years after the fact. "But things had changed, and she could not give me any more trouble. I showed her my divorce papers, which convinced her immediately. I also told her I was a changed man since I came to Chicago and married Lil."

He warned Daisy, "No more boisterous barrelhouse stuff. [I] am trying to cultivate myself. Now we can be the very best of friends, and if there is anything that I can do within my power I will gladly do it."

"That's fair enough," Daisy said. "Because, after all, you and I have been together for over three or four years."

"So that was that," Louis told himself.

As it turned out, that was *not* that. Daisy remained in Chicago, apparently with Louis's tacit approval, and she repeatedly attempted to rekindle their former passion. She turned up at odd moments in his daily routine, trying to catch his attention, practicing her wiles on him, always keeping her razor at the ready. "She and I would go to a tavern and have a few nips together, and she told me that she wouldn't ever stop loving me, no matter if we are not together," Louis recalled. "After all, I am the only man she'll ever love as long as she lives."

Whether they became lovers again Louis did not record, but Daisy clearly felt sufficiently loyal to him to remain in Chicago, and he acknowledged some indebtedness to her by giving her small amounts of money from time to time. He also tried to hide the presence of his first wife from his second. Both women, as he knew, could be very headstrong, as Daisy soon demonstrated. "Daisy got into a whole lot of trouble in a tavern one night," Louis wrote. "It was some guy (colored) talking about me. In other words, he was justa 'panning' me. Daisy happened to be sitting there—she didn't like it, in other words, she resented it—so she took it up. She went over to the guy and told him, 'Louis Armstrong is my ex-husband, and I don't like the way you talked about him. After all, you don't know him that well.' The fellow was half drunk, and said something to Daisy she did not like. The argument got real hot, and this drinking guy pulled out his big knife and Daisy always carries her razor, and they both turned out the joint, cutting on one another." In the end, "the ambulance had to come get both of them."

Daisy's wounds were serious enough to put her in the hospital for two weeks. When she recovered, she finally returned to New Orleans, her face bearing "a few scars," and her heart no doubt more deeply damaged by her ill-advised adventure in Chicago, her marriage to Louis, and her entire sad life. Louis never spoke to her again, except in passing. Every so often she would appear in his life and try to get his attention for a few fleeting moments, and each time she appeared before him, she looked older and more beaten down. The last time he saw her, he noted, "Her hair has turned gray."

ouis and Lil's renegotiation over the way Oliver handled Louis's salary inspired the others members of the band—the Dodds brothers, Dutrey, and Johnson—to review their situations. They had waxed a lot of sides, and they had been led to believe they would receive royalties. It did not occur to them that the record companies were extremely casual about meeting their obligations to pay the outstanding sums; instead, they became convinced that Joe Oliver had received the money and was withholding it from them. "Nobody saw the royalty checks but Oliver," Baby Dodds said. "They were in his name and had to be cashed by him. We had an argument when some of us wanted to see the checks. In our mind that showed guilt although we did not know for sure what the real story was."

The situation worsened when the musicians discovered that Joe was also retaining a portion of their salaries, as he had in Louis's case. "Johnny Dodds found out that Joe had been collecting $95 for each member of the band while he'd been paying us $75," Lil said. "Naturally, he'd been making $20 a week a piece off of us for who knows how long. Johnny and Baby threatened to beat Joe up. So Joe brought his pistol every night to work in his trumpet case in case anything happened." Whenever she was up on the bandstand performing, Lil was terrified, and while she played, she made sure to keep an eye on Joe, or on the trumpet case, in case shooting broke out. It was a very unhappy time for the Creole Jazz Band.

At last, the Lincoln Gardens engagement came to an end. Perhaps the best that could be said of the band at this point was that no one killed anyone else. Relief came in the form of the prospect of a brief tour. King Oliver "received an offer from a big booking office downtown," said Louis. "So the night after we finished the job, Joe called a meeting with the band and told them about the swell contract he had just signed. Told them about the salary, etc., which was very good. But when he told them they had to be traveling, the whole band backed out except Lil and me."

The irony was immense. Louis and Lil were supposed to be rebels, and the other members of the band loyalists, but now the Armstrongs were the only ones to remain with Papa Joe, and the other musicians, still convinced they had been cheated, ditched him. "Joe had to engage a whole new band to go on the road. Well, that wasn't so hot because those new players didn't understand our own way of playing like Johnny Dodds, Baby Dodds, Bill Johnson, Honore Dutrey, but we did the best we could, considering the situation."

Louis and Lil remembered the tour as a happy and lucrative interlude.

"I danced, took a lot of solos, you know, helped the old man out. After all, I was in there with him with all my heart because I loved Joe Oliver and would do anything in the world to make him happy, and he really did appreciate my effort. Our tour was a big success even though things were like they were. Then, too, the fellows who replaced the ones who didn't go were all top-notch musicians, such as Buster Bailey, who is now playing with John Kirby's orchestra and Rudy Jackson, who was the ace tenor man in those days."

Even as she outwardly displayed loyalty to Oliver, Lil never stopped scheming to get Louis away from him. When the tour ended, and they had been paid, she made her move.

"When we came back, I said to Louis, 'Now, look, we're married now—see, I don't want you playing second trumpet, you got to play first.' "

"Play first? Where am I going to play first?"

"You'll have to quit Joe and find you a job playing first."

As Lil recalled, Louis "didn't like the idea at all. Oh, no." But she was adamant as only Lil Hardin could be.

"You can't be married to Joe and married to me, too. Now, if you're going to stay with me, you have to play first."

"Well, what do you want me to do?" Louis asked.

"I want you to give him a notice."

Louis finally gave notice to Joe, and expected that his wife would give notice too, but Lil informed him, "I'm going to stay. One of us has got to be working."

King Oliver was surprised, as well. "Louis gave me his notice," he said to her, "and you didn't give me yours."

"No," she told him, "I'm not quitting."

Now Oliver was baffled, or pretended to be. "Why's Louis quitting?"

"I think you have to ask him. I don't know why."

Lil, of course, was playing dumb; she could be as sly as old Joe. "Oh, such lies, huh?" she exclaimed as she recalled the exchange.

As she usually did, Lil got her way, but at a cost. Louis was out of a job, and despite the reputation he had made during his year-and-a-half in Chicago, he seemed as insecure as ever. He fretted that his wife was working, and he was not. "Now, what am I gonna do?" he wailed.

Lil was never short of answers. "Just go out. Go out every day and look around. Go hang around the musicians. Find out who needs a trumpet player."

L ouis took her advice—what choice did he have?—but his early forays proved a bitter disappointment. He wanted a position in a high-class band. Although King Oliver's Creole Jazz Band had proved a sensation at the Lincoln Gardens and a particular favorite of white musicians, it was a little rough around the edges. Louis set his sights on bands with more social cachet, and of all the black orchestras in Chicago at that time, none was more high-toned than Sammy Stewart's outfit. Louis went to see the great Sammy Stewart. What a fine gentleman he was, dressed in fine clothes. And very well-spoken, too. Very flattering. When Mr. Stewart chuckled, he made a sound like a martini rattling in a silver shaker. Oozing charm, he said that he had heard of Louis Armstrong, hadn't everyone? And then he chuckled in his special way. In the presence of this refined gentleman, Louis became nervous, and when he was nervous, he lowered his head and looked straight ahead, his whole body seeming to droop. Finally, he got up his nerve to ask Mr. Stewart if he needed a trumpet player in his band, rather, his *orchestra*.

The chuckling stopped. Sammy Stewart turned to look at Louis, and what he saw was not the most brilliant trumpet player in Chicago, but a dark-skinned black man. Sammy Stewart, who was light-skinned, had no use for such a man in his band. He knew that his entree into Chicago society depended on his having only Creoles and light-skinned blacks in his outfit, and Louis, on the basis of his color, would never do. Sammy Stewart didn't bother to explain these fine distinctions and social hypocrisies to the naive young trumpet player, he simply executed a half turn and snapped at him, "No, I don't need anybody."

The rejection stunned Louis. It hadn't occurred to him that other band-leaders would not want to hire him the moment he left King Oliver. He was slow to realize that most bandleaders, and not just Sammy Stewart, were not benevolent teachers and father figures, they were often sons of bitches. They would bully, they would take their cut off the top, and never reveal how much they were keeping; they had countless ways to intimidate and control the men in their band. King Oliver was a pushover, slow and sentimental compared to an operator like Sammy Stewart, as Louis belatedly understood. He trudged home in a deep funk, wondering if he had destroyed his career by leaving the Creole Jazz Band for this mad scheme to become a soloist.

When he got home that night, he told Lil what had happened in Sammy Stewart's office that day. "He didn't even have the courtesy to speak, or say anything. All he did is snap at me."

"Oh, don't worry about him. Pretty soon he'll be eating at your feet," Lil said.

Despite her bravado, Lil was shaken. "I'm just talking, you know?" she remembered of that disquieting moment. She kept her misgivings to herself and sent her Louis out again in search of a job.

The next opening he heard about was with Ollie Powers, who was assembling a new band. He remembered Powells vividly from his courting days with Lil, and the time he gave Powells a dollar to play some of his favorites.

Powells offered him a position as first trumpet in the new band. This was the first time Louis had ever held that rank, and he was delighted and relieved to be employed once again. Within days he was blowing nightly at the Dreamland, Lil's old stomping ground. As far as Lil was concerned, the moment Louis became first trumpet, he came into his own as a performer. "That's when Louis started playing and showing what he had in himself, because as long as he was with King Oliver, he was playing second to Joe and trying to play Joe's solos, which he couldn't play, because it wasn't his style at all." Yet Louis yearned, even now, to return to Oliver's band. "Joe Oliver broke his band up and went into the Plantation Cafe at 35th and Calumet Avenue, as a featured cornetist," Louis wrote. "He sent down to New Orleans [for] Barney Bigard, Luis Russell, Albert Nicholas, Paul Barbarin." Louis was all set to join that group when without warning, his career took off in another direction.

"Fletcher Henderson had sent for him to come to New York to play with him at the Roseland," said Lil, with evident relief. And "Smack" Henderson was *the* outstanding bandleader in Harlem. The happy accident in timing rescued Louis from another stint with King Oliver, trying to recapture a past that was now irretrievably gone. Both Louis and Lil detected the hand of fate in the offer from Henderson coming at the time it did. Louis had mishandled a previous offer from Henderson, when he said he would go only if he could bring Zutty Singleton along, and Smack had turned him down flat. Now here he was, calling on Louis again, ready to bring him to New York, and make him *first* trumpet.

On the heels of Henderson's offer, Sam Wooding, another Harlem bandleader, also got in touch with Louis. "Armstrong was the man I wanted," Wooding related. "He was recognized to be the greatest then, and we sent a wire to make him an offer. I was paying good money in those days, one hundred dollars a week, and I know I could have had a shot at Louis. He would have taken it, too. Unfortunately I missed him." Instead, Louis opted for less money and more prestige. "Fletcher Henderson paid him $55 a week," Lil recalled. "The only statistics I remember is money: Fletcher paid him $55 a week. So Louis came alone."

Before leaving Chicago, he had to make a final break with Joe Oliver. "When I explained to the King that it was my one big chance to see New York, where the people really *do things*, he dug me (I knew he would) and released me so I could 'knock it.' " He took the next train bound for New York and the Fletcher Henderson Orchestra. Louis had changed the musical scene in Chicago during his two-and-a-half years there, and he was about to wreak the same joyous musical havoc on New York, where the opportunities for lasting fame were far greater than they had been in the Gem of the Prairie.

9.

T.N.T.

hen I arrived in New York I had to go straight to rehearsal," Louis recalled. "And don't you know when I got into the rehearsal I felt so funny. I walked up to old 'Smack' and said, 'Er, wa, I'm that boy you sent for to blow the trumpet in your band.' And 'Smack,' all sharp as a Norwegian, with that hard-hitting steel gray suit he had on, said, 'Oh, yes, we're waiting for you. Your part's up there' (meaning the bandstand). I said, 'Yassuh,' and went on up there with my eyes closed. When I opened them I looked square into the faces of Coleman Hawkins, Don Redman, Kaiser Marshall, Long Green, Escudero, Scotty, Elmer 'Muffle Jaws' Chambers, and Charles Dixon.

"They all casually looked out of the corner of their eyes. You know how they do when a new man joins a band, they want to be real friendly right off the bat. But they'd rather hear you play first. I said to myself, 'These boys look like a nice bunch of fellows, but they seem a little stuck up.'" So began Louis's introduction to the star musicians comprising Fletcher Henderson's orchestra—an orchestra he would come to revolutionize in the months ahead. For Louis, this was more than just a new job in a strange city; it was his first taste of a momentous cultural and social phenomenon known as the Harlem Renaissance.

Louis's arrival in New York at the end of October 1924 coincided with the exact moment the Harlem Renaissance burst into the national consciousness, and Harlem itself started jumping. His timing was impeccable. Once again he was part of a wave of immigration, not the broad-based movement of blacks from the South to Chicago, but a far more specialized influx of talent into Harlem. Within a few years—months, actually—Harlem became the newest center of black culture. This was a somewhat unexpected development, since Harlem was far removed from the centers of American black life and was in many ways an atypical black community. For decades, Harlem was known as a tranquil white bourgeois oasis stretching from the northern boundary of Central Park all the way up to 168th Street. When Irving Berlin struck it rich writing songs, for instance, the first thing he did was to move up to swell digs in Harlem. Even after it became known as the center of black life in New York, Harlem was still largely white-owned. "Harlem was beautiful in those days," said Milt Hinton, the venerable jazz bassist who made the pilgrimage from the South to Chicago and New York. "Everything on Seventh Avenue was real sharp and very clean. . . . Plenty of whites came uptown every night to see black performers in Harlem. People have talked about white mobsters owning nightclubs in Harlem. But I saw many bars and nightclubs which were owned by blacks. There were fantastic after-hours places catering to performers who'd start their day after the rest of the world had been sleeping for hours."

As Hinton suggests, Harlem was a place of striking contradictions, for its Renaissance was driven by a unique combination of black and white intelligentsia, as well as entrepreneurs (read "gangsters") seeking to extol and exploit the talents and attitudes found there in Harlem. At the high end of the spectrum, art and literature flourished. The new magazine *Opportunity*, under the stewardship of Charles Johnson, proclaimed its intention to "encourage the reading of literature both by Negro authors and about Negro life, not merely because they are Negro authors but because what they write is literature and because the literature is interesting." *Opportunity* was soon beckoning a new wave of young black intellectuals and artists to Harlem, and they in turn publicized it as something new and hot. The Harlem Renaissance also attracted many white participants and cheerleaders. They included figures as diverse as Sinclair Lewis, Dorothy Parker, Pearl Buck, Van Wyck Brooks, George Gershwin, Hart Crane, Eugene O'Neill, and Dubose Heywood. Many of the whites were jazz musicians who also savored the Harlem scene in those years: Bix Beiderbecke, Hoagy Carmichael, and Jack Teagarden. They, too, contributed to the Renaissance even as they drew sustenance from it. When the white, Iowa-born music critic Carl Van Vechten came to New York, he gravitated toward Harlem and tried to capture its ethos in his novel, *Nigger Heaven* (1926). For many whites, the book became the image of Harlem, a place of style, swagger, sophistication, and unpredictable romance.

The Harlem Renaissance gave blacks a voice, stature, and respectability, but, at the same time, they realized how alienated they were from white America. In celebration and in protest, they expressed the manifold implications of blackness: beauty, anguish, fear, subversiveness, striving, enjoyment, entertainment, music, and art. In the midst of this ferment, Heywood Broun, the white newspaper columnist, predicted the arrival of the "supremely great negro artist" who would personify the Harlem Renaissance. Such a man, wrote Broun, "could catch the imagination of the world, would do more than any other agency to remove the disabilities against which the negro race now labors." Not only that, but "this great artist may come at any time." Of all those who played a role in the Harlem Renaissance, Louis Armstrong most closely answered to this description.

The flourishing nightlife in Harlem made up its other, less lofty side. Prohibition remained the law of the land, but it simply did not exist in Harlem. The availability of liquor drew whites uptown to this place of mounting fascination, where they could relax, drink, get a girl, gamble, gawk, and generally pretend to be something they weren't: hip and black. Whites called the area around 133rd Street, where many of the nightspots clustered, "the Jungle." You could find just about anything in the Jungle: black-and-tan clubs, dancing waiters, transvestites on display. There, almost anything went on in public: drinking, of course, but also smoking marijuana and lurid sexual displays. Visitors gravitated to two nightspots—the Cotton Club and Connie's Inn—that would become as important to the development of jazz in the 1920s and 1930s as the brothels and honky-tonks of New Orleans had been in the previous decades. In years to come, Louis would become familiar with each place, and so fond of Harlem that it became his adopted community. New Orleans would always be the home of his memories and dreams, but New York became the city of his everyday life.

Like everything else about Harlem, the Cotton Club was brand-spanking-new, having opened its doors in late 1923. In no time, it had become the best-known jazz club in Harlem, if not the country, partly because it admitted white patrons only. Although the Cotton Club became synonymous with Harlem, many blacks who actually lived in Harlem hadn't heard of it, and even if they had, they couldn't gain admission. Interracial couples were not merely barred but risked a beating if they so much as appeared before the club's terrifying-looking bouncers. Even W. C. Handy, the blind "father of the blues," was shut out one night when he tried to listen to his own compositions being performed within. In many ways, the segregationist policies of the Cotton Club in its heyday were far worse than the customs Louis had left behind in New Orleans.

Inside the club itself, a crowd of about seven hundred white patrons celebrated night after night, drawn by its light-skinned, "high yellow" chorus girls; they were, as the endlessly repeated slogan promised, "Tall, tan, and terrific." From the start, the Cotton Club was an expensive, swanky place calculated to appeal to its wealthy clientele who arrived in their limousines. Its shows owed more to the lavish Broadway spectacles popularized by the impresario Florenz Ziegfeld than they did to the raw honky-tonks of New Orleans or the boisterous dance halls of Chicago. A typical Cotton Club presentation featured lavish staging, elaborate costumes, and scores composed by accomplished Broadway composers such as Harold Arlen, but the club still had an energy that exceeded the decorous bounds of the Broadway stage. Feathers flew, thighs flashed, and drums pounded to simulate an "African" intensity and sensibility. When the evening was over, the exhausted black performers retreated to their tiny dressing rooms, and the white patrons sped home in their chauffeured limousines with fond memories of their wild night in Harlem.

Nearby, Connie's Inn, which became almost a second home to Louis, favored music over spectacle. Located in a basement on Seventh Avenue, close to another Harlem landmark, the Lafayette Theatre, Connie's Inn was somewhat better integrated into the surrounding community. The proprietors, Connie and George Immerman, had, in a previous incarnation, managed a popular Harlem delicatessen, and Fats Waller—the "harmful little armful" himself—worked there as a delivery boy in his youth. Outside Connie's Inn, the Tree of Hope spread its boughs. It was said that rubbing its bark was sure to bring luck, and legions of entertainers and musicians came there to touch wood and find work. And they often did, because bookers sought them out in that exact location. At other clubs such as Smalls' Paradise, jazz musicians honed their skills, but whites rarely ventured further afield than Connie's Inn. *Variety* advised, "There are one or two other 7th Avenue rendezvous which may be possessed of more native color, but not considered very healthy as a general thing for the white trade." In fact, some whites were baffled by the music they heard up in Harlem. Rudy Vallee, the whitest of white crooners, remarked after a visit, "Truly, I have no definite conception of what 'jazz'

is, but I believe the term should be applied . . . to the weird orchestra efforts of various colored bands up in Harlem. . . . These bands
have a style all their own, and at times it seems as though pandemonium
has broken loose. Most of the time there is no distinguishable melody."
That was not at all the way Vallee learned to sing at Yale. Within a few
years, however, he revised his opinion of jazz, and even wrote an introduction to Louis's first autobiography, in which he claimed, "the author and I
have a great deal in common." He also asserted, "I believe I was among
the first to recognize his genius." Both comments pleasantly astonished
Louis.

Despite the brilliant musicians they employed and the revolutionary
music they presented, the Harlem clubs were not exactly benign institutions. The mob ran many of them. Louis had remained oblivious to organized crime in New Orleans, but now that he was in New York, he had to
deal with a deadlier variant. "To most whites, the ginmills of Harlem mean
only one thing, the underworld," said Milton "Mezz" Mezzrow, a white
saxophonist and drug dealer who deeply identified with blacks. "There's a
world of difference between the ofay underworld and the colored underworld," he explained in his eccentric memoir, *Really the Blues*. "You see, all
of Harlem—the whole colored race, in a sense—is one great underworld,
because practically all of these people are shoved to the bottom of the pile
and kept there on account of the one thing they have in common, the
pigmentation of their skin." Mezzrow's assessment of organized crime's
influence over Harlem's nightclubs was painfully accurate.

In its previous incarnation, the Cotton Club had been known as the
Club DeLuxe, a nightclub run by Jack Johnson, the boxing champion.
When he ran out of money, Johnson, who was black, brought in Owney
Madden, notorious bootlegger and gangster, as a partner. Madden's blood
money gave the DeLuxe's successor, the Cotton Club, its sparkle. Over at
Connie's Inn, the Immermans were fronting for Dutch Schultz, possibly the
most loathsome gangster of the Prohibition era. Nominally a bootlegger,
Schultz trafficked in murder, bribery, and corruption of every sort. A relentlessly hostile personality, he hated everyone—"He was a vicious,
pathologically suspicious killer who kept his people in line through sheer
terror," said Willie Sutton, the bank robber. Now that Louis was in New
York, it was only a matter of time until he would have to confront Schultz
and other gangsters like him.

. . .

ouis was not yet a celebrity in New York. Few people outside the jazz world had heard of him. The reputation he'd acquired from his recordings quickly dissipated. Furthermore, the New Orleans-style music he played was considered rude and unsophisticated, in other words, a liability. Harlem favored the polished style of his new boss, Fletcher "Smack" Henderson. He was unlike any other bandleader Louis had encountered: sophisticated, college-educated, easygoing to the point of diffidence. He was a man about town in his immaculate suits, his fine hair smoothed back from his ample forehead in a flawless flowing arc, and he was light-skinned, which enhanced his social acceptability among whites and even among blacks. Born in Cuthbert, Georgia, on December 18, 1898, Smack was only two-and-a-half years older than Louis, yet he was already famous. Even more remarkably, his background wasn't in music, it was in chemistry. He received his degree in that field from the University of Atlanta over the opposition of his parents, who considered chemistry too hazardous a profession for their son. There was music in his family—his mother taught piano, his father was a school principal—but Smack evinced no interest in music or jazz until he arrived in New York. He arrived in 1920, just four years before Armstrong, not to pursue music, but to get an advanced degree in chemistry at Columbia University. The hand of destiny intervened when he casually found work as a song plugger and demonstrator with the Pace-Handy Music Company, a job similar to Lil Hardin's first position in Chicago. The following year, Harry Pace went out on his own to launch Black Swan Records, and he took Smack with him. He quickly went from a song plugger to accompanist to conductor of the Black Swan Troubadours, the label's in-house orchestra. On the side, he performed with the Harlem Symphony and as a vocal accompanist.

Black Swan had another rising star in its stable, a sultry and mellifluous young blues singer named Ethel Waters, who belonged to the Black Swan Troubadours. Pace decided to send Ethel Waters and the Troubadours on tour, accompanied by Smack leading a small band christened the Black Swan Jazz Masters. When Smack's parents heard about the plan, they were appalled. To allay their fears, Pace obligingly brought the Hendersons up north to meet Miss Waters, who made a favorable impression on them, and the tour, now much delayed, finally got underway.

There were some wild times on that tour, incidents that confirmed his parents' worst fears. When they were not performing, the men often visited brothels in the various cities in which they played. In Louisville, Garvin Bushell, the clarinetist, so endeared himself to a madam that she kidnapped the lad and held him hostage. Garvin escaped in time for the band's Chicago engagement, but shortly afterward he and Gus Aiken, the trumpeter, were arrested outside another brothel and sent to jail. It fell to Smack, as the bandleader, to negotiate the release of his musicians from jail. He managed it, but discipline was never his strong suit. At the same time, he found the going rough with Ethel Waters, who kept trying to get him away from the symphonic music that came so easily to him and to imbue him with the spirit of the blues.

The education of Fletcher Henderson, musical and otherwise, continued as the tour headed south, to New Orleans, minus half the band, who wanted nothing to do with Louisiana and its reputation for mistreatment of blacks. They preferred to work their way back to New York, playing the dining car of a train in exchange for transportation. Smack found replacements willing to venture into New Orleans, where, despite everything, his band scored a huge success during their engagement in the Lyric Theatre and in radio broadcasts originating from it. It was now early 1922, and it is likely that Smack first heard Louis Armstrong play the trumpet at this moment. Louis did not leave the city for Chicago until July, and the club where he was performing, the Elite, happened to be just two doors from the Lyric, where the Black Swan artists held forth. Having lost his trumpeter in Chicago, Fletcher was so impressed by Louis's playing that he invited him to join up with him then and there.

Afraid to leave New Orleans, Louis temporized. He said he would go only if Smack took both him and his friend, the drummer Zutty Singleton. Of course, it was Louis that Henderson wanted, and no one else, so the offer evaporated. Had Louis joined Henderson's band at this point, his career might have taken off faster than it did. Instead of rambling around Chicago and recording for little one-horse outfits like Gennett, he would have gone straight to New York and the center of the Harlem Renaissance. He would have recorded for Black Swan, and his star would have risen along with Fletcher Henderson. He would have been an "overnight" success. But Louis never regretted the meandering course his career took: "I still had a lot to learn about jazz playing and there in New Orleans . . . I was living and working all the time around men who could teach me what I needed. Often it's better, I am sure, to come on a little slowly. You'll probably last a lot longer." Experience bore out Louis's assessment. By the time he did get to New York to join Fletcher Henderson's Orchestra, he had been strengthened and toughened by his two years in Chicago, and he was a different musician, and a different person, far more daring and self-confident.

After Louis declined the offer, and Smack returned to New York, he always remembered the remarkable hornman he'd heard in New Orleans. From then on, Henderson's career soared. He seemed to be everywhere, performing with his orchestra; accompanying the most famous blues singers of the day, including Bessie Smith and Ma Rainey; issuing records under the Black Swan label; and hiring young musicians. Two of his discoveries—Coleman Hawkins and Don Redman—became famous in their own right. Redman's skill as an arranger flourished during his time with Henderson. Redman and Smack started by picking out stock arrangements of popular show music, which Redman then adapted to suit the orchestra. Jazz arrangements still allowed plenty of room for improvisation. They tended to be casual affairs, indications of chords and harmonies and instrumentation; thus, the musicians referred to them as "charts" rather than "scores." In keeping with the musical fashion of the times, he built up the saxophones into an entire section, and then he went one step further by writing not just harmonies but intricate solos for the saxophones. Through his charts, a talented arranger such as Redman could exert an awesome influence over a band's sound, more, even, than the conductor.

By 1923, Henderson had won a reputation as a new style of jazz musician, polished, aloof, even inscrutable. His orchestra's sound, thanks to Don Redman's charts, contained the seeds of what would later become the most influential trend in popular music—"swing." Henderson didn't seem to realize or acknowledge the extent of his orchestra's influence and reputation. Asked about the origins of his musical style, he shook his head and smiled, but had nothing to say on the subject. Meanwhile, a black newspaper described his outfit as "the greatest, not at all like the average Negro orchestra, but in a class with the good white orchestras." Paul Whiteman exclaimed to the band members after hearing Henderson, "If Fletcher was a white man, he would be a millionaire." Although Whiteman's assessment seems a slap in the face, he meant it as high praise, and it contained a good deal of truth. The same could be said of many other black entertainers and artists, including Louis Armstrong.

Smack's standing increased once again when he took up residence at the Roseland Ballroom, at Broadway and 51st Street, in the heart of Manhattan. To play the Roseland was an unmistakable sign for the Fletcher Henderson Orchestra—because it was the preeminent dance hall in New York, or, for that matter, the country. This was the era of ballrooms; they were springing up in cities across America. Admission to the Roseland cost about a dollar, there were plenty of taxi dancers on hand, and everyone was welcome—everyone who was white, that is. The sole exceptions were the black musicians who came to listen to their colleagues; they were permitted on the premises as long as they remained in a special area, out of sight of the white patrons. Henderson's nine-member orchestra replaced a group of New Orleans musicians led by Armand J. Piron. The homesick Southerners yearned to return to New Orleans, and once they did, Henderson and his men took over on September 8, 1924. At the outset of the engagement, the cornetist, the talented but erratic (i.e. hard-drinking) Joe Smith, failed to keep pace with the others. His departure prompted Smack to invite Louis Armstrong to join the orchestra at this moment.

As he surveyed his new colleagues, Louis became terribly anxious. For all the musical sophistication he'd acquired in Chicago and with Fate Marable, he still preferred to play by ear, with only a cursory glance at written notes. Now he had to contend with an *arrangement*. "Where I had come from I wasn't used to playing in bands where there were a lot of parts for everybody to read. Shucks, all one in the band had to do is to go to some show and hear a good number. He keeps it in his head until he reaches us. He hums it a couple of times, and from then on we had a new number to throw on the bands that advertised in the wagons on the corner on the following Sunday. That's how we stayed so famous in New Orleans—we had a new number for the customers every week—and now I am in New York getting ready to join the biggest best band in New York. We played the first number down. The name of the tune was 'By the Waters of Minnetonka.' Still nobody said anything."

Henderson's concern about Louis's reading ability and musical refinement increased when he gave him his part, a "new arrangement of a medley of beautiful Irish waltzes." Louis seemed to stare at it in disbelief: "I had just left Chicago, where the way we used to do it was just take the wind in, and take what's left and blow out—and now I got to watch this *part*." He never was one to dwell on technique or fret unnecessarily about breath control or embouchure, but these charts confused him. "Now, those parts were well marked with all the dynamics of the music, and at one point the orchestration was indicated as *fff* with a diminuendo down to *pp*," by which Henderson meant, simply, that Louis's part was to go from very loud to very soft, with no opportunity to improvise or surprise.

"The band followed these notations and was playing very softly, while Louis still played his part at full volume. I stopped the band and said, 'Louis, you are not following the arrangement.' "

Taken aback, Louis insisted he was "reading everything on this sheet."

"But Louis, how about that *pp*?" Smack asked. Why wasn't he playing softer at that point?

"Oh, I thought that meant 'pound plenty.' "

Everyone on the stand burst into laughter, and according to Smack "there was no tension after that." Though he still relied largely on his ear and his memory, Louis quickly mastered the arrangements.

Next, he had to contend with a change in instrument. He started out playing cornet, but to Smack and the other members, the instrument sounded too shrill. Elmer Chambers and Howard Scott, the two other trumpet players, took Louis to a music store where he bought himself a trumpet. Until this time, Louis primarily played the larger, bolder cornet, but the cornet was going out of style, and the Fletcher Henderson Orchestra was determined to stay at the forefront of musical trends. Now that Elmer, Scott, and Louis all had trumpets, Smack was satisfied. The change of instrument didn't bother Louis at all—he knew how to make the trumpet sing and sting and soar as well as any cornet. He said he simply felt awkward holding a fat cornet while the others had sleek trumpets. He was even experimenting with the trombone, playing it during rehearsals, but he decided not to pursue it and never recorded with it.

"Finally I cut loose one night while we were down at the Roseland Ballroom and all the boys just couldn't play for watching me," Louis said, a boast confirmed by band member Howard Scott. "Louis played that opening night at Roseland, and my goodness, people stopped dancing to come around and listen to him. He was scared at first. He said, 'How am I doing,

Scottie?' I said, 'Listen, just close your eyes and play what you feel in your body, in your heart, in your mind. Just let it go, Louis. Be yourself, that's all. Forget about the people. So he did. And they could hear him out in the street, and we were told that there were people passing by that stopped, listening to him. He was so loud. Well, that was the first night. The next night, you couldn't get in the place. Just that quick, it had gone all around about this new trumpet player at the Roseland."

Louis's over-the-top style of playing and improvising upset the orchestra's equilibrium, and the other musicians struggled to match his furious pace. Henderson observed, "There were a lot of serious musicians in that orchestra of mine, and they were a little too stiff at first for Louis's taste. Finally, a fight developed between the trombonist and the bass player, and they had their coats off and were really going after each other before I quieted them, and this eased everything for Louis. For the first time he said, 'Oh, I'm gonna like this band.' "

After that incident, Louis quickly became known as a hardworking and reliable member of the orchestra, but his colleagues mocked his utilitarian manner of dress. "When he first came, we kidded him a lot about his thick-soled shoes and his long drawers," said Kaiser Marshall, the drummer. "He had to take so much about those drawers that he finally said to me, 'All right, I'll take them off, but if I catch cold in the winter time I'll blame it on you.' " While Louis sent his money straight to Lil in Chicago, the other fellows in the orchestra spent lavishly on their wardrobes, boasting that their shoes cost $110, and spats were *de rigueur*.

Whatever he lacked in sartorial style he made up for in musical panache. The keening emotional quality of his solos began to influence the others members of the orchestra, who were emboldened to interject more expressiveness and feeling into their playing. He learned from them, as well. Had Louis continued to play as Oliver did instead of joining a dance band, he would have been in danger of becoming passé. Instead, he straddled two musical worlds, one foot firmly in the New Orleans jazz and minstrel traditions, the other tentatively exploring the sophisticated new arena of dance bands. The tension between these two extremes would define his musical personality.

Louis saw himself as not just a musician, but an entertainer, a stage personality, and he tested the limits of the Henderson organization whenever he could. He often mugged his way through numbers, totally at variance with the stone-faced members of the orchestra. He was also dying to sing, if only Smack would let him. Louis found an opportunity. Thursday nights at the Roseland were given over to vaudeville. Ruby Keeler, Bing Crosby, and George Raft (a tap dancer at the time) were among the young stars who came to prominence on these occasions. Finally, one Thursday, Louis offered himself up to the audience as a singer. Kaiser Marshall described how Louis fared that night: "We got Louis out on the stage and he did 'Everybody Loves My Baby, But My Baby Don't Love Nobody But Me.' He sang it and he played it on the trumpet; the crowd surely went for it. He had the idea he wasn't in competition for the prize, but they made him come out and line up with the other acts, and when they held the money over his head the applause was so loud that there wasn't any question about it; he just walked off with first prize. From then on they used to cry for Louis every Thursday night, and he would play his horn and sing his songs."

The singing was just the beginning. He loved taking the audience into his world, and introducing them to a repertoire of imaginary characters based on stock minstrel figures and his memories of New Orleans. One of his favorite creations was the Preacher. How Louis loved to imitate preachers, and satirize their avarice and lechery. He'd shout, he'd jump, he'd deliver mock sermons. He'd don sunglasses and robes for his act, and use his low, asphalt voice to spine-tingling effect.

As it became apparent that he was going to be spending some time with the Fletcher Henderson Orchestra, he took an apartment in Harlem. He believed he was all but invisible to whites, but that he'd become well-known to New York's black population. "Nobody much on Broadway had ever heard of me," he remarked, "but Harlem saved my life." He made the most of the neighborhood. On a night off from the Roseland, he ventured over to the Savoy Dance Hall, where he took a trumpet solo. As he blew, he told himself he'd finally made it to "Harlem's biggest and finest ballroom." He went over so well that he was invited back for a second night. "Was I proud!"

As his reputation spread, Duke Ellington repeatedly brought his orchestra down to the Roseland to hear Louis blow. "When Smack's band hit town and Louis was with them, the guys had never heard anything just like it," said Duke. "There weren't the words coined for describing that kick. And Louis was no exception, he carried his horn round just like everybody else," said Duke. "Everyone on the street was talking about the guy." Absent were the insolent opponents who had tried to humiliate him in Chicago. Rex Stewart, a formidable trumpet man in his own right, said that "he was so tough on trumpet that nobody dared challenge him. Come to think of it, I don't remember ever seeing him at a session. He didn't come to us—we had to go to him. I shall never forget the scrambling to get to one tiny window backstage at Roseland Ballroom, just to catch Satchmo putting the 'heat to the beat' with Fletcher Henderson." After hearing Louis, Stewart "went mad with the rest of the town. I tried to walk like him, talk like him, eat like him, sleep like him. I even bought a pair of big policeman's shoes like he used to wear and stood outside his apartment waiting for him to come out so I could look at him. Finally, I got to shake hands and talk with him."

Armstrong imitators soon found that hitting the high notes wasn't as easy as Louis made it look. "You used to see more trumpet players with a little patch over their lip," said Howard Scott. " 'Say, what's the matter with you, fellow? What did you do, hit yourself? Cut your lip?' 'Oh, no, man, I was just practicing.' Come to find out they were trying to hit those high notes Louis hit. And Louis hit them with ease. They were trying to squeeze them out. They'd split their lips and everything. I never believed in that. I believe: be yourself and be natural and you're much better appreciated. See, Louis was natural."

Being "natural" did not prevent Louis from being extremely careful about his precious lip. He knew that without it, he was nothing, and he lived in permanent fear of splitting it, as his imitators frequently did. That was one reason why he wanted to blow *and* sing—to give his overworked chops a rest. He experimented with lip salves, and when he found a concoction he judged effective, he did not hesitate to recommend it to other players, who were eager to try anything that Louis recommended. One of them, Roy "Little Jazz" Eldridge, recalled what happened when he applied Louis's special salve: "I put that shit on my lip, and I couldn't play for a week! It was good for him, but it didn't work for me *no* kind of way!"

These were giddy days, Louis bouncing back and forth between being a nobody downtown and a somebody uptown. He was also recording again. Immediately after his arrival in New York, he recorded with Fletcher

Henderson's orchestra for Regal, Columbia, and Pathé. On October 7, 1924, they recorded "Manda" and "Go 'Long, Mule"; and the following week, they produced four more sides: "Tell Me, Dreamy Eyes," "My Rose Marie," "Don't Forget You'll Regret Day By Day," and "Shanghai Shuffle." To be sure, these recordings showcased the orchestra and Don Redman's sparkling arrangements more than Louis, who was let loose for only a few bars here and there. Yet even within these limitations, his sound is unique, distinctive, and once again, way ahead of the musicians surrounding him. The early recordings he made with the orchestra demonstrate two things: that he made his trumpet sing and that he did not fit into the confines of this decorous-sounding orchestra. He sounds as if he exists within his own musical universe.

The following month, November, Louis and the orchestra returned to the studio, strutting their stuff for Banner, Columbia, and Vocalion. Redman's arrangements were better than ever, but Louis's pyrotechnics seemed out of place. As the other members of the orchestra were hitting the right notes and staying on the beat, Louis, in his all-too-brief solos, was exploring the wonder of hitting the wrong notes, or the unexpected notes. He hit notes an octave higher or lower than the ear anticipated, or several notes away from the "correct" notes. He spilled notes at the "wrong" time, a trifle early or agonizingly late. His notes made listeners work to fill in the gaps he deliberately left in the music. In this way, Louis improvised an alternate structure that suggested the melody, but expanded it infinitely. By exploring harmonics and tinkering with the rhythm, he prefigured the outlines of jazz improvisation for decades to come. Even bebop, the new type of jazz that flourished after World War II and threatened to render Louis's approach obsolete, is based on the daring ear games he interjected into these seemingly harmless, toe-tapping tunes.

In late November, a deeply skeptical Henderson allowed Louis to make his first vocal recording. "About three weeks after he joined us he asked me if he could sing a number," Henderson said. "I know I wondered what he could possibly do with the big fish horn voice of his, but finally I told him to try it." The song was that reliable hit of the day, "Everybody Loves My Baby," usually sung by a female vocalist. To be on the safe side, the orchestra also recorded an instrumental version to make sure there would be at least one decent take. Considering that Louis was destined to become the most influential vocalist in jazz, and keeping in mind the almost unbearable passion he brought to his singing, the recording amounted to very little—just Louis shouting in that guttural voice of his at the end of the song. One can almost see Smack smiling inscrutably as he listened to the result, as if to say, "I told you so."

Louis never waxed another vocal with Fletcher Henderson's orchestra, but throughout the following year, on at least nine separate dates, he recorded with them as a trumpeter. One of the tunes immortalized during this period was a composition Louis himself had helped to compose, "Sugar Foot Stomp" (recorded on May 29, 1925, for Columbia). This was actually his signature number from his days with King Oliver's Creole Jazz Band, the "Dippermouth Blues." Redman's arrangement updated the song, which now sounded as though it had shed its threadbare overalls for a stylish tuxedo. Louis delivers his "wah-wah" solo with offhand dignity rather than a mocking rasp, suggesting he had belatedly discovered this was actually a terribly elegant song. Smack himself considered this one of the best recordings the orchestra ever made, if not *the* best, and it became the one most associated with the still-developing sound of New York jazz. None of the glory or credit devolved on Louis, however, and it is no wonder he felt overlooked and underappreciated.

Despite his mounting dissatisfaction with Fletcher Henderson's orchestra, Louis's last recordings with the unit came as a revelation. He remains his inimitable and illimitable musical self, but the orchestra and its once stolid hornmen have been transformed into something shiny and new. On earlier recordings, one can practically see the musicians tapping their toes to the rhythm. Now, they are infinitely looser; actually swinging. By the time they recorded "T.N.T."—October 21, 1925, a bit more than a year after Louis's arrival—they sound positively hip. Joe Smith, who rejoined the band, sounds so good one might think it was Louis blowing—which is precisely the effect Joe Smith intended.

During the winter of 1924–1925 Louis was busier than ever before. He was playing and recording with Fletcher Henderson, and taking brief gigs in Harlem, and he launched a new career as an accompanist for blues singers. In January 1925, he hit the very top, recording with the celebrated Bessie Smith.

Bessie Smith was a phenomenon, and everyone was in awe of her,

Louis included. She was larger than life, an unpredictable, volcanic, mesmerizing presence. Her voice had an unmatched power to move listeners, and she was well aware of her gift. Before a concert, she often explained that she was "going to walk me one tonight." That meant that she was going to focus her singing ability and strength on one member of the audience, usually a man, and send him into a trance with it, and when he was in this trance, he would "walk"—that is, stagger toward her, as if approaching a highly sexed deity. When he awoke, he would have no memory of the incident. Walkers were frequent at her concerts, and she took them as proof of her power.

Bessie's status as a recording star was of very recent vintage. In 1923, her debut record sold seventy-five thousand copies for Columbia and raised public awareness of the race record phenomenon. Part of the reason for her success was her remarkable diction. Listeners could understand every word, every syllable, and every drop of feeling she brought to her songs. She never treated words casually, and for this reason she was capable of making innocuous lyrics into something dark, bitter, and soulful. Gunther Schuller, the jazz performer, composer, and critic observed, "Bessie's fine microtonal shadings, the various 'flatnesses' with which she could color a pitch in relation to a word or vowel, the way she could move into the center of a pitch with a short, beautifully executed scoop or 'fall' out of it without a little moaning slide; or the way she could hit a note square in the middle— these are all part of a personal, masterful technique of great subtlety, despite the frequently boisterous mood of her language."

Offstage, she was tough as nails. She stood six feet tall and took no lip from anyone, especially her husband, a detective named Jack Gee, who was considerably smaller than she. "She looked like she could pick Jack Gee up by the collar with one hand," a friend of theirs remarked. At night, she would lie in bed with a butcher knife and hiss to her husband, "When you go to sleep I'm going to kill you. I'm going to stick you with the knife, man." Jack would reply, "You start over here, I'm going to blow your brains out."

Bessie had a variety of lovers, male and female. She spent a great deal of time in the company of Richard Morgan, whom she had known ever since her youth in Birmingham, Alabama. He became one of the leading bootleggers on Chicago's South Side, which automatically made him a leading figure in the community. "Although he was not himself a musician," wrote Bessie's biographer, Chris Albertson, "one might say he was a patron of the arts," for he spent much time in the company of jazz musicians, and he bought his young nephew, Lionel Hampton, the vibraphonist, his first marimba and his first set of drums. Bessie and Morgan loved to entertain musicians, and Louis, in his Chicago days, had been one of their regulars. He was completely in his element in these parties, but Lil, who accompanied him, felt lost in the crowd. It was Bessie, not Louis, who dominated these affairs. She was, at the time, better known than he, and her personality was even more powerful than his.

Louis found the singer's charismatic presence intimidating. "Bessie Smith was a very quiet woman—didn't bother nobody. But, God, don't mess with her," he said. "She had a quick temper. Made a lot of money, though. A cat came up to her one day, wanted change for a thousand-dollar bill. Trying to see if she had it. Bessie said, 'Yeah.' She just raised up the front of her dress and there was a carpenter's apron and she just pulled that change out of it. That was her bank."

Like Louis, Bessie eventually made her way to New York, and the two reunited there to record on January 14, 1925. Even here, she continued to dominate Louis, as she did nearly everyone else. From the moment she entered the Columbia Studio at Columbus Circle, she made it plain this was *her* record date, and *she* would be in control. As far as she and Columbia Records were concerned, Louis Armstrong was Fletcher Henderson's latest discovery—an accomplished sideman, to be sure, but he did not sell records. Bessie Smith sold records, and that made all the difference. She was the star, "the Greatest and Highest Salaried Race Star in the World," according to her publicity.

Despite the potential for conflict, Louis and Bessie developed an uncanny rapport and collaborated flawlessly. Louis treated her voice as a gem requiring the finest setting he could conjure from his horn. Their very first number, "The St. Louis Blues," drew strength and conviction from Bessie's sour, plangent rendering of Handy's lyrics, in contrast to Louis's delicate filigrees. His thin, liquid tone perfectly complemented her smoky voice. Their performance *is* the blues—straight, no chaser—and this recording became an indisputable classic.

They waxed four other numbers that day: "Reckless Blues," "Cold in Hand Blues," "Sobbin' Hearted Blues," and "You've Been a Good Ole Wagon." Each one has an enduring fascination, and "Sobbin' Hearted

Blues" is especially noteworthy because both Bessie and Louis really bend the rhythm here, getting so far behind the beat that they seem to be daring each other to new extremes, and Louis's replies on the trumpet match Bessie's singing so carefully that the result sounds more like two people singing than a vocalist and instrumentalist trading phrases. The recordings were released to acclaim, adding luster to the reputations of both artists. Most everyone applauded Louis's sensitivity as an accompanist. But Bessie herself was unimpressed by his horn playing. Even their peerless performance of "St. Louis Blues" left her indifferent to his tone and musical instincts. She said she preferred Joe Smith, even though his playing bore Louis's unmistakable stamp. Still, none dared to question her judgment. Bessie lived in her own world, musically, and there was no room for anyone else.

After Bessie Smith, Louis went on to accompany an ever-expanding roster of other distinguished blues singers, including Ma Rainey and Alberta Hunter, Margaret Johnson, and Clara Smith. Between October 1924 and May 1925, scarcely a week went by that he was not in the studio backing one singer or another.

There was more. In addition to all his other gigs, he was recording regularly with Clarence Williams, the New Orleans composer and music publisher who had never paid him the twenty-five dollars he once promised for Louis's composition, "Shimmy Like My Sister Kate." These days, Williams was the leading black music publisher, and a wealthy man. At the peak of his fame, a journalist caught up with him and asked, "Mr. Williams, if you were a white man, you'd probably be worth a million dollars today, wouldn't you? Think hard now, wouldn't you rather have been born a white man?" Williams responded with a roar of laughter and said, "Why, I'd never have written the blues if I had been white. You don't study to write blues, you *feel* them."

Williams's entrepreneurial instincts prompted him to assemble the Clarence Williams Blue Five. The shifting personnel included many of the best-known names in the volatile New York jazz scene. Most, like Louis Armstrong, were recent arrivals, or transients. Their number included Sidney Bechet, Louis's old friend and rival from New Orleans; Don Redman, Henderson's arranger; Buster Bailey, another Henderson saxophonist; Coleman Hawkins; Buddy Christian, a New Orleans banjoist; and Clarence himself, at the piano. This group was innovative because it performed not before a live audience but in the studio, before a microphone; thus the band easily accommodated personnel that changed from one record date to the next. At times, the Clarence Williams Blue Five suddenly expanded into the Blue Seven and then contracted again to its original size. Furthermore, the band rarely, if ever, played "the blues," but the name proved to be good marketing. Despite his soaring reputation, Louis did not have star billing; pride of place usually went to Eva Taylor, a blues singer of moderate talent and immense vibrato who happened to be married to Clarence Williams.

Louis put aside his reservations about Williams's business practices long enough to record some wonderfully endearing tunes with the Blue Five during that busy winter. Williams allowed him more leeway than Henderson did, and the recordings reveal Louis at ease and flourishing with like-minded musicians. The Blue Five's most popular record came early in their sequence of recordings—it was a version of "Everybody Loves My Baby," sung competently by Eva Taylor. At the end, Louis drives the song over the top with a cornet solo of spiraling power. One instant, his throbbing notes are menacing, the next, they are comic, and the ambiguity makes his solo compelling. Louis achieves his darker emotional cast by forgoing his customary clarion tone in favor of rasping notes, as if he were playing a slide trombone. He even descends into "dirty tone," almost panting through his horn. In Louis's hands, the result is brassy and coarse, but brilliantly calculated—a model of the art of concealing art.

Lightning struck again on January 8, 1925, when Armstrong and Bechet dueled on "Cake Walking Babies from Home," a light tune concocted by Williams and a few other collaborators. Sidney and Louis had recorded this same tune only three weeks earlier, backing Alberta Hunter, with another pickup outfit known as the Red Onion Jazz Babies. On that occasion, Bechet seemed firmly in command, but now, Louis pulled ahead of his jealous rival by imitating Eva Taylor's vocal and then surpassing and transforming it into something strange, new, and wonderful on his horn. For perhaps the first time since his arrival in New York, he displays increased confidence and technique, especially near the end of the song, when he digs down deep and comes up with a classic New Orleans flourish, a repeat stop-time phrase (pausing at the beat, then unexpectedly resuming), but Louis trills so quickly that he turns this near-gimmick into a bravura musical climax. This was Louis's third recorded masterpiece in his brief but extremely busy career in the studio.

. . .

In what little free time he had, Louis visited various Harlem nightclubs, listening to other musicians. His vantage point was usually of the stage door, since these were "whites only" institutions. One night at the Cotton Club, a chorus girl named Fanny Cotton caught his eye. He came back again and again to watch her, summoned the nerve to introduce himself, and they soon became friends. Their routine was always the same. He waited for her each night, and as soon as she got off work, the two of them retreated to a Harlem gin mill, where their relationship flowered in the darkness over drinks.

Not much is known about Fanny, and Louis wanted it that way. One of the few people to whom he confided any information about the affair—years after it had ended—was his friend Robert Goffin. Although he was usually nakedly revealing about his relationships, especially with women, he was unusually circumspect concerning, even apologetic about, Fanny, for he knew that she jeopardized both his marriage to Lil and his nascent career as a trumpet virtuoso. Louis was so caught up with his own needs that he did not stop to wonder about what Lil might be doing while she was alone in Chicago. For Louis, the concept of fidelity was infinitely elastic; wherever he went, he heard Black Benny's whispered admonition to make sure he always had more than one woman. It is not surprising that the twenty-four-year-old Armstrong found himself a girlfriend in Harlem; he was a fast-rising star, living alone, far from Lil. Behind all his fierce blowing and strutting in New York, he was enmeshed in an intricate power struggle with her, and both love and success were at stake. Although his affair with Fanny appeared to lessen his dependency on Lil, in the manner prescribed by Black Benny, it actually diminished his leverage in his marriage. So he cringed at the thought of Fanny rather than rejoicing in their romance.

No matter how often he sought solace in Fanny's arms, Louis continued to long for Chicago and for Lil. He wrote to her frequently, and daydreamed about forming his own band in Chicago. Finally, on May 31, 1925, the marathon stint at the Roseland ended. Luck seemed to favor Louis when Henderson obtained a long gig for the orchestra in Chicago, where he could mend his fraying relationship with Lil, but at the last minute the booking fell through. In its place, Henderson scheduled a series of one-night stands throughout New England over the course of the entire summer. At the beginning of June, Louis and the rest of the orchestra took a train to Lawrence, Massachusetts. The center of a railroad hub, the city served as their base throughout the season, and they made excursions from it to their gigs in New Hampshire, Maine, and Connecticut. They played dates as varied as Smith College in Northampton, Massachusetts, and the Catholic Youth Club in Manchester, New Hampshire. In Woonsocket, New Hampshire, Smack let Louis pull out all the stops during a rendition of "Hard-Hearted Hannah," spilling out one chorus after another from his shimmering trumpet, electrifying and astounding the young audience.

During the summer months, the orchestra resided in boardinghouses in Lawrence. Louis lived alone, apparently self-sufficient, enjoying a brief return to innocence. "Was quite a thrilling experience to have most of my days off and we would go swimming," he wrote in a 1943 memoir. "Buster Bailey was exceptionally good at swimming. He would swim all the way across that river [the Merrimac] in Lawrence, Mass. Of course, I am not too bad myself at swimming. In fact, it is one of my favorite hobbies, outside of typing. I love that also." Whenever the band's schedule took them to Boston, Louis trysted with Fanny, who came up from New York to see him. Their affair became so serious that he promised to marry her if she would only stay with him on the road. She left anyway, and Louis remained with the orchestra for the balance of the summer, yearning for Fanny, fearful of Lil.

Shortly after Labor Day, the entire orchestra returned to New York, where they began a new engagement at the Roseland, beginning on October 4. As he walked the streets of Harlem, all Louis could think about was Fanny, who had retreated to Pittsburgh. He had no idea when or if he would see her again. One night, when he was saddened, forlorn, momentarily defeated by the contradictory promptings of his heart, he wandered into a gin mill on 131st Street, ignored the prostitutes and the other musicians, and proceeded to drink himself into oblivion.

"I'd rather drink muddy water, Lord, sleep in a hollow log . . . I'd
rather drink muddy water, Lord, sleep in a hollow log . . . Than to
be up here in New York, treated like a dirty dog."

By now, Lil sensed that something was seriously wrong with her husband. As always, she was determined to remake his career to her satisfaction.

Tired of urging Louis by letter, she took the train to New York to see for herself what in the world had become of him.

The first thing she did after arriving was to check Louis's billing in the orchestra. To her dismay, she discovered he had none. In fact, one of the few times his name appeared in an advertisement for the orchestra, it was near the bottom of the roster, in microscopic type, and misspelled: "Lewis Armstrong." His lack of status was an embarrassment, but, as she recalled, "I didn't say anything but to myself." Instead, she told Louis, "You are situated all right. I'm going on back to Chicago." If she knew anything about the way her man was carrying on with Fanny, she did not let on, nor did she allow any hints to escape about her own extramarital activities.

Off she went, scheming to lure her husband back to her side and to put him properly in the limelight, where she believed he belonged. Back in Chicago again, she went directly to the Dreamland, where she had held court at the time she met Louis.

"I want to put a band in," she told the manager, Bill Bottoms.

"Who you got?"

"I got some good musicians, but I want to bring my husband back from New York. I want him to be featured and I want $75 a week for him."

"Well, nobody else is getting but $55."

"I know, but he's coming back and he's coming back from New York and I want $75. And I want his name out there in front."

"I think you're crazy," Bottoms argued, "nobody knows a thing about that guy yet."

"Never mind, you just put it up there. They know me and they'll come in," Lil insisted.

She persuaded him to manufacture a sign that announced:

LOUIS ARMSTRONG, THE WORLD'S GREATEST TRUMPET PLAYER

Having successfully concluded her negotiations, she wrote to her husband, "You can give Fletcher your two weeks' notice and come on back home because I got a job for you for $75 a week." Louis did not believe it was possible she had been able to get him that kind of money, and he told Lil he would stay on with Henderson. Despite the many reservations Louis subsequently expressed about his time with Henderson, Lil believed that her husband "kind of liked playing with Fletcher. He wasn't anxious to be a star. He just enjoyed playing, and he thought I was crazy. All that name stuff—putting his name out front—it was real silly. So, he said, he wasn't coming back."

Lil remained adamant. "I've already got the job, and if you're not here by this date, then don't come at all," she told Louis.

His recollection of the negotiation was much more succinct: "She finally got tired and made a squawk at me that I should quit Fletcher's Band and come home to her in Chicago." His resentment over her "squawk" is understandable because his return to Chicago meant bidding farewell to Fanny. He had no idea when he would see her again, but she continued to occupy his thoughts.

Lil still did not know of Louis's new love. Instead, she was consumed with his lack of star billing. Eventually she persuaded him that he was not as successful or happy in New York as he thought he was. Thirty years later, he recollected his experience with Fletcher Henderson's orchestra with resentment. "The whole time I was in his band he'd only give me 16 bars to get off with, but he'd let me hit those high notes that the big prima donnas, first-chair man, couldn't hit," Louis wrote. "As far as Fletcher was concerned he wouldn't let me sing nothing. All the singing I did before I joined Fletcher went down the drain. . . . Fletcher was so carried away with that society shit and his education he slipped by a small-timer and a young musician—me—who wanted to do everything for him musically. I personally don't think Fletcher cared for me too much anyway."

The disagreement between Louis and Smack stemmed from their different ideas of jazz. For Henderson, jazz was light, polite music for dancing and socializing. It was, above all, elegant, and not intended as a means of self-expression or, God forbid, experimentation. Smack was uncomfortable with rebellious musicians. He wanted to codify jazz and market it as a reliable, known quantity. When he hired Louis Armstrong, he thought he was getting a highly skilled trumpet player, not a man determined to reinvent jazz.

In the end, Louis justified what became a crucial career move on the basis of loyalty to Lil. "I had to choose between my wife and Fletcher's Band. After all, I chose being with my wife. So I put Fletcher on notice. Fletcher was very nice about it. He told me, 'I hate to see you leave the band, but after all I do understand your situation. Well,' he said, 'You can always come back whenever you get ready.'

"That's just what I wanted to hear him say, although I never went back. I always felt I'd return to the band someday. I had 'wedged' in there just that much. All the boys in the band hated to see me leave, and I hated like hell to leave them, too."

Now that he'd finally summoned the courage to give notice, he sent Lil a telegram. It read, simply, "I WILL BE THERE."

Smack threw a grand farewell party for Louis at Smalls' Paradise at Seventh Avenue and 135th Street. (Of all the major nightclubs in Harlem, only Smalls' welcomed black patrons.) At the party, the boisterous Armstrong tested Smack's easygoing nature to the limit, and beyond. "We had a special reserved table," Louis wrote of that night, "and the place was packed and jammed, and after Fletcher made his speech and I made my little speech—most of my speech was thanks to Fletcher for the wonders he had done for me—the whole band sat in and played several fine arrangements for the folks.

"After we finished playing we went back to our table and started drinking some more liquor. I got so drunk until Buster Bailey and I decided to go home, and just as I went to tell Fletcher Henderson good-bye as I was leaving New York for Chicago the next morning, I said, 'Fletcher, thanks for being so kind to me, an, er, wer, er, wer,' and before I knew it, I puked directly on Fletcher's bosom, all over his nice clean tuxedo shirt. Oh! I'd gotten so sick all of a sudden.

"I was afraid Fletcher would get sore at me, but all he said was, 'Aw, that's all right, Dip (my nickname at that time).' Fletcher told Buster Bailey to take me home and put me to bed, so Buster did.

"The next morning, my headache and all, I boarded the train for Chicago."

IO.

BIG BUTTER AND EGG MAN

When he reached Chicago and discovered that Lil had billed him as "The World's Greatest Trumpet Player," he was appalled.

"Girl, are you crazy?" he said. "What do you mean, calling me the world's greatest trumpet player? And I bet you I don't get $75 dollars a week."

Lil said, "I bet you do."

She showed Louis the contract she had obtained for him. He took a look at it and shook his head, muttering, "Well, I think you're crazy."

Lil didn't care what he thought, now that he was here, with her. She knew him far better than he knew himself. In his later years, Louis learned to accept the title of "the world's greatest trumpet player" with aplomb, but now he was embarrassed, afraid he might be laughed off the stage for making such a claim and failing to live up to it. He maintained that he wasn't the greatest trumpet player in the world—the title surely belonged to someone else—but his experience, ability, and thanks to Lil, positioning, all conspired to offer him the job. Within two weeks, the Chicago *Defender* picked up Lil's slogan for Armstrong, and promoted him as such to Chicago. The paper's music critic, Dave Peyton, who was also a bandleader, wrote, "Louis Armstrong, the greatest cornet player in the country, is drawing many 'ofay' musicians to the Dreamland nightly, to hear him blast out those weird jazz figures. This boy is in a class by himself."

Although Louis returned to instant acclaim in Chicago, things were not quite so marvelous as they seemed. He received star billing at the Dreamland Cabaret, but he was, in reality, a member of Lil Hardin Armstrong's band. She was the leader, and made more money than he did. As for her band, it was simply not the same caliber as Fletcher Henderson's Orchestra.

Even marriage could not deafen his ears to its shortcomings. "She had a nice little swing band, but not like Fletcher's, somehow," he wrote, carefully judging his words. "Lil's trumpet man quit her band, so she gave me the job. I held the job down a long time, and during the time I was there, playing in Lil's band, I became more popular every night and was the talk of Chicago." In fact, the group had begun to sound a little old-fashioned, and Louis's horn blew new life into it.

Not everyone greeted him with open arms. Across the street from the Dreamland, who should be playing but Joe Oliver, at the Plantation, on 35th and Calumet. Oliver was not pleased about his former protégé returning to compete with him for audiences. There was no cordial reunion between the two men, no jam sessions, no feasts of red beans and rice. Instead, Oliver sent word of his intentions: "Close those windows or I'll blow you off 35th Street." The grudge became public knowledge, and jazz aficionados made a point to drop in on both Louis and old Joe, to avoid offending one or the other. The concentration of jazz clubs—and there were others along 35th Street—became a magnet for customers, white and black. "Unless it happened in New Orleans I don't think so much good jazz was ever concentrated in so small an area," said Eddie Condon, a young man drawn to the sound of the bands, and who became a bandleader himself. "Around midnight you could hold your instrument in the middle of the street and the air would play it. That was music."

Louis moved right back into the fine home Lil had purchased on 44th Street, all eleven rooms of it, and happily picked up where he had left off with Clarence, his adopted son. All at once, he was a somebody again—a big butter and egg man here in Chicago—with a status and prestige he had never been able to attain during his frantic months in New York with Fletcher Henderson. The change of city, and the reunion with Lil, his son, and the roster of musician friends he left behind did him a world of good. His confidence returned. No longer was he a young man searching for a reputation, or a riff, or an artistic identity. Now he knew who he was, as a trumpeter if not yet as a man, and the realization propelled him into the busiest and most productive phase of his entire career. Until this point in Louis's life, crowded with incident though it is, significant events and turning points occur at regularly spaced intervals; he moved from the Waif's Home to marriage to Chicago in neat, if unplanned succession. From this moment on, the intervals shrink drastically. Where years and months and weeks once separated key events, Louis now passes milestones in his own life, and in the history of jazz, every few weeks, or even every few days.

S oon after he started blowing in Lil's band at the Dreamland, Louis heard that Okeh Records in Chicago was planning to throw together a small group of New Orleans musicians for some recordings. There were no rehearsals to speak of, and no preparation. For a flat fee of fifty dollars apiece, musicians would just come into the Okeh studio and blow. On the strength of this casual offer, the single most influential combo in the history of jazz—the Hot Five—was born. Exactly who at Okeh was responsible for overseeing the Hot Five has never been determined. Richard M. Jones, a scout, booked the dates, but his involvement probably ended there. E. A. Fern, the Okeh boss in Chicago, also took credit for the Hot Five, but it is apparent that the company's attitude toward the group was *laissez-faire*. In this vacuum, Louis's recent experience with the Clarence Williams Blue Five in New York stood him in good stead for the Hot Five dates, since it, too, was strictly a studio group. After their first haphazard assembly, the Hot Five, in various incarnations, continued to record sporadically for the next four years, releasing dozens of singles and becoming the most listened-to band in the history of jazz.

The lineage of the Hot Five reached all the way back to Louis's boyhood. The group consisted of Kid Ory, his one-time employer and fellow construction worker from New Orleans, on trombone; Johnny Dodds, the brilliant clarinetist from the Creole Jazz Band; Johnny St. Cyr, another New Orleans musician, on banjo; Lil on piano; and Louis himself on the cornet, but also singing and talking more than ever. As the name suggested, this was a small group, only five musicians, with, incredibly, no drums, no tuba, and no violin.

Technically, Okeh was still in the Stone Age, making acoustic recordings with horns placed in front of the other instruments. Musically, though, the conditions were ideal. When they got into the Okeh studio for the first time, on November 12, 1925, Louis—unbridled after years of being restrained by tyrannical bandleaders—led the band in a genial, collaborative manner. "Our recording sessions would start this way," Kid Ory recalled. "The Okeh people would call up Louis and say they wanted so many sides.

They never told him what numbers they wanted or how they wanted them. We would get to the studio at nine or ten in the morning. We didn't have to make records at night, with the lights out, or get drunk like some musicians think they have to do before they can play. . . . If we were going to do a new number, we'd run over it a couple of times before we recorded it. We were a very fast recording band. In fact, the records I made with the Hot Five were the easiest I ever made. We spoiled very few records, only when one of us would forget the routine and didn't come in when he was supposed to. Even then, we'd try to cover up. After we'd make a side, Louis would say, 'Was that all right?' And if one of us thought we could do it over and do it better, why Louis would tell them to do it again, and so we would do it over."

Each musician has his say in these recordings, but Louis marks all the songs with the stamp of his ebullient personality. The emotional tone is fresh and new, veering between leering humor and pathos, and there is nothing conventional here, only the odd mixture projected directly from Louis's fevered psyche. Though not yet wholly in the groove, he is close. The other musicians had all come great distances in the past couple of years, making the band sound even more tight and lean. Lil's piano playing is now confident; no wrong notes mar her performance. Kid Ory plays with an amusing swagger. And Johnny Dodds's clarinet, always burning and sinuous, now melds perfectly with Louis's cornet, and any sense of a struggle between these two instruments that might have once occurred has vanished. The music they play seems as off-the-cuff as ever, but the breaks are the results of thousands of hours of performing. They are still "improvised," but just barely, and feel perfectly gauged.

From the first tune they waxed, "My Heart," credited to Lil, it was apparent that the band functioned perfectly right out of the box. The issued take is crisp and flawlessly played—no mean feat in the days before splicing—and the musicians bounce happily off one another. Lil's piano playing is heard to good advantage, and Louis's stop-time solos, though commanding, are never overpowering. He has developed a nifty way of goosing the song along with his distinctive rat-*tat*-ta-tat attack, a figure that would reappear throughout his career and become his musical signature. From "My Heart," they proceed to a slower, bluesier, "Yes! I'm in the Barrel," a nonsensical title for this sardonic, sinuous mating of Louis's horn and

Johnny Dodds's licorice stick. But it was the third song they recorded that day, "Gut Bucket Blues," that put the Hot Five on the map. For a start, the song had a funky name—a gut bucket collects the discarded innards of a fish—to which it lived up. After some introductory subliminal banjo strumming, Louis, acting as the master of ceremonies, introduces each member of the band in turn, in his distinctive, hoarse voice. Chanting and cheerleading his way through the song, his rasp punctuates the music, the guts of the "Gut Bucket Blues." *"Aw, play that thing, Mr. St. Cyr, Lawd, you know you can do it!"* Louis shouts. St. Cyr answers with banjo, and Louis responds with what will become, in time, his battle cry, *"Everybody from New Orleans can really do that thing—hey! hey!"* Then he moves on to his wife, urging her, *"Aw, whip that thing, Miss Lil, whip it, kid!"* As she whips right along, he encourages her *"Aw, pick that piano, gal,"* and she continues brilliantly. When Kid Ory takes his trombone downtown, Louis cheers him on, *"You can really blow that thing,"* and next tells *"Mr. Johnny Dodds, Aw, do that clarinet, boy!"* and Dodds begins to wail. Then, in an amusing about-face, Kid Ory speaks up—*"Aw, do that thing, Papa Dip"* (meaning Dippermouth)—and Louis obliges with a brilliant keening solo, completely at odds with his coarse shouting. Quicksilver and delicate, it is a kind of musical pointillism, as Armstrong skips over the melody, blowing every other note, every third note, making the listener's ear and imagination race to fill in the gaps, while his horn dances ahead on a shimmering abstract musical beam, rattling out the musical ideas so rapidly that they must have bypassed his conscious mind and come straight out of his boisterous, fertile unconscious.

With this song-plus-comedy routine, the Hot Five concluded their first day's work in the studio, collected their fifty bucks apiece, and went their separate ways. "When we made the [records], we didn't have any expectation that they would be as successful as they became," said Kid Ory, but, "Times were good, and people had money to buy records. . . . The Okeh people gave away a picture of Louis to everyone that bought one of the records. When they did that, sales went way up, because Louis was popular." Okeh issued the three tunes, and "Gut Bucket Blues" naturally grabbed the lion's share of attention. Soon after, all over Chicago, bandleaders were imitating Louis, and introducing their musicians one at a time to audiences. The device became a staple of dance band show business stage craft, and though it seems always to have existed, Louis Armstrong was the first to "do that thing."

His star burned brighter and brighter as the weeks passed. "I became so popular at the Dreamland that Erskine Tate from the Vendome Theatre came to hire me to join his symphony orchestra. I like to have fainted," Louis recalled of that moment in December 1925. The Vendome had been constructed in 1887, originally as a dance hall and social center, until it was gutted by a fire. By 1919, the place had been renovated, and it reopened as a theater with Tate leading a quintet in the pit. Over the years, his group expanded into an orchestra known as "Erskine Tate's Little Symphony" when it performed overtures to movies, and as "Erskine Tate's Jazz Syncopators" when it performed by itself. The prospect of working with Tate and the orchestra gave Louis pause because, as he explained, "Erskine Tate had a twenty-piece orchestra playing at a moving picture house called the Vendome Theatre, located at 31st and State streets in Chicago. In those days they [showed] silent films instead of the talkies. His orchestra would furnish the music for all the scenes in the film, and when the picture would break the orchestra would play overtures, and they'd finish up with a red hot number. Then, *black out*. Then the picture would start over again. And for anyone to play in Tate's band was really something." For Louis, Tate's orchestra was something because it favored symphonic music, and he feared he couldn't meet their standards.

Lil, of course, had other ideas. "Boy," she said, "if you don't get out of this house and go down there to Erskine Tate's rehearsal, I'll skin you alive."

"Well, all right. I'll go," Louis reluctantly replied.

"I went down there, and the opening night was a sensation. I remember the first swing tune we played, called 'Spanish Shawl.' "

With this success, Louis's anxieties about performing with a symphonic orchestra evaporated. At the Vendome audiences beheld Louis's full range as an entertainer: the peerless trumpeter, the vocalist, the clown, and even the actor. The basic show at the Vendome began with Erskine Tate's Little Symphony playing a light interpretation of a symphonic warhorse, and then Louis took over. He would emerge from the pit, gleaming trumpet in hand, his white handkerchief flashing against his black tuxedo, bringing cheers, whistles, catcalls, and applause from the audience. He had a funny way of carrying himself on stage, very different from the way star attractions such as Bill Robinson strutted. Louis would turn his back to the audience, hang his head, as if he were hiding, and then spin around and begin to blow once he was into the music. Raising his head and his trumpet higher and higher, as the spirit filled him, he would begin *sending*, and he felt the audience responding. No matter how frivolous the song, there was a burning emotional urgency to his playing that electrified audiences. Louis made an indelible impression on his fans, who expected great things of him. On one occasion, another musician, Doc Cheatham (who eventually metamorphosed into a venerable presence in the jazz world) substituted for Louis on cornet at the Vendome. The spotlight picked him up, and the audience reflexively started screaming, until they got a closer look. "You could just measure the diminishing of the screams, right down to nothing, and I'm up there playing like a fool," Cheatham remembered of that bitter night.

While performing at the Vendome, Louis made a huge impression with a new number, "Heebie Jeebies," his variation on a tune by Boyd Atkins. As its lyrics make clear, the original version was simply another attempt to exploit the dance craze:

> *"I've got the Heebies, I mean the Jeebies . . . Talkin' about a dance—the Heebie Jeebies . . . You'll see girls and boys . . . Faces lit with joy . . . You will like it . . . It's the Heebie Jeebies dance."*

Louis, with his love of wordplay, sang his own wacky, swinging interpretation of the tune, astonishing his audience. "Before he hit the second note they were swaying back and forth in their seats all the way to the last row," wrote William Russell, one of the first jazz scholars. "He kept that up for a while and as suddenly picked up a little megaphone and in a husky voice poured forth the words of the song with all the warmth of the Southland. He took another vocal chorus, not with words but with a guttural mouthing of incoherent nonsense, supplemented with unearthly grimaces." Now, the song sounded more like this:

"Say I've got the Heebies, I mean the Jeebies . . . Talkin' about, the dazza heebie-jeebies . . . Eef, gaff, mmmff, dee-bo, duh-deedle-la-bahm . . . Rip-bip-ee-doo-dee-doot, doo . . . Poppa's got to do the heebie-jeebie's dance . . ."

Russell offered an academic interpretation of Louis's stunning vocal technique. "This hair-raising hokum had about it a chilling fascination, all the more because the steady beat helped to create a background for Armstrong's rhythm which itself added to the suspense." Yet this is not an adequate explanation of the *"Eef, gaff, mmmff, dee-bo, duh-deedle-la-bahm . . . Rip-bip-ee-doo-dee-doot, doo"* that punctuates Louis's "Heebie Jeebies." What were those words? What was he doing up there, singing nonsense syllables in the middle of the song, and smiling so proudly while he did it? What he was doing, of course, was scat singing. It was a trick as old as minstrelsy, but Louis would soon be among the first to record scat, and it sounded so startlingly original that audiences thought he had invented it.

For years, stories circulated that Louis dreamed up the technique when the sheet music slipped off the stand in the middle of recording this song, and he spontaneously substituted nonsense syllables while the band played on. Though charming, the story made no sense—if Louis had lost his way, he would simply have made another take. In addition, he scats throughout the recorded version of "Heebie Jeebies," long before he reaches the point at which he supposedly dropped the music. And finally, he was scatting well before the recording was made. The clearest explanation of the origins of scat singing come from Louis himself. In 1970, he told William Russell, "We used to do that in the quartet going down the street"—when he was a thirteen-year-old boy in New Orleans. "Scat-do-beep-dah ba. Some of those old comedians used to do that." Louis's scat routine might also have had some Jewish influence. Phoebe Jacobs, a friend of Louis's, recalls, "One day I heard Louis talking with Cab Calloway, the bandleader, about scatting, and Louis said he got it from the Jews 'rockin,' he meant davening"—that is, praying and swaying. "But Louis never talked about this in public, because he feared people would assume he was making fun of Jews praying, which wasn't his intention at all. So he kept it to himself."

Even though he didn't invent scat singing, Louis did have the brilliant notion of merging it with jazz, and this seemingly innocuous little innovation revolutionized jazz singing, for it freed singers, who were quick to take up the gimmick, to develop distinctive nonsense lyrics and rhythmic patterns, and to improvise with their voices just as musicians did with their instruments. All at once, the vocalist was liberated from the music to think and perform creatively, which was, of course, the essence of jazz.

Curiously, Louis was oblivious to the musical innovations with which he startled both audiences and musicians. To his way of thinking, he was just trying to sing from the heart—as he had learned from the Karnoffsky family—and to spice it up with antics inspired by the spasm bands whose odd mixture of singing, dancing, chanting, and acrobatics he had seen on the streets of New Orleans. He wasn't trying to launch a musical revolution—that happened accidentally. Despite his acute observations about personal matters in his various autobiographical writings, the one subject Louis generally avoids is his own music and technique. This lapse is due, in part, to his tendency toward self-deprecation, but it also derives from his deeply felt and profoundly intuitive approach to performing. He rarely *described* what he did; he simply went ahead and did it. He taught himself a few basic music theory concepts, and horn technique, and the rest was simply beyond expression. Very occasionally, Louis admitted to an awareness of bars, measures, and choruses—especially when referring to the length of his solos—but mainly steered clear of terminology and all that lay behind it. Instead, when he discussed musical terms, he referred to "whipping it," "blowing it," "picking it," "swinging it," and "playing that thing." If he needed to communicate what he meant more precisely, he illustrated with his instrument, or his voice, or body language.

Lil, more highly trained if less original, gave a clearer account of the musical challenges her husband struggled with. "While he was at the Vendome," she said, "he was supposed to make this F on the end [of a song]. Do you know people would come to two and three shows to see if he's ever going to miss that F? He never missed it. But it started worrying him. He said, 'You know, people keep coming down there expecting me to miss that F.' I said, 'Yeah, well come on and make some G's at home.' So then he would be hitting G's at home all day. So, psychologically, I was right. If you can hit G at home, you won't worry about an F at the theater."

Louis also displayed his extra-musical tricks at the Vendome. As soon as he finished playing his horn, he would go into a full-blown version of the comic routine with which he had teased audiences in New York. He turned his back, put on a long preacher's coat and a pair of sunglasses, then faced the expectant audience and explained that the Reverend Satchelmouth—another one of his nicknames—would commence to sermonize. As Russell described his act: "He proceeded with throaty stuttering to announce his text. If anyone asked Louis about the voice, he said, 'I got a cold.' Exhorting his flock, he thrust his chin out, looking for some response from the brothers and sisters. He always got it. Then his voice went really low—he'd fulfilled his ambition to sing bass by then—and when the congregation was ready for the light, he whipped out the cornet and gave it to them." The crowd loved it. In fact, the audiences came to see Louis perform and left as soon as he finished, even before the motion picture began. Unlike the movie, he spoke to his audience in a language they understood, a black, southern language, simultaneously mocking and warm. Everything about Louis was exaggerated: the sound of his horn, the size of his grin, the big lips and white teeth, the mugging, the popping and rolling of his eyes, the weird gyrations. He was completely extroverted, withholding nothing, relentlessly driving every comic point home.

By the early months of 1925, Louis had become, in his words, "Quite a figure at the Vendome, especially with the gals." One young woman in particular, Alpha Smith, caught his eye. "I met Alpha during the time I was working there. Alpha was a little cute young girl, 19 years [old], when she used to come to the Vendome Theatre twice a week. . . . Alpha used to sit in the front row every time she came, and she would sit right where I could get a good look at her. And she had big pretty eyes. Anyway, I couldn't keep from diggin' her." Before long, Louis started talking to her after the show, and she became his regular backstage date. Of course, when Lil was around, Louis kept his distance from Alpha, but when he was alone, he constantly spent time with her. "I tried to keep from wedging into Alpha too deeply, know I was still married to Lil, and Alpha was so young and fine with it." It is not hard to fathom Alpha's appeal. She was pretty, apparently sweet, young, and undemanding. Until this time, Louis had fallen in love with older women—Irene, Daisy, and Lil—who initiated him into the rites of manhood and then dominated him until he felt the need to flee their grasp. He had proposed marriage to Fanny and even conducted a dangerous dalliance with Daisy in Chicago, in order to free himself of Lil's control. Alpha presented his best chance to attain this goal. She was, in contrast to the other women in his life, six years younger than he, a girl really, a fan who wanted to indulge her fantasies about him.

Even without the distraction of Alpha, it was now clear that Louis's marriage to Lil had run into trouble. "I thought about how Lil had been running around with one of the Chicago pimps while I was at work," he wrote. "So as we Colored people say, 'What is good for the goose is good for the gander,' meaning if Lil could enjoy someone else's company, I could, too. Ever since I was a little boy in New Orleans hanging around those old hustlers and pimps down there (and they all liked me very well) they used to tell me, 'Not one woman, no matter how pretty or sweet she may be. Anytime she gets down wrong and ain't playing the part of a wife, get yourself somebody else also, and get another woman much better than the last one at all times.' " Hearing again the whisper of Black Benny's advice, Louis decided he was going to do just that.

"Alpha commenced inviting me to her house. Alpha was a fine gal. She was a poor girl, not near as fortunate as Lil was when I first met her: maybe the one reason why Lil and I didn't make a good go of married life together. Alpha was working for some nice white people out in Hyde Park, taking care of their little baby. Mrs. Taylor [Alpha's employer] thought lots of Alpha. In fact, she practically raised her. I used to go out to her job in the afternoon and Alpha would fix some of the most dee-licious meals for me while Mr. and Mrs. Taylor would be downtown shopping. Alpha and I would straighten up the house perfect by the time the Taylors returned.

"One night the Taylors came home and Alpha and I were in their parlor, having a grand time playing records, dancing, opening one of their choice bottles of whiskey. They were surprised at first. Then Alpha introduced me to them. She said, 'Mr. and Mrs. Taylor, I want you to meet my new boyfriend. His name is Louis Armstrong. He's the cornet player in Erskine Tate's Orchestra down at the Vendome Theatre.' Mr. and Mrs. Taylor were very nice to me, and seemed to be very happy for Alpha. It seemed as though all the rest of Alpha's boyfriends turned out to be no-good ones, so the Taylors saw a bright future for Alpha by taking me for her sweetheart. Even if I was a married man."

It is unlikely that Alpha's employers had ever heard of Alpha's boyfriend, or registered the significance of Erskine Tate's Orchestra. They were white, and he was a star among blacks. In hindsight, it seems extraordinary that the man who would become the most important and influential performer in twentieth-century American music was helping the maid with her domestic chores and conducting a backstairs romance. To people like the Taylors, Louis Armstrong wasn't a figure of great significance; he was "a colored musician" who might make a nice match for their maid.

The romance developed quickly, as Alpha took him ever deeper into her life. "Alpha had me come to her house in Chicago and meet her mother, Mrs. Florence Smith. From the first introduction I could see right then and there that I could like her and would like to be around her. She was so friendly and pleasant and could tell some of the funniest jokes. Right off the bat I fell for Alpha's mother and tried to stay as long as I [could] whenever I was invited to their apartment."

Some might see Louis as a reckless and selfish philanderer, a man who would use a woman as long as she could help him, and discard her when their relationship became vexed, or she had given him all she could. In fact, he was engaged in a massive internal struggle. Music, he found, was much simpler to conquer and master than women. They were infinitely beguiling, but also infinitely troubling. Over Louis's reminiscences of his love life hovers the shadow of guilt and uncertainty—feelings that never tainted his decisive horn playing. Obscurely but insistently, he doubted his worth as a lover, and felt he was destined to disappoint the women with whom he became intimate, just as his father had disappointed his mother. Although needy and dependent in his relationships with women, he was rarely callous or calculating. He was a man to whom women were at least as important, and probably more important than men, and in his relationships with women, which held vital importance for him, Louis revealed his flaws as well as his aspirations. His work life was populated with men, and his dealings with them were conventional, straightforward, and professional. With women, his needs were far more complex: he wanted a lover, a wife, a fan, a mother, a muse, a companion, and not surprisingly, he was never able to find one woman who fulfilled all these roles. Although his romance with Alpha thrilled him, it also tormented him, and he wondered what was driving him away from Lil and into Alpha's arms. "I must have been seeking some kind of comfort and life," he reflected.

His pain is apparent as he describes the domestic strife with which he had lived since his return to Chicago. "Lil and I had one of the finest homes in Chicago at the time I was sweethearting with Alpha, but with all that swell home Lil and I had, there was no happiness there. We were always fussing and threatening to break up. If I sat on the bed after it was made up, why, Lil would go into fits, and poor Clarence, my adopted son, with his nervous self, used to almost jump out of his skin when Lil or Lil's mother would holler at him. Most of the time it was uncalled for. Lil and her mother had some bad tempers, and it would make my blood boil when I'd see them abuse my son Clarence. Whenever they—especially Lil—would holler at me, I'd tell her just where to go. I'd say, 'Aw, woman, *Go to Hell!*' "

Although he inevitably viewed their relationship through the lens of his own needs, Louis described matters pretty much as they stood. Lil could be disloyal and difficult. By her own description, she was often "nasty when the mood came over her." She was given to scheming and controlling, yet her manipulations, when taken to their logical conclusion, were destined to frustrate her, because she would inevitably lose control over her man once he became as independent as she encouraged him to be. That painful process of separating was exactly what was happening now, and was especially difficult for Louis because he was accustomed to women running his life for him. When he was a boy, his mother and sister held the reins, and now Lil and *her* mother were doing the same. To be sure, Lil had been exceedingly generous to him. She gave him confidence when he needed it, she made him a home, and she encouraged him to become a solo performer, a gift that became the basis for his career as a jazz musician, artist, and entertainer. But now, as he approached his twenty-fifth year, Louis was slowly outgrowing the role of the eternal son. He was infuriated when his wife and mother-in-law turned their sharp tongues on his defenseless adopted son. Not to mention that Lil had at least one lover that he knew about, and a pimp, at that.

In contrast, young Alpha looked up to him. She didn't try to tell him what to do. Unable to renegotiate his relationship with Lil, he found in Alpha everything he was missing at home: comfort, admiration, and freedom from responsibility. Furthermore, Alpha seemed not to mind that her famous boyfriend was married, and her behavior suggests that she realized that if she remained unfazed by it, he wouldn't stay married much longer, and would become hers alone. Louis's habitual passivity with women, even with the much younger Alpha, lent strength to her romantic strategy. As their relationship continued, it presented Louis with new variations on the old themes of his heart. Soon both Alpha and her mother were ministering to his needs, just as Lil and *her* mother had before them, and his mother and sister, before that.

As the romance between Louis and Alpha flowered, the Hot Five reunited in Chicago's Okeh Studio on February 26, 1926—only one day, but what a day it was. They recorded six sides, three of them among the most influential songs that Armstrong ever waxed. Recording conditions were still primitive and confining. "We were only allowed two minutes and forty-five seconds per record," Johnny St. Cyr recalled of that session. "We could not play at ease as the musicians do now as we had no microphones then, and we had to play into a horn which was attached to the recording machine. There were several of them, one to the piano, one to the reeds, and one to the brass, and one to the banjo. I would be sitting on a small ladder, or on several packing cases stacked on top of one another. Boy! We did it the hard way, but it was fun." Their sense of fun made it into the grooves. First, there was Lil's version of "Georgia Grind," on which she tried to sound as naughty as she could, her voice robust and penetrating but utterly lacking in the bawdiness suggested by the lyrics. When Louis takes over the vocal, he all but shouts her down with his hoarse rasp. Next, there was a great New Orleans polyphonic jamboree called "The Muskrat Ramble," credited to Kid Ory, but the original name was "The Old Cow Died and Old Brock Cried," the tune Buddy Bolden wrote and played with his band in New Orleans shortly after the turn of the century. The Hot Five give it the full, ripe treatment, even working in a delirious musical quotation from the "Tiger Rag." It was all so much fun, more fun than any other music.

Then, there was Louis's own "Cornet Chop Suey," the title referring to his long-standing affection for Chinese food. His latest masterwork, "Cornet Chop Suey" was a showcase for his growing assurance on the cornet. Here he played the melody with an elegant, subtle vibrato, then displayed his skill at creating a spare, bracing cadenza. Furthermore, he uses *all* registers here, unlike so many ensuing trumpet virtuosi, who tended to concentrate on the upper or middle range.

All of these tunes became essential entries in the Armstrong canon, but the song with the greatest impact the Hot Five recorded that day was "Heebie Jeebies," in which Louis recorded his scat singing for the first time. The resulting platter found its way into the homes of aspiring singers, male and female, around the country, many of them just children at the time. Billie Holiday, Ella Fitzgerald, and Bing Crosby, among others, listened to Louis singing and scatting and decided this was what they would do when they grew up; they would sing jazz just like this new musical phenomenon, this wonderful black icon whom everyone adored, Louis Armstrong. Decades later, scat singing was still shaking up the jazz world, as singers enlarged upon the idea and used their voices to mimic and replace instruments, a technique known as "vocalese." All of these far-flung developments came from Louis's apparently childish babbling.

Despite the strain on the relationship between Louis and Lil, the rehearsals and recordings proceeded smoothly at Okeh that day, and Louis won high marks from his colleagues. He was, said St. Cyr, "a wonderful bandleader. One felt so relaxed working with him, and he was very broadminded. He always did his best to feature each individual in his combo. It was not Louis Armstrong, it was the Hot Five, if you get what I mean." The collaborative nature of the enterprise makes it nearly impossible to assign credit for the songs, no matter whose name was officially listed as composer, especially since many of the tunes were adaptations of older models. Even when Louis wrote an original song, he left it to Lil to put on paper—"Louis would play the melody and Lil would write it down fast as Louis played," said one musician who observed them in action. This *modus operandi* gave Lil the impression that she was not just Louis's transcriber but also his collaborator. Eventually, the impression hardened into a conviction that prompted Lil to haunt Louis in court for years to come.

The next day, February 27, Okeh staged a promotional concert at the Coliseum at 15th and Wabash designed to feature its race recording artists. Alberta Hunter, King Oliver, Clarence Williams, and Eva Taylor were all there, but the company gave pride of place to Louis Armstrong. Okeh came up with a promotional gimmick to promote the sale of its records: "The Okeh Record Company will demonstrate to the gathering how phonograph records are made from the ground up, just as it is done in their own studios. When the record is finished it will be played to the crowd."

Several weeks later, Okeh released the recordings from the second Hot Five session. With that, the group, especially its *de facto* leader, Louis Armstrong, instantly became names to be reckoned with not only among those who purchased race records, but in mainstream popular culture. By the time it had been on sale a few weeks, "Heebie Jeebies" had sold over forty thousand records. *Everybody* heard the "Heebie Jeebies," and everybody repeated the expression. "You would hear cats greeting each other with Louis's riffs when they met around town," Mezz Mezzrow said. " '*I got the Heebies*,' one would yell out, and the other would answer, '*I got the Jeebies*,' and the next minute they were scatting in each other's face." Mezz played his copy of the song for his pal Bix Beiderbecke, now making his presence felt in Chicago, and described the intoxicating effect it had on Louis's young acolyte: "Bix kept chuckling as the record played over and over, and his long bony arms beat out the breaks. . . . Soon as it was over he grabbed it from the machine and tore out of the house to wake up everybody he knew around Hudson Lake and make them listen to it." With the success of "Heebie Jeebies," the Hot Five achieved national recognition and became the most famous jazz band in the land, even though they had never performed live, in front of an audience.

As the winter gradually yielded to spring, Louis and Lil's extraordinary musical and marital partnership deteriorated. The other members of her band at the Dreamland, where he continued to perform, bestowed a new, intolerable nickname on him, "Henpeck." Lil was upset by the destructive effect this treatment had on her husband: "It embarrassed him and he became so hard to get along with at home and on the bandstand. I would get ready to start the band off and he'd have all the musicians on one side, telling them a damn joke. And I got after him about it, and he said, 'Well, if you don't like it, fire me.' " Louis ascribed the musicians' carping to jealousy. "The guys who called me Henpeck were broke all the time. And I always had a pocket full of money. All of those conniving, inquisitive, two-faced people started interfering in our personal love and business." He still professed loyalty to his wife: "Everything she bought for me was the best, her suggestions were all perfect." No matter, his marriage hovered on the verge of collapse. "Whenever we'd break up, we'd draw all our money out of the bank and split it up."

Of course, Alpha was always hovering in the background. "I kept on visiting Alpha and her mother down where they lived, in one of the poorest districts in Chicago, 33rd and Cottage Grove Avenue, in a very dingy apartment with a wooden bathtub," Louis wrote. "They had a big ol' tom cat named 'Sit,' and that big sumbitch used to jump on the windowsill of the room where I was sleeping and scare the hell out of me. But with all that dinginess I would sleep there more nights with Alpha than I went home." Alpha's mother, Florence, made him feel more than welcome in the little apartment, and he was happy to keep her company. In return, she would "see that I had my correct meals while Alpha was at work. After meals, Mrs. Smith used to tell my fortunes by cutting a deck of cards. She was very good at this sort of thing. I offered to set her up in business at it, but she didn't have the time. I liked Mrs. Smith because she was the type of woman who has been around and seen everything."

In time, Louis felt so comfortable at the Smiths' that he brought Clarence along to try out the new domestic arrangement. "The first night I took Clarence down there to meet Mrs. Smith, Mr. Woods (Mrs. Smith's husband), and Alpha, Clarence was so glad over it. Just the idea [that] he could talk free without someone hollering at him and ridiculing his affliction. He didn't have to put on airs with a certain spoon for this and a certain fork for that. As well as Clarence loves to eat, I love to see him eat. He could eat at Mrs. Smith's house to his little heart's content. I could see the joy in Clarence's eyes when he looked around at me and said as he bit on a nice hot biscuit, 'Pops (that's what he calls me),' he said, 'This is where I should be living instead of staying out there with Lil.' Well sir, I was speechless for a moment. Then all of a sudden I smiled at him and said, 'Yes, Clarence, you are right. And here is where you are going to stay, right here along with Mrs. Smith."

The next day, Louis made a conclusive break with Lil. By this point, he wrote, "Alpha had fallen deeply in love with me. . . . I immediately moved Clarence's bags and baggage—all his clothes and mine. We both moved down to 33rd and Cottage Grove Avenue with Mrs. Smith and Mr. Woods and Alpha. Hooray."

. . .

The breakup of his marriage to Lil had immediate consequences for Louis, who left her band at the Dreamland. Still performing regularly at the Vendome, he wanted a job to replace his Dreamland gig, and his first thought was to reunite with Joe Oliver. Old Joe still held forth at the Plantation, but the consensus among Chicago's musical fraternity was that his best days were behind him. His chops were gone, and everyone could hear it. Louis rejoined him anyway.

At that moment, Louis happened to find himself one afternoon at the headquarters of the musicians' union, Local 208, at State and 39th. The fellows hung out on the second floor there to look for work, but also to play cards, trade gossip, shoot pool, and drink. There, he began talking with a good-looking, rail-thin young pianist, Earl Hines. One thing led to another. Hines got himself in front of a keyboard, Louis pulled out his horn, and they began making music. "I always remember that first tune we played together," Hines said in his autobiography. "It was 'The One I Love Belongs to Somebody Else.' I knew right away that he was a giant. Nobody could play the horn the way he played it."

Soon after, Hines asked Louis, "Why don't you come on over with us young fellows?"

"I already promised Joe Oliver," Louis replied.

"Yeah, but you would do better to come with us." By "us," Hines meant Carroll Dickerson's more youthful and lively orchestra over at the Sunset Cafe. The timing of Hines's offer was perfect. Louis thought about it for a moment, and decided exactly what to do. He left Oliver yet again, and, beginning on April 10, 1926, made the Sunset his new performing home.

Located at 35th Street and Calumet, the Sunset was a black and tan owned by Edward Fox and Sam Rifas. It had been in business for nearly five years, managed by a brash young promoter named Joe Glaser. In his words, "The Sunset had the cream of the black-and-tan shows, and there wasn't a big name in colored show business that didn't work for me at one time or another. I spent more money on my shows than the Cotton Club. . . . We never had any small groups there. Besides the band we had twelve chorus girls, twelve showgirls, and big name acts. The place sat about six hundred people and we had a high-class trade—not like some of the other joints—the best people. There were lines for every show, and, mind you, we charged admission just to get in—from a dollar twenty to two-fifty or so—depending on how business was."

What Glaser lacked in polish, he more than made up for with his irresistible *chutzpah*. "I always admired Mr. Glaser from the first day I started working for him," Louis wrote in 1943. "He just impressed me different than the other bosses I've worked for. He seemed to understand colored people so much. And he was wonderful to his whole show and band. [He] would give us nice presents. And don't you think for once that Mr. Glaser didn't 'pitch a bitch' when things were not jumping right. I did not know about managers like they have nowadays. I don't think Mr. Glaser was thinking about it, either, or else he would've signed me up then."

Glaser immediately began billing Louis Armstrong as "The World's Greatest Trumpet Player," putting his name in lights. With characteristic overstatement, he insisted that he, not Lil, was responsible for being the first to bill Louis this way. Even Louis, in a rare lapse of memory, agreed with Glaser on this point. Louis's muddled version of this matter points up his reluctance to acknowledge Lil as the mastermind behind his very successful scheme. Now that he was separated from her, he transferred his dependency to Glaser and gave him credit for everything—credit that Glaser gladly took. Not so incidentally, Glaser despised Lil, kept her as far from Louis as possible, and did whatever he could to poison Louis's feelings about her.

At first glance, Joe Glaser seemed far less malignant than his Harlem counterparts, such as the vicious Dutch Schultz. True, he pledged allegiance to Al Capone, but Glaser and his musicians looked on Capone as a benefactor rather than a tyrant, which in a sense he was. Louis Armstrong and his musical colleagues had little to gain from legitimate authority—in short supply in Prohibition Era Chicago—so they found unlikely but powerful allies, such as the Capone syndicate. In general, individual musicians, while terrified of Capone's murderous reputation, found Al to be charming in person, as did Louis, who described him in utterly unique terms: "He was a nice little cute fat boy—young—like some professor who had just come out of college to teach or something." "Professor" Al tipped generously, and more importantly, he supplied liquor to the speakeasies, bars, and nightclubs that employed jazz musicians. Without Professor Al, many people, including jazz musicians, would be out of a job.

Louis Armstrong and the Sunset Cafe proved to be a perfect fit. "Although the club was on the main stem of the Negro neighborhood, it drew white as well as colored. Sometimes the audience was as much as 90 percent white. Even the mixing of white girls and colored pimps seemed to be an attraction," Hines recalled.

There was also a pronounced gangster element at the Sunset, but Louis, accustomed to being employed and protected by mobsters, didn't think twice about that. Capone's men ensured the flow of alcohol, and their presence reassured many whites. Nonetheless, police raids at the Sunset were a fact of life. "We would all have to get into the patrol wagon every night," Hines said. "All we did was sign up and go back to finish the rest of the night. I stood up in the wagon so often on those trips, I finally decided to *run* and get a seat when the police came." This was the Prohibition Era, after all, which meant that nothing was prohibited.

For a brief interval, Louis frantically raced from the Vendome to the Sunset, where he played, with intermissions, from seven o'clock in the evening until three o'clock in the morning. The crushing schedule took its toll, though, and not long afterward Louis ended his astonishing run with Erskine Tate to devote his energy to the Sunset and to recordings. Initially he shared performing responsibilities at the Sunset with a band led by the violinist Carroll Dickerson. With the exception of Honore Dutrey, a veteran of King Oliver's Creole Jazz band, all the musicians in the unit were strangers.

Louis quickly became a fixture at the Sunset, and soon supplanted the group's nominal leader. Dickerson drank so much that Glaser fired him and changed the name of the band from the Carroll Dickerson Orchestra to Louis Armstrong and his Stompers. Billing notwithstanding, Louis was a bandleader in name only. Glaser, always ready to "pitch a bitch," managed the orchestra; Earl Hines served as music director; and Percy Venable, the best-known black floor-show director in town, supervised a complex whirl of singers, dancers, showgirls, and even the obligatory Charleston contest on Friday nights.

Hines felt so proprietary about this band that when Louis wasn't around, he referred to the Stompers as *his* band, with considerable justification. This did not trouble Louis; true to form, he was glad to let someone else assume these responsibilities. Very quickly, Hines became Louis's pianist and, more than that, his current musical mentor, so what might have been a professional rivalry evolved into collaboration and friendship. Louis also respected Hines musically: he was an absolutely wonderful pianist, with a fluidity and ability to improvise that far exceeded Lil's stodgy technique. As their friendship deepened, they became, said Hines, "inseparable," and Earl was drawn in by the trumpeter's irresistible personality. "He was a very happy-go-lucky guy, and we used to have so much fun, telling jokes. . . . He was called 'Satchelmouth' and I was called 'Gatemouth.' We were very close and when we were playing we would steal ideas from each other. Or rather, I'd *borrow* an idea from him and say, 'Thank you.' A lot of people have misinterpreted the whole thing and said that I just got my style from Louis, but I was playing it when I met him."

Unlike so many other inhabitants of Louis's world, Hines wasn't a product of the tonks and racism of New Orleans. Raised in Pittsburgh, Pennsylvania, home to a thriving black community, he was a different breed of cat, with a confident, take-it-as-it-comes attitude toward everything, including music. He could make his piano mimic the trumpet, and eventually became known for his "trumpet-style" playing. Through his newest disciple, Louis's influence now spread beyond the horn to other instruments as well.

Louis and Earl pursued their interest in women together. "We started what we called a Christmas Fund, putting all the money made on the floor into it," Hines said. By Christmas, "We had three or four hundred dollars apiece to spend. We went around buying our girlfriends presents. We had a lot of fun going in those department stores, picking out lingerie and things we thought a girl would like, and all the time hoping we'd get a present in return!" The chief beneficiary of Louis's largesse was, of course, Alpha, but even as Louis describes his pride in bestowing gifts on her, it becomes painfully apparent that he came to feel she was taking advantage of his generosity. "Now I was making nice money so I had a good chance to buy Alpha some nice things with my extra money Lil didn't know about. I bought Alpha a very lovely overcoat—the first and finest she'd ever had. I paid $90.00," he remembered, an enormous sum at the time. "It was a very heavy blue coat, very plain, and a nice lamb collar, but not too big. She really did look smart in it. . . . She had lovely taste in clothes, even before I was really able to buy her a lot of fine clothes, furs, and diamonds galore.

She was, as a young girl, very neat and clean and always loved the best. If Alpha was going downtown to buy a couple of dresses and she didn't have enough money to get two good ones, she'd come home with that one good one. She did not have a whole lot of clothes when I met her, but what few she did have was good. And was she innocent—my, my, my. To believe that Alpha turned out in later years to be a no-good bitch, why, I am still flabbergasted, surprised as ol' Hell."

Louis's following was strongest among the blacks of Chicago, but he had other fans whose white faces made them conspicuous in the crowd. They started showing up at the Dreamland as soon as he returned to Chicago, and they followed him to the Sunset. They were young kids with smooth cheeks and neat clothes, who had gone to school together at suburban Austin High, and became known as the Austin High Gang. In their bow ties and tweed jackets and crisp shirts, they formed jazz combos, defied their teachers and parents, and flocked to the clubs on the South Side to hear their hero, Louis Armstrong. "All the young musicians in town would come to hear Louis," Glaser bragged. "Benny Goodman, Muggsy Spanier, and the rest. I used to let them in free. Hell, they were kids and never had money." The scene was oddly reminiscent of the Second Line down in New Orleans—the kids trailing after a funeral band, blowing their toy instruments—except these kids were ambitious, and they were white. There were lots of others, too: Jimmy McPartland, Eddie Condon, George Wettling, and Milton "Mezz" Mezzrow.

Mezzrow was the most sinister of this straitlaced bunch because he used his job as a clarinetist to cover for his *real* occupation, which was dealing drugs to jazz musicians, including his friend and advocate Louis Armstrong. He was also the most intriguing because he wrote an entire book, *Really the Blues*, about his experiences selling drugs and playing jazz. ("My, what a wonderful piece of literature that is!" Louis proclaimed. "*Really the Blues* is *felt.*") Though incredibly vivid, the book is a chilling self-portrait of an opportunist, junkie, and proto-hipster. Mezzrow began life as the youngest child of a pharmacist, and made his first dough from selling bootleg booze to get himself to Mexico. Once there, he discovered marijuana. He tried it, liked it, and decided to sell it in New York and, later on, in Chicago. "I did no pushing," he coyly explained, "I just stood under the Tree of Hope, my pokes full up, and the cats came and went, and so did all my golden leaf. Overnight I was the most popular man in Harlem. New words came into being to meet the situation: *the mezz* and *the mighty mezz*, referring, I blush to say, to me and to the tea [marijuana] both; *mezzroll*, to describe the kind of fat, well-packed and clean cigarette I used to roll. . . . Some of those phrases really found a permanent place in Harlemese, and even crept out to color American slang in general."

While many other jazz musicians saw Mezzrow for what he was—a pusher—he had a remarkable hold over Louis. "Ever since I was first introduced to him," he naively wrote of Mezzrow, "he impressed me as some kind of a god, who was sent down here from Harlem to serve, to prove that there are such things as Human Beings. Right off the reel— that's what I dug in old Mezzrow!" Louis was so crazy about this parasite that he compared him to Joe Oliver, of all people. When he looked at Mezzrow's cold-blooded visage, he thought he saw "the same *warmth* that was in Joe Oliver's eyes."

For all his vices, Mezz was an accomplished clarinetist, and his services were much in demand by New Orleans musicians. He even recorded some creditable sides with *le grand maître du clarinet* (as the French would soon call him), Sidney Bechet. According to Louis, Mezz "was just as good on his clarinet at that time as anyone who played clarinet in those days—very, very good. Of course, there were Johnny Dodds, Lawrence Dewey, Jimmy Noone, all HELLIONS on the clarinet, who had just arrived in Chicago and were blowing up a storm. . . . Those boys weren't in Chicago a hot minute before Mezz was sitting in with them, blowing like mad, like he always did, blowing a whole flock of good blues."

The two of them spent hours talking jazz, which Mezzrow discussed in terms that Louis appreciated. "Mezz would explain every little iota of meaning in jazz," Louis said, "every little beat of the drum, riff of the piano, the changes in the blues, and every little phrase that he thought would benefit those Austin High School lads."

The only thing Louis neglected to mention was the pungent smell of pot that hung over these discussions, as Mezzrow slowly, surely, and seductively got Louis habituated to the drug. Marijuana was not merely a diversion for Louis, it became an obsession, an inspiration, and a necessity. "I smoked it a long time," he wrote, "it's a thousand times better than whiskey. It's an assistant, a friend, a nice cheap drunk, if you want to call it that, very good for asthma, relaxes your nerves." It was so important in his life that in his later years, when he began to prepare a third volume of memoirs for publication, he planned to call it *Gage*, his preferred nickname for marijuana. By that time, his manager was Joe Glaser, who was understandably horrified by the prospect of his star client going on record advocating the use of an illegal substance. Glaser suppressed the manuscript and possibly destroyed parts of it, but Louis's introduction survives; in it, he went to great lengths to describe all that the drug meant to him and to extol its beneficial properties. "The first time I smoked marijuana, or 'gage,' as they beautifully call it sometimes, was a couple of years after I had left Fletcher Henderson's orchestra," he wrote. "I was actually in Chicago when I picked up my first stick of gage, and I'm telling you I had myself a ball. That's why it really puzzles me to see marijuana connected with narcotics, dope, and all that kind of crap."

One of Louis's Chicago friends recalled that the trumpeter was exposed to marijuana for the very first time during his gig at the Savoy, when he was standing in the back of the theater on a hot day. He was approached by a white arranger, who said, "I got a new cigarette, man. It makes you feel so good." Explaining that the special cigarette had helped cure him of pneumonia, the arranger lit the reefer, took a drag, and offered it around. There were no takers—except for Louis. He responded to it right away. It made him feel good, relaxed, and he liked the way it smelled, too. There was no way it could be bad for him, like dope. To his way of thinking, "Dope addicts, from what I noticed by watching a lot of different cats, felt they could get a much bigger kick by jugging themselves in the ass with a needle—heroin, cocaine, or some other ungodly shit." But marijuana "never did impress me as dope because my mother and her church sisters used to go out by the railroad tracks and pick baskets full of pepper grass, dandelions, and lots of weeds similar to gage, and they would bring it to their homes, get a big fat slice of salt meat—and make the most dee-licious pot of greens."

Louis was not entirely misguided about the relative harmlessness of marijuana, for it was often safer and cheaper than bootleg booze. In the jazz world, Prohibition meant thirteen endless years of imbibing hootch, moonshine, needle beer, and any other poison with an alcoholic content. Louis saw firsthand the devastating consequences of cheap bootleg booze on the jazz musicians who stayed up all night, every night, drinking the rotgut provided by the house, which was, inevitably, the worst available. "You should be 'shamed of yourself, young as you are, drinking all that whiskey," he scolded a fellow musician. "If you don't quit acting the fool with that juice, they gonna be giving you flowers, and you won't even smell 'em." Louis was in search of a safer high, and as far as he could tell, weed had no ill effects. It even seemed to help the music flow.

The fellowship surrounding the use of marijuana also appealed to Louis, and helped him overcome the lingering shyness that clung to him offstage. "Jazz musicians are so glad to see one another they'll call one another almost any kind of name (but affectionately) just to get that good handshake. After all this knowing each other, why, out of a clear sky a stick of gage would touch the palm of my hand or the tip of my finger. I was never born to be a square about anything, no matter what it is." Pot made him feel relaxed, hip, one of the gang, and he never tired of romanticizing it. "We all used to smoke marijuana," he wrote near the end of his life, "and called ourselves the Vipers. Yeah. It's a thrill to think back to those beautiful times and the wonderful cats who congregated to light up some of that good shuzzit—meaning, good shit."

Louis's developing taste for marijuana suited Mezzrow perfectly, who supplied him with a potent strain direct from Mexico. It became an integral part of his life, and vital to his way of thinking, but more than that, essential to his music. Louis was still on a steep curve, and his continually improving musical and vocal skills were captured on recordings made without the help of marijuana. (As Kid Ory pointedly remarked, the early Hot Five recordings were waxed in the morning, when everyone was sober and could think straight.) Once Louis started using reefer regularly, he decided it helped his music, his performing, his entire state of mind. The records he made before marijuana entered his life demonstrate that he was doing fine without it; after he began smoking, he simply got better and better.

Although there is no dramatic distinction between his pre- and post-marijuana recordings, Louis *thought* he heard a world of difference. The reason for this might have been the effect marijuana can have on hearing. Under the right circumstances, it can sharpen and amplify sounds, making them seem to bounce around. Marijuana can also give music a three-dimensional, almost sculptural quality, which explains why it helped to relax the hyperactive entertainer and stimulate his musical flights of fancy, both on his trumpet and in his singing. He made a point of blowing weed before he recorded or performed, and when he came out high and astonished his audiences, he assumed the pot must be responsible. He even encouraged his musicians to get high right along with him, and many did.

Once Mezz became known as the dealer to the trendsetting Louis Armstrong, the clarinetist's little sideline became a booming business. Mezzrow had no qualms about dealing; it was his way of rebelling against white, middle-class Austin, "a sleepy-time neighborhood big as a yawn and just about as lively, loaded with shade-trees and clipped lawns and a groggy-eyed population that never came out of its coma except to turn over," as he put it. Placid Austin seemed an unlikely breeding ground for a new wave of jazz musicians, but, as Mezzrow described in his ripest prose, this is just what happened. "Before they even collared their diplomas at Austin High they had all been swept up and carried away by the tidal wave of hot music that was searing and singeing its way from the Gulf of Mexico up to the Great Lakes. . . . These juvenile cats were gone with it; they meant to pave the way for that flood from the Mississippi delta." After listening to jazz on the radio, they went to Chicago to hear it live. "They heard the real jazz too, coming up from the South Side like a heartbeat," said Mezz. "Joe Oliver taught them how to cut their musical eye-teeth; Jimmy Noone and Johnny Dodds helped them dig their gut-bucket ABC's; Louis Armstrong riffed and scatted them through many an after-hours lesson in night school, until they were all honor students." To complete their education, Mezzrow taught them to smoke marijuana.

For Mezzrow and his students, jazz wasn't just a new form of music, it was a way of life, it *was* life. "The sprawling world outside, they found, was raw and bubbling, crude, brutal, unscrubbed behind the ears but jim-jam-jumping with vital spirits; its collar might be grimy and tattered, but it was popping with life and lusty energy, ready for anything and everything, with a gusto you couldn't drown. And jazz, the real jazz, was its theme song." The boys from Austin were, Mezzrow summarized, "a high-spirited, eager, try-anything bunch of kids, these teen-age refugees from the sunny suburbs, as frisky as a herd of prancing fillies, and yet they still had their dead-serious side, pledged body and soul to the gospel of jazz, and they formed the nucleus of a great crew of jazzmen who have gone down in history as the Chicagoans. . . . They may have been a drag and a headache to their mothers, but they were sure a jumping joy to me."

All the cats—Mezz, the Austin High Gang, and especially Louis—were in the thrall of Bix Beiderbecke, who continued to drink and blow with a frightening intensity—he seemed to be consuming himself right in front of them. Other musicians especially admired Bix's bell-like tone. "Like a mallet striking a chime," said Hoagy Carmichael. "Like a girl saying yes," said Eddie Condon. Bix's style was more subdued than Louis's. Where Louis inhabited the melody, Bix floated under and over it. There was something spectral about Bix's musical meanderings, as if he were listening to the music of the spheres rather than the other fellows in the band. He possessed incredible facility, and could fire off notes with stunning alacrity, then soar above a phrase like a hawk wheeling around in a clear blue sky. He eschewed some of the more obvious New Orleans tricks, such as dirty tone, and there was a subtle classical influence in his phrasing that reminded listeners that the cornet was the first cousin of the French horn. He had a distinctive habit of throwing sour bits of avant-garde music into jazz, which at first sounded unlistenable, but soon became second nature. Jazz absorbed everything else, so why not avant-garde music? "Over and over he would play the peculiar 'modern' music that was like a signpost to him, showing him where he thought he had to go—Stravinsky's *Firebird*, Dukas's *The Sorcerer's Apprentice*, Debussy's *Afternoon of a Faun*," Mezzrow recalled. Then, just to keep his listeners guessing, he began composing on the piano, devising his introspective, haunting "In a Mist." No one knew what had inspired him to do it, but Bix was always a mystery.

He left Chicago in 1926, and joined up with the enormous Paul Whiteman in New York. He eventually returned to Chicago as a featured soloist with Whiteman's orchestra. Louis was dying to see what had become of his old friend from the riverboat days, and how Mr. P, as Louis referred to Whiteman, compared to the likes of Erskine Tate. He attended the very first show, and what a spectacle it was. "As soon as I bought my ticket, I made a beeline to my seat because the band was already on, and the next number that came up was a beautiful tune called 'From Monday On.' My, my, what an arrangement that was. They swung it all the way . . . and all of a sudden Bix stood up and took a solo, and I'm telling you, those pretty notes went all through me. Then Mr. Whiteman went into the Overture by the name of *1812*, and he had those trumpets way up into the air, justa' blowing like mad, and my man Bix was reading those dots and blowing beautifully, and just before the end of the overture, they started to shooting cannons, ringing bells, sirens were howling like mad, but you could still hear Bix. The reason why I saw through all those different effects that were going on at the ending—well, you take a man with a pure tone like Bix's and no matter how loud the other fellows may be blowing, that pure cornet or trumpet tone will cut through it all."

Even better than hearing Bix play was the chance to blow with him again. "When Bix would finish up at the Chicago Theatre at night, he would haul it over to the Sunset where I was playing and stay right there with us until the last show was over and the customers would go home." But that was only the beginning. "Then we would lock the doors. Now you talking about jam sessions, huh, those were the things, with everyone feeling each other's note or chord, and blending with each other instead of trying to cut each other. We tried to see how good we could make music sound, which was an inspiration and play some of the sweetest things, real touching."

On June 16, the Hot Five reconvened to launch four tunes into the world, including Lil's funky evocation of romantic revenge, "Droppin' Shucks." A week later, they returned to the Okeh studios, waxed four more, and during that second date, Louis led the ensemble in one of their wittiest, most ironic compositions, "The King of the Zulus." Kid Ory's trombone moans and Louis's cornet never sounded fatter and warmer than it does here, but what is truly extraordinary about the song is the way it stops dead in the middle for a comedy routine. A man from Jamaica (Clarence Babcock), speaking furiously in a West Indian dialect, interrupts a barbecue, and becomes a source of amusement to everyone present. "*Mahn, I come from Jamaica and I don't mean to interrupt the partee but one of me countrymen tell me there's a chittlin' rag going on heah!*"

Few who heard this breathtakingly "new" jazz of the Hot Five realized that Louis was actually reviving an old minstrel show routine. James Weldon Johnson, the black poet, explained, "The Negro songs then the rage were known as 'coon' songs, and were concerned with jamborees of various sorts and the play of razors, with the gastronomical delights of chicken, pork chops and watermelon, and with the experiences of red-hot 'mammas' and their never too faithful 'pappas.' " These stereotypical images were vivid presences in Louis's imagination, but he conjured them with a sardonic wit suggesting that he had moved into new musical and social realms.

After they wrapped up the day's recording, the Hot Five made the sole public appearance of their career. The occasion was another promotional concert at the Coliseum, staged by Okeh records. Richard M. Jones booked the entire race record roster: King Oliver, Erskine Tate, not to mention the "king of them all, Louis Armstrong, world's hottest jazz cornetist." Louis was quoted as saying, "The old cornet is just itchin' to make blue music, mister, so I just can't stay away." The *Defender* ran an eight-page take-out promoting the concert, which was supposed to culminate in a rendition of "Cornet Chop Suey" by no fewer than twenty-one jazz orchestras. Even though that gargantuan performance failed to materialize, ten thousand people attended and finally heard the fabled, elusive Hot Five play their hits before their very ears. Louis, predictably, brought the house down.

In August, while the city of Chicago simmered in the heat, Louis's love life, surprising and unpredictable as ever, entered a strange new phase. He took a three-week-long vacation—not with Alpha, with whom he had been living—but with Lil. No matter how tight he became with Alpha and her mother, even living with them and asking them to take care of Clarence, he had never made the decision to divorce Lil. Both financial and emotional reasons made him reluctant to sever his relationship with his second wife. Her force of personality was as strong as ever, and they continued their musical collaboration in the recording studio. On a practical level, he still needed her; in fact, he could not afford to walk away from Lil. Alpha, quite unlike her predecessor, was content to take Louis's money or gifts without giving anything in return—she was an expensive habit. Although Louis earned walking-around money from his record dates and Sunset engagement, it was Lil who owned the big house on 44th Street, and Lil who claimed credit for many of the songs they recorded, because she had transcribed them. Through all these stratagems, she kept her hold on Louis.

Interested, as always, in real estate, Lil purchased a second home, a lakefront summer cottage in Idlewild, Michigan, where she invited Louis to join her. He leapt at the offer because it meant he could swim, his favorite form of exercise. "The lake was about a mile across and I could make that easy. But Lil wouldn't go swimming with me. I had dunked her in the water just for fun when we had spent a day once on Lake Michigan, and I guess I must have scared her too bad, without meaning to." If Lil had planned to woo her wayward husband back during their summer idyll, she was disappointed. When the three weeks ended, he returned to Chicago, Alpha, and his engagement at the Sunset.

Great things were happening at the Sunset Cafe during this time. Percy Venable, the floor-show director, who was perpetually on the lookout for something new, concocted a new routine for Louis and a popular female vocalist of the moment, May Alix. The number was built around a comedy song Venable had written, called "Big Butter and Egg Man." In the parlance of the day, a big butter-and-egg man was a small-time big shot, able to spend lavishly on inexpensive items, and the song called for Louis to boast to his girl about what a substantial butter-and-egg man he was. It seemed foolproof.

Venable's staging of the song called for Louis to go out on the floor of the Sunset and sing right along with May, but the prospect petrified him. It was one thing to shout into a horn in the recording studio, quite another to act out a little musical drama with May in front of an audience. He kept forgetting the lyrics. Earl Hines instantly diagnosed Louis's seizure as a case of puppy love. May was awfully good-looking and not a bit shy herself.

On the opening night, Louis suffered the performer's nightmare: he completely blanked out. "He didn't know whether to sit down, stand up, or what," said Hines, observing from the piano, "but May got a kick out of it and had fun with him, and the whole house cracked up." In subsequent performances, May tried her best to coax the lyrics out of him. She would sing out, "I want a butter-and-egg man," and wrap her arms around him, as he visibly melted, and "everybody in the band would get up and shout, 'Hold it, Louis! Hold it!' " Finally, Louis shouted out the lyrics and worked up a crazy, endearing little monologue that he inserted in the middle of the song:

> . . . *I'm your big butter and egg man, but I'm different, honey, I'm from way down in the South . . . Now listen, baby, I'll buy you all the pretty things that you think you need . . . As long as I can keep this cornet up to my mouth . . . Oh, I'll play you a little butter and*

*cheese, and if you say please, I'll even hit high C's . . . 'Cause I'm
your big butter and egg man . . . Come here, baby, kiss me! . . .
Big butter and egg man from way down in the South!*

His confidence on the rise, Louis spent much of his time fending off all
manner of hornmen who dropped into the Sunset to challenge him. Joe
Oliver, growing truculent with age, strode into the Sunset one night with a
piece called "Snag It" under his arm and dared Louis and the second
trumpet, Natty Dominique, to sight-read it. The duo managed it until the
break, whereupon they fell apart. "Practice it," Oliver snorted, "and when
you learn it, let me know." He departed, leaving a demoralized and enraged
pair of hornmen behind him. Louis immediately took Natty down to the
kitchen to rehearse. At the next intermission, they sent for the King, to
show him they had mastered the number. As soon as they finished, they
looked expectantly at Oliver, but all he said was, "At last, you've made it,"
and then he walked out.

For a while, Louis's biggest threat came not from Oliver but from
within the ranks of his own orchestra—specifically from the second trumpet, his comrade-in-arms Natty Dominique. Nique, as he was known, had
begun to play *exactly* like Louis, especially during the "Big Butter and Egg
Man" number.

During one intermission, Louis took his imitator aside and said, "Listen, Nique, don't do that. That's a bad idea you have, playing like I play."

Nique went home and sulked, but as he thought things over, he came to
the conclusion that Louis was right, that he would be better off playing in
his own style. His chance arrived when Louis took a two-week vacation
from the Sunset. During that interval, Dominique did develop his own
style, what he called a "driving trumpet," and earned himself the nickname
"The Driver." He admitted to a colleague, "I was angry at Louis once, he
didn't know it. He told me not to copy him. And I'm proud today that I'm
not playing like Louis Armstrong."

When Louis returned to the Sunset, he made a beeline for the second
trumpet player and asked, "Nique, how you made out?"

Natty said, "I know they all come here to hear you, but I'm glad I
don't copy you anymore and I promise you I'll never copy after you as long
as I live."

"I know you were peeved that night," Louis admitted.

"Louis, I was so angry."

Louis complimented Nique's playing, appraised his distinctive drive, and then the two of them went up on the bandstand to play. After twenty-five choruses of "Poor Little Rich Girl," Louis was still going strong, but Nique was exhausted—his poor lip "gave down."

"Louis Armstrong will kill you," he told himself, "he's got a powerful lip. That's the reason why he's gonna be great as long as he has breath in his body." Defeated but respectful, Nique just sat down, put his trumpet in his lap, and, along with everyone else, listened to the man blow.

Louis remained a fixture at the Sunset for the balance of 1926, and all the way to February 1927. Meanwhile, he continued to function as a sideman for various blues singers. Once in a great while, he reassembled the Hot Five for more bravura recordings. It was as though he used the infrequent Hot Five sessions to show what he had learned during the previous weeks and months at the Sunset and the other venues around Chicago where he had been performing. On November 16, 1926, the Hot Five, amplified by May Alix, waxed a version of "Big Butter and Egg Man" based on the vaudeville skit Louis had been singing and blowing at the Sunset, along with several other irresistibly upbeat virtuoso turns: "Jazz Lips" (a stop-time tour de force), "Skid-Dat-de-Dat" (more scatting, of course, and far more extreme than "Heebie Jeebies"), and "Sunset Cafe Stomp." A week later, with Henry Clark sitting in for Kid Ory on trombone, they took down "You Made Me Love You" and "Irish Black Bottom," solidifying their reputation as the best-known, most influential, and, owing to their nearly total lack of public appearances, most mysterious band in jazz.

The Hot Five soon expanded to take advantage of recent developments in technology. Beginning in 1925, Victor and Columbia, the leading record companies, switched to a new electrical recording process developed by Western Electric. The electrical system was far from perfect; in fact, the compression of the dynamics meant the earliest electric recordings were notably inferior to the best acoustic platters, but ultimately, the process offered vastly improved frequency response and fidelity. Improving in small increments, electric recordings remained the standard process for over sixty years, until the introduction of digital technology. By 1926, Okeh and most other record companies had completed the transition to electric recordings. Now bands could record with more or less the same instrumentation they deployed in performance; they could sound, at last, like themselves. Furthermore, the sound quality of record players increased dramatically, and for the first time, listeners were able to hear a relatively lifelike reproduction of a jazz band in their homes.

Turning electric, the Hot Five became the Hot Seven on May 7, 1927. In fact, Okeh now billed the group as "Louis Armstrong and His Hot Seven." The additions were a tuba player and, in a brilliant stroke, the resourceful, if difficult Baby Dodds on drums, playing beside his brother Johnny, who continued on the clarinet. Finally, the new technology allowed these instruments to be heard. The musicians' fledgling efforts, "Willie the Weeper" and Louis's own, aptly titled "Wild Man Blues," took the group to new heights, as they blended the relentless drive of current nightclub music with the by now slightly archaic tempo and rhythms of New Orleans-style jazz.

The Hot Seven sessions on May 10 ("Alligator Crawl," "Potato Head Blues"); May 11 ("Melancholy," "Weary Blues," "Twelfth Street Rag"); May 13 ("Keyhole Blues," "S.O.L. Blues"); and May 14 ("Gully Low Blues," "That's When I'll Come Back to You") showed the group falling increasingly under Louis's musical thrall. Even when the other musicians are playing, they sound more and more like him in their phrasing, and their beguiling combination of drive and relaxed swing. The songs are brief, most of them under three minutes, or just a few seconds over—due to the mechanical limitations of the records themselves—but they are best heard in groups, as parts of a larger whole, for they are united by their jaunty spirit, and the musical themes that Louis explores in one tune are often echoed in another. Although the musicians were earning more at these dates than they did at the start of the Hot Five, the money was still not interesting. They were playing more for fun, and despite the popularity of the records, had no sense they were leaving a musical legacy, or that these records surpassed all other jazz recordings of the era. The regard in which these tunes came to be held in later years startled the band, since they took them pretty much for granted, and didn't think too much about them at the time they were recording.

A casual air may have permeated the sessions, but nothing was random. A case in point is the "S.O.L. Blues." "S.O.L." means "shit out of luck." This was Louis's composition, and his title was of course a joke, his way of seeing how much he could sneak past the Okeh Record Company to the public, and on this occasion, he succeeded. Yet there was actually another, even more inside joke, because the first theme was actually Louis's freewheeling adaptation of an old New Orleans tune played by bands when they were victorious in a cutting contest. The traditional title was not "Shit Out of Luck Blues"; old-timers knew it instead as, "If You Don't Like The Way I Play, You Can Kiss My Fucking Ass."

Baby Dodds praised Louis's relaxed, confident style in the studio. "He would tell each of us when to take a solo or when not to, and who would come in at different times. We weren't a bunch of fellows to write down anything. That would have made it too mechanical," Dodds recalled. "If I would even ask him a question about playing he'd say, 'Go ahead, you know what to do.' "

By this time, Louis's recorded performances had begun to attract the interest and respect of collectors and musicians alike. The Melrose Music Company transcribed his solos and cadenzas on his records and gathered them into two books, *125 Jazz Breaks for Cornet* and *50 Hot Choruses for Cornet*. "Throughout the world the name of Louis Armstrong is known to thousands of musicians," Melrose advised its customers. "Many of the greatest hot men we have today, men who have made enviable reputations as recording artists, will tell you they conceived many of their tricks and ideas from the Armstrong style of playing." In conclusion, the publisher urged, "If you want to get hot and stay hot, memorize these breaks. They will prove invaluable to jazz cornetists as they may be used in playing any and all dance melodies." In one instance, though, Melrose inadvertently sowed confusion by crediting the solo on "Wild Man Blues" to Armstrong and Jelly Roll Morton. This was a song Louis had recorded twice—once with the Hot Seven for Okeh, and again for Brunswick with Johnny Dodds's own band, the Black Bottom Stompers—and Melrose relied on the slightly superior Stompers version. When the book appeared, Louis was astonished by the erroneous credit, for he did not consider himself the song's composer, nor was Jelly Roll, to the best of his knowledge. The song and transcription were presented as a collaboration between the two men, yet, "I never played any gigs nor jobs with Jelly," Louis explained, "and we didn't make any records together. Jelly was always somewhere else, like California. I never knew Jelly Roll in New Orleans." Despite the confusion, Louis's fame and influence on the horn spread, on record, in performance, and now in print.

. . .

What a man of contrasts Louis had become! At the Sunset, and in his other gigs around Chicago, he was the most accessible of performers, giving the impression that he would do absolutely anything to please the audience, even to the point of dancing the Charleston and making a fool out of himself. On record with the Hot Five and Hot Seven, he became invisible, aloof, commanding, even chilling. The disparity between these two aspects of Louis enhanced his growing mystique in an age enthralled with newly minted celebrities.

The only break in his relentless recording and performing schedule occurred in December 1926, when an illness sidelined him for several weeks. Once he recovered, he pushed himself as hard as he always did, almost as if he were still driving that old coal cart. In April 1927, Louis's engagement with the Erskine Tate Orchestra concluded, and he immediately joined a similar enterprise at the Metropolitan Theater, Clarence Jones's Orchestra, while continuing his primary gig at the Sunset. With Jones, Louis dazzled audiences with his rendition of Puccini's *Madame Butterfly*. The piece began with a violin solo, and then a trombone lament, and in the words of the Chicago *Defender*, "now comes the big punch and Louis Armstrong delivered the knockout wallop with that famous jazz version of his on the butterfly song. After this rendition the applause was deafening for at least five minutes. Flowers by the basket were showered on the new music makers at the Metropolitan Theater."

Later on, Louis indulged his taste for the ridiculous while working with Jones. He was reunited with his pal from New Orleans, the drummer Zutty Singleton, and the two of them played off each other like two kids. They worked up a vaudeville skit around the number "I Ain't Gonna Play No Second Fiddle" in which Louis came on stage in a funny little hat, weaving drunkenly and singing, and then a big fat washerwoman—played by Zutty in drag, with floppy pillows under his dress—rushed out of the audience right into the orchestra. Zutty rushed on stage and threw himself at Louis, which of course created a ridiculous spectacle. The crowd roared with delight until the fellows suddenly got down to business. Louis picked up his trumpet, Zutty went to his drums, and they beat out a pretty tune. And then, as always happened at the Sunset Cafe, the movie began . . .

Meanwhile, in July 1927, Louis played a two-week engagement at

Blackhawk's Restaurant, an all-white establishment in the Loop. It would be stretching a point to say that Louis Armstrong was integrating the Chicago music scene, but he was starting to test conventional thinking about where a black jazz musician should or should not perform. By playing consistently for white audiences as well as black, Louis built an ever-expanding base of young fans—acolytes really—who learned to appreciate subtler human qualities lurking behind his broad, larger-than-life persona. Max Kaminsky, an aspiring young trumpeter, recalled the extraordinary first impression that Armstrong made on him. "From listening to his records I already had some inkling of the warmth and power of the man, but I was totally unprepared for that remarkable penetrating awareness underneath the genial, easygoing manner. All his senses seemed to receive impressions of you; you feel he's not so much sizing you up as opening his mind to you." And when he started to play, said Kaminsky, "Louis's dazzling virtuosity and sensational brilliance of tone so overwhelmed me that I felt as if I had stared into the sun's eye."

At the same time, Louis's antics made a huge impression on the black youngsters who would regularly sneak into the Sunset, or the Metropolitan, or wherever he was playing. They would gaze at him with wonder, for though he was plainly adult size, he seemed to be one of them. Charlie Carpenter remembered his first sight of Louis, this "fat guy with the cornet" cavorting at the Sunset, singing and blowing his way through "Big Butter and Egg Man" with May Alix, so light-skinned she looked almost white. He hung around the Metropolitan day after day, hoping to catch sight of his idol, and eventually Louis noticed him. "Why do I always see you standing out here? Don't you ever go in?"

"I'd like to," said the boy, "but I don't have the dime." That was the price of admission.

"Come with me," Louis said. He led young Charlie to his dressing room, and asked if he was hungry. Sure, the kid said, but he wanted to see the show more than he wanted to eat, so they made a deal that they would go out for a meal afterward. They went straight to a Chinese restaurant—still Louis's favorite cuisine after red beans and rice—and Charlie tried to order chop suey, the only Chinese dish he'd ever heard of. No, no, Louis told him, "You don't want chop suey. Get something good like shrimp egg fooyung." The kid had never heard of it, but never mind, Louis ordered it for them both. Charlie tried it, and loved it. They were fast friends from then on, and Charlie became practically a surrogate son to Louis, who displayed his generosity in all sorts of ways. "My father was never able to give me the kind of pocket money Louis just threw at me," Carpenter said. "He even paid for my graduation picture from high school."

One time, Charlie brought Louis out to Hyde Park High to play at, of all things, a high school dance—"and in those days he played ten choruses of 'Tiger Rag' at a very fast tempo." Louis took one look at the band's young drummer and figured the kid would be lucky to last three choruses.

"I play 'Tiger Rag' way up here," he said gently, illustrating the tempo by clapping his hands. "Do you think you can keep up with me?" The little drummer said sure, of course he could. "Well," said Louis softly, "you can always slow it down." They started in playing, and incredibly the kid kept going. He constantly dropped the tempo, but Louis considerately slowed down along with him, coaxing him all the way to the tenth chorus. When they finally wheezed across the finish line, he gave the gutsy kid a hand.

His incredible run of luck suddenly snapped when Mayann, his mother, came up to visit.

"Mother stayed down in New Orleans about two years and she had taken sick. I had to send for her to come to me in Chicago again," Louis explained. "She suffered with the hardening of the arteries—a drastic thing to have. I did everything in my power to save Mayann. I gave her the finest doctors, and the whole time she was in the hospital it cost me over $17.00 a day. I didn't care what it cost, as long as I could save Mayann.

"That was the year of 1927 when she died. I buried her at the Lincoln Cemetery just outside Chicago. I've never cried in my life before, even when Mayann was dying, and grabbed my hand and said 'God bless you, my son, and thank God I lived to see my son grow up to be a big successful young man.'

"Then she passed away.

"The undertaker took her body to the chapel, and the moment that really touched me was when the sermon was finished and the undertaker began to cover up her coffin. I let out plenty of tears, and I just couldn't stop crying and Mayann was laying there looking so natural, just as though she was just taking a nap. I never forgot what Mother told me before she died. She said, 'Son, carry on. You're a good boy. [You] treat everybody right, and everybody white and colored loves you. You have a good heart. You can't miss.' "

Mary Albert Armstrong lived just forty-one years. Her life began in the dregs of the Civil War, and ended in the bright lights of modern-day Chicago. She had grown up in a world stifled by the oppressive memory of slavery, but lived long enough to see the glimmer of a new role for blacks in society, a role her son was struggling to make his own. Her passage through life had not been easy; she had endured hard times for most of her days. But if Mayann bent under the weight of circumstances, she never broke. She loved fun, and finery, and, most of all, her son. Mayann was no one's idea of a conventional mother, but it was from her that Louis derived his love of spontaneity, his enjoyment of people, his appetite, and his lack of envy of those who were born more fortunate than he. In short, it was Mayann who provided the human capital that sustained him throughout his life.

In November 1927, Louis's engagement at the Sunset ended, as did his gig with the Clarence Jones Orchestra. For eighteen months, these exhausting performances had served as his financial mainstay and claim to fame. Now, after working eighteen-hour days, he was suddenly out of work.

Constitutionally incapable of laying off, he hastily convened the original Hot Five, complete with Kid Ory, and on December 9, 10, and 13, the group made five recordings, each one displaying a gemlike precision and durability. One of them, "Hotter Than That" (credited to Lil Hardin, though Louis no doubt contributed heavily to the finished product), is the summa of what the Hot Five was trying to accomplish. No other song they waxed better displays their virtuosity, their balance, and their lyricism, and it is the first fruit of Louis's maturity. The song starts off fast, and gets still faster as it goes. When Louis starts blowing, he rattles off a succession of quicksilver arpeggios. His playing is all the more scintillating because he seems to have finally understood that he need not blow his brains out in the recording studio to be heard. On this number, diminished volume results in increased sensitivity and facility. He follows up his cornet solo with scatting, but at a higher level than anything he had done previously. A new warmth and lyricism creeps into his voice, supplanting the old

familiar hoarseness and shouting, and there is a sense of power held in
abeyance that makes his scatting more persuasive. Beyond his remarkable
vocal tone, Louis's scatting tightens into the same pointillist patterns he
had been blowing on his cornet. He hits notes over, above, and around the
melody, suggesting it by indirection. At this point, the guitar, played not
by Johnny St. Cyr, but Lonnie Johnson, also a product of New Orleans,
becomes prominent, chasing Louis's scat along the melody and picking up
his soft wails. He echoes them—you can practically see him smile with *dee-
light* as he does this—and after the two of them chase each other a bit, the
song rushes headlong to its conclusion. Although Louis manages to imitate
both his own cornet and Johnson's guitar, "imitation" is hardly the right
word, for his voice suggests the essence of each instrument, and the feat is
all the more haunting as a result. By the time he fires off the closing
cadenza, only one question remains: "Is there anything this man cannot
do?"

Louis, of course, would reach even greater heights, but without the
original members of the Hot Five. These December sessions were the last
for the founding members of the group. From then on, the Hot Five or
Seven (there was even, briefly, a Hot Four) became a generic term covering whatever musicians Louis happened to surround himself with in the
studio that day.

Even as the Hot Five grew increasingly accomplished and confident,
Louis's against-the-odds career unraveled. With time on his hands, he
took to sitting in with Sammy Payton's band at the Persian Palace, playing
his big hits, such as "Big Butter and Egg Man." Payton's drummer at the
time happened to be Louis's comrade-in-clowning Zutty Singleton. Louis
told Zutty he was thinking of starting his own band, and perhaps touring
the South. After all, Louis told himself, he had been the "leader" of the
band at the Sunset, Louis Armstrong and his Stompers. There, though, he
had enjoyed the support of the club, especially Joe Glaser, and he later
admitted, "that's how you get carried away." Zutty, albatross-like, gave his
friend the same advice he had given him back in New Orleans, advice that
had initially prevented Louis from joining Fletcher Henderson's orchestra:
let's stick together, and if anyone wants one of us, they must hire both of

us. Without a wife or a manager on whom to depend, Louis agreed to
Zutty's suggestion, and brought Earl Hines into the deal. Earl, like Zutty,
was brimming with misplaced confidence. Why don't we open up our own
joint? Why let the owners of those places get rich off our backs? We'll be
the ones to get rich this time, he told the others. All they needed was
financial backing, and for that they looked to bighearted Louis, who happened to have more money than the other two fellows. Louis went for it.

So began the worst career decision Louis ever made.

He sought the advice of Lil, with whom he maintained an arm's length
relationship, and the two of them went looking for a location. After only
two days, they settled on a building, Warwick Hall, just off Forrestville
Avenue. The lease was fiendishly expensive, $375 a month, a year's guaran-
tee required, but Louis took it lock, stock, and barrel. After all, he was the
leader now, a big butter and egg man, and liable for all expenses. Next, he
assembled a group of musicians, including Earl and Zutty, and called the
group the Hot Six. Assuming their reputation would attract audiences, he
decided to forgo publicity and promotion, but this turned out to be a
serious mistake. Furthermore, on the night the Warwick opened, a much
larger club only two blocks away, the Savoy Ballroom, also opened its
doors for the first time, and monopolized business. Opening night at the
Warwick, meanwhile, proved to be a dismal failure. Earl, Zutty, and most
of all Louis played until they were exhausted, but failed to rouse the
indifferent patrons.

After only a few nights, everyone connected with the venture realized
the Warwick would never work, not while the Savoy and its renowned
electric billboard, featuring preening peacocks, attracted everyone in sight.
It was painfully apparent that the sleek new Savoy was the club where an
artist of Louis's caliber should have been performing. Said Hines, "I don't
know what happened, but we like to starve to death, making a dollar or a
dollar-and-a-half apiece a night." Lil had no idea how to fix the problem,
nor did Alpha.

The three musicians decided to shut down the Warwick before they
lost any more money, and on the final evening, after locking up, they
walked to Louis's car, a Hupmobile, only to discover it had been stolen.
Louis found his car the next day, stripped of its valuable parts. He arranged
for it to be towed to a garage, where the manager lent him a yellow Ford

roadster with letters on the doors, spelling out the garage's name. In time, the yellow Ford became a familiar sight on Cottage Grove, where Louis and Alpha lived, a symbol of Louis's reduced circumstances. To make matters worse, he was in debt to the owners of the Warwick for nineteen hundred dollars. He defaulted on the lease, and the Warwick's owners sued him. Lil refused to help discharge the debt, and Alpha remained content to relieve him of every spare dime he had.

And so it happened that he was Shit Out of Luck.

S . O . L . BLUES

anuary 1928 was dawning, it was bitter in Chicago, and thanks to his misadventure with Zutty Singleton and their little orchestra, Louis had nothing to show for his efforts to revive his career but another case of the shorts. There he was, The World's Greatest Trumpet Player, and he was unemployed, shit out of luck. "Earl, Zutty, and I stayed out of work so long until it was impossible for me to get my car out of the shop, even after it was fixed," Louis wrote. "Things got so tough with us until fifteen cents looked like fifteen dollars. But we did not lose our spirit, and we all kept that good ol' clean shirt on every day, and ol' Earl Hines kept the big fresh cigar in his mouth every day. Zutty and I both admired that." He added, "You'd be surprised to know how happy we were." Perhaps they were, but only in retrospect.

There they were, three jazz musicians, two of them geniuses at what they did, and one of them the most significant figure in the history of jazz, yet "the three of us would go anywhere as long as we felt that we could make a few dimes and dollars," Louis wrote. "We still had our expenses to keep up at home, and money had to come from some place, so we rented this dance hall on the West Side. It was a very small place, but it was enough to make a piece of money. Only one thing: the darkies"—Louis's expression—"were so bad over there."

"The little joint was doing fine, with Earl (piano), Zutty (drums), and myself (trumpet) playing the music. I shall never forget the upright piano Earl was playing. We had a pretty nice crowd. We three had just been saying how nice it's going to be after the dance, and we'd divide up some pretty nice money for a change." But trouble soon arose. "Come intermission time, in walked a drunken darkie, pulled out a .45 pistol, and leveled it directly at us on the bandstand. Well sir! UMP.

"The crowd scattered everywhere. That left the hall rather clean, so this drunken darkie could get a good view at us on that little bandstand. Now when he raised his pistol again as if he really was going to shoot at us, we were so scared that Earl Hines tried to go through his upright piano, and heaven knows where Zutty and I went, but I know we came off that bandstand right away. Somebody went and found the cops from somewhere out that way, and they chased that black 'sumbitch' downstairs, and this drunken guy ran under a house, and the cops shot up all under the house and filled that guy full of holes. Of course, I was rather sorry to hear about that part of it, but later on I heard that this spade had some trouble over there with some cops the week before and he killed one of them. So as we put it, Death was really on him."

Even for Louis, who had lived constantly with hardship and thought nothing of it, this was no way to make a living. He should have succeeded brilliantly with this band, for his timing was perfect: 1927, the apogee of the Roaring Twenties. All around him, other major jazz figures were coming into their own. A few months earlier, for instance, a semiobscure bandleader from Washington, D.C., named Edward Kennedy Ellington began an engagement at the Cotton Club that would run for five years. True, he wound up at the Cotton Club on a fluke—Owney Madden, who owned the Cotton Club was shuffling bands around—but Ellington at the Cotton Club in 1927 turned out to be the right man at the right time in the right place. As a result of his consistent success there, Ellington rose to national and then international prominence. This was one great band; it was big and powerful and sounded like a locomotive whizzing along at a hundred miles an hour, precisely following every nuance and curve of the music.

Louis lacked Ellington's skill in handling people and finances, which were essential to the smooth running of an orchestra. He could *front* a band better than anyone else, but that didn't mean he could *lead* a band. He had always left that chore to others, to King Oliver at the Lincoln Gardens, or Lil at the Dreamland, or Okeh Records (with the Hot Five), or Joe Glaser at the Sunset. He was happy to sacrifice his independence just to be rid of the burden of responsibility. Louis's reluctance to lead a band shaped his career as surely as his virtuosity with his horn. It meant that someone else always ran the band for him—even if the band was called "Louis Armstrong and His Orchestra"—that someone else controlled his finances, managed his career, and managed *him*.

During the first half of 1928, Louis labored strenuously to repair his shattered career. In February, he returned to the Clarence Jones Orchestra at the Metropolitan Theater, clowning on stage between the picture shows. In March, he belatedly began performing precisely where he should have been all along, at the shiny new Savoy Ballroom, in an orchestra conducted by Carroll Dickerson. He was the violinist whom Glaser had dismissed from the Sunset for drunkenness, but Dickerson had managed to pull himself together, and when the Savoy changed bands, the management hired him to lead one of their two house orchestras. Louis figured Dickerson would rekindle the spirit that had once made the Sunset jump. "Carroll had all of the ol' timers rejoin him," Louis wrote. "Of course, Earl Hines couldn't make it. He had just given Jimmy Noone his word to play in his little four-piece combination down at the Apex nightclub on 35th Street, so Carroll hired Gene Anderson on piano. . . . With Gene, Zutty, Fred Robinson, Homer Hobson, Jimmy Strong, Bernadine Curry, Crawford Worthington, Peter Briggs, Mancy 'Peck' Carr, Louis Armstrong, and Carroll Dickerson—if I have to say it myself—we made up one of the damnedest bands there was." Louis became so fond of some of these fellows—Singleton, Robinson, and Carr, in particular—that he enlisted them in the Hot Five.

Since the Savoy had two bands going, often playing head to head, every night was a cutting contest, and Louis relished his musical triumphs there. "We took it into the Savoy Ballroom and battled ol' Clarence Black's band down to a low gravy," he boasted. "After all, Black's band didn't have anything but that one number called 'I Left My Sugar Standing in the Rain,' and after he'd finished playing that one, he was finished as far as breaking it up was concerned. And there we were with all of those good tunes we'd just finished recording, so it all turned out just fine. Then we became the favorite band of the house."

In June, Louis returned to the studio with a vengeance, and in the space of a few days, made musical history. These recordings were remarkable musically, and they were more widely distributed than Louis's previous discs. In 1926, Columbia had purchased Okeh, which meant that all at once Louis was recording for one of the two dominant record companies, a company with the resources to market his records across the country and keep them available for as long as people wanted to buy them. So the stakes were high when, on June 26, he accompanied Lillie Delk Christian, a blues singer who seemed to be everywhere at the time, on four tunes, including "You're a Real Sweetheart" and "Last Night I Dreamed You Kissed Me." The next day, he reassembled the Hot Five in the Okeh studios for the group's most important sessions. The only carryover from the original Hot Five was Louis Armstrong himself. The band now included Fred Robinson on trombone, Jimmy Strong on clarinet, Mancy Carr on banjo, and Zutty Singleton on drums. Most importantly, Earl Hines replaced Lil on the piano. Gone was her strenuous, literal-minded pounding, so different from Hines's imaginative musicianship. Hines unleashed broken chords and delicate improvisations with elegance. Even better, he modeled his phrasing and attack on Louis's style of trumpet playing, and the two of them bounced off each other with breathtaking dexterity. The musical interplay between these two formed the nucleus of the Hot Five's latest incarnation.

This new Hot Five—which actually consisted of six musicians— sounded more mellow than its predecessors, largely because Louis insisted everyone smoke some of that good shuzzit before they began recording. By the time the musicians played, everyone was pleasantly stoned, Louis most of all. What a day they had: "Fireworks," "Skip the Gutter," and "A Monday Date." The last was an accidental masterpiece. They needed a song and a title, and as Louis and Earl discussed their upcoming gigs, Earl reminded Louis not to forget their next date, Monday. They passed the phrase back and forth and felt it rolling nicely off the tongue. When they recorded it, they dreamed up a gimmick. Earl opens on the piano, then Louis interrupts him, asking to be invited to play along, then chides Earl, telling him that if he had himself a pint of Mrs. Searcy's gin, (Mrs. Searcy was a local bootlegger), he wouldn't act so cocky. Then the ensemble takes up the music, and at the end, Louis blows his horn solo over, around, and under the melody, carrying it off with complete confidence. The performance was so offhand, yet so sophisticated—a blend of musical brilliance and realism characteristic of jazz.

The next day, June 28, the Hot Five recorded, among other tunes, "West End Blues." If a single recording could be said to represent the peak of Louis's art, it would be the "West End Blues." Like many of his other masterpieces, the tune (this one by Clarence Williams) was unremarkable on its own. King Oliver had recorded it a few weeks earlier, and the earth had not moved. In Louis's hands, "West End Blues" became a tapestry of pain, joy, and transcendence through musical artistry. He starts off with what would become the most famous horn solo in jazz, a nine-measure opening cadenza of such dizzying difficulty that for decades aspiring horn players would struggle to imitate. It is a summons to the soul, dignified and daring. Once the horn has gotten the listener's attention, the song shifts gears, slows down, and dawdles along, until Louis begins scat singing in a light, delicate voice, trading phrases with the clarinet, and trolling in the lower registers. Then, without explanation or apology, Louis takes a second solo, holding a note for so long that it pierces through the fabric of the music like a gleaming arrow. With brilliant timing, he finally lets go of it and allows the piece to reach a grateful, satisfying conclusion with a shudder of Zutty's cymbals. When the band finished recording "West End Blues," there were smiles all around; the Hot Five knew they'd done something exactly right.

Louis outdid himself on this recording, but he endured rumors that he'd stolen the opening cadenza. Muggsy Spanier, an Armstrong disciple, claimed that Louis learned the cadenza from Joe Oliver. If Oliver had played the cadenza or anything like it, however, he never recorded it. Furthermore, phrases similar to the cadenza appear throughout Louis's compositions; there are echoes of it in his early "Dippermouth Blues." In "West End Blues," he strung distinctive phrases together into one long musical sequence. Lil took Louis's side in this controversy, insisting that Oliver never played the famous cadenza because *she* had taught it to Louis. Exactly how she accomplished the trick without playing the trumpet she never explained.

The masterpieces kept pouring forth from the Okeh studios. On June 29, the Hot Five continued their streak with "Two Deuces," which was virtually a continuation of "West End Blues," and "Squeeze Me." "Squeeze Me" starts out as a poky drag, but then Louis enters with a lengthy cornet melody, accompanied only by the banjo, building in intensity until he begins to scat the melody he just played on the cornet, competing with and outdoing himself. "Squeeze Me" reveals Louis Armstrong the vocalist, and his command of *two* instruments—his horn and his voice.

Although an enormous, nonmusical *bonk!* mars the song's finale, Okeh issued it anyway. For all its recent advances, the recording studio remained primitive, and the sensitive new microphones amplified mistakes as well as musical nuances.

The supercharged Hot Five reconvened once more that summer, on July 5, and did not return to Okeh's Chicago studio until December, when they created more musical miracles. There was "Basin Street Blues," with its intense, off-center rhythm that prefigured swing by a decade or so, and "Beau Koo Jack" (the title was slang for "lots of money"). "Weather Bird," an improvised duet between Louis and Earl, stands as their finest collaborative effort. On December 7, they recorded "Muggles," Louis's paean to his drug of choice and a concatenation of solos that would influence so many other musicians. "Tight Like This," the final masterpiece of this period, is enlivened with bawdy bantering between Louis, in his baritone, Earl, in falsetto. No one had ever made music like these recordings, and no one, not even Louis, would ever manage to again.

For all their artistry and influence, the 1928 Hot Five recordings occupied only a small fraction of Louis's time and attention. He expended most of his energy on live performances, especially with Carroll Dickerson's orchestra at the Savoy Ballroom. He got a boost when the Savoy started broadcasting the performances over the radio, giving listeners who never dreamed of venturing into sinful Chicago, let alone a South Side dance hall, their first taste of jazz and Louis Armstrong. There is no evidence that Louis received extra pay for these broadcasts, but the exposure led to his receiving offers to perform at dances, at parties, and, for the first time since he had left Fate Marable's orchestra, aboard a riverboat. He accepted a lavish fee of a hundred dollars a day and expenses for this gig, which required him to travel to St. Louis. What seemed a simple proposition quickly turned into a nightmare. Playing aboard the *St. Paul* with the Floyd Campbell band, he became enmeshed in a heated battle with a rival outfit, the Alphonso Trent band, and the spectacle drew so many customers, perhaps as many as five thousand, that the riverboat nearly sank and was forced to return to St. Louis ahead of schedule. Louis immediately returned to Chicago, and he never again performed on riverboats.

Through all the blowing, his musical style continued to evolve. Where he had once used his horn and voice to bring a new rasp and edge to jazz, he now veered toward a polite, even sweet big band sound inspired by Guy Lombardo, of all people. The white bandleader's unflappable sound had become all the rage among the jazz musicians of New Orleans. The exchange of musical influences worked both ways, as Lombardo and his band, in search of inspiration, often dropped in on Louis. In the process, Louis became quite a figure to the Lombardo musicians. On September 21, 1928, Louis and Zutty Singleton paid a visit to Lombardo at the whites-only Granada Cafe, and, according to the *Defender*, the pair of them were "wined and dined until the wee hours of the morning." At first glance, Lombardo's stately rhythms seemed antithetical to Louis's exuberant approach to music, but Louis had many different styles. He blew, he sang, he improvised, he played the melody, he hit two hundred high C's in a row. But he understood that jazz could be relaxed and soothing as well. "That band plays the tune, they put that melody there and it's beautiful. You can't find another band that can play a straight lead and make it sound that good," he said of Lombardo. In years to come, jazz critics and Armstrong fans disparaged Lombardo's influence, especially his simpering saxophones; they wanted Louis to sound like Louis, not like a white bandleader. Louis himself disagreed with this view. To his ears, the New Orleans sound had become tired. The next big thing in popular music was the big band; and for the moment, Lombardo had the big band sound. Always eager to expand his range, Louis wanted to incorporate the new sound into his many-faceted performing style.

In the fall of 1928, Louis's former employer, Fletcher Henderson, came through Chicago, and he offered the trumpeter a position with his band. Louis had no desire to go back to working for the supercilious Smack, but he used the offer to get the Savoy management to increase his salary to a mighty two hundred dollars per week. He remained there for the rest of the year, playing sweeter and earning more money than ever. The good times were back for Louis, and at the Savoy he was in the thick of things.

He was at the peak of his musical abilities, when, in January 1929, he developed a sudden enthusiasm for basketball. Louis wrote, "The Savoy Ballroom was doing all the business in town. They even had a basketball team named after the place, and what a team. They were so good they played some of the best teams in the U.S.A. They'd always have a basketball game first, then the dance would start." Inevitably, Louis was drawn into the games.

"The manager of the Savoy Ballroom decided a week before the big game came off that he would let each of the bands pick out a team from the band and play a game of basketball before the big teams went on—sorta give the customers a good laugh—and by the time the big [game] started everybody would be in good humor. I am telling you it was some fun for us all. Clarence [Black's] band was made up of young boys, and our band was made up of ol' timers and hustlers. Quite naturally we dissipated a little more than those young cats. Clarence's boys would go into the park every morning, run for miles, getting all that good fresh air, and all we were doing was going out every night lushing, staying up all night.

"Well, sir, the night of the dance and the basketball game [arrived]. Clarence Black's boys were dressed just like real basketball players. Clarence Black himself, a tall, lanky fellow, even had on knee guards, like the real players, and we had on all kinds of suits, and I was weighing 230 pounds at the time. So was Tubby Hall, Clarence Black's drummer. We couldn't get a suit to fit us, so Tubby and I had to wear our own bathing suits. The minute we all ran out on the floor, just like real players, the crowd went wild with applause. The game started, and those young cats of Clarence Black's nearly ran us crazy trying to get ahold of the ball. . . . Oh, what fun we had. There wasn't but one basket made in the whole game, and one of Clarence Black's boys made that one. . . . We were so tired we just dropped down on the floor, lifeless. . . . But we had to finish the game anyway, and it looked like the time would never come to quit. But it all ended up swell, with the score 2-to-0 in favor of Clarence Black's band. I did not know that basketball took up so much wind and energy."

After catching his breath and changing into his tuxedo, Louis arrived in front of the Savoy, where a crowd greeted him with frenzied shouts. The young men in the audience lifted him in the air as he shrieked in fear, discomfort, and delight. A near riot ensued as they began to fight over him, tugging him this way and that, bearing his bulky form in a jerking, swaying procession to the bandstand. Once there, they pushed him up the stairs and finally set him down, so he could begin blowing. Instead, he collapsed into a chair, bewildered by the scene he had inspired. He mopped his face with his white handkerchief, trying to recover from the ordeal of celebrity and adulation. Somehow, he got through the set that evening and limped home, but when he went to bed, he was so excited and sore that he could not sleep. For once, he had exerted himself too much. "I was in bed sick a whole week with flu from all of that sudden exposure. Honest, I thought I was going to die," he wrote. "Every bone in my body was aching."

The good times, the excitement, and the acclaim didn't last long.

Once Louis had paid the back rent on the Warwick misadventure and given Alpha the clothes and trinkets she regularly demanded, he was faced with another case of the shorts. Worse, by the spring of 1929, the Savoy was no longer the hottest spot in town. "Business began to get slow," Louis noted, "just like any other amusement that opened up in Chicago—go real big for a while, then, ka-blip, the bottom would drop out. So Mr. Fagan, the owner, would come to us with a hard luck story every week, and the way he would lay this story on us, we couldn't leave him. After all, we were troupers. But it looked liked Mr. Fagan was laying that hard luck story on us a little too often, and payments on our home were way past due. Zutty and I would talk it over every night, and we would say to each other, if Fagan comes with no money this week, we were sure to quit. Again, the usual thing would happen, no money. I was still signed up with the Okeh Record Company, but Mr. Fern turned my contract over to Mr. Tommy Rockwell, who was stationed in New York. And at the same time Mr. Fagan was coming up short with our money. Mr. Rockwell sent for me to come to New York immediately to make some records."

Charming, hard-drinking, Rockwell had the furious conviction of a born promoter. He was in his early twenties when he worked for Okeh, and he then launched a parallel career as a booker in partnership with Cork O'Keefe, who marveled at his partner's tin ear. "Tom Rockwell couldn't carry two notes of a melody, completely tone deaf," said Cork. Indeed, he couldn't even remember the names of songs." Nevertheless, Rockwell put his imprint on the trumpeter's career. Recognizing Louis's appeal to both black and white audiences, Rockwell developed a firm idea of the types of tunes he should record for Okeh—not the blues typical of race records, but popular ballads, romances, and Tin Pan Alley hits.

He began repositioning Louis Armstrong as a solo act. Rockwell had scant interest in the band backing Louis. As far as he was concerned, the only thing that mattered was getting Louis out front, blowing and singing. This meant the end of Louis's career as an ensemble player, the format that had given rise to all the wonderful Hot Five and Hot Seven recordings. This was a crucial step in his evolution as a performer; prior to Rockwell, Louis emphasized jazz, blues, and vaudeville material. His material was idiosyncratic, and reached right back to his New Orleans roots. After Rockwell, Louis moved away from the by now antiquated polyphony of New Orleans jazz toward the avowedly simple musical formulas of Tin Pan Alley and, later, of Hollywood. Rockwell had no interest in musical innovation; he wanted Louis to perform predictable, lucrative hits. Louis was happy to go along with Rockwell's formulas, just as he had been happy to go along with the ideas put forward by all his previous mentors.

Rockwell consummated his relationship with Louis by arranging for the trumpeter to appear in a Broadway musical, *Great Day*. At the time, Vincent Youmans was riding the crest of his popularity as a purveyor of light, bright, sophisticated musical comedies. Acting as his own producer on this occasion, he had come up with an idea that seemed a natural for Louis Armstrong, a romantic musical comedy set on an antebellum plantation near New Orleans. Louis yearned to make a name on Broadway, and *Great Day*, scheduled to open in October 1929, held out the possibility that he would, at last, achieve his goal. "When I received Mr. Rockwell's telegram in Chicago I showed it to Carroll Dickerson, Zutty, and the rest of the band boys. We were so attached to each other we hated like hell to break up our band." Louis was so comfortable with his musical colleagues that he mistakenly assumed that Mr. Rockwell, and even Mr. Youmans, would be delighted to have them all in the show.

In the midst of these negotiations, Louis was distracted by his romantic problems. In recent months, his affair with Alpha had cooled. He realized that she looked to him primarily for material things, and he had grown resentful about always laying out for her. And Alpha, he felt, gave nothing in return. Lil, although exasperating and domineering, had been generous with him personally and musically; they had formed an attachment that would outlive the changed circumstances of their marriage. Louis acknowledged that Lil, for all her contrariness, was a woman of genuine accomplishment, intelligence, and substance, all symbolized by her big house on 44th Street. In contrast, neither Louis nor Alpha owned any such possessions. It was all he could do to keep his Hupmobile running. More importantly, he could never hope to relate to Alpha in the area that mattered most to him: music.

He had even less in common with Fanny, the chorus girl to whom he had once proposed, but that was the essence of her appeal: she offered the prospect of escape from his romantic quandary. Although he spent nearly all his free time with Alpha, he hadn't forgotten about Fanny, and had been in touch with her occasionally. He had even seen her when she came through Chicago, but the visit had to be short, before Alpha noticed. To his surprise, she announced she was going to Paris to appear in a show. Louis was ambivalent about her decision. Even though he urged her to forget him, he began to miss her keenly. He loved Fanny when he couldn't have her, and she loved him when he was distant. They vowed that one day he would come to Europe, find her, and make her his own.

To be sure, he enjoyed playing the big butter-and-egg man with Alpha and her kind, lavishing gifts on them, and enjoying their attention in return, but in other moments, he felt the lack of an emotional center in his life, especially now that his mother was dead. There was an underlying sense of sadness and confusion about him, as he dashed from the arms of one attractive woman to another. He had found his calling, but he seemed to have lost himself in the process. Moving from one big, hard-driving city to another, he had no idea when, or even if, he would recover.

While Louis was absorbed in the complications of his love life, Tommy Rockwell waited impatiently. "Mr. Rockwell wired me again to come to New York right away," Louis wrote. "The band and I held a private meeting. I told them, 'Well, fellows, you all know how well I love you all, and you boys love me too. What say if we have our cars fixed up, and Mr. Rockwell has just sent me enough money, and I can give each man in the band $20 to eat and help buy gas, and we'll all go to New York together?' They all jumped in the air with joy and said that's great, and it makes us very happy to know that you're not going to leave us, and we'll still be together. I told them when we get to New York and Mr. Rockwell won't have anything for us to do, we'll just take ourselves a job because we have a band good enough to get a job any place.

"So finally we had the four cars overhauled. I got my Hupmobile out of the shop. Carroll Dickerson bought a secondhand Marmon. Gene Anderson had a little Essex, and Fred Robinson had a brand-new lightweight car—forget the name. Anyway, we left Chicago. All of our friends were on hand to wish us luck." Lil graciously "lent" them twenty dollars apiece to make the journey east.

So began a great adventure—and misadventure, as the fellows drove east, in search of fame. It was May, the weather was warm and lovely, and the twenties still had a few months more to roar before economic paralysis struck the nation. But Louis and the rest of the fellows were still broke. As soon as he hit the road, Louis realized that conditions were better than they'd seemed in Chicago. "It was nice for us to see the welcome we got everywhere," he wrote. "They had heard us over the radio and we found we had quite a reputation. They wouldn't let us spend money for anything. We would go to a cabaret and sit in with the local band for a few numbers and eat and drink with them, and there wouldn't be any check to pay. All the 'cats' were glad to see us. We took our time; we didn't have a job to do, so we didn't care about hurrying and just lazed along from one town to another, having real good fun. We stopped in Detroit and Dayton and Cleveland and other places, and when we got to Buffalo we decided we would like to see Niagara Falls, so we drove on out there." Soon they were sorry they'd ever heard of Niagara Falls, since they had the wrong directions and proceeded to drive two hundred miles back toward Chicago before they realized anything was amiss. There was nothing to do but turn around and drive two hundred miles the other way. When they reached Niagara Falls, said Zutty, "It was all just ice and fog and snow. The falls were all frozen over. You could only hear the gurgling underneath." They drove on to New York—what else could they do?—and soon enough they were all laughing about it. How fine it was to be footloose for a few days, with the prospect of New York looming. Louis would soon turn twenty-eight, and this meandering idyll, punctuated by impromptu gigs, was the closest he had ever come to a vacation.

At last we hit New York. Zutty and I were in my car. In fact, Zutty did pretty well near all the driving. I did most of the sleeping. We had lots of car trouble on the way there. Our gas line gave us lots of trouble, and we kept stopping to fix the damn thing all the time. The minute we were crossing 42nd Street and Broadway my radiator cap blew off, and steam was going every place, and we were embarrassed. The cops came over and saw we had a Chicago license on our car and asked us, 'Hey there, have you boys had shotguns in that car?' We gladly said, 'No, Suh, Boss.' He smiled and went away. In those days the gangsters were very popular in Chicago. . . .

"We all finally arrived in Harlem, everybody suffering with the 'shorts,' meaning we were all broke. So I immediately went down to Mr. Rockwell's office. He certainly was glad to see me. He said, 'Louis, I've just arranged to put you in the *Great Day* show.'

"I said, 'Fine, Mr. Rockwell, but I brought my band with me, and you'll have to book us some place.' Mr. Rockwell hit the ceiling. 'Band? I did not send for your band. I sent for you only.'

"I said, very calmly, 'Just the same, Mr. Rockwell, we're here now. I just couldn't leave my boys. I know you can book us some place. Another thing—we all need money, so you'll have to let me have money to keep us eating, room rent and our laundry until we go to work. After all, they must hold their heads up and stay sharp, because they're all sharp cats and can play their asses off.' "

While the matter hung in doubt, Louis traveled to Philadelphia, to join *Great Day*, then in rehearsal. The show was in a state of chaos, as Youmans, trapped into functioning as his own producer, hired and fired with abandon. Within days, the trumpeter was out of the show, and Louis's Broadway hopes remained as remote as ever. As it turned out, Louis was well rid of the show, which continued to limp along until its New York opening in October, and then closed after just thirty-six performances.

At liberty again, Louis returned to New York and resumed negotiating with Tommy Rockwell. His case of the shorts persisted, and he moved in with his friend Wellman Braud in Harlem. Braud, from New Orleans, played bass in Duke Ellington's Orchestra. In fact, Louis wound up living there for the duration of his stay in New York. "Next morning, Braud gave Louis some money and he distributed it to the boys," Zutty recalled of that anxious moment. "Then he got some from Rockwell. Lucky we all had good clothes. We started hanging around the Rhythm Clubs. We changed the name of the band from Carroll Dickerson to Louis Armstrong, figuring that was the big name. We hung around for a few days. Then Duke Ellington had to open at the Audubon Theatre in the Bronx. He couldn't make the first show, so they sent our band up there. Letha Hill was on the bill, and while we were playing she would look around at Louis, doing all that fancy blowing behind her. When it came to us, we played 'St. Louis

Blues.' When we got through it, all the musicians in the pit were standing up looking at Louis . . . and I saw something I'll never forget as long as I live. When he finished, even the band in the pit stood up and applauded for him." The performance served noticed that an exceptional orchestra had come to town, led by an extraordinary trumpeter.

On June 1 and 2, directly after their Audubon debut, the band played the Savoy Ballroom—the New York Savoy, not the better-known Savoy in Chicago—where they confirmed their prowess. On the strength of that success, they won an audition for the most powerful Broadway impresario of the era, Florenz Ziegfeld Jr. Then in the twilight of his opulent career, he was renowned as the producer of the annual *Follies*, which had been appearing in annual editions for nearly two decades. Two years earlier, he had launched *Showboat*, the most influential of all musicals. Now he was planning a new spectacular, *Show Girl*, scheduled to open in the Ziegfeld Theatre on Broadway in July. A typical Ziegfeld extravaganza, the production glittered with big names; George Gershwin was writing the score, Ruby Keeler was set to star, Jimmy Durante was in the cast, and the plot was the usual Cinderella story of a poor girl's ascent to fame in show business. All Ziegfeld needed was an authentic jazz orchestra to perform with the show. Louis Armstrong and his Orchestra, as the fellows now called themselves, played for Ziegfeld himself, and then held their breath for several days, only to discover that he preferred Duke Ellington. Once again, Broadway eluded Louis Armstrong. (*Show Girl*, with Ellington, went on to become a modest hit on Broadway.)

Despite the rejection, Louis had reason to rejoice. "Finally Mr. Rockwell gave in and gave me all the money I wanted, and inside of two weeks we had a job in Connie's Inn in Harlem, at 131st Street and 7th Avenue," he wrote. "That club and the Cotton Club were the hottest clubs in Harlem at that time, and Harlem was really jumping. All the white people would think it was a real treat to spend a night up in Harlem." Louis started his new gig at Connie's Inn on June 24, 1929, and the Depression that had begun to make itself felt in Chicago had yet to arrive in Harlem. On his first trip, five years earlier, Louis had been a very young man, just twenty-three, but now he was a seasoned performer, far more confident in front of an audience, and unwilling to be reined in by any bandleader. He loved the Harlem scene, and he observed it closely, a participant in and a witness to the Jazz Age—the age of jazz—the age he had unwittingly but unmistakably helped to invent. "In the audience, any old night, would be famous actresses and critics and authors and publishers and rich Wall Street men and big people of all kinds, being gay and enjoying the hot swing music and the fast-stepping floor shows," he said of these heady days.

The guys and dolls who flocked to Connie's Inn to hear him were high rollers, the biggest butter-and-egg men he'd ever seen. "My, the money they spent in those days in those Harlem clubs!" he marveled as he totaled up the costly rites of Prohibition. "A gentleman and a lady would have to spend from forty to sixty dollars for one evening, without spending money for wine. It was during Prohibition and the clubs could not sell liquor, although the waiters and the captain often took a chance and cleaned up selling it undercover at terrible prices—ten dollars for a pint and so on. So most of the people would bring in their own drinks in flasks and buy bottled soda or ginger-ale at one dollar apiece for a little 'splits' bottle, good for one tall drink. They would pay three dollars for an order of chicken á la king or a seafood Newburgh, forty cents for a black coffee and so on—and all of that on top of a cover charge of perhaps seven to ten dollars." Louis could only shake his head in amazement at what rich folks spent their money on. He, on the other hand, was conditioned to live frugally, except when it came to women, when he couldn't help himself. Instead of expensive booze, he smoked his weed, ten cents a reefer, supplied by Mezz, and no hangover in the morning. He wheedled his meals from the kitchen at Connie's Inn. He was content to drift along on the fringes of the underworld with the gamblers, dealers, gangsters, and hookers he knew so well.

None was more devoted to Louis than Dutch Schultz, the one-man crime wave. As a silent partner in Connie's Inn, he decided he had to meet the hot young trumpeter who was causing such a sensation. Late one evening, he planted himself at the bar and asked one of his flunkies to arrange an introduction. If Louis was frightened to meet Schultz, he gave no hint of it and readily shook the man's cold-blooded hand. "We see your picture in the *Daily News* all the time, Mr. Schultz," he said.

"Yeah," Schultz replied, "people are startin' to bug me for my autograph." He introduced Louis to a young white musician he'd taken under his wing, Harry Gibson. Harry played the piano in a band at one of Schultz's speakeasies in the Bronx, and he worshiped Louis Armstrong. Louis beamed at the young musician who was so plainly in awe of him.

"Gimme some skin, Pops," said Louis.

"Me and the guys in the band dig you blowin' through the window all night long," Harry said.

Louis laughed his ripe, resonant laugh. "I heard about you cats. It's a ball playin' for musicians. You boys keep listening out there. You'll be in the big time before you know it."

Harry was now more enthralled than ever with Louis, and he came back again and again with Dutch Schultz to hear Louis blow. And when Louis took him backstage to the tiny "bandroom" cluttered with half-empty bottles of Canadian Club whiskey, Harry thought he'd died and gone to heaven. Instead of offering him a drink, Louis picked up a reefer the size of a cigar, lit up, and sucked in the sweet fumes. Harry couldn't believe his eyes. "It just about blows my top when Louis passes it over to me," Harry remembered. "I take a couple of big tokes. Louis laughs, points his finger at me. 'That boy's gonna do all right in the music business.' " Later on, Louis offered this advice to Harry: "I like blowin' on gage a lot better than booze. But remember, man, it ain't the reefer or the likker that's playing jazz. It's you, just feeling a lot better listening to it."

Finally, Louis got to make his long-awaited Broadway debut. On the strength of his success at Connie's Inn, he found himself performing on Broadway, not on stage, but as the star musical performer in the orchestra of a musical revue, *Hot Chocolates*, staged by Connie Immerman. The show—underway before Louis came aboard—had opened to acclaim at the Hudson Theatre on Broadway on June 20. It brought well-deserved attention to its principal creators, the lyricist Andy Razaff and Fats Waller, who instantly won Louis's affection. Waller was a many-faceted jazz entertainer: a clown and a virtuoso; a stride pianist of genius—stride being the predominant style in Harlem; a composer; a singer; and a storyteller. He was a complete entertainer. Louis believed that Waller and he were kindred spirits. The two met when Connie moved the band from the Hudson Theatre uptown to Connie's Inn, replacing them with new musicians on Broadway. "And then we showed up," Louis said, and for once, the band's timing was perfect. "We got the job, and were we lucky! Coming into the big town like that and landing plump into one of the top spots in all New York, all in a month."

Hot Chocolates was an agglomeration of skits and showstoppers; chorus girls were "Hot Chocolate Drops," chorus boys were "Bon Bon Buddies," and they all participated in vignettes of Harlem street life. The show was especially memorable for one of Waller's songs, "Ain't Misbehavin'." "From the first time I heard it, that song used to 'send' me. I woodshedded it until I could play all around it," Louis said. "I was all ready with it and it would bring down the house, believe me!" Each time he heard the audience's applause, he silently thanked his new manager, Tommy Rockwell, for having snared him this precious gig. "I tell you, I have been lucky, and I have had a good manager, which I think is a good combination for anybody in show business to have." He was in show business at last, and Tommy Rockwell had gotten him there.

The good times rolled for a few months longer. He was at the peak of his powers now, and never blew better than he did at this moment in his career. Rockwell kept him incredibly busy with overlapping bookings. He appeared twice at Harlem's Lafayette Theatre, in June and in October, electrifying audiences and critics alike. At the end of his first engagement at the Lafayette, the *New York Age* commented, "Never before in the history of Harlem theatricals has any artist received a reception comparable to that accorded Louis Armstrong at the Lafayette Theatre. The audience . . . cheered as this most remarkable of all cornetists drew from his golden trumpet music such as has never been heard before."

Louis seemed to be performing everywhere at once, uptown in Harlem, downtown on Broadway, and in the recording studio. He would show up at small nightclubs and jam, or engage in ferocious cutting contests. He would play before a crowd of whites only, and then he would play exclusively to blacks, evoking equal enthusiasm from both. He'd blow, he'd sing, he'd tell stories, he'd dress up in a frock coat to preach a mock sermon. News of Louis Armstrong's conquest of New York traveled back to Chicago, where he was considered a hometown favorite. The *Defender's* music critic, Dave Peyton, came to Harlem to see for himself how Louis was doing. He even stayed with Louis at Braud's Harlem digs. Peyton was eager to portray the trumpeter as a black hero and a Chicagoan who had conquered New York, and his observations confirmed his expectations. "Chicago's own Louis Armstrong and his orchestra are the current rage in New York," he advised the *Defender*'s readers. "They have taken the city by storm. They have things their own way and to this writer they are playing better than ever before."

To demonstrate New York's wholehearted acceptance of Louis, Peyton made a point of describing his friend's standing among his white colleagues. "The white musicians of New York tendered Louis a banquet several weeks ago and presented him with a handsome wristwatch, engraved thusly: 'To Louis Armstrong, the World's Greatest Cornetist, from the Musicians of New York.' Truly they are wild about Louis and his Chicago Orchestra." Peyton was right; Louis *was* the rage in Harlem. His stage persona, his use of a blinding white handkerchief, his sharp suits (no more secondhand apparel or "police shoes" for him), and his penchant for marijuana all inspired imitators. Mezz Mezzrow noticed that legions of young men in Harlem started clasping a handkerchief in their hands, in emulation of Louis, and "all the raggedy kids . . . were so inspired with self-respect after digging how neat and natty Louis was, they started to dress up real good, and took pride in it, too, because if Louis did it, it must be right."

As Louis's dealer, Mezz enjoyed unlimited access to his idol, whom he worshiped with erotic fervor. "Every day, soon as I woke up about four in the P.M., I would jump up to Louis's apartment and most of the time catch him in the shower," he wrote. "I would sit there watching him handle his razor, sliding it along with such rhythm and grace you could feel each individual hair being cut, and I'd think it was just like the way he fingered the valves on his horn." The biggest thrill Mezz ever had occurred when he brushed up against Louis as he was blowing his horn one night, "and goddamn if I didn't feel his whole body vibrating like one of those electric testing machines in the penny arcade that tell how many volts your frame can stand. Louis really blew with every dancing molecule in his body."

Louis's pride in himself and his music was a daring statement in an era in which black entertainers came in predictable categories—minstrel show clowns, blues singers, or tap dancers. Despite their relatively small numbers, they wielded a large influence over American popular entertainment. Far and away the most popular act in any medium at this moment was the radio show "Amos 'n' Andy," broadcast each evening at seven o'clock on NBC. The whole country seemed to pause to hear the show. President Calvin Coolidge was a faithful listener, and when George Bernard Shaw returned to England from a visit to the United States, he stated, "There are three things I'll never forget about America: the Rocky Mountains, Niagara Falls, and 'Amos 'n' Andy.' " Of course, the creators and stars of the show, Freeman Gosden and Charles Correll, were white and southern, and their show was the wireless equivalent of a blackface act. They portrayed black stereotypes, yet they infused their sketches with a gentle humor and warmth so that Amos and Andy came to represent Everymen, and listeners naturally identified with their little trials and foibles.

In contrast to these ersatz blacks, Louis Armstrong was the genuine article, and he took his inspiration from the commanding pride and showmanship of Bill Robinson. To Peyton, and other black critics, here at last was a man who was authentically black and did not pander to white expectations of black behavior, yet had the respect and affection of whites. The black press began to view Louis Armstrong as more than a musician, he was a symbol: a black man making his way in white America while remaining true to himself and his people.

Once again, the good times evaporated. *Hot Chocolates* ended its run after six successful months and 219 performances. At the same moment, "My band stayed down in Connie's Inn for over six months, then the guys commenced to making 'late time,' especially Bernadine Curry (alto sax), Jimmy Strong, and Carroll Dickerson," he wrote. The performers' frequent tardiness aroused the ire of their boss. "Connie gave us two weeks' notice. The band broke up the minute we came out of Connie's Inn. Some of the band boys went back to Chicago. Carroll, Zutty, and Gene Anderson stayed in New York. I stayed also. I did a single act the rest of 1929 and the beginning of 1930."

Louis's changing fortunes led to a painful rift with Zutty Singleton. Louis had long felt that he had carried the drummer, paid his bills, gotten him jobs, and had come to the conclusion that Zutty was prepared to take advantage of him indefinitely. Encouraged by his manager, Tommy Rockwell, Louis broke up the band. Zutty countered by claiming that Connie's Inn wanted him even if Louis did not. To hear Zutty tell it, Louis was so infatuated by the prospect of a solo career that he brushed off his old friend. "Louis told me how much money he had a chance to make and everything like that. And that's when I told Louis, I said, 'Well, Louis, friendship is one thing and business is another.' " Still, Zutty was outraged, and so was his wife, Marge Creath. Zutty's hurt over Louis's rejection became the cross she bore. "Zutty was so crazy about Louis and loved Louis so much," she recalled, "I have to tell Zutty all the time, 'He don't give a shit about you, so forget him. I get sick of you talking about Louis, Louis, Louis." When he later heard Louis perform with another band, Zutty told his former friend that it was positively the worst band he'd ever heard. Louis replied, "I don't even hear them."

Another event greatly affected Louis's career at this moment: the onset of the Depression. Black Tuesday, October 29, 1929, had come and gone; the stock market had crashed; the Depression had settled in; and no one knew how bad it would get or how long it would last. Most everyone lived in disbelief and denial that such a thing had occurred. It would take years for the full economic and social effects of the Depression to be felt, and it would strike hardest of all in Harlem because blacks were among the most vulnerable to the consequences of an economic reversal. Family income in Harlem sank from $1,808 in 1929 to $1,019 in 1932, a drop of slightly more than 40 percent. The economic underpinnings of black life—black burial societies and banks—went under or sold out at bargain rates to large, white institutions.

The economic collapse meant the end of the Harlem Renaissance, and one uptown jazz club after another fell on hard times. The Cotton Club, the best-known, most prosperous venue of all, was under a death sentence and finally expired in 1936. There was still plenty of jazz to be heard in Harlem, but it was found in speakeasies and at rent parties rather than at lavish nightclubs. Black musicians who had become celebrities in Chicago and Harlem lost their jobs and fell into obscurity. Hardly a musician of Louis's generation was unscathed. Sidney Bechet, the brilliant, resentful clarinet player with whom Louis had dueled on record, was working as a tailor to support himself. Baby Dodds was driving a taxi instead of playing his drums. Kid Ory, Louis's longtime friend and favorite trombonist, managed a chicken farm during the hard times. Fletcher Henderson suffered a broken collarbone in an automobile accident in 1928, and was never quite the same. He toured with his band after his recovery, but had lost the polish and zip for which he was known. He presided over an unruly, ever-changing cast of characters until his band deteriorated and finally broke up in 1934, long after his popularity had waned.

Bix Beiderbecke, the only other musician to rival Louis on the cornet, fell deeper into the bottle. By the end of the decade, his fund of musical invention began to suffer, and he appeared with the Paul Whiteman Orchestra less and less often. Whiteman eventually discharged him from the orchestra, and told him to return when he could. He reappeared in the early months of 1931, but he soon resumed drinking, harder than ever. He made a few recordings with such old friends as Hoagy Carmichael and Bud Freeman, and burned his candle at both ends at wild parties. His best-known fan during this time was another burnt-out case, Babe Ruth. The slugger was so big and Bix's apartment so small, that Ruth took the doors off the hinges so that he could pass from one room to another. These two dying embers of the Jazz Age endlessly drank and talked about music and baseball.

Hoagy Carmichael, who was as close as anyone to Bix, urged the cornetist to get out, get some exercise, quit drinking, and start eating. Bix tried. He tried to get a band together to tour Europe, but then he happened to catch a cold. The cold turned into pneumonia, and on August 7, 1931, Bix died. He was just twenty-eight years old.

The older generation of musicians fared even worse. Bunk Johnson, Louis's first teacher, disappeared from New Orleans. No one knew what had become of him. King Oliver, the man who had given so much of himself to Louis, also fell on hard times. He came to New York, but his old-fashioned ensemble approach to music had failed to attract audiences or backers. He made records, many of them distinguished, but he was now known as the bandleader who had once employed Louis Armstrong. In 1931, Victor Records canceled his contract, and his principal source of income was gone. He retreated to the South, where, hampered by deteriorating health, he played one-night stands with pickup bands, harvesting a legacy of undeserved bitterness.

New Orleans, too, was a very different place now. Funky Butt Hall, where Louis first heard jazz as a small boy, had become a church. The spacious parks where Buddy Bolden and Freddie Keppard and Joe Oliver and other musicians had entertained audiences in open-air concerts became nothing more than memories. No one, not even Louis Armstrong, had any idea Buddy Bolden was still alive. After a quarter century of incarceration in the insane asylum at Jackson, Louisiana, he died on November 4, 1931. The cause of death was listed as "arterial sclerosis." He was fifty-four years old and had not had contact with the outside world since being committed in 1907. To the end of his life, he had no idea what had become of the music he had let loose on New Orleans and the rest of the country, no indication of its development, its flourishing, and its widespread acceptance. Bolden did not even have the benefit of a traditional New Orleans jazz funeral. There was no notice of his passing in the *Times-Picayune*, and no musicians attended his last rites. When his sister was unable to pay for the maintenance of his gravesite, his remains were disinterred and reburied in a common grave. Although his musical legacy is ubiquitous, his final resting place is as obscure as he had been in the last years of his life.

The Depression would mean profound changes for Louis. It would test his mettle, and his ability to endure hard times while remaining a working musician. His initial strategy of survival was to get as far away from New York and Chicago as he could. "I had a friend who ran on the [rail]road from New York to California," Louis wrote, "And he would always tell me he could get a pass for me at any time I should see fit to go out there, and always I would ask him, 'What's out there?' not knowing that I was as popular as I actually was in California with the white people mostly." The idea of going all the way to California intrigued Louis, but he was frankly afraid to go because of the color of his skin. "Naturally, in those days, the minute a colored man gets off a train anywhere West or South, he would have his head whipped worse than a kettle drum"—not by whites, Louis explained, but by a Red Cap (a black porter), as a stern warning.

In May 1930, Louis overcame his trepidation, packed his horn, and boarded a transcontinental train bound for Los Angeles. This was an unauthorized journey. He left Alpha behind in Chicago, and Lil—not to mention Fanny, who was somewhere in Europe. His manager, Tommy Rockwell, hadn't lined up any gigs for him. For once he was not traveling with his usual cadre of New Orleans musicians. He told himself he had enough money not to "cop a beg"—beg for work—"unless I was actually satisfied and willing."

On his arrival in Los Angeles, he checked into the Dunbar Hotel on Central Avenue and 42nd Street, well-known for its black show business clientele. He discovered there was quite a scene here in L.A., and the Dunbar was right in the thick of it. There were prize-fighters strolling along Central Avenue, one of whom, Gorilla Jones, walked a lion cub on a leash. There were black movie stars, such as Clarence Muse and Stepin Fetchit. Stepin Fetchit, as his stage name suggests, earned his living portraying humiliating black stereotypes, but along Central Avenue he was hailed as a celebrity and world-class hell-raiser. When he went to work, he made himself conspicuous by arranging for a motorcade of five Cadillacs, three for friends, one for his clothes, and the last for the great man himself. Watching the spectacle, Louis no doubt began wondering what his chances of making it in motion pictures might be, now that the talkies were fully established.

Catching the mood of Los Angeles, Louis tried to dress the part of a celebrity. He considered getting a conk—straightening his hair. As it happened, the Dunbar Hotel's barber, Jimmy Brown, was considered the best in the business, and he conked the hair of many black entertainers and musicians. Louis was uncertain about whether or not to get a conk. It was a popular practice, but he'd heard horror stories about the procedure. "The barber had to use real lye mixed up with some kind of stuff that looked like putty," he explained, "and if he puts this stuff into your hair and if he's a split second late getting to the washbowl, man, that lye is liable to burn all of your head and make a gang of great big sores." Ultimately, Louis decided against a conk. Instead, he preferred to "be sharp, feel sharp, stay sharp." He kept his hair neatly trimmed and heavily pomaded.

It was in this barbershop that he got to talking with a fan known as Soldier Boy, whose real name was Luther Gafford. Soldier Boy would do anything for Louis, and made it his mission to find him work at a good club. He presented Louis to Frank Sebastian's Cotton Club in Culver City, and Louis was hired to front the club's resident band, led by Leon Elkins. Sebastian was a handsome Italian-American who was generally well-liked by the musicians he employed. Despite its derivative name, this West Coast Cotton Club had a flavor all its own. It was located next to the MGM lot, which meant that the movie crowd—everyone from stars to bit players to directors—frequented the place, making it an excellent showcase for Louis's talents.

To accommodate the new star who had suddenly appeared in his midst, Frank Sebastian changed the band's name to "Louis Armstrong and His Sebastian New Cotton Club Orchestra." Louis immediately took to the new musicians. "These boys had something on the ball musically that I had not witnessed, such as endurance, tones, perfect sense of phrasing, and the willingness and the spirit that the Eastern or the Southern Musicians used to have before they got to Broadway and became stinkers, looking for power and ego, the desire to do practically anything but enjoy their first love— which is their instrument." Louis's assessment was accurate; this was one terrific band. "In the band were such fine players as Lawrence Brown on trombone and Lionel Hampton on drums. I discovered the greatness of those two youngsters the very first day I went to rehearsal. Lionel was so young and vivacious (still is) on those drums, and he had taken a liking to me, and I felt the same way about him. He was one of the swingingest drummers I had ever seen in my life, and he was playing some little bells he kept beside his drums, and he was swinging the hell out of them, too, like I had never heard in my life."

Louis made a name for himself as soon as he started blowing at the New Cotton Club. The critic for the Los Angeles *Evening Herald*, W. E. Oliver, could not find words sufficient to express his admiration: "Louis Armstrong is the most extraordinary trumpeter I have ever heard. He not only expands his cheeks to produce his silver notes, but his neck, also. He can give a perfect imitation of a bullfrog's throat swelling out and in as he hits notes unbelievably high and pleasing. In addition, he is one of the best showman I have seen at the head of an orchestra. He has only a husky voice to supplement his trumpet in his musical offering. But he has a sure-fire personality and a native instinct for blues in addition." Celebrities turned out to admire the Armstrong phenomenon. Oliver counted "no less than five stars with big parties sitting and listening to this artist and his musi- cians" the night he visited the club. D. W. Griffith dropped in, and Bing Crosby, twenty-six years old, came by frequently to observe Louis with a professional, admiring eye. Crosby became an ardent admirer and cham- pion, and subtly adapted Louis's singing to his own, more restrained man- ner. Crosby never scatted in the zany way Louis did, but he did drop in a few nonsense syllables here and there.

Each night, Louis entertained, at most, several hundred patrons of the Cotton Club, but regular radio broadcasts of his show reached an audience of thousands. Years later, young jazz musicians in Los Angeles recalled their amazement on first hearing Louis play. Among them was an aspiring young hornman named Buck Clayton, who became intrigued with the way

Louis made a "gliss" on his trumpet. "A gliss means to slide from one low note to a high note without any in-between notes, in other words like a trumpet would do," Clayton explained. Clayton couldn't figure out how Louis made his gliss. In search of Louis's secret, Clayton talked his way backstage at the Cotton Club and found his hero holding court in the dressing room, his head covered with a white handkerchief. With the intensity of youth, Clayton beseeched Louis to demonstrate how he produced that gliss. At that, Louis opened his instrument case, pulled out his horn, and gave it to Clayton to examine. The young man studied the horn and mouthpiece; it was a standard issue Conn, nothing special about it.

"I'll show you how I do it, but if we were down in New Orleans, I wouldn't," Louis said. Down there, he explained, "I'd put a handkerchief over my valves so nobody could see how I did it, but you follow me and I'll show you." Before he went any further, he gave young Clayton a funny-looking cigarette, "not the kind that I had been used to seeing." Louis lit up and took a toke, and, grinning as he sat on the toilet, handed it to Clayton, who puffed on it, too. By the time they smoked the entire reefer, Clayton's mind was teeming with his mother's dire warnings about the dangers of drug addiction. "But with Louis Armstrong I would have done anything." Finally, a very mellow Louis got around to demonstrating the trick behind the gliss for his newest initiate: "You push your valves half way down and tighten up your lips, then you'll be able to make a gliss." That was all there was to it. Louis went off to play his set.

When Clayton arrived home that night, "I got down on my knees and I prayed to God. I said, 'Oh God, now that I am a dope addict, please forgive me.' " He shook off his fear, and before long, Clayton was making those glisses himself. And he never became a dope addict.

On the strength of his musical ability and the Cotton Club's proximity to MGM, Louis landed a role in a movie, *Ex-Flame* (1931), a domestic drama fleshed out with several songs. This was his first appearance in a film, and as such an artifact of considerable significance. Unfortunately, the film had only a brief commercial run, and received only a few tepid reviews. " 'Ex-Flame' is funny, said *Variety*, "whether intended or no." In an ominous foreshadowing of his entire movie career, Louis did not have a dramatic role here; he simply appeared as part of a "colored jazz orchestra." Few reviews singled him out for mention, and worse, no prints of the picture survive. The inauspicious beginning did not prevent Louis from returning to the movies, again and again, throughout his career.

Around this time, Louis's own ex-flame, Lil, came out to California to stay with him, and, if she could, to win him back. Each night at eleven she tuned into the radio broadcasts from the Cotton Club to listen to the man with whom she had invented jazz less than a decade earlier. She also resumed instructing him as best she could. "One night," she recalled, "they were playing 'Tiger Rag' and at the end, Louis makes a high note, but this night, he just kept on going and kept on going, and when he hit the highest note, he hit it an octave higher than it's supposed to be. I couldn't believe my ears, so I jumped up and ran to the piano and hit the note to make sure that was it. So when he came home that night, I said, 'Do you know what you made tonight?' He said, 'Yeah, the fellows told me I made something different.' I said, 'Yes, you made something different.' Then when I showed him what it was, he was astonished himself.' "

Although she rekindled their musical rapport, Lil's plan to win him back was doomed. She blamed his success in Los Angeles for his lack of interest in resuming their relationship. "Louis had become very popular there, and I don't know, he had changed his way of thinking of a lot of things. And I hadn't changed. So he told me I was a little bit too old-fashioned. So I said, 'Well, I think it's best you go your way and I'll go my way and we'll remain friends that way.' He thought I was joking, but I wasn't joking. I wasn't joking at all." In fact, their problems were more complicated than Lil let on. She had brought her boyfriend to California. Louis wryly described him as "the man she claimed traveled with her from New York to massage her hips, to keep them from getting too large— UMP." Once Louis discovered her secret, Lil lost all hope of repairing their marriage. "She sure must have thought I was a damn fool. Sho' nuff, as if I didn't know her hips are sure to ignite from the friction. I found out this guy and Lil had been going together and he'd been spending my money for years." So much for Lil's being "old-fashioned."

Nor was Lil the only woman pursuing him. He was also receiving frequent cables from Fanny, who was in Paris, imploring him to join her there. This was a drastic move, and one that Louis was not prepared to take. There was more. Alpha was writing him regularly from Chicago, and boasting that she had just been hired as a chorus girl in a nightclub in Cicero, Illinois, the home of the Capone syndicate. She was waiting and hoping he would be enticed to return to her, but Louis stayed on in California. Alpha hopped a train for the West Coast without telling Louis, who discovered her in his dressing room one night after he had completed a set. "The Lord must have sent her out there to me, as surprised as I was," Louis wrote. All at once, he realized he had an escape from Lil's infuriating machinations.

"Now after she arrived, she got scared and thought that I'd get sore with her for coming out there," Louis wrote of Alpha. "But I was so glad to see her again, because I hadn't seen her for months and months. I just couldn't help but say to her, 'Now that you are here you might as well stay and I'll find you a room'—which I did." Lil was unaware of her rival's presence in Culver City. All she knew was that Louis was pulling away from her, because, she told herself, he was getting so damned "popular." Once she realized he had lost interest in her, Lil returned to Chicago in a car paid for by Louis, who stayed on with Alpha.

Louis maintained his equilibrium throughout these comings and goings. He played brilliantly, and recorded stunning performances for Okeh: "I'm a Ding Dong Daddy from Dumas," "Body and Soul" (the recording launched this song as a warhorse of the jazz repertoire), "Just a Gigolo," and "If I Could Be with You One Hour Tonight." His sublime indifference to his domestic travails was evidence of a man so deeply immersed in his work that he scarcely noticed who happened to populate his life.

With Lil gone, Louis gave himself over to gage. "It makes you feel good, man," he once explained to John Hammond, the record producer, who disapproved of marijuana. "It relaxes you, makes you forget all the bad things that happen to a Negro. It makes you feel wanted, and when you're with another tea smoker it makes you feel a special kinship." He was proud to be a Viper—a member of the fraternal order of the weed. Vipers were *not* the same as drug addicts, Louis insisted. A dope addict "stays dirty-grimy all the time. Show most addicts a bucket of water and they'll run like hell to keep it from touching them. But a viper would gladly welcome a good bath, clean underwear and top clothes—stay fresh and on the ball." Vipers, said Louis, came from "all walks of life that smoked and respected gage."

Not everyone respected gage as much as Louis did. One night, between sets, he was in the parking lot of the Cotton Club, sharing a joint with Vic Berton. Vic was a white drummer who had recorded with Red Nichols, a white trumpet player who idolized Louis Armstrong and found stunning, though short-lived success with his group, The Five Pennies. Louis took a liking to Vic, and the two of them were sealing their friendship by sharing a joint. They were loose, minding their own business, "having lots of laughs and feeling good enjoying each other's company," Louis said. "Just then two big healthy dicks (detectives) came from behind a car, nonchalantly, and said to us, 'We'll take the roach, boys.' "

Louis was stunned. "Vic and I said nothing. So one dick stayed with me until I went into the club and did my last set." As soon as it ended, the detective arrested him.

On the way to the station, Louis and the detective had a little "heart-to-heart talk." The trumpeter was amazed to hear the man say, "Armstrong, I am a big fan of yours and so is my family. We catch your program every night over the radio. In fact, nobody goes to bed in our family until your program is over."

Louis was relieved to hear his captor talking this way. Being arrested by a fan meant he probably wouldn't get roughed up, which was what he feared most. Surer of himself, he leaned over to the dick and said, "Since you and your family are my fans, they'd be awfully sad if anything drastic would happen to me, the same as the other thousands of my fans. So please don't hit me in my chops." If his jaw were broken, his career would be over.

The detective blinked and replied, "Why I wouldn't think of anything like that."

"That's all I wanted to hear," Louis told him. "OK, let's ride."

Along the way, he filled the sympathetic dick's ear. "I'm not a criminal," he explained. "I respect everybody, and they respect me. And I never let 'em down musically."

"Hell," said the dick, "You ain't doing any more 'n' anybody's doing. It's when they get caught. . . ." The dick then admitted Louis never would have been arrested had not a jealous bandleader working at a nearby club not tipped off the police. "He dropped a nickel on you," said the dick, meaning that the rival had dropped a nickel in the telephone, called the police, and ratted on Louis. The dick even said that when he and his partner learned they had to arrest Louis Armstrong, of all people, "it broke our hearts." By now Louis was so relaxed he forgot he was being busted—until the dick mentioned that conviction for possession of marijuana carried a six-month jail sentence.

They arrived at police headquarters, "and the minute we came through the door they all recognized me right away. . . . Oh boy, were those guys glad to see me. They gave me one look (with glee) and said, 'What 'ta hell are you doing here this time of night away from the club?' So we yakity yakity while I was being booked."

Despite the apologies, bonhomie, and adulation he received at the police station, Louis, unprotected and unconnected, was jailed without bail to await his trial for possession of marijuana. Frank Sebastian, whom Louis had considered a supportive boss, immediately replaced Louis with another singing trumpeter named Red Mack. "On the radio, he sounded so much like Louis that many people hardly knew the difference," Buck Clayton noted.

This was Louis's most serious confrontation with the law since his arrest for firing a gun. Unlike that boyhood experience, he saw no good coming from this encounter. "I spent nine days in the Downtown Los Angeles City Jail, in a cell with two guys who were already sentenced to 40 or 45 years for something else. Robbery, pickpocket, or whatever they were in for, didn't make any difference to me, and they cared less as to what I was in for." Still, he felt physically vulnerable in prison, especially when his cellmates began to fight, and one of them warned, "Move out the way, Pops, we don't want to hurt them chops." Then they went at it, and one bit off the other's finger. The fight continued until a guard separated them. Incredibly, Louis grew rather fond of these two, and once he got know them, discovered they were "intelligent" and "highly educated." He remarked, "It was actually a drag for me when I had to leave them in their cell and go to trial."

When Louis entered the courtroom, he found quite a scene. There were lawyers, there were men claiming to manage him, there were even journalists who'd come all the way from Chicago to write about his arrest and predicted he would serve the full six-month sentence. There was also a fellow sent by Tommy Rockwell to help get Louis out of this jam. His name was Johnny Collins. He was a fat, surly white man with a potbelly. At first, Louis took him to be a lawyer, but he was actually a manager and a fixer. That day, he did his job well. After all the hoopla, Louis wrote, "the judge gave me a suspended sentence, and I went to work that night. Wailed like nothing happened."

Far from getting him fired or blacklisted, the arrest and attendant publicity had boosted his popularity, and he had a ball on the bandstand. Movie stars were coming up to him, joshing, telling him that when they read that Louis Armstrong was caught with maryjane, they thought he'd been discovered with a girl. "Woo boy—that really fractured me." Not only that, but the two dicks who had arrested him came every night just to hear him blow the house down.

Louis was back on top of the world. Johnny Collins, the man who had appeared from nowhere and claimed to be Tommy Rockwell's emissary, was his manager now. As the price of extricating Louis from his legal trouble, he demanded a significant cut of the trumpeter's weekly paycheck. Collins remained a man of mystery. Some jazz musicians repeated the groundless story that he once practiced with an old Chicago law firm, Collins and Collins. More likely, he was a small-time hoodlum who was trying to use his hold over Louis Armstrong to advance his own interests. Carrying on as though he were the manager of the entire Cotton Club orchestra, Collins made himself unpopular with the other band members. He even called a rehearsal on Easter Sunday, and when Lawrence Brown, the trombonist and a minister's son, said he couldn't make it, Collins replaced him with a movie studio musician. Brown found a safer haven in Duke Ellington's Orchestra. Louis regretted losing Brown, but, for the moment, remained oblivious to the damage his new manager was capable of inflicting on others.

It was now March 1931 and Louis's gig at the Cotton Club was winding down. Soon, he would have to leave California's sunshine and all that fabulous gage for Chicago's brutal chill. After the club's closing-night celebration, he boarded a train to Chicago. Louis did not have a place of his own there, but Lil, still hoping for a reconciliation, invited him to stay with her. On the Sunday morning he arrived, he went directly to her house on 44th Street.

To Lil's dismay, Louis took advantage of her hospitality but did not reciprocate her interest. "Had a sleep up into the afternoon," he recalled of his sojourn under her roof, "then had my supper while listening to some of my records. Lil was out visiting some place." This time, she realized she had lost him for good. Their marriage finally came to an end. "We separated in August 1931," she noted matter-of-factly. They were not yet divorced, though, and Louis could not marry Alpha, which was precisely what Lil intended.

In the days after his return to Chicago, more than a few people were surprised to see Louis Armstrong walking freely about the streets of Chicago. Everywhere he went, people would say to him, "but I thought you were in jail." The newspaper articles predicting he would receive six months in jail had not been followed by accounts of his suspended sentence. The erroneous impression remained that he was behind bars in Los Angeles. Instead, Louis was blowing once again. Johnny Collins, who had come to Chicago with Louis, quickly found him a gig at the Regal Theater. It seemed he had landed on his feet, thanks to his new manager.

At the conclusion of the brief Regal gig, Louis began fronting a large new band comprised of old musical comrades, mostly from New Orleans, men whose names he loved to recite: "Charlie Alexander (piano), Zilner Randolph (trumpet), George James (alto sax), Al Washington (tenor), Preston Jackson (trombone), Tubby Hall (drums), Lester Boone (alto sax), Johnnie Lindsay (bass), Mike McKendrick (banjo), and myself (trumpet)." Although the band bore Louis's name, he was, as before, the leader in name only. Zilner Randolph, who also played trumpet, had actually assembled the musicians. Louis was happy to let him run the show. "Now, this is your band," Louis told "Randy" one night, as he asked him to "pick out a set." Randolph made his choice, and prepared to lead the band. "I always give them a signal to get ready," Randolph said. "One—that means for everybody to get in position. And I stomped off, sitting down. One, two, three four. Louis hollered, 'Get up from there,' and the people were all standing, looking, and that embarrassed me. 'Get up from there and stand in front of the band!' I jumped up and commenced directing the band. I had charge of the band from then on." The experience of leading the band and then playing the trumpet *after* Louis unnerved Randolph. To make matters worse, the other musicians—whom *he* had hired, glared at him resentfully—and when he approached them to say hello, "everybody would scatter." Despite the disrespectful treatment he received from his colleagues, Randolph continued to enjoy Louis's confidence and support.

This was the first group of musicians backing Louis that came in for serious criticism. Many of his fans, as well as jazz aficionados, didn't take to them at all. They longed for Louis to resume the rough-and-ready antics of his Hot Five recordings. But Louis was delighted with the band and its sound. "Now there's a band that really deserved a whole lot of credit they didn't get," he wrote. One of the band's chief characteristics—and the reason it didn't get the respect Louis believed it deserved—was that it played "sweet" instead of "hot." Nor did the musicians improvise much. This wasn't Randolph's doing; all the fellows in the band were still in the thrall of Guy Lombardo. As soon as their set ended, they would rush down to the dressing room, turn up the radio, and groove to Guy's music. This was a significant instance of white music influencing black, rather than the other way around, but Louis didn't see matters in white or black terms. He simply declared, "I like that sound," and he would adapt it to his style. On April 20, 28, and 29, 1931, Louis wrote, his new band "made some of my finest recordings with me. I can right now remember some of them as follows: 'Sleepy Time Down South,' 'When Your Lover Has Gone,' 'Between the Devil and the Deep Blue Sea,' 'I Got Rhythm,' 'Stardust,' 'Wrap Up Your Troubles in Dreams,' 'Lonesome Road,' 'Laughin' Louie,' 'All of Me,' 'I Surrender, Dear,' 'Kickin' the Gong Around,' 'World on a String,' 'Gotta Right to Sing the Blues'—aw, hell, I would be here all night jottin' down the names of these fine recordings." Many of these songs were essential entries in the growing Armstrong canon.

It was remarkable that he was back in the studio at this moment. The boom in race records, which had done so much to boost his popularity, was over, a casualty of the Depression. In fact, the record industry had collapsed. In 1921, sales had reached $106 million, and, in the process, brought Louis Armstrong, Bessie Smith, and hundreds of other performers before the public. Throughout the 1920s, sales had slowly declined, and by 1931, they had slumped to $17 million. Devastated, record companies canceled or refused to renew recording contracts, and limited their artists to one take only (unless defective), instead of the customary three, four, or five takes. The new controls meant that alternate takes—now prized by collectors—became very rare.

Louis survived commercial disaster because he continued to follow Rockwell's advice and recorded mainstream hit songs, no matter what their source. Even so, Louis rendered these familiar tunes with a repertoire of idiosyncracies. He favored compelling, bizarre vocals over the trumpet virtuosity on which he had previously relied. He would pepper the lyrics with in-jokes, asides, comments, and nonsense syllables; he would throw his voice like a ventriloquist, sing in a light tenor, then swoop down to a deep growl. His distinctly African-American voice, imbued with southern dialect and inflections, came as a pleasant shock to many white listeners. And it was certainly recognizable. No one else sounded like him, simultaneously crude and sophisticated. Part of the reason for the looseness and wackiness of these latest recordings was that Louis, along with the other band members, was stoned when he made them. Indeed, they were so high that the band might as well have been called "Louis Armstrong and his *Vipers*."

It was also apparent that he reveled in his blackness, in black language and the bits of black experience that he tossed into his songs, and he wanted everyone to get hip to it along with him. He would sing, scat, kid the other musicians, and even address the instruments. "Watch out there, saxophone," as he mugged "lightly, lightly, and politely," through "Chinatown, My Chinatown." In these ways, Louis left a distinctive imprint on songs that were often banal. He was always close to vaudeville, imitating Al Jolson when the mood came over him. In his version of "The Lonesome Road," he ignored the tune altogether in favor of performing as "Reverend Satchelmouth Armstrong" in tandem with "the little Creole member," John Lindsay:

> *LINDSAY: Now, Sisters and Brothers, we want to pick up a good collection here tonight for Brother Armstrong. Come on with it if you're coming. Oh, you dog!*
> *ARMSTRONG: And if you ever get it, Brother Lindsay, please don't put it in your pocket, will you?*
> *LINDSAY: Amen. . . .*

ARMSTRONG: Look out now, Brothers and Sisters, I thank you for your little offering. Of course, it could have been better. A few dollars more would have gotten my shoes out of pawn. But nevertheless I'm in love with you. [Woman shrieks.] Hold that, Sister, but get offa my foot.

The most controversial tune to come out of the April sessions was "When It's Sleepy Time Down South." As written, it was a dreamy evocation of southern plantation life. The lyrics laid it on thick, with banjoes "ringing" and mammies "singing," and "soft winds blowing though the pinewood trees," and complacent, happy "darkies" singing and "dancing to the break of day." Even at the time, the song sounded old-fashioned and troubled some listeners, but Louis didn't see it as a retrograde political statement. For him, "When It's Sleepy Time Down South" was thirty-two bars of musical magic, a tone poem evoking a beautiful, tranquil South that existed only in show business. In making the song his own, Louis added a spoken introduction that challenged the tune's simple meaning.

. . . There's a guy comin' up the street, look like he's from my home town . . . Look like ol' Charlie Alexander, man . . . Well, I believe it is . . .

". . . How long you been up here, boy? . . ."

". . . Oh, I been up here about . . . about a year-and-a-half . . ."

". . . A year-and-a-half? . . . Man, I been up here a long time myself. . . . I'm goin' back home . . ."

His preamble made "When It's Sleepy Time Down South" into a commentary on the experiences of blacks, who, like himself, who had come to Chicago in search of economic opportunity, and had found it. Once the Depression struck, their horizons shrank, and they paused to take stock of their gains and losses and discovered that material rewards carried a spiritual price. Louis worked all of these complex emotions into a bittersweet musical reverie and made it his signature song. He recorded it dozens of times, and he performed it thousands of times. He considered "When It's Sleepy Time Down South" the perfect way to ingratiate himself with audiences. It offered him a chance to sing, to explore the higher registers of his instrument, and to introduce the members of his orchestra. Then, with the chorus softly swelling behind him, he lulled his audience into a pleasant state of stupefaction.

Once Louis completed his recordings, Collins booked Louis and the orchestra into a nightclub called the Showboat. The opening night was a great event. The festivities were broadcast over radio station WIBC, and the show stretched on for hours as one bandleader after another came by to "say a few words in favor of Louie Armstrong." Yes, *Lou-ie*. The bandleaders were white, and, as he noted, "all the white folks call me Louie," a quirk he cheerfully accepted. In fact, most everyone at the Showboat, except the band, was white, since the nightclub was firmly in white territory, the Loop. Playing in the Loop—as opposed to the South Side, scene of numerous black and tans—didn't bother him a bit. He considered Chicago his hometown.

There was another, nastier side to the Showboat. It was filled with telephones, and it doubled as a bookie joint. Gangsters were everywhere, placing bets by day and leaving big tips by night. Mike McKendrick, the banjo player, packed a .45 and served as the band's straw boss, charged with keeping the other musicians in order, but even he was unable to protect the star of the show from outside interference. As soon as he started the Showboat engagement, Louis received threats and demands for money. When he ignored them, he was approached by two local hoodlums, Joe Fiore and Emmet Ryan, who demanded he pay six thousand dollars, or they would take him for a ride. As everyone in Chicago knew, that meant they would murder him. Louis shrugged off the threats and continued to blow.

The pair of extortionists decided the price they had placed on Louis's life was too steep, so they lowered it to five thousand. Louis continued to ignore them. With comical ineptitude, they lowered it again, to four thousand dollars, and Louis continued to play. Three thousand. More playing. Two. Still no dice. By the time Fiore and Ryan dropped their price to one thousand dollars, Louis had ceased to pay attention, and the pair of them were soon arrested, along with the man who put them up to their job, a music publisher named Milton Weil, who was part-owner of a rival nightclub. The story made the Chicago dailies. JAIL MUSICIAN FOR BLACKMAIL OF ARMSTRONG, proclaimed one, describing Louis as a "world famous cornetist and orchestra leader." Another speculated on Weil's motive for trying to shake down such a popular figure. By way of explanation, Weil said he was "only trying to get him to change managers." This remark suggested that the culprit was a manager with a real grievance against Louis Armstrong, a manager who felt the trumpet player had double-crossed him, a manager like Tommy Rockwell.

In New York, Rockwell was furious over Johnny Collins's hold over Louis. As far as he was concerned, Johnny Collins was *not* Louis Armstrong's manager. Louis's description of the situation reveals his own confusion over his management. He thought Johnny Collins had "some deal . . . made with Mr. Tommy Rockwell, my other manager." But on second thought, he wasn't so sure. "Damn—come to think of it, I sure had a manager's fit." Louis had no idea his "manager's fit" had placed him in harm's way. "Funny how I did not know that Johnny Collins and Rockwell were having a feud over my contract, why and for what I've never found out to this day," he remarked. But he did realize someone was pushing him, and the more he was pushed, the more stubborn he became, even to the point of risking his life. "All I know is, whoever was the 'gang' in New York sent gangsters to Chicago where I was working and tried their damnedest to frighten me into quitting the job and come to New York to open at Connie's Inn again, and I felt that as dirty Connie had fired me and my band, I did not want any part of those people ever again. I am just that way. If you kick my ass once you can bet I won't come back if I can help it. And Connie's Inn was going down by degrees, and at that time I was the rage of the nation. But nay, nay, never, no Connie's Inn."

Louis knew the identity of the "gang" in New York: it was Dutch Schultz, the homicidal bootlegger and part-owner of Connie's Inn. No one, not even Capone, dared interfere in Dutch Schultz's dealings. Louis was on his own. He expected repercussions, and he was not disappointed.

SONG OF THE
VIPERS

O ne night the gangsters started a fight in the Showboat in Chicago, right in front of where I was standing, playing my trumpet. I mean, they were really fighting worse than a bunch of spades. One of the gangsters took a chair and hit a woman over the head with it and the chair crumbled up all in little pieces. Some of the pieces hit my horn, but *that* could not make me leave the bandstand. The captain must go down with the ship. Then, too, things like that never frighten me. I've seen so much of that bullshit during my days of playing music."

This time, he was subjected to harsher treatment. "Ain't but one incident at the Showboat that kind of got me, and it happened one night as we were justa playing and the people were all dancing and having a ball. Our dressing room was located on the same side of the bandstand, a pretty large one at that. I usually blow my trumpet with both of my eyes closed, and as I was blowing I felt someone touching me very quietly, speaking in a whisper. It was a big, burly gangster saying, 'Somebody wants you in the dressing room.'

"So I said, 'Sure, I'll go as soon as I finish this dance set.' And I didn't pay any attention to it.

"So after the set was over, I ran lickety-split to my dressing room to see who it was. I rushed to the door thinking it was one of the cats, but there was a white guy with a beard. He spoke first—'Hello,' kind of sarcastically.

"I still ain't hep to the jive. I said 'hello' very pleasantly.

" 'Do you know who I am?' "

" 'Why, er, no. No, I don't.' In fact, it really didn't matter. As long as he talked about music I just knew he and I were going to really run our mouths.

"Then this guy said, 'I am Frankie Foster.'

"At first, I didn't pay any attention. Then it dawned on me what he said, and I turned cold as I took a double look, as I said to him, 'What did you say your name was?'

"By this time he had his big pistol, pulling it out, as he said, 'My name is Frankie Foster,' and he said he was sent over to my place to see that I catch the first train out to New York.

"I still tried to make it appear he ain't frightening me. I said, 'New York? Why, that's news to me. Mr. Collins didn't tell me anything about it.'

"Frankie Foster said, 'You're a bad sumbitch. Oh yes, you're going to New York to work at Connie's Inn, and you're leaving tomorrow morning.' And he flashed his big ol' pistol and aimed it straight at me with my eyes as big as saucers and frightened, too.

"I said, 'Well, maybe I *am* going to New York.'

"Then Frankie Foster said, 'OK. Now you and me are going to the telephone booth and you'll talk.'

"By this time anything he ordered me was alright because it's no trouble at all for a gangster to pull the trigger, especially when they have you cornered and you disobey them, sooooooo we went to the phone with a gun in my side, and sure enough, someone said, 'Hello,' a familiar voice, too, yes sir, I'd know that voice if I heard it a hundred years from now." To the end of his days, Louis has never revealed the speaker's identity, but he was, in all likelihood, someone connected to Dutch Schultz. "The first words he said to me were, 'When are you gonna open here?'

"I turned around and looked directly into Frankie Foster's face and said, 'Tomorrow morning.' "

Upstairs, the band members knew something had happened to Louis, and they were alarmed. Mike McKendrick, the straw boss, told them not to leave the club. "Just stick close right here like nothing is happening," he advised, and then he added, "Pops can get hurt behind this action." McKendrick conferred with Collins, who urged silence: "Don't tell anybody anything about Louis, you just don't know if they ask you."

Rockwell denied that he had inspired the terror. He claimed he just happened to be passing through Chicago at the time, and four thugs ordered *him* to leave town in four hours—or else. Rockwell's reaction was to gather four "friends" and pay a call on Louis at the Showboat, but he said he was unable to see his former client and in the morning took the train back to New York. He insisted that he knew nothing about the Connie's Inn contract, although his actions strongly suggested that he was trying to enforce it.

Moving swiftly to defuse the crisis, Collins hustled Louis out of Chicago within hours of the confrontation with Frankie Foster. He instantly canceled the Showboat engagement and sent the band on the road, where Louis, unharmed, rejoined them. Together again, they went on to play an exhausting series of one-night stands throughout Illinois, Ohio, Kentucky, West Virginia, and always one step ahead of the mob.

Wherever they went on this tour, they encountered hard times. They played the Royal Theater in Baltimore, located in a black neighborhood suffering badly from the Depression. "When we arrived in the town it was as cold as well-digger's you-know-what. Freezing. Well, I heard about these people who were too poor to get coal to keep themselves and their kids warm, so I went to the coal yard, ordered a ton of coal and had the company deliver it to the lobby of the Royal Theater. Then I had all of the folks who needed coal to help themselves. It made them very happy. And they made it their business to come backstage and thank me—of course, it caused me to stick out my chest with pride. I came up through life the hard way just like these folks."

As the weeks passed, the band moved from one town to the next, growing wearier after each gig. The prospect of an entire week in one place—Detroit's Graystone Ballroom—came as a huge relief. Still, as long as Armstrong's orchestra could get bookings, they took them, however far-flung they were. A steady series of gigs was all that mattered. After Baltimore and Detroit, the tour took them to Milwaukee and Minnesota, and finally, in a daring move in mid-June, they accepted an engagement in a city Louis hadn't seen in nine long years—New Orleans.

The manager of the Suburban Gardens in New Orleans proposed a three-month engagement. Ever since Louis had left the Crescent City he had been spreading the gospel of jazz wherever he went, and in the process he had made New Orleans world famous. Despite his obsession with New Orleans in his music and his reminiscences, he had avoided the city. Part of the reason for his staying away was emotional; his extended absence was his way of separating himself from the protracted struggles of his youth. He had found himself as a musician in New Orleans, but he had won recognition, respect, and fame up north. As a black man, he could go places and do things up north that he could never do in New Orleans. It was only now, after nine years' absence, that Louis felt secure enough in himself to return home.

The other half of the rationale behind the New Orleans engagement was more expedient. The pressures that the mob could apply against him—whether directly, or through Frankie Foster—extended all the way from Chicago to New York. He knew it was hopeless to stand up to the likes of Capone or Dutch Schultz or Owney Madden; if he wanted to blow on their turf, he had to do so on their terms. New Orleans offered a temporary respite from these concerns and, he hoped, an opportunity to consolidate his position as the trumpet king on his *own* turf.

Louis was going home, but he was also entering the South, where segregation ruled, and the Depression had only served to increase racism. It looked so beautiful and lush, yet it was filled with hatred. Louis assumed he would be welcomed by the city's blacks, but he doubted that whites in New Orleans would want any part of him. He was also unsure about what to do with Alpha, who was traveling with him on the road. She wasn't from the South, and so she wouldn't know what to expect when she arrived down there. He had wanted to marry her before they got to New Orleans, thinking they could greet the city as husband and wife, but his divorce from Lil had not yet come through. Lil didn't want him back; she just didn't want to let him go. All these worries troubled his train ride back home, yet he couldn't help but be seduced by the familiar sights sliding past his windows, the swamps and bayous, the Spanish moss and lonely shacks, the magic, mysterious, and sinister landscape of Louisiana.

To Louis's eye, nothing had changed. "We reached New Orleans early in June, and the last of the magnolias were still on the trees, the smell of them in the air," he wrote of his return. He wondered if he'd been forgotten during his absence, but "when our train pulled into the old L.& N. Station out by the Mississippi, at the head of Canal Street"—the same terminal from which he had departed with his fish sandwich years before—"I heard hot music playing. I looked out of the car window and could hardly believe what I saw. There stretched out along the track, were eight bands, all swinging together. . . . As soon as I got off the train the crowd went crazy. They picked me up on their shoulders and started a parade down the center of Canal Street. Those eight bands almost bust the town open, they made so much noise." His sister, Mama Lucy, was there to greet him. A brief hush fell over the crowd as Johnny Collins came forward, guiding Alpha by the arm—a white man escorting a black woman—but the moment passed, and Louis got into an open car at the head of the parade. As he moved along Canal Street, he surveyed a crowd composed of blacks and whites alike, a sight unprecedented in New Orleans, and one that alarmed Louis as much as it pleased him. He thought he saw familiar faces in the crowd—boyhood friends now grown up; adults from his youth now grown old; maybe even Irene, one of his first loves, or someone who looked like her. All of a sudden, two faces stood out with iron clarity: Captain Jones and Peter Davis. Still in command of the Waif's Home and its marching band, the two men had come out to greet the most renowned pupil ever to have survived their regimen. Louis promised them he would visit, and the parade into his past continued, as he caught glimpses of Parish Prison, the Fisk School, and the church that had superseded Funky Butt Hall. When they reached the Astoria Hotel, he had a brief reunion with his razor-wielding first wife, Daisy Parker, and continued to move through crowds of people and policemen, one of whom shook his hand. After the bands finally broke up he and Alpha went to his hotel room to reflect on the day's momentous events. "All in all," said Louis, "I think that day was the happiest day in my life."

The next day, Louis kept his promise to visit the Waif's Home he had left seventeen years before. Wanting to look his very best for the grand occasion, he wore a new cream-colored suit, white shirt, red tie, and, to ward off the heat, a straw hat. The staff had organized an elaborate welcoming ceremony for their hero, but Louis's enthusiasm and restlessness overwhelmed their plans. Before anyone realized what was happening, he had found an old friend from his days at the Home, Louis Duplan, who now worked there as a handyman. The two of them went off to the kitchen to devour a meal of red beans and rice, as if no time at all intervened since their days as inmates.

After the impromptu meal, Louis wandered up the stairs of his old dormitory, found his old bunk—second row, third bed—jumped on it, pulled up the sheet, and closed his eyes. With his stomach full, and overwhelmed with the events of the last twenty-four hours, he drifted off into an afternoon nap. Present-day inmates slowly gathered round to gape and gawk at the sleeping hero who had traveled far afield and conquered the great white world and now returned to their midst, once again and always a member of the Waif's Home.

I n the nine years he had been away, Louis had changed greatly. New Orleans, however, was still New Orleans, and the deprivation imposed by the Depression had only served to increase racial animosity in the city. The exhilaration he experienced on returning to his hometown was short-lived, for racial problems and Dutch Schultz's influence followed him all the way home.

Without warning, the American Federation of Musicians expelled the members of Armstrong's orchestra from its ranks "for continuing to play with Armstrong after he had been expelled for not fulfilling a contract with a New York nightclub"—Connie's Inn. Louis and the other members of the band immediately realized that Tommy Rockwell—who was subverting Louis's New Orleans engagement in order to gain revenge on Johnny Collins—was behind their union's peculiar behavior. If Rockwell thought he could win his prize trumpeter back with threats and intimidation, he was mistaken. The orchestra had nothing to gain from the union, and Louis was determined to perform in any event.

The situation became even uglier. "We're called down to the local Union and questioned," recalled Preston Jackson, who was in Louis's New Orleans band. "There wasn't anything to be done about it but then they's making announcement over the air about 'the niggers comin' down to New Orleans and taking the white musicians' jobs.'" Wherever Louis's band went after that, they were shadowed by a car bearing four strange and grim-looking white men.

Louis refused to be intimidated. He and his band intended to play their engagement at the Suburban Gardens as planned, the first black orchestra to do so. "Opening night came and the place was packed," Louis recalled. "All of New Orleans high society was there. The Suburban Gardens had its own radio program. They had a mike in front of the bandstand, which used to broadcast only for white bands. There was a lot of excitement in the air." Outside the Suburban Gardens, ten thousand blacks, excluded from the concert because of their race, awaited the black phenomenon who had grown up in their midst. Louis remembered that many of them "gathered outside right along the levee, hoping to catch the music through the open windows. I'll never forget that sight. And the club was just as packed inside, five thousand people or more, they said. And among them were people I'd grown up with, white boys you understand, I used to play games with on the empty lots after school, and they were calling me by name, pleased to see me again."

When it was time to introduce Louis Armstrong and the orchestra, the white announcer refused. "I can't announce that nigger man," he angrily declared.

Collins appeared at Louis's side, explaining what had just occurred. Louis's reaction was instantaneous. "I turned to the boys on the bandstand and said, 'Give me a chord.' I got an earsplitting chord and announced the show myself. It was the first time a Negro *spoke* on the radio down there." There were many ways to signify, and Louis Armstrong had just found a new one. Amid the poison of racial animosity, Louis managed to make good music, and even to enjoy himself.

After that night he was a hero to blacks—and even to some whites—in New Orleans, and they filled the Suburban Gardens to hear the native son they knew from recordings and newspapers. One of his younger fans, Sherwood Mangiapane, who had been collecting Armstrong recordings since he was a child, caught Louis right at the start of his engagement. "He came out dressed different from the rest of the band," Mangiapane remembered. "Louis had on a sport outfit like a brown coat, light tan pants, and during the night he would change three or four times. He always looked so neat. He would introduce the tune and he'd beat the band with his foot or his hand and they'd start. He just ate up everything, he just owned that place, I'm telling you I could hardly stand it." Once the band settled in, they managed to accommodate themselves to the club's segregation policy; in this respect it was exactly like the Cotton Club or Connie's Inn up north.

Louis spread his good fortune among his fans and hangers-on with careless abandon. At six o'clock each evening, a line of people stretching half a block formed outside his hotel. When Louis appeared, he walked among his fans, smiling and distributing money to anyone who came by and asked for it. He visited the Waif's Home, donated radios to the current inmates, posed for pictures, and grinned as if he were more amazed than anyone else by what had become of him in the years since he had left the place.

He sponsored a local baseball team comprised largely of members of the Zulu Social Aid and Pleasure Club, the black burial society. The team renamed itself "Armstrong's Secret Nine." Louis bought them brand-new uniforms and looked fine himself—decked out in two-tone shoes, white trousers with dark stripes, dark jacket with a handkerchief peeking out of the breast pocket, striped tie, and soft hat, leaning lightly on a baseball bat, one wrist encircled with a bracelet—in the photographs taken to commemorate the occasion. The uniforms helped morale, but they also got in the way. "One Sunday," a club member recalled, "they were playing a tight game and they were behind by one run and a fellow got thrown out at third base, and when he came over to the dugout everybody jumped all over him, yelling, 'Why didn't you slide?' And he said, 'What, and dirty up my pretty white suit?'"

Louis's fame even extended still further. A tobacco company named a cigar after him, the Louis Armstrong Special. Louis was so proud of this honor he mentioned the cigar in his November 1931 recording of "Lonesome Road" in which he describes Charles Carpenter—a young friend from Chicago—as "smoking a Louis Armstrong Special Cigar," which was exactly what Carpenter was doing in the studio as Louis recorded the song.

At that moment, Lil, of all people, showed up in town, accompanied by her current boyfriend, and they checked into the same hotel as Louis and Alpha. Louis was furious with Lil, but he wanted to avoid a confrontation. She had other ideas. One day, around noon, she entered his hotel room while he was sleeping. To his dismay, he woke to find her there, haranguing him about Alpha and his career. She wanted him, but she also wanted to destroy him. Finally, late in the afternoon, Lil took her leave of an exhausted Louis, who stayed behind to recover his strength in preparation for his evening performance.

That night, he went down to the lobby to retrieve his car, only to discover someone else had taken the keys and driven off. He learned that "Mrs. Armstrong"—as Lil still referred to herself—had taken his car, and was driving back to Chicago in it, accompanied by one of the hotel's handsome young bellboys.

Even after Lil's departure, more trouble awaited him at the Suburban

Gardens. One evening, while Louis was backstage, and Zilner Randolph was leading the band in a waltz, a white woman, obviously drunk, danced erratically in front of the band, and then suddenly grabbed Randolph's hand. The bandleader struggled unsuccessfully to free his hand and return to the business of conducting before he and the rest of the band were lynched for violating a racial taboo. Preston Jackson, who was from New Orleans, was so scared by this incident, that "my teeth began to chatter." Jackson also noticed, however, that the whites in the audience were smiling, some of them actually laughing, at Randolph's obvious terror. Finally, he managed to free his hand from the white woman who unthinkingly endangered his life, and the band completed their set, all of them utterly terrified. When they went backstage, "Louis asked what's the matter, and I said, 'Man, a white woman not only grabbed Randolph by the hand she wouldn't turn him loose.' Then the manager follows up and says: 'It's all right, boys. Everybody knows it was none of Randolph's fault.'" As Randolph explained, "You had to be very careful down there with them people. They didn't understand."

Racism again plagued Louis and his band at the close of his Suburban Gardens engagement. Louis agreed to give a free concert for the city's blacks at an army base, and on the day of the big event, hundreds of them congregated there in expectation of a fine time. They had come in cars, in horse-drawn carriages, and some had even come in wagons pulled by oxen. When Louis and the orchestra arrived, they were confronted with a locked gate. Dancing, they were told, was not permitted at a United States Army base. The situation grew heated when the National Guard was called in and drove away the bitterly disappointed crowd with drawn bayonets. Louis turned to Collins for help, a white man to talk to the other white man and find out what the problem was. Collins asked around and saw there was nothing to be done. With no promoter standing to profit from the engagement, there was no one to whom Collins could appeal. The crowd dispersed gradually, on foot, plainly angry and cursing at Louis Armstrong, one of their own who had so unexpectedly let them down. As the band drove away from the army base, Louis wept.

On the way back to the hotel, he told Johnny Collins to let him out of the car, and he went stumbling in the direction of Jane Alley, where his grandmother Josephine still lived. Jane Alley was there, and so was the Chinaball tree, from which Josephine had plucked her switches to thrash her grandson, but the whole scene had shrunk. The neighborhood where he had spent the first years of his life differed from his memories. The air smelled foul, and trash littered the yard. He searched in the dark for his grandmother's house, but couldn't find it. All at once, he realized he was lost. What he really wanted was to find his grandmother and press a fat roll of bills into her hand, but he was disoriented, alone, and suddenly feeling defeated. It was time to get back to his hotel, to Alpha, and his current life. No taxis frequented this part of town, so he caught the nearest streetcar, paid his fare, and took his seat in the Colored section.

In September, Louis and the band, accompanied by Johnny Collins and his wife, embarked on a bus tour of the South. Even in the Depression they attracted huge crowds along the way—twelve thousand people came to see them perform in Houston. They played Dallas, Tulsa, Oklahoma City, then returned to Dallas. There, they ran into Joe Oliver, on tour with a pickup band, but Louis and his former mentor hardly spoke. The tour moved on relentlessly.

In Memphis, the local driver refused to allow Louis and the band on his bus. "I didn't know it was going to be like this," he complained, meaning he hadn't realized the band was black. "Well now, one of the musicians was smoking a cigarette in a long fancy holder," said Louis, "and this somehow didn't please the man, and he kept looking at my trumpet man Zilner Randolph who had some sort of French beret on. Zilner began to make it pretty clear he wasn't standing for any of this shit. I said to Mike McKendrick, 'Go off and phone Mr. Collins and he'll sort this mess out.' I'd seen this kind of scene before."

Instead of Collins, they were met by the police. They immediately eyed Louis perched on the arm of a seat in which a white woman was sitting. She was Johnny Collins's wife, and she had been traveling through the South with the band, helping to make travel arrangements. The sight of a black musician talking easily and openly with a white woman so infuriated one cop that he asked his partner, "Why don't you shoot him in the leg?" Fortunately, no one took aim at Louis that night, but more policemen came aboard that bus. "It looked like half the Memphis police force met us there," observed Preston Jackson.

"All right you niggers, get out here," the police ordered. "You're in

Memphis now, and we need some cotton pickers, too." With that, they took all the musicians into custody.

"Just as we're being hauled into the police wagons," said Louis, "Mike McKendrick came running round the corner—I can see him now, his coat all flapping. He was quick, but so was the rest of the band, nobody waved or shouted or did anything, and Big Mike kept on running."

Down at the jailhouse, the mood turned even uglier. Once the desk sergeant had recorded everyone's name, a policeman hissed, "You ain't gonna come down to Memphis and try to run the city. We'll kill all you niggers."

"By now, a few of the band were really worried, and so was I, for them," Louis remembered. The police didn't need an excuse to make good on their threats, and Louis knew that some of the musicians were hardly model citizens. "See, I knew that one of the guys sometimes carried a .45 and another had a regular pimping scene going for him that didn't want too much questioning," he later recorded. The police locked the men two to a cell. Louis and his valet, "Professor" Sherman Cook, were thrown together. The Professor, terrified, immediately confessed to his boss, "Now look, Louis, I've got something in my pocket that could mean trouble," and promptly pulled out a "great big joint all neatly wrapped."

"Hey, man," Louis said, "we can't be in any more trouble than we are in right now," and so, "We lit up and smoked our way out of trouble. Now when the other cats in their cells caught the smell of the stuff they all started shouting out about passing it around, but old Cook and myself, we demolished the evidence." But they were still in jail, and scheduled to perform the next day. Luckily, Mike McKendrick, whom the police had overlooked, contacted Johnny Collins and told him the whole story. Collins in turn reached the Palace Theatre in Memphis, where they were to play. The management bailed out Louis and the orchestra on condition that they also make a radio broadcast.

That night, the Palace gig went off without incident, and the following morning, they made their live broadcast, as promised. Cops were milling around everywhere, keeping an eye on things. Louis stood before the microphone, leaned into it and said, "Ladies and gentlemen, I'm now going to dedicate this song to the Memphis Police Force." The band swung into it, hard, and he began to sing, *"I'll be glad when you're dead, you rascal, you . . . Oh, I'll be glad when you're dead, you rascal, you. . . ."*

When the band finished, the cops rushed right over. Terrified that Louis's little joke would get them all killed, the musicians tried to run, but there was nowhere to go. As the cops closed in, Louis and the orchestra braced themselves for the worst. Instead, they were confronted with smiles of delight. "You're the first band that ever dedicated a tune to the Memphis Police Force," the officers exclaimed. Weak with relief, but also shaken by this bizarre and unexpected turn of events, the band carefully backed away, got on the bus, and got the hell out of Memphis.

For the next six months, Louis and the band were on the move. They played St. Louis, Columbus, Cincinnati, Chicago, and Cleveland. During their stop in Philadelphia, Louis's old friend and dealer, Mezz Mezzrow, now strung out on heroin, came to see him perform. The spectacle made an indelible impression on his memory: "Louis began playing 'Rockin' Chair', his specialty. The great big wailing notes came shuddering down to us through the floor, each one a-tremble with strength and mastery. All those unbelievable little runs, strung out like diamond pendants by Louis's terrific artistry, full of sobs and bellylaughs, trickled down into our ears." Mezz was accompanied by Zutty Singleton, the drummer whom Louis had left behind, and the mingled feelings of admiration and regret overwhelmed the two men as they listened to Louis blow. Tears filled their eyes. "I leaned over towards him," said Mezz, "his head on my shoulder and mine on his chest, and while we stood there hugging each other we just cried and cried."

From Philadelphia, the orchestra went to Washington, D.C., Baltimore, New Haven, Jersey City, and Boston. Then, in a daring move, Johnny Collins booked Louis at the Paramount-Publix Theatre on Broadway in New York. Both Louis and his manager hoped to sidestep conflict with the mob by avoiding Connie's Inn and the Harlem scene, but Tommy Rockwell found them nonetheless. Vindictive as ever, Rockwell joined with Connie Immerman to sue Louis for breach of contract. Louis countersued, coaxed by the intransigent Collins, but the legal action scuttled his Broadway engagement.

With time to kill, Louis made two short films in New York. Considered utterly ephemeral at the time, they have taken on new resonance as artifacts of the way black performers have been treated by the movies. In one, he appeared as a guest star in a Betty Boop cartoon, singing "I'll Be Glad You're Dead, You Rascal, You." In the cartoon, a live-action shot of his head is suspended against an animated sky. The disembodied head sings and pursues a fleeing, perspiring cartoon character. In the other short, he portrays a mythical trumpeter in a place called Jazz Heaven. Here, Louis, knee-deep in soap bubbles, wearing a leopard skin and a three-foot-high headpiece, picks up his horn and blows so brilliantly that the ridiculous setting fades before the burning conviction of his trumpet solo. His costume, preposterous as it is, reveals his arms and chest, and one can see the intense physicality of his playing, all the muscles of his upper body working to produce his sound. In the process, he converts parody into an impressive spectacle.

Checkmated by his adversaries in New York, Louis and the orchestra returned to Chicago for a few more engagements. A short time later, in March 1932, the band broke up, a casualty of Rockwell's machinations, Depression economics, and Louis's restlessness. Eager to try a different tack, and seeking refuge from his career and management troubles, Louis returned to California, and threw himself into playing with Les Hite's Band at the New Cotton Club. Unfortunately, this proved to be a brief respite. He needed something *completely* different. With Collins, Louis hatched a daring idea for a tour that would take him far from the Depression and the gangsters plaguing his career, and bring him to the attention of an entirely new audience.

Throughout the early months of 1932, reports of the phenomenon known as Louis Armstrong regularly reached England. His recordings circulated widely throughout the country, and the Chicago *Defender*, so heavily invested in his career, had been urging him to consider a foreign tour for some time. The paper's English correspondent, Ivan H. Browning, wrote, "If Armstrong comes to England and brings his real band (and not a lot of substitutes) he certainly can't miss." Finally, while he was completing his return engagement at the New Cotton Club, Louis decided to accept whatever English bookings Collins could get. Perhaps he would find abroad the stability and respectability that eluded him in his own country.

Despite all his touring, and the popularity of his recordings, Louis's life was still in disarray at this time. Alpha provided scant emotional security; she was his girlfriend, nothing more or less. He did not own a home, and he drove a secondhand Buick. He never seemed to have enough money, for

Collins had a way of frittering away the receipts. So it was in a mood of desperation that Louis, Alpha, Johnny Collins, and Collins's wife sailed aboard the SS *Majestic* from New York on July 9. He was to open at the London Palladium, the famous variety theater, nine days later.

Jazz had been drifting from America to English shores since 1919, when Sidney Bechet astonished foreign audiences with his clarinet playing. Bechet had been followed by dozens of other American artists, black and white, and they had drawn varying reactions from audiences and journalists. The Armstrong style was known to British audiences in part because Nat Gonella, a self-described "raving fan" of Louis, made a career of imitating his idol. Parlophone, the English record company, kept thirty-eight of his recordings in circulation, and a small, fierce group of jazz loyalists in London were devoted to him. None of these fans ever thought they would actually get to see Louis Armstrong play live. Once it became known that he *was* coming to England, they were immediately concerned about the impression he would make on audiences outside of the capital city. The country's leading dance band and jazz publication, the *Melody Maker*, predicted: "In the provinces, or even in the suburbs, we fear that Louis would be too much for the general public."

The *Majestic* docked at Plymouth on July 14, and the Armstrong party disembarked amid great confusion, for they were expected at Southampton, not Plymouth. They hastily boarded a train to London, leaving behind most of Louis's wardrobe. On the train, Dan Ingman, a zealous reporter from the *Melody Maker*, stumbled from car to car, in search of his quarry, until at last he came upon "a young coloured boy and girl. The latter, chic, fashionably dressed and entirely charming, and the former a small, slight fellow with an enormous white cap and a long biscuit coloured blanket coat." Ingman paused to ask the young couple if they knew the whereabouts of Mr. Armstrong. Suddenly, Johnny Collins appeared and declared that they *were* Mr. and Mrs. Armstrong. "I nearly collapsed!" Ingman recalled. "From his photograph I had been expecting a six-footer . . . at least thirty-five years of age. And this boy—! I hardly believed it. That is, not until he spoke; there was no chance of mistaking that voice!"

Ingman hastily introduced himself and inquired as to where the Armstrongs would be staying in London, only to learn that Mr. Collins hadn't thought to make any reservations. When they arrived at Paddington Station, Ingman dashed into a phone booth and began calling one prominent hotel after another, but as soon as these establishments heard that he wished to reserve a room for "coloured" guests, they all said, "Sorry, sir, we're full up." Finally, on the ninth try, Ingman managed to find a room for the world's greatest trumpeter at the Howard Hotel, in Norfolk Street, just off the Strand. The Armstrong party immediately piled into a taxi, and when they arrived were cordially received by the hotel management.

Soon after they had settled in, a journalist named Percy Brooks approached Louis and greeted him with the name "Satchmo." Louis was momentarily perplexed—he had never heard *that* name before. He quickly realized, though, that the designation was an English corruption of one of his many nicknames, "Satchelmouth," and it instantly became his favorite and best-known alias. Friends still called him "Gate," "Dippermouth," and especially "Pops," but the world hereafter would know him as "Satchmo."

Across the length and breadth of London, posters heralded his Palladium engagement. They promised "Louis Armstrong and His New Rhythm Band, Presented by Johnny Collins" on a bill rounded out with a "Scottish comedian, Continental dancers, and comedy jugglers." The accompanying illustration of Louis went beyond caricature; it depicted a monkey wearing a tuxedo and appearing to rise up on two legs to blow a trumpet. (Louis carefully preserved the appalling image in a scrapbook he had lately begun to maintain.) All the ballyhoo—ranging from offensive to cautious to profoundly admiring—ensured that his two-week-long engagement at the Palladium sold out. Collins hastily assembled a band built around a core of musicians imported from Paris: Charlie Johnson on trumpet, Joe Hayman on saxophone, Peter Du Conge on clarinet, and Maceo Jefferson on guitar. Although Armstrong already knew Johnson and Du Conge, who was, in fact, from New Orleans, they had next to no rehearsal time, and he had to indoctrinate strange musicians as well. "There were several colored French musicians and I had to talk to them through an interpreter," Louis recalled, "but . . . all swing men can talk together and understand each other through their music, so we got along fine."

The imported musicians were scheduled to arrive at Victoria Station, where Louis planned to greet them and lead them straight into rehearsal. At the same time, a music critic and jazz enthusiast named Robert Goffin was making his way to the train station. Goffin, a Belgian, had first heard Armstrong's records back in 1928 and was moved to write a book, *Aux Frontières Du Jazz*, about the amazing new music from America and its

greatest exponent, Louis Armstrong, to whom he had dedicated his work.
Goffin loved jazz and revered Armstrong: "In the wonderful simplicity of
jazz songs, I have rediscovered poetry in its purest state; the prophetic
sobbing of popular tunes has gone straight to my heart. . . . To discover
jazz, one must go to the poems of Langston Hughes, and feel the syncopated pulse beating in the solos of Louis Armstrong or in the irrational
outbursts of the 'St. Louis Blues.' "

Goffin, clearly, was not a dispassionate critic, but a fan, and he was
determined to meet his hero. Intensely excited, he spotted a black man who
could only be Louis Armstrong amid the crowds at Victoria Station, fought
his way to his idol, introduced himself, and presented Louis with a copy of
his book. When Louis saw the inscription, which Goffin carefully trans-
lated—"To Louis Armstrong, the Real King of Jazz"—he kissed it, and a
friendship was born. "Ten minutes later he was calling me 'Gate,' "Goffin
said. By now the other musicians had arrived from Paris, and they merrily
went off to the rehearsal hall, *tout ensemble*.

They practiced until late at night, and Goffin was lost in a reverie of *le
vrai jazz*, transfixed by the sight of Louis blowing. It was one thing to listen
to Louis on recordings, quite another to see him at work, in the flesh. "It
was unbelievable," Goffin remembered. "He shut his eyes, flourished his
trumpet, twisted his handkerchief, sang in tears, climbed up to hit notes
with his neck and cheek so distended that I thought they would burst. What
a revelation that was!" Just then Johnny Collins showed up, roaring drunk,
and turned the festive gathering into an ugly scene. He fell into a shouting
match with Louis, who was understandably disgusted with his manager's
behavior. Collins finally stormed away, only to shatter a plate-glass window
as he tried to walk through it. Said Goffin, "He flattened his cigar and his
nose in almost equal proportions."

The day of his London premiere, Monday, July 18, 1932, Louis suffered
one trauma after another. The problems began in the afternoon, when he
was resting in his hotel room with Alpha. Answering a knock on the door,
he found Fanny Cotton, his former girlfriend, awaiting his open arms.
Louis backed away and awkwardly introduced Fanny, to his "fiancée,"
Alpha Smith. Fanny wilted, asked to use the phone, placed a brief call, and
departed as mysteriously as she had arrived. Alpha was not so easily pla-
cated. The spectacle of an old lover having the temerity to come all the way
to London to find her Louis aroused all her suspicions. Matters went from

bad to worse when they arrived at the Palladium that evening, and she caught sight of Fanny lurking in a taxi outside the theater.

Minutes before Louis was scheduled to perform, Alpha's jealousy reached a fever pitch. Enraged and hysterical, she sprang at Louis and grabbed him by the neck, trying to strangle him in his dressing room. He freed himself from her grasp, but she then fastened her hand on the black satin lapel of his tuxedo and ripped with all her strength. Her shrieks echoed backstage, and when the stage manager came running to investigate, he found the star fending off his girlfriend's blows. She had already torn off his lapel, and, even more seriously, was trying to bust him in the chops— his entire livelihood—at this crucial moment in his career. Stunned by the scene before him, the manager announced that the curtain was rising. Louis knew that the audience was awaiting him—"so here's what I did. With a mighty punch I knocked her out and then I laid her down on the couch and got out fast." He quickly exchanged the coat Alpha had torn for another, snatched up his trumpet, plucked a white handkerchief, and dashed up on stage to greet the acclaim he had traveled three thousand miles to hear.

At that moment, wrote the *Melody Maker*, "Louis popped out in front of the curtain and took his bow. And what applause there was. His first number was 'Them There Eyes,' his second 'When You're Smiling,' his third (dedicated 'to the musicians') 'Chinatown, My Chinatown,' and his last, 'You Rascal, You.' Each one was received with tumult. The packed house absolutely rose to it." They rose all right—to leave. By the time he finished his set, the place was half empty. The evacuation of the Palladium occurred on each night of his run. What made the rush to the aisles all the more remarkable was that the audience consisted mainly of jazz enthusiasts, or people who thought they were, but their impressions of Louis Armstrong came from records alone, those three-minute-long sides that constrained his exuberance. Seeing him in motion before their eyes—joking, jiving, dancing, blowing, and singing—came as a complete shock. In the United States, the Jazz Age, which Louis had helped to invent, was over, but in England, it had not begun until this evening. Said one startled observer, "The sweating, strutting figure in the spotlight hitting endless high notes had only a tenuous and intermittent connection with the creator of the intensely moving music of 'West End Blues' and 'Muggles'." To be sure, Louis's act took some getting used to. When he introduced that chestnut, "Tiger Rag," for instance, he would rush around the stage, slapping his arms and shrieking, "That tiger's traveling fast, gonna take a few choruses to catch him—lookout!" Then he proceeded to play the song so fast that the band couldn't keep up with him. American audiences adored these vaudeville hijinks, but they baffled rather more staid English spectators.

At the intermission, Louis sought the privacy of his dressing room, where Alpha, who had regained consciousness, greeted him indifferently. He now had to submit to the indignity of a gaggle of "admirers" who came to call on him, and to ask if he had doctored his trumpet in order to achieve those astounding notes. As ever, Louis graciously submitted his instrument for examination, and demonstrated again and again that it was an ordinary trumpet in the hands of an extraordinary entertainer and artist.

After the performance, Louis, Alpha, Collins, and Goffin repaired to a music club called the Monseigneur for a nightcap. With closing time only minutes away, Collins ordered no fewer than thirty large mugs of ale, downed six in swift succession, and under Louis's watchful eye, appeared to lapse into unconsciousness. As Louis and Goffin bantered, Collins drunkenly muttered, "Can you fight?" When Goffin answered affirmatively, Collins suddenly shouted, "Then I won't pay!" With that, Collins collapsed. "We had to carry Collins off like a sack of potatoes," Goffin wrote, "and Armstrong signed for the check." So ended the exhausting, eventful London debut.

Over the course of the next few days, the British press pounced on the Armstrong phenomenon and subjected the musician to intense scrutiny and analysis. To the English, Louis was exotic, unexpected, and deeply challenging, and he engendered strong reactions. At the high end of the spectrum, the *Melody Maker*, the British jazz enthusiasts' house organ, hailed him as the savior of popular music, the "Great Man" and proceeded to take credit for discovering and bringing "this coloured trumpet wizard" to the attention of the English public. Louis's appearance at the Palladium "vindicated everything that THE MELODY MAKER had ever said in the aggrandisement of modern dance music." In fact, the magazine's staff was so impressed by Armstrong that they went to the trouble to broker agreements between Collins and the managers of provincial theaters, so that he would be able to tour the provinces—ready or not—once he completed his Palladium stand. At the low end of the spectrum, Hannen Swaffer, the *Daily Herald*'s critic, gawked at Armstrong's stage show, which he considered beneath contempt. Only "pale aesthetes" and "the young Jewish element" displayed enthusiasm for the trumpeter. True, he was "the most amazing performer the stage has seen for months . . . he caresses his trumpet like a lover, making it do things I never heard a trumpet do before." Swaffer half expected, half feared Louis would make his trumpet ejaculate on stage. Not only that, but his stage appearance physically repelled Swaffer: "Armstrong is the ugliest man I have seen on the music-hall stage. He looks, and behaves, like an untrained gorilla. He might have come straight from some African jungle and thereafter to a slop tailor's for a ready-made dress suit, been put on the stage and been told to sing." Undaunted, Louis took care to save Swaffer's commentary in his scrapbook.

Another critic, under the *nom de plume* Bass Clef, tried to explain calmly that Armstrong's "screeches" were not the wonders some misguided enthusiasts claimed they were because "such screeches can be heard in a bandroom" when a musician mischievously decides to "torment his pals." As far as Bass Clef was concerned, Louis played the trumpet in a wholly unnatural way: "The strain put on the lips by producing the 1400 double vibrations per second required for the high G which Armstrong features leaves the lips so impoverished that they are unable to perform properly, even when he descends to normal registers. His tone is thin or harsh, according to the dynamics, and his intonation poor. He breaks all the tenets and principles laid down by orthodox teaching and he attempts to defy Nature."

Yet another anonymous critic was appalled not by Louis's blowing but by his singing—or, as this detractor described it, "savage growling . . . as far removed from English as we speak or sing—and as modern—as James Joyce." Having lumped Louis with that other benighted modernist, the critic advised his readers to "have no more of this attitude that that gentle little negro, Louie Armstrong, is the world's master. He is, as I can testify, an extraordinarily nice person. But there are Englishmen who are at least just as talented." The reviewer concluded that Louis might be a genius, of sorts, but "his genius is barren. . . . It can give birth to no developments in music proper in the same way that Ellington's can and does." His scrapbook growing daily, Louis saved this rant as well.

A few mainstream critics managed to put aside their reservations about Louis's excesses and embraced him. Most of them realized a genius was in their midst, and he was transforming the jazz idiom. Dudley Leslie, a correspondent for the *Evening Mail*, counseled, "Adore it, or deplore—do whatever seems natural, but at least try to realise you are criticising the music of to-morrow, not the polkas of Victoria."

After his tumultuous fortnight at the Palladium, Louis exchanged his imported French musicians for a "ten-piece band of white swing-men" and began a tour of the British Isles. He had played with whites before, but only on a casual basis, late at night, when Bix or Hoagy or Mezz sat in with his band. This was the first time he had fronted an all-white band in a formal engagement. The combination of an American soloist with an English band made Louis's strong music rather more palatable for English audiences, and for the next four months, he performed with this orchestra in cities such as Glasgow, Nottingham, and Liverpool. Wherever he went, Louis, clearly enjoying the attention he received, endeared himself to all, while the boorish and drunken Collins alienated anyone who crossed his path. Just before one provincial engagement, Dan Ingman reported that Collins flew into one of his rages when Louis, resplendent in his tuxedo, was preparing to perform. "Where's the dough?" Collins demanded of the theater's promoter. "If I don't get the dough, Louis don't play." The promoter immediately proffered a check, but Collins insisted on cash. While Louis looked down at his feet, the promoter went to the box office and returned with several bags of silver. "There's your money," he informed Collins. (Ingman thought to himself, "He doesn't know how to count it.") Only then was the star permitted to blow for the paying customers. Ingman, for one, was enormously impressed by Louis's demeanor: "Everything he did was right in an embarrassing situation for which we were all responsible to a degree."

Meanwhile, Louis trailed an ever-growing legend. The Glasgow *Sunday Mail* claimed he earned £1,100 a week (and traveled with 130 suits and forty-eight trunks). In fact, Louis and the entire band made about £500 a week on this tour, and only a fraction of that amount went to the star himself. The leader of his English group, the pianist Billy Mason, actually earned more than Louis did. In comparison, Paul Whiteman, the so-called King of Jazz, was paid more than three times as much at the time, and Duke Ellington's Orchestra received twice as much. Louis's meager wages offered further evidence of Collins's incompetence.

Despite all the stresses imposed by the tour, Louis always comported himself with aplomb. He never wasted breath responding to his race-baiting critics or even to defend his type of music. On stage, he was always genial, no matter how many customers hissed him or stormed up the aisles in the midst of his performance. He was blowing, so he was happy. Even better, he was a free man. Although the press savaged him, no one arrested him in England, or threw him into jail, or threatened to shoot him in the leg, or called him "nigger." He moved about this foreign country as he pleased—quite unlike the United States. Even before he finished the tour he planned to return the following year.

Leaving England in late October, Louis and Alpha, reconciled for the moment, spent a week sightseeing in Paris and then sailed for New York. They arrived there on November 2, 1932, the day Franklin D. Roosevelt was elected President, and four days later, Louis, looking relaxed and fit after his ocean voyage, returned to work. He performed at Harlem's Lafayette Theatre, where he was brilliant as always, and went on to play other dates throughout the East, always on the move, constantly performing, never resting, not even for a day.

December found him in New Jersey, recording for his new company, Victor. The change, engineered by Johnny Collins, touched off a nasty dispute, as Okeh, now part of Columbia, attempted to exercise a year-long option on Louis. Collins, in his typically clumsy fashion, ignored Okeh's demand and was promptly faced with a lawsuit and an injunction to prevent Louis's recording for the Victor label. Blustering his way through these complications, for which he was to blame, Collins hired a band to accompany Louis. The musicians included Chick Webb, a first-class drummer, and Mezz Mezzrow, who had partially recovered from the effects of his heroin addiction.

When he arrived at the Victor studio, Mezz discovered that the months of touring had taken their toll on Louis: "He had a terrible sore lip, in addition to being dogtired, and that day he had played five shows and made two broadcasts. . . . I didn't see how poor old Pops was going to blow note one." At 1:30 in the morning, Louis and the other musicians drove to a red brick church in Camden, New Jersey, the site of the Victor studio. "This is funny, ain't it, Mezza, jammin' in an ole church," Louis said. "Where else should Gabriel Blow?" Mezzrow replied.

They got down to work under the direction of Eli Oberstein, the Victor recording manager, with Louis trying to baby his lip through the session, and Mezz trying to remember what it felt like to play the clarinet. As the night wore on, the other musicians became impatient with the two of them, especially Mezz, who they thought had no business discussing arrangements with Louis. Louis, on the other hand, felt perfectly comfortable relying on Mezz. After they had hashed out the head arrangement for "That's My Home," Mezz recalled, "Louis stomped off and started the band, this time for a test record. . . . What a thrill I got when that revised bass part came thumping out loud and forceful. The moment Louis finished playing his lead passage, he tore his horn away from his lips, came running over to me bubbling with joy, and exclaimed, 'From now on, Mezz is my musical director!' The tension in that room snapped like an overstretched elastic band." Buoyed by Louis, everyone clicked into gear. They recorded "Hobo, You Can't Ride This Train," a tune Louis had never seen until the moment the sheet music appeared on the stand in front of him. "Now what am I gonna do with this?" he plaintively asked Mezz. "I don't know nothin' 'bout no hoboes, any more'n this songwriter did." Mezz quickly filled him in on hobo lore, and Louis expertly took it in and spat it back out as his spoken introduction to the song. The more he sang, the stronger he became. "You just couldn't hold down old Pops."

Soon after, though, during a New Year's Eve engagement in Baltimore, Louis teetered on the brink of exhaustion. His damaged lip, said Mezz, "was so bad, all raw and swole up, that he just sat and looked at it all day in the mirror, all the time applying some lip salve . . . so it wouldn't be agony for him every time he blew into his horn. To make things worse, he kept picking at the great sore with a needle." Mezz shuddered at the sight, and Louis explained, "I been doin' this for a long time you know, got to get them little pieces of dead skin out 'cause they plug up my mouthpiece." Despite the horrendous condition of his lip, Louis took his trumpet and a supply of white handkerchiefs, and went on stage, where a full house, a large orchestra, and a line of chorus girls awaited him.

Mezz held his breath and listened. "He started to blow his chorus, tearing his heart out, and the tones that came vibrating out of those poor agonized lips of his sounded like a weary soul plodding down the lonesome road, the weight of the world's woe on his bent shoulders, crying for relief to all his people. . . . There were tears in all the eyes around me, tears for what Louis was preaching on that horn, tears for wonderful, overworked, sick and suffering Louis himself, the hero of his race. Everybody knew that each time that horn touched his lips, it was like a red-hot poker to him." At the climax, "Louis slid slowly, oh so slowly up into one of those high-gliding wails, moaning his way along." Just as Mezz thought Louis would crack, the trombone man, Charlie "Big" Green, burst into tears and fled backstage. Next the whole band started crying, which naturally set off the chorus girls, but Louis stayed out there, horn to his lips, trying to get all the way up to high F. Determined to hit that note at all costs, he attacked it "with the last breath of life left in him . . . Louis clutched and crawled and made that high F on his knees, just barely made it, in the last nerve-slashing second." When the audience drowned him out with cathartic applause, he just stood, "holding his horn and panting, his mangled lip oozing blood that he licked away." Slowly, his head rose, and the audience, already beside themselves, saw that he was smiling. He bowed, and then he was gone.

"Tough scuffle" he said hoarsely to Mezz in his dressing room, as he sat there, his tuxedo soaked with sweat, mopping his face, "but that's all in life."

Not long after this extraordinary performance, Mezzrow stepped down as Louis's "musical director" and returned to New York and his heroin addiction. Louis, meanwhile, kept up a frenetic pace throughout the winter and spring of 1933, traveling with Zilner Randolph, performing night after night. Nothing seemed to matter to him but work—touring, performing, recording, blowing, singing. Irving Kolodin, the music critic for the New York *Sun*, caught him at the Lafayette Theatre in Harlem one February night and was astounded by the frenzy and skill of Louis's act:

> *"He announces 'When You're Smiling,' and . . . backs off, downstage left, leans halfway over like a quarter miler, begins to count, (swaying as he does) 'one, two, three'. . . . He has already started racing toward the rear where the orchestra is ranged, and he hits four, executes a slide and a pirouette; winds up facing the audience and blowing the first note as the orchestra swings into tune. It's mad, it's meaningless, it's hokum of the first order, but the effect is electrify-*

*ing. . . . His trumpet virtuosity is endless—triplets, chromatic ac-
cented eerie counterpoints that turn the tune inside out, wild sorties into
the giddy stratosphere where his tone sounds like a dozen flights in
unison, all executed with impeccable style and finish, exploits that
make his contemporaries sound like so many Salvation Army cornetists."*

From New York, Louis fled to Chicago, where, he told his pals at the *Melody Maker,* "I am . . . enjoying myself to the highest. The first thing I had for supper the first day I arrived in the ol' home town was a big pot of good red beans and rice, ha, ha, ha. I had to pull myself up from the table, ha ha. And then I went and heard 'Ol Father Hines get off for me last night. And boy did he play that piano? He made that piano say 'Goodness Gracious!' Honest!"

To be sure, there were some great times back in Chicago. Louis was high much of the time, and whenever he went into a Victor studio that April, he seemed transported, almost in a trance. He was working with a small group of Vipers: Zilner Randolph, Teddy Wilson, Scoville Brown, and a young tenor saxophonist named Albert (later, "Budd") Johnson. On April 24, they confirmed their Viper status by waxing "Laughin' Louie" under very special circumstances. "We wouldn't allow anybody in the recording sessions," Budd Johnson recalled, "because Louis would like to get high, and he'd like for the band to get high. So he says, 'We're going to record 'Laughin' Louie' today, gentlemen. I want everybody to smoke a joint.' . . . We were floating when we made that 'Laughin' Louie' and Louis played that trumpet like a bird."

He proceeded to take the Vipers on tour. The band trooped through Louisville, Indianapolis, and Omaha. When they got to St. Louis, Budd Johnson recalled, "We got up on the bandstand, and when I looked on the music rack, lo and behold, all of the racks were filled with reefers, and I'm saying to myself, 'What the devil is this?' " When Louis emerged from his dressing room, "six little guys . . . walked up to the bandstand and said, 'Louis Armstrong, Pops,' and you know, he was a great greeter, I don't think nobody could greet anybody more beautifully than Louis Armstrong, even if he didn't know you, so he says, 'Yeah, man, what's happenin' here?' and the man says, 'We want to present you with this,' and they held out their arms, and it was a great big joint rolled in the form of a baseball bat. It must have been about a foot long. And they had taken a fountain pen and punched holes in it to read: TO THE KING OF THE VIPERS FROM THE VIPERS CLUB OF ST. LOUIS."

No matter how high he became, Louis never stopped. His stage antics and energy astounded even the musicians who played with him every night. Just before leaving St. Louis, they got into a cutting contest with a local band called The Crackerjacks, and their trumpeter, Hal Baker, stood up and started to imitate Louis playing 'Shine,' foolishly trying to outdo him. Baker was hitting G's and ended on a high C. "Well, this kind of upset Pops," said Budd. "He said, 'Can you imagine that? What is he trying to do?' Well, when they came off the stand, Louis called 'Shine.' He hit 250 high C's—I counted 'em—and ended on a high F that you wouldn't believe. It just shook the rafters in the place."

After that, Louis made "Shine" into his tour de force, murdering his lip but delighting audiences. "We used to get out in those little towns in the Midwest where people didn't know him too well," said Harry Dial, who beat the drums on the tour. "He'd hit as many as 350 High C's on 'Shine.' I used to count them. He'd make me so mad on 'Tiger Rag' that I wouldn't know what to do. He'd want me to ride the cymbals on the last three choruses. I'd grab the cymbal around the eighth chorus and start riding it, and by the end of the tenth it would sound good to him and he'd hit with one finger, which would mean one more chorus . . . and he'd play ten more choruses. . . . That guy worked me to death."

The exhausting tour with the Vipers ended on July 1, but only a week later Louis was in Philadelphia, doing five or six shows a day in a vaudeville house patronized mainly by blacks. Even here, far from the danger zones of New York and Chicago, mobsters calling themselves "bodyguards" confronted him in his dressing room one day. Suspecting trouble, Louis played his set and went directly from the stage to the nearest police station, where he asked the cops to keep him in custody, lest those grim-looking "bodyguards" bust his lip. Eventually Johnny Collins rescued him from this jam, but one thing was now clear: Louis Armstrong couldn't play anywhere in the United States without fearing for his safety. Once again, it was time for a quick exit, pursued by gangsters. Collins booked him a suite aboard the SS *Homeric*, bound for London, where, if not critically accepted, he would at least be out of harm's way.

The previous winter, "something very odd had happened in England"—in the words of one of his British admirers. The normally sane *Daily Express* ran the headline: "Man With Iron Lips Killed by His Art" and explained that Louis Armstrong, who had recently dazzled audiences in Great Britain, "died suddenly in a nursing home in New York, a victim to the terrific strain which his art put on him." At the time, Louis was considerably more famous in England than in the United States, and the *Daily Express* was flooded with questions about the incredible circumstances surrounding his passing. Though the source of the story was never confirmed, the press informed the public, in time for his return to British shores, that reports of Louis Armstrong's death were greatly exaggerated.

He was scheduled to open at the Holborn Empire in London on August 5, 1933, and sailed at the end of July, accompanied by Alpha and Johnny Collins. By now his relationship with his manager, always contentious, had entered its final throes. John Hammond, the record producer, also happened to be aboard the *Homeric* for the crossing, witnessed Collins's loathsome behavior. "One night he got very drunk in Louis's stateroom while I was upbraiding him for his use of the word 'nigger' and for his shabby treatment of Armstrong. Who was, after all, Collins's bread and butter," Hammond wrote. "The manager became so furious he took a swing at me. Somehow . . . I managed to counter his punch and knock him on his behind. I think Louis never forgot that fight. It was probably the first time a white man had thought enough of him to fight someone who abused him." A child of privilege, Hammond liked to portray himself as a two-fisted champion of civil rights, and this scene flattered his vanity—but, contrary to his own speculations, it made no impression on Louis.

Shortly after they arrived in London, Johnny Collins went on another drunken rampage. He packed up and left England without Louis, but with Louis's passport, just to make his client's life even more difficult. Their relationship had always been dreadful, so Louis was understandably relieved to be rid of the man. Collins had worked him like a dog, but he had little to show for all his years of incessant blowing but a bulging scrapbook and a badly damaged lip. He certainly did not have the money befitting his star status, but for once Louis's modest financial circumstances were not entirely his manager's fault. The concept of saving money was alien to Louis, who generally spent whatever cash he had on Alpha and anyone else who asked for a handout. Louis picked up checks, paid hotel and restaurant bills, and never worried about where the money came from. Collins's bullying, exploitative mismanagement had allowed Louis's spending to cross the line from casual to reckless.

To fill the void left by Collins, Louis turned to Jack Hylton, an English bandleader and promoter, to function as his manager. Although this was a temporary arrangement, Louis's choice made a strong statement about American managers. Tommy Rockwell, Johnny Collins, Dutch Schultz—he wanted no part of them or the various mobs infesting Chicago, New York, or any other big American city. Fleeing predators rather than debts, Louis was poised to go into exile to remain out of their reach. The prospect of living abroad permanently was very much in the air, as numerous jazz musicians, fed up with the same poisonous mixture of gangsters and racism that had bedeviled Louis, went abroad to pursue their careers, where they could live and work without fear. Sidney Bechet, the best known of the expatriates, was busy establishing himself as a clarinet star in Paris, and would eventually become much better known in Europe, truly a giant of the jazz world, than he was in the United States, where his reputation slowly faded.

For a time, Louis relaxed, and he found myriad ways to make London his second home. He took up residence in the Astoria Hotel. With his white imitator, Nat Gonella, trailing along as his sidekick, he frequented small restaurants in Wardour Street—the Bag o'Nails or The Jigs Club—and feasted on his beloved red beans and rice. In Greek Street, close to his hotel, he found various Chinese restaurants to his liking. He held court in his hotel room for visiting jazz musicians. His relationship with Alpha was placid for the moment—no more fistfights and scenes—and she went everywhere with him. Everyone took her to be his wife, although they still had not wed.

Louis opened at London's Holborn Empire on August 5, 1933. Twelve days later, his father Willie died in New Orleans of acute gastroenteritis, complicated by pneumonia. At the time of his death, Willie Armstrong resided at 3817 Melpomene Street, and he was still employed at the turpentine plant where he had worked most of his adult life. He was forty-nine years old. Louis hadn't seen him since boyhood and did not attend the funeral.

Louis's geographical and emotional distance from this milestone high-lighted his astonishing trajectory—how he had risen from the lowest level of a caste-ridden society in a provincial city, abandoned by his father, and cared for by relatives with no interest in music, to international promi-nence, revolutionizing the entire field of jazz, and by extension, contempo-rary music. He had accomplished all this on his own, in the face of intense economic pressure and social discrimination. And he was only thirty-two years old.

In October, Louis undertook a Scandinavian tour. Unlikely as it seemed, he had developed a fanatical following in these northern countries, where numerous "Hot Clubs" of jazz aficionados endlessly discussed his record-ings and his approach to music and life. In Denmark, especially, he was treated like a major star. Ten thousand people turned out to greet him when he arrived at the Copenhagen train station. "All I remember is a whole ocean of people all breaking through the police lines and bearing down on us until I got afraid we were going to get stomped underfoot," Louis wrote. He thought the crowd of faces, every single one of them pale white, had assembled to greet someone else, but they were there for him. "They pushed a big trumpet, all made out of flowers, into my hands and put me into an open automobile and started a parade." Within minutes, the crowd tore apart the floral trumpet, as Louis rode off in triumph, and when he reached his hotel, he was mobbed again by autograph seekers, and by Danish women begging him for a kiss.

He performed eight times in Copenhagen's Lyric Park and proved so popular in Denmark that he made a movie there, a valuable record of his performing style at that moment. He was obviously high when he went before the cameras; mugging, grinning, and wagging his head, but his playing style was dramatically simplified. He was still reaching for the impossibly high F's and G's with his trumpet, but instead of spattering countless notes across the stage, he played a straight melody. The bold, unadorned, declamatory style, masterfully paced, proved an effective con-trast to his busy and bizarre antics. His horn seemed to be his master.

From Denmark, Louis traveled to Stockholm. Alpha was constantly at his side, keeping her eye on him. For once, he welcomed her attentions. "When I was in Sweden a young, cute little newspaper reporter came up while I was autographing one of my little teenage fans' books," he later wrote. "He said to me, 'Hey, Louie Armstrong, how do you like our Swedish women?' I looked up at him and said, 'Man, my wife has the best Smorgasbord in the world.' He cut out very swiftly."

In November, Louis resumed playing in London, this time for the Prince of Wales. When he stopped to think about it, it was incredible how he'd come all the way from driving a coal cart in New Orleans to this particular eminence in the space of sixteen years. If only his mother had been alive to see it. He continued to perform in London right through to the end of the year. Then, when he was blowing away at the Holborn Empire one night, "my lip split, blood all down in my tuxedo shirt, nobody knew it. Just bowed off the stage and didn't go back for four months."

In truth, the injury and the prospect of enforced rest came as a relief. In January 1934, Louis declared in a newspaper interview that he had worked for ten years without a break—actually, it was closer to fifteen—and he needed rest. His lip damage provided the ideal excuse to avoid any professional commitments. Throughout the winter he moved around London, attending concerts, nightclubs, and plays, always with Alpha. For once, he seemed content *not* to work. Johnny Collins finally resurfaced in New York and sent a telegram declaring he was "Still all for you." He included a list of fancy engagements he had lined up for his former client back in New York, and closed with the exhortation, "Telegraph time of your arrival." Louis read it, crumpled it, and tossed it away, muttering, "Never, never, never."

Collins was not the only manager whose entreaties he resisted. Jack Hylton, who supposedly was handling him now, planned to pair Louis with Coleman Hawkins, who had emerged from Fletcher Henderson's orchestra to become the most stylish saxophone player of the day. The two virtuosi were supposed to have a gala concert at the Hippodrome on April 22. Hawkins arrived in London, was duly lionized by the English press, but then Louis—who never failed to appear at an engagement no matter how hard he had been working, or how tender his lip, or how wretched the conditions or the pay—refused to blow with the Hawk.

Everyone in England was mystified by his stubborn behavior, and Louis, appearing tranquil enough, blamed the managers for trying to cajole both men into playing in a concert neither wanted. "So you see, it was all bullshit from the start," he remarked. The ignominious affair ended his tenuous relationship with Hylton, and he signed up with yet another English manager, Audrey Thacker. He did not, however, resume a full schedule. This wasn't the United States, he told himself, and no thug was going to force him at gunpoint to blow or else. For once, he wasn't going to do anything he didn't want to do. Tired and even disgusted with the music business in general, Louis went deeper into exile.

May 1934 found Louis in Paris, enjoying himself with Alpha, avoiding the recording studio and the concert hall, jamming with musicians when he pleased. "I just lazied around Paris for three or four months," he explained of that fallow period, "had lots of fun with musicians from the States— French cats, too. And I'd do a concert now and then." There were rumors that he had lost his gift, that his lip was shot, that he had had a breakdown, that gangsters were out to kill him, but none of this speculation proved true. He was living with Alpha in a flat in the rue de la Tour Auvergne, socializing with other expatriate members of American cafe society, many of them black—Josephine Baker, Bricktop, Bobby Jones, and Arthur Briggs— taking his ease at the Café Boudon, nursing apéritifs, observing the scene. It seemed to him that life had never been this good back in the United States. He acquired a stature in Paris that he had never attained at home. Here he was an artist, not a "colored entertainer."

It began to look as if he had entered a permanent semiretirement and might never return to America. If he never performed again, made another recording, or blew another note, his reputation as the most innovative and influential of all jazz musicians was secure. At the same time, he knew that jazz musicians often burned out or blew themselves out at an early age, and he wondered how much more his lip could take. If he were going to survive, he would have to find a way to preserve himself. Though he was only in his midthirties, he had felt like an old-timer. To counter the effects of aging, he dieted strenuously under Alpha's supervision. He boasted that he lost 105 pounds under her regimen, and his weight was down to 165 pounds. Alpha, he said, weighed just 112. "We were two cute little people," he noted.

. . .

A newly energized Louis started to rebuild his career. In October 1934, he assembled a group of musicians, mostly members of the band from his first London engagement, and in a Paris studio they recorded not for Columbia or Victor, but for Brunswick, an independent label, in an apparent violation of his other recording contracts. No matter how convoluted the business aspect of this session, he waxed some astonishing sides, including two deliciously fruity renditions of "On the Sunny Side of the Street." The most memorable tune to emerge from that session, however, was Louis's own "Song of the Vipers," a lyrical, haunting celebration of jazz and marijuana. (Louis made sure that his French band inhaled deeply before recording.) Louis scats his way through the tune, almost keening at several points, and his performance concludes with a transcendent horn solo. The entire song has a visionary quality reminiscent of the sweet sorrow suffusing "West End Blues," but it is freer and looser, and seems to extend all the way to the gates of paradise. Transported, Louis plays the music of the spheres. Brunswick released this daring experiment in the United States, but it was on sale for only a few days before the company realized what the title indicated and promptly withdrew it from stores. Not for decades would this recording—one of Louis's best—become available again.

On November 9 and 10, 1934, he performed at the prestigious Salle Rameau in Paris. There, his over-the-top showmanship, fueled by thick sticks of marijuana, enthralled the audience from the first note but baffled the man from the New York *Herald*, Marshall Sprague. "At the start, his disadvantages seemed appalling," the critic observed. "His conversation was entirely in Negro dialect and was lost not only to the French but to many of the English as well." But once Louis got going, Sprague softened slightly and decided that Louis's aggressively contemporary style of singing actually "traces back in a straight, unbroken line to the yearning and colorful emotionalism of the pre-Civil War Negro slave." In the end, Sprague remained "faintly disturbed by the suspicion that jazz, unlike conventional forms, is the musician's, not the composer's, sole creation." This discovery was hardly news to Louis or his audience, who loved the show. Their reaction delighted him: "I had to take so many bows until I wound up taking 'em in my bathrobe."

The reemergence of Louis Armstrong attracted a French promoter, N. J. Canetti, who quickly assembled a tour for Louis and his Parisian band, accompanied by an alluring dancer. Canetti dispatched the group on a brief winter tour of Belgium, France, and Italy. New Year's Eve found them in Lausanne, Switzerland, and Louis remembered that "We went over the Alps into Switzerland by bus. . . . We saw Italian soldiers way up on the mountain sides moving along on skis. They went very fast." His career, too, was going fast, regaining momentum, and wherever he went, the Europeans embraced him. There were banquets and receptions held in his honor, and he was repeatedly hailed as *le Roi du Jazz*. European jazz critics accosted him whenever he performed; they followed him to his dressing room and engaged him in lengthy discussions about this new American music and his role in it. All these Hot Clubs, and all these terribly earnest record collectors throughout Europe and Scandinavia, wanted to know exactly who had recorded with him on long forgotten record dates or how he had thought up the cadenza for "West End Blues." The "experts" seemed to know more about him, or at least his recordings, than he knew himself! Without quite realizing it, Louis had become the musical symbol of the Primitivist and *art nègre* movements sweeping the European art world. He ignited the imagination of the French critic Hughes Panassié, who became the latest convert to the cult of Louis Armstrong. In 1936, Panassié wrote, "I do not think I am making too strong a statement when I say that Louis Armstrong is not only a genius in his own art, but is one of the most extraordinary creative geniuses that all music has ever known."

Even as foreign critics celebrated his African ancestry and musical influences, they remained oblivious to the myriad European influences in jazz—all those French quadrilles, Italian melodies, and Spanish rhythms that Louis had learned back in New Orleans. They knew little about New Orleans and its music, Creole musicians, marching bands, and musical funerals. Had Louis's foreign admirers realized that he came straight out of that city's well-established musical and cultural traditions, they would have understood that he was not an isolated phenomenon. Contrary to their assumptions, his type of music really wasn't "art" in the modernist sense— something singular, apart from society—but actually belonged to daily life, to nightclubs and brothels, to funerals and parades and picnics and other everyday events.

Amid the acclaim, Louis's lip problems returned to plague him, and he was forced to withdraw from various European engagements. Canetti threw up his hands and canceled the rest of the tour, which would have taken Louis all the way to North Africa. In the pages of the *Melody Maker*, Canetti railed against his recalcitrant star, claiming he had taken Louis to see a doctor about his lip injury and that the trumpeter was simply using his condition as an excuse to hold back. The *real* reason he refused to perform, Canetti insisted, was that Louis felt overshadowed by his pianist, Herman Chittison. Canetti also complained that Louis's arrangements featured "his own pompous and anything but musical finales." This was a poor justification for canceling Louis's tour, since audiences were attracted to Louis for precisely that reason. Canetti climaxed his attack by suing his former client for breach of contract.

Not knowing which way to turn, Louis fled Europe as impulsively as he had arrived. On January 24, 1935, he and Alpha sailed for New York aboard the SS *Champlain*. He was confident he could pick up the pieces of his American career, but quickly discovered he had spent so much time abroad that people at home were asking, "Whatever became of Louis Armstrong?"

13

PUBLIC MELODY
NUMBER ONE

No sooner had Louis disembarked in New York than business troubles engulfed him. In France, Canetti pursued his breach-of-contract suit. In England, Thacker insisted Louis honor a year-long contract. And on American shores, Johnny Collins reared his ugly head the moment Louis arrived. Enraged by Louis's refusal to return to his fold, Collins obtained a measure of revenge by preventing the trumpeter from keeping an engagement with the Chick Webb Orchestra at Harlem's Apollo Theater, the center of black show business. As soon as he arrived in New York, Louis seemed to have been banished. American managers—the very word had become an irritant—were unimpressed by Louis's status as *le Roi du Jazz* in France, or by the fact that he'd played for the Prince of Wales. In America, the "king of jazz" was not Louis Armstrong, it was Paul Whiteman. In a gesture of Jim Crow jazz criticism, Whiteman admitted that Louis Armstrong was "a definite outstanding character in the field of colored musicians and entertainers"—but no more than that.

Unable to work, and needing a place to stay until he found his footing, Louis contacted his old friend and dealer, Mezz Mezzrow. Mezz now lived in Jackson Heights, Queens, and was still struggling with his heroin addiction. Occasionally he sold gage, but not with the old gusto. He yearned to think of himself as a musician, not an addict, but whenever he tried to practice the clarinet "the opium would make me fall asleep." When Louis, fresh from his European triumphs, appeared before Mezz, he reminded the clarinetist of all he prized in life.

As soon as they reunited, a Broadway producer offered Mezz a thousand dollars to obtain Louis's services, and the producer promised to make

Mezz Louis's business manager. Intrigued, Louis and Mezz went to talk things over with the producer, but soon discovered Mezz had no part of the deal after all. Shattered, Mezz tore up the thousand-dollar check as Louis dragged him from the office. Later, in the car, Mezz broke down in tears as he cursed his fate, swearing that he'd rather be an honest-to-God musician than a dealer. Still, he couldn't bring himself to tell Louis about his heroin habit.

"Don't worry," Louis told him, "I'll go back to Chicago and rest my chops for a while, and you go to work on some arrangements for me and we'll start out together." He laid out a grand scheme—Louis fronting for Mezz's band, and then, "when your name gets big enough you can go start your own band."

Mezz wanted to explain that nothing would make him happier, but the words wouldn't come. He simply could not bring himself to confess his addiction.

When they got back to Jackson Heights, Louis, in a fit of magnanimity, wrote to Local 802 of the Associated Musicians of New York to state that henceforth Mezz Mezzrow would be his "manager and musical director." Mezz felt he had duped his best friend, yet "bad as I felt, I couldn't help smiling." Louis proceeded to give Mezz a thousand dollars. "We're going to make plenty more and I'm stickin', I won't need it," he blithely explained. The idea was for Mezz to use the money to pay the rent, stop selling gage, and start managing his new client, Louis Armstrong. Not only that, he told Mezz to get cracking on some new arrangements. Mezz put up a show of resistance when it came to taking the money, but ultimately relented when his friend shoved five hundred dollars into the bureau. By the time Louis left, he believed he had hired himself a new manager, a man he could trust, who knew how to write arrangements, and who, if he ever stopped crying, could even play the clarinet. Although Louis displayed endearing loyalty by attempting to place his affairs in Mezz's hands, the gesture also showed how thoroughly muddled his thinking had become on the subject of managers.

At the end of January 1935, Louis left for Chicago. No one greeted him with flowers or marching bands when he arrived. It was all very far from his days in London, performing for the Prince of Wales, or his weeks in Paris. He quietly took an apartment on South Parkway and spent time frolicking with two dogs he had acquired, Peter and Rags, and trying out his fancy English suits in the raw winter weather. He revived his friendship with Zutty Singleton, the drummer he left behind in Harlem.

He visited Lil, still in the house on 44th Street they once shared. Instead of welcoming him, she sued him for six thousand dollars, insisting he owed her "maintence." He didn't have the money, needless to say. While he was abroad, she had pursued her own career now as a bandleader; she was recording, as well, under the name "Lil Armstrong." Although a decade had passed since their passion ended, they had not completed their divorce. Lil continued to stall, to retain her influence over Louis.

Occasionally, he emerged from his enforced retirement to play one-night stands, including a ceremonial gig with the Duke Ellington Orchestra, but his future remained in doubt. He awaited word from Mezz back in New York, but nothing materialized. "There was the biggest chance in my life, dangling right in my face," Mezz wrote of that awful moment. "I had to straighten out, right quick. I sat down and went to work on some arrangements for Louis, and I ran straight into that brick wall again. . . . I couldn't keep my attention on the notes, couldn't even stay awake. I wasn't breaking the habit. It was breaking me."

Finally, in May 1935, after four tedious months of laying low in Chicago, Louis Armstrong returned to performing full-time, playing the old familiar songs with the old familiar bands at the old familiar places, but everything was different. He was under new management—yet again—but this time, his choice of manager was more than a business decision, it was a new way of life. The man who ran his life now was named Joe Glaser.

To hear Joe Glaser tell it: "Louis came back from England, he was broke and very sick. He said, 'I don't want to be with anybody but you. Please, Mr. Glaser, just you and I. You understand me. I understand you.' And I said, 'Louis, you're me, and I'm you.' I insured his life and mine for $100,000 apiece. Louis didn't even know it. I gave up all my other business, and we went on the road together." This was the same Joe Glaser who had managed the Sunset Cafe during Louis's glory days there almost ten years earlier, the man whom Louis always felt understood "colored people."

But to hear Louis tell it, the balance of power was somewhat different. It was Glaser who had fallen on hard times: "I could see he was down and

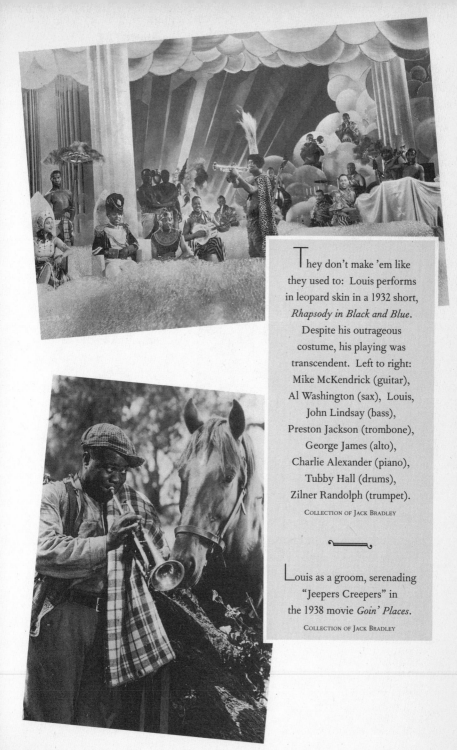

They don't make 'em like they used to: Louis performs in leopard skin in a 1932 short, *Rhapsody in Black and Blue*. Despite his outrageous costume, his playing was transcendent. Left to right: Mike McKendrick (guitar), Al Washington (sax), Louis, John Lindsay (bass), Preston Jackson (trombone), George James (alto), Charlie Alexander (piano), Tubby Hall (drums), Zilner Randolph (trumpet).

COLLECTION OF JACK BRADLEY

Louis as a groom, serenading "Jeepers Creepers" in the 1938 movie *Goin' Places*.

COLLECTION OF JACK BRADLEY

Louis as Hollywood's version of a superstitious bandleader in the fanciful *Pennies from Heaven* (1936), starring his friend Bing Crosby. ARCHIVE PHOTOS/FRANK DRIGGS COLLECTION

Another Hollywood image of Louis Armstrong, this time as the Devil's assistant in the 1943 musical *Cabin in the Sky*. Although he filmed a lavish production number, Lena Horne grabbed most of the attention, and much of his role in this groundbreaking movie was left on the cutting room floor. COLLECTION OF JACK BRADLEY

Louis, blowing, and James Stewart, trying to blow, at the time of *The Glenn Miller Story*, in which they appeared together. COLLECTION OF JACK BRADLEY

Louis and Martha Raye in the controversial *Artists and Models* (1937). Her provocative, gyrating hips generated a chorus of criticism. As a result, Louis's future interactions with women on screen were held to a minimum. THE MUSEUM OF MODERN ART/FILM STILLS ARCHIVE

Louis looks on admiringly as his erstwhile teacher, Bunk Johnson, tries to prove he is still a trumpet "king." Louis helped to rescue Bunk from years of obscurity, to the point of raising money to provide the older man with a new set of teeth. ARCHIVE PHOTOS/ FRANK DRIGGS COLLECTION

Louis and the All Stars at their peak, in Paris, 1949. The small group made lots of money and drew large crowds, but many complained their predictable format curbed Armstrong's innovative style. Left to right: Cozy Cole, Jack Teagarden, Louis, Arvell Shaw, Barney Bigard, Earl Hines. ARCHIVE PHOTOS/ FRANK DRIGGS COLLECTION

Lucille Wilson, Louis's fourth wife, as a chorus girl in the Cotton Club in New York, 1940. Louis called her his "Brown Sugar." ARCHIVE PHOTOS/ FRANK DRIGGS COLLECTION

Louis and Lucille marry, 1942. Although they had their share of quarrels, and Louis occasionally strayed, they remained together for the rest of his life. ARCHIVE PHOTOS/FRANK DRIGGS COLLECTION

Louis clowns with Lil, his second wife, when she visited him backstage during the 1950s. Although their marriage had ended years earlier, she never got over him and died while performing at a memorial concert in his honor. HOGAN JAZZ ARCHIVE, HOWARD-TILTON MEMORIAL LIBRARY, TULANE UNIVERSITY

Louis and Lucille, his fourth wife, carry on backstage before a concert. Louis often paraded naked around his dressing room. ARCHIVE PHOTOS

SWISS KRISSLY

SATCHMO-SLOGAN
(Leave It All Behind Ya)

Shock value: Louis displays himself and his devotion to the herbal laxative Swiss Kriss. He gave away packages of the medicine to everyone he met and distributed hundreds of copies of this picture to startled friends and fans. COLLECTION OF JACK BRADLEY

Louis in front of his home in Corona, Queens, New York. He was now world famous, yet he refused to live like a celebrity. COLLECTION OF JACK BRADLEY

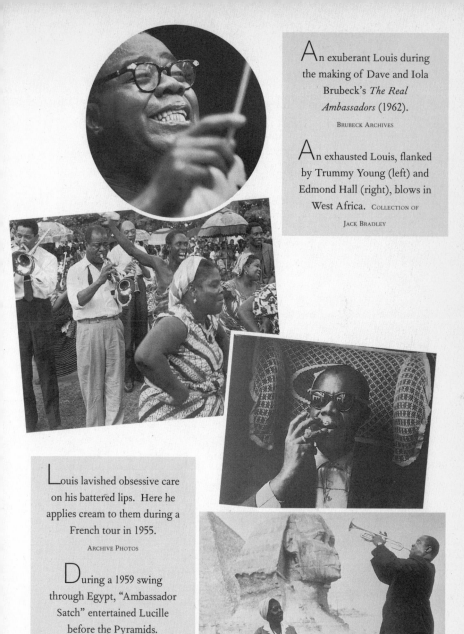

An exuberant Louis during the making of Dave and Iola Brubeck's *The Real Ambassadors* (1962). BRUBECK ARCHIVES

An exhausted Louis, flanked by Trummy Young (left) and Edmond Hall (right), blows in West Africa. COLLECTION OF JACK BRADLEY

Louis lavished obsessive care on his battered lips. Here he applies cream to them during a French tour in 1955. ARCHIVE PHOTOS

During a 1959 swing through Egypt, "Ambassador Satch" entertained Lucille before the Pyramids. ARCHIVE PHOTOS

A melancholy Louis at age seventy, practicing the trumpet at home, against the doctor's orders, shortly before his death in 1971. ARCHIVE PHOTOS

out. He had always been a sharp cat, but now he was raggedy ass. I told him, 'I want you to be my manager.' He said, 'Oh, I couldn't do that. I'm stony broke.' "

"That doesn't make any difference," Louis recalled saying. "You collect the money. You pay me one thousand dollars every week free and clear. You pay my band, the travel and the hotel expenses, my income tax, and you take everything that's left." In any event, the two men joined forces.

Joe Glaser awakened ancient memories in Louis, who saw in him a combination of the toughness of his one-time guardian, Black Benny, and the scruples and protectiveness of the Karnoffsky family, who had virtually adopted him when he was a child. Beyond that, Glaser was the father he had never had. "He's my daddy," Louis said near the end of his life. "He's been my daddy for forty years, and we ain't never gonna die, not one of us, so he's gonna be my daddy for forty more years." Such was Louis's view of Joe Glaser, but it was shared by no one else.

To many people, Joe Glaser was an awful man, which was his chief qualification for managing the most talented and influential—but also the most prodigal—of all jazz musicians. Said Max Gordon, the owner of the Village Vanguard, a New York jazz club: "Joe Glaser was the most obscene, the most outrageous, and the toughest agent I've ever bought an act from." Said George Avakian, the brilliant Columbia record producer who worked with Louis, "Joe was a professional tough guy. He put on a very tough front. He was a tough man and he believed in being pretty abrupt with people because that's the way he got things done. He was coarse. He talked very rapidly and he didn't want to listen very much to anyone else's ideas." Said George Wein, the producer of the Newport Jazz Festival, which became a showcase for Louis: "Joe Glaser had this wonderful ability to lie with total impunity. You know, there aren't many people who can do that. Joe Glaser didn't care what he said. If you called him and asked, 'Joe, why did you do this? Why can't I get this?' he'd say anything he wanted to say, he had total impunity, as long as somebody was asking a question he didn't want to hear or didn't care about." And these were people who *admired* Glaser.

There were many questions Joe Glaser didn't want to hear, questions about his "business associates," questions about his past. In the ten years since they had worked together, Joe Glaser had been eking out a marginal existence as a pimp and quasi-hoodlum, expending much of his time and energy trying to avoid prosecution and jail for arrests stemming from his unusual sexual tastes. Glaser's tale is often sordid, but is worth recounting because his association with Louis Armstrong made him one of the most important forces in American popular music and culture—certainly the most important impresario and manager in the jazz arena. Despite the influence he came to wield, no one knew much about him. Throughout his life, he muzzled the press, and the world saw little beyond his gruff façade. "You don't know me," a typical Glaserism ran, "but you know two things about me: I have a terrible temper and I always keep my word." (The first part of that claim was certainly true.) The laudatory obituaries that appeared at the time of his death in 1969 barely hinted at what lay behind the façade.

He came from Chicago, a son of Russian-Jewish immigrants. His father, George, was a doctor, and Joe was raised to be a doctor, too, but as a young man he drifted into *la vie bohème*, Chicago-style. His run-ins with the law began when he was managing the Sunset Cafe, where he first met Louis; in October 1926, the Chicago *Tribune* identified him as part of a "gigantic conspiracy" to bribe policemen in connection with his duties at the Sunset. Even more interesting were his associates—Jack Zuta, "Jew Kid" Grabiner, "Lovin' Putty" Anixter, and Jim Genna—all of them notorious bootleggers and racketeers in Prohibition-era Chicago. To judge from the company Glaser kept, it was apparent that he was fronting for the Capone syndicate. On Christmas Day, 1926, he was arrested at the Sunset and charged with violating Prohibition in a highly publicized raid staged by Chicago's Chief of Detectives, William "Shoes" Schoemaker.

Glaser the bootlegger and small-time fixer was one thing, but Glaser the pimp was quite another. On January 22, 1927, he was convicted of running a "disorderly house"—a brothel—for which he was fined a sum of one hundred dollars. Glaser appealed. He then made the classic pimp's mistake; he got involved with the girls he ran—very young girls. Six months to the day after his conviction for running a brothel, he was indicted for rape; the complainant, Dolores Wheeler, was just fourteen years old. Facing the prospect of a long jail sentence, Glaser turned to a powerful gangland connection, Billy Skidmore, for help in beating the rap. Skidmore was a venerable fixer in Chicago, who brokered deals between the police and the Capone syndicate. He had been a fixture since the turn of the century, and now he stepped forward to post bail for Glaser, amid rumors that he had arranged bribes to get the police to drop the charges. The bribes, if any, failed to work, and Joe had to live with this lurid accusation hanging over his head.

Glaser also developed a parallel career as a fight promoter in Chicago, with ties to the Capone syndicate, which controlled the major professional bouts in town. Newspaper reporters discovered that "promoter" meant "fixer." Glaser supplied Vern Whaley, who wrote for the Chicago *Evening Post* with the names of the next day's winner and, occasionally, the round in which they would achieve their knockout. "I always wrote a boldface precede on my stories, picking the probable winners," Whaley recalled. "I had a sensational record, thanks to dear old Joe Glaser." For a time, Glaser prospered under the Capone aegis, but then a character named Eddie Borden came to him, asking for backing to start a boxing magazine. Glaser, who worked out of a two-room office in the Loop, gave Borden the use of one room, and Borden proceeded to write a story describing how his backer, Joe Glaser, was fronting for the Capone syndicate. Glaser immediately ran Borden out of town, but the damage was done. Hot-tempered and profane, Glaser gradually came to realize that stories about his syndicate affiliations might help him more than hurt him. If people thought he was close to Capone, they would be impressed, intimidated. Never again would he have to resort to compromise or reason, he could bully and bluster his way through any of his dealings—except the rape charge.

Glaser's long-delayed rape charge finally came to trial on February 10, 1928. The case was tried in a single day, and the jury took only forty-five minutes to reach its decision. The Chicago *Defender* gave the story front-page play: "Found guilty of attacking Dolores Morgan Wheeler (white), a 14-year-old schoolgirl, Joseph G. Glaser (white), was sentenced to 10 years by Judge Harry B. Miller." Glaser knew there was but one way to avoid jail; he married his victim. A year later, the Illinois Supreme Court overturned his conviction. He later explained away Dolores Wheeler's extreme youthfulness to a friend. "She wore make-up and seemed to be in her twenties," he said. "In fact, it was her mother who pointed her out to me and encouraged my interest in her."

Six weeks after the rape conviction, he was arrested again, for a similar offense. This time, he picked up seventeen-year-old Virginia Sherman in the Plantation (across the street from the Sunset), brought her back to his apartment with another girl. When he attacked Virginia, her girlfriend ran screaming into the street and attracted the attention of police, who found Glaser with the girl and arrested him. Relying on his syndicate connections, Glaser contrived to beat this rap as well, though his troubles were by now so widely publicized that many musicians were under the impression Glaser had actually done hard time. As the years passed, his rap sheet lengthened. In January 1930, yet another woman brought a paternity suit against him. And in April 1935, he was indicted for receiving stolen liquor in connection with his interests in various mob-infested nightclubs.

Such were the "business interests" Joe Glaser sacrificed to manage Louis Armstrong.

Louis didn't care whether Glaser was a pimp, pedophile, rapist, bootlegger, or racketeer. He had grown up among people like Glaser, and had learned long ago that they often had their uses, and even their good sides. The appeal of "raggedy ass" Joe Glaser was that he was exactly what Slippers, the honky-tonk bouncer in New Orleans, had long ago advised Louis to seek in a manager: *"Be sure and get yourself a white man that will put his hand on your shoulder and say, 'This is my nigger.'"* For that reason, the ugly stories about Glaser didn't bother Louis in the slightest. "He was a crude sonofabitch, but he loved me and my music. . . . The white man was Joe Glaser."

Glaser's arrival on the scene was especially well timed because Louis was in difficult straits. He was nearly broke, having just sold his beloved Buick to raise four hundred much needed dollars. Besides his wardrobe and his trumpet, the car had been his only significant possession. His business affairs were an unbelievable mess. No fewer than three ex-managers were suing him for assorted contract violations, as was Lil for her six thousand dollars. His recording contracts were another quagmire; at various times he had run afoul of both Columbia and Victor. Louis needed help badly, and he knew it. He was in danger of drifting off into debt-laden obscurity, like so many other jazzmen in the Depression, but Glaser vowed he would not allow that to happen. To the extent that he could ever redeem his own sins, he would do so through the vehicle of Louis Armstrong.

Within weeks of becoming Louis's manager, Glaser dealt with his client's problems, one by one. First, he took over the management of Louis's band from Zilner Randolph. From then on, he hired, fired, paid the musicians, and made transportation arrangements and hotel reservations. Next, he arranged for Louis to give a carefully rehearsed interview to *Down Beat*, a Chicago-based jazz publication, and the resulting article read like a press release from the office of Joe Glaser. It was Glaser's way of serving notice that he, not Johnny Collins, was now the man to see concerning "The World's Greatest Trumpeter."

"MY CHOPS WAS BEAT," SAYS LOUIE, "BUT I'M DYIN' TO SWING AGAIN"
ARMSTRONG TO OPEN SERIES OF ONE-NIGHTERS

Louie Armstrong and his newly formed orchestra began a tour of one-nighters, opening at Indianapolis the first week in July. Joe Glaser, Louie's newly acquired personal manager, is handling the details of the bookings.

Louie Armstrong, king of the trumpet, whose freak lip and "hot" solos have amazed and delighted musicians for ten years will definitely resume his career the first week in July.

"My chops was beat, when I got back from Europe," said the leather-lipped and balloon-lunged Louie. "My manager worked me too hard, and I was so tired when I got back that I didn't even want to see the points of my horn. And 'pops,' [Collins] he wouldn't even let the 'cats' come 'back-stage' to visit me, and you know I am always glad to see everybody. . . .

Armstrong has been resting in the Chicago home of his mother-in-law waiting for his contract to expire.

His inactivity and seclusion has [sic] started a score of rumors that he had "lost his lip," that he had a split lip. . . . Musicians all over the world wondered what the real truth was in Louie's "solitude."

"My chops is fine, now," Armstrong said, "and I'm dying to swing out again."

Next, Glaser turned his attention to Lil. He intuitively recognized that no other individual had as strong a hold on his client as she did. He took a virulent dislike to her, and schemed to keep her away from Louis and to poison his mind against her. For example, when the sheet music for "Struttin' with Some Barbecue" was published, with Louis credited as composer, Lil claimed the song was actually a collaboration between the two of them in their days with Joe Oliver. She asked five thousand dollars in exchange for her rights, but Glaser told Louis that she demanded one hundred thousand dollars. (It would be decades until Louis discovered that Glaser had lied to him about the amount.) Glaser also tried to get Lil to stop advertising herself as "Lil Armstrong" in her concert appearances. And as for her "maintence" suit, she could paper her bedroom ceiling with it, for all Joe Glaser cared. Louis was not to pay her a penny of alimony.

Joe proceeded to make short work of claims lodged by Louis's former managers. He paid Johnny Collins five thousand dollars for Louis's contract, and as for the cagier Tommy Rockwell, that was the beauty part, for Glaser and Rockwell already had a relationship. In fact, Glaser rented space in the Tommy Rockwell-Cork O'Keefe booking agency in New York, and he made sure to keep Rockwell happy and far from Louis. As for the irate managers Louis had left behind in Europe, Glaser decided Louis wouldn't be returning to Europe for a good long time, despite the acclaim and prestige that had accrued to him overseas.

On July 1, as soon as he had put these arrangements into place, Glaser went on the road with Louis, smoothing the way himself and learning the music management business day by day, dollar by dollar, mile by mile, note by note. His presence was absolutely necessary since the tour covered the South. "We had two white guys with us—the bus driver and Joe Glaser," said Pops Foster, the bass player on that tour. "If you had a colored bus driver back then, they'd lock him up in every little country town for 'speeding.' It was very rough finding a place to sleep in the South. . . . You rented places in private homes, boardinghouses, and whorehouses. The food was awful and we tried to find places where we could cook. We carried a bunch of pots and pans with us." On July 21, the tour bus reached New Orleans, where Louis belatedly fulfilled his promise to perform free for the region's impoverished blacks. For six days, he played at the Golden Dragon, a theater patronized by blacks. For the first three nights, there was a one-dollar charge to hear him from ten p.m. until three a.m; the balance of the week was free to all. In September, the tour worked its way north, to New York, where Louis was supposed to keep another broken date, this time at the Apollo Theater in Harlem.

When they arrived in New York, Glaser discovered that the musicians had run into union troubles, and they were not allowed to perform in the city. Furiously impatient, he returned to Chicago, fired them all, and hired another band acceptable to the New York union. The new outfit was Luis Russell's Orchestra. Russell's background was very quirky. When he was seventeen, he won a lottery in Panama, took his winnings, and came to New Orleans. He played piano with King Oliver for a while, and by 1927, at the age of only twenty-six, he was leading his own band in New York, comprised mostly of New Orleans musicians, many of them recruited from Oliver's band. A chameleon when it came to musical styles, Russell soon discarded New Orleans polyphony in favor of the smoother, plusher, broader big-band sound. He dabbled in composing and arranging, which led to his hit, "The Call of the Freaks." The tune was everywhere in 1929. For a brief time in the early 1930s, he performed with Louis Armstrong; but the two had gone their separate ways until Glaser reunited them. It seemed like a good fit—both musicians had roots in New Orleans and extensive experience with more harmonically sophisticated big-band styles. Louis liked the idea, too: "I enjoyed all the moments I spent with Luis and his band, maybe because the boys were mostly from my home. The warmth, the feelings, the beat—everything was there. They were all down to earth also in that band. I loved them regardless of what the critics said about it."

The critics did indeed have a different point of view. Most said this was the worst band Louis Armstrong ever fronted and that his years with Luis Russell, which covered most of the thirties, represented the nadir of his career. They also complained that he ran out of fresh musical ideas and was content to recycle his virtuoso trumpet solos from the late 1920s, and that the musical value of what he was doing now was just about nil. Louis paid no heed to the cavils. He was happy with Russell's outfit mainly because they followed his lead and let him do exactly what he wanted, no matter how extravagant. In return, he indulged the band's shortcomings. He knew that some of them were inferior, "but so long as they could hold their instruments correct[ly] and display their willingness to play as best they could, I would look over their shoulders and see Joe Oliver and several other great masters from my home town."

While pairing Louis with a new orchestra, Glaser negotiated his client out of his "exclusive" recording deals and turned to a feisty new firm, Decca. The year before, Jack Kapp, a veteran record producer, had founded Decca. It was the first of a new breed of record company. Columbia and Victor belonged to the vanished record boom of the 1920s; Decca was a child of the Depression. Kapp's idea was to make records very cheaply and sell them very cheaply, for only thirty-five cents. He lured some big names to the label, notably Bing Crosby and the Mills Brothers, and he let them do their thing, as long as it was commercial. By October 3, Louis was in New York, recording with his new band for his new label. That first date included "I'm in the Mood for Love," "You Are My Lucky Star," "La Cucaracha," "Got a Bran' New Suit," and, significantly, Louis sang on all four sides.

He would remain with Decca for the next seven years, and although the tunes he recorded during that period were often standards, his performances displayed utter conviction tempered with a new maturity. He backed away from his derring-do on the trumpet, but his singing was better than ever—mellow, articulate, filled with humor and sentiment. It contained echoes and hints of his former idiosyncracies, the demented laughs and Viper babblings; now he used them all in the service of the melody. As ever, he influenced and inspired younger musicians, yet no one sounded like him; the moment Louis started singing, his voice was unmistakable.

His life began moving incredibly fast. On October 29, Louis and his new orchestra began a four-month stand at his old Harlem stomping ground, Connie's Inn. Much had happened since Louis last blew there: Connie Immerman was dead, and the gangsters who had alternately tried to force him to perform there or to stay away were in retreat now that Glaser was calling the shots. No longer did armed thugs show up in Louis's dressing room to shake him down, threaten his life, or run him out of town; he had a thug of his own, managing him.

His return to the fabled Harlem nightspot after an absence of six years was an occasion for excitement and curiosity. Musicians flocked to see how well he could blow after all his troubles and his long absence, and for many, seeing him again after all these years was a source of amazement. Rex Stewart, the cornetist, caught his act and recalled the power of the moment Louis appeared on stage, "immaculate in a white suit. Somehow, the way the lights reflected off his trumpet made the instrument look like anything but a horn. It looked as if he were holding a wand of rainbows or a cluster of sunlight, something from out of this world. I found out later that I was not the only one who had the strong impression of something verging on the mystical in Louis's entrance. . . . He blew a searing, soaring, altissimo fantastic high note and held it long enough for every one of us musicians to gasp." At the end of the show, "swarms of women kept rushing the stand for his autograph. They handed him everything from programs to whiskey bottles to put his signature on. One woman even took off her pants and pleaded with him to sign them."

He obliged them all, of course. Louis finished his triumphant engagement at Connie's Inn with his reputation greatly enhanced and moved on to the Metropolitan Theater in Boston, where he and the orchestra pulled in an astonishing eight thousand dollars a week. Until the Glaser era, Louis and his various bands had always ranked near the bottom of the major touring groups in terms of earnings; now, thanks to Glaser's muscle, they hovered near the top. For the first time in his life, Louis was making more money than he spent. Glaser kept him on a generous allowance, and whatever he didn't run through, Glaser kept in trust. When word of Louis's robust salary circulated among other black musicians, they flocked to Joe Glaser, seeking his strenuous representation, so both men were making money.

Louis spent the balance of 1936 on the road. Glaser sent him everywhere—New York, Chicago, Detroit, Kansas City, Savannah, St. Louis—zigzagging across the country, revisiting each of these cities several times. Whenever his musicians ventured south, Glaser made a point of joining the band, but he couldn't change the region's rigid racial codes. "Lots of times we wouldn't get a place to sleep," Louis recalled. "So we'd cross the tracks, pull over to the side of the road and spend the night there. We couldn't get into hotels. Our money wasn't even good. We'd play nightclubs and spots which didn't have a bathroom for Negroes. When we'd get hungry, my manager, Joe Glaser, who's also my friend, Jewish and white, would buy food along the way in paper bags and bring it to us boys in the bus who couldn't be served." Louis's only break from work that year occurred in May, when he underwent a tonsillectomy. As soon as he recovered, he was back on the road with Luis Russell and the orchestra.

Glaser wanted to build his client into a motion picture star as well as musician, but he found it nearly impossible to penetrate Hollywood's racism, which was as unyielding as anything Louis had encountered in New

Orleans. Glaser did manage to land him a part in an offbeat movie, *Pennies from Heaven*, a musical starring Louis's admirer, Bing Crosby, but Louis's role, as written, makes one cringe.

In the picture, Crosby plays a wandering troubadour who resolves the difficulties of the less fortunate and, later on, inherits a haunted mansion that he converts into a nightclub. At this point, Louis appears, casually dressed, and the two of them launch into some banter dwelling on black inferiority and subservience when Bing invites Louis to perform at the new club for a salary of ten percent of the business.

"Is that enough?" Bing asks.

"Well, yes. And no," Louis replies. "There's seven men in the band. And none of us knows how to divide ten percent up by seven. So if you could only make it seven percent . . ." Bing laughs his hail-fellow-well-met laugh, and agrees. Louis exclaims, "I told them cats you'd do the right thing."

Later on, Louis redeems himself through music when he appears on stage in a gloomy cafe, singing "Skeleton in the Closet," shivering and shaking as a moving skeleton approaches him, and Lionel Hampton beats the drums.

When the movie opened in December 1936, *Variety* singled out Louis for praise: "Best individual impression is by Louis Armstrong, Negro cornetist and hi-de-ho expert. Not as an eccentric musician but as a Negro comedian he suggests possibilities. He toots his solo horn to a nice individual score." It was clear that Louis had "possibilities" for the screen, but making music for the movies posed a problem for a performer as spontaneous as he. Louis couldn't just sing his song while the cameras rolled, he had to run through it *twice:* once on the set before the cameras, and again in a studio, lip-synching before a microphone. Movies exaggerated even the slightest shift of an eyebrow, and on the screen, Louis's exaggerated body language seemed distorted. The process of lip-synching, which covered a multitude of sins for a conventional performer, actually put him at a disadvantage.

The following year, Glaser found Louis a part in a Paramount comedy, *Artists and Models*, starring Jack Benny and Ida Lupino. The trumpeter was to perform in a dreamlike musical sequence set in Harlem, but without realizing what he had done, Glaser had entangled Louis in a nasty racial imbroglio. In the controversial sequence, billed as the "largest negro number ever filmed in Hollywood," Martha Raye, a white actress known for her ingratiating, anything-for-a-laugh antics, appears in a tight satin dress, her skin darkened to a bronze tint. Louis then appears on screen, resplendent in a suit, and begins to blow, while Raye bumps and grinds out her interpretation of black sensuality. All the while, she sings about dangerous music that will *"sneak right up on you . . . And kind of put the finger on you . . . so look out for Public Melody Number One."* Later in the song, Louis puts down his trumpet and growls, *"Ain't no use hidin' . . . I'm going to take you ridin' . . . Look out for Public Melody Number One."* The witty number, written by Harold Arlen and Ted Koehler, was intended to portray the outlaw, irresistible music known as jazz as "Public Melody Number One." On the screen, though, it looked as if Louis meant to seduce Martha Raye with that music. He was certainly making her hot, judging from the way she swayed those luxurious hips as he blew his horn. The inflammatory element in this scenario was that Louis Armstrong was black, and Martha Raye was white.

Reviewers gagged at this breach of the movies' strict racial code. "While Miss Raye is under cork, the intermingling of the races isn't wise," *Variety* judged, "especially as she lets herself go into the extremest manifestation of Harlemania torso-twisting and gyrations. It may hurt her personally." The controversy boiled throughout the summer of 1937. Joseph Breen, the man responsible for enforcing the strict production code on behalf of the studios, received letters warning of the perils of this scene. In Atlanta, after the mayor, school superintendent, and other elected officials previewed the movie, they conveyed their collective horror to Breen's office. "For a white woman to act with negroes is a most certain offense to the South," they warned. "For *ANYONE* to act in as obscene a manner as Miss Ray does, in this scene, would offend taste anywhere, but in the good South, and with negroes, it will certainly be her finish. . . . No one has a keener contempt for a white woman who descends to their level than the negro himself." And Dolph Frantz, the managing editor of the *Shreveport Journal*, elaborated on this point for the benefit of Adolph Zukor, Paramount's chairman: "For negroes and whites to be shown in social equality is offensive in this part of the country, where the races have nothing socially in common." Frantz went on to explain to Mr. Zukor that "there is a color line, and it will always be drawn, and when negroes and white persons act together there will always be a bad reaction."

The implications of the critical backlash were that Louis couldn't appear in a scene with a woman or interact socially with whites on screen. The only way around these obstacles was for him to portray a musician, performing in a specialty number that had nothing to do with the rest of the film. The bitter lessons of *Artists and Models* were never lost on him or Glaser, and Louis would conform to these strictures throughout his movie career, right up through the 1960s. Yet within these absurd and cruel restrictions, he occasionally devised moments that transcended the shabby circumstances surrounding him.

In 1938, he found himself in another stereotypical role, as a stable hand—whom everyone fondly calls "Uncle Tom"—in the Warner Brothers comedy, *Going Places*. This was a Dick Powell vehicle, with Anita Louise playing the female lead, and a very young Ronald Reagan portraying her son. Louis's contract, dated August 10, 1938, called for him to receive twenty-five hundred dollars a week for the first two weeks, and, if necessary, an additional two thousand dollars for a third week. The studio looked to him to participate in a "darkie jam session" with other black performers, and they got what they wanted. From the moment moviegoers saw the display ad, showing Louis cutting up with the Dandridge Sisters, a popular black vocal group, they knew there would be no mingling between the races in the picture. Whites would have their place, and blacks would have theirs—in the nursery, the scene of the movie's big musical number, "Mutiny in the Nursery," in which Louis, the singer Maxine Sullivan, and the Dandridges perform.

The film's great gimmick was that a racehorse named Jeepers Creepers runs wild *except* when Louis, the affable groom, sings to the animal. In one striking sequence, he croons a tune—"Jeepers Creepers," composed by Harry Warren—named after the horse. The extraordinary thing about the scene was the heartfelt way Louis sings to that horse, and the way the horse, apparently bewitched, responds to his voice. His singing is so endearing he seems to charm the animal. On the strength of his performance, the song earned an Academy Award nomination, and given the harsh social climate in which *Going Places* was made, the recognition seems like a minor miracle.

As a result of these three roles, Louis's movie career, though severely restricted by racism, was big enough to propel him into the front ranks of the handful of black performers in Hollywood, exactly as Glaser had planned. Even so, moviegoers who thought they were seeing the "real" Louis Armstrong on screen were mistaken; they witnessed only a distorted impression of the performer as he tried to fit into stereotypical "darkie" roles. Movies robbed Louis of the one element he always retained on stage and in his recordings—his dignity. Of all the facets of his career, his movie roles cast him in the least admirable light. Hollywood capitalized on his— or Joe Glaser's—worst instinct: the desire to please at all costs.

During this period of movie-making, recordings, and live performing, Glaser made sure that his client branched into a new field: network radio. On April 9, 1937, Louis substituted for Rudy Vallee as the host of a popular radio series sponsored by Fleischmann's Yeast, broadcast over the CBS Network. In so doing, he became the first black to host a sponsored, national broadcast. Only six years before, a white announcer in New Orleans had refused to introduce him over the air, and now, for a time, he had his own radio program. This was a milestone, to be sure, but what is often overlooked is that his exuberant radio broadcasts bombed. Louis and his orchestra, said *Variety*, "sounded like a boiler factory in swingtime, and, as such, could only be recommended to the most incurable addicts of Harlem stomp music in its most blatant pitch. . . . Family tuner-inners, except swing-bitten youngsters, will be startled by the noise, even though the bandsmen are acknowledged experts in their particular field. Armstrong's throaty, almost unintelligible announcements do not help, either, and he should refrain from singing." Despite such heavy criticism, Louis continued to cross the color lines and racial barriers typical of American society in the Depression Era. But as his movie and network radio appearances demonstrated, he often had to stoop to conquer.

In addition to obtaining lucrative bookings, Glaser also took care to *publicize* Louis Armstrong, something that Collins had never thought to do. Articles about Louis appeared in the mainstream white press at the same time he resurfaced as a performer. The October 1935 issue of *Esquire* ran a provocative account of Louis's life story in pseudo-black dialect. The following month, the style-setting magazine *Vanity Fair* ran a full-page portrait of Louis by Anton Bruehl, who photographed Louis in a dramatic, glamorous pose befitting a movie star. Several months later, *Vanity Fair* ran a flattering article pairing Louis with Fritz Kreisler, the violinist, in an imaginary dialogue. And there was more image-building to come.

In 1936, Glaser struck a deal for Louis to write his first book, a brief autobiographical reminiscence. Ever since he had left New Orleans, he had been typing letters and stories to friends, and his powers of written expression, to say nothing of his facility with a typewriter, had grown steadily. Working with an amanuensis, Horace Gerlach, he poured forth tales of his formative years—New Orleans and Joe Oliver and Fate Marable, and even his first wife, the passionate, violent Daisy Parker—but he naturally eased over the many rough parts of his early years. Gerlach was a twenty-five-year-old pianist who unfortunately attempted to tidy up Louis's ramblings for publication. He made Louis's erratic prose conform to standard written expression, and in the process robbed it of charm and bite. It is also likely that he added stories to flesh out Louis's tale, further compromising the account's authenticity. The second, much briefer, part of the book was devoted to a musical analysis of Louis's playing style, complete with simple transcriptions of solos for various instruments contributed by star white musicians such as Benny Goodman, Tommy Dorsey, and Bud Freeman. The musical analysis was nonsense—a profoundly intuitive musician, Louis never discussed his songs in terms of "rhythmic counterpoint" and "melodic obbligatto" as the book did—but the learned discussion undoubtedly added to his stature, as did Rudy Vallee's obsequious forward. Published on November 7, 1936, under the title *Swing That Music*, dedicated to King Oliver and Bix Beiderbecke, among others, the book was calculated to increase Louis's standing with white audiences, and it accomplished its goal. But it was also a whitewash. As if to make amends, Louis would return again and again to his life story, recounting it in increasingly revealing terms until he succeeded in laying bare the truth.

Although Louis was active on so many fronts during the middle and late 1930s, he still devoted 90 percent of his time and energy on his staple: endless touring with his orchestra. Crisscrossing the country in a weary bus, he wowed them at the Roxy, the Cotton Club, the Apollo, whatever city he happened to be in that night. That was where the reliable money was, and that was what Mr. Glaser told him to do. He never tarried in Hollywood for more than a month, movies were just another gig, and then it was back on the road with Alpha and the fellows, reinforcing his reputation as "The World's Greatest Trumpeter." His was a life of one-night stands.

To ensure the smooth operation of Louis's tours, Glaser sent orders: *no marijuana.* He was appalled by the way Louis and the band carried on and smoked in public. Didn't they realize how vulnerable they were to arrest? Louis refused to listen to reason, so Glaser shouted, and Louis refused to listen to shouting. One witness to the standoffs recalled, "Glaser would scream and Louis would say, 'Fuck you.' " Of all the issues they confronted, this was the one on which they would never agree. In the end, Louis refrained from getting high on the bandstand, but *no one* was going to stop him from smoking his good shuzzit in private, in his dressing room—not even Mr. Glaser.

Glaser had seized the reins of Louis's out-of-control career and spurred it on at a breakneck pace. Most managers considered their jazz and dance band musicians to be talented amateurs who basically wanted to go out and play in front of an audience, have a good time, and get drunk, but Glaser took Louis seriously—not as an artist, for Joe didn't care about "art"—but as an *act,* and one that required constant care. Always looking for the sure thing, the next booking, Glaser encouraged Louis to smile, damn it, smile. Yet for all the frantic activity Glaser scheduled for his client, a certain predictability crept into Louis's act. Few jazz enthusiasts would point to his work with the Luis Russell Orchestra or his Decca recordings as highlights of his career, and his early movies now seem at best a curiosity, at worst an embarrassment. Rather than breaking new ground, Louis started to codify and reinforce his earlier accomplishments, and he continued this process for the rest of his days. One can rejoice in the hard-earned, long-overdue financial rewards he was reaping, but something was lost in the process, a quality of innocence and exploration. One of the delights of Louis's early career was its unpredictability, as he caromed from New Orleans to a Mississippi riverboat to Chicago and Harlem, absorbing influences along the way from mentors and friends and Lil, his second wife. Amid that semichaos, he had produced dozens of works of genius that revolutionized American popular music and culture. Abroad, he had given America a sound, a voice, and a face—*his* face—and called the tune to the Jazz Age. It was becoming clear only now how far-reaching his legacy was, how lasting his innovations. Louis continued to evolve as an artist and entertainer under Glaser's regimen, but at a much slower pace. There would be no more chaos, nothing would be left to chance, and everything would be safe, predictable, and profitable.

. . .

ouis had occasion to judge the combined effect of his talent and Glaser's commercial drive during a swing through the South in September 1937, when a chance encounter demonstrated to him just how far he had come. In Savannah, Louis happened to go shopping for food, and approached an elderly, stooped pushcart peddler. He tapped the man on the shoulder and said, "I want a sack of potatoes." The old man with the pushcart turned around, and Louis looked straight into the face of the King—Joe Oliver.

He knew Joe had lost his Victor recording contract and had fallen on hard times, scrapping around for gigs in southern towns beaten down by the Depression. He also knew that Joe's chops weren't what they had been in his heyday, that teeth and gum trouble had impaired his blowing, but he hadn't realized it had all reduced his mentor to pushing a cart through the streets of Savannah. The fall of Joe Oliver from his high estate was as emblematic of the fate of New Orleans jazz musicians as Louis's ascent to fame. In Louis's opinion, Joe took a wrong turn when he refused a long engagement at the Cotton Club, allowing Duke Ellington to slip in and make the club his own.

Joe's reluctance to make a name for himself in New York always baffled Louis, who, as he looked back over his career, realized that it was *essential* to have the New York exposure, the New York connections and cachet. "They tried to get Joe to come to New York when he got hot, but he wouldn't come," Louis said. "And all the time the cats were coming out from New York with those big shows and picking up on what he was playing. Joe Oliver was *the* man in Chicago. But he came to New York too late. When he got there everybody was playing him. Even I had been there long before him. And it was all his own fault, too, because he had Chicago sewed up." Instead, Oliver returned to the unforgiving South, to Savannah, Georgia, where he worked with pickup bands, looking backward, trying to revive the old times and the old music, while Louis was always pushing forward.

Joe's decision to remain in the South led to one miserable experience after another. His old touring bus broke down, and he missed many gigs. When he managed to get the bus running again, it was badly damaged in an accident, and by the time he could pay for repairs, his gums were so bad he couldn't play his horn. Finally, he suffered the nightmare of every hornman—he lost he teeth. At the end of 1935, he wrote his niece, "Thank God I only need one thing and that is clothes, I am not making enough money to buy clothes as I can't play any more. I get [a] little money from an agent for the use of my name and after I pay room rent and eat I don't have much left." In 1936, he rallied a bit and resumed his tour, but this time, his bus broke down for good, stranding him in Mississippi. It took him most of the year to work his way back to Savannah, trying to revive his name and career, dealing with small-time bookers, and making ends meet with the pushcart.

Louis gave Joe all the money in his pockets, a hundred and fifty dollars or so, and told his mentor to go buy himself a new suit of clothes. He took up a collection among the other members of the band—Pops Foster, Red Allen, Paul Barbarin—for old Joe's sake. "That night we played at a dance, and look over and there's Joe standing in the wings," Louis remembered. "He was sharp like the old Joe Oliver of 1915. He'd been to the pawn shop and gotten his . . . suits and all—Stetson hat turned down, high-button shoes, his box-back coat. He looked beautiful and he had a wonderful night, just listening to us—talking."

The next day, Louis and the band resumed their tour, leaving Oliver behind to fend for himself. Their largesse helped ease Joe's burden only temporarily, and he once again struggled in isolation. In years to come, Louis's cavalier treatment of his mentor attracted considerable criticism, not all of it justified. Until their meeting in Savannah, Louis, like most everyone else in the jazz world, had no idea what had become of Joe Oliver. And until very recently, had his own financial difficulties. Time and circumstance, not Louis Armstrong, had conspired to topple the King from his throne.

Occasionally Oliver did get gigs, but only in small towns; he was afraid to play the big cities, where he was known, afraid to compete with his own reputation. He didn't want people who remembered him as the King to see him in his present condition, playing with amateurs and barely able to blow. He had to curtail even these humble engagements when his health deteriorated. He returned to Savannah, watching his existence ebb, and trying not to become bitter. He developed a persistent cough and began to contemplate the cold fact of his mortality. "I am not the one to give up quick," he wrote his sister from his boardinghouse at 508 Montgomery Street. "I always feel like I've got a chance. I still feel I'm going to snap out of the rut I've been in for several years." He found a dentist, and got himself fitted for false teeth, but he ran short of money again. "I've started a little dime bank saving," he told his sister. "Got $1.60 in it and won't touch it. I am going to try to save myself a ticket to New York." When the pushcart got to be too strenuous, he found work as an attendant at a pool hall at 526 West Broad Street, opening the place at nine in the morning, closing it at midnight. The manager, Connie Wimberly, recalled telling him, "Go ahead and do what you can, sweep up now and then, and I'll give you something when I can." She had no idea he had ever been the King of anything

A once-great jazz man who had dazzled New Orleans and Chicago; one of the founders of jazz; a bandleader and cornetist who made 168 recordings, with forty-nine songs to his credit, Joe Oliver was now living in obscurity. "Pops, breaks come to cats in this racket once in a while and I guess I must have been asleep when mine came," he lamented. "I've made lots of dough in this game but I didn't know how to take care of it . . . I have helped to make some of the best names in the music game, but I am too much of a man to ask those that I have helped to help me."

Oliver developed high blood pressure. He obtained medical treatment for a while. Then, he wrote, "I am unable to take treatments because it cost $3.00 per treatment and I don't make enough money to continue my treatments." He was afraid his heart was giving out on him. "Should anything happen to me will you want my body?" he asked his sister. "Let me know because I won't last forever and the longer I go the worse I'll get." Finally, in February 1938, he was forced to admit the end was approaching. "I may never see New York again in my life," he told his sister. "Don't think I am afraid. . . . I am trying to live near[er] to the Lord than ever before. So I feel like the Good Lord will take care of me." Two months later, on Sunday, April 10, Joe Oliver died in his room.

Louis always believed his teacher, mentor, and father figure died of a "broken heart." The medical cause, according to his death certificate, was a cerebral hemorrhage, aggravated by arteriosclerosis. He was fifty-two years old. His sister paid for his remains to be shipped up north, to New York, "in a very cheap box," according to the undertaker, for his funeral.

Joe Oliver died believing he was forgotten by a world that had gradually beaten him down. He was wrong. A week later, the Savannah *Tribune* ran his obituary:

'Daddy' Jazz Music Passes
King Oliver, Noted Band Leader
FOUND DEAD IN BED
Was The Discoverer of Louis Armstrong

The paper further noted that "he remained here living on the scant royalties he received from the sales of the phonographic records his top-notch bands had made." In New York, the *Amsterdam News* also took note of his passing, describing the funeral he received in New York, where a leading minister, Adam Clayton Powell Jr. officiated, and Louis himself played the trumpet in a program underwritten by the Negro Actors' Guild.

Many big names turned out to pay their last respects to Joe Oliver. W. C. Handy and Clarence Williams were there, as were all of Joe's relatives, but Louis found the ceremony crass and impersonal, not at all like the splendid New Orleans funeral to which King Oliver, of all people, was entitled. Louis was certain Joe would have preferred a real New Orleans-style sendoff, complete with music and feasting and dancing in the streets. "It would have been nice if they'd had a parade for him," Louis said, "but instead they took him into the chapel across from the Lafayette—that big rehearsal hall in Harlem. I didn't like the sermon the preacher [Adam Clayton Powell Jr.] gave." Apparently, Reverend Powell took the occasion to moralize about all the money Oliver had squandered in his lifetime, which infuriated Louis. "Just because the Guild buried him was no reason for rubbing it in," he complained. "The Guild isn't supposed to say that; that's what we donate our services for when they give benefits."

Never fond of the clergy, Louis considered ministers to be con artists and bullies who used the prestige of the pulpit to fleece their followers. Several months after Joe Oliver's funeral, he went into the studio and, in a startling departure, recorded a growling monologue delivered by "Elder Eatmore," a pompous hypocrite who accuses his congregation of floating a rumor that he had stolen his Thanksgiving turkey. In this nonmusical skit, Louis sounded serious, menacing, even angry, not at all comic. "Any of you that throws rocks at me, I'm gonna throw them back at you," the Elder warns, "and when I start throwing, friends, I shall miss nobody."

Not long after Joe Oliver's death, Louis reached another turning point in his life. On September 30, 1938, he divorced Lil, after more than fourteen years of marriage, two of which had been more or less conventional, and twelve of which were tormented. They hadn't lived together since he was a young man, but Lil had never been willing to let go of him, even during the last five years when newspapers regularly referred to Alpha as "Mrs. Armstrong." In the divorce decree, Lil charged Louis with deserting her in 1931; at the same time, she waived her claim to alimony.

Days later, on October 11, while on tour in Houston, Louis married Alpha Smith, with one of the members of the band, Pops Foster, acting as best man. The long-postponed marriage brought him neither stability nor happiness. Indeed, the wedding actually marked the beginning of the end of their relationship. There is evidence that he was chasing another woman at the time; her name was Polly Jones, and the following year, she filed a thirty-five thousand dollar breach-of-promise suit, alleging that Louis had promised to marry *her* as soon as he got his divorce from Lil. She was too late—Alpha had finally claimed her prize, and Louis, normally so generous toward nearly everyone in his life, had few kind words for his third wife. "Alpha was all right," he managed to say, "but her mind was on furs, diamonds and other flashy luxuries and not enough on me and my happiness. I gave her all the diamonds she *thought* she wanted, but still she wanted other things. She went through all my money and then walked out." Behind the harmonious image they projected, "We had some real spats. She'd get to drinking and grab that big pocketbook of hers and hit me in my chops with it. Then I'd want to go over after her and beat her a while, but some of the cats would grab me and say, 'Don't hit her, Pops.' "

Soon after marrying Alpha, Louis Armstrong began an engagement at the Cotton Club in New York—an engagement that would further complicate his love life. This was not the old Cotton Club in Harlem, but a new, downtown version that occupied the top floor of a large building at Broadway and 48th Street, near Times Square. The new Cotton Club abolished the gaudy floor shows of its predecessor. There were still plenty of chorus girls, though they wore fewer feathers and more clothes, and one of the girls—dark-skinned, with a round face, full-figure, and large eyes—caught Louis's fancy one night. She was "swinging in the front line every night, looking beautifuller 'n' beautifuller every night direct[ly] in front of me," Louis wrote. "Standing there directing the band and blowing my solos on my trumpet whenever it was time for me to blow 'n' wail, . . . me diggin' those cute little buns of hers. Hmmm." Her stage name was "Brown Sugar," but in real life, she was Lucille Wilson.

From the start, Louis was powerfully attracted to Lucille. "Maybe her color had something to do with my falling in love with Lucille," he theorized. "Ever since I was old enough to feel a desire for women I've been drawn to those of darker hue. Lucille was the first girl to crack the high yellow color standard used to pick girls for the famous Cotton Club chorus," he boasted. "I paid strict attention to her when she was working in the chorus at the Cotton Club." She impressed him not as a gold digger, like Alpha, but as innocent, sensible, and responsible. Lucille was twenty-four, the daughter of a small businessman (her father owned a fleet of cabs), and the product of a fairly strict Catholic upbringing in Corona, Queens. Her childhood was nothing like Louis's exotic youth; she spent her early years in a closely knit, middle-class family. Also unlike Louis, who lived as he pleased, she was thoroughly bourgeois. She was working at the Cotton Club not out of a desire to be in show business but because her father had suffered financial reversals in the Depression. "With her salary she had to help take care of her family, which consisted of her mother, her two brothers, Jackie and Sonny, and a sister, Janet," Louis learned. She augmented her modest salary by selling cookies to the members of the cast, Louis included. "She would be a very busy young girl trying to get dressed and put on her first show, and get rid of the cookies, which she would bring down from Harlem."

Louis offered to buy her entire supply. Lucille accepted, "which took a big load off her mind," and he distributed them to schoolchildren in Harlem. But more than cookies were at stake here. Louis was in love. "It seemed to me that Lucille was the ideal girl for me." During one of her regular visits to Louis's dressing room, "I just couldn't hold back the deep feeling and the warmth that I had accumulated for her ever since I first laid eyes on her in the front line on the Cotton Club floor." And so he said,

"Lucille, I might as well tell you right now, I have eyes for you, and have been having them for a long time. And if any of these cats in the show [are] shooting at you, I just want to be in the running."

She looked at Louis and laughed, and they started dating, ducking into movies between their shows at the Cotton Club. In the magical early hours of the morning, he took her on long drives through Harlem in "that big long rust-colored Packard car that Mr. Glaser bought for me, and boy it was sharp. It was the hottest car in town, and the talk of the town. Bob Smiley, my right hand man, a tall, good looking, six-foot brownskin cat, used to drive that fine long Packard while Lucille + I would sit in the backseat and she looking just like a li'l ol' doll and me sharp as a wedding (you know what) and happier than two peas in a pot (pod to you)."

While Louis and Lucille toured Harlem in the shiny Packard, the tangible proof of his newfound material success, Alpha tried to put the best face on the situation, devising a game in which she fined her errant husband five dollars whenever he came home late. Louis gladly paid the amount and continued to court his Brown Sugar.

The courtship proceeded by fits and starts because Louis was in demand and constantly on the road throughout 1939. Joe Glaser had hit upon the nifty idea of pairing Louis with the idol of his youth, Bill Robinson. Robinson was past his prime now, well over sixty, but he was as elegant, gracious, amusing, and well dressed as ever, and could still tap circles around people half his age. A program featuring both Louis *and* Bill Robinson, whose show business skills complemented each other so neatly, appeared to be a surefire proposition—and it was.

Robinson first joined the Armstrong forces during Louis's Cotton Club engagement, and the acclaim the two old pros received there led to almost a year of bookings. They started off the New Year at New York's Strand Theater in a presentation bursting with show business razzle dazzle. Louis performed with Russell's fourteen-man orchestra before a backdrop depicting a huge trumpet topped by a crown, constantly proclaiming him as the "king of the trumpet." His blowing alternated with skits and songs by several other entertainers, all of them black, including the Dandridge Sisters. The highlight of the show, second only to Louis's trumpet, was Robinson's stylish tapping. Louis wrapped up every show by playing the hit songs he had popularized in his movies, "Jeepers Creepers" and "Skeleton in the Closet." There was no room for experimentation or improvisation. It was safe, it was sure, it was the big time. In February, they went on the road, playing Baltimore, Kansas City, Hartford, Buffalo, Chicago, Indianapolis, Atlanta, Madison, St. Paul, Miami, Dayton, Cleveland, and smaller towns in between. At the end of their run, the troupe returned to New York, and, on October 7, 1939, Louis again took center stage at the Cotton Club. "It would be kinda nice to stick around the Apple (meaning New York) this winter," he mused in a letter to a friend, "but in case we don't, it won't make any difference because we're so used to the Road. We've been traveling so long. We're an orchestra that's on the go all the time. We ain't fixing to sit around New York, waiting for something to turn up. I should say not. When I was a kid, my Grandmother used to say to me that the only person that makes money sitting on his ass is a shoemaker." Louis got his wish, this time, and he spent the next seven months in the Apple, blowing nightly at the Cotton Club.

During his months in New York, Louis became involved in a Broadway play that seemed destined to restore the prestige and critical acclaim missing during his recent tours. He had been there before, trying to make a name for himself on Broadway while performing in a nightclub, and had never quite established himself as a star on the Great White Way. The idea still held appeal for him, and this time, seemed to have found a worthy vehicle: Shakespeare. In fact, it was a musical adaptation of *A Midsummer Night's Dream* entitled *Swingin' the Dream*, set in Louisiana in 1890, and performed by a mostly black cast in the most prestigious venue on Broadway, the huge new Rockefeller Center Theater. Everyone involved in this ambitious undertaking was prominent: Gilbert Seldes and Eric Charell adapted Shakespeare's comedy; Jimmy Van Heusen wrote the score; Walt Disney designed the settings; Benny Goodman and his sextet performed. Butterfly McQueen was cast as Puck; and "Moms" Mabley would play Quince. Louis Armstrong would play Bottom the Weaver, attired in a bright red fireman's uniform.

The enterprise, so filled with promise, opened on November 29, but from tepid applause that greeted the final curtain, it was apparent that something had gone terribly wrong. "At one moment you hear genuine pentameters in the style and sometimes the original wording of the bard," said a reviewer, "at another you hear anti-climactic lines like 'go fly a kite' which are appropriate neither to Shakespeare nor to the New Orleans 1890 setting into which the story has been dumped." In *Down Beat*, Leonard Feather, an English critic fast becoming an influential jazz writer in the United States, naturally focused on Louis: "Armstrong, playing only occasional snatches of trumpet and betraying that the doubling between the show and the Cotton Club is too much for his weary lip, nevertheless walks away with honors. From the moment he enters in the red fireman's suit as 'Bottom' and calls 'Peace, Brother,' until the final scene in which you learn Pyramus kicked the bucket, Louis is the same brilliant actor." But even he could not rescue the show; *Swingin' the Dream* lasted only thirteen performances. Feather spoke for many when he called the overambitious production a "hell of a fine nightmare."

Once again, Louis failed to crack Broadway, but he continued playing at the Cotton Club. Later in 1940, he undertook yet another marathon coast-to-coast tour. Everything was as it had been, no harm done, iron-lipped Louis could go on like this forever, singing and blowing his brains out. While he was the same, popular music changed dramatically. On the cutting edge of nearly everything a dozen years earlier, Louis—and all that he embodied musically—stood in danger of becoming passé. When he had emerged in Chicago nearly two decades earlier, jazz was poised to become a national phenomenon, and he had been in the right place at the right time. To many audiences, Louis Armstrong *was* jazz, and jazz *was* popular music. Louis proved the point by launching one hit tune after another—more than any other performer. But jazz wasn't the new thing anymore. The new thing was "swing."

The birth of the swing craze is usually traced to a series of appearances by Benny Goodman, the Chicago-born clarinetist, at the Palomar Ballroom in Los Angeles in 1934. Goodman had been on the circuit for quite some time, playing "hot" before noticeably cool audiences. It was only when his style became more elegant, restrained, and disciplined that he began to attract throngs of enthusiastic youngsters who considered jazz old-fashioned, something their parents had played on the Victrola back in the days of Calvin Coolidge and Prohibition. Goodman's influence instantly spread across the country because his performances at the Palomar were broadcast live, and the three-hour difference meant that the music he played on the

West Coast reached East Coast living rooms at the dinner hour, peak listening time. Suddenly, other swing bands came to prominence: Tommy Dorsey, Harry James, Glenn Miller. Many of the swing-era bands were white, but there were important black swing bands as well. Duke Ellington, who had experimented with swinglike rhythms, added swing players to his band, and out in Kansas City, Count Basie slowly built an orchestra whose swing rhythm section was unrivaled. Swing was everywhere, and in 1938, Benny Goodman capped its rise with a triumphant concert in Carnegie Hall.

Though easy to identify by ear, "swing" is notoriously difficult to define. In general, it means an attack on the notes *surrounding* the beat, not on the beat itself. In 4/4 time, this means the accents fall more or less on the second and fourth beats rather than on the expected first and third. Swing's accents create a number of subtle effects. They impart a propulsive quality to the music, reminiscent of the rhythm of a train. They also *imply* the beat rather than express it, and the technique causes the ear to anticipate it. Swing permits rhythmic sophistication of a high order and gives performers, especially singers, an arsenal of devices to beguile the listener. They can fall behind the beat, or get ahead of it, or do one and then the other, and in the process establish a delicate but compelling rapport with the audience.

Although the rise of swing pushed Louis aside, one of the great ironies surrounding its acceptance was that he'd been one of the first musicians ever to swing. There are elements of swing in his earliest solos with King Oliver, and also in his Hot Five recordings, which anticipated Benny Goodman by a dozen years or more. One can hear swing's influence in his solos with the Fletcher Henderson Orchestra. He wrote about "swinging" his songs in Chicago as early as 1925. And in his 1931 recording of "You're Driving Me Crazy," he instructs the band to "swing." In nearly all these cases, Louis swings—but the band backing him does not. In fact, his irregular "swing" rhythms give his early solos their distinctive modern sound. The old marching bands of New Orleans, the nightclubs of Chicago, and the early Harlem bands—all the places where he served apprenticeships—didn't swing. Yet, in his solos, Louis did. His feeling for swing developed gradually during his years blowing behind Joe Oliver, on second trumpet. The King played the melody, emphasizing the beat in a resolutely unswinging fashion, while Louis found a place for his horn inside the music, filling

in behind Joe. In the process of complementing Joe Oliver, Louis anticipated swing. Eventually, his improvisations acquired crucial importance;
they were the real, essential jazz, incubating behind the melody, back of the
beat.

To all of Louis Armstrong's musical innovations—the jazz solo, scatting, vocalese, "glissing"—swing must be added, even though others
claimed credit. No matter, it all went back to Louis. In his "Mahogany Hall
Stomp," dating from 1929, his trumpet break features expert swing, and his
subsequent recordings helped popularize the notion of swing among jazz
musicians even before it acquired a name. "The number of musicians who
have assimilated his ideas must run into the hundreds," *Down Beat* remarked in 1938. "As a vocalist, too, he has had great influence, as is attested
by numerous singers who have some of the vocal effects for which he is so
well known." In short, Louis was the most influential musician still at work.
Yet he no longer seemed as daring and original as he once had. It wasn't
that he sounded like everyone else; everyone else sounded like *him*.

As the Big Bands refined swing, perfecting it, polishing it, making it
tighter and tighter, Louis was getting looser and looser. He could still turn
out the occasional hit, and in 1938, he made the first jazz recording of
"When the Saints Go Marching In," transforming a traditional song into a
standard. Increasingly, though, Louis traded on nostalgia, performing hit
songs he had introduced in movies, novelty numbers, and the familiar
"When It's Sleepy Time Down South." His journey into the past led him
to record swing versions of his Hot Five classics, such as "West End Blues"
and "A Monday Date"—songs ingrained in the cerebral cortex of every
jazzman. But Luis Russell's orchestra couldn't hope to emulate the velocity
and dazzle of the Hot Five musicians, and Louis's solos came off as poor
imitations of his brilliant originals. He seemed to lack both musical inspiration and the ability to make his horn pulse with life and emotion. Those
famous cadenzas, once razor-sharp, now sounded limp, vague, tired. Rather
than reigniting interest in his old hits, the new Decca recordings furnished
disturbing evidence of his decline. In an assessment of the recordings, *Down
Beat*, normally his number-one fan, ran a headline asking, HAS LOUIS ARM-
STRONG PASSED HIS PEAK AS A JAZZ LEADER? And another trade publication,
Music and Rhythm, ran a condemnation of Louis's latest recordings under
the headline, LOUIS ARMSTRONG STOPPED BEING GOD BACK IN 1932.

Simultaneously, a new generation of musicians originally inspired by

Louis threatened his eminence. *Down Beat* began running polls of the "best" jazz musicians and bands. In 1937, Louis Armstrong, "the world's greatest trumpeter," came in third. The trend became worse with time. Meanwhile, his acolytes were on the rise. Roy Eldridge was doing incredible things on his horn, especially in the middle register. Rex Stewart was "glissing" his way to prominence. Bunny Berigan, a white trumpeter who revered Louis, was also in ascendance. Each was poised to snatch the title of "The World's Greatest Trumpeter" from Louis. And there were still other musicians, many of them managed by Joe Glaser, who were exploring new realms in jazz—realms that Louis had discovered and then, as age and popularity overtook him, neglected.

Entering his fortieth year, Louis seemed destined to enter an irreversible decline, and jazz, once the soul of an age, doomed to fade along with him. Appearances were deceiving. Jazz was changing and maturing, but it was more than a musical fad that had outlived its day; it was attracting sophisticated audiences, and these new partisans began to have a profound, transforming effect on the music itself. They acknowledged that Louis's lip was not what it once was, but that was beside the point. The new audiences looked to him as the personification of their music: the musician's musician, the trumpeter's trumpeter, the singer's singer, the Viper's Viper—the quintessence of jazz.

14

WHAT DID I DO
TO BE SO
BLACK AND BLUE?

For Louis, the new and surprising direction jazz was taking became clear when he received a letter from his old teacher, Bunk Johnson, at the beginning of 1939. No one had heard from Bunk in years, and no one knew what had become of him. He was even older than Joe Oliver, and, Louis was delighted to discover, still alive. Now he was writing to his famous former pupil, Louis Armstrong, to say he needed a new set of teeth.

"Dear Friend," he began, "Your old boy is down and in real deep need for an upper plate and also a bottom plate and cannot make money enough to have my mouth fixed. . . . I drive a truck and trailer and that pays me $1.75 a day and that do not last very long. . . . Let your friend Bunk hear from you as I cannot blow any more."

Later in the letter, Bunk alluded to the troubles he had endured during the last ten years, and they were formidable. He had been touring rural Louisiana with a group of minstrels, the Black Eagles Band, but in 1931 they were involved in an ugly brawl. Bunk's teeth were knocked out, and the band's leader, Evan Thomas, was killed. After leaving New Orleans he had worked odd jobs for several years and wound up in New Iberia, a bayou town in the Cajun country north of the Crescent City. To make ends meet during the Depression, he taught children in a program administered by the Work Progress Administration and occasionally whistled at a local carnival. Other times he drove a truck for the Konniko Rice Mill. Eventually, he came to the attention of a wealthy white patron, Weeks Hall, who lived in a stately mansion known as The Shadows. Weeks Hall was as much of an eccentric as Bunk, and the two became friends—such was Weeks's way of challenging local racial codes—and he treated Bunk to meals and not a few drinks. Bunk passed his days in conversation with Weeks, possibly helping out around the mansion in return for his meals. His was truly a life lived in The Shadows, and it seemed certain that his career as a musician was finished.

Meanwhile, two young literary fellows in New York, Frederic Ramsey Jr. and Charles Edward Smith, inspired by their enthusiasm for the jazz of the twenties, persuaded Harcourt, Brace, where Ramsey worked, to publish a book about the origins of the music they loved. They received $250 between them as an advance and enlisted a jazz enthusiast, musicologist, and violinist named William Russell to help assemble the book. The three of them comprised an American version of the numerous European Hot Clubs that had sprung up to collect jazz records, and whose members venerated the jazzmen from New Orleans, especially Louis Armstrong. Of the three men, Bill Russell would become the first of a new breed, the jazz historian. In time, jazz historians would be legion, and would outnumber authentic jazzmen at about a two-to-one ratio, but for the moment Russell had the field to himself. "I was one of the real nuts," he reminisced happily, "a lunatic record collector."

Russell started collecting Jelly Roll Morton recordings. Although he treasured them, the racial divide in New Orleans was such that he had no idea that he and Jelly Roll came from the same city. He progressed to Louis Armstrong, then to Sidney Bechet, Clarence Williams, and on down the list of New Orleans greats. "All the people I liked were from here," he said. Record collecting was easy in those days, and cheap. New jazz issues cost only thirty-five cents, and the old ones went for practically nothing; the Salvation Army sold them for a penny a piece. Russell went up to New York to study Chinese music at Columbia University, but he remained a zealous "hot" collector, trying to amass every single side Louis Armstrong ever made. Often he ventured up to Harlem, not far from Columbia, to hear his idol blow. Russell came to the attention of Ramsey through his own record collecting, and he was assigned, at a fee of about forty dollars, to write three chapters for the book, which would be called *Jazzmen*. It was to be the first significant book about the history of jazz and, in some ways, is still the best and least solemn work of its kind.

When Russell came to Chicago in the fall of 1938, he conducted as many interviews as he could with New Orleans jazzmen, including Baby Dodds, who told him all about his experiences with Louis Armstrong, but also mentioned Louis's teacher, a man named Bunk Johnson, who had never recorded. Baby made Bunk sound extremely tantalizing. "You should hear him play 'Maryland, My Maryland,' " Baby told Russell. "What a lip that guy has." Baby added that Bunk was "still as unreliable as ever," and other musicians also warned Russell that Bunk would never get anywhere "as long as the story gets around that he was just like in the old days," meaning that Bunk was still inclined to drink. Intrigued, Russell went on to interview Zutty Singleton, Clarence Williams, and Sidney Bechet. These were revolutionary conversations; jazz was serving as a meeting ground between blacks and whites.

In the process, Russell was receiving a remarkable education in the overlooked history of New Orleans. He, and a few other critics and historians, mostly self-appointed, were discovering that jazz was more than a popular form of music—it was a path to important elements in the black experience, and the black mind and imagination, a place unknown to most whites. The deeper Russell went into this subject, the more he realized that "jazz" covered a great deal of territory, not just music; it tapped into a world, generally invisible to white society, of astonishing richness, subtlety, and variety. Jazz served as a conduit into and out of that world, a language pregnant with meaning and feeling. As they learned to decode that language, Russell and others like him were delighted, amazed, and grateful.

Now embarked on a quest to find Bunk Johnson, Russell tracked down Lil Hardin Armstrong, still living in Chicago, and she remembered that Louis had always raved about Bunk to her, and said he was *the* man. Lil said she didn't know if Bunk was still alive—he had disappeared years before—but she thought Louis might know.

Finally, Russell caught up with Louis in New York on January 18, 1939, during his engagement at the Strand Theater. They met in Louis's dressing room, with Alpha in attendance. She immediately handed Russell a copy of *Hot Jazz*, the book by Hughes Panassié, and a Decca catalog featuring Louis's latest recordings, but he brushed them aside. He wasn't interested in swing, and he wasn't a music critic, as Alpha had thought. He was interested in nuts and bolts, in piecing together the history of jazz as best he could, and learning how it was passed down from one player to the next. Louis and Russell began by discussing the old-time New Orleans jazzmen, and Russell played records from his collection, then listened to the jazzman's impressions, writing as fast as he could. Soon Louis was reminiscing about his days as a sideman for Ma Rainey, and the fellows from the

Fletcher Henderson Orchestra, Buster Bailey and Don Redman. It was getting to be a long time since they had made that *good* music. Russell kept pressing, asking about New Orleans. What about Buddy Bolden? Louis thought maybe he had heard Bolden blow, couldn't be sure. "I was very young," he explained. Russell continued to throw out names—Freddie Keppard, Emanuel Perez, and finally, Bunk Johnson.

At the mention of Bunk's name, Louis became "excited," "incoherent." He seemed to have been waiting thirty years for someone to ask him about Bunk, and finally someone had. "The fellow they ought to write about is Bunk," he told Russell. "Man, what a man! How I used to follow him around. Parades. Funerals. He could play funeral marches that would make you cry!"

"What style did he play?" Russell asked.

Louis put his fingers up into the air to imitate Bunk's trumpet style. "Man, what a tone he had! He used his band like I do. Used the same kind of fingering. I might say he played a swing lead." Louis illustrated by singing. By now Russell was avid to reach this unknown living legend, the man who had taught Louis Armstrong. "Does he still play?"

"No," said Louis, "he lost his teeth."

By now, Russell was incredibly excited. It sounded as if Louis had recently *talked* with Bunk, and sure enough, Louis explained that he had just received a letter from Bunk, asking for a new set of teeth.

Hearing all this from Louis's lips, Russell knew he just had to meet this fabled Bunk Johnson himself. He wanted to move beyond talk; he wanted Bunk to play again, so Russell could hear that tone Louis raved about, hear those funeral marches that could make a man cry. Thus he conceived a scheme to find Bunk, get the man some teeth and a horn, and *record* him. Then the world could finally hear the man who had taught Louis Armstrong. It would be like bringing Buddy Bolden back from the dead.

Russell wrote to Bunk Johnson in care of the Postman in New Iberia, Louisiana. The letter found its way to its recipient, and, to Russell's delight, Bunk responded with amazing accounts of long-ago events. "Now here is the list about that jazz playing," Bunk wrote, " 'King' Buddy Bolden was the first man that began playing jazz in the city of New Orleans, and his band had the whole of New Orleans real crazy and running wild behind it. Now that was all you could hear in New Orleans, that King Bolden's Band, and I was with him. That was between 1895 and 1896 . . ." Bunk had a way of penciling himself into crucial events in the history of jazz, and it was difficult to prove—or disprove—many of his claims. To hear Bunk tell it, he was the missing link between the late, legendary Buddy Bolden and Louis Armstrong. Even when his accounts were exaggerated or self-serving, he was full of insights: "Now here is the thing that made King Bolden's band the first band to play jazz. It was because they could not read at all. I could fake like 500 [tunes] myself, so you tell them that Bunk and King Bolden's band were the first ones that started jazz in that city or any place else." Bunk was not the first to have spoken of Bolden. Three years earlier, in *Swing That Music*, Louis himself had paid tribute to the man, which only lent credibility to Bunk's claims.

Bunk also positioned himself as the chief inspiration of the young Louis Armstrong. "While I would be playing with brass bands in the Uptown section, Louis would steal off from home and follow me. During that time Louis started after me to show him how to blow my cornet. When the band would not be playing, I would let him carry it to please him. How he wanted me to teach him how to play the blues. . . . And now you are able to go ahead with your book."

The letters Bunk wrote to Russell began circulating in the New York jazz world even before *Jazzmen* was published. They fascinated everyone who saw them. *Down Beat*, which published several excerpts, was moved to comment, "Perhaps soon we will all have the opportunity to hear the man to whom we owe an unpayable debt of gratitude—the man who taught Louis Armstrong and thereby indirectly influenced the whole scope of modern swing music—Bunk Johnson."

In return for Bunk's help, Russell and his collaborators raised sixty dollars from their friends, enough to buy him dentures. The plates were far from perfect and hurt like hell whenever he wore them, so he decided he would wear them only when he was playing, which he planned to do as soon as he got himself a trumpet. A secondhand trumpet was found in a pawnshop and sent to Bunk, but he did not yet feel secure enough to play in public. He remained in New Iberia, practicing, and trying to recapture some of his old musical magic.

In the course of looking for Bunk Johnson, Russell had done a superb research job, and late in 1939, *Jazzmen* appeared, drawing heavily on his pioneering work. It was a trove of information, some of it newly discovered, much of it long forgotten, about Clarence Williams, Bix Beiderbecke, Bunk Johnson, and of course, Louis Armstrong. Within a short span of time it became the Bible of jazz cultists, a one-of-a-kind poetic evocation of Storyville and the origins of jazz. Louis embraced the book. As soon as he read an advance copy in October, he wrote to Russell from the Harlem hotel where he was preparing for his lengthy Cotton Club engagement. "You are really a swell cat, indeed" he told Russell. "All of us Spades just love you, Brother Russell." Adding helpfully, "P.S. 'Spades' means colored folks." As for the book itself, it was "Absolutely wonderful. . . . And those stories about [the] New Orleans red-light district are absolutely perfect. . . . And the first-class information about me driving that coal cart is oh, so true." In fact, the overall accuracy of the book was what impressed him most. "I've just finished reading page 132 where it said Johnny Dodds broke down and couldn't say a word in the recording horn while we were making 'Gut Bucket Blues,' and, boy, that is the actual truth. Wait till Johnny sees this article. Man, it'll bust his konk. In fact, everything that's inserted into your book is the truth, so help me."

Louis then picked up the saga of Bunk Johnson, thanking Russell for raising the money to get Bunk's "chops fixed." "Honest, Gate," Louis wrote, "that's something we will be talking about for the rest of our lives." He also wanted to get Bunk a new trumpet, not just a pawnshop special. He hadn't forgotten about it, he explained, "I just haven't had the time to go over to Rudy Muck's place and intercede—Ump—Diddat come outa me?" He promised to have Rudy "send Bunk a trumpet right away." In closing, Louis proclaimed "Brother" Russell "a real sender, if there ever was one," and signed it as he did all his letters, evoking his fondest memory of New Orleans, "Red Beans and Ricely Yours."

Louis's claims to the contrary, *Jazzmen* did have its share of distortions and downright inaccuracies that would be recycled for decades to come. Many originated with Bunk, on whom the book's editors relied uncritically. Russell judged Bunk "the ideal successor to the throne of King Bolden," which was stretching a point. Bunk was certainly a presence in the New Orleans musical scene of his day, but hardly the dominant figure. Russell also vividly described Bunk's playing style—"He had an unprecedented sense of swing and feeling for the low-down blues and gutbucket style, yet a tone unrivaled in its beauty"—but he had yet to hear Bunk actually blow.

For all its inaccuracies, though, what is most remarkable about *Jazzmen* is how contemporary it feels today. There is still nothing else quite like it.

Word of the book—and Bunk's appearance in it—trickled back to New Iberia, where Bunk was talking his way back into the music world. Unlike Joe Oliver, who had willed himself into obscurity and died—as Louis said, of a "broken heart"—Bunk wasn't shy about asking for help in getting another chance. He wrote to Frederic Ramsey Jr., offering to sell pictures of himself, five dollars for six portraits. Ramsey obliged, and, after a time, Bunk wrote back to explain why the pictures were taking so long: "We have no colored studios. This is a Cajun town, and, in these little country towns, you don't have a chance like the white man, so you just have to stand back and wait until your turn come. That is just the way here. So please do not think hard of me. Think hard of the other fellow." He added that "I want to become able to play the trumpet once more, as I know can really stomp trumpet yet." Evidently, Louis hadn't gotten around to sending that trumpet, or it had failed to reach Bunk, because he asked, in closing, "You tell Louis to please send me a trumpet, as he told me he would, and you all do your best for me."

Everyone did. Through his letters and his influence on *Jazzmen*, he became a symbol in New York of the lost world of jazz, and Russell and others like him were determined to recapture the glorious, rollicking past that Bunk personified. That same year, 1939, another serious book about jazz appeared: Wilder Hobson's *American Jazz Music*, which also accorded traditional jazz new respect while avoiding the tendency of European critics to romanticize it out of reality. However, none of these critics and historians expressed an interest in the future of jazz; they believed the future of jazz lay in its past. Even Louis sounded suspiciously modern to the purists, who were inclined to blame him for the demise of New Orleans jazz and, worse still, for becoming a Hollywood-style celebrity. These learned, well-meaning traditionalists soon became known as "moldy figs." At the same time, a number of new jazz clubs were springing up around New York that featured small, "New Orleans-style" jazz bands rather than big swing bands. Jazz was now a distinct entity: no longer synonymous with popular music, yet increasingly in the grip of the "moldy figs." Only Louis successfully straddled these two worlds—by confounding his educated, well-meaning fans even as he obliged them with "traditional" playing.

On May 27, 1940, hoping to capitalize on the interest in traditional, small-band jazz, Decca reunited Louis with Sidney Bechet (on soprano saxophone), and Zutty Singleton, among other New Orleans musicians. The idea was to play good old-fashioned New Orleans-style jazz: "Coal Cart Blues," "Down in Honky-Tonk Town," and a Buddy Bolden tune, "2:19 Blues." Bechet, a genius but a prickly personality, had been drifting from one city to the next, receiving acclaim, getting into fights with his colleagues, and then moving on. In accordance with this pattern, he approached the Decca sessions with optimism and then succumbed to paranoia. He labored under the mistaken impression that Alpha had organized the session and was even responsible for the arrangements. Bechet believed that he had stumbled into a conspiracy to make him sound bad. "Louis's wife had written down the important things I was to do," he recalled, "and I played them that way. And they'd been written down the same way for Louis, but when it came time to actually record Louis done nothing like what was written for him; it was like he was a little hungrier; he began to take runs different from how we had arranged. I don't mind that. He can change his mind. What I don't understand is why he didn't come to me first and tell me he wasn't going to go along with the parts that had been written." According to Bechet, these takes were ruined when Louis unexpectedly began talking at the end.

They tried again, and this time, Bechet recalled, "Louis . . . seemed like he was wanting to make it a kind of thing where we were supposed to be bucking each other, competing instead of working together for that real feeling that would let the music come new and strong." To give the knife one last twist, Bechet remarked, "The funny thing is that I can remember Louis years ago when he was so timid you'd have to urge him to get up and play when there was some *regular* bucking kind of session going on." Fueled by jealousy, Bechet complained that Louis had succumbed to the star syndrome and abandoned real jazz. "A man now, he's not just a musicianer any more. He's got himself a name and he's got to perform up to that name. . . . He's got to be a personality." Bechet made an exception in the case of Buddy Bolden: "If a man can really play where the music is, he's entitled to all the personality they'll give him." In the case of others— Bechet didn't mention Louis by name, but he was plainly referring to him—"If the personality get to come first, that's bad for the music." For Bechet, this attitude ruined the recordings they made that day. "You can have every tub on its own bottom all right, but that don't make real music."

Not surprisingly, the sides resulting from the 1940 small-band session revealed Louis struggling with those around him, but he hadn't tried to outdo or subvert Bechet. According to others present at the session, Louis was polite and deferential toward the clarinet master, and the recordings reveal that he held both his blowing and his singing in check, while Bechet indulged himself. In fact, Bechet, despite his complaints, delivered an incredible performance, while Louis's was merely credible, and Luis Russell's, on the piano, lamentable. In the end, these recordings furnished additional evidence that Louis was losing his glow.

Bewildered by Louis's apparent inability to play the "traditional" music of youth, the "moldy figs" wondered whether he had outgrown jazz. He had not, of course. Louis was simply not the traditionalist of the "moldy figs'" imaginings; he was a revolutionary, as demonstrated by his Hot Five recordings. If anything, Decca had reached too far back in time. Rather than plunging Louis into his New Orleans era, when he was struggling to make a place for himself in the music world, the company should have set their sights on his Chicago years, when he was in his first flowering, and beginning to break jazz out of its boundaries with his scatting and wild solos.

All the while, Bunk remained in New Iberia, practicing his trumpet with his new dentures. Finally, in 1942, he did make his first recording, when an engineer from Victor captured Bunk's sound on a portable machine. It was primitive, but it was enough to lure Bill Russell to Bunk's door. The day Russell appeared, Bunk was barefoot, hacking away at the weeds in the yard with a scythe, and tending to his pet monkey. Russell fell under his spell. They started talking about the old days back in New Orleans with Louis Armstrong. "Anybody that thinks they can outplay Louis, send them around to me," Bunk advised. "If I can't outplay 'em, I can talk 'em to death."

Russell persuaded Bunk to return to New Orleans to record and to emerge from years of isolation and neglect. In the jazz world, his reappearance was greeted as the equivalent of the Second Coming. To back Bunk, Russell arranged for an outfit containing such stalwarts as Baby Dodds, and, in subsequent sessions, Shots Madison. As they were preparing, Bunk fell back into his old ways and began wandering off to the saloons. When he resurfaced, his head was clouded, and the group had to wait for him to sober up enough to blow. Patient for a time, Russell managed to record quite a bit of music, including a number of blues and marches, until Bunk went off on another bender. Russell finally had enough of this behavior and paid Bunk, who promptly spent his earnings in a week of drinking before skulking back to New Iberia and sobriety.

How good was Bunk? It was a matter of some controversy. There were those who swore he was as great as they came, and there were others who considered him aptly named, close to an outright fraud. Of course, he was well past his prime and handicapped by dentures when Russell made his recordings, and they were consequently a very uneven lot. On some numbers, especially traditional marching band pieces, Bunk sounds stiff, almost amateurish, but on others, when playing the blues, he displays the extraordinary clarion tone Louis had raved about, as well as a sense of rhythm so compelling it makes the drums almost unnecessary. Overall, Russell's microphone had captured the wreck of a once great musician.

Imperfect though they were, these recordings proved sufficient to launch Bunk on a long tour that took him to San Francisco, Boston, and of course, New York, where the Bunk Johnson revival was in full flower. For a man who had spent the better part of a decade in a Louisiana backwater, it was quite a comeback. He appeared on NBC radio, recorded for Decca, and played with Sidney Bechet, as truculent as ever. The Bunk craze peaked in 1945, with his engagement at the Stuyvesant Casino in New York. His appearance there earned reverent publicity in *The New Yorker*, *Time*, and even *Vogue*. Just about everyone wanted to be part of the Bunk phenomenon. Virgil Thompson, the critic and composer, insisted that Bunk was the "greatest master of the blue or off-pitch note I have ever heard," a statement that said more about Thompson's lack of exposure to jazz than about Bunk's ability.

Despite the ballyhoo, ticket sales for Bunk's Stuyvesant Casino gig were disappointing and his playing irregular. The engagement was marred by his frequent disappearances and benders. Jazz musicians who heard him play wondered what all the excitement was about. Barney Bigard, the New Orleans clarinetist who played with Ellington's orchestra, considered Bunk "pathetic to begin with. People just capitalized on him." Even Louis, who had done so much to call attention to Bunk, disavowed him. "Bunk didn't actually teach me anything," he said, making an about-face. "He didn't show me *one* thing."

Through all the controversy, Bunk remained unfazed. He still talked a good game, telling critics and aficionados alike what they wanted to hear, and he appeared to be in good shape, thin, elegant, and well-dressed, but the drinking had taken its toll, and he looked considerably older than his sixty-odd years. "I do not know when I will become old now," he said. "The only things I know that's old are my clothes. They get old, not Bunk." To the end he remained an enigmatic, controversial figure. He died in 1949, eulogized as the last great trumpeter of the early days of jazz.

With Bunk gone, it fell to Louis Armstrong to carry on the grand old traditions of New Orleans.

With or without Louis, the traditional jazz movement continued to gain strength, especially with the approach of another World War. Americana, including jazz, became precious to a bewildered public clinging to traditions. Louis and his orchestra were swept up in the passion for homegrown music and toured almost constantly during the war years. By now he had finally outgrown Luis Russell, who remained with the orchestra but yielded leadership to Joe Garland, a tenor saxophonist better able to keep pace with Louis's demanding sets.

With the arrival of war, the venues changed. Instead of the ballrooms, dance halls, nightclubs, and theaters to which Louis was accustomed, he now played in gymnasiums, at colleges and high schools, and, especially, on or near military bases, where GIs, mostly segregated by the military, their tastes unclouded by critics' cavils, were hungry for his music. Out on the road, liberated from the restraints of swing, Louis demonstrated that he could still ignite the excitement of his earliest years of blowing in Chicago and Harlem. Although Glaser always managed to find a booking some-where for Louis Armstrong and His Orchestra, their fees declined sharply, barely covering the expense of transporting, feeding, and sheltering the band. No matter. Louis played as energetically as ever, inspired by the energy he felt emanating from the crowd, especially when they were young and dancing. He would play sets running about thirty minutes, as many as three or four a night.

Among his most memorable appearances of this era was at Fort Barran-cas, near Panama City, Florida, at the end of September 1941. Days later, Louis described the scene in detail in a letter to Leonard Feather, the jazz writer, or "Feathers," as Louis called him. Louis first entertained the white soldiers, and, in recognition of efforts at morale-boosting, received a medal in the form of crossed cannons from the commanding officer, Colonel Lloyd C. Magruder, who asked Louis what he would do with them. "I laid that fine thankful smile of mine on him and said, 'Man, them's gold. I'm going to put them away in my safe deposit box. I shall never part with them.' . . . When they pinned that Official Coast Artillery Insignia on my lapel, I was almost in tears."

After the ceremony, the chaplain and Private George Grow, who was white, escorted Louis to the post hospital. "And, Feathers, you've never seen anything like the way those soldiers, colored and white, all brightened up at the sight of me. . . . The doctors and nurses told me that some of those patients [who] hadn't been on their feet in weeks were up this day and smiling when they found out I was coming to visit them. . . . I signed a whole gang of autographs, including one on the cast of a soldier confined to his bunk with a broken back. This young feller said that he's never gonna part with that cast, even after he's well and out of the army. He expects to send it home to his parents when he comes out of it. I inscribed Louis Satchmo Armstrong on it for him." He led the invalid soldiers in a rendition of "When the Saints Go Marching In," and when the singing ended, they all devoured lemonade and sandwiches. "One of the colored patients wanted a few bars of 'Watcha Know, Joe,' so I laid it on him lightly before I departed."

As soon as he completed his official duties on the post, "I went out to town to play for the colored dance that night. I was so wringing wet." His new friend, Private Grow, followed Louis to the dance, where mayhem struck. "Those spades commenced to fighting like cats and dogs. Ooooowee! I ain't never seen the like in all my born days, honestly. The fight started so quick and everybody started towards the bandstand, and the cop—to quiet it all down—pulled out his pistol as if he were really going to shoot and didn't look like he cared where he was going to shoot," he wrote Feather. "I looked around and George was standing way back there by Smoothie (Frank Galbreath, my get-off trumpet man), justa running his mouth with Smoothie and watching the Battle Royale. As long as he was 'allreet' I was 'sausagefried' (meaning satisfied). I'm telling you, between watching those bottles flying up into the air [and] the policeman with his gun in the air, and every time he went to put it back into his satchel look like the gun would be pointing directly at me—Ump—between all of that and watching and seeing that nothing happens to my guest and figuring out the maneuverings of that heat and those notes from my trumpet, I'm telling you I was a very busy man, indeed. But it all ended up in fun."

When it was over, at two in the morning, Louis went back to his hotel room. He changed out of his perspiration-soaked clothes, met Alpha, and, along with the rest of the band, got on the bus, which drove through the night to the next gig in the next town, where Alpha searched for a laundry to clean her husband's clothes quickly. "She has that routine down to the last frazzle," Louis boasted. "She even learned my routine of how to keep plenty of handkerchiefs . . . and also how to take good care of those fine vines"—clothes.

Segregation was still the rule wherever they performed in the South. In Atlanta, they played an auditorium with chicken wire down the middle to separate white from black patrons. Finding a place to eat or sleep or even to go to the bathroom was a constant problem. On stage, Louis and his band were stars; offstage, they were second-class citizens. Glaser tried to protect his musicians by reserving a private railway car for them down south, but often the military took over the cars, stranding the band in small southern towns where unexpected groups of black men were likely to wind up in jail. "They'd put us off in a little one horse town, milk trains ran through and they would pass us by," John Simmons, a band member, recalled. "We'd try to sleep on these wagons, and an express train would come through and throw cinders everywhere." To avoid depending on the railroad, Glaser arranged for a bus to carry his men from one date to the next.

When they reached New Orleans, Louis was able to indulge himself. While the driver, "Shanghai," was "taking his beauty nap," Louis and the band treated themselves to "some good ol' gumbo feelay, as they call it down here," followed by "raw oysters on the half shell and a dozen fried. . . .'Twas a light dinner but so delicious." Since he was in a Creole restaurant, he started to reminisce about the good old days, and how "those Creoles . . . would not let the Uptown boys [blacks] pass Dumaine and Claiborne without putting up a fight or getting sapped up. Of course, ever since I was a youngster my mother always told me, 'a good run is better than a bad stand any time.'"

The journey into his past continued that night, when Louis arrived at the Rhythm Club for their engagement. Who should be there but "Mr.

Morris Karnoffsky himself, and his wife," who "enjoyed themselves and our music to the highest." After the show, Louis fell to reminiscing with his old boss: "He and I talked about the good ol' days when I was just a kid working on his coal wagon with him selling coal to the sporting class of people down in the red light district . . ." Those days were gone, long gone, he realized. "I went sightseeing I passed through these places where the red light district used to be and they have built some of the most beautiful homes there one would ever want to see. Why, you'd hardly recognize the ol' landmarks," he wrote with mingled pride and regret.

He even had time to see "my Grandma, Mrs. Josephine Armstrong," and his sister, Mama Lucy, on this trip. They, too, talked about the past, especially since "my sister and I are the two what's left of the Satchmo family." Resuming their good-natured sibling rivalry, they laughed about the time young Louis finally got himself a job at Matranga's and proudly gave his mother the salary he had earned, all of fifteen cents. When he awakened his little sister out of a sound sleep to tell her about his achievement, she sneered, *Blow all night for fifteen cents.*" Before he left New Orleans, he made sure to "lay a little scratch" [money] on both women, and of Mama Lucy in particular, he said, "I greased her mitts real heavy."

The most important thing on Louis's mind these days, besides music, was food—or rather, dieting. "I've been forty pounds overweight for almost five years now," he lamented. "I picked up all of this excess weight when I was playing downtown at the New Cotton Club on Broadway. When I would get off from work, me and my gang would go uptown to Harlem to a little restaurant that used to run all night, and they had red beans and rice, pig ears, hog maws, pig tails, greens, and all that real honest-to-goodness home cooking, and me being a down home boy, I'd latch on real heavily, to my regret." To remedy the problem, Alpha clipped diets from fashion magazines (especially the one that Louis renamed *Vague*) and tried to place her exuberant husband on a strict regimen. Alpha herself lost weight—"got streamlined," as Louis put it—and now she was "streaming" all the cats in the band. "You should see them getting their grapefruit juices, etc., together when we hit these towns, and they're eating more sensibly, too. . . . All they had to do was cut out all of their starches and stop eating at night." He boasted in a letter to Leonard Feather that "By the time you see me, I should be rather streamlined myself because I sure am getting rid of that excess weight. And boy, if I ever get back down to my normal weight, which is around a hundred and seventy-five, at most, . . . that would strike me very pretty."

ouis's declarations of love and devotion to Alpha notwithstanding, their marriage was in serious trouble. His earnings in decline, he could no longer lavish jewelry and furs on her as he once had, and playing the role of Mrs. Louis Armstrong had gradually lost its allure. She had had enough of laundering her husband's handkerchiefs and tending to his wardrobe, of one-night stands, and all-night bus rides. She left him to complete the tour by himself, and when she rejoined him in Detroit, everything was different. "After a few nips too many," Louis wrote, for once agitated and bitter, "she began spilling her guts. She don't love Louis Armstrong and hasn't for a long time, because she is now going with Cliff Lehman, the drummer in Charlie Barnett's band. Ha ha. Surprised? Well, I ain't. I am one of the cats that's from the old school. I always become surprised when a woman does right and not when she does wrong."

Word of the breakup of his third marriage appeared in Walter Winchell's column, and on January 19, 1942, Louis felt impelled to write to the columnist with the *real* story. "No doubt this letter will floor you," Louis warned, and he proceeded to supply more details concerning his wife's transgressions with "this ofay boy." For example, Alpha had boasted to Louis that Lehman had paid her gas bill. "Brother Winch," Louis wrote, "can you imagine my wife bragging about this lad paying a few lousy gas bills when I've given her THOUSANDS and THOUSANDS of dollars for furs, diamonds, jewelry, etc. It really kills one, doesn't it?" Even worse, "she proudly admits that it was Cliff Lehman who took her away from me." Now all Louis could say was, "Thank God. If I could only see him and tell him how much I appreciate what he's done for me by taking that chick away from me." Then he began to rant, "And to think that I have to go to court and fight a no good woman like Alpha after traveling up and down the road working awfully hard blowing my little Satchmo trumpet, sending all of my money to Alpha, who stays here all the time in that fine and beautiful apartment that I've furnished for her, and all she has been doing is BALLING. I am telling you, Pops, it's a hard pill to swaller, but man, I can take it." Louis charged Alpha with desertion, and divorce was inevitable.

Although Louis was genuinely aggrieved, he was not quite the innocent injured party he made himself out to be. Alpha's desertion freed him to resume his stalled courtship of Lucille Wilson, his lovely young "Brown Sugar." His cynicism about women evaporated, replaced by the euphoria of unfolding love. One night, he reached out and took her "cute little beautifully manicured hand" and inquired:

"Can you cook red beans and rice?"

At first she laughed, and then, "it dawned on her that I was very serious."

"I've never cooked that kind of food before," said the very northern Lucille. "Just give me a little time and I think that I can fix it for you."

That was all Louis wanted to hear. "How about inviting me out to your house for dinner tomorrow night?" he suggested.

She stalled for time, but not too much time, and two days later, he appeared at her house, "with bells on, also my best suit." He met Lucille's family, who "impressed me right away as the kind of relatives that I could be at ease being around for the rest of my life." The Wilson family was deeply suspicious of Lucille's celebrated suitor, however. They all knew that Louis was much older—over forty, in fact—and had already been married *three* times. They knew that he was on the road nearly all the time, faced with the distractions and temptations that such a life entailed. What kind of home could he provide for Lucille? On the other hand, he *was* Louis Armstrong, a hero to blacks and whites alike, charming, generous, rich by their standards, and sincerely in love with Lucille. He was also hungry. He loved her red beans and rice. "I am sure that Lucille had never witnessed any one human being eat so much," he recalled, "especially at one sitting." It looked like a match. But on the verge of proposing marriage to Lucille, he was called away to Los Angeles for a near-emergency.

Throughout the spring of 1942, the American Federation of Musicians, under the direction of James C. Petrillo, had been threatening to call a ban on recordings. No one knew how long the ban, if enacted, could last. It would mean, though, that Louis could no longer make new recordings. Desperate to open new avenues of exposure for his client, Joe Glaser arranged for Louis to appear in a series of four "soundies." These were four-minute short subjects based on his recent hits: "When It's Sleepy Time Down South," "(I'll Be Glad When You're Dead,) You Rascal, You," "Swingin' On Nothin'," and the notorious ode to a happy-go-lucky shoeshine boy, "Shine," which Louis, through some musical sleight of hand, had contrived to turn into an affirmation of black identity. Louis hadn't appeared in a motion picture in four years, since his success in *Goin' Places*, and the soundies, shown in theaters around the country, reaffirmed his presence in Hollywood, and led to his receiving an offer in an upcoming motion picture based on the Broadway hit, *Cabin in the Sky*. On April 30, 1942, he signed a contract with Metro-Goldwyn-Mayer to appear in the movie. Along with five other musicians, he received a two-week guarantee of seventy-five hundred dollars, and they would each be paid two thousand dollars for a third week, if required. Shooting was scheduled to begin in August.

Glaser's move proved shrewd, for, in August, Petrillo did call a recording ban, instantly throwing 130,000 union members out of work. The strike became a disaster for the musicians, who collectively lost over four million dollars in pay, and a boon for record companies, who devised numerous strategies for circumventing the strike even as their expenses plunged. For popular musicians who could no longer record, such as Louis Armstrong, touring assumed paramount importance, followed closely by live radio appearances, and, of course, the movies.

To keep his client working until August, Glaser lined up months of dates for Louis and the band in Montana, Idaho, and Minnesota. After weeks on the road, the men became touchy and suspicious of one another. Many resented Louis's "valet," Bob Smiley, who, they decided, was actually Joe Glaser's snitch. According to this theory, Smiley reported back to the boss on the behavior of the men, especially their use of alcohol and drugs. Resentment against Smiley mounted, and then one day on the bus he got into a fight over a seat with the drummer, Big Sid Catlett. When Big Sid found Smiley sitting in his seat, he warned, "I ought to knock you down," and Smiley stood up and dared him. Big Sid knocked Smiley out with one punch, astounding the fellows on the bus. Louis, who sat watching the whole thing, didn't want anything to do with the brawl. "Let 'em fight," he said. Meanwhile, Velma Middleton, the band's new singer, became hysterical. "They're fighting! They're fighting!" she shrieked, and the bus driver nearly drove off the road. Finally, Louis took matters into his own hands, declaring that when they reached Chicago, Catlett would be fired, and so would another musician, John Simmons. This edict infuriated Simmons, who insisted that he had had nothing to do with the brawl.

The bus stopped, and the men got off to cool down, Simmons in the lead. He stood by the door, waiting for Louis to show his face, and planning to "pop him right in the mouth," ruining his chops. He got ready to slug Louis, but just then felt these big arms drop around him, and heard Big Sid, growling in his ear. "You hit that man in his mouth, you'll never play another note of music in your life. You'll be blackballed for life." Simmons tried to shrug off Big Sid, but the incident ended without any harm coming to Louis.

At this point, Louis called a brief halt to the tour to fulfill his obligation to appear in *Cabin in the Sky*. During the band's layover, Catlett and Simmons returned to New York, while Louis arrived in Los Angeles to perform in what promised to be his first substantial dramatic part in a film.

No movie project had ever begun so auspiciously for Louis. With its all-black cast, *Cabin in the Sky* had electrified Broadway when it opened in 1940. A pseudo-folktale about greed, lust, and redemption, it was part of a new wave of "serious" productions on Broadway featuring black characters and a black ethos. Though dated by today's standards, the production was far removed from minstrel stereotypes. The story, by Lynn Root, describes the travails of Petunia, portrayed by Ethel Waters, and her charming, ne'er-do-well husband, "Little Joe," whose addiction to the sporting life, and a girlfriend, brings disaster on nearly everyone close to him. The reverent Petunia prays to the Lord to give her errant husband another chance. What ensues is a battle between the Lord and Lucifer for Little Joe's soul. Just when Little Joe appears to be climbing out of the lush life of sin, he falls back and, trying to save him during a brawl, Petunia is shot. In the show's most striking sequence, Petunia and Little Joe arrive at the Pearly Gates, where this good and faithful woman persuades the Lord to forgive her husband and admit them both to Heaven. Vernon Duke's score and George Balanchine's choreography helped make the Broadway version a hit, and Arthur Freed, M-G-M's musical specialist, began the process of adapting *Cabin in the Sky* to the screen. Louis didn't get the plum role of Little Joe in the movie—it went to Eddie "Rochester" Anderson—but he did land a nice part as one of Lucifer's assistants, as well as a chance to blow in a big production number based on a rousing song by Harold Arlen and Yip Harburg, "Ain't It the Truth."

The movie would be a Hollywood landmark, the first all-black musical. Freed vowed to market it not as a race picture but as a musical designed to appeal to everyone. He obtained the best talent he could find: Louis Armstrong, Duke Ellington, Ethel Waters, and Lena Horne, cast as Little Joe's dynamite girlfriend. Elmer Rice wrote the screenplay, Vincente Minnelli would direct, and George Balanchine supervised the choreography. To Freed, *Cabin in the Sky* marked the coming of age of the Negro in Hollywood. No more would performers of color be relegated to peripheral roles of domestics and comics—or so he hoped. Freed also wanted to sell tickets to his movie by building it into an event and was moved to powerful rhetoric. "Upon its success or failure will stand the future of the race in the greatest medium of the world," he insisted.

Rehearsals began at the end of August, and Minnelli shot the picture swiftly, from August 31 through October 28. Although the story portrayed "rustic" characters, he gave the *mise-en-scène* the high-gloss finish typical of an M-G-M musical. To make the point that it was an all-black story, he filmed every scene in sepia, which was, given the story's otherworldliness, not a bad decision. Louis had two big scenes, one dramatic, the other musical. In the dramatic scene, he portrayed the Trumpeter, a comically demonic figure who plots mischief in the Hotel Hades. The scene really belongs to Rex Ingram, a powerful screen presence as the devil, but Louis remains compelling throughout. He constantly clutches his trumpet, but it remains a prop in this scene. His big chance to show off musically comes in the movie's big production number, "Ain't It the Truth," in which he attempts to teach right from wrong to Little Joe's girlfriend, Lena Horne. Minnelli staged it as an all-singing, all-dancing extravaganza, complete with delirious sepia devils gyrating provocatively in Hell. The sequence was intense, over-the-top, and destined to be controversial. It would have been the film's highlight, except that the studio cut it completely from the movie.

With his major contribution consigned to the cutting-room floor, Louis Armstrong was mentioned only in passing, if at all, in reviews when *Cabin in the Sky* opened on April 9, 1943. Brooks Atkinson of the *New York Times* gave it the equivalent of two thumbs up, and *Variety* echoed Freed's party line: " 'Cabin' is a worthwhile picture for Metro to have made, if only as a step toward Hollywood recognition of the place of the colored man in American life." Relegated to a bit part, Louis was overshadowed by an impossibly sexy Lena Horne, whose singing and dancing evoked the passion and eroticism of her role. "Lena Horne is a definite click, both vocally and dramatically, as the fatal Georgia Brown, while Louis Armstrong has merely a few moments on the trumpet and a couple of lines," *Variety* commented.

The movie went on to do good business, even though theaters in the South refused to show films portraying blacks in anything other than the smallest roles. Everyone was relieved that the movie avoided minstrel stereotypes and lived up to Freed's promises, but its most pungent and memorable five minutes—with Louis Armstrong jiving with the happy devils in Hell and proving yet again that the devil really does have all the good tunes—were never shown to the public.

As soon as Louis completed his chores for *Cabin in the Sky*, he turned back to his band, replacing the troublesome Simmons with Charles Mingus, who would emerge within a few years as the most talented bass player in jazz. Mingus was as unstable as he was brilliant; he was often paranoid about life and about whites, occasionally with good reason, and he had little patience with his new leader. He admired Louis's work on the trumpet, but couldn't abide his mugging and "Tomming," as he called it. Mingus was a serious musician and wanted to be taken seriously, and he was upset by the spectacle of Louis grinning and joking and capering across the stage like a vestige from a minstrel show. Eventually he left the band to pursue his own brilliant, idiosyncratic musical vision.

Louis hardly noticed Mingus's arrival and departure. He spent most of his time daydreaming about his Brown Sugar, Lucille. The only obstacle to marriage was his finally obtaining a divorce from Alpha. He appeared to testify in a Chicago court on September 29, 1942, at the ungodly hour of ten o'clock in the morning. He was under great strain, exhausted and giddy. He later wrote that he had been up the entire night preceding his court appearance, "having one drink after another, no sleep and juiced (drunk)," so that "by the time I got to the courthouse . . . I was very hoarse and could only whisper." All he wanted was to go back to his hotel room and get some rest, but the sight of his "Brown Sugar" in the courtroom cheered him greatly. He was touched that Lucille had come to Chicago just to "dig my trial and be with me. Just then, the judge turned to me and commenced asking me a few questions. My voice sounded so bad the judge looked straight at me and said, 'Look here, young man, have you caught a cold?' I said, 'No, Judge. It's just the sawmill voice that all my fans said I have.' The judge gave a little chuckle and immediately said, 'Divorce granted.'" On October 2, 1942, the Superior Court of Cook County, Chicago, formally dissolved the marriage of Louis Armstrong and Alpha Smith Armstrong.

Things were happening very fast. He had to play a gig that night in Chicago, and then another one in St. Louis, but all he could think about was how badly he wanted to marry his Brown Sugar. For her sake, he gave up a collection of erotic movies he had amassed. He had carried these reels with him on the road to help fill the lonely hours, but they did not belong in the new life he was arranging for himself. In a gesture of true friendship, he conferred the treasured reels on his colleague Jack Teagarden, the trombonist.

On the train to St. Louis, he confessed his love for Lucille to Velma Middleton, the singer. A large, spirited young woman, Velma—"bless her"—said she was from St. Louis, and that Lucille and Louis could get married right in her home. Even better, she said, "My mother belongs to a large church in St. Louis and her pastor is a fine man loved by the whole congregation." Velma was certain he would be delighted to perform the ceremony.

Louis and Lucille set a date for the wedding, October 7, but complications soon arose. "Lucille is Catholic and I am a Baptist," Louis wrote. "We went to several priests, and they all turned us down and would not o.k. our marriage license. The time was getting near, and Lucille and myself were getting desperate . . . but we could not give up. Then all of a sudden it dawned on Lucille and me that after all we are both deeply in love, which priests or any human could understand. So we decided to forsake all others and go on with the wedding." Lucille's mother arrived in St. Louis, unperturbed by the religious issue and gave her blessing.

At the last moment, they found a clergyman willing to perform the ceremony, Rev. John E. Vance of the Washington Tabernacle Baptist

Church in St. Louis. On their wedding day, "I bought a beautiful orchid and pinned it on Lucille," Louis recalled. "That was the first orchid I'd ever bought in my life. . . . We made a very good-looking couple, with me down to my fighting weight. Very slim. I had on a sharp, hard-hitting gray suit. Luis Russell and his boys all looked nice and had a real good time. All the liquor 'n' everything they wanted."

There was no time for a honeymoon. That night, Louis and the band played, as scheduled, at the Tune Town Ballroom in St. Louis, and as soon as that engagement ended, they began six months of one-night stands. Meanwhile, said Louis, "I sent Lucille and her mother back to New York to wait until I returned from my long trip. I had no fear." But he did have a good chortle when, two weeks after the wedding, the minister who performed the ceremony was sued for divorce by his wife. "Well sir," Louis wrote, "she caught the Reverend in a peculiar position with one of the young Church sisters who sing in his Church choir. That certainly did strike us all as funny. But I did not have any fear of something like that ever happening to Lucille and me. We had too much sincere love and devotion." He vowed that this, his fourth marriage, would be his last, that he and Lucille would never seek a divorce. "I guess I could be called a three time loser," he mused. "The first three marriages started out fine, but look how they ended! But I never gave up the search for the kind of mate who could bring me the happiness I needed and the relaxation I craved. When Lucille came along I knew she was it, the right one. I think a man instinctively knows when he's got the right woman."

Given that Louis had finally found marital bliss on the fourth try, it may seem odd that he resumed his tour immediately after his wedding. In fact, his return to the road was evidence of his life's priorities, which always remained clear. He repeated them often: *First comes my horn, and then Lucille. But the horn comes first.* His attitude wasn't a result of callousness or even dedication to the cause of music; it had simply evolved through years of conditioning. From the time he was seven years old, delivering coal for the Karnoffsky family, he had always worked hard—worked to eat, to feed his family, to live. He was incapable of being lazy, or even taking a vacation. No matter how far he had come as an artist, entertainer, and celebrity, his mind-set remained that of an old-fashioned New Orleans musician who played "music for all occasions" and who measured his success by how far ahead he was booked. To have six months of bookings, as he did at that moment, was a sign of status and good fortune, neither of which he was about to spurn.

Lucille joined Louis on the road so they could spend their first Christmas together, only to discover what a gypsy her husband was. She bought a small Christmas tree to decorate their hotel room, and when he came back from his gig at about three in the morning, he was so startled by the sight of the tree and its twinkling lights that he was, for once, speechless. "I gave him his Christmas present," Lucille said, "and we finally went to bed. And Louis was still laying up in the bed watching the tree; his eyes just like a baby's eyes would watch something." She offered to turn the lights out, but he said, "No, don't turn them out. I have to just keep looking at it. You know, that's the first tree I ever had." When she heard that, Lucille became, as she put it, "all swollen up inside." She was astonished at her globe-trotting husband, and remarked that "it seems to me that in forty years a person would have at least one tree."

The next day, they were to leave for Kansas City. Lucille remembered that, "I figured Christmas is over. . . . I'll leave the tree. So Louis said, 'No, don't leave the tree. Take the tree with you.' And he had me take the tree on those one-nighters. Before I even unpacked a bag I had to set that tree up, his Christmas tree. . . . I kept that first little tree until way after New Year's, putting it up every night and taking it down every morning, in a dozen hotels. And then when I did take it down for the last time, Louis wanted me to mail it home."

This wasn't how Lucille planned to spend the rest of her life. She found no intimacy in strange hotel rooms, with their awkward twin beds. "My, my how Lucille and I suffered every time we did the vonce (sex, you know). We had to tie those beds by the bed posts in order to have little happiness while we were wailin'. Sex, ya dig?" Knowing his bride was unhappy, "I came to a conclusion that I must set Lucille down. . . . I figured if we want the comfortable happiness that I seek with that girl, she must stay home." Instead of buying Lucille jewelry and furs, he wanted to buy her a house in which they could do the vonce in the manner to which he was accustomed. "Our home must be our castle, where we could pleasantly lock our bedroom door at inventory time," in other words, "Sex."

Louis duly sent Lucille back to New York, and with her husband's salary regularly coming in from Glaser's office, she began to look for a suitable dwelling somewhere in the city. She decided to avoid the obvious choice, Harlem, because it contained too many temptations for Louis: nightclubs and chorus girls, bars, and all-night restaurants. Instead, she looked in Corona, Queens, a quiet residential neighborhood. She came across a house owned by a white family she had known since she was a girl; she had even gone to school with one of their children. As it happened, they were planning to move, said Louis, "and when they found Lucille came all the way from Harlem out to Corona looking to buy a house, why, they were so glad to know that she liked their house, and she told them that she would buy it." The neighborhood was mostly white in those days, but a few blacks were moving in. Like Lucille, they were leaving Harlem in search of a quiet, stable neighborhood. In time, Corona and a neighboring area, St. Albans, would become home to many jazz musicians, writers, and other members of the black intelligentsia. Lucille paid thirty-nine hundred dollars for the house, and Glaser arranged for the payments to be deducted from his client's earnings. Louis knew nothing about the transaction until it had been accomplished.

The tour finally ended in March 1943, and Louis returned to New York. He took his bags off the bus, said good-bye to the fellows in the band, hailed a taxi, and gave the driver the strange address in Corona: 34-56 107th Street. It was a long drive out to Queens, at least half an hour, and along the way Louis became concerned. He was going to his new home, his *first* home, but he had no idea how to get there. He had never been to Corona. "The cab driver finally found the house. He looked around to the back of the cab and said to me, 'OK. This is the place.'" They pulled up in front of an imposing, three-story house on a quiet middle-class residential street. There were steps in front, a yard to the side, and a garage. It had been built in 1925. "*One* look at that big *fine* house and right away I said to the driver, 'Aw, man, quit kidding and take me to the address I'm looking for.'" It was late, he was "tired as old hell," and he was in no mood for jokes. But the driver insisted this was the place. "I got up enough courage to get out of the cab and rang the bell. And sure enough the door opened and who stood in the doorway with a real thin silk nightgown, and her hair in curlers?" It was Lucille, of course, inviting him into their home. "To me she looked just like my favorite flower, a red rose. The more Lucille showed me around the house, the more thrilled I got. Yeah. You hear? I felt very grand over it all."

When talk of the house in Corona and Louis's plans for a happily-ever-after with his Lucille circulated around the jazz community, certain musicians rolled their eyes. They knew the musician's life; you were on the road three hundred days a year or more, and they also knew that Louis was the most hustling cat out there. He lived to play, and he hated to stay home. Besides, women threw themselves at Louis, and being human, he didn't always avoid them. Despite his indiscretions—and there would be several—the big house in Corona signified that Lucille was now "Mrs. Armstrong" in a way that Alpha, the perpetual girlfriend, had never managed. Everything about the house was settled and proper; it seemed to be the stately residence of a doctor or funeral home director, not a jazzman's pad. After the magical moment when Louis first realized this would be *his* house, he was rarely there, since for the rest of his life, he continued to tour for as many as fifty weeks a year. Instead, it was Lucille's house, and she decorated it with loving care, and all the money her husband could afford to send her through Glaser's office. Occasionally Lucille joined her husband on the road, but most of the time, she stayed in Corona, where she maintained the house as a shrine to Louis Armstrong and to their marriage.

D-Day came, followed by V-E Day and V-J Day, but he was so busy performing and touring that he hardly noticed these momentous events. He was married, he was happy, he was paying the mortgage, and Mr. Glaser kept him working constantly. Nothing else mattered.

il, meanwhile, followed her ex-husband's progress, even though several spouses and nearly twenty years intervened since they had been intimate. She performed with a band and as a soloist, always as "Lil Armstrong," until the new waves in popular music finally swamped her. She then launched an entirely new career in New York, as a clothes designer. She held a fashion show, complete with champagne and *paparazzi*—all very unusual in wartime, and remarkable for a black woman in those days. This event was her way of bidding adieu to music and launching a new career, but as the champagne flowed, the guests asked Lil to sit at the piano and *play* something. At a stroke, Lil's new career was demoted to a hobby, a personal passion, and she returned to music.

. . .

Louis returned to New Orleans in February 1946, just in time for Mardi Gras. "My band boys, the Northern ones, have never seen anything like our Mardi Gras in their whole lives," he exclaimed, and neither had Lucille, who came along to spend an uproarious day with him. He had a wild time, especially because he rode on one of the floats belonging to Zulu Social Aid and Pleasure Club, the burial society to which he belonged. "You should have seen me bowing and waving to the folks and cats as they cheered at the sight of me, their home boy." Meanwhile, he was savoring an invitation from the Zulus to officiate as their Mardi Gras King in the near future.

The float made stops along the way, where the Mardi Gras King and his courtiers (including Louis) fortified themselves. "I got so full of champagne I thought I was seeing two floats with a gang of Kings and Satchmos on it. Honest to goodness," he wrote, "we were having so much fun we almost forgot we had to go to Mobile and play that night. Velma and I had to beg the King of the Zulus and his boys to let us cut out so we could catch that 3:20 train to Mobile, Alabama, and we just did make it." He slept off the effects of the champagne during the ride. The train arrived in Mobile at 8:45, "and we hit at nine. Now you can see we were some *maneuvering* set of cats, huh?"

This latest visit to New Orleans left Louis more determined than ever to complete a memoir of his remarkable childhood there. Unlike most jazz musicians, who were noticeably reticent once they stepped off the bandstand, Louis's exuberance spilled over into his letters and hastily written reminiscences. He had been tossing off autobiographical fragments for twenty years by this point, and his powers of expression had steadily improved. It had been over a dozen years since *Swing That Music* had appeared, and he wanted to tell a fuller and bawdier story of his youth. He still felt the need of a ghostwriter to help him convert his autobiographical fragments into an actual book, but this time, he wanted to work with someone who, he believed, understood him and his music better than Horace Gerlach. He had just the man in mind.

In 1940, Robert Goffin, the Belgian critic who had hailed Louis in his 1928 book *Aux Frontières du Jazz*, fled his country immediately after the Nazis parachuted into it. He had come to New York and located his hero in his dressing room at the Paramount Theater. "If you need money," Louis told him, "don't you ask anyone else but old Satchmo."

Goffin burst into tears. "He was the only one of my friends who had given a thought to what my situation might be," he wrote of Armstrong. "Jazz meant a lot to me at that tragic moment of my life." Over the next few years, while Goffin tried to reconstruct his life in the United States, Louis kept his word, frequently wiring his friend payments of fifty dollars to help him along. Louis was nearly always on the road when he sent money, but he made sure to confirm that Goffin had actually received the funds. When he could not get this assurance, he fired off telegrams and letters to alert Goffin that money awaited him. Sometimes, "the money came back," and when that happened, it was gone. "Dear Pal Goffin," Louis wrote, "you know how I am with money. The sooner I get my hands on it the faster I spend it. Tee hee. So accept this hundred and I'll send the other 'before a black cat can lick his behind.' Haw haw haw."

In the end, Louis gave his beleaguered friend five hundred dollars and asked nothing in return except that Goffin function as his amanuensis. Wherever he was on the road, Louis would send Goffin stories about prostitutes and pimps, about his Grandmother Josephine and Black Benny, about Irene and Daisy and Frankie Foster, and much more. He told Goffin to go ahead and make a biography out of these materials. They laid big plans. First there would be a book about Louis's early life, and then a movie. In Hollywood, Louis had met Orson Welles, and they had discussed the possibility of the boy genius filming the jazzman's life story. He had pleasant daydreams about casting possibilities. They obtained a contract from a publisher, Allen, Towne & Heath, and the dream came closer to being a reality.

When the book, titled *Horn of Plenty*, was published in 1947, it was immediately apparent that something had gone wrong with the project. A large part of the problem was Goffin's lack of familiarity with the United States, to say nothing of his uncertain grasp of the English language. Louis had supplied him with hundreds of pages of fully realized writing: dialogue, dates, and explanations for the general reader. It hardly needed an intermediary. Goffin took these pages, added dialogue where none was necessary, and inexplicably left out good material. Even worse, he decided to write this dialogue in dialect. For instance, he invented a scene in which a loud noise startles the infant Louis, who begins howling, and his mother turns to his father and says, " 'Tain't no two ways 'bout it—we's gwine leave dis head mizzable dump!" To which Willie replies, "Yo' sed it, May Ann." May Ann then observes that, "Yo' makin' nuf money now, an' ah kin wohk. We saves up and mebbe fun' us a place on Perdido Street." These disastrous exchanges went on for many embarrassing pages. Critics took Goffin to task for his literary horrors, and even though Louis had collaborated on the book, *Horn of Plenty* was discredited.

The book's questionable reputation obscured two significant facts. First, nearly everything in its pages, with the exception of the obviously contrived dialogue, closely followed Louis's manuscript. Second, Louis often spoke—and wrote—in a southern black idiom, not because he was unsophisticated or incapable of producing standard English, but because he relished black idiom. To be sure, Louis's genuine speech was vastly different from Goffin's notion of black dialect. He could be vastly eloquent, perceptive, ironic, and downright funny, for he loved to play with language almost as much as he loved to play music. Unfortunately, Goffin didn't take Louis at his own word, and the resulting biography suffered greatly.

By the time *Horn of Plenty* appeared, Orson Welles's enthusiasm for adapting the project had evaporated, but Hollywood still displayed an interest in a movie featuring Louis Armstrong. United Artists decided to make what promised to be a *real* jazz movie: *New Orleans*. It would be set in that city in 1917, the year Storyville closed and its music became a national commodity. For the sake of authenticity, a unit filmed Kid Howard's Brass Band leading a funeral and parade in New Orleans. The studio contacted Joe Glaser and hired Louis Armstrong, "The World's Greatest Trumpeter," along with another Glaser client, Billie Holiday, whom Glaser billed as "America's No. 1 Song Stylist."

The movie's attempted realism crumbled when the producers played the recording of the "authentic" New Orleans marching band for Louis and a number of other jazz musicians. All of them, Louis included, burst into laughter when they heard the archaic sound. Far from being authentic, the music was a hodgepodge of wrong notes and out-of-tune instruments; no one who played *that* way could expect to earn a living. These were stylish musicians, who knew their way around many types of music, not just jazz. More importantly, jazz itself had evolved dramatically in the previous thirty years, with Louis as the principal catalyst. So much for the film's spurious authenticity; given the spontaneous nature of jazz, the authentic style was whatever happened to be going on at the time. The producers were chagrined, but declared that there was no going back.

More serious problems soon presented themselves. McCarthyism had come to Hollywood. Gone were the idealism and liberalism underpinning movies such as *Cabin in the Sky*. Once again, blacks found themselves consigned to peripheral roles, even in *New Orleans*, a movie intended to celebrate their music and history. The producer, Jules Levey, and the screenwriter, Herbert Biberman, knuckled under to right-wing pressures, and what had begun as a re-creation of the early days of jazz metamorphosed into a melodrama about the romantic and career quandaries of a white opera singer played by Dorothy Patrick. Most of the remaining jazz elements featured Woody Herman, the white clarinetist whose ties to New Orleans were tenuous, at best.

Matters worsened, if that were possible, once filming began. Billie, who was to sing three tunes in the movie, was assigned a role as a maid, which meant she appeared in a domestic's uniform. "I'd fought my whole life to keep from being somebody's damn maid," she recalled of this demeaning episode. "After making more than a million bucks and establishing myself as a singer who had some taste and self-respect, it was a real drag to go to Hollywood and end up as a make-believe maid." She was furious at Glaser for subjecting her to this indignity. At the same time, she was slipping into the thrall of heroin, and the dulling effect of the drug on her appearance and performance was apparent to all.

As shooting proceeded, the script kept changing, reflecting Senator Joseph McCarthy's increasing sway over Hollywood. The screenwriter, Herbert Biberman, who became notorious as one of the "Hollywood Ten" (industry figures suspected of Communist sympathies), was jailed. Under intense pressure, the studio continued to tone down the movie. Jazz was pushed to the background; snatches of Armstrong classics were heard, but only as incidental music, while the preposterous opera story took center stage. As for Louis himself, he appeared stiff and ill-at-ease in the scenes in which he portrayed a character only vaguely inspired by the real Louis Armstrong. He introduced a song that later became identified with him, "Do You Know What It Means to Miss New Orleans?" but it was lost amid the murky, nonsensical plot. In his scenes with white actors, tension is palpable; there is no interracial contact, not even a handshake. "In the original script, Louis's band was slated to appear on the same bill as Woody

Herman's at the big stage concert," said Red Callender, who played the bass in Louis's band in the movie. "We had our tuxedos and everything, filmed it, but thanks to McCarthyism it was never shown."

The ninety-minute, black-and-white film opened in July 1947 to tepid reviews, yet in spite of everything Louis remained an object of fascination to reviewers. "The only saving grace of this colorless, lifeless, unimaginative story of jazz is, of course, Louis Armstrong and his band," said the New York *Daily News* critic. "Armstrong and jazz are synonymous and he tells the story single-handedly—with his music." Most commentators echoed her sentiments. With no studio support, the film did little business and soon disappeared. What had begun as the definitive jazz movie of the era ended as a curiosity and a reproach to the forces that had subverted it. *New Orleans*, once Louis's biggest and best hope in the movies, was quickly forgotten.

I f any good came from this cinematic fiasco, it was that Louis reconsidered the music he was playing. He had slowly been slipping behind the musical curve for years, throughout the swing era, and he now came to the conclusion that he would be best served—and happiest—playing the kind of music he knew best and loved best, and musical fashion be damned. For any other popular performer, a decision to leave the mainstream could be suicidal, but because Louis incarnated jazz, he brought to it unequaled authenticity and conviction. Only he could have pulled off this maneuver which, at first, even Joe Glaser refused to countenance. For once, though, Louis felt strongly enough to challenge his manager on the subject. "My boss, Mr. Glaser, is so anxious that I make good," Louis confided to Leonard Feather at the end of 1946, "[that] he will send someone from his office—someone who doesn't even know how we play, or what we play. He will suggest that we play this tune or that tune because he thinks we can do a better job, or some jive. Quite naturally that will take all the heart out of all of us. . . . I readily see Mr. Glaser's side of the situation, but it's no good. That alone almost made me say (musically) to hell with it all."

Soon after, on February 8, 1947, Louis found relief from this frustrating situation when he signed on with a sextet, Edmond Hall's Cafe Society Uptown Orchestra ("He's that ace clarinet man in New York, a grand player"). Glaser was very uncomfortable about the idea of an A-list client playing with a small group, and insisted that for the second half of the evening Louis perform with his own, sixteen-piece unit. They were engaged to play at New York's Carnegie Hall, the temple of high culture at 57th Street and Seventh Avenue. Carnegie Hall was a long way from the Basin Street brothels and New Orleans street parades, but jazz had been gaining respectability throughout the 1940s, thanks to an alliance among the "moldy figs," a new breed of historically aware critics (including Feather), and the legions of fans they educated and attracted. The celebrated nightclubs of Harlem where jazz had once been played were long gone, dance halls such as the Savoy and Roseland were passé, and promoters found that by staging concerts in Carnegie Hall, or even the Metropolitan Opera House (where Louis had performed one night in 1944) the music became endowed with sufficient respectability to appeal to white audiences.

The shift away from parades and brothels and nightclubs to concert halls did have an effect on the music. Jazz had long been functional, music for all occasions, for singing, crying, talking, smoking, and especially, dancing. Now that it had come to Carnegie Hall, it became a *concert*, where the audience sat still and quietly listened. This was an ideal way to display jazz to maximum advantage, but it was not a setting designed to encourage musicians to interact or experiment. This scene suited Louis just fine, however. He was no longer interested in developing anything new; he preferred instead to reach back to the good old-fashioned music he knew. His Carnegie Hall date with the Edmond Hall group proved a rousing success with the audience. More importantly, it demonstrated that Louis was most at home playing New Orleans-style tunes with a small, New Orleans-style band (or one vaguely reminiscent of the Hot Five) rather than a large "swing" orchestra.

The newly invigorated Louis attracted the fanatical devotion of a publicist and jazz buff named Ernest Anderson, who vowed to make it his life's work to stage Louis Armstrong concerts in the small-band format, playing traditional tunes. Ernie loved jazz, and he had made a name for himself promoting Eddie Condon concerts; Condon evoked the spirit of the Jazz Age without ever quite being the genuine article. But Ernie knew that Louis was the real thing, and he, like so many others, was wholly in the thrall of the man and the music. A large part of Louis's appeal these days went way beyond the music he performed, which had grown slightly wheezy and repetitive. Instead, the fascination lay in the entire *world* he created and transported with him wherever he went, an environment comprised of music, sex, marijuana, and hazy memories of Storyville permissiveness. It was a world of boundless fellowship, where members of all races were welcome, in which the audience mattered as much as the musicians. In this world, Louis functioned as the master of ceremonies; he called the tune, and let the good times roll. Ernie Anderson wanted to be in the thick of the excitement, so he insinuated himself into Louis's entourage and struck up a friendship with his hero.

Through a contact in Glaser's office, now called Associated Booking Corporation, Ernie learned that ABC was getting just $350 for Louis and the entire, sixteen-man orchestra on a weeknight, and $600 on a Saturday. To compensate for the small fees, Glaser often booked the orchestra into one-nighters as much as six hundred miles apart. Ernie sought to rescue Louis from these straits, and with this in mind, presented him with the idea of playing in a small—and therefore less expensive—group, emphasizing the traditional tunes he had played at the Carnegie Hall gig. Louis leaped at the idea, but added a caveat: "I can't do this unless Joe Glaser wants me to." Ernie knew just how abrasive and foulmouthed Glaser could be, but he could be pretty gruff himself when he had a mind to, so he decided to see what he could do.

"I got a cashier's check at my bank made out to Joe Glaser for $1,000," Ernie wrote. "Then I went up to Joe's luxurious office on Fifth Avenue and Fifty-Seventh Street. He had one of those upper floors of a white marble skyscraper. The next obstacle was his waiting room. There were seats along four walls and they were forever occupied. Here sat band leaders, vaudeville acts, managers, mostly all black. They were all convinced to a man that lives depended on getting a few minutes with Joe Glaser.

"Then the door of the waiting room opened to reveal Joe, holding the check. He seemed to be in a purple rage. He threw a hostile glare at me and shouted, 'What are you trying to do, you jerk?' I was deeply offended by this, but I remained calm and said, 'That's for Louis for one night without the band.' After all, I knew Joe Glaser well enough to know that he was never going to give up that check."

Glaser reluctantly admitted Ernie into the inner sanctum. The decor featured a large and disconcerting wall hanging of black musicians singing away happily on the old plantation and paying homage to their white master. No one knew why Glaser had this monstrosity hanging in his office, if he intended it as an ironic commentary on his position, or as an expression of the way he really felt about the musicians he handled. Standing before this alarming scene, Glaser scowled while Ernie outlined his plan to present Louis at New York's Town Hall at midnight on May 17, with a small band—just six men—comprised of stars of the jazz world. This wouldn't be just another gig, Ernie assured Glaser, the concert would be a great jazz event. Glaser kept throwing out arguments to knock down the plan, but then he looked at the check, and Ernie mentioned he knew how low Louis's fees had sunk. That got a rise out of Joe, but Ernie said, "If this works as I think it will, instead of $350 a night for Louis, you'll be getting $2,500 a night." Check still in hand, Glaser agreed to the plan.

By the time of the concert, Anderson had assembled an all-star lineup of musicians at fees ranging from sixty to seventy-five dollars per man. They included Bobby Hackett, a white trumpeter whose sweet tone Louis adored; Jack Teagarden, the Texan trombonist whom Louis had known ever since the old days in New Orleans; George Wettling and Big Sid Catlett on drums; Dick Cary on piano; and, for a while, Sidney Bechet. His psyche as convoluted as ever, Bechet withdrew shortly before the event, but Tea proved an able anchor.

Anderson deployed all his promotional skills to advertise the concert, and the critics and jazz writers came out in force. He also arranged for the concert to be recorded—not as easy as it seemed in the days before tape machines became common, and engineers still relied on wax discs—and paid part of the expense out of his own pocket. And he made sure Joe Glaser had the best seat in the house.

Although the concert sold out quickly, Louis gave no sign of anticipating anything special. In fact, on the evening of the performance, he refused Anderson's offer of a rehearsal. No, Louis said, there was no need; they were all fine musicians. All they had to do was go out in front of the audience and play together, and that is precisely what they did. Of course, the music was a little rough-edged at first, as the musicians tried to get familiar with one another, and Louis announced the tunes simultaneously to the audience and to the band. After the fellows played "Cornet Chop Suey" and "A Monday Date" to warm up, Louis asked for "Big Butter and Egg Man," a surefire crowd-pleaser, but Dick Cary, the pianist, introduced the song by repeating "A Monday Date," utterly confusing the rest of the band, and some of the audience, except for Louis, who gently blew along with Dick, covering any sense of a "mistake," until, after nineteen bars of the wrong song, he growled at the pianist, "Butter and Egg Man." Cary still didn't get it, and Louis finally stepped up to the mike and announced, "Now we're going to play some 'Big Butter and Egg Man' for ya." Cary finally got the idea, and launched into the introduction to the right song. Louis laughed, and the audience laughed, and everyone understood this was the real thing, unrehearsed—it just happened.

Thereafter, Louis took it as it came, performing unadorned versions of "Muskrat Ramble" and "Royal Garden Blues" and an incredibly fruity version of Hoagy Carmichael's "Rockin' Chair" with Jack Teagarden, the two of them singing back and forth in liquor-sodden brotherly love, and the more they played, the hotter they got, and Louis, freed of the restraints of swing, cut loose, growled and traipsed across the stage and generally enjoyed himself so much that the audience had no choice but to join in the fun, because the concert sounded exactly as everyone imagined grand old-time New Orleans honky-tonk jazz would sound, better than Bunk Johnson, better than any of the revivalists, because only Louis was old enough to have been there at the inception, but young enough and strong enough to be blowing it still. For once, he didn't sound like a pale copy of himself, but the real thing, the man who made up jazz, the leader of the Hot Five, the protégé of King Oliver.

There was nothing new in this concert. Louis never exceeded the audience's expectations, but he didn't need to. All he had to do was live up to their image of him, of the way he once was. And he did it brilliantly. Every note he blew was amplified by history, and by the time he finished the twenty-song set, he had transformed his career, thrown off the harness of swing, and reinvented himself in the small-band, "traditional" format. The Big Band was dead. Long live Louis Armstrong.

Louis carved himself a unique niche in the music world that night, and he stayed there for the rest of his career, playing the old tunes over and over. It was fortunate that he triumphed as a newly minted traditionalist, for he had no where else to go musically but back in time. His retrospective was an admission that his days in the mainstream of popular music had ended. Despite the success of the Town Hall concert and new impetus it gave to Louis's floundering career, Glaser remained deeply skeptical about the small-band format. On the one hand, he was delighted to pay fewer musicians, but on the other, he knew that the audience for jazz, as opposed to popular music, was limited. He wanted Louis to be where the money was, and the critics be damned.

In the face of Glaser's opposition, a chorus of jazz figures—Ernie Anderson and Leonard Feather among them—urged him to package Louis with a group of all-stars, similar to the Town Hall format. When Glaser finally bowed before the inevitable, he determined to make some money out of the situation and went around signing up the men for long-term commitments. Jack Teagarden, for instance, agreed to a seven-year contract, the longest allowable length. On the face of it, the contract seemed to be a good deal, for it guaranteed him five hundred dollars a week, a good living for a jazzman, but poor Tea had so many debts that he took home only ninety dollars a week after all the deductions. As a result, he was often demoralized and complained, "If I don't have enough to buy a pint of Four Roses every day I'm going to quit playing."

Since Glaser no longer toured with the band, he employed a road manager to keep his men in line. His real name was Pierre Tallerie, but the musicians all called him Frenchy, and he was, to quote Barney Bigard, "the 'real ass-hole' of the bunch." Dick Cary called Frenchy "one of the slimiest sonsofbitches I ever knew." It wasn't just that Frenchy was Mr. Glaser's snitch, although that was reason enough to hate him, but he had a penchant for causing trouble. One time he repeated something to Big Sid Catlett, the drummer—something that Louis had supposedly said—and Catlett became so enraged that he began choking Louis. Finally he came to his senses and was so upset with himself that he started to cry. On another occasion, Frenchy told Glaser that Cary, who took sedatives, was a drug addict. This naturally enraged the pianist, who knew that the story, though false, could prompt Glaser to fire him. Such was Frenchy's brand of malice. Still, the musicians stayed with the unit because Glaser paid them consistently and paid them well. They all realized that he, not Louis, made the decisions, a strategy that freed Armstrong to concentrate on his music while Glaser acted as the lightning rod for discontent.

On August 13, 1947, Louis Armstrong and the All Stars debuted at Billy Berg's, a Los Angeles nightclub. Now that Barney Bigard had come aboard as the clarinetist, the group was even stronger than it had been at Town Hall. Bigard had played with Ellington's orchestra for years and had just enough continental elegance to leaven Louis's declamatory style. The engagement became a bona fide event. The jazz world finally ceased obsessing about Louis's playing ability and emphasized the scope of his accomplishments and influence. *Down Beat*—whose polls had repeatedly consigned Louis to musical purgatory—suddenly rehabilitated him. "Nearly everyone agrees that Louis Armstrong is the outstanding figure in the history of jazz. The greatest trumpeter, the greatest vocalist, the greatest showman, the greatest influence, just the greatest," the magazine now insisted. "You hear frequently that single-handed Louis shaped the whole course of jazz, that without Armstrong jazz would today be something quite different from what it became, that his hand is apparent everywhere and not one of his successors is completely free from a debt to him. All this is perfectly true." *Time* was more succinct: "Louis Armstrong has forsaken the ways of Mammon and come back to jazz."

The favorable publicity was sufficient to launch the All Stars on a coast-to-coast tour—a very lucrative tour, as it happened. Ernie Anderson's prediction that Glaser would be able to get twenty-five hundred dollars a night for his men proved too conservative, for Louis and the group could command as much as four thousand dollars a night. Later in the year, Louis and Mr. Glaser added Velma Middleton, the singer who had recently toured with Louis. Her presence raised eyebrows among purists, who disdained her antics. Velma was as large as a barn, nearly three hundred pounds, and she sang, danced, and did splits, as well. She pulled Louis into endless vaudeville routines about her big "Dusenbergs," and the critics and jazz commentators, who felt so emotionally tied to Louis, complained that she was ruining the sanctity of the jazz. Glaser and Louis couldn't have cared less. Once again, they were having fun and making money and pleasing most of the customers in nightclubs and concert halls. "Armstrong can take an insipid pop tune, shake it around in his enormous mouth, and somehow let it out in a gravel voice that makes it sound like a comedy epic," said the man from the New York *Daily News*, after the All Stars again rocked Carnegie Hall in November 1947. "He doesn't drive with his trumpet quite as hard as he used to. But his veiled tone, the true melody of his breaks and turns, and the musical good humor and sentiment of his phrasing are as beautiful today as they were when he was twenty years ahead of his time."

As if to formalize and even canonize his musical style, Louis began listening to recordings of himself, starting with this Carnegie Hall concert. He undertook this practice quite by accident, when he heard Ernie Anderson play a bootleg recording of the evening's music. The next day, he bought two tape recorders for his personal use, and took them wherever he went. "From that time until the end of his life he saw to it that every performance he did was recorded," Anderson said. "Then later that night if you happened by Louis's digs you'd hear what he had played that night. He studied those shows. . . . Louis played those tapes over and over. Sometimes he'd playfully add a little narration to them." In the process, he committed the entire evening's "spontaneous" music to memory. For this reason, he never needed to rehearse, because each evening became a rehearsal for the next. This self-study gave his playing complete conviction, because he always knew exactly what he was doing. At the same time, it restricted his music growth, and eliminated the possibility of experimentation and improvisation. Everything in his music now came down to a marvelous, beguiling formula. To many, especially younger audiences, "jazz" meant something entirely different from Louis's traditional minstrel-inspired singing, blowing, celebration of New Orleans, and endless choruses of "When It's Sleepy Time Down South." His act, and all the Jim Crow social baggage it carried, was an embarrassment to the more socially aware and sophisticated musicians known as the boppers.

Now that he was regarded as the leading exponent, indeed, the *inventor*, of traditional New Orleans jazz, Louis didn't pay these detractors any mind. He was nearly fifty, and had made all his major choices: the type of music he would play, the manager he would trust, the home in which he would live, and, finally, on the fourth try, his life's companion. His life was complete in all major respects, and he had consolidated his position as the king of jazz—or had he?

15.

HIGH SOCIETY

or nearly a decade now, an entirely new style of jazz had been evolving, a style that Louis didn't even want to think about. Bebop. The biggest thing to hit jazz since the old days in New Orleans, bop featured several new elements, most of them developed not in New Orleans or Chicago, but in Harlem. There, musicians congregated in after-hours clubs such as Minton's and Clark Monroe's Uptown Theatre and jammed the night away, experimenting with harmonic theory through endless trial and error, all of it in the greatest possible contrast to the conservative, traditional music espoused by the "moldy figs" and Louis Armstrong. Their music wasn't quite avant-garde, but it pointed in that direction with distinctive innovations. There was the "flatted fifth"—simply flatting the fifth note of the scale. (Said Eddie Condon, the preeminent "moldy fig," on hearing the result: "We don't flat our fifths, we drink 'em.") There was "playing on the changes"—improvising on the chords, rather than the melody. The idea was to build a song on chord changes derived from standard tunes, the more harmonically advanced the better. This element involved far more complex rhythms in the solos, which became faster and more demanding technically than Louis had ever imagined. The vast increase in speed all but eliminated the old, relaxed New Orleans polyphony. Bop was energetic, tense, precise, sophisticated, and difficult. It wasn't functional like the old jazz; there was no such thing as a bop funeral, or a bop parade, or even bop dancing.

Bop revolutionized trumpet playing. For the first time, its adherents found a way to blow that did *not* emulate Louis Armstrong. John Birks "Dizzy" Gillespie became the symbol of the new wave of trumpeters. His instrument even looked different. He'd started out playing a conventional trumpet, but at a party one night it became bent. The bell, instead of extending forward, pointed upward. Dizzy came to prefer the contorted horn because he could blow and look at the music without the bell getting in the way, and since the bell was now close to his ears, he could hear himself much more clearly over the music. He wanted to patent his accidental invention but discovered that a nineteenth-century inventor had registered a claim. Dizzy even gave this new style of music its name. Instructing his band, he would sing the lines for the men—do, do, dee, biddy, oh, bo, dee, oh, bop, she, doo—and a customer who happened to be listening thought Gillespie was telling his men to play a song called "Bebop." Gillespie was so taken with the new name that he gave it to the song, which came to represent this entirely new type of jazz. It was bebop, or bop.

Gillespie was not the only innovator. Charlie Parker—also known as "Bird"—was a saxophonist who made the pilgrimage from Kansas City to New York, where he heard Art Tatum, the greatest jazz piano virtuoso, play the piano. Tatum's technique was so awesome that classical musicians who heard him breathed a sigh of relief that they didn't have to compete with his speed and his harmonic inventions, or the way he threw off dense clusters of notes in improvised formations. Parker was so crazy about Tatum that he became a waiter in the restaurant where Tatum was playing just to hear that music every night. After listening to Tatum, Parker had a brilliant insight: musicians could derive improvisations not from the melody of a song, but from the chords, and they could thereby make up their own melody. This meant the jazz performer was, more than ever, the composer. Parker took the tune "Cherokee" and deconstructed it, forsaking the melody for the chords and harmonies, entering the twilight domain of jazz, and the result was bop.

Parker proceeded to explore harmonies contained in other tunes, played the changes, and turned them all into bop. Of course, it took a keen musical intellect and great technique to reinvent songs this way, but Parker was endowed with both. He wasn't a big celebrity like Louis; he was wrapped up in his instrument, and the music was all that mattered. He played in nightclubs, the Apollo, and all the other jazz venues, but he was not a show business-style entertainer, he was an innovative, tormented musician. Bop was far more challenging, provocative, vital, and demanding than Louis's rather simple conception of jazz as good music for a good time. The boppers were committed to extending the limits of jazz, and one of the bonds they shared was an intense desire to distance themselves from the old-time New Orleans musicians, particularly Satchmo. As far as they were concerned, he was an old Uncle Tom, laughing and telling naughty jokes and carrying on as if he were in a minstrel show. He was, to their way of thinking, an embarrassment, and they began criticizing him publicly. Dizzy took Louis to task for his "plantation image," and boppers in general detested Louis's nostalgia for the South. They were self-consciously northern, urban, and intellectual; Louis's theme song, "When It's Sleepy Time Down South," was the antithesis of all they believed in.

Another young bopper, Miles Davis, who had arrived in New York in 1944 to study at the Juilliard School of Music was contemptuous of Louis and even of Dizzy. "I hated the way they used to laugh and grin for audiences. I know *why* they did it—to make money and because they were entertainers as well as trumpet players. They had families to feed. Plus they both liked acting the clown," he explained. "I was younger than them and didn't have to go through the shit they had to go through to get accepted in the music industry. They had already opened up a whole lot of doors for people like me to go through. . . . I didn't look at myself as an entertainer like they both did. I wasn't going to do it just so that some non-playing, racist, white motherfucker could write some nice things about me."

Louis could take only so much of this abuse. He didn't just turn a deaf ear to bop, he actively campaigned against it. It is not hard to understand why bop bewildered him. He had come up in the old school of New Orleans jazz, where melody was king. But now, he complained, "When they tear out from the first note and you ask yourself, 'What the hell's he playing?'—that's not for me. Personally, I wouldn't play that kinda horn if I played a hundred years; you don't have to worry about me stealing those riffs." He wouldn't, and he *couldn't*. That was the other thing about bop that bothered him terribly. He lacked the technique and the musical training to play on the changes even if he had wanted. His playing style was getting slower with the years, more conservative, and bop was going like mad in the other direction. He couldn't pretend to recast himself as a bop musician as he once had as a swing musician. Although boppers followed Louis in the broadest sense, as jazz soloists, and as performers who were also composers, bop was one musical development that was destined to pass Louis by. For the only time in his career, Louis lashed out at his young new rivals and became ever more strident in his criticism. Bop, he claimed, ruined jazz, and everything he had done to popularize jazz, because it took it away from the simple pleasure of melody that always gave jazz its accessibility and appeal.

Louis demonstrated the durability of his traditional approach by example. With the All Stars, he continued to perform almost every night of the year. American critics, seduced away by the boppers, were no longer paying attention, but audiences were, and Glaser was able to send Louis and the band abroad for his first foreign tour in fourteen years. He arrived in Paris on February 21, 1948, and spent a week visiting with French Hot Clubs and jazz enthusiasts who had tended the Armstrong flame throughout the dark war years. To them all, Louis was the sound of America, the sound of freedom and celebration and triumph over fascism. In Nice, he performed at an international jazz festival organized by Hughes Panassié, the jazz critic who had been among the first to take him seriously. Even on foreign shores, he continued to rail against the boppers back home and all their excesses. In his suite at the Negresco Hotel, an exasperated Louis gave his musical credo its fullest articulation in a lengthy, all-night conversation with friends.

He began by extolling the timeless virtues of jazz. "I always think of them fine old cats way down in New Orleans—Joe and Bunk and Buddy Bolden—and when I play my music, that's what I'm listening to. The way they phrased so pretty and always on the melody, and none of that out-of-the-world music, that pipe-dream music, that whole modern malice. . . . You got to like playing pretty things if you're ever going to be any good blowing your horn. These young cats now, they want to make money first and the hell with the music. And then they want to carve everyone else because they're full of malice, and all they want to do is show you up. . . . You get all them weird chords which don't mean nothing and first people get curious about it just because it's new, but they get tired of it because it's really no good and you got no melody to remember and no beat to dance to." More than style was involved; the contest between Louis and the boppers was generational warfare. Discussing younger musicians resisting his influence, Louis became choleric. "Look at them young cats too proud to play their horns if you don't pay them more than the old-timers," he snorted. "'Cause if they play for fun they aren't king no more. So they're not working but once in a while and then they play one note and nobody knows if it's the right note or just one of them weird things where you can always make like that was just the note you were trying to hit." He talked this way for hours, until daybreak, when his road manager reminded him they had to leave to catch a plane, but Louis had one last thing to get off his chest. "You make a pretty tune and you play it well and you don't have to worry about nothing. If you swing it, that's fine, and if you don't, well look at Lombardo and Sinatra and they're still not going hungry. We'll be around when the others are forgotten."

No matter what Louis said, the boppers couldn't be written off that easily. They had become the center of a cult that extended far beyond jazz. They were laying down the soundtrack for the emerging Beat Generation, for Allen Ginsberg and Jack Kerouac and other writers and seekers after hidden truths who fastened onto the boppers' introverted, sullen attitude and manner of dress and their language—"cool" and "gone" and "crazy." The boppers also popularized goatees, sunglasses, and berets, accoutrements that Louis found ridiculous. In a new version of "The Whiffenpoof Song" designed to skewer the boppers, he rasped, *"They constitute a weird person-nel! . . . Let them beat their brains out till their flatted fifths are gone . . . They are poor little lambs who have lost their way."* He dedicated his derisive "Whiffenpoof Song" to Dizzy Gillespie, who endured the criticism and considered it a backhanded compliment. "Armstrong never played our music, but that shouldn't have kept him from feeling or understanding it," he remarked. "Pops thought it was his duty to attack! The leader always attacks first; so as the leader of the old school, Pops felt that it was his duty to attack us. At least he could gain some publicity, even if he were over-whelmed musically."

The boppers brought more than their berets and flatted fifths to jazz. Alcohol and marijuana lubricated Louis's jazz world, but among the young boppers, heroin—far more dangerous and expensive—was the drug of choice. According to one survey, at least half of all bop musicians had tried heroin, at least a quarter of all bop musicians were addicts, and one-fifth of boppers had died as a result of their addiction. The highly publicized arrests of a few musicians for possession of the drug tarnished the reputations of all bop musicians, whom promoters and record labels considered unemployable addicts, or potential addicts. Charlie Parker, the bopper's bopper, was also the junkie's junkie, the archetypal man with a golden arm. Parker's habit devoured his money. So strong was the grip of his addiction on his psyche, he pawned his horn and was reduced to playing on a cheap plastic saxophone. After setting fire to his hotel room while nodding off, Parker was confined to the Camarillo State Mental Institution in California for most of a year. Heroin dealers meanwhile whistled the introduction to his song "The Mooche" to announce they had junk to sell. In the jazz world, Parker's name became synonymous with heroin the way Louis's name had once been with marijuana, but the effects of heroin were far more lethal than weed. Louis lived on, performing nightly, but Parker succumbed to his addiction in 1955. He was just thirty-four years old.

No wonder Louis felt threatened by the onslaught of bop. He had been drawn into a huge cutting contest aimed at redefining jazz and lost. From now on, jazz *was* bop. To his credit, he did not remain an implacable enemy of bop, but gradually arrived at a détente, playing with Gillespie, and then with others; to no one's surprise, his style melded beautifully with theirs— after all, it had come from him. At the end of the transition to bop, Louis was seen as an elder in the jazz world, not a has-been. He was still much too volatile to be consigned to the ranks of the "moldy figs." Even after the entire landscape of jazz had changed, his turf remained secure.

here's a thing I've dreamed of all my life, and I'll be damned if it don't look like it's about to come true—to be King of the Zulus' Parade. After that, I'll be ready to die," Louis declared.

In February 1949, it looked as if he would at last achieve his dream, provided that Joe Glaser did not interfere. Two years earlier, Louis had reached an understanding with the Zulu Social Aid and Pleasure Club that he would appear as their king during Mardi Gras—for honor rather than a fee. Once Glaser heard about the arrangement, he treated it as just another gig and tried to extract as much money as possible from the Zulus for Louis's appearance. "Joe Glaser was more interested in trying to promote Louis commercially and financially than he was in Louis being king, and this had always been the desire of Louis, to be king," said a club member, Jim Russell. Shortly before the 1949 Mardi Gras, the two sides came to terms, and Louis began to prepare for what promised to be his wildest appearance ever in his hometown. Learning of his impending appearance, *Time* magazine chose to place him on its cover, and with the issue of February 21, 1949, Louis Armstrong (whom the magazine insisted on renaming Louis *Daniel* Armstrong) became the first jazz musician to receive a cover story. His face, now universally recognizable, appeared in a joyful illustration, wearing a colorful jeweled crown suggesting that he was not only the King of the Zulus, but of the trumpet and the jazz world at large.

The *Time* cover confirmed Louis's singular place in popular music even as the boppers assailed it. The magazine took pains to celebrate his early accomplishments—innovations it had ignored or deprecated at the time. *Time* noted questions surrounding Louis's appearance as King of the Zulus, because, "among Negro intellectuals, the Zulus and all their doings are considered offensive vestiges of the minstrel-show-Sambo-type Negro. To Armstrong such touchiness seems absurd, and no one who knows easygoing, nonintellectual Louis will doubt his sincerity. To Jazz King Armstrong, lording it over the Zulu Parade (a broad, dark satire on the expensive white goings-on in another part of town) will be the sentimental culmination of his spectacular career, and a bang-up good time besides." The lengthy story also provided a useful introduction to his youth. He waxed nostalgic about Joe Oliver, railed against the depredations of bop, paid tribute to Mr. Glaser and to Lucille, and mused about the persistence of racism in postwar America. "I know where the discrimination is, so I avoid those cities," he said, choosing his words with care. "Anyone who goes huntin' for discrimination is a glutton for punishment." About prostitution, marijuana, Glaser's mob connections, Louis's writing, or the wilder side of jazz, not a word was said. For *Time*, it was sufficient to portray Louis as the clown prince of jazz.

As the magazine appeared on newsstands, a chartered bus bearing Louis Armstrong and the All Stars headed for New Orleans. His arrival was heralded by a barrage of outrageous publicity:

NEW ORLEANS TIMES-PICAYUNE
Head Hunters on the Loose

New Orleans, February 27. The most ferocious assemblage of African bushmen ever to set sail from the Dark Continent will invade New Orleans for the annual Zulu Parade on Mardi Gras. . . . Reports are that the tribesmen, whose king is to be Louis "Satchmo" Armstrong, intend to "kill a few" along the line of the march. But a review of the moist and liquefied history of the Zulus would imply that their victims are to be bottled products—exclusively. . . . A profusion of tom-toms and musical notes will adorn the first float, bearing the king—the notes symbolizing the musical talent which has earned for Armstrong a nationwide reputation as a hot trumpet man and band leader. The second float will contain the queen and her maids, and the third will present the Zulu Babies, a group of warriors incongruously wearing baby bonnets.

Louis reveled in the attention, no matter what form it took. Upon his arrival In New Orleans, he was greeted by Mayor DeLesseps Morrison in his crowded City Hall office. A white mayor chatting amiably with a black man: this was a highly unusual tableau for the Crescent City. "Satchmo," said the mayor, with a politician's wink at the throng, "I read in *Time* where it said all you wanted was to be King of the Zulus, and you were ready to die."

"Yes, Mayor, I do remember saying those words, but it ain't no use for the Lord taking me *literally*." The crowd laughed along with Louis as the mayor presented him with the key to the city.

Later that day, he retreated to his hotel room to rest. "No sooner had I fallen asleep," Louis wrote, "than I felt something crawling around my chops." He awoke to find a member of the Zulus making him up in preparation for the parade: "white stuff around my lips, eyes, in fact, everywhere he could swerve a brush. As much as I was not accustomed to this creepy feeling, I did remember my stepfather having the same stuff put on his face some 20 years before I was the King." Relaxing, Louis dozed again until Earl Hines, who had recently joined the All Stars, came into his hotel room. "When Lucille pointed toward me, with all this jive on my face, Earl's eyes got big as saucers. 'WHAT THE HELL IS THAT?' he said so loud he awakened me."

As the starting time approached, Louis donned his costume: a wig, red velvet tunic, yellow grass skirt, black tights, and a crown adorned with red feathers. His broad visage concealed behind white face and stark black lines around his lips and eyes, he was a grotesque sight, almost unrecognizable. Scepter in hand, accompanied by a retinue of female assistants, Louis mounted the Zulu float, where he joined other Zulu dignitaries. Throughout the daylong journey, he waved to the two hundred thousand revelers and tossed coconuts in their direction. The coconuts were another Carnival tradition, and Louis was equipped with an arsenal of two thousand, each painted with a gold-and-silver face. It was his responsibility to distribute these prized Mardi Gras souvenirs to appreciative members of the crowd, trying to be as gentle as possible about it. "I happened to look up on a porch where a young man was justa yelling at me, 'Come on, Satchmo, throw one of those fine coconuts up here.' The coconut hit the tip of his finger and fell down on a brand new Cadillac. Gee. I just turned my head, as if nothing happened."

The float proceeded through the heart of New Orleans, and Louis, from his perch, "saw straight down Claiborne Street for miles, seemingly, and the whole street was blocked with people waiting for the parade to come their way, but instead, the float turned in the other direction, and all of those people made one grand charge toward the float." As the afternoon waned, the float, burdened by Big Sid Catlett, the All Stars' drummer, and Velma Middleton, the group's three-hundred-pound vocalist, "commenced to crumbling to pieces." By day's end, it had fallen apart, and Louis, having relived a good chunk of his life in the space of a few hours, was utterly exhausted. He was supposed to ride a barge across the basin, but he contrived to find a double to take his place for that leg of the journey while he rested and communed with his French champion, Hughes Panassié, who had journeyed to New Orleans to be with his hero on this special occasion.

That night, Louis and the All Stars were scheduled to participate in a gala Mardi Gras performance at the Booker T. Washington Auditorium. After all the acclaim, only five hundred people showed up to hear Louis perform. Interest in Louis Armstrong, the celebrity, now outstripped enthusiasm for the music he had championed throughout his life. Among those who did attend, there was one woman who demanded to be admitted for free; she claimed to be "Mrs. Louis Armstrong." Everyone knew this woman was *not* Lucille, who was already inside. Undaunted, she ordered anyone who would listen to tell Louis that "Mrs. Armstrong" was waiting outside. Louis finally appeared, took one look at her, and said, "Let her in." The woman was Daisy Parker, his first wife, the knife-wielding prostitute who, in her own fashion, still loved him. That night, Louis performed with two Mrs. Armstrongs in attendance.

It had been a grand party, but Mr. Glaser gave his client no opportunity to rest. The next day, Louis, Lucille, Panassié, and the All Stars, all of them mightily hung over, left New Orleans by bus to begin a brief series of one-nighters throughout the South. Louis confided to his typewriter that he was grateful that the French critic remained blissfully unaware of the delicate, demeaning racism with which the All Stars had to contend during these southern engagements.

By March 10, he was in Las Vegas, where he performed for several weeks at the Flamingo Hotel. "I am just now getting myself together after the big day down there," he wrote to Mayor Morrison of New Orleans. "I was so beat for my youth when I left New Orleans I slept all the way to Jackson, Miss., where we played a dance the very next night after Mardi Gras, then continued one nighters in Tulsa, Oklahoma, Dallas, Texas, then Las Vegas, here at this fine Flamingo Hotel. . . . Honest, Mayor, I see so much money shot across the table here I kinda get swimming in the head, but we're not allowed, thank God, because I never was lucky in gambling. We used to play a little African golf (shoot craps for pennies) in which once or twice I surprised May Ann (my mother) with a whole sack of pennies, but I've found out since then that a person cannot work and gamble, too."

Louis Armstrong and the All Stars spent the next nine years very much as they had spent the previous two. They were nearly always on the road, and they performed over three hundred nights a year in auditoriums, concert halls, nightclubs, in cities big and little, and on college campuses. Not every show was greeted by a big, sellout crowd, but Louis didn't care. The smaller the audience, the longer and harder he would blow. One night in 1951, he found himself booked into Basin Street, a New York jazz club, and by the third set only a dozen people remained in the audience. Louis blasted the faithful out of their seats with his horn, and when he was done, he even picked up their checks. About once a year, the All Stars embarked on a foreign tour lasting several weeks. Their destinations included Europe, Japan, and Australia, and in most places, they were thronged with well-wishers. During one tour of Australia, for instance, Louis and the band performed twenty concerts in ten days, each one sold out, with audiences varying in size from twelve thousand to twenty-six thousand. Louis Armstrong was an instantly recognizable celebrity in the United States, but abroad, the man was revered. Still, he had no interest in becoming an expatriate, and always returned home to Queens for brief respites between tours.

In his spare time, he pored over the scrapbooks painstakingly compiled by Ernie Anderson, while playing the tapes Ernie had made of the All Stars's various performances. Although Louis lovingly preserved the tapes, he took a scissors to the scrapbooks and pasted dozens, then hundreds, and eventually thousands of pictures of himself and the band on the walls of his study. To Ernie's dismay, he discarded the reams of prose written about him.

He experienced a new sensation: contentment. With Glaser managing his business affairs and Lucille his home, he was free to concentrate on his music. "I don't want a million dollars," he insisted to Gilbert Millstein, a *New York Times* journalist who befriended him. "With a lot of musicians, money made a fool out of them. They forget about the life they love, standing on the bandstand. They're famous and can't play music for watching the box office to see how many people came in. I don't give a damn how many come in. If it was one or two thousand. . . . I'm not looking to be on no high pedestal. I'm just appreciating what I'm doing, you know. . . . I think all I can do is play the way I feel."

His fiftieth birthday, celebrated on July 4, 1950, became the occasion for a celebration of Louis Armstrong and his musical legacy in the mainstream press. *Down Beat* devoted most of an issue to a ripe, show business-style tribute to him. He marked the occasion performing before celebrities at Bop City, a popular New York nightclub and declared, "My chops are in A-1 triple groovey condition."

He became increasingly obsessed not only with his chops but with his entire physical condition, to which he ministered with a variety of home remedies. His valet, Doc Pugh (the "Doc" was strictly honorary) maintained a small pharmacopoeia to minister to Louis's needs and to maintain his strength with vitamins. Glaser's personal physician, Dr. Alexander Schiff, joined Louis's entourage, the better to keep an eye on Glaser's prize client. Louis drank little but continued to smoke marijuana in the form of fat, hand-rolled cigarettes known as bombers. He used a powerful gargle called Oral Pentecresol, recommended by Bing Crosby, but instead of diluting it with water, as prescribed, Louis took it straight. He lavished understandable care on his battered lips. He bathed them in witch hazel every day and continued to apply the same potent, numbing salve he had been using for decades. To observers, it seemed impossible Louis could blow at all with his disfigured lips, but he believed that given enough care his chops would last indefinitely. "Sure, my lips are scarred up—I been playing that horn 50 years—but they're *relaxed* all the times, and that's it. If your lips swell up a fraction on the mouthpiece, you're in trouble with your notes."

Louis's obsession with health didn't end with his chops. He became enamored of the writings of the physical fitness guru Gayelord Hauser, who recommended small daily doses of an herbal laxative known as "Swiss Kriss" to cleanse and regulate the bowels. For years, Louis had been devoted to a liquid laxative called "Pluto Water," to the point of signing letters "Am Pluto Wateredly Yours," but now he switched his loyalty to Swiss Kriss, which he took in triple doses, morning, noon, and night. More than that, he gave absolutely everyone he encountered little cellophane packages of Swiss Kriss and urged them to take it immediately to clean themselves out. He gave it to his friends, to journalists, and to photographers. On tours of Europe, he offered it to puzzled, polite diplomats and heads of state. He enclosed the cellophane packets in his letters, and generally behaved as if he were on a twin mission to alert the world to jazz and to Swiss Kriss. The idea of taking a powerful laxative made others uncomfortable, but not Louis, who flaunted his fascination with Swiss Kriss and his bowel movements, which he discussed with pride.

Since his weight continued to fluctuate, he combined Swiss Kriss with an idiosyncratic diet in which he tried to interest the world. He wrote and distributed a flyer promoting weight loss "The Satchmo Way." His ebullient prose belied some of its dubious, idiosyncratic advice:

At Bedtime
Your first dose will be real heavy, in order to start blasting right away, and get the ball to rolling. After you get over your surprises and whatnots, you'll be very happy. The first week, take a tablespoon of Swiss Kriss. Put it into your mouth and rinse it down with a glass of water. Fifteen minutes later, drink a large glass of water. Don't eat no food before going to bed. . . .

Supper Time
You can eat from soup to nuts. Eat as much as you want to. Please see that you have, at least, either sliced tomatoes (with lemon juice) or

your favorite salad. All kinds of greens are good for the stomach, so eat to your satisfaction. Of course, the less you eat is in your favor, hmm?

Comments 'n' Stuff

It's a known fact, while eating your meals, if you feel yourself getting full, it's in your favor to leave the table with a satisfactory stomach. . . . Don't get frantic because you have to trot to the bathroom several times when you first get up (awakened). P.S. You won't need an alarm clock to awaken you, no-o-o-o. Relax, if you feel a little tired from the swinging actions of dear old Swiss Kriss. Ha ha. P.S. In case you're wondering how much Swiss Kriss do I take, well, even though I've always taken a heaping tablespoonful every time I go to bed to rest my body, I shall do the same every night for the rest of my life. Because, when you and Swiss Kriss get well acquainted, then you'll dig he's your friend. . . . P.S. When the Swiss Kriss Company give me a radio show, my slogan will be, "Everybody, this is Satchmo speaking for Swiss Kriss. Are you loosening?" Wow.

As a combination joke and self-promotional stunt, he arranged to print thousands of cards with a photograph of him sitting on a toilet, his pants down around his knees, smiling, as if glimpsed through a keyhole. Underneath the startling photograph was the legend, SATCHMO SAYS, 'LEAVE IT ALL BEHIND YA!' He sent copies to his friends and to the press who alternately enjoyed his earthy humor and rolled their eyes in disbelief at his antics. He printed it on his stationery, on the front of the envelopes, and when *Life* ran the picture in its glossy pages, protests were raised that the magazine thereby insulted both Louis Armstrong and the Negro, but Louis didn't mind in the least.

Over the years, changes in personnel subtly affected the All Stars's vibrant sound. Jack Teagarden, Louis's soulmate, eventually left, and was replaced by the younger and more vibrant trombonist Trummy Young. The great Big Sid Catlett, in poor health, yielded the drums to Cozy Cole, a bundle of rhythmic energy, though not endowed with Catlett's inventiveness. Cole eventually turned over the skins to Barrett Deems, billed, in typical Glaser fashion, as "the fastest drummer in the world." Not every departure was amicable. When Earl Hines decided to leave the All Stars, Louis fired off a salvo: "Hines and his ego, ego, ego. If he wants to go, the hell with him. He's good, sure, but we don't need him. What really bothers me is losing Jack. That Teagarden, man, he's like my brother." Despite the occasional flare up, the All Stars were remarkable for their consistency, especially in the volatile jazz world. Returning to the All Stars after a five-year-long hiatus, Barney Bigard, the clarinetist, was astounded to find that the group was still playing "Indiana" precisely as they had before his departure.

Louis's personal life remained equally unvaried. His marriage to Lucille continued to bring him the stability long missing from his life. Joe Glaser directed all his professional activities, driving him at the same grueling pace as always, despite Louis's advancing years, and he controlled the Armstrong family finances. He kept both Lucille and Louis on monthly stipends, which occasioned frequent disputes. Lucille was supposed to spend no more than $350 on her Saks Fifth Avenue charge account, and if she exceeded it, Louis heard about it from his manager. Glaser usually kept Louis supplied with a $1,000 bankroll, as well as the occasional $2,000 bonus, which Louis instantly sorted into envelopes and distributed to a large number of camp followers, needy cases, and the occasional girlfriend. In one burst of generosity, he splurged on $500 television sets for various elderly acquaintances, and to pay for them he borrowed $2,500 from a Broadway loan shark known as Fat Morris. For this loan, Louis had to pay $250 a week in vigorish, and his finances, always casual, collapsed under the strain. Frenchy, privy to all secrets, reported the situation to Mr. Glaser, who became apoplectic and hastily paid off Fat Morris. "Now Louis," he said, "it's very kind and thoughtful of you to hand out all these free sets, but we have to draw the line some place." Glaser offered to supply sets to whomever Louis specified, but the discovery of his little scheme proved sufficient to embarrass Louis from pursuing his project.

Glaser tolerated these antics because Louis continued to be Associated Booking's biggest draw. When promoters wanted to book Louis, Glaser would generally tell them he would be unavailable for months, but if they took one of Glaser's lesser acts now, they could count on having Louis later. Using this formula, Glaser boosted himself and his company to new heights of prosperity. He drove a blue Rolls-Royce now, and lived in a lavishly decorated apartment on 57th Street, in midtown Manhattan. He continued to conduct affairs with very young girls, whom he paid associates to locate. But he was rarely seen in the company of a woman. "You know," he once lamented to an acquaintance, "I'm the only man who's been around the world without getting laid." He was also infatuated with show dogs, Schnauzers in particular, and owned a pair of prizewinners, Trumpet and Trinket. His temper still flashed, but he often apologized in the form of a letter or a gift. Glaser earned the loyalty of those who worked for him, because he did more than any other manager to keep jazz musicians working. While rumors of his shady past continued to circulate, he looked exactly like what he was, a highly successful businessman.

In 1953, Glaser made a rare but conspicuous managing misstep when he arranged a six-week tour for Louis and Benny Goodman. The Big Band All Stars, as the new unit was known, generated a million-dollar advance sale, but the notoriously strict Goodman tried to keep the irrepressible Louis Armstrong at bay, beginning with mandatory rehearsals. Louis had no use for rehearsals and took an intense dislike to Goodman. "I remember you in Chicago," he said, "when you were sitting under Jimmy Noone, trying to learn something. Now your head's got fat." Wherever they performed, Louis outplayed and outclowned Benny. While the clarinetist was on stage, audience members milled about the lobby, smoking, until Louis began to blow, when they returned to their seats. While Benny played his standard forty-minute set, Louis stretched his out to well over an hour. One night, when they were supposed to close the show by playing together, Benny announced Louis, who refused to appear on stage. Benny was so furious that when he got backstage he took a glass of Scotch and soda and hurled it at the wall. He complained bitterly that Louis clowned on stage with Velma Middleton rather than playing honest-to-God music. Eventually, Benny became ill, entered a Boston hospital with suspected heart trouble, and the tour ground to a halt, to the relief of all concerned.

Several years later, Goodman came to the conclusion that the disastrous tour was actually Joe Glaser's fault, and he decided to make amends by inviting Louis and Lucille to dinner. "Are you crazy?" Louis said to his wife. "I don't want to have dinner with that motherfucker."

Louis's ideas about music, jazz, and performing were by now fixed, and most nights he played tunes drawn from a repertoire of about two dozen jazz standards. This was fine with Glaser, who wanted his musicians to play nothing but hits, and Louis was happy to oblige. He opened each set with "When It's Sleepy Time Down South," and proceeded through a predictable mixture including "Basin Street Blues," "Indiana," "When the Saints Go Marching In," "Rockin' Chair," "Muskrat Ramble," and "Back o' Town Blues." Despite the air of predictability surrounding them, Louis's performances continued to sparkle. Although he was more disdainful than ever of developments in jazz—developments he had once embodied—he continued to be an ingratiating, amusing, and, on occasion, dazzling performer. The great irony of this phase of his life was that the less interesting his music became, the more widespread was his acceptance. In the public mind, Louis Armstrong was synonymous with jazz, even though he no longer had much to do with the current jazz scene. While the condition of his aging chops varied from night to night, and he was bedeviled by a fearsome callus that had formed on his upper lip, the legacy of years of blowing too long and hard, his singing acquired new authority and conviction. Time had taken its toll on his facility with the trumpet, but it had burnished his instantly familiar voice. Indeed, part of the appeal of his persona was the contrast between his vaudeville hijinks and his mellow crooning, suggesting that a new, rather more dignified Louis Armstrong was struggling to emerge from the shadow of the all-too-familiar clown.

Wherever he went, Louis held court in his dressing room, where he attracted the most varied entourage in show business. "He'd be sittin' down in his underwear with a towel around his lap, one around his shoulders, an' that white handkerchief on his head, and he'd put that grease around his lips. Look like a minstrel man," said Danny Barker, the jazz guitarist, of the spectacle. "And in the room, you see maybe two nuns. You see a streetwalker dressed all up in flaming clothes. You see a guy come out of a penitentiary. You see a blind man sitting there. You see a rabbi. You see a priest. Liable to see maybe two policemen or detectives. You see a judge. All of them different levels of society in the dressing room and he's talking to all of 'em. 'Sister So and so, do you know Slick Sam over there? This is Slick Sam, an old friend of mine. . . .' 'Slick Sam, meet Rabbi Goldstein over there, he's a friend of mine, rabbi good man, religious man. Sister Margaret, do you know Rabbi Goldstein? Amelia, this is Rosie, good time Rosie, girl used to work in a show with me years ago.' " The party went on into the night, right through to the dawn. Even Clarence, Louis's adopted son, now fully grown, joined the entourage. "I see no reason why I should expect him to go out and get a job," Louis said of Clarence. "He has a tendency to be rather nervous. I am sure it came from that fall. I always see that he is with people who understand him and know how to treat him and keep him happy." In practice, that meant keeping Clarence close to him, a part of his wonderful world. Everyone, saint and sinner (since he was both, he drew no distinctions), was welcome to it. Many came to visit, and some wanted to dwell there with him forever.

Throughout the early and mid-1950s, Louis continued to mine his receding youth for nuggets, both musical and literary. During his spare hours in unfamiliar hotel and dressing rooms, his typewriter was his constant companion. When he was alone, he didn't blow, he typed, his mind infused with potent marijuana. And when he typed, he inevitably turned to reminiscing about the good ol' days in New Orleans, and the lost world of Mayann, Black Benny, Joe Oliver, and the other unforgettable characters of his early years.

Of course, his tale was not quite in keeping with the carefully tended "Satchmo" persona he projected. It contained too much blood and sex, too many prostitutes and flashing knives to be consistent with the wholesome image America showed to itself in the fifties. The legacy of slavery, the havoc it had wreaked on black families, and the continuing oppression of the black man were all terrifyingly vivid, because they were real. As he recaptured his struggles on paper, Louis saw in his own life and in the lives of those he had known cause for anger and resentment, but also for celebration, mirth, and love. Amassing fragments of autobiographical manuscript, he increasingly felt a sense of mission about recording his actual life story for posterity, for he wanted people to know him as he was, not as they perceived him through a lens clouded by bigotry or sentimentality.

For several years, specimens of his writing had been appearing in an eclectic mix of publications: an account of his most recent trip to Europe in genteel *Holiday*, a raw childhood reminiscence in hairy-chested *True*, his delirious letters in *Down Beat* and *Esquire*, a rambling account of his marriages in *Ebony* ("Why I Like Dark Women"), even a critique of a biography of Jelly Roll Morton in *The New York Times Book Review*. These were all written by Louis himself, not ghostwriters. "I have to write between shows," Louis explained to a friend in February 1952, "and you can imagine, trying to write, and shaking hands with your fans at the same time. . . . So you can tell everybody that Ol' Satchmo has octopus hands. I have my tape recorder right here by my right side [and] pretty near all of my recordings, on reels, so when I listen to my records I can get food for thought, since I'm writing my life story . . . I'd gladly live it over again, if I had the chance. In fact, I'm looking forward to another year before I die. Hmm. Who said something about dying?"

Despite the solemn implications of the deed, he was now caught up in writing his life story. By the standards of the jazz world, Louis had lived a long and full life and had reached a great age. So many of the great horn players had died young, and now that Louis was past fifty, he became attuned to the whisper of mortality. Before he went, he urgently needed to tell the truth of his New Orleans childhood, in his own words, without a meddling, if well-meaning ghostwriter.

On he typed with his "octopus hands," tossing out an anecdote here, a chapter there, and by 1952 had completed several hundred typewritten pages covering his life until he left New Orleans in 1922. He anticipated this would be the first of two volumes. It was strong stuff, tales of whores and knife fights and pimps—too strong, perhaps, for an American publisher— but in postwar France, where he was idolized, his autobiographical manuscript instantly found a publisher, Editions René Julliard, whose translator, Madeleine Gautier, deftly converted Louis's unsophisticated, eloquent prose into congenial, colloquial French. "*En 1900, anneé de ma naissance,*" the book began, "*mon père, Willie Armstrong, et ma mère, May Ann—alias Mayann—habitaient une petite rue dénommeé James Alley.*" *Ma Nouvelle Orléans*, as the book was called, was published on October 1, 1952. Thus it was that Louis first told the full story of his youth in a foreign tongue.

On the strength of its success in France, Louis's book finally found an American publisher, Prentice-Hall, willing to bring out the lurid tale in the language in which Louis wrote it. Two years later, in 1954, *Satchmo: My Life in New Orleans*, appeared in the United States and was quickly acknowledged as an essential document about both Louis and the origins of jazz. It was, in many places, inconsistent, repetitive, and disorderly, but it was nonetheless a remarkable account—pure Satchmo. He took great pride in the book and began typing a sequel covering his years in Chicago, his experiences with Joe Oliver at the Lincoln Gardens, and his discovery of that wonder drug, marijuana. He showed the pages he had typed to Glaser, pages discussing marijuana and the mob, and Glaser, who had no desire to draw unwanted attention to his own transgressions or Louis's, destroyed them.

Rather than encourage Louis in the risky business of writing, Glaser sold him six ways from Sunday. He kept Louis Armstrong and the All Stars constantly on the road, racing from one gig to the next. Then there were the movie roles, about one a year, mostly in forgettable flicks, with Louis and the All Stars appearing as themselves, playing a specialty number, and briefly heating up the movie. The film appearances added little to Louis's stature, but they were extremely lucrative. For seven days' work on *The Strip* (1951), the All Stars received twenty thousand dollars for blasting out such staples as "Basin Street Blues" and "When the Saints Go Marching In." For appearing in *Glory Alley*, Louis received twenty-five thousand dollars. In 1953, Louis played himself in *The Glenn Miller Story*, starring James Stewart. He spent two days on the set, led the All Stars in a bang-up rendition of "Basin Street Blues," and collected five thousand dollars for his trouble. Even in that brief time, he made a memorable impression on Stewart, who solicited advice on how to prevent sore lips caused by blowing the trombone. "Yeah, daddy," Louis shot back. "When you go home tonight, have your old lady sit on your face." Next morning, Stewart gave Louis the high sign.

Only in *High Society* was Louis able to make more than a token contribution to the proceedings. His appearance came as an afterthought, yet the entire film coalesced around his charismatic presence. *High Society* started to take shape in the early months of 1956, when Sol Siegel, a veteran producer, began to package Philip Barry's society comedy, *The Philadelphia Story*, as a musical for M-G-M. Siegel enticed Cole Porter to write the score, and he signed Bing Crosby, Grace Kelly, and Frank Sinatra to reenact roles memorably performed by Cary Grant, Katharine Hepburn, and James Stewart in the 1940 screen version. As the project gathered momentum, the setting shifted to Newport, Rhode Island, another society haven, but also, since 1954, the home of the country's leading jazz festival. It was hard to imagine a more unlikely setting for a boisterous gathering of

jazz musicians than aristocratic Newport, but one of the town's most prominent citizens, Louis P. Lorillard, heir to the tobacco fortune and a jazz
enthusiast, lent his backing and his financial support to the endeavor.

Lorillard and his cronies had the good sense to bring in a talented
young promoter, George Wein, who ran a nightclub, Storyville, at the
Copley Square Hotel in Boston, and could deal equally well with the Newport blue bloods and the jazz world. From the start, Wein faced formidable
negotiating challenges, for once jazz musicians and their managers learned
who was backing the project, they asked for huge sums. Wein patiently
explained that the Newport Jazz Festival was a nonprofit venture, but on
the other hand, he needed stars to attract audiences—stars such as Louis
Armstrong—which meant he had to deal with Joe Glaser. Wein also had to
contend with the wealthy and powerful Newport residents who were aghast
at the prospect of a jazz festival in their pristine summer colony. "They'll
never be able to do anything about it," Wein insisted in 1955, "because the
Festival is backed by one of their most respected members, Louis Lorillard,
who will fight for his convictions even at the expense of being branded a
traitor to his own class." Despite these many obstacles, Wein managed to
make the Festival a fixture, partly because his own tastes in jazz leaned to
the traditional and show-bizzy. He favored the venerable Louis and Ella
and Duke over younger, more experimental cats, and this was just fine with
the audiences who came to Newport.

Taking his inspiration from the Festival, Sol Siegel signed Louis Armstrong and the All Stars to appear in *High Society*. For once, they spent
more than a matter of hours on the set; Louis and the other musicians
devoted twenty-three working days to the project, and Glaser received
seventy-five thousand dollars for the entire band. Their fee was modest in
comparison to the two hundred thousand dollars that Crosby and Sinatra
each received. Siegel had all his pieces in place, and although they appeared
to be mismatched, a respectable movie began to take shape. Louis was
external to the bittersweet love story at the heart of the movie, but the
script accorded him pride of place. He appears as himself, a black man in a
white world, a musician among playboys and socialites and sets the tone for
the movie in an opening vignette in which he and the All Stars, crowded
into a taxi on the way to Newport, sing the "High Society Calypso," the
most charming sequence in the entire picture. Throughout, Louis has no
realistic social interaction with anyone else, except in a musical context, and

the All Stars remain a closed society, permitted to mingle with whites until the party ends, and they disappear into their own world.

Bing Crosby came closest to crossing the color lines drawn in the script. Crosby had been Louis's friend and student for twenty years, and their rapport is apparent in all their scenes. Crosby conveys the impression that he genuinely appreciates Louis's art, and when they sing a duet, "That's Jazz," he shows that he understands it.

High Society opened in August 1956. The production surpassed Louis's other movies, yet it suffered by comparison with its esteemed source material, *The Philadelphia Story*. Crosby's performance left reviewers cold. "He strokes his pipe with more affection than he strokes Miss Kelly's porcelain arms," said Bosley Crowther in the *New York Times*. But all the critics applauded Louis Armstrong. "It is bulging-eyed Louis Armstrong whacking out 'That's Jazz' with Bing Crosby, blasting a hot wedding march, and jingling a 'High Society Calypso' who steals the show and provides its best punch," said one reviewer, echoing a universal sentiment.

When Louis finished work for *High Society*, he went back into the recording studio. Although the All Stars had been performing constantly since 1947, they had spent little time in front of a microphone during their first seven years. All that changed in 1954, when Glaser developed a novel strategy for dealing with record labels. Instead of signing Louis to long-term contracts, the common practice, Glaser moved his client from one company to another, often for a single album. After his years with Decca, Louis suddenly found himself ricocheting between RCA and its archrival, Columbia. The recording company executives loved Louis but loathed his quasi-hoodlum manager, who played them off one another. Still, they knew they had no choice, and during the mid and late fifties, Louis Armstrong and the All Stars turned out a series of spectacular albums, largely as a result of talented producers who were knowledgeable about jazz and sympathetic to Louis's aims.

George Avakian, of Columbia Records, was the most talented of all, the smartest and most creative producer to record Louis. A gentle man, educated at Yale, his face framed by a carefully maintained beard, Avakian possessed an impeccable ear and an infatuation with state-of-the-art technology. He exploited the full potential of splicing, of multitrack recording, and, the moment it became available, stereo. His recordings were slick and beguiling, with wonderful sound, and his collaborations with Louis would hold to the same high standard—once he got past Glaser. Avakian succeeded because, he said, "Glaser was aware of the fact that his performers had to do something different. Otherwise, they'd get into a rut."

Glaser let Avakian have his way with an idea for a long-playing record called "Louis Armstrong Plays W. C. Handy." This was, of course, an ideal fit between performer and composer, for Handy's tunes, most of them as old as jazz itself, included "St. Louis Blues," "The Memphis Blues," and "Beale Street Blues." Preoccupied with Louis's touring schedule, Glaser gave Avakian and the Columbia engineers only three days in Chicago with Louis and the All Stars to record the entire album—July 12, 13, and 14, 1954. Avakian found it impossible to reach Louis to discuss the program in advance of the recording session. The All Stars were on the road, criss-crossing the country, and unavailable for consultation, but when Louis arrived in the studio, he scanned the list and said, "OK. I'm ready. Let's do them."

"He had not worked out specific routines," Avakian said. "He just had the first choruses worked out, and he made sure the guys knew exactly what changes they were going to play. He let me set the routines, because, he said, 'You know how it is, we go out on the road, we play each tune in the same sequence, and it's easy for us to get through the work.' And so he let me use my imagination on some of the sequencing." Avakian tried to banish Velma Middleton, whose singing and clowning with Louis continued to annoy the jazz cognoscenti, but Louis insisted she was family, so Velma stayed. Once the All Stars completed the sessions, Avakian took the tapes back to New York, where he spliced and edited the performances until they gleamed. Every note was clear and correct. Louis's horn had never been recorded better, so brassy you could almost taste it, and the microphones captured the rasp of his voice together with a warm resonance that made it seem he was singing softly in your ear.

The album functioned as a superb showcase for Handy's bittersweet art, and Avakian invited the elderly composer to the Columbia offices to hear the tapes as they were being edited. As Handy listened, there were "tears streaming from his sightless eyes." Louis, who was also there, tried to put Handy at ease. "Ain't no work, making records like this," he told the composer. "Them old time good ones, they play themselves, Mr. Handy. You get to blowing those beautiful changes right, and you have to play good. We was just having a ball, that's all." Here and there, Louis had taken liberties with Handy's music and lyrics, but his performances on "St. Louis Blues" and "Beale Street Blues," to name but two, stand as the definitive recordings of these tunes. Avakian was delighted with the result, which he believed would be remembered as the most significant and enjoyable album of his career. When it was released, the sales and critical reception were the best Louis had received in decades.

In September 1955, Avakian cajoled Louis into recording a tune that a number of other musicians had turned down, Kurt Weill's "Mack the Knife," from *The Threepenny Opera*. This was a dark, violent nightmare of a song, but it reminded Louis of the thugs he'd known and admired as a child in New Orleans, and he agreed to record it. Glaser allowed one night for the project. Louis entrusted the arrangements to his valet, Doc Pugh, who promptly lost them. Without preparation, Louis needed six takes spread over several sessions to get through the song. Avakian adroitly spliced them together, and the recording eventually sold over a million copies. It was on every jukebox in the land, until it was eclipsed by Bobby Darin's version. Louis's audiences began screaming for him to play the new hit, but Doc Pugh managed to lose the arrangements again. Finally, Louis promised an audience in Miami that he would play "Mack the Knife" the following night. "After the show," Avakian said, "he goes to the cashier, gets two rolls of dimes, goes down to the coffee shop with the musicians and the sheet music and starts pouring dimes into the jukebox, and he tells the guys, 'Copy out your part.' The following night, he's finally able to play his smash hit."

In stark contrast to Louis's casual approach to music, Glaser continued to rule the All Stars with his iron-fist-in-iron-glove style of management. George Avakian, alert to the adulation and prestige jazz received abroad, urged Glaser to send Louis on a more ambitious foreign tour, but Glaser always said, "No, they can't pay money."

Avakian replied, "Joe, what do you need the money for? It's an opportunity to do something that nobody has ever done before."

"I can get $10,000 a night for him here," Glaser countered.

"Joe, the money doesn't count, this is what he should do!"

As Glaser continued to stonewall Avakian, Dizzy Gillespie and Benny Goodman, among other musicians, demonstrated there was much favorable publicity to be had performing behind the Iron Curtain. Finally, Glaser decided to outdo everyone and send Louis and the All Stars on a three-month tour of West Africa and Europe. Sponsored by the State Department, the tour was trailed by a crew from CBS News, who planned to assemble the footage into an installment of Edward R. Murrow's news program, *See It Now*. As it happened, Murrow had absolutely no feeling for jazz, and Louis made him ill at ease. Nonetheless, the correspondent known for bringing Senator Joseph McCarthy to his knees remained suavely professional as he grilled Louis at six o'clock one morning in Paris, while the CBS cameras rolled:

> MURROW: *Now what's this rock-and-roll stuff? I don't dig that at all.*
> ARMSTRONG: *Well, it's the essence of gutbucket, see what I mean? It's the essence of things we did, but we didn't tear up seats in the theater. The people sat down and listened to what we played. Now you take the youngsters, they figure in order to be on the ball, they gotta take a razor and cut seats, and well, they didn't enjoy music like that in those days. . . .*
> MURROW: *Now, what's "cool?"*
> ARMSTRONG: *Cool? In my estimation, it's a cat that's playin' a trumpet, and he's too lazy to hit the high notes.*
> MURROW: *Now, what's "bop?"*
> ARMSTRONG: Bop? *What is that?*
> MURROW: *I don't know, I'm asking you.*
> ARMSTRONG: *A passin' fancy, that's it. . . .*
> MURROW: *Now, what's a "cat?"*
> ARMSTRONG: *Cat? A cat can be anybody from the guy in the gutter to a lawyer, doctor, the biggest man and the lowest man, but if he's in there with a good heart and enjoyin' the same music together, he's a cat.*
> MURROW: *Well, you know, listening to you tonight, I think I became a cat for the first time.*

In May 1956, Louis Armstrong, the All Stars, and the CBS news crew arrived in Accra, the capital of Ghana, where a crowd of ten thousand greeted them. After all these years, Louis was accustomed to acclaim, but the welcome in Accra was something special. "After all, my ancestors came from here and I still have African blood in me," he said. He was particularly struck by the resemblance he bore to the Ghanaians; it was more than the color of skin. His features, his physique, even his facial expressions appeared distinctly Ghanaian. Like many descendants of slaves, Louis had no firm idea of his ancestors' origins, but it was true that many slaves came from this part of Africa, and Louis was now persuaded he had found his roots. It was exhilarating to be a black man in a black land, not part of the minority for once, but a member of the overwhelming majority.

Louis's open-air concerts in Ghana drew crowds intrigued by the arrival of the best-known black American celebrity. His first performance, on May 24, drew a throng estimated at one hundred thousand, far more than would have turned out to see him in the United States, where he was ubiquitous and taken somewhat for granted. "Women left their kitchens with babes on their backs to pay homage to Mr. Armstrong," the *New York Times* remarked. The local police were fearful that Louis's hot jazz would provoke a huge riot. "When you play fast," a police chief warned him, "these natives can't stand it. They'll riot all over the place from joy." "OK, Daddy," Louis said, "I'll give 'em a little slow beat. You know, that ol' four o'clock in the morning music." With that, the All Stars launched into the most soporific song in their repertoire, "When It's Sleepy Time Down South," which quelled any restiveness. After the performance, said the *Times*, "crowds lined the streets and a mile-long procession followed Mr. Armstrong to his hotel."

There were other great moments. At Gold Coast University, he performed before a gathering of seventy tribal chiefs, whose drummers played fantastic rhythms for him. After listening to the beat, he put his gleaming trumpet to his lips, and began to improvise the wildest "Stomping at the Savoy" ever heard, while a university dean, still dreading the prospect of a riot, admonished Louis to keep it low and slow. Louis responded by mopping his face with a white handkerchief. It was ninety-seven degrees, and he was feeling the heat as well as the beat.

On another occasion, he performed before the Prime Minister of Ghana, Kwame Nkrumah. He had acquired a taste for jazz as a college student in the United States, but could not afford to see Louis in person. Now, only months from taking his country to independence, Nkrumah helped promote the popularity of jazz in Africa, bringing the music back to its roots. Louis rose to the challenge of this performance brilliantly, and chose "What Did I Do to Be So Black and Blue?" as his centerpiece. Transfixing the audience with this musical commiseration and celebration of their blackness, Louis sang with unequaled intensity before the man who was in the throes of creating an independent African nation.

The entire tour was a resounding success. Wherever he went, Louis displayed a deft touch for uttering apparently artless but carefully meditated messages of goodwill and peace. He seemed to conquer the world effortlessly with a melody and a grin.

When he returned home from the tour, George Avakian assembled a jazz concert at Lewisohn Stadium in New York City on July 14, 1956. Dave Brubeck, a member of the Columbia roster, opened the program, and Louis, playing with full symphony orchestra conducted by Leonard Bernstein, closed it. Afterward, Louis had a story to tell about working with a classical musician such as Bernstein. "He said, 'Now, when you get to this cadenza, and you get a little nervous, well, just shorten it.' I said, 'Okay, daddy.' Well, I warm up at home. I hit the stage, I'm ready. From the first rehearsal on, we wailed. Well, from then on, he got confidence; it don't take long for a person to relax once they hear me go down with the arrangement. After that, he got himself straightened. After the performance he liked to shake my hand off."

Glaser got a double bounce from the African tour and subsequent concert. CBS presented a half-hour account of Louis's travels on Murrow's *See It Now*, and subsequently released it as an hour-long documentary, *Satchmo the Great*, which received encouraging reviews and helped build Louis into an icon of the era, the personification of freedom, "Ambassador Satch." Despite the hype, serious American jazz partisans took Louis's warm reception abroad as proof of the bigotry and artistic barrenness of the United States during the McCarthy era. Foreigners, they insisted, understood America and its artists better than Americans did. "Louis and Dizzy now roam the world, our best 'ambassadors,' sponsored by a State Department that only yesterday shunned jazz and all music like the plague," wrote Rudi Blesh, in a representative outburst. "To everyone except Americans, jazz and the spirituals are *the* American music because they express what America stands for or, at least, once stood for. . . . Here is the universal language of freedom and hope." But it was a language spoken more widely abroad than at home.

This latest development in jazz was remarkable. What had begun as a highly idiosyncratic music blending black and white elements, developed by self-taught musicians in the country's most eccentric city, New Orleans, traveled up the Mississippi River to Chicago, where recording companies and radio stations disseminated it across the country. The moment it went national, jazz drastically altered popular music. But when it hit New York, it changed yet again, underwent further refinements, and split into two strands—traditional and progressive. Even more surprising, the State Department, a branch of government not generally recognized as a hotbed of music appreciation, saw fit to spread jazz to those parts of the world that were most hostile to the United States. Though still suspect in its homeland, the voice of an oppressed minority, jazz now became the Sound of America for the rest of the world, the music of freedom, celebration, and happiness, a symbol of a nation of vastly different ethnic groups blending into the most wonderful noise ever heard. This was the trajectory of jazz, the music first heard in the brothels, funeral processions, and honky-tonks of New Orleans only sixty years before.

All of this globe-trotting and spreading the gospel of jazz took a considerable toll on Louis's marriage. He became increasingly insistent that much as he loved Lucille, his horn still came first. To make matters worse, during the brief intervals that he was at home, he occasionally indulged in hijinks that were not exactly to her taste. He had long ago relinquished his collection of stag films, but he still enjoyed soft-core pornography in written form. He typed out lengthy pornographic narratives, "Doctor Ulrich," "Tortures of Love," and "Exercises in Love," all of them adapted from stories that he had come across in his reading. "Moving the plump thighs apart, he closely examined the delicious, full lipped cunt: soon his finger was inserted and found the firm barrier to further progress," ran one typical passage from "Doctor Ulrich." "Then he drew it out, and patted the full growth of hair about the Mound of Venus, while contemplating the lovely lines beneath, was impelled to kneel before that altar and press his lips lovingly on the tender spot." Louis did not simply read these stories to himself—he invited Lucille and various friends to recite sections of the story aloud. He hugely enjoyed bawdy joshing and storytelling, dirty limericks, and lewd jokes of all types, but Lucille emphatically did not. She hadn't grown up among the prostitutes of Storyville, and didn't share her husband's fascination with erotica.

When his schedule allowed him to spend a week or two in the same place, she often joined him, and hidden tensions erupted into the open. "A lot of times I would leave him, I would say, 'I just can't take this anymore and I think I'll go home,' " Lucille admitted. "And as soon as I'd get home, [Louis would say], 'When the hell are you going to get back here?' And I'd say, 'Well, I think you need to be by yourself a little while.' When I'd get back, I don't know what happened, but the boys would always tell me, 'We're so glad you're back, we've been catching hell.' " Still heeding Black Benny's increasingly irrelevant advice about having more than one woman at all times, Louis felt entitled to extramarital involvements, and he tried to cajole Lucille into looking the other way. He fooled himself into thinking she was content to let him to stray. "Know what I always tell my Lucille?" he said to a friend. " 'Pay no mind to all them chippies, honey. You just remember you my one an' only missus.' "

In fact, Lucille minded these dalliances very much, and they were not always as superficial as he pretended. They filled in the empty places of life on the road, as well as the empty places in his heart. For years, Louis had wanted a child of his own. He loved Clarence like a son, but he wanted a biological heir as well. Barney Bigard, the All Stars's clarinetist, recalled that Louis "had a little gal called 'Sweetie,' and she got pregnant, but not by Louis. But Louis thought it was by him, because she was telling him that. Oh, he was proud. He was going to be a daddy. He had a bag, and all the change he had in his pocket, plus dollars, he'd put it in his bag. I asked him what he was doing that for. He said, 'That's for my kid when it's born.' By the time this kid was born, that bag was stuffed with coins and dollars and five and tens. So he gave it to the little gal. He was walking around like a peacock. He started talking to Lucille. He said, 'Lucille, how'd you feel if you adopt my kid?' She said, 'What kid?' He said, 'My kid. I got a baby by Sweetie.' She said, 'Who told you you got a baby by Sweetie? You better not bring no baby around here. You couldn't make a baby with a pencil. Now you're talking about your kid. She done fool you, and she's got a boyfriend. He must have done it, and he's telling her to tell you that you're the father.' She said, 'You sure are stupid.' " With those words, Lucille shattered the elaborate delusion he had devised about his girlfriend's child. In years to come, he wistfully maintained the hope of having a son or daughter of his own, but this episode taught him that it was better to love his women wisely than too well.

As Louis suffered the pangs of thwarted fatherhood, George Avakian made elaborate plans for a series of "Louis Armstrong Plays——" recordings. Fats Waller, Jelly Roll Morton, Joe Oliver, and so on—Avakian intended Louis to run the gamut of jazz figures—but he was able to record only the "Satch Plays Fats" album before Glaser demanded more money from Columbia, and the company balked. "I was very upset about it," Avakian said of this painful episode. "Glaser was saying, 'You put Louis on the map with those albums and "Mack the Knife," ' " yet when the time came to continue, he treated Columbia and me as though we were trying to cash in. Louis wanted to do those projects, but he said, 'Well, you're going to have to deal with Mr. Glaser. I want to do it, but, after all, he's done for me, I have to do whatever he wants.' Louis was really sad about it." Predictably, Joe Glaser was untroubled by loyalty or gratitude. "Louis is going to record for the highest bidder from now on. He's not going to sign any more exclusive contracts," he told Avakian.

The next thing Louis knew, he was working without the All Stars for another producer, Norman Granz, at a new record label devoted solely to jazz, Verve, in a brief, brilliant collaboration with Ella Fitzgerald, the supreme jazz vocalist. At a stroke, Louis left mainstream popular music, where Glaser usually positioned him, for the small, high-octane world of "pure" jazz. He was among the cultists now, those who saw jazz as an art form, not a bawdy, minstrel-influenced branch of popular entertainment. Verve reflected the discriminating taste of its founder, ruler, and presiding genius, Norman Granz. Twelve years earlier, Granz had made his name promoting swinging jam sessions at the Los Angeles Philharmonic and other classy venues. "Jazz at the Philharmonic" soon became Granz's specialty, his way of dignifying what he perceived as the neglected artistry of African-American artists. Thus was the race record reborn as artistic jazz. Granz made no concessions to Jim Crow practices still afflicting the jazz world. He included antidiscrimination clauses in contracts and fervently championed his artists such as Ella Fitzgerald, even as he made a fortune from their music. In a 1957 article, *Esquire* called him "The Jazz Millionaire."

After years of managing jazz musicians and promoting concerts, Granz launched a series of record labels, culminating with the creation of Verve in 1956. At Verve, Granz presented his musicians in austere settings designed to highlight their abilities, offering up their compositions as if they were gleaming jewels arrayed on a background of black velvet. Jazz had already made it from New Orleans's streets and brothels to the nation's nightclubs, dance halls, and theaters; Granz's mission was to elevate it to the status of art in opera houses and symphony halls. Something was gained in the process—jazz gained stature in the eyes of critics and cultists, who were delighted that musicians such as Ella Fitzgerald and Art Tatum were getting the respect they deserved. But something was lost—the fun and spontaneity of jazz were in danger of disappearing amid the musical mastery. One of the traditional charms of jazz was its lack of pretension, its come-as-you-are approach to music. Granz upset that balance by distributing instructions titled "How to Act at a Jazz Concert." "Sure, it's O.K. to get excited and applaud and even cheer . . . your favorite trumpeter on 'Perdido' or 'Cottontail' or 'Flying Home,'" the program warned, "but why not keep quiet when these same artists play 'Body and Soul' or some other beautiful ballad. . . . And another thing, shouting for numbers you want to hear isn't necessary. RELAX! BE PATIENT!" This side of Granz drove people crazy, his self-importance and relentless one-upmanship. He was usually right, and he never let anyone forget it.

For the time being, Louis was on his own in Granz's kingdom. Without the All Stars, without the Satchmo persona, without the mask of the entertainer, vaudeville clown, grinning Uncle Tom, and all the other *shtick* on which he'd always relied. Louis was stripped to the essentials: his voice, his instrument, and his soul. "Ella and Louis" was recorded on August 15, 1956, in Los Angeles. A year later, Granz reunited the two in "Ella and Louis Again." Each record contained spare, masterful renditions of love songs at relaxed, almost soporific tempos. Their most daring work together, recorded in the course of a single day, August 18, 1957, was an adaptation of George Gershwin's 1935 opera, *Porgy and Bess*. Over the years, dozens of black entertainers and musicians have reinterpreted this work, but Louis and Ella brought special poignancy and clarity to its melancholy harmonies.

In reality, Louis didn't have the vocal range or the training to handle the score, but what he lacked in technique he more than made up for in authenticity. All the albums Louis made for Granz turned out to be highly distinguished efforts. What might have been an occasion for suffocating seriousness became instead a revelation of the dignified, reflective, occasionally somber side of Louis Armstrong. The performances were also emotionally rich, largely because he worked so beautifully with Ella. Her plush voice complemented the deep, even tragic rumble in which he sang. For all their restraint, these were the most dramatic, haunting performances Louis had ever recorded.

As far as Glaser was concerned, restraint was just the problem. These Verve albums, elegant as they might be, were *collaborations*, and while Louis didn't exactly take a back seat to Ella, he wasn't the unchallenged star, either. To Glaser's way of thinking, Louis was *twice* the performer anyone else was, because he both sang *and* blew his horn. The truth was that Louis's lip troubled him throughout the Verve recordings. He had cleverly disguised the handicap by singing more than blowing, and when he did blow, he didn't push it or reach for notes. In the end, his understated trumpet work underscored the importance of his vocals. Still, the mellow approach to the material made him sound ancient, as if he might lay down his horn at any time and walk off into the sunset. Glaser didn't want an introverted Louis, he wanted a star belting out those hits. He pulled Louis out of Verve as soon as Granz's "artistic" recordings were done. It was time to get Louis back to basics, back to the All Stars and their reliable hits— time to put the happy Satchmo mask firmly back in place. He soon found the ideal vehicle.

At the end of 1956, Glaser moved his client back to Decca for a grand, multidisc retrospective of Louis Armstrong's entire career. It would be a "musical autobiography" recorded under the direction of Milt Gabler, a producer who had worked comfortably with both Glaser and Armstrong since 1950. The reasons behind the change of label weren't quite as straightforward as Glaser pretended. At the time, he claimed to be able to obtain as much as fifty thousand dollars for a Louis Armstrong album, yet he told Gabler that he would be willing to cut the price in half simply because he, Joe Glaser, liked Milt. This may have been the case, but the real reason was that Glaser wanted Louis to be the centerpiece rather than share the limelight with a composer or a producer's schemes. Before he became a record producer, Gabler had run the Commodore Record Shop on 42nd Street, a location well known to jazz collectors. He was a true believer in jazz and in Louis Armstrong, whom he had known for twenty years and revered for as long as he could remember, and he was as concerned with promoting the Satchmo image as Joe Glaser was. With his simple, self-effacing approach, Gabler was able to lure Louis back to Decca.

Gabler did have one novel suggestion for the project: he wanted Louis to narrate brief introductions to the songs. The idea had worked well with a Bing Crosby retrospective, and Glaser was encouraged to let Louis try the same thing, if only because the narration called attention to his client. Based on his previous experiences recording the All Stars, Gabler was also concerned with the effects of Glaser's constant overbooking. "They were tired, always tired, and I wanted them fresh," Gabler recalls, "so I told Joe Glaser, 'I don't want you to book them in New York City while we're doing the album. The only job they'll have will be the recording session, and I'll pay the men double to make up for their not working at the club at night.' " Gabler offered full price—fifty thousand dollars—for the arrangement, and Glaser naturally agreed.

Gabler scheduled the first sessions, for December 11, 12, 13, and 14, 1956, in Decca's Studio A, at 50 West 47th Street in New York. Working from circumspect arrangements commissioned for the occasion, Louis and the All Stars, augmented with several brass musicians and Edmond Hall on clarinet, played tunes drawn from the entire spectrum of jazz and Tin Pan Alley standards: "If I Could Be with You," "Lazy River," "I Can't Give You Anything But Love," "On the Sunny Side of the Street," "I Can't Believe That You're in Love with Me," "Body and Soul," "When You're Smiling," "Some of These Days," "I Surrender Dear," "Georgia on My Mind," "Mahogany Hall Stomp," "High Society," "Memories of You," and "Them There Eyes." On January 23, 24, and 28, 1957, they returned to record "Hotter Than That," "Gut Bucket Blues," "Weary Blues," "Potato Head Blues," "Cornet Chop Suey," "Mandy Make Up Your Mind," "Wild Man Blues," "Gully Low Blues," "Everybody Loves My Baby," "Heebie Jeebies," "King of the Zulus," "Frog-i-more Rag," "Georgia Grind," "Snag It," "Canal Street Blues," "Dippermouth Blues," "You Rascal You," "Knockin' a Jug," "See See Rider," "Reckless Blues," "Trouble in Mind," "Courthouse Blues," among many other songs.

The marathon recording sessions seemed to take nothing out of Louis, who was, if anything, invigorated by the music, not to mention the food and libations Gabler had cleverly arranged to be available to the musicians at all times. Louis had recorded these tunes before, but his familiarity with them only increased the stakes, for the unspoken truth was that each time Louis had returned to these songs, especially the celebrated titles he had recorded with the Hot Five thirty years earlier, he had failed to recapture their freshness, and had inadvertently tarnished their luster in the process. In only a very few instances was a later Armstrong recording preferable to an earlier version, but under Gabler's direction, he was able to reinterpret his classics with new mastery and confidence. For years, Louis had been haunted by the ghost of his younger, faster, sleeker self, the Louis Armstrong of the Hot Five, whose lengthening shadow obscured the middle-aged Louis Armstrong of the present day. But in these sessions, he managed the considerable feat of reversing years of decline and lived up to, and, in many instances, even surpassed those youthful, zany Hot Five-era performances. His latest recordings of "Dippermouth Blues," and "Georgia Grind," to name but two examples, showed that he was still capable of devising solos equal to those that had made him famous, and his singing, honed through three decades of experience, was clearly superior to anything he had accomplished in the 1920s, when he shouted or scatted, but rarely *sang*. His latest performances were so eloquent that the rather stilted introductions to the songs, written by Leonard Feather, proved distracting and were eventually dropped in rereleases of the collection.

One telling omission from the retrospective was "West End Blues," with its famous, bruising opening cadenza. In a recent live recording, he had mangled this sacred tune, but this exception was insignificant in the face of his overall accomplishment. Much of the jazz world had long since written him off, insisting he was doing nothing new and couldn't hope to live up to the musician he once was. Louis proved them wrong. He had devised the vocabulary of jazz, and these newly minted recordings—the four long-playing discs that made up Decca's *Satchmo: A Musical Autobiography*—became the definitive textbook of his art.

For a performer who had supposedly ceased to be interesting twenty-five years earlier, Louis had been extraordinarily productive in recent months. He had published his memoirs, starred in *High Society*, toured

West Africa in the capacity of "Ambassador Satch," launched a hit record ("Mack the Knife"), made several peerless recordings with Ella Fitzgerald, and recorded his "musical autobiography." Even more remarkably, he had done all this in addition to his usual touring with the All Stars and guest appearances on television variety shows. Then, in the fall of 1957, Louis did something that seemed so out of character that his career nearly blew up in his face. He was getting tired of playing the world-famous minstrel known as "Satchmo." Times were changing, and so was he, and faster than anyone imagined.

The first sign of trouble occurred in February 1957. Louis was playing a concert in Knoxville, Tennessee, before a segregated audience: two thousand whites, a thousand blacks. While he played "Back o' Town Blues," someone tossed a stick of dynamite at the theater. No one was hurt in the explosion, and Louis deadpanned, "That's all right, folks, it's just the phone." Over the years, he had performed before some unruly crowds, especially in the South. Knives had flashed, shots had been fired, but a bomb—that was something new and ugly. It was later discovered that a local militant group, the White Citizens Council, who sought to protest the theater's accommodating both races, had been responsible. Inevitably, Louis was asked if he would stop touring, and just as inevitably, he replied, "Man, I'll play anywhere they'll listen."

But that was not the case in July, when he was scheduled to make his annual appearance at the Newport Jazz Festival. On his arrival, he was informed that since the Festival was celebrating his birthday, he would have to appear in each set. Furthermore, since Ella Fitzgerald was also appearing at the Festival, Velma Middleton, the All Stars's vocalist, couldn't go on. "I'm playing with my band and my singer and none of this other shit," Louis declared. Even Joe Glaser couldn't make him back down. Louis ranted for hours, and when photographers stalked him, he turned to them, wearing only a head rag, and ordered them to keep clear of his dressing room. Eventually he appeared on stage, played a spirited set with the All Stars (including Velma) and old friends such as Kid Ory and Jack Teagarden, and left, trailing streams of controversy.

The crisis came on September 19, when Louis and the All Stars arrived in Grand Fork, North Dakota, for a performance. Before he went onstage, he happened to catch television coverage of the school desegregation crisis in Little Rock, Arkansas. He learned that Governor Orval Faubus was using the National Guard to prevent desegregation, and he saw pictures of black children walking fearfully to school as a crowd of whites heckled them; and he watched footage of a white man spitting in the face of a black girl.

At the moment, Louis was preparing to embark on another international goodwill tour in the guise of Ambassador Satch, the personification of the American dream, and the American way of life and all its freedoms, but after watching these traumatic events in Little Rock, he was damned if he was going to stand up and grin hypocritically before foreign audiences, pretending that his country was the land of the free with equality for all. "The way they are treating my people in the South, the government can go to hell," he told a reporter as he shaved in his North Dakota hotel room. "It's getting so bad, a colored man hasn't got any country." He laced into President Dwight Eisenhower, whom he called "two-faced," with "no guts." As for Faubus, Louis dismissed him as an "uneducated plow boy." The international goodwill tour was off. "The people over there ask me what's wrong with my country, what am I supposed to say?" His logic was irrefutable, but in the South, such words were tantamount to a lynching, and in show business, they were suicide.

Yet Louis was merely giving voice to what so many other blacks and jazz musicians had always felt. But Louis? *Satchmo?* No one could believe it, not his fans, not those who knew him well, not Joe Glaser, not even Lucille. For a time, it was widely assumed the reporter had fabricated Louis's angry remarks, but he had diligently submitted the quotations to Louis for approval. And Louis had signed off on them and added, in his own writing, "Solid." There could be no doubt about their accuracy. His remarks, widely repeated over the next few weeks, seemed destined to destroy his career. The newspaper columnist Jim Bishop wrote, "I checked the newspaper files to see what Louis Armstrong had done for the people of his race. I haven't found anything. And now I ask the musician himself: 'What have you done for your people, except hurt them?' " Bishop called on the public to boycott Louis's performances and to avoid his television appearances. Nor were whites the only ones who trashed him. Sammy Davis Jr. lamely argued that Louis wasn't talking on behalf of all blacks, only himself ("Who cares about Sammy Davis Jr.?" said Glaser), and Adam Clayton Powell, Harlem's best-known politician, added his voice to the chorus of criticism.

Frenchy, Louis's white manager, tried telling the press that Louis was just shooting his mouth off. Louis countered with a clarification: "My people—the Negroes—are not looking for anything. We just want a square shake. But when I see on television and read about a crowd in Arkansas spitting on a little colored girl, I think I have the right to get sore." He then fired Frenchy, calling him a "menace to the colored people." Now that Louis had sunk his teeth into this issue, he wouldn't let go. He remained contemptuous of Faubus and said he would rather play in the Soviet Union than in the state of Arkansas. When Eisenhower dispatched federal troops to Arkansas to enforce integration, Louis fired off a telegram to the President: "If you decide to walk into the schools with the little colored kids, take me along, Daddy. God Bless you."

Louis's repeated outbursts attracted the scrutiny of the Federal Bureau of Investigation. Looking for signs of subversion or Communist affiliations in his actions and remarks, the FBI began to maintain a secret file on Louis Armstrong. As FBI files go, Louis's wasn't much. There was an unsubstantiated report concerning his use of marijuana in the Flamingo Hotel in Las Vegas. There were newspaper clippings concerning his remarks about Eisenhower and integration, and there were letters sent to the FBI Director, J. Edgar Hoover, both for and against Louis Armstrong. Reviewing the file, Hoover suggested that "Armstrong's life is a good argument against the theory that Negroes are inferior," and let the matter rest. Nevertheless, the mere existence of a secret FBI file indicated that Louis's outspoken defense of integration had reverberated at the highest levels in Washington and brought him under suspicion.

As time passed, he became even angrier, and New Orleans was his next target. Throughout his life, Louis had been exasperated by the racial codes enforced in the city where Jim Crow was born, but he loved the place deeply and realized that racism in New Orleans was never as simple and monolithic as it seemed. Still, a Louisiana law prohibited integrated bands like the All Stars from performing. Even after the law was ruled unconstitutional in 1956, the state continued to enforce it. No longer willing to tolerate intolerance, Louis refused to play in Louisiana at all. He would play in the Soviet Union, in Africa, across Europe and the United States, spreading the gospel of jazz throughout the world, but he would not play in his hometown. A prophet without honor, he was fully aware of the symbolic significance of this refusal. "I don't care if I ever see that city again," he insisted. "They treat me better all over the world than they do in my hometown. Ain't that stupid? Jazz was born there and I remember when it wasn't no crime for cats of any color to get together and blow."

Despite Louis's new militancy, his Uncle Tom reputation persisted, much to his disappointment. "I think that I have always done great things about uplifting my race, but wasn't appreciated," he wrote in 1969, near the end of his life. "I am just a musician, and still remember the time as an American citizen I spoke up for my people during a big integration riot— Little Rock, remember? I wrote Eisenhower. My first comment or compliment, whatever you would call it, came from a Negro boy from my hometown, New Orleans. . . . As we were sitting down at a table to have a drink he looked straight at me and said, 'Nigger, you better stop talking about those white people like you did.' Hmmm. I was trying to stop those unnecessary head whippings at the time, that's all."

The dire predictions that Louis had destroyed his career never came to pass. Radio stations refused to play his records, fearing that he was too controversial, but he was back on the road, touring, always touring, and a year later, everyone (except Louis) had pretty much forgotten what the ruckus was about. At the beginning of 1959, he returned to Hollywood to perform in Paramount's biographical movie, *The Five Pennies*, which traced the career of Red Nichols, an early white jazz trumpeter. He received a generous salary—fifty thousand dollars for eleven days' work—in what seemed to be another tepid Hollywood product confining him to a cameo appearance. Matters turned out differently, for the star, Danny Kaye, yielded to no one in his affection for Louis, and, as a result, *The Five Pennies* contained Louis's strongest movie performance. Indeed, the whole movie was surprisingly good, permeated with the darkness and ambiguity of a Hitchcock thriller.

Kaye portrays Nichols as a rube from Utah who is possessed by quixotic ambition. He thinks he could become the greatest horn player of all time, yet he is terribly insecure. He takes his girlfriend, played by Barbara Bel Geddes, to a Harlem speakeasy to see Louis perform, and admits to her over a teacup of moonshine that Louis Armstrong already *is*. Louis plays "St. Louis Blues" with the All Stars, and Kaye tries to join in, but he is too drunk. When he sobers up, he holds his own with the great Armstrong, playing a hot version of "The Battle Hymn of the Republic." Later, Kaye does a hilarious imitation of Louis's mannerisms and gravelly voice, and Louis in turn mimics Kaye's imitation.

The story darkens when Nichols's daughter contracts polio, and he renounces his career to care for her. In a scene that Hitchcock might have directed, Kaye goes out to the Golden Gate Bridge in the middle of the night and instead of jumping hurls his cornet into the dark waters. This martyrdom is simultaneously his finest and his lowest moment. Time passes, and even his precious daughter, for whom he sacrificed his career, professes to have only a vague memory of her father's former fame. "There was Bix, there was Louis, and there was me!" he proclaims, but no one believes him. Although the movie ends with an obligatory comeback by Red Nichols, its disturbing message lingers long after the music fades.

In the spring of 1959, when he was finished with his work on the movie, Louis and the All Stars embarked on another long, profitable, and exhausting tour of Europe. There seemed to be no reason why he couldn't go on this way indefinitely. He continued to be the indestructible man, iron-lipped Louis, until the night of June 23.

16

DIDN'T HE RAMBLE?

ouis was in Spoleto, Italy, that night for a performance, and became seriously ill. Alerted, Dr. Schiff found him on his knees, grasping the bed, and immediately called an ambulance. During the ride, Louis said, "I don't know why they are taking me to the hospital. I'm fine," but the physicians who examined him described his condition as "grave." In the hospital, he ran a fever of 104 degrees, and an attendant was about to give him an injection of penicillin, to which he was allergic, when Dr. Schiff ran into the room and shattered the syringe.

As the news that he was stricken spread to newspapers worldwide, everyone around Louis went into denial. Dr. Schiff declared that his patient had not suffered a heart attack; the diagnosis, he said, was pneumonia. The Italian doctors concurred. Louis simply refused to believe that after all the Swiss Kriss he had ingested to cleanse his bowels and marijuana he had inhaled to relax his mind, he could possibly have had a heart attack. Nevertheless, that was precisely what had happened to him. Even when forced to confront the truth, he disputed its meaning. "Man, a heart attack is nothing but so much *gas* accumulated and bubbled over," he said.

Under the cover story that he was recovering from a bout of pneumonia, Louis remained in the hospital until the end of the month. From Spoleto, he went to Rome, where he visited St. Peter's and rested in his hotel room, still insisting that he had not had a heart attack. He flew home to New York and stunned everyone by appearing, unannounced, in the middle of a concert at Lewisohn Stadium on July 4, his ceremonial birthday. "If there had been a roof, it would have been blown off," said the reviewer from the *New York Times*. He blew for fifteen minutes or so, taking it easy with tunes like "When It's Sleepy Time Down South," and after his brief set ended, he declared, "I didn't come here to prove I'm not sick. I came just to play." By September, he was back on the road with a limited performing schedule, and seemed so much his old self that he managed to convince everyone that the heart attack had never occurred.

In the months to come, people close to Louis would question the wisdom of Joe Glaser's working his renowned client almost to death. Louis went along with the plan; as far as he was concerned, if he was too feeble to stand up in front of an audience and blow, he might just as well be dead. Accordingly, Glaser booked more movies and record dates and television appearances, and everything was as it had been before the heart attack, except that Louis was tired all the time. He was often late for engagements, and sequestered himself in his dressing room with Dr. Schiff, rather than holding court as he once had. No longer an energetic jazz sprite, he began to age quickly and visibly. His eyes became rheumy, and when he wasn't on stage, blowing and beaming, he seemed frail, far older than his fifty-eight years. Only his smile remained unchanged, electric as ever.

He tried to resume his former pace. In October 1960, he returned to Ghana with the All Stars, dancing and carrying on with Prime Minister Nkrumah, but the tour failed to recapture the spontaneous ebullience of his first visit. In Nigeria, a crowd of fifteen thousand assembled to see him and departed well before the end of his set. The following week, in the Congo (now Zaïre), he received a warmer reception, as local dignitaries swapped their normal Western attire for more exotic garb, including spears and headdresses, and the good times returned for a while. He hobnobbed with Moïse Tshombé, who would soon be the country's leader, and even criticized Tshombé to his face, to the consternation of the other band members, who knew Tshombé's reputation and feared he would poison Louis. But the two of them got along like a house on fire, and even after Tshombé was arrested and charged with the murder of his political adversary, Patrice Lumumba, Louis remained loyal to his pal. "I pray each night they won't kill him," he said. "That cat was *so* nice to me. Kept me in his big palace and all, fed me good, stayed up all night gassing. I had this little tape recorder that cost me several big bills and Tshombé dug it so much I laid it on him."

Throughout the tour, he took grief from no one. When the All Stars swung into Beirut for a performance, Trummy Young said, "some newspaper guys came in the basement dressing room and said, 'How come you're going to play for them damn Jews in Israel?' So Louis looked at them, and he said, 'Let me tell you something. When I go down there, the first thing they are going to ask me is, 'How come you played for them damn Arabs?' That horn, you see that horn? That horn ain't prejudiced. A note's a note in any language.' " Sure enough, when he arrived in Israel, journalists posed the same question, and Louis gave them the same answer. "So ain't none of you no better than the other one," he lectured, as the All Stars laughed in delight at his *chutzpah*.

Armstrong would return to Africa, but shortly before the All Stars left, at the beginning of 1961, Velma Middleton, the oversized, lively singer whom Louis loved and the critics despised, suffered a stroke while performing. She was taken to a local hospital, and Glaser ordered the band to continue the tour without her. She lingered for a brief while, and then word came that Velma had died in the hospital. Shock and dismay spread among the All Stars, and Barney Bigard remarked bitterly, "I'll never forgive Joe Glaser and Louis for that, because they said it would take too many people to lift her on the plane to France. I said to myself, 'This woman gave her all, and they just leave her in some little African town.' "

Louis returned to the United States and was soon back on the road with the All Stars, whose ranks now included Velma's replacement, Jewell Brown.

Several months earlier, in April 1960, Glaser unexpectedly pulled Louis off the road for a unique recording event. He was to collaborate with the other great survivor of the Jazz Age, Duke Ellington. Although Ellington was as active and energetic as Louis, the only other figure in the jazz world to equal him, the two maintained only a cordial, arm's-length relationship. Duke had his orchestra, Louis his All Stars, and the two units went their separate ways. Even now, their collaboration was carried out under curious circumstances.

The celebrities did not record for a major label, as might be expected. Instead, they circumvented their contracts to record for tiny Roulette Records, a label whose boss, Morris Levy, was later revealed to have strong ties to organized crime. Fortunately, a credible producer was in charge, Bob Thiele, who enlivened Roulette during its brief heyday. "The miasmal hoodlum atmosphere at Roulette Records was so heavily oppressive that it was often difficult for me to concentrate on the musical matters that were my direct and only responsibilities," Thiele said later. "Everyone was diligently circumspect about my 'civilian' status and left me alone, even though every day I felt I was trapped in a grade B gangster epic." Glaser allowed Louis and Duke just two days, April 3 and 4, to make their recordings.

Despite the discouraging circumstances, Thiele worked wonders with his aging and fatigued stars, who, for all their experience, were insecure about the collaboration. He struck a balance by persuading Louis to perform songs written by Duke, and he convinced Duke to play the piano backed not by his own orchestra but by the All Stars. For this recording, the lineup consisted only of Barney Bigard on clarinet, Trummy Young on trombone, Mort Herbert on bass, and Danny Barcelona on drums.

The musicians convened in the RCA studios in New York, and although he managed to smile for photographers, Louis was uncomfortable. His lip was down, and worse, he was recording material that was new to him. Duke, meanwhile, was suffering from a persistent headache. No matter. Their performances were perfect—there is no other word to describe them. Louis sang and blew his way through the Ellington standards, "C Jam Blues," "I'm Just a Lucky So and So," "Cottontail," "Drop Me Off in Harlem" (with updated lyrics), and "It Don't Mean a Thing." The session closed with "Azalea," a song Duke had written years before, thinking of Louis, a tune mixing memory and desire. Duke had recorded some of these numbers dozens of time, but with Louis on board, they sounded fresh and different. He treated every syllable and note, no matter how simple, as if it contained essential truths, and in the process, demonstrated his uncanny knack for transforming familiar material into something special. Fatigue and acceptance of mortality are present in his voice, but so is a lifetime of experience. When he was done, Louis didn't bother to assess the quality of the recordings, which resulted in two albums. To him, it was just another recording date, perhaps best forgotten. Late that afternoon, he was back on the bus, nursing his sore chops with ointments and salves, as he hurried to another live performance.

Racism continued to plague him even now. On a tour that took him through Connecticut, he asked the driver to stop so he could use the bathroom. It was a sunny Saturday afternoon. "I was stunned when the owner of a restaurant, clearly on the basis of race, refused him use of otherwise available facilities," said Herb Snitzer, a photographer who accompanied the band. "I will never forget the look on Louis's face. Hero that he was, world-famous, a favorite to millions of people, America's single most identifiable entertainer, and yet excluded in the most humiliating fashion from a common convenience." Among the most visible and popular of all blacks, he was still, after all these years, condemned to this treatment—not in Louisiana, Alabama, or Mississippi, but in Connecticut.

Back in New York, Glaser was still contending with the southern promoters who canceled Louis's dates when they realized he performed with an integrated band. At the same time, another hot Glaser client, Dave Brubeck, suffered the cancellation of an entire southern tour once promoters discovered that his band was not all white. Brubeck became indignant on behalf of both himself and Louis and wanted to compose a work addressing the cruel irony of the American ambassador to the world who could not use a rest room in his own land. "I had read about what Louis Armstrong had done on his tours," Brubeck said, "and it seemed that jazz, stemming from World War II, had become a real symbol of freedom for many Europeans. I felt that real jazz had never been presented in a Broadway show. So my wife, Iola, and I thought of the idea of the musicians themselves being on stage and playing themselves, and they would get into a cultural exchange program." To star in their musical, the Brubecks wanted Louis Armstrong, "the epitome of jazz, not only to us, but to Europeans." They set to work and wrote the score and libretto. At one point, Louis would be called on to declaim, *They say I look like God. Could God be black? My God. If both are made in the image of Thee, could Thou perchance a zebra be?*" It was a solemn and high-minded work, not really in Louis's rambunctious vein, but it belonged to the moment when Civil Rights came to the top of the national agenda.

The Brubecks took their idea to Glaser, who represented them all. Joe had no interest in sticking Louis in a Broadway show, which would prevent him from touring and tie up all his time, but a recording might be a possibility. Even there Joe had his doubts, for he still was looking exclusively for hits, and *The Real Ambassadors*, as Brubeck called his work, did not promise to be a toe-tapping jamboree. Still, he couldn't just stifle his two important clients. He suggested that Brubeck find Louis and talk it over with him. Brubeck caught up with his star in a Chicago hotel, and talked his

way past several gatekeepers into Louis's suite, where he anxiously presented his idea. To his delight, Louis endorsed it. "What I want you to do
is go play all these pieces on the piano and put them on tape, and I will
learn them," he said to Dave. He also wanted Brubeck to print the lyrics in
large type. Louis would then paste the lyrics to the mirror and memorize
them while he shaved. He went around telling people, "Brubeck's written
me an opera."

With Louis on board, Brubeck dashed back to New York to nail down
a recording date with his label, Columbia, which also viewed the project
with skepticism. Like Glaser, the company wanted hits, and though it
agreed to the project in the end, it devoted scant resources to the making or
the selling of the album. Louis came off the road in September 1961 to
record it with an orchestra and the singer Carmen McRae. Time was short
as always, but to Brubeck's surprise, "Louis was prepared. It's amazing how
well he did and how musical that guy is. When the time came to sing
harmony, where we had written Louis to sing the lead, Carmen said, 'Pops,
please, you sing the harmony and let me sing the lead.' Without any
rehearsal, he jumps right in and does it. He was amazing to work with."

Despite the optimism and idealism surrounding the project, the resulting album attracted little attention—in part because Columbia did not promote it, and in part because it was unlike anything else Louis had done. It
was, truth to tell, obvious and a bit strained. Nonetheless, *The Real Ambassadors* enjoyed a reprise the following year, at the Monterey Jazz Festival.
Glaser meddled as usual, and refused to allow the performance to be filmed
or recorded. To complicate matters further, the Brubecks wanted Louis to
dress the part of an ambassador, with a top hat. At first he balked, but then
relented, and when he made his entrance and heard the applause, he paused
at Dave's piano and whispered, "Am I hamming it up enough to suit you,
Pops?" Unlike the stiff recording that had preceded it, the performance
itself, according to those present, was moving and deeply felt. This was the
only live performance of *The Real Ambassadors*.

Joe Glaser appeared to be in full control of Louis's career at this point,
but he was, in reality, engaged in a losing battle with the mob. People
in the entertainment industry were aware of his former associations with the
Capone syndicate in Chicago, and Glaser helped to keep the rumors alive,

but there was much more to the story. Glaser kept in touch with Al Capone's stylish successor, Murray "The Camel" Humphreys, who now ran the Chicago syndicate. Humphreys's every move was shadowed by the FBI, and many of his supposedly secret business meetings were surreptitiously recorded by enterprising FBI agents. Among those tracking Humphreys was FBI agent William Roemer, a charter member of J. Edgar Hoover's "Top Hoodlum Program" in Chicago. In this capacity, Roemer listened to thousands of hours of conversation picked up by the hidden microphone nicknamed "Little Al," after Al Capone, planted in Celano's Custom Tailor Shop at 620 North Michigan Avenue. The tailor shop served as the Outfit's headquarters. "One day in 1960," Roemer said, "Murray The Camel Humphreys and an associate, Frankie Strongie Ferraro, were discussing bringing an entertainer to Joe Glaser because they had an association with him and felt he could properly represent the performer. Humphreys had a working relationship with Glaser. He could present a situation to Glaser and get what he wanted from Glaser."

Glaser's mob connections occasionally had a direct bearing on Louis's engagements. In Philadelphia, he was unhappy about having to play at Ciro's, a nightclub owned by hoodlums. He was accustomed to dealing with gangsters, and while he didn't let his resentment show as he grinned and signed autographs, he ultimately got his revenge. "Louis is the king of scat. With an extra twist," said a musician who sat in with him. "Somehow, in the middle of these choruses he manages to keep saying, 'Kiss my ass, kiss my ass, kiss my ass.' Over and over. I hear it plain as day but nobody in that bunch digs what he's putting down. He's looking right at them, smiling his famous smile, scatting. 'Kiss my ass, kiss my ass.' "

Glaser's control over Associated Booking faltered when Sidney Korshak, one of the most feared men in the entertainment industry, entered his life. Like Glaser, Korshak came out of Chicago, where he, too, had formed ties to the Capone syndicate, but then Korshak headed to Los Angeles, where as a labor lawyer and power broker he moved in the highest circles in Hollywood. At the same time, he maintained a close relationship with the Chicago syndicate, according to the FBI. William Roemer, who supervised the FBI's file on Korshak, confirmed that the lawyer's direct link to the Chicago mob was Gussie Alex, who was Murray Humphreys's first lieutenant. "Korshak always did what the mob told him to do," Roemer said, and he recalled something Alex once said to Korshak: "You're our guy, we raised you up. When we call, you call us." (For the record, Korshak denied he knew Alex, though he did admit that their wives, both models, were friends.) In a 1976 exposé of Korshak, the *New York Times* reported: "Federal officials contend that he has been involved in such activities as bribery, kickbacks, extortion, fraud and labor racketeering." The IRS had been on his case since 1942. He was even responsible for successfully blackmailing Senator Estes Kefauver, who at the time was leading a congressional inquiry into organized crime in Chicago, by photographing the senator in bed with a woman "supplied by the Chicago underworld."

Given this reputation, no one wanted to get on the wrong side of Sidney Korshak, not even Joe Glaser. When Korshak decided to bring Associated Booking and its roster of famous artists into his sphere of influence, Glaser had no choice but to acquiesce. In 1962, he assigned control over the agency, the nation's third largest, to both Korshak and himself. No one realized that Glaser had actually taken a much more powerful partner into the business. To the outside world, it seemed that Sidney Korshak was, at most, the company's legal counsel. When Joe Glaser died in 1969, Korshak demonstrated his authority by assuming complete control over ABC.

Since the entire transaction was conducted in secret, it is highly unlikely that Louis or any other ABC client realized how large a role Korshak played in the company. Given Louis's lifelong affinity for hoodlum-managers, it is unlikely he would have minded even if he had known.

Throughout this period, Louis continued to blow, but as the 1960s turned confrontational and shrill, his brand of jazz came to sound like distant music. The British invasion and the rise of rock and roll in 1963 pushed him to the periphery of the popular music world he had dominated so many decades ago. To make matters worse, jazz was becoming more specialized and losing its audience, just as he had prophesied in 1947. The few vital musicians who were around, people such as Miles Davis and John Coltrane, were taking jazz to a level of sophistication that Louis couldn't hope to match. They were pushing the limits and setting new standards for hipness, while he was blowing endless choruses of "When It's Sleepy Time Down South" and "Back Home in Indiana." It seemed that his day had passed.

At the end of 1963, Glaser directed Louis to record a song. It was just a demo, no guarantee that it would ever be released. The tune, "Hello,

Dolly," came from a musical by the same name, which had yet to open. The music publisher wanted to enlist Louis to record it simply as a way to plug the show, which had nothing to do with jazz. On December 4, 1963, Louis and the All Stars went into the studio. Louis found the song lifeless and trite, and in a last-minute effort to inject some zip into the proceedings, the recording company dubbed a banjo introduction. Louis promptly forgot about the session and went back on the road.

When Glaser heard the demo, he exclaimed, "It's a fucking hit!" and pushed like mad to get the song released. The demo tape eventually found its way to David Kapp, who ran his own label, and he swiftly released it. Jazz purists gagged when they heard "Hello, Dolly." It supplied further proof, if any were needed, that Louis had lost all connection with the jazz world. Its provenance was suspect, for it came from a Broadway show, and the recording contained a banjo and strings, both of which marked it as a novelty number, at best. What the purists didn't realize—though Glaser did—was that "Hello, Dolly" was Louis's best single in donkey's years. The vocal featured exquisite timing, and Louis's trumpet playing contained a striking, improvised passage. In addition, the song had excellent self-promotion possibilities, for Louis changed a lyric to include his name: "This is Louis, Dolly." Not "Lou-ie," but "Lou-*is*," the way he always pronounced his own name. By drawing himself into the tune, he turned it into a paean to the long-lost persona of Louis Armstrong, who had so much history behind him, and who was still out there singing and blowing.

Hello, Dolly!, the musical, opened on Broadway in January 1964, and it became a major hit. Louis's demo recording followed suit. It appeared on the charts in February, and on May 9 the song astounded the music industry, to say nothing of the jazz world, by reaching the number-one spot for one gorgeous week, at a time when the Beatles and other British rock groups were thought to have an absolute lock on the charts.

Louis missed all the hoopla. He was on the road, playing Puerto Rico, when Glaser's office called down to tell the All Stars to start playing their new smash hit "Hello, Dolly." The musicians, Louis included, were perplexed. They didn't even have the music. "Any you guys remember this damn tune?" Louis gently inquired. No one did. They raced all over San Juan trying to find the sheet music, without success, and finally a copy arrived from New York, and the band learned it. The first time they played it, in San Juan, they were a bit skeptical about whether it was a bona fide hit, but when the audience made Louis take eight curtain calls, they damn well knew Glaser was right: it really was a fucking hit.

Kapp capitalized on the success of "Hello, Dolly" by hauling Louis back into the studio for an album consisting of remakes of earlier hits, and in June, the album also reached the number-one position. Louis basked in the glow of his sudden, unexpected popularity. He was all over the radio, and all over television, on *The Ed Sullivan Show*, and just about every other variety and talk show. Later, he appeared in the movie, singing "Hello, Dolly" to Barbra Streisand, his version of the song largely responsible for building the Hollywood version of the show into yet another hit. At sixty-three, after years of riding the bus, touring, blowing, and singing, in good times and bad, Louis enjoyed a personal triumph the likes of which he had never expected to see.

The only problem with Louis's hit was that it supplanted his earlier, more distinguished work in the public mind. For millions, especially younger listeners, "Hello, Dolly" was their first exposure to Louis Armstrong. They knew him not as the heroic and volatile personification of jazz, but as the charming old man who sang "Hello, Dolly" in that funny, gravelly voice. He had succeeded in reinventing himself at the cost of obscuring his earlier achievements. The audience he won with "Hello, Dolly" overlooked his discography, one of the biggest and richest in the business. Since his first sessions with King Oliver, he had recorded over a thousand tunes, some many times over. There were nearly a hundred versions of his "When It's Sleepy Time Down South," for instance, and more than fifty renditions of "When the Saints Go Marching In." He recorded "Basin Street Blues," "Muskrat Ramble," and "Mack the Knife," to name but a few, more than forty times each.

Despite his unequaled longevity and fertility, not to mention his recent number-one hit, record label executives remained skeptical about his appeal. Shortly after "Hello, Dolly," Bob Thiele, who had produced the distinguished Armstrong-Ellington albums, came to Louis with a ballad called "What a Wonderful World." Louis instantly fell in love with the song, and he agreed to record it with Thiele, who was now at ABC Records. For once, Louis didn't play his horn, he simply sang. Since the recording required the added expense of strings, cellos, and other musicians, he even agreed to forego his usual advance and work for scale—$250.

When the company president, Larry Newton, heard the recording, he hated it. He hated Armstrong, the song, and Thiele. A distraught Glaser offered to buy the recording from ABC Records, but Newton insisted on releasing it without any promotion. It sold fewer than a thousand copies, while "Hello, Dolly" had sold millions. In England, however, "What a Wonderful World" quickly sold six hundred thousand copies and went to the top of the charts, and its popularity spread to other countries as well, everywhere except the United States. Newton predictably did an about-face and demanded that Louis make an entire "What a Wonderful World" album for five hundred dollars. When he heard that, Glaser told Thiele, "You tell that fat bastard to fuck himself and give us twenty-five thousand dollars for eight more sides." Newton returned the compliment, saying that Glaser could go fuck himself, too.

Ultimately Glaser prevailed and Louis recorded the album for the full twenty-five thousand dollars. When it was released, Newton was showered with accolades for his brilliant and innovative exploitation of Louis Armstrong. But the song didn't find a wide audience in America until it was featured on the soundtrack of the movie, *Good Morning, Vietnam*, more than twenty years later.

Louis's enhanced popularity and income during the mid-1960s had little effect on the way he lived. By this point in his life, he was who he was, and he was damned if he was going to change to suit anyone, not even his wife Lucille. Not surprisingly, she had become impatient with their modest house in Corona, Queens, and yearned for the lush green expanses of suburban Long Island. With Glaser's help, she located a posh dwelling complete with swimming pool, not far from Jackie Robinson's home, but Louis wouldn't have any of it. "We're right out here with the rest of the colored folk and the Puerto Ricans and Italians and the Hebrew cats," he said of life in Corona. "We don't need to move out in the suburbs to some big mansion with lots of servants and yardmen and things. What for? What the hell do I care about living in a 'fashionable' neighborhood? Ain't nobody cutting off the lights and gas here 'cause we didn't pay the bills. The frigidaire is full of food. What more do we need?" Asked why he didn't live in Beverly Hills with other celebrities, Louis carefully explained that he never felt a part of Hollywood. He had been to a few Hollywood parties, and people were polite to him, but frequently someone who'd had a few too many would come up to him and say, "You know, I used to have a colored mammy." He didn't consider the movie stars his friends, not even those who admired or imitated him. "Even though I've played with a lot of them—Danny Kaye, Sinatra—I don't even know where they live," he said. "In fact, I've never been invited to the home of a movie star, not even Bing's." He knew he would never feel at home in Hollywood.

He liked to do his own shopping, to visit the local barbershop, to buy ice cream cones from the Good Humor Man for the kids in the neighborhood every afternoon at 3:15. Sometimes, the kids came into the living room and watched television with him in the late afternoon; he favored Westerns. "We've seen three generations grow up on our block," he said, looking back over his twenty-odd years in Corona. "White and black, and those kids when they grew up and got married, their children still come around to our house and visit their friends Louis and Lucille. That's how close they feel towards us." This, he knew, was the way life should be.

Kids weren't the only visitors to the house in Corona. Jazz musicians and critics frequently dropped in on Pops, even at the price of participating in his obsession with Swiss Kriss. His old nemesis Dizzy Gillespie, who lived nearby, became a friend and frequent visitor. Diz realized Louis was still the hippest cat in jazz; he had never been the Uncle Tom of the boppers' imaginings. He had risked everything when he had taken on Ike over school desegregation in 1957, and although the public at large quickly forgot the controversy, the jazz world remembered his stand. Musicians like Diz, and even Miles, came to understand how much they owed to Louis's music and his career. Diz would come by, usually with Clark Terry, the trumpet player, and they would say, "Pops, we came to get our batteries charged."

Inside, the rooms were large and immaculate, and the bathrooms resplendent, with mirrors and gold-plated fixtures. In the den, Louis stored his mammoth collection of reel-to-reel tapes of the All Star performances. He owned almost none of the records he had made; the live music held more appeal for him. In his spare time, he decorated the tape boxes with bold collages of photos and headlines clipped from newspapers, and later he compiled a 175-page catalog of his tape collection. Lucille, for her part, furnished the living room in contemporary French decor, and she continued to cook for Louis in the large kitchen, which was equipped with an oversized stove. She hung paintings by Leroy Neiman on the walls. A blowup of

Louis's 1935 *Vanity Fair* portrait hung over the fireplace. And she made sure to display their marriage license in the hallway.

Meanwhile, Louis's sister lived on in New Orleans, proudly and defiantly remaining in a shabby neighborhood. Mama Lucy was nearly a foot taller than her brother, with the same rumbling voice and stubborn independence. "I got my grave, my tombstone, and my funeral's all paid," she declared. "I don't need no help from no one, no how." She refused to take money from Louis, and she actually sent him food to make sure he was eating enough up north. Photographs of him were displayed throughout her home. There was little love lost between Lucille and Mama Lucy, though the older woman did admit, "My brother was married four times, but he has only one wife." On hearing that remark, Lucille said, "You know, that was the first time Mama Lucy ever said anything nice about me."

Beneath the superficial tranquillity of Louis's life, his iconoclastic spirit boiled away. He refused to hobnob with the wealthy and powerful, black or white. On learning that Howard University wished to confer an honorary doctorate on him, he sighed and lamented, "Where were they forty years ago when I needed them?" And in 1969, when Richard Nixon, newly elected president, dispatched an emissary to invite Louis to the White House, Armstrong gave short shrift to an honor few would refuse. "Fuck that shit," he said. "Why didn't they do it before? The only reason he would want me to play there now is to make some niggers happy."

He was ambivalent about living this *haute bourgeois* existence with Lucille. They fought occasionally in front of friends. Once they got into a scuffle on a train, and Louis became so enraged he drove his fist through the glass window. Afterward, he muttered dark words about divorcing Lucille, and even mentioned the idea to several friends. "If I had to make a choice between my wife and my little trumpet," he told William Russell, the jazz critic, "I'll take my little trumpet." Russell added, "He really meant it." Once he had finished ventilating his rage and frustration with the constraints of marriage, and Lucille's unwillingness to embrace the wilder side of life, he returned to speaking of her in tender, passionate tones. "We're *still* married and still at it. Yes, Lord, it's ALL SEX," he wrote in 1969. "Can you imagine these kids of my neighborhood at my home listening and grinning as I was telling them about Aunt Lucille's and my beautiful life together? I commenced to calling Lucille 'Moms.' My Moms. She's so attentive, and she reminds me and does a lot of things just like my mother, May Ann. And since she passed in 1927, it seems as if Lucille has features just like Mayann. Some of Lucille's ways and little gestures are just like my mother."

During the late '60s, Louis was beset with minor ailments, but he kept touring with the zeal and humility of a young cat trying to make a name for himself. The man who refused to play the White House came to Iowa in 1968 to perform at Grinnell College. "Nearly two-dozen intellectuals and artists were on campus to participate in a series of discussions and to receive honorary degrees, yet the college refused to award one to Armstrong," wrote the jazz critic Gary Giddins, who, as a Grinnell student, had been responsible for inviting Louis to the campus. "Outside the gymnasium where he performed, a handful of students picketed because they wanted a rock group." Giddins was even more disquieted when he approached the great man of jazz: "There he was, an old man in a loose tuxedo, his brown coloring tinctured with gray, his eyes slightly rheumy, the scar on his upper lip alarmingly raw." On stage that night, though, "he appeared transfigured. The ashen color was gone, the eyes blazed, the smile blinded. . . . His huge tone was as gold and unspotted as ever."

Many of Louis's admirers wondered why he drove himself this way. He didn't need the money, he had every accolade that could come the way of a jazz musician, his reputation as a cultural force and jazz icon was secure. Why did he do it? "People are quick to forget you if you don't keep your name before the public," he insisted, evoking the tragic end of his mentor, Joe Oliver. He didn't want to become just a name in the history books, an occasion for nostalgia; he was determined to blow till he dropped. Glaser still drove him at a cruel pace. After all these decades, Louis was still doing one-nighters, as he always had. It was the life he knew, and it was the routine that Joe Glaser knew. Louis occasionally quoted Bert Williams's lament, "In show business, you've got to die to prove that you're sick," but then he would pick up his horn, and for an hour or two he would forget about the inescapable fact of his mortality. So he hauled himself to Las Vegas, or Atlantic City, to play for jaded audiences, and was transported the moment he began to blow.

Despite his ebbing strength, he kept devising ways to inject new energy into the material he performed. In 1968, he recorded his most surprising album, "Disney Songs the Satchmo Way," a children's collection bursting with affecting vocals and surprising solos, all of them recorded when Louis was obviously fatigued and uncomfortable. Even so, his rendition of "Chim Chim Cher-ee," for instance, showed that he still had the power to invest a familiar song with haunting emotional urgency and musical finesse.

n September 1968, he appeared in the office of his doctor, Gary Zucker, short of breath. When Dr. Zucker ordered him to proceed directly to Beth Israel Hospital. Louis could not bring himself to enter the hospital. Unable to let go of life and all its pleasures, he dropped out of sight for two weeks. He spent his time in Harlem, carousing, seeing old friends, being himself, denying his mortality. Meanwhile, his condition worsened, and his limbs swelled ominously. Eventually, he was forced to go to Beth Israel. His heart and his kidneys were failing. He was suffering from a lifetime of very hard living, of driving himself incessantly, of gaining and losing weight, not to mention more than forty years of marijuana. Chronic use of the drug that Louis insisted was necessary to his well-being leads to lung disease, mild depression, and disorientation—all of which plagued him now.

Rest and treatment in the form of diuretics helped him to regain his health, and he was able to go home, only to return to Beth Israel in February 1969 with more heart and kidney problems. This time, he stayed for two wrenching months. He underwent emergency surgery to clear his lungs of fluid, and his doctors tried to make him understand that he could no longer return to his old life of one-nighters; in fact, he couldn't even blow his horn anymore. It was too hard on his weakened lungs. These restrictions were more than Louis could bear. "He made it abundantly clear that the only thing that was important was to make music," said his doctor. "If he couldn't make music, then he was through."

Even Joe Glaser was telling his star client that it was time to retire.

Before he could enforce his will, Glaser suffered a debilitating stroke in the elevator of his office building. He was taken to Beth Israel for treatment. Louis was still there, undergoing treatment, but Lucille decided not to tell him about Glaser, for fear of upsetting her husband. He found out anyway, when Dizzy Gillespie came to visit Louis and mentioned he was going to give blood for Mr. Glaser.

"Blood for Joe Glaser for what?" Louis asked.

"Why, man, Joe Glaser's sick as a dog right around the corner in the hospital here."

Incensed, Louis insisted on visiting Glaser, and was taken in a wheelchair to see his manager, who lay in a coma in an intensive care unit. Louis returned from the visit badly shaken. "He didn't know me," he said to Lucille.

As Louis continued to languish in his hospital room, he sought consolation in memories of his youth, of Storyville and its prostitutes, his mother and sister and boyhood friends. On March 31, 1969, Louis, "ill in his bed at the Beth Israel Hospital," as he described himself, penned an affecting memoir of his days with the Karnoffsky family, and, making an associative leap, dedicated the piece to the dying Joe Glaser, "the best friend that I've ever had. May the Lord bless him, watch over him always." He signed it, "His boy and disciple who loved him dearly, Louis Satchmo Armstrong."

Glaser never awoke from his coma. He died on June 6. His passing was a devastating blow for Louis, who faced the prospect of living on without the spiritual father who had filled such a large void in his career, and in his heart. He recovered sufficiently to go home, and tried to make the best of what was left of his life. Looking back on this terrible period in July, Louis wrote to a friend, "It was a toss up between us, who would cut out first. Man, it broke my heart that it was him. I love that man, which the world already knows. I prayed, as sick as I was, that he would make it. God bless his soul. He was the greatest for me and all the spades that he handled."

Associated Booking continued to manage Louis's career and finances. He resumed a limited performing and recording schedule, singing, but not blowing, always conscious of his health, and growing increasingly dependent on the doctors who tended to him. Every appearance he made now had the air of a valedictory about it. In May 1970, he returned to the studio to record an album entitled "With Friends." The friends included some of the leading lights of jazz, many of whom had either disdained or evolved far beyond him. Eddie Condon, Miles Davis, and Ornette Coleman were there; old friends like Bobby Hackett came along; even a few jazz critics, such as Stanley Dance, turned up—all of them backing Louis in a chorus. Even George Wein joined in. The event was a bit show-business sappy, but everyone realized that Louis wasn't going to be around forever, and they wanted one last memory of him, a memory he was happy to supply.

On his ceremonial seventieth birthday, July 4, 1970, he sat for an introspective, somber interview with the *New York Times*. He sounded as if he had come to terms with the prospect of his own death. "I think I had a beautiful life. I didn't wish for anything I couldn't get, and I got pretty near everything I wanted because I worked for it." He talked about his own funeral, visualizing it as a traditional New Orleans sendoff. "They're going to enjoy blowing over me, ain't they?" he remarked. "Cats will be coming from California and everywhere else just to play. . . . If anybody plays a bad note, Lucille'll slap 'em right in the face. She'll take care of that for me. I don't want no part of it. Once I cut out, forget it. It'll be good if I get to the Pearly Gate upstairs. Saint Peter will have all those good things written down. He ain't got no business with the bad things up there. . . . I listen to my idols, I ain't going to worry about their personals, their living. Just the music, that's all I'm interested in. . . . You have to have something to die with, Pops."

Later that summer, George Wein organized a birthday tribute to Louis at the Newport Jazz Festival. The occasion proved bittersweet, because Louis was very frail by this time, emaciated and unable to climb a short staircase without a boost. In rehearsal, he looked distinctly retired, puttering around in his shorts and a white baseball cap with the visor turned to one side. His voice was, if possible, more gravelly than ever, and doctor's orders forbade him from blowing. Troubled by the memory of Louis's famous ruckus at Newport back in 1959, Wein was attentive to his star's needs, but they disagreed on the staging of the show. Louis wanted to come out singing "When It's Sleepy Time Down South," just as he always did, to demonstrate that nothing had changed, he was still the same, but Wein urged Louis simply to walk out on stage and stand beneath a spotlight, unannounced, to what Wein was certain would be an ovation. The idea made Louis nervous. What if no one recognized him? What if they didn't applaud? Ultimately, Wein got his way, and when Louis appeared on stage after a series of trumpet tributes, the effect was electric. He did look transformed, straight and strong in an impeccable bronze-colored suit, his cufflinks gleaming, and for the time being, he was still the king of the trumpet, and the king of jazz. He sang "Mack the Knife," and his gruff voice glided through surprisingly mellifluous passages. His horn was gone, but his voice was still going, and his timing remained as startling as ever. Once again, he *was* the music.

Invigorated by his success at Newport, he planned a comeback. Against doctor's orders, he began practicing the trumpet, but only in the bathroom, where he thought no one would hear him. In September 1970, he played a two-week stand in Las Vegas with a reconstituted All Stars. The good times, it seemed, were back. He was on the road again, spending October in England, and December in Vegas. In February 1971, he went on network television, singing "Pennies from Heaven" with Bing Crosby. He recorded "The Night Before Christmas." There was no more talk of dying.

At home, feeling cocky, he spent his time answering the voluminous mail elicited by his illness and remarkable comeback, stuffing his letters into envelopes imprinted with the infamous photograph of Satchmo on the toilet. To a friend he wrote, "Your boy Satchmo is getting pretty sassy these days. Blowing his black ass off. I knew I could, all the time. My fans and friends, quite naturally they'd be a little uneasy about things, but as for me, they're my chops. I wear them 24 hours a day, and I keep them in good trim." He was still in love with his Lucille, in his slightly crazy way: "We shares everything in life from soup to nuts, especially the latter. Ha. Ha. Ya dig?"

In March, he played a two-week engagement—"just another hustle"— in the Waldorf-Astoria's Empire Room. Before his first show, his doctor, Gary Zucker, issued a dire warning: "You could drop dead while you're performing."

"Doc, you don't understand. My whole life, my whole soul, my whole spirit is to blow that horn," Louis said. "I've got to do it."

On opening night, he received a devastating review. After he read it, he turned to Joe Sully, a representative from his manager's office, and asked, "But you'll still book me, huh, Joe?"

As soon as the engagement ended, he returned to Beth Israel, having suffered another heart attack. The press kept watch over Louis, and bulletins about his condition regularly appeared in the papers. He underwent a tracheotomy to ease congestion in his lungs and bronchial tubes, and in mid-June, he went home again to recover whatever was left of his health.

For a time, he seemed to rally. On his ceremonial birthday, July 4, 1971, television crews and interviewers came to visit him in Corona. In a soft voice, with Lucille at his side, he declared his intention to resume performing as soon as he was able. The next day, he told the All Stars to prepare for a rehearsal. He had another gig coming up, and he was very excited about it.

At 5:30 the next morning, July 6, 1971, Louis Armstrong died at his home, in bed, in his sleep.

His last rites in New York were splendid and dignified, but nothing like the festive jazz funeral he had imagined for himself. The roster of "honorary pallbearers"—including the likes of John Lindsay, the Mayor of New York City; Johnny Carson; Earl Wilson, the gossip columnist; Dick Cavett; and Merv Griffin—sparked controversy. People in the jazz world wondered what these prominent white figures had to do with Louis, or with jazz. His body reposed in an open coffin at the Seventh Regiment Armory at Park Avenue and 66th Street in Manhattan. An estimated twenty-five thousand mourners waited in line to pay their last respects. Again, there were rumblings in the jazz world because many of the musicians who had known Louis in the old days couldn't afford to come to New York to say good-bye. On July 9, his funeral took place at the Corona Congregational Church. He was buried in Flushing Cemetery.

Two days later, an old-fashioned raucous jazz funeral took place in New Orleans. An immense parade in Louis's honor wound its way through the streets of the city, streets that he had celebrated in his music. The Onward Brass Band, successor to the marching bands in which Louis had played as a young man, pounded out the old familiar tunes: *"Oh, didn't he ramble? . . . He rambled everywhere . . . He rambled till the butcher cut him down . . ."*

Amid the clamor attendant on his death, Lil Hardin, Louis's second wife, went overlooked. Lil still lived in the house at 421 East 44th Street in Chicago, where she and Louis had once spent so many happy hours, and played so much music. The years had done nothing to lessen the tie she felt to him, and she still considered herself Mrs. Armstrong.

Several weeks after his death, on August 28, 1971, she emerged from semiretirement to play in a televised memorial concert at the Civic Center Plaza, an outdoor arena in Chicago. After waiting impatiently for her turn, she was introduced to the crowd and began to play the "St. Louis Blues" as if it were still 1924, and she was the same "Hot Miss Lil." She exuded joy and smiled broadly as the music poured forth. Then, suddenly, she began gasping for breath and collapsed in front of the audience. She had suffered a massive heart attack.

With cameras mercilessly bearing down on the scene, a rescue worker attempted mouth-to-mouth resuscitation, and finally an ambulance took her to a nearby hospital. Doctors tried to revive her, without success, and pronounced her dead. To some, the manner of her passing seemed grotesque, too public, while others considered it altogether fitting that Lil died performing in honor of her late husband.

Louis left an estate valued at $530,775. The amount was formidable for a jazz man, but it was hardly the millions people supposed he had amassed. Joe Glaser, for example, was a far wealthier man and left an estate valued at more than $3,000,000. For decades, rumors had circulated that Glaser had stolen Louis blind. Associated Booking insisted that was not the case, that the agency took a standard 15 percent fee. Lucille, for her part, affirmed that Joe Glaser always kept half of Louis's earnings.

Louis's will, dated February 10, 1970, bequeathed nearly all his assets to his wife. Clarence and Mama Lucy each received five thousand dollars. Louis had never legally adopted Clarence, and he lived on in obscurity. After her husband's death, Lucille stayed in the house in Corona, Queens, preserving it as a memorial to her husband. During the ensuing decade, she received royalties averaging seventy-three thousand dollars a year, and her assets approached a million dollars. She was now wealthy, but she lived as she always had, devoted to her husband's memory, no matter what trials he had put her through during their years together.

At the beginning of October 1983, she journeyed to Boston to attend a fund-raising concert at Brandeis University in honor of her late husband. She suffered a seizure in her hotel room and died at Beth Israel Hospital in Boston on October 5, at the age of sixty-nine. Lucille was buried beside Louis, as if to maintain an everlasting vigil over his restless spirit.

Acknowledgments

This is the first biography I have written in which my opinion of my subject kept improving as I worked. This circumstance made the book a unique pleasure to research and write. As I discovered, to explore Armstrong's life and career is to mine the history of jazz. And the history of jazz is in many ways, perhaps even essentially, oral history. Therefore, I am especially obliged to those individuals who spoke with me, often several times, about various aspects of Armstrong's life and career for this biography.

Chris Albertson
Richard Allen
Ernest Anderson
George Avakian
Jack Bradley
Dave Brubeck
Iola Brubeck
Jim Collum
Roger Dickerson
Frank Driggs
Milt Gabler
Milt "Judge" Hinton
Morris Hodara
Phoebe Jacobs
Mollnye Karnofsky

Floyd and Lucille Levin
Marian McPartland
James T. Maher
Fate Marable Jr.
Wynton Marsalis
Dan Morgenstern
Joseph Muranyi
Albert Murray
Louis Panassié
William F. Roemer Jr.
Arvell Shaw
Clark Terry
George Wein
Vern Whaley

Many other interviews contributed to this work. The mother of all jazz oral histories, the Smithsonian Institution's Jazz Oral History Project, housed at the Institute of Jazz Studies at Rutgers University in Newark, New Jersey, proved especially helpful. Those on which I have drawn include:

Danny Barker
Barney Bigard
Lawrence Brown
Buck Clayton
Cozy Cole

Joe Darensbourg
Albert "Budd" Johnson
Milt "Judge" Hinton
Teddy McRae
Russell "Big Chief" Moore

Zilner Randolph

Howard R. Scott

John Simmons

Zutty Singleton

Trummy Young

Throughout my research on this book, the Institute of Jazz Studies proved to be a source of continual enlightenment. I owe a profound debt to the Institute's Director, Dan Morgenstern, who was generous with his time, guidance, and insights. Those acquainted with his authoritative writings about jazz in general, and Armstrong in particular, will immediately realize how fortunate I am to have had the opportunity to learn from him. I frequently consulted the Institute's library, based on the holdings of Marshall Stearns, a leading scholar and historian of jazz. The Institute also contains the remarkable series of letters from Armstrong to Leonard Feather, the jazz critic and composer, written primarily in the 1940s, when Louis was honing his formidable literary and storytelling gifts. Thanks also to Don Luck and the rest of the Institute's staff.

In New Orleans, I was able to learn much about Armstrong and the origins of jazz at the Hogan Jazz Archives at Tulane University, where Bruce Raeburn, the Director, Alma D. Williams, the Associate Curator, and Diane Rose were generous with their time and expertise. Of particular value was the Hogan's collection of oral histories. Accounts from the following proved helpful to this book:

Lillian Hardin Armstrong

Louis Barbarin

Paul Barbarin

Peter Bocage

Steve Brown

Frank Cary

Lee Collins

Warren "Baby" Dodds

Tony Fougerat

Albert Glenny

Monk Hazel

Preston Jackson

Mrs. Joseph Jones

John Joyce

Nick LaRocca

Charlie Love

Manual Manetta

Bill Matthews

Punch Miller

Stella Oliver

Kid Ory

Joe "Babe" Phillips

William "Baba" Ridgley

William Russell

Zutty Singleton

Dr. Edmund Souchon

Muggsy Spanier

Johnny Wiggs

Also of considerable importance was the Historic New Orleans Collection, specifically, the William Russell Collection in the Williams Research Center. William Russell, a pioneering jazz historian in New Orleans, conducted a number of interviews with jazz figures in 1938. Some of this material provided the basis for Russell's contribution to *Jazzmen*, published in 1939, but much of his work concerning Armstrong has not appeared before. The interviews from this trove included:

Lillian Hardin Armstrong

Louis Armstrong

Johnny Dodds

Preston Jackson

Richard M. Jones

Clarence Williams

Zutty Singleton

In addition, I would like to thank Richard B. Allen, the dean of New Orleans jazz historians, for his advice. Roger Dickerson, the distinguished composer and teacher, provided me with an account of the creation of his *Requiem* for Louis Armstrong. Peggy Scott Laborde, of WYES-TV, New Orleans Public Television, furnished leads and documentaries. I also wish to acknowledge the New Orleans Museum of Art, and Preservation Hall, where I spent many happy hours listening to traditional New Orleans jazz. Don Marquis, Curator of the jazz collection at the Louisiana State Museum in New Orleans and the author of *In Search of Buddy Bolden*, was generous with his collection, time, and expertise. Steve Steinberg located a rare print of *New Orleans*, the 1947 movie starring Louis and Billie Holiday.

I wish to thank Phoebe Jacobs, the Executive Vice President of the Louis Armstrong Educational Foundation, for her encouragement and long-standing support of this biography, and for facilitating my research. Phoebe also spoke with heartfelt conviction about both Louis and Lucille Armstrong in my interviews with her. I also wish to thank David Gold, the Foundation's President, for his advice.

The Louis Armstrong Archives, at Queen's College/City University of New York, is dedicated to disseminating information contained in its collection. My thanks to Michael Cogswell, Director of the Louis Armstrong Archives, for introducing me to its many resources, and to the staff for assisting me during my visits.

Many other music historians, archivists, and experts were helpful. At the Library of the Academy of Motion Picture Arts and Sciences, Sam Gill and his staff provided information about Armstrong's extensive movie career. At the USC Cinema-TV Library, Ned Comstock, with whom I have had the pleasure of working in the past, located Armstrong material in various special collections, including the Arthur Freed Collection. At the Library of Congress in Washington, D.C., Patricia Willard, the Gershwin Consultant in Jazz and Popular Music, offered valuable advice and commentary. Miles Kreuger, the President of the Institute of the American Musical, brought his encyclopedic knowledge of show business to bear on Armstrong's extensive movie career. Thanks also to Professor Vivian Perlis of the Oral History Collection of American Music at Yale University and to Lawrence Gushee of the University of Illinois at Urbana-Champaign for sharing their insights. Dr. Bruce Charash provided information about the potential effects of Armstrong's chronic marijuana use. The Bentley Historical Library, University of Michigan, supplied the Gingrich-Armstrong correspondence. In addition, I found useful material in various divisions of the New York Public Library: the Lincoln Center Library for the Performing Arts, the Schomburg Center for Research in Black Culture, and the Maps Division. I would also like to thank the New York Society Library; the Northwestern University Library, Special Collections, R. Russell Maylone, Curator; the FBI's Information Resources Division, which supplied Louis Armstrong's confidential file; the Fisk University Library, Special Collections, where Beth House assisted me; and the Chicago Crime Commission, which furnished records concerning the early career of Joseph Glaser, Louis's manager.

In addition, Allie Barnicoat brought to my attention the role her father, Ernest Anderson, played in Louis's career. Thanks to Dr. David Berger, as well. 'Captain' Jack Bradley, the leading collector of Armstrong materials, opened his home and vast collection to me, and tried against all odds to persuade me that original 78s really *do* sound better than compact discs. Irakli de Davrichewy proved helpful. Daniel Dolgin was, as always, a font of friendship and wisdom. Darrell Fennell offered gleaming insights into jazz history and welcome encouragement. The list of recordings that he compiled for this book emphasizes the many facets of Louis's vast musical legacy. Gary Giddins, the distinguished jazz writer and author of the ebullient *Satchmo*, dispensed advice and enthusiasm. Joe Kraus uncovered material about the elusive Joseph Glaser in Chicago. James T. Maher, coauthor of *American Popular Song*, again proved himself to be a generous friend, sharing his profound knowledge of the American musical scene with me, including his files on Lillian Armstrong. Albert Murray was brimming with insights, ideas, and irresistible enthusiasm on the subject of American music and culture. Lynn Meyers and Michael Schulman of Archive Photos helped me to locate photographs, as did the Museum of Modern Art/Film Stills Archive, where Mary Corliss and Terry Geesken assisted me yet again. George Wein, the impresario of the Newport Jazz Festival, provided me with hours of rare footage of Louis Armstrong in concert, in rehearsal, and reminiscing. Thanks also to Jon Binder, Shelley Finkel, Lizzie Hutton, Anne Johnston, T. George Harris, Tom Selz, John Steiner, Jeff Taylor, and Dempsey Travis.

I am grateful for the assistance and persistence of several talented research assistants: Sarah Amelar, Lesley Alderman, and Richard Livsey in New York, and Amy Handelsman in Los Angeles. In New Orleans, Daniel "Froggy" Meyer's scholarly sleuthing contributed much to this book's account of Louis's New Orleans years.

This is the third book on which I have worked with genealogist Marsha Dennis, and I can think of no one else who could make a research visit to the Queens County Courthouse as entertaining and informative as she did. Antonia Martin, a founder of the African American Genealogical Society, assisted in tracing Louis's roots. Jaymie Meyer painstakingly transcribed my recorded interviews. My wife, Betsy Bergreen, also researched with a will, and in dozens of ways, large and small, she made it possible for me to complete this work and even gave me the very cool computer on which I wrote it.

There were others who were crucial to the process of seeing this book into print. My literary agent, Andrew Wylie, once again showed why he is so good at what he does. I also wish to thank Bridget Love, who was always there. My thanks to all the others at the Wylie Agency who labored on behalf of this book.

At the brand-new Broadway Books division of Bantam Doubleday Dell, I worked with two highly capable veterans. Bill Shinker, Broadway's Publisher, shared my enthusiasm for this project right from the start and made me feel at home in his new house. My editor, John Sterling, proved to be enthusiastic and perceptive—just as I hoped he would be. Special thanks to Victoria Andros for her rigorous, sensitive line editing. I also wish to acknowledge Kathy Spinelli, Trigg Robinson, Maggie Richards, Jennifer Swihart, and the rest of the Broadway team.

LIST OF RECORDINGS

COMPILED BY DARRELL K. FENNELL

This selection of Armstrong's recordings is intended to give a sense of the broad range of his legacy and to call attention to his significant collaborations and record company affiliations. For each session listed, all masters on which Armstrong performs are identified. Sessions are grouped to illustrate Armstrong's musical associations and therefore are not in strict chronological order.

Abbreviations and symbols: *arr.*-arranger, *as*-alto sax, *b*-string bass, *bar*-baritone sax, *bcl*-bass clarinet, *bj*-banjo, *bs*-bass sax, *c*-cornet, *c.*-circa, *cel*-celeste, *cl*-clarinet, *clo*-cello, *Cm*-C melody sax, *d*-drums, *db*-doubles on, *eb*-electric bass, *fl*-flute, *flg*-flugelhorn, *g*-guitar, *gfs*-goofus, *hwg*-Hawaiian guitar, *hm*-harmonium, *inst*-instrumental version, *LA&HO*-Louis Armstrong and His Orchestra, *md*-musical director or conductor, *o*-oboe, *p*-piano, *perc*-percussion, *prob.*-probably, *r*-various reeds, *ss*-soprano sax, *so*-sits out, *sw*-slide whistle, *t*-trumpet, *tb*-trombone, *ts*-tenor sax, *tu*-tuba or sousaphone, *v*-vocal, *vib*-vibraphones, *vla*-viola, *vln*-violin, *wb*-washboards, *?*-not universally accepted, *[. . .]*-occasionally plays or doubles on, +-Armstrong vocal; ++-Armstrong duet with Velma Middleton; *-Armstrong sings but does not play trumpet or cornet.

The original labels are listed for studio recordings, but matrix numbers have not been included. Sessions with recording dates shown in *italics* have been released on compact disc. Pieces on which Armstrong received composer or other copyright credit are shown in SMALL CAPS. Parenthetical numbers—e.g. (16-18)—next to musicians indicate on which titles the musician played. Musicians without parenthetical numbers play on all numbers in the following set or group of sessions.

ARMSTRONG AS SIDE MAN

King Oliver's Creole Jazz Band. Joseph "King" Oliver (c, md) Armstrong (c), Honore Dutrey (1-31) or Ed Atkins (32-35) (tb), Johnny Dodds (1-31) or Jimmie Noone (32-35) (cl), Paul "Stump" Evans (20-23) (Cm), Charlie Jackson (17-31) (bs); Lil Hardin (p, arr), prob. Arthur "Bud" Scott (not Bill Johnson) (1-9), Arthur "Bud" Scott (10-16) or Johnny St. Cyr (20-35) (bj), Warren "Baby" Dodds (d):

April 5, 1923, Richmond, Indiana (Gennett): 1. Just Gone; 2. CANAL STREET BLUES; 3. Mandy Lee Blues; 4. I'm Going Away to Wear You Off My Mind; 5. Chimes Blues. • *April 6, 1923*, Richmond (Gennett): 6. WEATHER BIRD RAG; 7. DIPPERMOUTH BLUES; 8. Froggie Moore;

9. Snake Rag. • *June 22(?), 1923*, Chicago (Okeh): 10. Snake Rag; 11. Sweet Lovin' Man; 12. High Society Rag; 13. Sobbin' Blues (Armstrong db sw). • *June 23(?), 1923*, Chicago (Okeh): 14. WHERE DID YOU STAY LAST NIGHT? 15. DIPPERMOUTH BLUES; 16. Jazzin' Babies Blue. • *September 1923(?)*, Chicago (Paramount): 17. Mabel's Dream; 18. Southern Stomps; 19. Riverside Blues. • *October 5, 1923*, Richmond, Indiana (Gennett): 20. Alligator Hop; 21. Zulu's Ball; 22. Working Man's Blues; 23. Krooked Blues. • *Early October 1923* , Chicago (Okeh): 24. Buddy's Habit; 25. TEARS; 26. I Ain't Gonna Tell Nobody; 27. Room Rent Blues; 28. Riverside Blues; 29. Sweet Baby Doll; 30. Working Man's Blues; 31. Mabel's Dream. • *October 15, 1923*, Chicago (Columbia): 32. Chattanooga Stomp. • *October 16, 1923*, Chicago (Columbia): 33. London (Café) Blues; 34. Camp Meeting Blues; 35. NEW ORLEANS STOMP.

With Fletcher Henderson. The collective personnel of Henderson's orchestra during Armstrong's one-year stay were: Fletcher Henderson (p, arr, md); Elmer Chambers, Howard Scott (1-30) or Joe Smith (31-40), and Armstrong (t), Charlie Green (tb), Don Redman (cl, as, [o, gfs, t?, ss], prob. Cecil Scott (1-2) (cl, as)), Buster Bailey (3-40) (cl, as, [ss]), Coleman Hawkins (ts, [cl, Cm, bar, bs]), Charlie Dixon (bj), Ralph Escudero (tu), Kaiser Marshall (d). All recorded in New York.

October 7, 1924 (Columbia): 1. Manda; 2. Go 'Long, Mule (arr. Redman). • *October 13, 1924* (Pathé Actuelle): 3. Tell Me, Dreamy Eyes; 4. My Rose Marie; 5. Don't Forget You'll Regret Day By Day; 6. Shanghai Shuffle. • *October 30, 1924* (Vocalion): 7. Words; 8. Copenhagen (arr. Redman). • *November 7, 1924* (Vocalion): 9. Shanghai Shuffle (arr. Redman); 10. Naughty Man. • *November 10 or 11, 1924* (Banner): 11. One of These Days; 12. My Dream Man. • *November 14, 1924* (Columbia): 13. The Meanest Kind of Blues; 14. Naughty Man. • *Mid-November 1924* (Banner): 15. How Come You Do Me Like You Do? 16. Araby. • *Late-November 1924* (Domino/Banner/Oriole): 17. Everybody Loves My Baby+ (*first recorded vocal by Armstrong*); 18. Everybody Loves My Baby (inst); 19. Naughty Man. • *November-December 1924* (Paramount): 20. Prince of Wails; 21. Mandy Make Up Your Mind. • *January 12 (?), 1925* (Banner/Ajax): 22. I'll See You in My Dreams; 23. Why Couldn't It Be Poor Little Me? • *January 23, 1925* (Columbia): 24. Bye And Bye; 25. Play Me Slow. •

January 30 (?), 1925 (Banner): 26. Alabamy Bound (arr. Redman); 27. Swanee Butterfly. • *February 4 (?), 1925* (Pathé Actuelle): 28. Poplar Street Blues; 29. 12th Street Blues; 30. Me Neenyah. • *April 18, 1925* (Vocalion): 31. Memphis Bound; 32. When You Do What You Do. • *May 19, 1925* (Columbia): 33. I'll Take Her Back If She Wants to Come Back; 34. Money Blues. • *May 29, 1925*: 35. SUGAR FOOT STOMP (arr. Redman); 36. What-Cha-Call-Em-Blues (arr. Redman). • *August 7, 1925* (Harmony): 37. I Miss My Swiss (arr. Redman); 38. Alone at Last (arr. Redman). • *October 21, 1925* (Columbia): 39. TNT (arr. Redman); 40. Carolina Stomp.

A S   V O C A L   A C C O M P A N I S T

During his first stay in New York, Armstrong, often with other musicians from the Henderson band, accompanied numerous blues and popular singers.

Ma Rainey and Her Georgia Jazz Band: Armstrong (c), Charlie Green (tb), Buster Bailey (cl), Fletcher Henderson (p), and Charlie Dixon (bj).

October 16, 1924 (Paramount): 1. See See Rider; 2. Jelly Bean Blues; 3. Countin' the Blues.

Eva Taylor with Clarence Williams Blue Five [or *Trio* (13)]: Armstrong (c), Aaron Thompson (1-2) or Charlie Irvis (3-12; 14-15) (tb); Buster Bailey (1-2, 7-12) or Sidney Bechet (3-10) (ss) [Bechet db cl 7-10; Bailey db cl on 7-10]; Don Redman (7-8; 14-15: cl, as; 9-10: cl, ss; 11-12: cl); Coleman Hawkins (14-15) (ts); Clarence Williams (p) and Buddy Christian (bj). All on Okeh.

November 11, 1924: 1. Of All the Wrong You've Done to Me; 2. Everybody Loves My Baby. • *December 17, 1924*: 3. Mandy Make Up Your Mind; 4. I'm a Little Blackbird Looking for a Little Bluebird. (*Armstrong's first record with Bechet.*) • *January 8, 1925*: 5. Cake Walking Babies from Home; 6. Pickin' on Your Baby. • *March 4, 1925*: 7. Cast Away; 8. Papa-De-Da-Da. • *October 6, 1925*: 9. Just Wait 'Til You See My Baby Do the Charleston; 10. Livin' High. • *October 8, 1925*: 11. COAL CART BLUES; 12. Santa Claus Blues. • *October 16, 1925*: 13. Santa Claus Blues (Williams and Clarence Todd v). • *October 26, 1925*: 14. Squeeze Me; 15. You Can't Shush Katie.

Alberta Hunter with the Red Onion Jazz Babies: Armstrong (c), Aaron Thompson (1-2) or Charlie Irvis (3-5) (tb); Buster Bailey (1-2) (cl) or Sidney Bechet (3-5) (cl, ss); Lil Hardin (p), Buddy Christian (bj). All on Gennett.

November 6, 1924: 1. Everybody Loves My Baby. • *November 8, 1924*: 2. Texas Moaner Blues. • *December 22, 1924*: 3. Nobody Knows the Way I Feel Dis Morning; 4. Early Every Morn'; 5. Cake Walking Babies from Home (Clarence Todd v).

Bessie Smith: Armstrong (c), Charlie Green (6-9) (tb), Fred Longshaw (hm: 1-2; p: 3-9). All on Columbia.

January 14, 1925: 1. St. Louis Blues; 2. Reckless Blues; 3. Sobbin' Hearted Blues; 4. Cold in Hand Blues; 5. You've Been a Good Ole Wagon. • *May 26, 1925*: 6. Nashville Woman's Blues; 7. Careless Love Blues. • *May 27, 1925*: 8. J. C. Holmes Blues; 9. I Ain't Gonna Play No Second Fiddle.

Among the other singers whom Armstrong backed during this period: Virginia Liston (*October 17, 1924*; Okeh); Margaret Johnson (*November 25, 1924*; Okeh) Sippie Wallace (*November 28, 1924*; Okeh); Maggie Jones (*December 9-10 and 17, 1924*; Columbia); Clara Smith (*January 7, 1925 and April 2, 1925*; Columbia); Trixie Smith (*February 9, 1925 and March 25, 1925*; Paramount). Armstrong's last recording before returning to Chicago in 1925 was under the name of "Perry Bradford's Jazz Phools." (Vocalion): Armstrong (c), Charlie Green (tb), Buster Bailey (cl), Don Redman (as), James P. Johnson (p), Charlie Dixon (bj), Kaiser Marshall (d), Perry Bradford (v): *November 2, 1925*, 1. Lucy Long; 2. I Ain't Gonna Play No Second Fiddle.

After moving to Chicago in November 1925, Armstrong again backed Sippie Wallace (*March 1, 1926 and May 6, 1927*; Okeh), Bertha "Chippie" Hill (*November 9, 1925, February 23, 1926 and November 23, 1926*; Okeh), Blanche Calloway (*November 9, 1925*; Okeh), and Lillie Delk Christian (*June 26, 1928, December 11-12, 1928*; Okeh).

In New York again in 1929, Armstrong with small group accompanied Seger Ellis (*June 4, 1929 and August 23, 1929*; Okeh) (*with Jimmy and Tommy Dorsey*) and Victoria Spivey (*July 10, 1929*; Okeh) (*with members of the Carroll Dickerson band*).

THE CLASSIC SMALL GROUPS

The Hot Five. In Chicago after the stint with Henderson, Okeh arranged for Armstrong to record with a group of established New Orleans players resident in Chicago (plus Lil Hardin). The group, originally the Hot Five, consisted of: Armstrong (c) and (t- by June 1926), Kid Ory (tb) [Henry "Hy" Clark replaces Ory on 23-24], Johnny Dodds (cl), Lil Hardin (p), Johnny St. Cyr (bj). Okeh recorded the group in Chicago.

November 12, 1925: 1. My Heart; 2. I'M IN THE BARREL; 3. GUT BUCKET BLUES+ (Ory v). • *February 22, 1926*: 4. Come Back, Sweet Papa (Dodds db as). • *February 26, 1926*: 5. Georgia Grind+ (Hardin v); 6. Heebie Jeebies+ (*arguably the first scat recording*); 7. CORNET CHOP SUEY; 8. Oriental Strut; 9. You're Next; 10. Muskrat Ramble. • *June 16, 1926*: 11. Don't Forget to Mess Around+ (Dodds db as); 12. I'm Gonna Gitcha+; 13. Droppin' Shucks+; 14. Who's It (Armstrong db sw). • *June 23, 1926*: 15. King of the Zulus+ (Clarence Babcock and Hardin v); 16. Big Fat Ma and Skinny Pa+ (Babcock v); 17. Lonesome Blues+; 18. Sweet Little Papa. • *November 16, 1926*: 19. Jazz Lips; 20. Skid-Dat-De-Dat+; 21. Big Butter and Egg Man+ (May Alix v); 22. Sunset Cafe Stomp (Alix v). • *November 27, 1926*: 23. WHO MADE ME LOVE YOU+: 24. IRISH BLACK BOTTOM+.

The Hot Seven. Nearly six months later, by adding tuba and drums, the group was augmented to a septet. The Hot Seven consisted of Armstrong (t), John Thomas (tb), Johnny Dodds (cl), Lil Hardin (p), Johnny St. Cyr (bj, g), Pete Briggs (tu), and Warren "Baby" Dodds (d).

May 7, 1927: 1. Willie the Weeper; 2. Wild Man Blues. • *May 10, 1927*: 3. Alligator Crawl; 4. POTATO HEAD BLUES. • *May 11, 1927*: 5. Melancholy; 6. Weary Blues; 7. Twelfth Street Rag. • *May 13, 1927*: 8. Keyhole Blues; 9. S.O.L. BLUES. • *May 14, 1927*: 10. GULLY LOW BLUES; 11. That's When I'll Come Back to You+ (Hardin v).

More Hot Five. Same personnel as before with Lonnie Johnson (g) added (8-9).

September 2, 1927: 1. Put 'Em Down Blues+; 2. Ory's Creole Trombone. • *September 6, 1927*: 3. The Last Time+. • *December 9, 1927*: 4. STRUTTIN' WITH SOME BARBECUE; 5. Got No Blues. • *December 10, 1927*: 6. Once in a While; 7. I'M NOT ROUGH+. • *December 13, 1927*: 8. Hotter Than That+; 9. Savoy Blues.

Other Small Groups. During the same period, evidently in violation of his contract with Okeh, Armstrong participated in several small group sessions (for Vocalion) based on the format of the Hot Five. The *May 26, 1926* date, nominally led by Lil Hardin (as Lill's [*sic*] Hot Shots), but in fact the Hot Five, produced Georgia Bo Bo and DROP THAT SACK. On *April 21, 1927* he recorded as part of Jimmy Bertrand's Washboard Wizards (with Dodds (cl), Jimmy Blythe (p) and Bertrand (wb)). On *April 22, 1927* a group recorded, under the leadership of Johnny Dodds (the Black Bottom Stompers), which consisted of Armstrong (c), Gerald Reeve (tb), Johnny Dodds (cl), Barney Bigard (ts), Earl Hines (p); Arthur "Bud" Scott (bj) and Warren "Baby" Dodds (d): 1. Weary Blues (*Armstrong's first recording with Hines*); 2. NEW ORLEANS STOMP; 3. Wild Man Blues (*recorded two weeks before the Hot Seven's version*); 4. Melancholy.

With Earl Hines. In 1928 Armstrong replaced Hardin with Hines (p) and used other personnel from the Carroll Dickerson orchestra (which Armstrong was fronting). The new group consisted of: Armstrong (t), Fred Robinson (so 16) (tb), Jimmy Strong (1-12; 17-20) (cl, ts), Don Redman (13-15; 18-20) (cl, as, [arr.-13, 15, 18-20]), Earl Hines (p, [cel 12]), Mancy Carr (1-12; 17-20) or Dave Wilborne (13-15) (bj), Arthur "Zutty" Singleton (so 16) (d). Okeh continued to record the group in Chicago.

> *June 27, 1928*: 1. Fireworks; 2. Skip the Gutter; 3. A Monday Date+ (Hines v). • *June 28, 1928*: 4. Don't Jive Me; 5. West End Blues+; 6. Sugar Foot Strut+. • *June 29, 1928*: 7. Two Deuces; 8. Squeeze Me+ (Hines, Carr v). • *July 5, 1928:* 9. Knee Drops. • *December 4, 1928*; 10. No; 11. Basin Street Blues+ (Hines, Carr v). • *December 5, 1928*: 12. No One Else But You+; 13. BEAU KOO JACK (arr. Hill); 14. Save It, Pretty Mama+. • *December 5, 1928*: 15. WEATHER BIRD (*Armstrong t and Hines p only*). • *December 7, 1928*: 16. MUGGLES. • *December 12, 1928*: 17. HEAR ME TALKIN' TO YA+; 18. St. James Infirmary+; 19. Tight Like This+ (Redman and Hines v).

In New York Again. In 1929 Armstrong moved to New York. Aside from several recordings accompanying vocalists, he recorded this small group and then abandoned the format for fifteen years. *March 5, 1929* (Okeh): Armstrong (t), Jack Teagarden (tb), Albert "Happy" Caldwell (ts), Joe Sullivan (p), Eddie Lang (g) and Kaiser Marshall (d): "KNOCKIN' A JUG" (*Armstrong's first recording with Jack Teagarden*).

FRONTING THE BIG BAND

While recording with the studio groups the Hot Five and Hot Seven in Chicago Armstrong continued to perform with big bands.

Erskine Tate's Vendome Orchestra. Armstrong (c?, t), James Tate (?) (t), Fayette Williams [or Eddie Atkins] (tb), Angelo (Alvin) Fernandez (as?, cl), Paul "Stump" Evans (as, bar), Norval Morton (ts), Teddy Weatherford plus another (p), Frank Etheridge (bj), John Hare (tu), Jimmy Bertrand (d, wb), Erskine Tate (md, bj?).

May 28, 1926, Chicago (Vocalion): 1. Static Strut; 2. Stomp Off and Let's Go.

Louis Armstrong & His Stompers. Armstrong, Bill Wilson (c), Honore Dutrey (tb); Boyd Atkins (cl, ss, as), Joe Walker (as, bar), Albert Washington (ts), Earl Hines (p), Rip Basset (g), Pete Briggs (tu), Tubby Hall (d).

May 9, 1927, Chicago (Columbia): Chicago Breakdown (*Armstrong's first record as leader of a big band uses the band he led at the Savoy Ballroom*).

Carroll Dickerson's Savoyagers. Carroll Dickerson (vln, md), Armstrong, Homer Hobson (t), Fred Robinson (tb), Bert Curry, Crawford Wethington (as), Jimmy Strong (cl, ts), Earl Hines (p), Mancy Carr (bj), Pete Briggs (tu) and Arthur "Zutty" Singleton (d). Recorded in Chicago (Odeon).

July 5, 1928: 1. Symphonic Raps; 2. Savoyagers' Stomp.

Luis Russell. Back in New York in 1929, Armstrong recorded with the Luis Russell band under the name "Louis Armstrong & His Savoy Ballroom Five." Armstrong (t), J. C. Higginbotham, (tb), Albert Nicholas, Charlie Holmes (as), Teddy Hill (ts), Luis Russell (p), Eddie Condon (bj), Lonnie Johnson (g), George "Pops" Foster (b) and Paul Barbarin (d). Recorded in New York for Okeh.

March 5, 1929: 1. I Can't Give You Anything But Love+; 2. Mahogany Hall Stomp.

Carroll Dickerson (as "LA&HO"). Armstrong, Homer Hobson (t), Fred Robinson (tb), Bert Curry, Crawford Wethington (as), Jimmy Strong (cl, ts), Carroll Dickerson (vln, md), Gene Anderson (p, cel), Mancy Carr (bj), Pete Briggs (tu), Arthur "Zutty" Singleton (d). Recorded in New York for Okeh.

July 19, 1929: 1. Ain't Misbehavin'+. • *July 22, 1929*: 2. Black and Blue+; 3. That Rhythm Man; 4. Sweet Savannah Sue. • *September 10, 1929*; 5-6. Some of These Days (5-+; 6-inst). • *September 11, 1929*: 7-8. When You're Smiling (7-+; 8-inst). • *November 26, 1929*: 9-10. After You've Gone (9-+; 10-inst).

Luis Russell (as "LA&HO"). Armstrong (t), Otis Johnson, Henry "Red" Allen (t), J. C. Higginbotham (tb), Albert Nicholas (1-9) or Thornton Blue (10-11) (cl, as), Charlie Holmes (cl, as, ss), Teddy Hill (ts), Luis Russell (p, md), Will Johnson (g), George "Pops" Foster (b), and Paul Barbarin (d). Recorded in Chicago for Okeh.

December 10, 1929: 1-2. I Ain't Got Nobody (1-+; 2-inst); 3-4. Dallas Blues (3-+; 4-inst). • *December 13, 1929*: 5-7. St. Louis Blues (5-+; 6-7-inst); 8. Rockin' Chair+ (Hoagy Carmichael v). • *January 24, 1930*: 9. Song of the Island (with 3 vln; Barbarin-vib; ?-d). • *February 1, 1930*: 10. Bessie Couldn't Help It; 11. Blue, Turning Gray Over You.

Willie Lynch (as LA&HO). Armstrong, Ed Anderson (t), Henry Hicks (tb), Bobby Holmes (cl, as), Theodore McCord (as), Castor McCord (cl, ts), Joe Turner (1-6) and Buck Washington (1) (p), Bernard Addison (g), Lovert Hutchinson (tu) and Willie Lynch (d, md). Recorded in New York for Okeh.

April 5, 1930: 1. My Sweet+; 2. I Can't Believe That You're in Love with Me+. • *May 4, 1930*: 3. Indian Cradle Song+; 4. Exactly Like You+; 5. Dinah+; 6. Tiger Rag.

Leon Elkins (as "Louis Armstrong & His Sebastian New Cotton Club Orchestra"). Armstrong (t), Leon Elkins (t, md), Lawrence Brown (tb), Leon Herriford, Willie Stark (as), William Franz (ts), Harvey Brooks (p), Ceele Burke (bj, hwg), Reggie Jones (tu), Lionel Hampton (d, vib). Recorded in Los Angeles for Okeh.

July 21, 1930: 1. I'm a Ding Dong Daddy+; 2. I'm in the Market for You+. • *August 19, 1930*: 3. I'm Confessin'+; 4. If I Could Be with You One Hour Tonight+.

Les Hite (as "Louis Armstrong and His Sebastian New Cotton Club Orchestra"). Armstrong, George Orendorff, Harold Scott (t), Luther Graven (b), Les Hite (as, bar, md), Marvin Johnson (as), Charlie Jones (cl, ts), Henry Prince (p), Bill Perkins (bj, g), Joe Bailey ([tu], b), Lionel Hampton (d, vib). Recorded in Los Angeles for Okeh.

October 9, 1930: 1. Body and Soul+. • *October 15, 1930*: Memories of You+; 3. You're Lucky to Me+. • *December 23, 1930*: 4. Sweethearts on Parade+; 5. You're Drivin' Me Crazy+ (Hampton v); 6. The Peanut Vendor+. • *March 9, 1931*: 7. Just a Gigolo+; 8. Shine+.

Zilner Randolph (as "LA&HO"; this band was originally directed by Mike McKendrick). Armstrong (t), Zilner Randolph (t, arr, md), Preston Jackson (tb), Lester Boone (cl, as), George

James (cl, ss, as), Albert Washington (cl, ts), Charlie Alexander (p), Mike McKendrick (bj, g), John Lindsay (b) and Alfred "Tubby" Hall (d). Recorded in Chicago for Okeh.

April 20, 1931: 1. Walkin' My Baby Back Home+; 2. I Surrender Dear+; 3. When It's Sleepy Time Down South+. • *April 28, 1931*: 4. Blue Again+; 5. Little Joe +; 6. You Rascal You+. • *April 29, 1931*: 7. Them There Eyes+; 8. When Your Love Has Gone+. • *November 3, 1931*: 9. Lazy River+; 10. Chinatown, My China Town+. • *November 4, 1931*: 11. Stardust+. • *November 5, 1931*: 12. You Can Depend on Me+; 13. Georgia on My Mind+. • *November 6, 1931*: 14. The Lonesome Road+ (Randolph, McKendrick, Lindsay v); 15. I Got Rhythm+. • *January 25, 1932*: 16. Between the Devil and the Deep Blue Sea+; 17. Kickin' the Gong Around+. • *January 27, 1932*: 18. Home+; 19. All of Me+. • *March 2, 1932*: 20. Love, You Funny Thing+. *March 11, 1932*: 21. Tiger Rag+; 22. Keepin' Out of Mischief+; 23. Lawd, You Made the Night Too Long+.

Chick Webb (as "LA&HO"). Armstrong, Luis Bacon, Louis Hunt, Billy Hicks (t), Charlie Green (tb), Pete Clark (cl, as), Edgar Sampson (as, vln), Elmer Williams (ts), Don Kirkpatrick (p), John Trueheart (g), Elmer James (tu, b) and Chick Webb (d), Mezz Mezzrow (bells on 2).

December 8, 1932, Camden (Victor): 1. That's My Home+; 2. HOBO, YOU CAN'T RIDE THIS TRAIN+ (*Charlie Green's last recorded solo*).

Armstrong Pickup Group. Armstrong, Charlie Gaines plus another (t), ? (tb), Louis Jordan, Arthur Davey (as), Ellsworth Blake (ts), Wesley Robinson (p), ? (bj, g), Ed Hayes (tu) and Benny Hill (d).

December 21, 1932, Camden (Victor): 1. Medley of Armstrong Hits (Part II) (When You're Smiling, St. James Infirmary, Dinah)+; 2. Medley of Armstrong Hits (Part I) (You Rascal You, When It's Sleepy Time Down South, Nobody's Sweetheart)+.

Zilner Randolph (as "LA&HO"). Armstrong, Elmer Whitlock, Zilner Randolph (t), Frederic "Keg" Johnson (tb), Scoville Brown, George Oldham (cl, as); Albert "Budd" Johnson (cl, ts); Teddy Wilson (1-12) or Charlie Beal (13-23) (p), Mike McKendrick (bj, dobro), Bill Oldham (b, tu) and Yank Porter (1-12), Sid Catlett (13-17) or Harry Dial (18-23) (d). Recorded in Chicago for Victor.

January 26, 1933: 1. I've Got the World on a String+; 2. I Gotta Right to Sing the Blues+; 3. Hustlin' and Bustlin' for Baby+; 4. Sittin' in the Dark+; 5. High Society; 6. He's a Son of the South+. • *January 27, 1933*: 7. Some Sweet Day+; 8. Basin Street Blues+; 9. Honey, Do!+. • *January 28, 1933*: 10. Snowball+; 11. Mahogany Hall Stomp; 12. Swing, You Cats. • *April 24, 1933*: 13. Honey, Don't You Love Me Anymore?+; 14. Mississippi Basin+; 15. Laughin' Louie+; 16. TOMOR-ROW NIGHT+; 17. Dusky Stevedore+. • *April 26, 1933*: 18. There's a Cabin in the Pines+; 19. Mighty River+; 20. Sweet Sue, Just You+ (Budd Johnson v); 21. I WONDER WHO+; 22. St. Louis Blues; 23. Don't Play Me Cheap+.

Louis Armstrong and His Orchestra. During an extended stay in Europe, Armstrong recorded in Paris (*October 1934*; Brunswick) with European and American musicians, including two from New Orleans (Tines and DuConge): Armstrong, Jack Hamilton, Leslie Thompson (t), Lionel Guimares (tb), Pete DuConge (cl, as), Henry Tyree (as), Alfred Pratt (ts), Herman Chittison (p), Maceo Jefferson (g), German Arago (b), Oliver Tines (d).

October 1934: 1. St. Louis Blues+; 2. Super Tiger Rag+; 3. Will You, Won't You Be Ma Baby+; 4. On the Sunny Side of the Street (Parts 1 and 2); 5. SONG OF THE VIPERS +.

Luis Russell (as "LA&HO"). On returning from Europe, Armstrong became permanently asso-ciated with Russell's big band and began his long association with Decca. The personnel of the band was: Armstrong, Leonard Davis (1-25) or Shelton Hemphill (26-74), Gus Aiken (1-25) or Henry "Red" Allen (26-40; 49-74) and Louis Bacon (1-40) or Otis Johnson (49-54) or Bernard Flood (55-74) (t), Harry White (1-19) or George Matthews (26-32) or Wilbur de Paris (33-40; 49-74), James Archey (1-16; 20-25) or Lawrence "Snub" Mosley (17-25) or George Washington (26-40; 49-74), and J. C. Higginbotham (26-74) (tb), Henry Jones (1-25) or Pete Clark (26-40) or Rupert Cole (41-74 [cl]) and Charlie Holmes (as), Bingie Madison (cl, ts), Greely Walton (1-25) or Albert Nicholas (26-40; 49-50) or Joe Garland (51-74) (ts), Luis Russell (p), Lee Blair (g), George "Pops" Foster (b) and Paul Barbarin (d [vib]) (1-48) or Sid Catlett (49-74) (d). All recorded for Decca in New York (or Los Angeles [33-40]).

October 3, 1935: 1. I'm in the Mood for Love+; 2. You Are My Lucky Star+; 3. La Cucaracha+; 4. Got a Bran' New Suit+. • *November 21, 1935*: 5. I've Got My Fingers Crossed+; 6. OLD MAN MOSE +; 7. I'm Shooting High+; 8. Falling in Love with You+. • *December 13, 1935*: 9. Red Sails in the Sunset+; 10. On Treasure Island+. • *December 19,*

1935: 11. Thanks a Million+; 12. Shoe Shine Boy+; 13. Solitude+; 14. I Hope Gabriel Likes My Music+. • *January 18, 1936*: 15. The Music Goes Round and Round+; 16. Rhythm Saved the World+. • *April 28, 1936*: 17. I Come from a Musical Family+; 18. Somebody Stole My Break+. • *April 29, 1936*: 19. IF WE NEVER MEET AGAIN+. • *May 18, 1936*: 20. Lyin' to Myself +; 21. Ev'ntide+; 22. SWING THAT MUSIC+; 23. Thankful+; 24. Red Nose+; 25. Mahogany Hall Stomp. • *July 2, 1937*: 26. Public Melody Number 1+; 27. Yours and Mine+; 28. RED CAP +. • *July 7, 1937*: 29. She's the Daughter of a Planter from Havana+; 30. Alexander's Ragtime Band+; 31. I'VE GOT A HEART FULL OF RHYTHM+; 32. Sun Showers+. • *January 12, 1938*: 33. SATCHEL MOUTH SWING +; 34. Jubilee+; 35. STRUTTIN' WITH SOME BARBECUE; 36. The Trumpet Player's Lament+; 37. I Double Dare You+; 38. True Confession+; 39. Let That Be a Lesson to You+; 40. Sweet as a Song+. • *May 13, 1938*: 41. So Little Time+; 42. Mexican Swing+; 43. As Long as You Live, You'll Be Dead if You Die+; 44. When the Saints Go Marching In+ (*Armstrong's first recording of the piece*). • *May 18, 1938*: 45. On the Sentimental Side+; 46. It's Wonderful+; 47. Something Tells Me+; 48. Love Walked In+. • *January 18, 1939*: 49. Jeepers Creepers+; 50. WHAT IS THIS THING CALLED SWING?+. • *April 5, 1939*: 51. HEAR ME TALKIN' TO YA+; 52. Save It, Pretty Mama+; 53. West End Blues+; 54. Savoy Blues+. • *April 25, 1939*: 55. Confessin'+; 56. OUR MONDAY DATE+; 57. If It's Good+; 58. ME AND BROTHER BILL*. • *June 15, 1939*: 59. Baby, Won't You Please Come Home?+; 60. Poor Old Joe+; 61. Shanty Boat on the Mississippi+. • *December 18, 1939*: 62. Poor Old Joe+; 63. You're a Lucky Guy+; 64. You're Just a No Account+; 65. Bye and Bye+. • *March 14 1940*: 66. Hep Cats' Ball+; 67. You've Got Me Voodoo'd+; 68. Harlem Stomp+; 69. Wolverine Blues; 70. Lazy 'Sippi Steamer+. • *May 1, 1940*: 71. Sweethearts on Parade+; 72. You Run Your Mouth, I'll Run My Business+; 73. Cut Off My Legs and Call Me Shorty+; 74. Cain and Abel+.

Major changes in the orchestra took place in 1941. Until the recording ban in 1942, it consisted of: Armstrong, Shelton Hemphill, Gene Prince (75-78) or Bernard Flood (79-82), Frank Gailbreath (t), George Washington, Norman Green (75-78) or James Whitney (79-82), Henderson Chambers (tb), Rupert Cole, Carl Frye (as), Prince Robinson, Joe Garland (cl, ts), Luis Russell (p), Lawrence Lucie (g), Hayes Alvis (b), Sid Catlett (d). The following were recorded for Decca.

November 16, 1941, Chicago: 75. When It's Sleepy Time Down South; 76. Leap Frog; 77. I Used to Love You; 78. You Rascal, You+. • *April 17, 1942*, Los Angeles: 79. Cash for Your Trash+; 80. Among My Souvenirs+; 81. Coquette+; 82. I Never Knew+.

During the recording ban (from August 1942 through late 1944), Armstrong toured with the orchestra (under the musical direction of Joe Garland), although there were many personnel changes. The band that recorded the Jubilee Broadcast (in *March* or *April 1943*, Los Angeles) and the Spotlight Bands Shows (on *August 17, 1943*, Dallas, and *December 7, 1943*, Houston) probably consisted of: Armstrong, Shelton Hemphill, Frank Galbreath, Bernard Flood (t), George Washington, Henderson Chambers and James Whitney (tb), Rupert Cole (as, cl), Joe Garland (ts, r, md), Albert "Budd" Johnson and Dexter Gordon (ts), Carl Frye and Prince Robinson (r), Luis Russell or Gerry Wiggins (p), Larry Lucie (g), Art Simmons or Charles Mingus (b), and Chick Morrison or Jesse Price (d).

After the ban, Armstrong signed with Victor and his big band consisted of: Armstrong, Ed Mullens, Ludwig Jordan (1-5) or Robert Butler (6-12), Andrew "Fats" Ford (1-7) or Thomas Gridder (8-12), William "Chieftie" Scott (1-5; 8-12) or Louis Gray (6-7) (t), Russell "Big Chief" Moore, Adam Martin (1-5) or Waddet Williams (6-7), Morman Powe (1-5) or Nat Allen (6-7) or Al Moore (8-12), Al Cobbs (1-5) or James Whitney (6-12) (tb), Don Hill (1-7) or Arthur Dennis (8-12), Amos Gordon (as), Joe Garland, John Sparrow and Eli "Lucky" Thompson (8-12) (ts), Ernest Thompson (bar, cl), Ed Swanston (1-5) or Earl Mason (6-12) (p), Elmer Warner (g), Arvell Shaw (b), Butch Ballard (1-5), Edmund McConnery (6-7) or James "Coatsville" Harris (8-12) (d), and Velma Middleton (v).

April 27, 1945, New York: 1. Linger in My Arms a Little Longer+; 2. Whatta Ya Gonna Do?+; 3. NO VARIETY BLUES++ (*first recorded duet with Velma Middleton*); 4. JOSEPH AND HIS BRUDDERS+; 5. BACK O' TOWN BLUES.++ • *October 17, 1946*, Los Angeles: 6. Endie+; 7. The Blues Are Brewin'+. • *March 12, 1947*, New York: 8. I Wonder, I Wonder, I Wonder+; 9. I Believe+; 10. WHY DOUBT MY LOVE?+; 11. It Takes Time+; 12. You Don't Learn That in School+.

THE ALL STARS

Pre-All Stars Small Groups. Although his working unit was the big band, Armstrong also recorded with a variety of small groups using traditional instrumentation, with smaller groups from his big band, or with studio pickup groups. What follows are examples.

October 1938, New York: Armstrong (t), Jack Teagarden (tb), Lawrence "Bud" Freeman (ts), Thomas "Fats" Waller (p), Al Casey (g), George Wettling (d):

1. Tiger Rag; 2. On the Sunny Side of the Street+; 3. Jeepers Creepers+; 4. I Got Rhythm; 5. The Blues+ (Waller, Teagarden v); 6. Honeysuckle Rose.

May 27, 1940, New York (Decca). Armstrong (t), Claude Jones (tb), Sidney Bechet (cl, ss), Luis Russell (p), Bernard Addison (g), Wellman Braud (b), Arthur "Zutty" Singleton (d):

1. PERDIDO STREET BLUES; 2. 2:19 Blues+; 3. Down in Honky-Tonk Town; 4. COAL CART BLUES +.

January 13, 1944, New York, Esquire All Stars. Armstrong, Roy Eldridge (t), Jack Teagarden (tb), Barney Bigard (cl), Coleman Hawkins (ts), Art Tatum (p), Al Casey (g), Oscar Pettiford (b), Sid Catlett (d) and Kenneth "Red" Norvo (5) (vb):

1. Basin Street Blues; 2. Stompin' at the Savoy; 3. Esquire Bounce; 4. Basin Street Blues+ (Teagarden v); 5. I Got Rhythm.

January 10, 1946, New York, Leonard Feather's Esquire All-Americans. Armstrong, Charlie Shavers (t), Jimmy Hamilton (cl), Johnny Hodges (as), Don Byas (ts), Duke Ellington (1) and Billy Strayhorn (p), Remo Pamieri (g), Grieg "Chubby" Jackson (b) and Sonny Greer (d):

1. Long Long Journey; 2. Snafu.

September 6, 1946, Los Angeles (Victor). Armstrong (t), Vic Dickenson (tb), Barney Bigard (cl), Charlie Beal (1-2) or Leonard Feather (3-4) (p), Allan Reuss (g), George "Red" Callender (b), Arthur "Zutty" Singleton (d):

1. I Want a Little Girl+; 2. Sugar+; 3. Blues for Yesterday +; 4. Blues in the South+.

October 17, 1946, Los Angeles (Victor) (*with musicians filming the movie "New Orleans"*). Armstrong (t), Kid Ory (tb), Barney Bigard (cl), Charlie Beal (p), Arthur "Bud" Scott (g), George "Red" Callender (b) and Minor "Ram" Hall (d):

1. Do You Know What It Means to Miss New Orleans?+; 2. Where the Blues Were Born in New Orleans+; 3. Mahogany Hall Stomp.

The 1947 concerts. In 1947 Armstrong began performing in the "All Stars" format. Three concerts charted his evolution in this direction. In the Carnegie Hall concert (*February 8, 1947*), half was given over to the big band and half to Armstrong with Edmond Hall's small group. At the Town Hall concert (*May 17, 1947*), Armstrong played exclusively in small group format with various combinations of: Armstrong, Bobby Hackett (t), Jack Teagarden (tb, v), Michael "Peanuts" Hucko (cl), Dick Cary (p), Bob Haggart (b), Sid Catlett (d). The pieces were among those that would end up in the All Stars's book, including Ain't Misbehavin', Rockin' Chair, BACK O' TOWN BLUES, and St. James Infirmary. On *June 19, 1947* these same horns (with Ernie Caceres (cl, bs) added and the rhythm section of Johnny Guarnieri (p, cel), Al Casey (g), Al Hall (b) and Cozy Cole (d)) recorded four pieces for Victor. The third concert, on *November 30, 1947*, at Boston's Symphony Hall, saw the All Stars fully formed with the lineup: Armstrong (t), Jack Teagarden (tb), Barney Bigard (cl), Dick Cary (p), Arvell Shaw (b) and Sid Catlett (d).

The All Stars. The debut of the group that would remain Armstrong's last working unit took place at Billy Berg's in Los Angeles, while Armstrong was filming *A Star Is Born*. The All Stars first recorded in Chicago for Victor.

October 16, 1947. Armstrong (t, v), Jack Teagarden (t, v), Barney Biagard (cl), Dick Cary (p), Arvell Shaw (b) and Sid Catlett (d): 1. A Song Was Born; 2. Please Stop Playing Those Blues, Boy; 3. Before Long; 4. Lovely Weather We're Having.

The All Stars underwent gradual personnel changes. Teagarden (1-13) (tb) was replaced by Russell Phillips (14-15) in early 1952, then Trummy Young (16-17; 20-103) (summer 1952-63), Joe Yukl (18-19) (Dec. 1953), Russell "Big Chief" Moore (104-113) (1965) and Tyree Glenn (114-122) [vib] (1965-end). Bigard (1-52) (1947-55; 60-61) was briefly replaced for a tour in late 1952 by Bob McCracken, then Edmond Hall (53-97) (1955-57), Michael "Peanuts" Hucko (98-101) (July 1958-60), Joe Darensbourg (102-113) (June 1951-February 1965), Eddie Shue (March-June 1965), Buster Bailey (1965-67) and Joe Muranyi (114-122) (mid-1967-end). Dick Cary's piano seat was taken by Earl Hines (1-13) (early 1948-51), Joe Sullivan (early 1952), Marty Napoleon (14-15; 18-19; 114-122) (1952-53; again 1966-end), Joe Bushkin (16-17) (April 1953), and Billy Kyle (20-113) (1953-64). Arvell Shaw (1-13; 16-52) (1947-56) was replaced as bassist by Dale Jones (14-15) (1948-52 and mid-1956; 1964-65), Milt Hinton (early 1952), William "Squire" Gersh (53-97) (1956-57), Mort Herbert (98-101) (1958-61), Irving Manning (1961), Billy Cronk (1962-May 1963). The last bassist was George "Buddy" Catlett (114-122) (1965-end). On drums

Sid Catlett was replaced by William "Cozy" Cole (1-19) in 1949, then Kenny John (20-23) (early 1954), Barrett Deems (24-97) in mid-1954, and Danny Barcelona (98-122) (late 1957-end). Occasionally additional musicians supplemented the group: Yank Lawson (87-89) (t), Milt Yaner (16-17), Dick Jacobs (16-17), George Dorsey [fl] (53-64; 66-71; 90-93), Hilton Jefferson (59-63; 65-71; 90-93) (as), Donald Ruffell (14-15), Sam Taylor (16-17), Babe Russin (18-19), Bud Freeman (20-21), Eli "Lucky" Thompson (53-63; 65-71), Shelton Powell (90-93), Eddie Miller (98-101) (ts), Dave MacRae (53-63; 65-71; 90-93) (bar, [bcl]); Everett Barksdale (16-17; 90-93), George Barnes (72-88), and Al Hendrickson (98-101), Art Ryerson (110-111) (g), Tony Gottuso (102-103), Glen Thompson (104-113) (bj, g), Gene Krupa (18-19) (d), Gary Crosby (51-52) (v), and Sy Oliver (53-71), Bob Haggart (72-83) (md, arr). Velma Middleton (1947-60), then Jewell Brown were the female vocalists.

April 26 and 27, 1950, New York (Decca): 1. Panama; 2. New Orleans Function; 3. 12th Street Rag; 4. That's for Me+; 5. Bugle Call Rag/ Ole Miss; 6. I Surrender Dear+; 7. Russian Lullaby; 8. Baby, Won't You Please Come Home (Teagarden v); 9. Fine And Dandy; 10. My Bucket's Got a Hole In It+ (Teagarden v). • *April 23, 1951*, Los Angeles (Decca): 11. Unless+; 12. A Kiss to Build a Dream On+; 13. YOU'RE THE APPLE OF MY EYE. • *April 19, 1952*, Denver (Decca): 14. I'll Walk Alone+; 15. Kiss of Fire+. • *April 21, 1953*, New York (Decca): 16. April in Portugal +; 17. Ramona+. • *December 29, 1953*, Los Angeles (Decca): 18. Basin Street Blues+; 19. Otchi-Tchor-Ni-Ya+. • *March 19, 1954*, New York (Decca): 20. Basin Street Blues+; 21. Otchi-Tchor-Ni-Ya+; 22. STRUTTIN' WITH SOME BARBECUE; 23. Margie (Young v). • *July 12, 1954*, Chicago (Columbia): 24. Loveless Love++; 25. Hesitating Blues++; 26. Aunt Hagar's Blues+; 27. Beale Steet Blues+; 28. Ole Miss+. *July 13, 1954*, Chicago (Columbia): 29. St. Louis Blues++; 30. Long Gone++; 31. The Memphis Blues+; 32. Atlanta Blues+; *July 14, 1954*, Chicago (Columbia): 33. Yellow Dog Blues+; 34. Chantez-les Bas+. • *September 1, 1954*, New York (Decca): 35. Muskat Ramble; 36. Medley: Tenderly/You'll Never Walk Alone. • *April 25, 1955*, New York (Decca): 37. Yeh!++; 38. Mm-mm++; 39. Baby, Your Sleep is Showing++; 40. Tin Roof Blues; 41. PRETTY LITTLE MISSY+. • *April 26, 1955*, New York (Columbia): 42. Honeysuckle Rose++; 43. I've Got a Feeling I'm Falling+; 44. Black and Blue+; 45. Ain't Misbehavin'+. • *April 27, 1955*, New York (Columbia): 46. Blue Turning Gray Over You+; 47. I'm Crazy 'Bout My Baby and My Baby's Crazy About Me+; 48. All That Meat and No

Potatoes++. • *May 3, 1955*, New York (Columbia): 49. Squeeze Me; 50. Keepin' Out of Mischief Now+. • *September 9, 1955*, Los Angeles (Decca): 51. Easy Street+; 52. Lazy Bones+. • *December 11, 1956*, New York (Decca): 53. If I Could Be with You+; 54. Lazy River+; 55. I Can't Give You Anything But Love+; 56. On the Sunny Side of the Street+; 57. I Can't Believe That You're in Love with Me+; 58. Body and Soul+. • *December 12, 1956*, New York (Decca): 59. When You're Smiling+; 60. Some of These Days+; 61. I Surrender Dear+; 62. Georgia on My Mind+; 63. Mahogany Hall Stomp; 64. High Society; 65. Exactly Like You+. • *December 13, 1956*, New York (Decca): 66. Song of the Islands+; 67. That's My Home+; 68. Memories of You+; 69. Them There Eyes+. • *December 14, 1956*, New York (Decca): 70. This Younger Generation+; 71. In Pursuit of Happiness +. • *January 23, 1957*, New York (Decca): 72. Hotter Than That+; 73. Gut Bucket Blues+ (Young v); 74. Weary Blues; 75. POTATO HEAD BLUES; 76. CORNET CHOP SUEY. 77. Of All The Wrongs You've Done to Me. • *January 24, 1957*, New York (Decca): 78. Two Deuces; 79. Mandy Make Up Your Mind; 80. WILD MAN BLUES; 81. GULLY LOW BLUES+; 82. Everybody Loves My Baby+; 83. Heebie Jeebies+ (Young v). • *January 25, 1957*, New York (Decca): 84. King of the Zulus+ (Young and Hall v); 85. Frog-i-more Rag; 86. Georgia Grind; 87. Snag It; 88. Canal Street Blues; 89. DIPPERMOUTH BLUES (Hall v). • *January 28, 1957*, New York (Decca): 90. You Rascal You+; 91. HOBO, YOU CAN'T RIDE THIS TRAIN+; 92. KNOCKIN' A JUG; 93. Dear Old Stockholm (*Armstrong and Kyle only*); 94. See See Rider (Middleton v); 95. Reckless Blues (Middleton v); 96. Trouble in Mind (Middleton v); 97. Courthouse Blues (Middleton v). • *October 8, 1958*, Los Angeles (Decca): 98. I Love Jazz (with choir); 99. The Mardi-Gras March (with choir); 100. Basin Street Blues+; 101. Otchi-Tchor-Ni-Ya+.

December 3, 1963, New York: 102. Hello, Dolly; 103. A Lot of Livin' to Do. • *April 18, 1964*: 104. It's Been a Long, Long Time; 105. A Kiss to Build a Dream On; 106. SOMEDAY; 107. Hey, Look Me Over; 108. I Still Get Jealous; 109. Moon River; 110. Be My Life's Companion; 111. Blueberry Hill; 112. You Are Woman, I Am Man; 113. Jeepers Creepers. • *August 16, 1967*, New York (ABC-Paramount): 114. Hellzapoppin'+; 115. Cabaret+. • *July 23, 1968*, Las Vegas

(ABC-Paramount): 116. Dream a Little Dream of Me+; 117. I Guess I'll Get the Papers and Go Home +; 118. There Must Be a Way+; 119. Give Me Your Kisses +. • *July 24, 1968,* Las Vegas (ABC-Paramount) (with unknown big band): 120. Hello Brother+; 121. The Home Fire+; 122. Fantastic, That's You+.

In addition, there are a number of recordings of Armstrong and the All Stars in performance. Among these are the following: *January 30, 1951* (Pasadena, Decca); *January 21, 1955* (Hollywood, Decca); *October 29, 1955* (Concertgebouw, Columbia); *December 20-21, 1955* (Milan, Columbia); *January 21, 1956* (Los Angeles, Columbia); *June 1, 1956* (Chicago, Columbia); *July 4, 1957* (Newport, Pablo); *July 1, 1960* (Newport, Omega); *April 24, 1962* (Paris, Europe1); *June 4, 1965* (Paris, Vanguard); *July 26, 1967* (Juan les Pins, Bandstand).

OTHER SETTINGS

Armstrong performed in a wide variety of settings including Hawaiian strings (*September 18, 1936* and *March 24, 1937*), Hollywood string orchestras (Sy Oliver, Gordon Jenkins, Russell Garcia, John Trotter, Billy May and others), gospel choirs (*June 14, 1938* and *February 4, 6, 7, 1958*), the Dukes of Dixieland (*August 3-5, 1959; May 24-25, 1960*), Guy Lombardo (*July 1966*), and even a country/western band. "Country and Western" with the Nashville Rhythm Boys, August 1970, Arco Embassy, was his last album. The following is a sampling of these special projects.

With The Mills Brothers. Armstrong (t, v), Harry Mills, Herbert Mills, Donald Mills (v), John Mills Sr. (v, [g]). Recorded for Decca.

April 7, 1937: 1. Carry Me Back to Old Virginia+; 2. Darling Nelly Gray+. • *June 29, 1937*: 3. In the Shade of the Old Apple Tree+; 4. The Old Folks at Home+. • *June 10, 1938*: 5. The Flat Foot Floogie +. • *June 13, 1938:* 6. The Song Is Ended+; 7. My Walking Stick+. • *April 10, 1940*: 8. W.P.A.+; 9. Boog-It+. • *April 11, 1940*: 10. Cherry+; 11. Marie+.

With Billie Holiday. Armstrong (t, v), Sid Cooper, Johnny Mance (as), Art Drellinger (ts), Billy Kyle (p), Everett Barksdale (g), Joe Benjamin (b), Jimmy Crawford (d), Holiday (v).

September 30, 1949, New York (Decca): 1. You Can't Lose a Broken Heart+; 2. My Sweet Hunk O' Trash+; 3. Now or Never+.

With Ella Fitzgerald. Armstrong recorded with her for Decca with big bands on *January 18, 1946* (Bob Haggart Orchestra); *August 25, 1950* (Sy Oliver Orchestra) and *November 23, 1951* (Dave Babour Orchestra). With Verve he cut the three following albums.

August 15, 1956, Los Angeles ("Ella & Louis"): Armstrong (t, v), Oscar Peterson (p), Herb Ellis (g), Ray Brown (b), Bernard "Buddy" Rich (d): 1. Can't We Be Friends?+; 2. Isn't This a Lovely Day?+; 3. Moonlight in Vermont+; 4. They Can't Take That Away from Me+; 5. Under a Blanket of Blue+; 6. Tenderly+; 7. A Foggy Day+; 8. Stars Fell on Alabama+; 9. Cheek to Cheek+; 10. The Nearness of You+; 11. April in Paris+. • *August 13, 1957,* Los Angeles ("Ella and Louis Again"): Armstrong (t, v), Oscar Peterson (p), Herb Ellis (g), Ray Brown (b), Louis Bellson (d), Ella Fitzgerald (v): 1. Don't Be That Way*; 2. I Won't Dance*; 3. I've Got My Love to Keep Me Warm+; 4. I'm Putting All My Eggs in One Basket+; 5. A Fine Romance+. • *August 23, 1957:* 6. They All Laughed*; 7. Autumn in New York+; 8. Stompin' at the Savoy+; 9. Gee Baby Ain't I Good to You?+; 10. Let's Call the Whole Thing Off+; 11. Love Is Here to Stay+; 12. Learnin' the Blues+. • *August 18, 1957,* Los Angeles ("Porgy and Bess"): Armstrong (v, t), Fitzgerald (1-4) (v) with orchestra of Russell Garcia: 1. Summertime+; 2. Bess, You Is My Woman Now+; 3. I Got Plenty O' Nuttin'+; 4. It Ain't Necessarily So+; 5. There's a Boat Dat's Leaving Soon for New York+; 6. A Woman Is a Sometime Thing+; 6. Oh Lawd, I'm on My Way+; 7. Bess, Oh Where's My Bess?+ (*Other songs by Fitzgerald and orchestra only*).

With Oscar Peterson. Armstrong (t, v), Oscar Peterson (p), Herb Ellis (g), Ray Brown (b) and Louis Bellson (d).

July 31, 1957, New York (Verve): 1. I Get a Kick Out of You+; 2. Makin' Whoopee*; 3. Willow Weep for Me+; 4. Let's Do It*. • *October 14, 1957:* 5. That Old Feeling+; 6. Let's Fall in Love+; 7. I'll Never Be the Same+; 8. Blues in the Night+; 9. How Long Has This Been Going On+; 10. I Was Doing All Right+; 11. What's New+; 12. Moon Song+; 13. Just One of Those Things+; 14. There's No You+; 15. You Go to My Head+; 16. Sweet Lorraine+.

With Duke Ellington. Although Armstrong never recorded with the full Ellington orchestra, Ellington sat in for Billy Kyle with the working All Star unit.

    April 3, 1961, New York (Roulette): 1. Duke's Place+; 2. I'm Just a Lucky So and So+; 3. Cotton Tail+; 4. Mood Indigo+; 5. Do Nothin' Till You Hear from Me+; 6. The Beautiful American; 7. Black and Tan Fantasy; 8. Drop Me Off at Harlem+; 9. The Mooche; 10. In a Mellow Tone; 11. It Don't Mean a Thing+; 12. Solitude+; 13. Don't Get Around Much Any More+; 14. I'm Beginning to See the Light+; 15. Just Squeeze Me+; 16. I Got It Bad+; 17. Azalea+.

What a Wonderful World. Joe Wilder, Clark Terry (t), Urbie Green, J. J. Johnson (tb), Sam Marowitz (cl, fl, as), Dan Trimboli (fl, as, ts), Jerome Richardson (cl, fl, ts), Raymond Stanfeld (bar), 12 strings, Hank Jones (p), Allen Hanlon, Art Ryerson, Willard Suyker (g), Russell Savakus (b), Grady Tate (d), Warren Hard (perc), Armstrong (v), choir, Tommy Goodman (md, arr).

    August 16, 1967, New York (ABC-Paramount): 1. The Sunshine of Love*; 2. What a Wonderful World*.

With Friends. Armstrong's next to last album (for Flying Dutchman) was a tribute by a number of "moderns" backing his singing.

The Real Ambassadors. Dave Brubeck's trio recorded a number of Brubeck compositions with Armstrong, his All Stars, and the vocalists Dave Lambert, Jon Hendricks, Annie Ross, and Carmen McRae in *September 1961.*

    May 26, 1970, New York. James Spaulding (fl), 9 vln, 4 vla, 4 clo, Frank Owens (p), Sam Brown, Kenny Burrell (g), George Duvivier, Richard Davis (d), John Williams (eb), Pretty Purdie (d), Armstrong (v), Oliver Nelson (md, arr): 1. Mood Indigo*; 2. What a Wonderful World*; 3. My One and Only Love*. • *May 27, 1970* [Gene Golden (perc) and Leon Thomas (6) (v) added]: 4. His Father Wore Long Hair*; 5. Everybody's Talking*; 6. The Creator Has a Master Plan*. • *May 29, 1970*, New York. Thad Jones, Jimmy Owens, Ernie Royal, Marvin Stamm (t, flg), Garnett Brown, Bill Campbell, Al Grey, Quentin Jackson (tb), Robert Ashton, Ray Beckenstein, Danny Bank, Jerry Dodgion, Billy Harper (r), Frank Owens (p), Sam Brown, Kenny Burrell (g), Chuck Rainey (eb), Pretty Purdie (d), Gene Golden (perc), and Armstrong (v). Vocals on 6 and 7: Carl Hall, Janie Bell, Ila Gowan, Matthew Ledbetter, Tasha Thomas. Added vocals on 7: Bobby Hackett, Miles Davis, Ruby Braff, Tony Bennett, Leion Thomas, Chico Hamilton, Eddie Condon, Ornette Coleman, Mike Lipskin, George Wein, Father Norman O'Connor, Stanley Dance and others: 6. Give Peace a Chance*; 7. We Shall Overcome*; 8. Boy From New Orleans*; 9. This Black Cat Has Nine Lives*.

SELECT BIBLIOGRAPHY

Albertson, Chris. *Bessie.* New York: Stein & Day, 1982.

Allen, Walter C. and Brian A. L. Rust. *"King" Oliver,* rev. ed. Chigwell, England: Storyville Publications, 1987.

Allsop, Kenneth. *The Bootleggers and Their Era.* Garden City, N.Y.: Doubleday, 1961.

Armstrong, Louis. *Ma Nouvelle Orléans.* Paris: René Julliard, 1952.

————. *Satchmo: My Life in New Orleans.* New York: Prentice-Hall, 1954.

————. *Swing That Music.* New York: Da Capo Press, 1993. (Originally published 1936.)

Asbury, Herbert. *The French Quarter: An Informal History of the New Orleans Underworld.* New York: Alfred A. Knopf, 1936.

Ashmore, Harry S. *Arkansas: A History.* New York: W. W. Norton, 1978.

Barker, Danny. *A Life in Jazz.* New York: Oxford University Press, 1986.

Bechet, Sidney. *Treat It Gentle.* New York: Hill and Wang, 1960.

Bergreen, Laurence. *Capone: The Man and the Era.* New York: Simon and Schuster, 1994.

Bigard, Barney. *With Louis and the Duke: The Autobiography of a Jazz Clarinetist.* New York: Oxford University Press, 1986.

Blesh, Rudi. *Shining Trumpets.* New York: Alfred A. Knopf, 1946.

Blue Book. New Orleans: s.n., 1908.

Bordman, Gerald. *American Musical Theatre: A Chronicle.* New York: Oxford University Press, 1986.

Brask, Ole and Dan Morgenstern. *Jazz People.* New York: H. N. Abrams, 1960.

Brenner, Teddy and Barney Nagler. *Only the Ring Was Square.* Englewood Cliffs, N.J.: Prentice-Hall, 1981.

Bultman, Bethany Ewald. *New Orleans.* Oakland: Compass American Guides, 1994.

Charters, Samuel B. and Leonard Kunstadt. *Jazz: A History of the New York Scene.* New York: Da Capo Press, 1981.

Chilton, John. *Sidney Bechet: The Wizard of Jazz.* New York: Oxford University Press, 1987.

Clayton, Buck. *Buck Clayton's Jazz World.* New York: Oxford University Press, 1987.

Collier, James Lincoln. *Louis Armstrong: An American Genius.* New York: Oxford University Press, 1983.

————. *The Making of Jazz: A Comprehensive History.* New York: Dell, 1978.

Condon, Eddie. *We Called It Music: A Generation of Jazz.* New York: Henry Holt, 1947.

Cooper, Ralph and Steve Dougherty. *Amateur Night at the Apollo.* New York: HarperCollins, 1990.

Crow, Bill. *Jazz Anecdotes*. New York: Oxford University Press, 1990.

Dance, Stanley. *The World of Earl Hines*. New York: Charles Scribner's Sons, 1977.

Davis, F. James. *Who Is Black?: One Nation's Definition*. University Park: Pennsylvania State University Press, 1991.

Davis, Miles and Quincy Troupe. *Miles: The Autobiography*. New York: Simon and Schuster, 1989.

Douglas, Ann. *Terrible Honesty: Mongrel Manhattan in the 1920s*. New York: Farrar, Straus and Giroux, 1995.

Eaton, Jeanette. *Trumpeter's Tale: The Story of Young Louis Armstrong*. New York: William Morrow, 1955.

Ellington, Edward Kennedy. *Music Is My Mistress*. Garden City, N.Y.: Doubleday, 1973.

Ellison, Ralph. *Invisible Man*. New York: Vintage Books, 1990.

Fox, Stephen. *Blood and Power: Organized Crime in Twentieth-Century America*. New York: Penguin Books, 1990.

Gara, Larry. *The Baby Dodds Story*. Los Angeles: Contemporary Press, 1959.

Giddins, Gary. *Satchmo*. New York: Doubleday, 1988.

Gillespie, Dizzy and Al Evans. *to BE, or not . . . to BOP: Memoirs*. Garden City, N.Y.: Doubleday, 1979.

Gioia, Ted. *The Imperfect Art*. New York: Oxford University Press, 1988.

Gitler, Ira. *Swing to Bop*. New York: Oxford University Press, 1985.

Gleason, Ralph J., ed. *Jam Session: An Anthology of Jazz*. New York: G. P. Putnam's Sons, 1958.

Goffin, Robert. *Horn of Plenty: The Story of Louis Armstrong*. New York: Allen, Towne & Heath, 1947.

———. *Jazz: From the Congo to the Metropolitan*. Garden City, N.Y.: Doubleday, Doran, 1944.

Goldblatt, Burt. *Newport Jazz Festival*. New York: Dial Press, 1977.

Gordon, Max. *Live at the Village Vanguard*. New York: St. Martin's Press, 1980.

Hadlock, Richard. *Jazz Masters of the Twenties*. New York: Macmillan, 1965.

Hammond, John. *Hammond on Record: An Autobiography*. New York: Penguin Books, 1981.

Hentoff, Nat. *The Jazz Life*. New York: Da Capo Press, 1975.

Hillman, Christopher. *Bunk Johnson: His Life and Times*. New York: Universe Books, 1988.

Hinton, Milt and David G. Berger. *Bass Line: The Stories and Photographs of Milt Hinton*. Philadelphia: Temple University Press, 1988.

Hodier, André. *Jazz: Its Evolution and Essence*. New York: Grove Press, 1956.

Hodes, Art and Chadwick Hansen, eds. *Selections from the Gutter: Jazz Portraits from "The Jazz Record."* Berkeley: University of California Press, 1977.

Holiday, Billie and William Duffy. *Lady Sings the Blues*. Garden City, N.Y.: Doubleday, 1956.

Jones, Max. *Talking Jazz*. New York: W. W. Norton, 1988.

Jones, Max and John Chilton. *Louis: The Louis Armstrong Story, 1900–1971*. New York: Da Capo Press, 1988.

Joy to the World: A Celebration of Satchmo. Los Angeles: Friends of the USC Libraries, 1973.

Kaminsky, Max and V. E. Hughes. *My Life in Jazz*. New York: Harper & Row, 1963.

Kennedy, Rick. *Jelly Roll, Bix, and Hoagy: Gennett Studios and the Birth of Recorded Jazz*. Bloomington: Indiana University Press, 1994.

Kenney, William Howland. *Chicago Jazz: A Cultural History, 1904–1930.* New York: Oxford University Press, 1993.

Lambert, G. E. *Johnny Dodds.* New York: A. S. Barnes, 1961

Lemann, Nicholas. *The Promised Land: The Great Black Migration and How It Changed America.* New York: Alfred A. Knopf, 1991.

Lewis, David Levering. *When Harlem Was in Vogue.* New York: Alfred A. Knopf, 1981.

Lomax, Alan. *Mister Jelly Roll: The Fortunes of Jelly Roll Morton, New Orleans Creole and "Inventor of Jazz."* Berkeley: University of California Press, 1973. (Originally published 1950.)

Longstreet, Stephen. *Sportin' House: A History of the New Orleans Sinners and the Birth of Jazz.* Los Angeles: Sherbourne Press, 1965.

Lord, Tom. *Clarence Williams.* Chigwell, England: Storyville Publications, 1976.

Marquis, Donald M. *In Search of Buddy Bolden: First Man of Jazz.* Baton Rouge: Louisiana State University Press, 1978.

McCarthy, Albert J. *Louis Armstrong.* New York: A. S. Barnes, 1961.

Meryman, Richard. *Louis Armstrong: A Self-Portrait.* New York: The Eakins Press, 1971.

Mezzrow, Mezz and Bernard Wolfe. *Really the Blues.* New York: Citadel Press, 1990. (Originally published 1946.)

Miller, Marc H., ed. *Louis Armstrong: A Cultural Legacy.* Seattle: University of Washington Press, 1994.

Murray, Albert. *The Blue Devil Nada: A Contemporary American Approach to Aesthetic Statement.* New York: Pantheon, 1996.

———. *Stomping the Blues.* New York: McGraw-Hill, 1976.

Nicholson, Stuart. *Billie Holiday.* Boston: Northeast University Press, 1995.

Ondaatje, Michael. *Coming Through Slaughter.* London: Macmillan, 1984.

Ostransky, Leroy. *Jazz City: The Impact of Our Cities on the Development of Jazz.* Englewood Cliffs, N.J.: Prentice-Hall, 1978.

Panassié, Hughes. *Hot Jazz: The Guide to Swing Music.* New York: M. Witmark, 1936.

———. *Louis Armstrong.* New York: Charles Scribner's Sons, 1971.

Pinfold, Mike. *Louis Armstrong.* New York: Universe Books, 1987.

Priestly, Brian. *Mingus.* New York: Da Capo Press, 1982

Ramsey, Frederick Jr. and Charles Edward Smith, eds. *Jazzmen.* New York: Limelight Editions, 1985. (Originally published 1939.)

Roemer, William F. Jr. *Roemer: Man Against the Mob.* New York: Donald I. Fine, 1989.

Rose, Al. *Miss Lulu White de Basin Street Nouvelle Orleans.* Paris: Gaston La Churie, 1991.

———. *Storyville, New Orleans.* University: University of Alabama Press, 1974.

———, and Edmund Souchon. *New Orleans Jazz: A Family Album.* Baton Rouge: Louisiana State University Press, 1984.

Russell, Bill. *New Orleans Style.* New Orleans: Jazzology Press, 1994.

Rust, Brian. *The American Record Label Book.* New Rochelle, N.Y.: Arlington House, 1978.

Sanjek, Russell. *American Popular Music and Its Business: The First Four Hundred Years*, vol. III. New York: Oxford University Press, 1988.

Schuller, Gunther. *Early Jazz: Its Roots and Musical Development.* New York: Oxford University Press, 1968.

————. *The Swing Era: The Development of Jazz, 1930–1945.* New York: Oxford University Press, 1989.

Shapiro, Nat and Nat Hentoff. *Hear Me Talkin' to Ya: The Story of Jazz as Told by the Men Who Made It.* New York: Dover Publications, 1966.

Shaw, Arnold. *Black Popular Music in America.* New York: Macmillan, 1985.

Smith, Alson J. *Chicago's Left Bank.* Chicago: Henry Regnery, 1953.

Smith, Jay D. and Len Guttridge. *Jack Teagarden: The Story of a Jazz Maverick.* New York: Da Capo Press, 1976.

Stearns, Marshall W. *The Story of Jazz.* New York: Oxford University Press, 1972.

Tallant, Robert. *Voodoo in New Orleans.* Gretna, Louisiana: Pelican Publishing, 1974.

Terkel, Studs. *Giants of Jazz.* New York: Thomas Y. Crowell, 1957.

Thiele, Bob and Bob Golden. *What a Wonderful World: A Lifetime of Recordings.* New York: Oxford University Press, 1995.

Travis, Dempsey J. *An Autobiography of Black Jazz.* Chicago: Urban Research Institute, 1983.

Westerburg, Hans. *Boy from New Orleans: A Discography of Louis "Satchmo" Armstrong.* Copenhagen: Jazzmedia, 1981.

Williams, Martin. *The Jazz Tradition.* New York: Oxford University Press, 1983.

KEY TO ENDNOTES

Abbreviations for archives and frequently cited sources:

ARCHIVES AND OTHER COLLECTIONS

CCC   The Chicago Crime Commission, Chicago, Illinois.

HJA   Hogan Jazz Archives, Tulane University, New Orleans, Louisiana

HNOC   William Russell Collection, Williams Research Center of the Historic New Or-
       leans Collection, New Orleans, Louisiana

IJS   Institute of Jazz Studies, Rutgers University, Newark, New Jersey

JOHP   Jazz Oral History Project, Institute of Jazz Studies, Rutgers University, Newark,
       New Jersey

JTM   James T. Maher file on Lillian Hardin Armstrong

LAA   Louis Armstrong Archives, Queens College/CUNY, Queens, New York

USC   USC Cinema-TV Library, Los Angeles, California

PUBLICATIONS

FR   Frederic Ramsey Jr. and Charles Edward Smith, eds., *Jazzmen*

GG   Gary Giddins, *Satchmo*

LAM   Louis Armstrong, *Satchmo: My Life in New Orleans*

LAS   Louis Armstrong, *Swing That Music*

MJ   Max Jones and John Chilton, *Louis: The Louis Armstrong Story*

MM   Milton Mezzrow and Bernard Wolfe, *Really the Blues*

NS   Nat Shapiro and Nat Hentoff, *Hear Me Talkin' to Ya*

NYT   *New York Times*

RI   Lillian Hardin Armstrong recorded interview, Institute of Jazz Studies, Rutgers
       University, Newark, New Jersey

ENDNOTES

OVERTURE

4 "it was a pleasure": *MJ*, pp. 224-5.
5 "Yeah, those were": Autobiographical MS, *LAA*.

6 "Every time I close": Armstrong, Louis, "Storyville—Where the Blues Were Born," *True*, November 1947.

1: PERDIDO STREET BLUES

9 the wealthiest city: Bultman, *New Orleans*, p. 47.
10 "The girls are": Longstreet, *Sportin' House*, pp. 110–1.
10 The system of maintaining: Ostransky, *Jazz City*, p. 18.
11 *"Now, if you's white"*: Douglas, *Terrible Honesty*, p. 397.
11 "The favorite dances": Goffin, *This Is Jazz*, p. 14.
12 French folk songs collided: *Ibid*, p. 19.
12 the number of free blacks: *New Orleans*, pp. 70–1.
13 In 1897: *Ibid*, p. 73.
14 until a baptismal certificate: For more on the discovery of Armstrong's baptismal certificate and his actual birthday, see Gary Giddins's account in the *Village Voice*, August 34, 1988, and *GG*, p. 48.
14 Although baptized as a Catholic: Certificate of Baptism, Louis Armstrong, *HJA*.
15 "When I was about four": Meryman, *Louis Armstrong*, p. 7.
15 "a row of Negroes": *GG*, p. 52.
15 "Toilets with wooden seats": Autobiographical MS, *LAA*.

15 "I remember one moonlit": *GG*, p. 52.
15 "churchpeople, gamblers": *LAM*, p. 8.
16 "Whether my mother": *Ibid*.
16 "One thing, everybody": *GG*, p. 53.
17 "Ever since I was": *LAM*, p. 10.
17 "did a whole lot": *Ibid*, p. 11.
17 "All the slaves came": Goffin, *Horn of Plenty*, p.29.
17 The way the old lady: *Ibid*.
18 "Them that kicks": *Ibid*, pp. 19–20. Goffin often dressed up Louis's genuine anecdotes with dialect. To focus on the stories themselves, I have, in rare instances, cut back on the obvious embellishments.
18 "Days I did not": *LAM*, p. 9.
18 Louis tired of being: *Ibid*, p. 10.
19 In the process, the name: Tallant, *Voodoo in New Orleans*, p. 9.
19 *"I don't want no black woman"*: Lomax, *Mister Jelly Roll*, p. 84.
19 Its rites included: Tallant, *Voodoo in New Orleans*, p. 29.
20 The reign of Marie: *Ibid*, p. 52ff.
20 While Louis watched: Goffin, *Horn of Plenty*, pp. 32–3.
22 "Listen here, Louis": *LAM*, pp. 13–4.

22 "Since I was the first": *Ibid*, pp. 14–5. In this book, Louis quotes the first sign as saying "For Colored Only," as well as the second sign, but it is clear from the sense of this story that he meant that the seats in the front of the car were intended for whites only. Thus, I have changed the wording of the first sign so that his sense becomes clear: "Colored" passengers had to sit in the rear of the trolley.

23 "Oh God, a very funny": *Ibid*, p. 16.

23 "Always remember": *Ibid*.

23 This was the Fred Staehle: Marquis, *In Search of Buddy Bolden*, p. 51.

23 He wandered: *LAM*, pp. 16–7.

24 "I was young": *Ibid*, pp. 17–8.

24 This was the Myles: 1900 Census, State of Louisiana, 15th Precinct, 3rd Ward, Enumeration District 32, sheet 8B, lines 57–62. Although this census dates from several years earlier, it is apparent that the Myles branch of the family lived in the house at 723 Jane Alley prior to Armstrong's birth, departed, and subsequently returned en masse.

There is some confusion about the spelling of "Myles." Armstrong, or various editors, spelled the name as "Miles," but as census reports make clear, the actual spelling is "Myles."

24 "They were about": *LAM*, p. 19.

25 "the Lord takes care": *Ibid*, p. 20.

25 "The man who": Autobiographical MS, *LAA*.

25 In reality, Willie Armstrong: 1910 Census, State of Louisiana, 3rd Ward, Enumeration District 39, 4A, lines 2–4.

25 "He made the chicks": *LAM*, p. 29.

25 "Down South, the iceman": *MJ*, p. 228.

26 "My mother Mayann": *GG*, p. 60.

27 "it seemed as though": *Ibid*, p. 59.

27 When he was six: Marquis, *In Search of Buddy Bolden*, p. 29. No Fisk School records from Armstrong's era survive, so there are no transcripts of his early schooling.

27 "In our neighborhood": *LAM*, p. 21.

28 One Sunday: Autobiographical Manuscript, *LAA*; *LAM*, p. 16.

2: MAHOGANY HALL STOMP

29 "It was like a phenomenon": *NS*, p. 3.

29 "people of color": *New Orleans*, p. 164.

30 In Louis's childhood: *Ibid*, pp. 178–83.

30 "I can remember the Mardi Gras": Louis Armstrong to Leonard Feather, June 29, 1953, *IJS*.

31 "with a big stick": *Ibid*.

31 "To watch those old timers": *Ibid*.

32 "Night before a funeral": Meryman, *Louis Armstrong*, p. 9.

32 "some bodies used to": *Ibid*.

32 At the wake of a deceased: *MJ*, p. 227.

33 "There were all sorts of honky-tonks": Russell, *New Orleans Style*, p. 136.

34 "So far as any of us know": *LAS*, p. 12.

34 "He blazed himself into": *Ibid*.

34 "When Buddy Bolden played": *FR*, p. 11.

34 "the Creole people are slow": Lomax, *Mister Jelly Roll*, p. 89.

35 Buddy Bolden was Uptown: *Ibid*, pp. 58–60n.

35 He could be heard over at: *FR*, pp. 15–6.

35 One night, down at the Mix: Marquis, *In Search of Buddy Bolden*, p. 81.

35 "Bolden used to put his horn": Interview with Kid Ory, April 20, 1957, *HJA*. This is actually Mrs. Ory's recollection, which Kid Ory then seconds.

36 "You was always hearing": Bechet, *Treat It Gentle*, p. 84.

36 "the most powerful trumpet": Lomax, *Mister Jelly Roll*, p. 60.

36 "*I thought I heard Buddy Bolden say*": Lomax, *Mister Jelly Roll*, p. 60.

37 "Buddy Bolden always had his cornet": Interview with Bill Matthews, March 10, 1959, *HJA*.

38 Finally, the men decided: *FR*, pp. 17–8.

38 In 1906, he started showing signs: Marquis, *In Search of Buddy Bolden*, pp. 117ff.

39 "McDonald Cemetery": Armstrong, Louis, "Scanning the History of Jazz," *Esquire*, December 1971.

40 "On Saturday nights": Autobiographical MS, *LAA*.

40 If a cat wanted to show respect: Meryman, *Louis Armstrong*, pp. 8–9.

40 "li'l ol' kid, selling": Louis Armstrong to Betty Jane Holder, February 9, 1952, *HJA*.

42 "The Karnoffsky family came": *GG*, p. 62.

42 "The bottoms of those buckets": Meryman, *Louis Armstrong*, p. 12.

43 When the French ceded control: *New Orleans*, p. 152.

43 An ordinance calling for: *New Orleans*, p. 152.

44 "From the South Side": Asbury, *The French Quarter*, p. 431.

44 "just like someone telling a joke": Autobiographical MS, *LAA*.

44 A single block in Storyville: Asbury, *The French Quarter*, p. 451.

45 "*Gimme a pig foot*": Longstreet, *Sportin' House*, pp. 221, 290.

46 "First, because it is the only district": Asbury, *The French Quarter*, p. 442ff; *Blue Book, passim.*

46 They featured harmonicas: Asbury, *The French Quarter*, p. 438.

47 "I was just": Armstrong, Louis, "Storyville—Where the Blues Were Born," *True*, November 1947.

52 Flamin' Mamie: *NS*, p. 11.

52 "creep joints": *Ibid*, pp. 6–7.

53 "unquestionably the most elaborately": *Ibid*, pp. 8–9.

53 "Lulu White was a famous woman": Armstrong, Louis, "Storyville—Where the Blues Were Born," *True*, November 1947.

54 "crazy deal": Meryman, *Louis Armstrong*, p. 13.

54 "Why, you should have seen": *NS*, pp. 12–3.

54 "They couldn't pay": Autobiographical MS, *LAA*.

55 "great asset to the junk wagon": *GG*, p. 64.

56 "One day when I was on the wagon": *Ibid*.

56 "I was relaxed singing": *Ibid*, p. 62.

58 "I was only seven": *Ibid*.

58 "Their food was always pure": *Ibid*, p. 57.

58 "I still eat": *Ibid*, p. 62.

58 "Of course, we are": Autobiographical MS, *LAA*.

58 "in an alley or in the street": *GG*, p. 61.

59 "The mulattos were": Pinfold, *Louis Armstrong*, p. 12.

60 Now that he was: Goffin, *Horn of Plenty*, pp. 44–45.

60 "Of the three": *LAM*, p. 24.

60 "You really heard music": *Ibid*, p. 23.

61 In 1895 or so: Gleason, *Jam Session*, p. 110.

61 "What you got": *Ibid*.

61 "King Bolden and myself": *FR*, p. v.

62 "I was having an itch": Bechet, *Treat It Gentle*, p. 91.

62 "he sort of hemmed": *Ibid*, p. 92.

63 "Buddy Bolden had the biggest": Russell, *New Orleans Style*, p. 136.

63 "Louis was eleven": Gleason, *Jam Session*, pp. 104–5.

64 "He'd stay behind the piano": Bechet, *Treat It Gentle*, p. 93. Bechet, who could be casual with dates, places this in 1913 or

thereabouts, but internal evidence strongly argues in favor of 1911, before Louis was sent to the Colored Waif's Home.

64 "Now I've just said a lot": *Down Beat*, June 1939.

3: AIN'T MISBEHAVIN'

66 "I remember running around": *MJ*, pp. 50–1.

66 "Since you want to start": *MJ*, p. 51.

67 That night, Louis planned: Meryman, *Louis Armstrong*, p. 14

67 "all of a sudden a guy": *LAM*, p. 34.

69 "door with little bitty": *MJ*, p. 52.

70 "In those days": Morris, Bob, "Cap Jones," *The Second Line*, May-June 1957.

70 Moved by their plight: Interview with Mrs. Joseph Jones, January 7, 1974, *HJA*.

70 "He was very firm": *Ibid*.

71 "I was so hungry": *LAM*, p. 38.

72 Each morning: Interview with Mrs. Joseph Jones, January 7, 1974, *HJA*.

73 "One day a couple of small": *LAM*, pp. 50–1.

73 "That shot, I do": *LAS*, pp. 2–5.

73 The director of the Home's: Scully, Arthur, Jr.,"The Building Nobody Wanted," *The Second Line*, July-August 1970.

74 "I felt real proud": *LAM*, p. 46.

75 "Louis came to me": "New Orleans Society Hall" (booklet), privately printed, New Orleans: 1951.

75 "People thought": Autobiographical MS, *LAA*.

77 "I remember Louis": *New Orleans Times-Picayune*, August 22, 1962.

77 "Louis, I know I can count": *LAS*, p. 18.

78 "I got up and after a while": *Ibid*, pp. 21–2.

78 "I loved Louis's style": Interview with Chester Zardis, Production file for "Satchmo in New Orleans," WYES-TV, *HJA*.

78 The larger New Orleans: Interview with Charlie Love, June 19, 20, 1958, *HJA*.

78 "I heard this trumpet": Russell, *New Orleans Style*, p. 177.

79 "all the whores": *LAM*, pp. 47–8.

80 "when the air was heavy": *LAM*, pp. 52–3.

81 "I did not even know": *LAM*, pp. 52–3.

81 "Mrs. Jones kissed me": *LAM*, p. 54. In *Swing That Music*, Armstrong says his mother came to get him, rather than his father, but in all his subsequent recollections, his father retrieved him.

81 "I shall never forget": "Louis Armstrong's Letter to his 'Daddy,'" *Second Line*, July 1976.

4: COAL CART BLUES

83 "tall nice looking Guy": *LAM.*, p. 54.

84 "Before I realized it": *MJ*, p. 233.

84 For the next three years: *LAM*, pp. 83–4.

85 "Liberty and Perdido": Autobiographical MS, *LAA*.

87 "All you have to do": *LAM*, p. 58.

87 "He got off at 12": Gleason, Ralph J. "God Bless Louis Armstrong," August 5, 1971.

87 "They fought each other": *GG*, p. 222.

88 "The Economy Hall": *Ibid.*

88 "Benny was a really different": *Ibid*, p. 221.

88 "six foot six": *NS*, pp. 52–3.

89 "He would have cleaned": *LAM*, p. 76.

89 "Benny was the musician's": *Ibid.*

89 "In the crowded places": *NS*, pp. 47–8.

89 "I was playing trumpet": Pinfold, *Louis Armstrong*, p. 25.

90 "If anyone made the mistake": *LAM*, p. 112.

90 "And when all the church sisters": Meryman, *Louis Armstrong*, p. 21.

90 "liked him so much": *Ibid*, p. 22.

91 "I don't think": *LAM*, pp. 79–80.

92 "Saturday the tonk stayed open": *LAM*, pp. 58–9.

92 a chore that Morris: Goffin, *Horn of Plenty*, p. 74.

93 "I loved it": *LAM*, p. 59.

93 "Son, always have": Louis Armstrong to Betty Jane Holder, February 9, 1952. *HJA*.

93 "Once when he was driving": *LAM*, p. 76.

93 "This surprised me because": *Ibid*, p. 61.

94 "we were always looking": *Ibid*, p. 64.

95 "Ain't nothin' tougher": Goffin, *Horn of Plenty*, pp. 92–7.

95 "They grabbed each other": *LAM*, pp. 74–5.

96 "My God, was I frantic": *Ibid*, p. 26.

97 "an idea popped": *Ibid*, p. 28.

98 "A large saw mill": LAM, p. 80.

98 "They were a little more jive proof": *Ibid*, pp. 80–1.

99 The day she gave birth: Goffin MS, *IJS*.

99 "The storm broke": *LAM*, pp. 83–4.

99 "Joe Oliver, Bunk": *Ibid*, p. 84.

99 "there wasn't anyone in the family": Goffin MS, *IJS*.

100 "Clarence became very much": *LAM*, pp. 83–8.

103 "I could go on talking": Armstrong, Louis, "Storyville—Where the Blues Were Born," *True*, November 1947.

104 "A lot of musicians": *MJ*, p. 234.

104 "On Sundays, the bands": Gleason, Ralph J. "God Bless Louis Armstrong," August 5, 1971.

105 "I suppose some would say": Russell, *New Orleans Style*, p. 163.

106 She spoiled Louis: Interview with Stella Oliver (Mrs. Joe Oliver), April 22, 1959, *HJA*.

106 "I prized that horn": *LAM*, pp. 99–100.

106 "For a time I worked": *Ibid*, p. 93.

107 "Why don't you try": Interview with Bill Matthews, March 10, 1959, *HJA*.

108 "The law commenced": Armstrong, Louis, "Storyville—Where the Blues Were Born," *True*, November 1947.

109 "A neccesary evil": Asbury, *The French Quarter*, pp. 451–2.

109 On the appointed day: *Ibid*, p. 453.

109 "The scene was pitiful": *NS*, pp. 63–4.

5: HOTTER THAN THAT

110 "The law dragged her down": *LAM*, p. 149.

110 "After Storyville closed down": Armstrong, Louis, "Storyville—Where the Blues Were Born," *True*, November 1947.

111 "When the hall was only": *LAM*, p. 106.

112 "the other room": Meryman, *Louis Armstong*, p. 19.

113 "Knowing how sensitive my people": *MJ*, p. 17.

113 They walked into a brightly: Goffin, *Horn of Plenty*, p. 88.

113 "At the end of the night": Louis Arm-

strong to Leonard Feather, October 10, 1941, *IJS.*

114 "They didn't bother with kids": Meryman, *Louis Armstrong*, p. 23.

114 "Around four or five": *Ibid*, p. 20.

115 "tough sportin' people": *MJ*, pp. 233–4.

115 "We all like": Armstrong, Louis, "Storyville—Where the Blues Were Born," *True*, November 1947.

116 "I don't see how": Meryman, *Louis Armstrong*, p. 23.

116 "I was too glad": *Ibid*, p. 19.

116 "They would wear real short": Louis Armstrong, "Satchmo": *Gent*, October 1957.

117 "Son," she said: *Ibid.*

117 "That goes to show": *LAM*, p.177.

118 At that moment, Slippers: *MJ*, p. 17.

118 "Everybody was buying": Armstrong, Louis, "Satchmo," *Gent*, October 1957.

119 "I had Caruso records": Meryman, *Louis Armstrong*, p. 24.

120 "She was as raggedy": *LAM*, p. 101.

120 "I had not had any": *Ibid*, p. 102.

121 "he was always": *Ibid*, pp. 100–1.

121 "old man Lala": Pinfold, *Louis Armstrong*, p. 26.

122 "real bad spade": Goffin MS, *IJS.*

124 "No sir": *LAM*, pp. 117–8.

124 "We were glad": *Ibid*, p. 120.

124 "I worked away furiously": *Ibid*, pp. 119–20.

125 He gave as his date of birth: Collier, *Louis Armstrong*, p. 72.

125 "When I could feel": *LAM*, pp. 124–34.

127 "There were many": Collier, *Louis Armstrong*, p. 71.

127 "Within two hours": *Ibid.*

128 "When he hired:" Anderson, Ernie, "Louis Armstrong: A Personal Memoir," *Storyville*, December 1, 1991.

128 possibly inspired by Kate: *Ibid.*

128 *"Why don't you keep off"*: Levin, Floyd,

" 'I Wish I Could Shimmy Like My Sister Kate': The First Recorded Hit of the Jazz Age," *The Second Line*, 1994.

128 "vulgar cooch dance": quoted in Anderson, Ernie, "Louis Armstrong: A Personal Memoir," *Storyville*, December 1, 1991.

129 In 1906, he discovered: Abbott, Lynn, "Brown Skin, Who You For?": Another Look at Clarence Williams's Early Career, *The Jazz Archivist*, December 1993.

129 When he heard Louis: Lord, *Clarence Williams, passim.*

129 *"I might be late"*: Levin, Floyd," 'I Wish I Could Shimmy Like My Sister Kate': The First Recorded Hit of the Jazz Age," *The Second Line*, 1994.

130 "I waited": Anderson, Ernie, "Louis Armstrong: A Personal Memoir," *Storyville*, December 1, 1991.

131 "noticed all those": *LAM*, p. 142.

131 "After all, we'd proved": *Ibid*, p. 143.

132 "He had on": Interview with William "Baba" Ridgley, April 11, 1961, *HJA.*

132 "he would bust out": Interview with Punch Miller, September 1, 1959, *HJA.*

132 "he always delivered": *GG*, p. 215; Rose, *New Orleans Jazz*, p. 197.

132 The Tuxedo Brass: *LAM*, p. 219.

133 "He told me": Interview with Joe "Babe" Phillips, March 25, 1957, *HJA.*

134 "I immediately dropped": *LAM*, p. 144.

134 "you could get your head": *Ibid*, p. 150.

134 "the Lord was": *Ibid*, pp. 146–7.

135 *"Won't-cha come"*: Goffin, *Horn of Plenty*, p. 129.

135 "As much as I've": *LAM*, p. 151–6.

137 "She really did": *GG*, p. 223.

137 "With my good sense": *LAM*, p. 159.

138 "many times she and I": *MJ*, p. 59.

139 "He was playing": Goffin Manuscript, *IJS.*

140 "In order to get": *LAM*, pp. 163, 234.

140 "lived for a whole week": Meryman, *Louis Armstrong*, p. 21; Goffin, *Horn of Plenty*, p. 120.

141 "I saw Daisy": *LAM*, p. 167.

141 "All of a sudden": *Ibid*, p. 179.

6: LAZY RIVER

144 "Fate was a very serious": LAM, p. 183.

145 "They didn't have": Interview with Danny Barker, April 1980, *JOHP*.

145 From this vantage point: Goffin Manuscript, *IJS*.

145 "Marable had worked": Gara, *The Baby Dodds Story*, p. 23.

146 It was so big: *LAS*, pp. 34–9.

146 "Hardy was blowing": Interviews with Monk Hazel, July 16, 1959 and with Tony Fougerat, June 8, 1960, *HJA*.

146 "There was a saying": *NS*, p. 76.

147 "Being a very apt": Goffin MS, *IJS*.

147 "He wanted me": *LAS*, pp. 34–5.

147 "Meanwhile, Joe Oliver: *Ibid*, p. 35.

147 "Fate had a way": *LAM*, pp. 184–5.

148 "I couldn't see anything": Panassié, *Louis Armstrong*, p. 9. Teagarden dates the meeting to 1921, but Louis says it took place in 1919. Teagarden also puts a trumpet in Louis's hands that night, when it was no doubt a cornet; indeed, Teagarden calls Louis a cornetist.

148 "The first time": *LAM*, p. 188.

149 "I will never": *LAM*, p. 189.

149 Long after the city's: Miles Davis, *The Autobiography*, pp. 14–5.

149 "Louis was so shy": *MJ*, p. 60.

150 "If one of us": *LAM*, pp. 183–4.

150 "Whenever Fate": Author's interview with Clark Terry.

150 After seeing this ritual: Author's interview with Fate Marable Jr.

151 "No gambling": Chevan, David, "Riverboat Music from the St. Louis and the Streckfus Steamboat Line," *Black Music Re-*

search Journal, Fall 1989; Gara, *The Baby Dodds Story*, p. 26.

151 "He would attend": Chevan, David, "Riverboat Music from the St. Louis and the Streckfus Steamboat Line," *Black Music Research Journal*, Fall 1989.

151 Streckfus was also determined: Chevan, David, "Riverboat Music from the St. Louis and the Streckfus Steamboat Line," *Black Music Research Journal*, Fall 1989; Gara, *The Baby Dodds Story*, p. 25. Chevan notes that the salary for musicians was thirty-five dollars a week, and no bonus.

152 "It gave us an altogether": Gara, *The Baby Dodds Story*, p. 2.

152 "Lodges and fraternal orders": Goffin, *This Is Jazz*, p. 53.

152 These spirited river-born Monday: Chevan, David, "Riverboat Music from the St. Louis and the Streckfus Steamboat Line," *Black Music Research Journal*, Fall 1989.

152 Finally, a year before Louis's: *Ibid*.

153 "It had a different": *Ibid*.

153 "loved our music": *LAM*, p. 187.

153 "I have always loved": *Ibid*, pp. 194–5.

153 "It was the first time": *LAS*, p. 51.

154 "After several numbers": Stearns, *The Story of Jazz*, pp. 163–4.

154 "He reported for band": Anderson, J. Lee, "Riverboats, Fate Marable and the Streckfus Family Matters," *Mississippi Rag*, July 1994.

154 "He used to wear jumpers": Russell, *New Orleans Style*, p. 20.

155 "If we weren't": Gara, *The Baby Dodds Story*, p. 3.

156 He added gadgets: Rudi Blesh interview with Baby Dodds, August 1944, *HNOC*.

156 Baby had been married: Gara, *The Baby Dodds Story*, p. 34.

156 "You can take": Rudi Blesh interview with Baby Dodds, August 1944, *HNOC*.

157 "We played 'Tiger Rag' ": *LAM*, p. 195.

157 "Bix was a raw–boned": *MM*, p. 79.

157 He had inherited: *FR*, pp. 145–148.

158 "We used to call white": Gara, *The Baby Dodds Story*, p. 25.

158 "Louis told Bix he didn't": *Ibid*, p. 24.

159 "gang of black": *LAM*, p. 206.

159 "Fate was the type": Author's interview with Clark Terry.

159 "But when we got": Gara, *The Baby Dodds Story*, pp. 24–5.

160 "The boll weevils": *LAM*, pp. 208–9.

160 "a pair of fat": *LAM*, p. 193.

160 "He had a cold": Gara, *The Baby Dodds Story*, pp. 25–6; Rudi Blesh interview with Baby Dodds, August 1944, *HNOC*.

161 "Come on, you cats": Gara, *The Baby Dodds Story*, p. 25.

161 "You couldn't get cool": *LAS*, pp. 55–6.

162 "An idea came": Anderson, J. Lee, "Riverboats, Fate Marable and the Streckfus Family Matters," *Mississippi Rag*, July 1994.

162 "We were the first colored": *LAM*, p. 189.

163 On they steamed: Chevan, David, "Riverboat Music from the St. Louis and Streckfus Steamboat Line," *Black Music Research Journal*, Fall 1989.

163 "Why is the jass": *Times-Picayune*, June 17, 1917; Rose, *Storyville, New Orleans*, pp. 106–7.

165 The ODJB polished: *NS*, pp. 60–61.

165 "The Negro did not play": Interview with Nick LaRocca, June 9, 1958, *HJA*; Author's interview with Milt Gabler.

166 "one of the most outstanding": Interview with Nick LaRocca, May 21, 1958, *HJA*.

166 "If Daisy would only": *LAM*, p. 213.

166 "went to Zatteran's": *Ibid*, p. 214.

167 "Pete Lala got mad": Russell, *New Orleans Style*, p.179.

167 "vice-City Hall": Goffin, *This Is Jazz*, p. 48.

167 "That was a swell job": *LAM*, p. 215.

168 "I could read music": *Ibid*, p. 68.

168 "One day Louis rehearsed": Gara, *The Baby Dodds Story*, p. 26; Anderson, J. Lee, "Riverboats, Fate Marable and the Streckfus Family Matters," *Mississippi Rag*, July 1994.

169 "To me, four beats": Gara, *The Baby Dodds Story*, p. 31.

169 "We were the stars": *Ibid*, pp. 31–32; Chevan, David, "Riverboat Music from the St. Louis and the Streckfus Steamboat Line," *Black Music Research Journal*, Fall 1989.

170 Just as he'd feared: *LAM*, pp. 221–2.

171 "After all, a cornet": *Ibid*, p. 223.

171 "Shots Madison and I": *MJ*, p. 19.

172 "and with that wide": *LAM*, pp. 223–4.

172 "I made up my mind": *GG*, p. 215.

173 He would be making: Meryman, *Louis Armstrong*, p. 28.

173 "because Joe Oliver and his boys": *GG*, p. 215.

174 "If you didn't have": Collier, *Louis Armstrong*, p. 13.

174 In time, Louis would find: *MJ*, p. 17.

174 "Joe Oliver is my idol": *LAM*, p. 228.

174 "Just then I boarded": *GG*, p. 215.

7: CHICAGO BREAKDOWN

175 "I arrived": *LAM*, p. 231.

175 "all the colored people": *Ibid*.

175 "hear the King's": Armstrong, Louis, "Scanning the History of Jazz," *Esquire*, December 1971.

176 "Somebody must have told Joe": *GG*, p. 216.

176 "Why I've not seen": Armstrong, Louis, "Scanning the History of Jazz," *Esquire*, December 1971.

176 They reached: *LAM*, pp. 234–5; *GG*, p. 216.

177 Although he admired: Meryman, *Louis Armstrong*, p. 29.

177 Joe made his cornet: *LAM*, pp. 239–40.

178 "first class resort": *Chicago Jazz*, p. 19.

178 "Lil believed in me": *LAS*, p. 71.

178 Shortly after the Civil War: *JTM*.

183 "I stopped and gazed": *Down Beat*, June 1, 1951.

183 "they had it all right": Lil Hardin Armstrong, *RI*.

183 "He sat down and played": *Down Beat*, June 1, 1951.

183 "My mother wouldn't": Lil Hardin Armstrong, *RI*.

184 "in no time": *Down Beat*, June 1, 1951.

185 "Jelly Roll sat down": *Ibid*; Lil Hardin Armstrong, *RI*.

185 "I'm really in for it": *Down Beat*, June 1, 1951.

185 "I learned all the popular": Lil Hardin Armstrong, *RI*.

186 "long, lanky": *Down Beat*, June 1, 1951; Lillian Hardin Armstrong, *RI*.

191 "teeming Negro street": Allsop, *The Bootleggers and Their Era*, pp. 180–1.

191 "Royal Gardens": Kenney, *Chicago Jazz*, p. 27.

191 Chicago had everything: *Ibid*, p. 14–5.

192 "supplying the needs": *Ibid*, p. 26.

192 "Chicago's musicians": *Ibid*, p. 14–5.

192 "Work together": *Ibid*, pp. 26–7.

193 The absence of law: Lemann, *The Promised Land*, p. 64

193 Black-and-tans employed: Kenney, *Chicago Jazz*, pp. 16–7.

194 "Atmosphere of sensuality": *Ibid*, p. 27.

196 "Things quieted down": Gara, *The Baby Dodds Story*, p. 40.

197 "You taken so long": Louis Armstrong to Isidore Barbarin, September 1, 1992, *GG*, p. 74.

198 "What really started": Crow, *Jazz Anecdotes*, pp. 207–8.

198 "He would be having valve": *NS*, p. 90.

199 "Freddie, he blew": Crow, *Jazz Anecdotes*, p. 208.

199 "A heavy drinker": *GG*, p. 80.

200 "I still remember the arrival": *NS*, pp. 100–1.

201 "'Gate' is a word": *LAS*, pp. 77–8.

203 "I had a secondhand": Lillian Hardin Armstrong, *RI*.

203 "I probably would have never paid": *Down Beat*, July 14, 1950.

204 "used to get so afraid": Lil Hardin Armstrong interview with William Russell, *HNOC*.

204 "He always said": Lil Hardin Armstrong interview with William Russell, *HNOC*; Lillian Hardin Armstrong, *RI*.

205 "got so disgusted": Lil Hardin Armstrong interview with William Russell, *HNOC*.

206 In his early reminiscences: Goffin, *Horn of Plenty*, pp. 169–70.

206 "did not know jazz": *GG*, p. 80.

207 "the boys in the band": Goffin MS, *IJS*.

208 "May Alix had one": Armstrong, Louis,

"Scanning the History of Jazz," *Esquire*, December 1971.

208 "I had Bill Johnson": GG, p. 76.

208 *"As he came out"*: *Ibid*, pp. 76–7.

209 "He did not wear old": *Ibid*, p. 34.

210 "No one could come up": Crow, *Jazz Anecdotes*, p. 207.

210 Without the burden of school: FR, p. 148.

211 "The first time I heard Bix": NS, p. 158.

211 Bix, in turn, brought: NS, pp. 141–2. Car-

michael dates his first hearing Armstrong to mid-1923, but internal evidence suggests that it took place in late 1922, soon after Louis became firmly established in the Lincoln Gardens.

211 "As I sat down": *Ibid*.

212 Chicago was really jumping: Armstrong, Louis, "Scanning the History of Jazz," *Esquire*, December 1971.

8: DIPPERMOUTH BLUES

215 In 1915: Kennedy, *Jelly Roll, Bix, and Hoagy*, passim.

217 "It was something": *Ibid.*, pp. 62–63.

217 "We'd rehearse it on the job": *Ibid*.

220 "the technician asked us": *Ibid*, p. 66.

221 *"For years, King Oliver's Band"*: FR, p. 74.

222 "You don't look right": Lillian Hardin Armstrong, RI.

224 "willfully deserting": "Louis Armstrong vs. Daisy Armstrong," Circuit Court of Cook County (Illinois), December 18, 1923. Queens County, New York, Surrogate Court.

225 "When Lil and I got married": Goffin MS, IJS.

226 "we all went to Louis's place": NS, pp. 94–5.

226 "I had the folks down": Goffin MS, IJS.

226 "When Lil and I had our home": *Ibid*.

227 "immediately grabbed": *Ibid*.

227 "Just as we": *Ibid*.

227 "She smiled all over": Armstrong, Louis, "Scanning the History of Jazz," *Esquire*, December 1971.

227 "To make her happy to go back": Goffin notebooks, IJS.

228 Mayann exchanged a few words: Goffin, *Horn of Plenty*, p. 180.

228 "Whenever Joe came": Collier, *Louis Armstrong*, p. 113.

228 "What does Louis think": Lil Hardin Armstrong interview with William Russell, HNOC.

229 "We had been kidding": Dodds, *The Baby Dodds Story*, p. 41.

229 "Quite naturally": Goffin MS, IJS.

230 "She and I would go": Goffin, *Horn of Plenty*, p. 183.

230 "Daisy got into": Goffin MS, IJS.

230 Daisy's wounds: *Ibid*; Goffin, *Horn of Plenty*, p. 182.

230 "Her hair": Goffin MS, IJS.

231 "Nobody saw the royalty": Kennedy, *Jelly Roll, Bix, and Hoagy*, p. 71.

231 "Johnny Dodds found out": Lil Hardin Armstrong, RI.

234 "He didn't even have the courtesy": Pinfold, *Louis Armstrong*, p. 39.

234 "Joe Oliver broke": Goffin MS, IJS.

235 "Armstrong was": Pinfold, *Louis Armstrong*, p. 39.

235 "Fletcher Henderson paid him": Lil Hardin Armstrong, RI.

9: T.N.T.

236 "When I arrived": *NS*, p. 204.

237 "Harlem was beautiful": Hinton and Berger, *Bass Line*, p. 55.

237 "encourage the reading": Lewis, *When Harlem Was in Vogue*, p. 97.

237 They included figures: *Ibid*, pp. 98–9.

237 "supremely great: Collier, *Louis Armstrong*, p. 210.

238 Even W. C. Handy: Lewis, *When Harlem Was in Vogue*, p. 209.

239 And they often did: *Ibid*, p. 210.

239 "There are one": Collier, *Louis Armstrong*, p.122.

240 "the author and I": *LAS*, p. xv.

240 Madden's blood money: Pinfold, *Louis Armstrong*, p. 43.

241 He arrived in 1920: Charters and Kunstadt, *Jazz*, p. 165.

241 To allay their fears: *Ibid*, p. 166.

242 It fell to Smack: *Ibid*, p. 167.

242 Having lost his trumpeter: *Ibid*.

242 "I still had a lot": *LAS*, p. 35.

243 Two of his discoveries: Charters and Kunstadt, *Jazz*, p. 170.

243 "the greatest": *MJ*, p. 95.

243 "If Fletcher was a white": Interview with Howard R. Scott, March 1979, *JOHP*.

244 Admission to the Roseland: Collier, *Louis Armstrong*, p. 120.

244 His departure had prompted: Charters and Kunstadt, *Jazz*, p. 173.

244 "Where I had come from": *NS*, p. 204.

245 "new arrangement": Collier, *Louis Armstrong*, p. 125.

245 Elmer Chambers and Howard Scott: Interview with Howard R. Scott, March 1979, *JOHP*.

245 even experimenting: Hodes, *Selections from the Gutter*, p. 85.

245 "Louis played that opening": Interview with Howard R. Scott, March 1979, *JOHP*.

246 "There were a lot": Crow, *Jazz Anecdotes*, p. 210.

246 "He had to take": Hodes, *Selections from the Gutter*, p. 85.

247 "We got Louis out": *Ibid*.

247 his favorite creations: *NS*, p. 221.

247 "Nobody much on Broadway": *LAS*, pp. 81–2.

247 "When Smack's band hit": *NS*, p. 205.

248 "he was so tough": Crow, *Jazz Anecdotes*, p. 211.

248 "You used to see": Interview with Howard R. Scott, March 1979, *JOHP*.

248 "I put that shit": Crow, *Jazz Anecdotes*. p. 211.

249 "About three weeks": Collier, *Louis Armstrong*, p. 133.

251 "Bessie's fine microtonal": Schuller, *Early Jazz*, p. 229.

251 "When you go to sleep": Crow, *Jazz Anecdotes*, p. 217.

252 "not himself a musician": Albertson, *Bessie*, p. 75.

252 "Smith was a very quiet": Crow, *Jazz Anecdotes*, p. 217.

252 "Greatest and Highest": Albertson, *Bessie*, p. 83.

252 They waxed four other: *Ibid*, p. 84.

253 "Mr. Williams, if you": *FR*, pp. 110–1.

255 Their routine was always: Goffin, *Horn of Plenty*, pp. 204–5.

256 Henderson scheduled: *Ibid*, p. 205.

256 In Woonsocket: *Ibid*, pp. 207–8.

256 "Was quite a thrilling": Goffin MS, *IJS*.

256 wandered into a gin mill: Goffin, *Horn of Plenty*, p. 208.

256 "I'd rather drink muddy": *FR*, p. 212.

257 "I didn't say anything": Lil Hardin Armstrong, *RI*.

258 "kind of liked playing": *Ibid.*

258 "The whole time": *MJ*, pp. 236–7.

258 "I had to choose": Goffin MS, *IJS*.

10: BIG BUTTER AND EGG MAN

260 "Girl, are you?": Lil Hardin Armstrong, *RI*.

260 "greatest cornet player": Pinfold, *Louis Armstrong*, p. 49.

261 "She had a nice": Goffin MS, *IJS*.

261 "Close those windows": Condon, *We Called It Music*, p. 132.

261 "Unless it happened": *Ibid.*, p. 133.

262 "Our recording sessions": *NS*, p. 110.

264 "When we made": *Ibid.*, p. 109.

265 "I became so popular": *GG*, pp. 84–5.

265 "Erskine Tate had": Goffin MS, *IJS*.

265 "Boy," she said: *GG*, p. 85.

267 "*Say I've got the Heebies*": Samuels, David, "The Satchmo Sound," *Civilization*, August-September 1996. Mezzrow, *Really the Blues*, pp. 119–20, offers somewhat different lyrics for both versions of "Heebie Jeebies."

267 "This hair-raising": *FR*, p. 129.

267 "We used to do that": Louis Armstrong interview with William Russell, May 5, 1970, *HNOC*.

267 "One day I heard": Author's interview with Phoebe Jacobs, December 1, 1995.

268 "While he was at the Vendome": Lil Hardin Armstrong, *RI*.

269 "He proceeded with throaty": *FR*, pp. 129–30.

269 "Quite a figure": Goffin MS, *IJS*.

273 "only allowed two minutes": St. Cyr, Johnny, "The Original Hot Five," *Second Line*, September-October 1954.

274 "wonderful band leader": *Ibid.*

274 "Louis would play": *NS*, p. 102.

275 "Okeh Record Company will demon-strate": Unidentified newspaper clipping, *LAA*.

275 "a few weeks": Samuels, David, "The Satchmo Sound," *Civilization*, August-September 1996.

275 "You would hear cats": *MM*, p. 120.

275 "Bix kept chuckling": *Ibid.*, p. 123.

275 "It embarrassed him": *MJ*, p. 109.

275 "The guys who called": *Ibid.*

276 "Whenever we'd break": *Ibid.*, p. 110.

276 "I kept on visiting": Goffin MS, *IJS*.

276 "I took Clarence": *Ibid.*

276 "Alpha had fallen": *Ibid.*

277 "I always remember": Dance, Stanley, "Earl Hines Remembers Louis," *Village Voice*, July 4, 1977.

277 He left Oliver: *MJ*, p. 110.

277 "The Sunset had": *NS*, p. 108.

278 "I always admired": Goffin MS, *IJS*.

278 "nice little cute fat boy": Meryman, *Louis Armstrong*, p. 36.

279 "Although the club": Dance, Stanley, "Earl Hines Remembers Louis," *Village Voice*, July 4, 1977.

280 "Now I was making": *GG*, p. 92.

280 "I bought Alpha": Goffin MS, *IJS*.

281 "All the young musicians": *NS*, p. 115.

281 "My, what a wonderful": Armstrong, Louis, "A Toast to Mezzrow and Joe Oliver," *Melody Maker*, January 10, 1953.

281 Mezzrow began life: Author's interview with Ernest Anderson, April 15, 1988.

282 "Ever since I was first": Armstrong, Louis, "A Toast to Mezzrow and Joe Oliver," *Melody Maker*, January 10, 1953.

282 "just as good": *Ibid.*

282 Louis neglected to mention: Hammond, *Hammond on Record*, p. 106.

282 "I smoked it": *LAA*.

285 "sleepy-time neighborhood": *MM*, pp. 103–6.

286 "Over and over he would": *Ibid*, p. 124.

286 "As soon as I bought": *NS*, pp. 158–9.

287 "The Negro songs then": Collier, *Louis Armstrong*, p. 87.

288 "The old cornet": *FR*, p. 134.

288 The *Defender* ran: *Ibid*.

288 "The lake was about": *LAS*, p. 83.

289 "He didn't know whether": Dance, Stanley, "Earl Hines Remembers Louis," *Village Voice*, July 4, 1977.

290 "Practice it": Russell, *New Orleans Style*, p. 152.

290 "I was angry": *Ibid*, pp. 150–2.

293 "He would tell each": Gara, *The Baby Dodds Story*, p. 72.

295 Blackhawk's Restaurant: Kenney, *Chicago Jazz*, p. 34.

295 "Why do I?": Dance, Stanley, "Earl Hines Remembers Louis," *Village Voice*, July 4, 1977.

296 "Mother stayed down": Goffin MS, *IJS*.

299 "I don't know what": Dance, Stanley, "Earl Hines Remembers Louis," *Village Voice*, July 4, 1977; Goffin MS, *IJS; GG*, p. 95.

11: S.O.L. BLUES

301 "Earl, Zutty and I": *GG*, p. 95.

301 "three of us would go": Goffin MS, *IJS*.

303 "Carroll had all": *GG*, p. 95.

303 "We took it into the Savoy": Goffin MS, *IJS*.

303 Muggsy Spanier: Interview with Muggsy Spanier, February 2, 1961, *HJA*.

305 Lil took Louis's side: William Russell interview with Lil Hardin Armstrong, *HNOC*.

306 He got a boost: *MJ*, p. 118.

306 Playing aboard the *St. Paul*: *Ibid*.

307 "wined and dined": Chicago *Defender*, September 22, 1928.

307 he used the offer: *FR*, p. 137.

307 "The Savoy Ballroom": Goffin MS, *IJS*.

308 he had exerted: Goffin, *Horn of Plenty*, pp. 255–6.

308 "I was in bed": Goffin MS, *IJS*.

309 "Business began": *Ibid*.

309 "Tom Rockwell couldn't carry": Collier, *Louis Armstrong*, p. 179.

310 "When I received": Goffin MS, *IJS*.

310 They vowed that one: Goffin, *Horn of Plenty*, p. 253.

311 "Rockwell wired me again": Goffin MS, *IJS; GG*, p. 106.

312 "It was nice": *Down Beat*, July 4, 1950.

312 "At last we": Goffin MS, *IJS; GG*, p. 106.

313 *Great Day*: Bordman, *American Musical Theatre*, *MJ*, p. 288.

313 he moved in: *FR*, p. 138.

313 "Next morning, Braud": *NS*, p. 171.

314 Now he was planning: Bordman, *American Musical Theatre*, p. 452.

314 played for Ziegfeld himself: William Russell interview with Zutty Singleton, *HNOC*.

314 "Rockwell gave in": Goffin MS, *IJS*.

314 new gig at Connie's: Goffin, *Horn of Plenty*, p. 260.

315 "My, the money": *LAS*, p. 90.

315 "We see your": Gibson, Harry, "Mahatma Satch," *Village Voice*, June 11, 1991.

316 "And then we showed": *LAS*, p. 91.

317 "Never before in the history": *New York Age*, June 29, 1929.

317 "Chicago's own Louis": Chicago *Defender*, July 1929.

318 "all the raggedy": *MM*, p. 212.

318 "Every day, soon as": *Ibid*, pp. 212–3.

319 "My band stayed down": Goffin MS, *IJS*.

319 "Louis told me how": Interview with Zutty Singleton and Marge Creath (Mrs. Singleton), *JOHP*.

320 Family income: Lewis, *When Harlem Was in Vogue*, p. 240.

320 Hardly a musician: Collier, *Louis Armstrong*, p. 168.

320 Henderson suffered: Ostransky, *New York Jazz*, pp. 212–3.

321 These two dying embers: *FR*, pp. 158–60.

321 Hoagy Carmichael: *NS*, p. 164.

321 The cold turned into: *FR*, pp. 158–60.

321 King Oliver: Marquis, *The Search for Buddy Bolden*, p. 143.

322 Bolden did not: *Ibid*, pp. 131–3.

322 "I had a friend": Goffin MS, *IJS*.

323 When he went to work: Clayton, *Buck Clayton's Jazz World*, p. 50.

323 Jimmy Brown: *Ibid*, p. 47.

323 "The barber had to use": Autobiographical manuscript, *LAA*.

323 "These boys had": Goffin MS, *IJS*.

324 "the most extraordinary": Los Angeles *Evening Herald*, July 30, 1930.

324 "A gliss means to slide": Clayton, *Buck Clayton's Jazz World*. p. 45.

325 " 'Ex-flame' ": *Variety*, January 28, 1931.

326 "they were playing": Lil Hardin Armstrong, *RI*.

326 "the man she claimed": Goffin MS, *IJS*.

327 All she knew: Goffin, *Horn of Plenty*, pp. 268–9.

327 "It makes you feel": Hammond, *Hammond on Record*, p. 105.

328 "having lots of laughs": *MJ*, pp. 133–8.

329 "on the radio, he sounded": Clayton, *Buck Clayton's Jazz World*. p. 47.

330 He even called: Interview with Lawrence Brown, July 1976, *JOHP*.

331 "We separated": Lil Hardin Armstrong, *RI*.

331 "Charlie Alexander": Goffin MS, *IJS*.

331 "Now, this is your band": Interview with Zilner Randolph, February 1977, *JOHP*.

332 "Now there's a band": Goffin MS, *IJS*.

332 As soon as their set: Interview with Zilner Randolph, February 1977, *JOHP*.

332 "made some of my": Goffin MS, *IJS*.

332 Throughout the 1920s: Sanjek, *American Popular Music*, p. 119.

335 Mike McKendrick: Collier, *Louis Armstrong*, p. 224.

335 "Jail Musician": Unidentified newspaper clipping, *LAA*.

335 "only trying to get": *MJ*, p. 143.

12: SONG OF THE VIPERS

337 "One night the gangsters": *GG*, pp. 120–5.

338 "Just stick close": Collier, *Louis Armstrong*, p. 225.

338 Rockwell denied: *MJ*, pp. 145–6.

340 "We reached New Orleans": Goffin, *Horn of Plenty*, pp. 275–280.

341 "All in all": *LAS*, pp. 96–7.

341 Before anyone realized: Goffin, *Horn of Plenty*, pp. 282–3.

342 "for continuing to play": *MJ*, p. 145.

342 "We're called down": Jones, *Talking Jazz*, p. 135.

342 "Wherever Louis's band": *MJ*, p. 147.

342 "Opening night came": *Ibid*, p. 148.

343 "I turned to the boys": Gleason, Ralph J. "God Bless Louis Armstrong," *Rolling Stone*, August 5, 1971.

343 "He came out dressed": Interview with Sherwood Mangiapane, Production file for "Satchmo in New Orleans," WYES–TV, *HJA*.

344 "One Sunday": with Jim Russell, Pro-

duction file for "Satchmo in New Orleans," WYES–TV, *HJA*.

344 A tobacco company: Jones, *Talking Jazz*, p. 138.

344 One day, around noon: Goffin, *Horn of Plenty*, pp. 287–8.

345 "my teeth began": Jones, *Talking Jazz*, p. 136.

345 "You had to be": Interview with Zilner Randolph, February 1977, *JOHP*.

345 Louis agreed to give: Goffin, *Horn of Plenty*, pp. 290–1.

345 On the way back: Goffin, *Horn of Plenty*, pp. 291–3.

346 "one of the musicians": *MJ*, p. 239.

346 "Why don't you shoot": Interview with Zilner Randolph, February 1977, *JOHP*.

346 "It looked like half ": *MJ*, p. 239.

347 "a few of the band": *Ibid*.

347 "Ladies and gentlemen": Jones, *Talking Jazz*, pp. 136–7.

349 "If Armstrong comes": Chicago *Defender*, April 26, 1930.

350 The Armstrong style: *MJ*, p. 159.

350 "In the provinces": *Ibid*, pp. 160–1.

350 "A young coloured": Ingman, William S., "England's Welcome to Louis Armstrong," *Melody Maker*, August 1932; *MJ*, p. 167.

351 "greeted him with the name": *MJ*, p. 48. Jones and Chilton cast doubt on how Armstrong acquired his nickname, but Louis always insisted that Brooks was responsible for christening him this way. It is also worth noting that Louis's middle name was never "Daniel," as was widely repeated for a time. He had many nicknames, but no middle name.

351 "There were several colored": *LAS*, p. 100.

352 "In the wonderful simplicity": Goffin, *Jazz*, p. 3.

352 "Ten minutes later": *Ibid*, pp. 125–6.

352 "It was unbelievable": *Ibid*, p. 126.

352 "He flattened his": Goffin, *Horn of Plenty*, p. 295.

353 "so here's what I did": *Ibid*, pp. 296–7; Panassié, *Hot Jazz*, p. 33.

353 "Louis popped out": *MJ*, p. 163.

353 "The evacuation": *Ibid*, p. 161.

353 "The sweating, strutting": *MJ*, p. 162.

354 "That tiger's traveling": Pinfold, *Louis Armstrong*, p. 80.

354 "We had to carry Collins": Goffin, *Jazz*, p. 127.

354 "coloured trumpet": *Melody Maker*, nd. Armstrong scrapbooks, *LAA*.

355 "pale aesthetes": *Daily Herald*, July 25, 1932.

355 "such screeches": Armstrong scrapbook, *LAA*.

356 "Adore it, or deplore": *Evening Mail*, July 22, 1932.

356 "ten-piece band": *LAS*, p. 100.

356 "If I don't": *MJ*, pp. 176–7.

356 claimed he earned: Glasgow *Sunday Mail*, August 14, 1932.

356 The leader of his English: *MJ*, p. 177.

357 Leaving England in late: *LAS*, p. 109.

357 "He had a terrible sore": *MM*, pp. 255–7.

358 "He started to blow": *Ibid*, pp. 259–60.

359 "*He announces*": *GG*, p. 116.

360 "I am . . . enjoying": Panassié, *Louis Armstrong*, p. 19.

360 "We wouldn't allow": Interview with Albert "Budd" Johnson, 1975, *JOHP*.

361 "We used to get out": Pinfold, *Louis Armstrong*, pp. 58–9.

362 Collins booked him: *MJ*, p. 175.

362 "Man With Iron Lips": Pinfold, *Louis Armstrong*, p. 83.

362 "One night he got": Hammond, *Hammond on Record*, p. 105.

363 His relationship with Alpha: *MJ*, pp. 177–8.

364 He was forty-nine: Death Certificate for Willie Armstrong, State of Louisiana, Divi-

sion of Archives, Records Management, and History, Baton Rouge.

364 "All I remember is": *LAS*, p. 112.

364 when he reached his hotel: Goffin, *Horn of Plenty*, p. 300.

365 "my lip split": Meryman, *Louis Armstrong*, p. 39.

365 "Still all": *MJ*, p. 181.

366 "So you see": *MJ*, pp. 182–3.

366 "We were two": Louis Armstrong to Leonard Feather, October 1941, *IJS*.

367 "At the start": New York *Herald*, November 11, 1934. Many accounts note that Louis performed at the Salle Pleyel, but as this notice makes clear, it was actually the Salle Rameau.

368 "We went over the Alps": *LAS*, p. 114.

368 "I do not think": Panassié, *Hot Jazz*, p. 64.

369 "his own pompous": *The Melody Maker*, January 26, February 2, 1935.

13: PUBLIC MELODY NUMBER ONE

370 "the opium would make": *MM*, pp. 271–2.

372 "Louis came back": *MJ*, p. 189.

372 "I could see he": Anderson, Ernie, "Joe Glaser & Louis Armstrong: A Memoir," *Storyville*, December 1, 1994.

373 "He's been my daddy": *NYT*, June 8, 1969.

373 "Joe Glaser was the most": Collier, *Louis Armstrong*, p. 270.

373 "Joe was a professional": Author's interview with George Avakian.

373 "Joe Glaser had this wonderful": Author's interview with George Wein.

374 "You don't know me": *NYT*, June 8, 1969.

374 "gigantic conspiracy": Chicago *Tribune*, October 10, 1926.

374 On Christmas Day: Chicago *Tribune*, December 26, 1926.

374 On January 22: Anderson, Ernie, "Joe Glaser & Louis Armstrong: A Memoir," *Storyville*, December 1, 1994.

375 "I always wrote": Vern Whaley to author, August 1, 1991.

375 Borden proceeded to write: Brenner and Nagler, *Only the Ring Was Square*, p. 2.

375 "Found guilty": Anderson, Ernie, "Joe Glaser & Louis Armstrong: A Memoir,"

Storyville, December 1, 1994; Chicago *Defender*, February 11, 1928; Joseph Glaser file, *CCC*.

375 "She wore make-up": Anderson, Ernie, "Joe Glaser & Louis Armstrong: A Memoir," *Storyville*, December 1, 1994.

375 Six weeks after: *Ibid.*

376 In January 1930: Joseph Glaser file, *CCC*.

376 "He was a crude": *MJ*, p. 17.

377 "*My Chops Was Beat*": *Down Beat*, June 1935.

378 "We had two white": Collier, *Louis Armstrong*, p. 277.

379 The new outfit was Luis: *GG*, p. 140.

379 The tune was everywhere: Schuller, *The Swing Era*, pp. 186–87.

379 "but so long as they": *MJ*, p. 194.

380 "immaculate in a white": Crow, *Jazz Anecdotes*, p. 91.

381 Louis finished his triumphant: *MJ*, p. 290.

381 "Lots of time": Pinfold, *Louis Armstrong*, p. 91.

382 "Is that enough?": Miller, *Louis Armstrong: A Cultural Legacy*, p. 164.

382 "Best individual impression": *Variety*, December 16, 1936.

382 The process of lip: My thanks to Dan Morgenstern for pointing out that Armstrong was ill served by lip-synching.

383 "While Miss Raye": *Variety*, August 4, 1937.

383 "For a white woman": Mrs. Alonzo Richardson to Joseph Breen, August 31, 1937, Library of the Academy of Motion Picture Arts and Sciences, Los Angeles.

383 "For negroes and whites": Dolph Frantz to Adolph Zukor, August 25, 1937, Library of the Academy of Motion Picture Arts and Sciences, Los Angeles.

384 Louis's contract: Warner Collection, *USC*.

384 "darkie jam session": Letter from Benjamin Glazer to Hal Wallis, August 8, 1939, Warner Collection, *USC*.

385 "sounded like a boiler": *Variety*, April 28, 1937.

387 "Glaser would scream": *GG*, p. 130.

388 In Savannah, Louis: Interview with Kid Ory, April 20, 1957, *HJA*.

388 "They tried to get Joe": *NS*, p. 187.

389 "Thank God I only need": *FR*, p. 87.

389 "That night we played": Meryman, *Louis Armstrong*, p. 49.

390 "I am not the one": Allen and Rust, *"King" Oliver*, pp. 178–9.

390 168 recordings: Ramsey, Frederick Jr., "King Oliver in Savannah," *Saturday Review*, March 17, 1956.

390 "Pops, breaks come": *NS*, p. 184.

390 "I am unable to take": *FR*, pp. 90–1.

390 "broken heart": *NS*, p. 188.

390 The medical cause: Allen and Rust, *"King" Oliver*, p. 179.

390 "cheap box": Ramsey, Frederick, Jr., "King Oliver in Savannah," *Saturday Review*, March 17, 1956.

391 Many big names: Allen and Rust, *"King" Oliver*, p. 182.

391 "Just because": *NS*, p. 188.

392 In the divorce: Lillian H. Armstrong vs. Louis Armstrong, Superior Court of Cook County, State of Illinois, September 30, 1938. Queens Surrogate Court, County of Queens, NY.

392 Days later: Louis Armstrong vs. Alpha Smith Armstrong, Decree for Divorce, Superior Court of Cook County, September 29, 1942.

392 There is evidence: *Down Beat*, December 15, 1939.

392 "We had some real": Armstrong, Louis, "Why I Like Dark Women," *Ebony*, August 1954.

393 "swinging in the front": *LAA*.

393 "Maybe her color": Armstrong, Louis, "Why I Like Dark Women," *Ebony*, August 1954.

393 She was working: Collier, *Louis Armstrong*, pp. 282–3.

393 "With her salary": *GG*, p. 141.

393 "which took a big": *Ibid*, p. 146.

394 "that big long": *Ibid*.

394 Louis gladly paid: *MJ*, p. 197.

394 Louis wrapped up: *Variety*, January 11, 1939.

395 "It would be kinda": Louis Armstrong to William Russell, October 3, 1939, Russell Collection, *HNOC*.

396 "Armstrong, playing": *Down Beat*, December 15, 1939.

398 "The number of musicians": *Ibid*, March 1938.

398 "Has Louis Armstrong": *Ibid*, July 1939.

398 "Louis Armstrong Stopped": *Music and Rhythm*, August 1941.

399 In 1937, Louis: Collier, *Louis Armstrong*, pp. 281–2.

14: WHAT DID I DO TO BE SO BLACK AND BLUE?

400 "Dear Friend": Gleason, *Jam Session*, pp. 111–2.

400 After leaving New Orleans: Hillman, *Bunk Johnson*, p. 46.

401 "I was one": Interview with William Russell, Production file for "Satchmo in New Orleans," WYES-TV, *HJA*.

401 When Russell came: A "Bunk Johnson" apparently accompanied Sippie Wallace, the Blues singer, in a 1924 recording, along with Sidney Bechet and Clarence Williams. If this was in fact the same Bunk Johnson, his rather limited exposure on this record had long been forgotten.

402 "You should hear": William Russell Collection, *HNOC*.

403 "I was very young": Louis Armstrong interviewed by William Russell, January 18, 1939, *HNOC*.

404 "Now here is the thing": *Down Beat*, June 1939.

404 "Perhaps soon we will": *Ibid.*

405 "You are really": Louis Armstrong to William Russell, October 3, 1939, Russell Collection, *HNOC*.

406 "He had an unprecedented": *FR*, p. 23.

406 "We have no colored": *NS*, pp. 69–70.

407 "Louis's wife had": Bechet, *Treat It Gentle*, pp. 175–6.

408 Not surprisingly: Chilton, *Sidney Bechet*, p. 124.

408 "Anybody that thinks": Hillman, *Bunk Johnson*, pp. 62–3.

409 "greatest master": Gleason, *Jam Session*, p. 115.

410 "pathetic to begin": Bigard, *With Louis and the Duke*, p. 88.

410 "I do not know": Gleason, *Jam Session*, p. 115.

411 "I laid that fine": Louis Armstrong to Leonard Feather, October 1, 1941, *IJS*.

412 "She has that routine": *Ibid.*

412 "In Atlanta, they": Interview with John Simmons, Washington, D.C., January 1977, *JOHP*.

412 "They'd put us off": *Ibid.*

412 "some good ol' gumbo": Louis Armstrong to Leonard Feather, October 1, 1941, *IJS*.

414 "No doubt this letter": Louis Armstrong to Walter Winchell, January 19, 1942, *HJA*.

415 "cute little": Autobiographical manuscript, *LAA*.

416 Along with five: MGM Internal Memo, April 30, 1942, Arthur Freed Collection, *USC*.

416 Petrillo did call: Sanjek, *American Popular Music*, pp. 217–23.

417 "I ought to knock": Interview with John Simmons, January 1977, Washington D.C., *JOHP*.

417 During the band's: Priestly, *Mingus*, pp. 18–9.

418 "Upon its success": *Pittsburgh Courier*, October 3, 1942.

419 "'Cabin' is a": *Variety*, February 17, 1943.

420 "having one drink": Autobiographical manuscript, *LAA*.

420 On October 2: Louis Armstrong vs. Alpha Smith Armstrong, Decree for Divorce, Superior Court of Cook County, September 29, 1942.

420 "My mother belongs": Autobiographical manuscript, *LAA*.

421 At the last moment: Marriage Certificate, Louis Armstrong and Lucille Wilson, Will of Louis Armstrong, Queens Surrogate Court. In his autobiographical manuscript,

Armstrong gives October 12 as his wedding date, but the actual certificate states the wedding took place on October 7.

421 "I bought a beautiful": Autobiographical manuscript, *LAA*.

421 "she caught the Reverend": Armstrong, Louis, "Why I Like Dark Women," *Ebony*, August 1954.

422 To have six months: Hentoff, *The Jazz Life*, p. 30.

422 "I gave him his": *Ibid*, pp. 26–7.

422 "My, my how Lucille": Autobiographical manuscript, *LAA*.

423 "and when they found": *NYT*, February 10, 1996.

423 "The cab driver finally": Autobiographical manuscript, *LAA*.

424 She then launched: *JTM*.

425 "My band boys": Louis Armstrong to Mrs. Church, March 10, 1946, *IJS*.

426 "If you need": Goffin, *Jazz*, p. 128.

426 "Dear Pal Goffin": Louis Armstrong to Robert Goffin, July 19, 1944 and various telegrams from 1944, *IJS*.

427 " 'Tain't no two ways": Goffin, *Horn of Plenty*, p. 10.

427 The movie's attempted: Pinfold, *Louis Armstrong*, pp. 102–3.

428 "I'd fought my whole": Holiday, *Lady Sings the Blues*, p. 119.

428 she was slipping: Nicholson, *Billie Holiday*, p. 153.

429 "In the original script": *Ibid*.

429 "My boss, Mr. Glaser": Louis Armstrong to Leonard Feather, December 21, 1946, *IJS*.

430 The newly invigorated: Author's interview with Ernie Anderson, April 15, 1988.

431 Ernie Anderson wanted: Author's interview with Dan Morgenstern, January 23, 1996.

431 "I got a cashier's": Anderson, Ernie, "Joe Glaser and Louis Armstrong," *Storyville*, December 1, 1994.

431 The decor featured: Hentoff, Nat, "Louis Armstrong and Reconstruction," *Village Voice*, May 26, 1992.

432 "If this works": Anderson, Ernie, "Joe Glaser and Louis Armstrong," *Storyville*, December 1, 1994.

434 "If I don't have": Interview with Dick Cary, July 8, 1991, *JOHP*.

434 "the 'real ass-hole' ": Bigard, *With Louis and The Duke*, p. 116.

434 One time he repeated: Interview with Dick Cary, July 8, 1991, *JOHP*.

435 "Nearly everyone agrees": *Down Beat*, November 5, 1947.

435 "Louis Armstrong has forsaken": *Time*, September 1, 1947.

435 "Armstrong can take": New York *Daily News*, November 17, 1947.

436 "From that time": Anderson, Ernie, "Joe Glaser and Louis Armstrong," *Storyville*, December 1, 1994.

15: HIGH SOCIETY

439 "plantation image": Gillespie, *to BE*, p. 295.

439 "I hated the way": Davis, *The Autobiography*, p. 83.

439 "When they tear": Panassié, *Louis Armstrong*, p. 51.

440 In Nice, he performed: *Down Beat*, March 10, 1948.

440 "I always think": *Ibid*, April 7, 1948.

441 "Armstrong never played": Gillespie, *to BE*, p. 296.

441 According to one: Nicholson, *Billie Holiday*, p. 137.

442 "There's a thing": *Time*, February 21, 1949.

444 "I read in *Time*": Louis Armstrong to Betty Jane Holder, February 9, 1952; *HJS*; *Variety*, March 9, 1949.

444 "No sooner had I": Louis Armstrong to Betty Jane Holder, February 9, 1952, *HJS*.

444 As the starting time: *Down Beat*, April 8, 1949.

445 "I happened to look": Louis Armstrong to Betty Jane Holder, February 9, 1952. *Hogan*.

445 Interest in Louis: *Down Beat*, April 8, 1949.

445 Among those who did: Interview with Jim Russell, Production file for "Satchmo in New Orleans," WYES-TV, *HJA*.

446 One night in 1951: Author's interview with Phoebe Jacobs, December 1, 1995.

447 To Ernie's dismay: Anderson, Ernie, "Louis Armstrong: A Personal Memoir," *Storyville*, December 1, 1991.

447 "I don't want": Liner notes for "Satchmo the Great," Columbia, CK 53580.

447 "My chops are": *Newsweek*, July 17, 1950.

447 He used a powerful: Anderson, Ernie, "Louis Armstrong: A Personal Memoir," *Storyville*, December 1, 1991.

448 "Sure, my lips": Gleason, Ralph J., "God Bless Louis Armstrong," *Rolling Stone*, August 5, 1971.

448 *"At Bedtime"*: Ibid.

450 "Hines and his ego": Collier, *Louis Armstrong*, p. 313.

450 "Now Louis": Anderson, Ernie, "Louis Armstrong: A Personal Memoir," *Storyville*, December 1, 1991.

451 "I'm the only man": Author's anonymous interview.

451 "I remember you": Bigard, *With Louis and The Duke*, p. 111.

451 Benny was so furious: Interview with Trummy Young, Washington, D.C., September 1976. *JOHP*.

451 Eventually, Benny: Hammond, pp. 312–22.

451 "Are you crazy": Jones, *Talking Jazz*, p. 120.

452 "He'd be sittin' ": Collier, *Louis Armstrong*, pp. 314–5.

453 "I see no reason": Goffin MS, *IJS*.

453 For several years: Armstrong's articles appeared in *True*, November 1947; *Holiday*, June 1950; *Newsweek*, July 17, 1950; *Esquire*, December 1951; *Ebony*, August 1954.

453 "I have to write": Louis Armstrong to Betty Jane Holder, February 9, 1952, *HJA*.

454 in postwar France: Panassié, *Louis Armstrong*, p. 29.

455 He showed the pages: Giddins, *Satchmo*, pp. 19–20.

455 For seven days': Arthur Freed Collection, *USC*.

455 "Yeah, Daddy": *GG*, p. 181.

456 "They'll never be": Goldblatt, Burt, *Newport Jazz Festival*, p. xiii.

456 For once, they spent: Arthur Freed Collection, *USC*.

457 "He strokes his pipe": *NYT*, August 10, 1956.

457 "It is bulging-eyed": *Mirror-News*, August 2, 1956.

458 "Glaser was aware": Author's interview with George Avakian, July 29, 1995.

460 "my ancestors": *Los Angeles Times*, May 24, 1956.

461 At Gold Coast: *Los Angeles Times*, May 25, 1956.

462 "Louis and Dizzy": Belsh, Rudi, *Shining Trumpet*, p. 359.

463 "Moving the plump": "Doctor Ulrich," *LAA*.

464 "A lot of times": Collier, *Louis Armstrong*, p. 284.

464 "Know what I": Smith and Guttridge, *Jack Teagarden*, p. 151.

465 "I was very upset": Author's interview with George Avakian, July 29, 1995.

466 "The Jazz Millionaire": Feather, Leonard, "Jazz Millionaire," *Esquire*, January 1957.

467 "fifty thousand dollars": Author's interview with Milt Gabler, January 22, 1996.

468 "They were tired": *Ibid.*

470 "Man, I'll play": *GG*, p. 160.

470 "I'm playing with": *Ibid*; *NYT*, July 5, 1957.

470 Before he went onstage: *MJ*, pp. 204–5.

471 "The way they are": *GG.* p. 160.

471 "I checked the newspaper": *Ibid.*

472 "My people": *Melody Maker*, October 12, 1957.

472 FBI files: FBI Files for Louis Armstrong, #100–438995, 87–114728, 62–522660, 44–24016–394. Files obtained by author under the Freedom of Information Act.

472 "I don't care": Pinfold, *Louis Armstrong*, p. 109.

473 "I think that I have": *GG*, p. 165.

473 He received: Paramount Production Files, *USC*.

16: DIDN'T HE RAMBLE?

475 "I don't know why": Collier, *Louis Armstrong*, p. 326.

475 "Man, a heart": King, Larry L., "Everybody's Louie," *Harper's*, November 1967.

476 "I didn't come": *NYT*, July 5, 1959.

476 In October 1960: *LA Times*, October 20, 28, 29, 1960.

476 He hobnobbed: Interview with Trummy Young, September 1976, Washington D.C., *JOHP*.

476 "I pray each night": King, Larry L. "Everybody's Louie," *Harper's*, November 1967.

476 "some newspaper guys": Interview with Trummy Young, September 1976, Washington D.C., *JOHP*

477 "The miasmal hoodlum": Thiele, *What a Wonderful World*, p. 94.

478 The musicians convened: Brask and Morgenstern, *Jazz People*, p. 97.

478 "I was stunned": Hentoff, Nat, "Louis Armstrong and Reconstruction," *Village Voice*, May 16, 1992.

479 "I had read about": Author's interview with Dave and Iola Brubeck, June 18, 1996.

481 "One day in 1960": Author's Interview with William Roemer, January 30, 1996.

481 "Louis is the king": Gibson, Harry, "Mahatma Satch," *Village Voice*, June 11, 1991.

482 "Federal officials": *NYT*, June 27, 29, 1976.

482 Since the entire: *NYT*, June 27, 29, 1976; Author's interview with William Roemer, January 30, 1996.

483 Louis found the song: Interview with Joe Darensbourg, April 4, 1984, *JOHP*.

483 He was on the road: Crow, *Jazz Anecdotes*, pp. 213–4.

485 There were nearly: *GG*, p. 197.

485 "You tell that fat": Thiele, *It's a Wonderful World*, pp. 4–6.

485 "We're right out here": "Louis Armstrong," *Ebony*, November 1964.

486 "You know, I used": Gleason, Ralph J., "God Bless Louis Armstrong," *Rolling Stone*, August 5, 1971.

486 "We've seen three": *GG*, p. 152.

486 "Pops, we came": Author's interview with Clark Terry, February 4, 1996.

487 "I got my grave": Author's interview with Phoebe Jacobs, December 1, 1995.

487 "Where were they": Author's interview with Clark Terry, February 4, 1996.

487 "Fuck that": *GG*, p. 168.

487 "If I had to": Interview with William Russell, Production file for "Satchmo in New Orleans," WYES-TV, *HJA*.

487 "We're *still* married": Autobiographical manuscript, *LAA*.

488 "Nearly two-dozen": *GG*, p. 44.

488 "There he was": *Ibid*, p. 47.

488 Louis occasionally quoted: Author's interview with Dan Morgenstern, January 23, 1996.

489 "He made it abundantly": Collier, *Louis Armstrong*, p. 328.

489 He found out anyway: *Ibid*, pp. 329–30.

490 "ill in his bed": Autobiographical manuscript, *LAA*.

490 "It was a toss up": Louis Armstrong to Little Brother Montgomery, July 29, 1969, *HJA*.

491 "I think I had": *NYT*, July 4, 1970.

492 "Your boy Satchmo": Louis Armstrong to Otis L. Neironter, February 21, 1971, *HJA*.

492 "You could drop dead": Collier, *Louis Armstrong*, p. 331.

493 Several weeks after: *NYT*, August 28, 1971; *Down Beat*, October 28, 1971; Albertson, Chris, "Lil Hardin Armstrong, A Fond Remembrance," *Saturday Review*, September 25, 1971.

494 Louis left: United States Estate Tax Return (Form 706) for Louis Armstrong, July 23, 1974, Surrogate Court, Queens County, New York.

494 Associated Booking insisted: Collier, *Louis Armstrong*, p. 330.

494 Louis's will: Last Will and Testament of Louis Armstrong, February 10, 1970, Index # 4560–1971, Surrogate Court, Queens County, New York.

494 During the ensuing: Last Will and Testament of Lucille Armstrong, Surrogate Court, Queens County, New York, File # 5722.

494 She suffered a seizure: *NYT*, October 5, 1983.

INDEX

Giddins, Gary (jazz critic), 488
Gillespie, John Birks "Dizzy" (trumpeter),
437–38, 441, 442, 459, 486, 489
Girod, Nicholas, 69
Glaser, Joe (promoter), 277–78, 279, 283, 298,
450–54
death of, 489–90
estate of, 494
as LA's manager, 372–88, 410, 431, 450,
456, 488
LA's music and, 429, 433–34
Mardi Gras and, 442, 443
movies and, 427
recordings and, 457, 465, 467–68, 477,
478, 482–83
tours and, 412, 416, 455, 459, 476
and organized crime, 480–82
as manager of other musicians, 399, 427,
428, 431, 451
Goffin, Robert, 167, 255, 351–52, 354, 425–27
Gonella, Nat (musician), 350, 363
Goodman, Benny, 281, 386, 395, 396, 451,
459
Good Morning, Vietnam (movie), 485
Gordon, Max (nightclub owner), 373
Gosden, Freeman, 319
Grant, Cary, 455
Granz, Norman (record producer), 466–67
Great Day (musical), 310, 313
Green, Charlie "Big" (trombonist), 359
Green, Kid, 137
Green, Long (musician), 236
Griffin, Merv, 493
Griffith, D. W., 324
Grinnell College, 488
Grow, Private George, 411–12
guns, blacks and, 66

Hackett, Bobby (trumpeter), 432, 490
Hall, Edmond (clarinetist), 430
Hall, Tubby (drummer), 186, 308, 331
Hall, Weeks (music patron), 400–401
Hammond, John (record producer), 327, 362
Hampton, Lionel (drummer), 252, 324
Handy, W. C., 181, 238, 391, 458
Harburg, Yip (songwriter), 418
Hardin, Dempsey, 179, 184, 188
Harding, Warren G., president, 195
Hardin, Lil. *See* Armstrong, Lil Hardin
Hardin, Will, 179
Hardy, Emmet (horn), 146
Harlem
the Depression in, 320
music in, 165, 437

Renaissance of, 236–40, 320
Harlem Symphony, 241
Hauser, Gayelord, 4, 448
Hawkins, Coleman (saxophonist), 236, 243,
253, 365
Hayman, Joe (saxophonist), 351
Hello, Dolly! (musical), 483
Henderson, Fletcher "Smack" (bandleader),
147, 234, 236, 241–45, 258, 307, 320
on LA, 246, 249
recordings by, 243
see also Fletcher Henderson Orchestra
Henry Ponce's honky-tonk, 33, 86, 92, 93,
119
Hepburn, Katharine, 455
Herbert, Mort (bassist), 478
Herman, Woody (clarinetist), 428–29
Heywood, Dubose, 237
Hill, Letha (musician), 313
Hines, Earl (pianist), 277, 279–80, 289, 298–
99, 301, 302, 303, 304, 444, 450
Hinton, Milt (bassist), 237
Hobson, Homer (musician), 303
Hobson, Wilder, 406
Holiday, Billie, 274, 427, 428
Holiday magazine, 453
Holyland, Detective Edward, 68
honky-tonk (tonk), 33, 63–64, 88, 134–35
Hoover, J. Edgar, 472, 481
Horne, Lena, 418, 419
Horn of Plenty (Armstrong), 426–27
Hot Chocolates (musical), 316–17, 319
Hot Clubs, 364, 368, 401, 440
Hot Five recording band, 262–64, 273–75,
284, 287–88, 291, 297–98, 304–306
Hot Four, 298
Hot Jazz (Panassié), 402
Hot Seven recording band, 292–93
Howard University, 487
Hughes, Langston, 191, 352
Humphreys, Murray "The Camel," 481
Hunter, Alberta (singer), 178, 253, 254, 274
Hyde Park High School, Chicago, 296
Hylton, Jack, as LA's manager, 363, 365–66

Immerman, Connie, 239, 240, 316, 319
Immerman, George, 239, 240
improvisation
bop and, 438
and reading music, 143
Ingman, Dan (reporter), 350–51, 356
Ingram, Rex (actor), 418
Irene (prostitute), 120–23

INDEX

Panassié, Hughes (critic), 368, 402, 440, 445, 446
parades, bands and, 78–80
Parker, Charlie "Bird" (saxophonist), 438, 441–42
Parker, Daisy (LA's first wife), 135–42, 147–48, 166, 168, 173, 190, 228, 229–30, 269–70, 341, 445
Parker, Dorothy, 237
Patrick, Dorothy (actress), 428
Paul Whiteman's Band, 209
Payton, Sammy (bandleader), 298
Perez, Emanuel (cornetist), 49, 133
Pete Lala's Cabaret, 47, 54, 121, 128
Petrillo, James C., 415–16
Petty, Reverend R. J., 179
Peyton, Dave (bandleader and music critic), 260, 317–18, 319
Phillips, Babe (musician), 133
piano, 54, 219
Picou, Alphonse (musician), 104, 133
Piron, Armand J. (violinist), 130, 244
plaçage, 10
Plessy vs. Ferguson (1896), 13
Porgy and Bess, 466
Porter, Cole, 455
Pouilly, Jacques N. B., 69
Powell, Adam Clayton, Jr., 391, 471
Powell, Dick, 384
Powers, Ollie (singer), 208, 234
Prentice-Hall Company, 454
Prohibition, 159–60, 194–95, 238, 278–79, 283–84, 315
prostitution, 42–46, 52–54, 108–109, 110–11, 114–16
Provenzano, as a Mafia faction, 87, 112
Puccini, Giacomo, 294
Pugh, Doc (LA's valet), 447, 459

quadrille, the, 40
quadroon balls, 9
quadroons, 9–10

race relations
  in Chicago, 192–93
  in New Orleans, 11, 14, 66, 342–43, 345–46
racism
  in the movies, 381–85
  touring musicians and, 346–48, 378, 381, 478–79
radio broadcasts
  by LA, 324, 335, 342–43, 347, 385
  of dance music, 306

of swing, 396
Raft, George, 247
Ragas, Henry (pianist), 165
ragtime, 33–34, 46, 163, 181
Rainey, Ma, 243, 253, 403
Ramsey, Fred, Jr. (writer), 401, 406
Randolph, Zilner (trumpetist), 331, 345, 346, 359, 360, 377
Raye, Martha, 383
Razaff, Andy (lyricist), 316
Reagan, Ronald, 384
Real Ambassadors, The, 479–80
Really the Blues (Mezzrow), 240, 281
Reconstruction, blacks in New Orleans and, 13
recording companies, 214, 241, 249, 291, 350, 367, 457, 484
  see also Columbia; Decca; Okeh; Verve; Victor
recordings
  albums
    "Disney Songs the Satchmo Way," 489
    "Ella and Louis," 466
    "Ella and Louis Again," 466
    "Louis Armstrong Plays W. C. Handy," 458
    "Real Ambassadors, The," 479–80
    "Satchmo: A Musical Autobiography," 468–69
    "Satch Plays Fats," 465
    "What a Wonderful World," 485
    "With Friends," 490
  ban on, by the musicians' union, 416
  of Bessie Smith, 251, 252–53
  of Bunk Johnson, 60–61
  the Depression and, 332–33
  of early jazz, 164, 213–15, 221–22
  facilities for, 213–14, 216–17, 262, 273
  of performances, 432
  technology of, 291, 457
records
  collectors and, 293, 401, 467
  influence of, 162, 273
Red, Buddy (nightclub manager), 223
Redhead Happy. See Bolton, Redhead Happy
Redman, Don (musician), 236, 243, 253, 403
  as an arranger, 243, 249, 250
Red Onion Jazz Babies, 254
Rice, Elmer (screenwriter), 418
Ridgley, William "Baba" (trombonist), 132, 133
riverboats, 144, 158, 161–63, 170, 306
Robichaux, John (bandleader), 89
Robinson, Bill "Bojangles," 208–09, 266, 319, 394
Robinson, Fred (trombonist), 303, 304, 311

Suburban Gardens (nightclub), New Orleans, 339, 342–45
Sullivan, Maxine, 384
Sully, John, 492
Sunday, Billy, 194
Sunset Cafe, Chicago, 277, 289, 291, 297
Sutton, Willie (bank robber), 240
Swaffer, Hannen (critic), 354–55
Sweden, LA in, 365
swing
    LA and, 396, 397–98
    origin of, 243, 396–97
Swingin' the Dream (musical), 395
Swing That Music (Armstrong), 211, 386, 404, 425

Talking Machine Journal (trade periodical), 221
Tallerie, Pierre "Frenchy" (road manager), 434, 472
Tate, Erskine (bandleader), 265, 288
Tatum, Art (pianist), 438, 466
Taylor, Eva (singer), 254, 274
Tchaikovsky, Peter, 286
Teagarden, Jack (trombonist), 148, 237, 420, 432, 433, 434, 449, 470
television, 460, 462, 484, 492
Terry, Clark (trumpeter), 150
Thacker, Audrey, as LA's manager, 366, 370
Thiele, Bob (recording producer), 477–78, 484
Thomas, Evan (bandleader), 400
Thompson, Lydia, 30
Thompson, Virgil, 409
Threepenny Opera, The, 459
Time magazine, 435, 442–43
Times-Picayune, 69, 163–64, 443–44
Toohey, Reverend J. M., 14
trombone, LA playing, 245
True magazine, 453
trumpet
    bop and, 437–38
    LA playing, 1, 245–46
    see also cornet
Tshombé, Moïse (prime minister of Zaïre), 476
Tuxedo Brass Band, 132–33, 172, 174
"25" (gambling joint), 49–50

union, labor. See American Federation of Musicians

Vallee, Rudy, 239–40, 386
Vance, Rev. John E., 420
Van Heusen, Jimmy (composer), 395
Vanity Fair (periodical), 385, 487
Van Vechten, Carl, 237
Variety (periodical), 128, 214, 239, 325, 382, 383, 385, 418–19
Venable, Percy, 279 (floor-show director), 279, 289
Vendome Theatre, Chicago, 265, 268–69, 279
Verve recording company, 465–66
Victor Records, 321, 357–58, 360, 380, 408
vipers, 327, 360–61
vocalese, 274, 398
voodoo, 14, 18–21

Wade, Clerk, 50–51, 112
Waller, Fats, 239, 316
Warren, Henry (composer), 384
Warwick nightclub, failure of, 299
Washington, Al (tenor), 331
Waters, Ethel, 241, 417
Webb, Chick (drummer), 357
Weill, Kurt, 459
Weil, Milton (publisher), 335
Wein, George (producer), 373, 456, 490, 491
Welles, Orson, 426, 427
Wettling, George (drummer), 281, 432
Whaley, Vern (reporter), 375
Wheeler, Dolores, 374, 375
White Citizens Council, 470
White, Lulu (madam), 53, 54, 110
Whiteman, Paul, 210, 243–44, 286, 321, 356, 370
White, Violet (music teacher), 179
Wickemeyer, Ezra (recording engineer), 217
Wiggins, Fred (music company manager), 215
Williams, Arthur P., 27
Williams, Bert, 488
Williams, Black Benny (drummer), 32–33, 50, 62, 88–92, 93, 97, 103, 133, 140, 155, 255, 373, 464
Williams, Clarence (pianist/entrepreneur), 54, 129–30, 253–54, 274, 305, 391, 402, 405
    recordings by, 401
Williams, Laurence (musician), 144
Williams, Nelly (Black Benny's wife), 90–91
Williams, Spencer, 135
Wilson, Earl (columnist), 493
Wilson, Judge Andrew, 68, 70, 80
Wilson, Lucille
    LA and, 393–94, 415, 419–21
    see also Armstrong, Lucille Wilson
Wilson, Teddy (musician), 360

Wilson, Udell (musician), 144
Wilson, Wila Mae (Daisy Parker's adopted
daughter), 170
Wimberly, Connie (poolhall manager), 390
Winchell, Walter, 414
Wooding, Sam (bandleader), 235
Work Progress Administration, 400
World War I, 125
World War II, music and, 410
Worthington, Crawford (musician), 303
Wynn, Wilhemina Bart (musician), 144

Youmans, Vincent (producer), 310, 313
Young, Trummy (trombonist), 449, 476, 478

Zardis, Chester, 78
Zeno, Henry (Harry), 32, 37, 47, 48–49, 50,
51
Ziegfeld, Florenz, Jr., 239, 314
Zucker, Dr. Gary, 489, 492
Zukor, Adolph, 383
Zulu Social Aid and Pleasure Club, 30, 344,
425, 442–45